THE Millennials

Americans Born 1977 to 1994

6th EDITION

THE Millennials

Americans Born 1977 to 1994

6th EDITION

The American Generations Series

BY THE NEW STRATEGIST EDITORS

New Strategist Press, LLC
Amityville, New York

New Strategist Press, LLC
P.O. Box 635, Amityville, New York 11701
800/848-0842; 631/608-8795
www.newstrategist.com

ISBN 978-1-940308-81-4 (hardcover)
ISBN 978-1-940308-82-1 (paper)
ISBN 978-1-940308-83-8 (pdf)

Printed in the United States of America

Table of Contents

Chapter 4. Housing

Chapter 5. Income

Chapter 6. Labor Force

Chapter 7. Living Arrangements

Chapter 8. Population

Chapter 9. Spending

Chapter 10. Time Use

Chapter 11. Wealth

Part Two: The iGeneration

Chapter 12. Education

Chapter 13. Health

Chapter 14. Housing

Chapter 15. Income

Chapter 16. Labor Force

Chapter 17. Living Arrangements

Chapter 18. Population

Chapter 19. Spending

Chapter 20. Time Use

List of Tables

Chapter 1. Attitudes

Chapter 2. Education

Chapter 3. Health

Chapter 4. Housing

Chapter 5. Income

Chapter 6. Labor Force

Chapter 7. Living Arrangements

Chapter 8. Population

Chapter 9. Spending

Chapter 10. Time Use

Chapter 11. Wealth

Part Two: The iGeneration

Chapter 12. Education

Chapter 13. Health

Chapter 14. Housing

Chapter 15. Income

Chapter 16. Labor Force

Chapter 17. Living Arrangements

Chapter 18. Population

Chapter 19. Spending

Chapter 20. Time Use

List of Illustrations

Part One: The Millennials

Chapter 1. Attitudes

Chapter 2. Education

Chapter 3. Health

Chapter 4. Housing

Chapter 5. Income

Chapter 6. Labor Force

Chapter 7. Living Arrangements

Chapter 8. Population

Chapter 9. Spending

Chapter 10. Time Use

Chapter 11. Wealth

Part Two: The iGeneration

Chapter 12. Education

Chapter 13. Health

Chapter 14. Housing

Chapter 15. Income

Chapter 16. Labor Force

Chapter 17. Living Arrangements

Chapter 18. Population

Chapter 19. Spending

Chapter 20. Time Use

Introduction

The Millennial generation—America's young adults—was once the new kid in town. No longer. The youngest Millennials turned 20 in 2014, and the oldest are in their mid-thirties. This sixth edition of *The Millennials: Americans Born 1977 to 1994* provides a demographic and socioeconomic profile of the generation that is, as of 2014, comprised entirely of adults.

Millennials ranged in age from 20 to 37 in 2014. They number 78 million and account for 25 percent of the total population—surpassing the Baby-Boom's 24 percent. A special supplement included in this book profiles the generation that follows Millennials—born in 1995 or later (the oldest turned 19 in 2014) and now comprising the nation's children. We call them the iGeneration, and their characteristics are only beginning to emerge. The end date for the iGeneration remains an unknown. There is evidence of a new Recession Generation forming, a consequence of the drop in births below the 4 million annual level beginning in 2010. A few tables in *The Millennials* show some of the demographics of the Recession generation.

The naming of new generations is the sport of marketers. Behind the effort, however, is a serious attempt to identify the shared characteristics of a group of people. By naming the generations, businesses and policymakers can make better sense of the chaotic jumble of 300 million-plus diverse and individualistic Americans.

The Millennials

The Millennial generation's beginning marked the end of the small Generation X, once known as the baby-bust generation. The oldest Millennials were born in 1977, when the long anticipated echo boom of births began. In that year, the number of births ticked up to 3.3 million. This followed a 12-year lull in births that is called Generation X. By 1980, annual births were up to 3.6 million. By 1990, they topped 4 million. Altogether, 68 million babies were born between 1977 and 1994. Since then, the number of Millennials has grown to 78 million because of immigration.

As is true with Boomers, the Millennial generation is defined by its numbers. When Millennials moved through the education system, schools were strained by rising enrollments. Colleges and universities that had been competing for scarce Gen Xers could pick and choose from among the best as applications soared. Millennials also made their mark in the housing market, the homeownership rate rising to record highs by the mid-2000s. Fortunately, few Millennials bought houses during the bubble, the majority of them avoiding the nation's overpriced real estate. In the future, these renters will be better positioned to buy at lower prices—if they decide they want to become homeowners.

Every generation of Americans is unique, shaped not only by its numbers but also by the historical moment. Millennials are no exception. Three characteristics have emerged to define the generation. One, Millennials are racially and ethnically diverse—so diverse, in fact, that in many parts of the country the term "minority" no longer has meaning for their peer group. Two, they are fiercely independent thanks to divorce, day care, single parents, latch key lifestyles, and the technological revolution that has made communication with family and friends instantaneous and continuous. Three, Millennials feel powerful—even in the midst of the economic downturn. Raised by indulgent parents, they have a sense of well-being not shared by Gen Xers. Optimistic about the future despite their trouble finding jobs and becoming independent, Millennials see opportunity where others see problems.

The Millennials: Americans Born 1977 to 1994 examines the young-adult generation as it goes to college, finds jobs, establishes households, becomes parents, and struggles to gain a foothold in the nation's increasingly fragile middle class.

The iGeneration

The special supplement on what we call the iGeneration examines the socioeconomic status of the nation's children. The generation that follows Millennials was aged 19 or younger in 2014 (born in 1995 or later). We look at these children from the perspective of their family, exploring family incomes, time use, and labor force status of parents, day care arrangements, the spending of married couples and single parents with children, and many other family characteristics. The supplement also includes school enrollment data, mobility statistics, and an examination of the health and well-being of high school students.

Soon the youngest generation will go to college, join the labor force, and begin to establish their own households. At that time, they will require a reference book devoted entirely to their unique socioeconomic characteristics. Until then, however, *The Millennials* provides a comprehensive look at both the nation's young adults and its children.

How to Use This Book

The Millennials: Americans Born 1977 to 1994 is designed for easy use. It is divided into 11 chapters, organized alphabetically: Attitudes, Education, Health, Housing, Income, Labor Force, Living Arrangements, Population, Time Use, Spending, and Wealth. The special supplement on the iGeneration is divided into nine chapters that examine the characteristics of families with children: Education, Health, Housing, Income, Labor Force, Living Arrangements, Population, Time Use, and Spending,

The sixth edition of *The Millennials* includes the latest data on the changing demographics of homeownership, based on the Census Bureau's 2013 Housing Vacancies and Homeownership Survey. It documents the steep decline in the homeownership rate of "first-time" homebuyers—adults aged

30 to 34. The Income chapter, with 2013 income statistics, reveals the struggle of so many young Americans to find a stable job that pays a living wage as the economy climbs out of recession. The Spending chapter reveals trends in the spending of young adults and families with children through 2013, and examines how their spending changed after the Great Recession. *The Millennials* includes the latest labor force numbers showing the decline in participation among teens and young adults. The Wealth chapter presents data from the Survey of Consumer Finances, which reveal the impact of the Great Recession on the wealth of householders under age 35, with a look at 2007-to-2013 trends—including statistics on education loans. The Health chapter has up-to-date statistics on falling birth rates, out-of-wedlock childbearing, and health insurance coverage. The Attitudes chapter, based on New Strategist's analysis of the 2012 General Social Survey, compares and contrasts the perspectives of the generations.

Most of the tables in *The Millennials* are based on data collected by the federal government, in particular the Census Bureau, the Bureau of Labor Statistics, the National Center for Education Statistics, the National Center for Health Statistics, and the Federal Reserve Board. The federal government is the best source of up-to-date, reliable information on the changing characteristics of Americans. By having *The Millennials* on your bookshelf you can get the answers to your questions faster than online. Even better, visit www.newstrategist.com and download the PDF version of *The Millennials* with links to each table in Excel, including all tables in the special supplement.

The chapters of *The Millennials* present the demographic and lifestyle data most important to researchers. Within each chapter, most of the tables are based on data collected by the federal government, but they are not simple reproductions of government spreadsheets—as is the case in many reference books. Instead, each table is individually compiled and created by New Strategist's editors, with calculations designed to reveal the trends. The task of extracting and processing data from the government's web sites to create a single table can require hours of effort. New Strategist has done the work for you, with each table telling a story about Millennials or the iGeneration—a story explained by the accompanying text and chart, which analyze the data and highlight future trends. If you need more information than the tables and text provide, you can plumb the original source listed at the bottom of each table.

The book contains a comprehensive list of tables to help you locate the information you need. For a more detailed search, see the index at the back of the book. Also at the back of the book is the glossary, which defines the terms and describes the many surveys referenced in the tables and text.

Each generation of Americans is unique and surprising in its own way. With *The Millennials: Americans Born 1977 to 1994* on your bookshelf, you will understand the nation's young adults and be ready for the generation that follows, still living at home, but soon to add its own stamp to the dynamic American culture.

CHAPTER

1

Attitudes

■ Only 22 percent of Millennials (aged 18 to 35 in 2012) are satisfied with their financial situation, well below the 40 percent of Older Americans who are satisfied.

■ Older Americans are the only generation in which the majority identifies itself as middle class, with 60 percent saying so. Only 36 percent of Millennials consider themselves middle class.

■ Most Millennials think they are better off than their parents were at the same age, and most also think their children will be better off than they themselves are today.

■ Only 32 percent of Millennials identify themselves as Protestant compared with 63 percent of Older Americans.

■ In 2012, the 62 percent majority of Millennials thought gays and lesbians should have the right to marry compared with only 43 percent of Boomers and 30 percent of Older Americans.

■ Among Millennials, 43 percent identify themselves as politically moderate, 29 percent as liberal, and 28 percent as conservative.

■ The 55 percent majority of Millennials favored legalizing marijuana in 2012 compared with only 42 percent of Gen Xers.

Television Remains the Most Important Source of News

The Internet is more important for Millennials and Gen Xers, however.

When asked where they get most of their information about current news events, 46 percent of Millennials say the Internet and 40 percent say television, according to the 2012 General Social Survey. Among Gen Xers, 40 percent name the Internet and 39 percent television.

Most Boomers and Older Americans say television is their most important source of news about current events. The Internet is the number-two choice for Boomers, and newspapers is number two for Older Americans.

Among Millennials, only 15 percent say they read a newspaper every day. Among Older Americans, the figure is 55 percent. One in four Americans never reads a newspaper.

■ The media preferences of younger generations are revolutionizing the news industry.

Media use varies sharply by generation

(percent of people aged 18 or older who name selected medium as their most important source of information about current events, by generation, 2012)

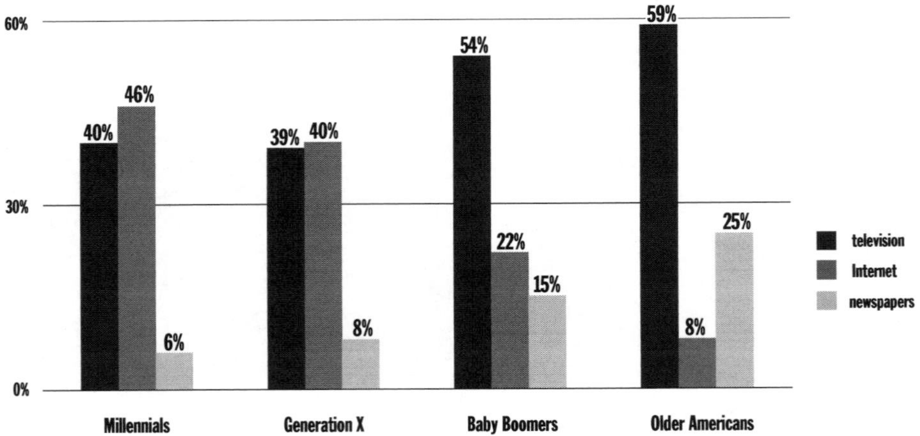

Table 1.1 Main Source of News, 2012

"Where do you get most of your information about current news events?"

(percent of people aged 18 or older responding by generation, 2012)

	television	Internet	newspapers	radio	other
Total people	**47.9%**	**30.0%**	**12.4%**	**4.7%**	**5.0%**
Millennial (18 to 35)	40.5	45.8	5.9	1.2	6.6
Generation X (36 to 47)	38.5	39.8	8.1	9.2	4.4
Baby Boom (48 to 66)	54.1	22.1	14.7	4.3	4.8
Older Americans (67 or older)	58.5	7.7	24.8	5.9	3.1

Source: Survey Documentation and Analysis, Computer-assisted Survey Methods Program, University of California, Berkeley, General Social Survey, 1972–2012 Cumulative Data Files, Internet site http://sda.berkeley.edu/cgi-bin/hsda?harcsda+gss12; calculations by New Strategist

Table 1.2 Daily Newspaper Readership, 2012

"How often do you read the newspaper?"

(percent of people aged 18 or older responding by generation, 2012)

	every day	few times a week	once a week	less than once a week	never
Total people	**26.7%**	**16.3%**	**15.7%**	**16.5%**	**24.8%**
Millennial (18 to 35)	14.8	18.0	19.3	20.3	27.6
Generation X (36 to 47)	22.8	12.7	17.0	18.8	28.8
Baby Boom (48 to 66)	31.0	17.7	13.2	16.4	21.7
Older Americans (67 or older)	54.9	14.9	9.2	3.1	17.9

Source: Survey Documentation and Analysis, Computer-assisted Survey Methods Program, University of California, Berkeley, General Social Survey, 1972–2012 Cumulative Data Files, Internet site http://sda.berkeley.edu/cgi-bin/hsda?harcsda+gss12; calculations by New Strategist

Internet Is Most Important Source of Science News

Television is number one for Boomers and Older Americans, however.

When asked where they get most of their information about science and technology, the largest share of the public now says the Internet (41 percent), followed by television (36 percent). Most Millennials and Gen Xers say the Internet is their most important source of science news, according to the 2012 General Social Survey. In contrast, a larger share of Boomers and Older Americans turn to television rather than the Internet for science news.

Most Americans, regardless of generation, disagree with the notion that "science makes our way of life change too fast." Fully 52 percent of the public disagrees with the statement, with little variation by age.

Sixty-one percent of Millennials believe in evolution. Among Gen Xers and Boomers, the figures are 59 and 56 percent, respectively. Among Older Americans, only 38 percent believe in evolution.

■ Older Americans are almost as likely to depend on magazines (13 percent) as the Internet (15 percent) for their science news.

Millennials are most likely to believe in evolution

(percent of people aged 18 or older who think the statement "human beings developed from earlier species of animals" is true, by generation, 2012)

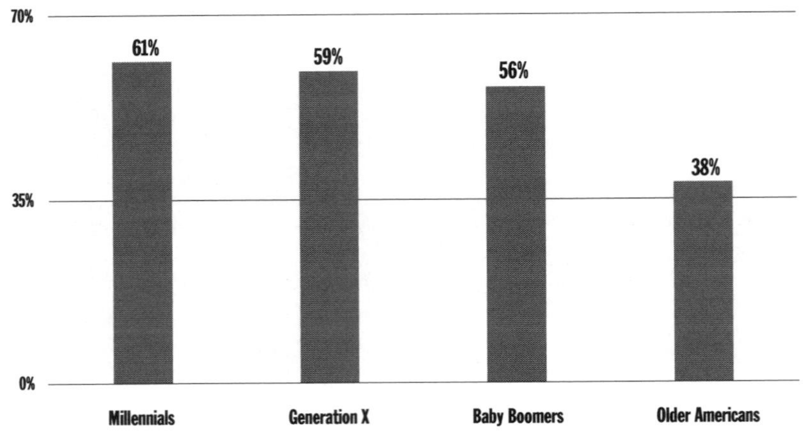

Table 1.3 Main Source of Information about Science and Technology, 2012

"Where do you get most of your information about science and technology?"

(percent of people aged 18 or older responding by generation, 2012)

	Internet	television	magazines	newspapers	radio	books	other
Total people	**41.5%**	**35.9%**	**7.0%**	**5.5%**	**2.8%**	**2.7%**	**4.6%**
Millennial (18 to 35)	59.8	25.8	1.5	3.2	1.0	2.7	6.0
Generation X (36 to 47)	51.6	25.4	8.7	4.5	2.9	2.5	4.4
Baby Boom (48 to 66)	33.4	41.9	7.7	5.8	4.1	2.4	4.7
Older Americans (67 or older)	14.7	54.8	12.7	9.9	2.9	3.9	1.1

Source: Survey Documentation and Analysis, Computer-assisted Survey Methods Program, University of California, Berkeley, General Social Survey, 1972–2012 Cumulative Data Files, Internet site http://sda.berkeley.edu/cgi-bin/hsda?harcsda+gss12; calculations by New Strategist

Table 1.4 Science Makes Our Way of Life Change Too Fast, 2012

"Science makes our way of life change too fast.
Do you agree or disagree?"

(percent of people aged 18 or older responding by generation, 2012)

	strongly agree	agree	disagree	strongly disagree
Total people	**9.8%**	**33.7%**	**52.5%**	**4.0%**
Millennial (18 to 35)	5.0	34.9	54.2	5.9
Generation X (36 to 47)	13.1	29.5	54.0	3.4
Baby Boom (48 to 66)	12.1	33.2	50.7	4.0
Older Americans (67 or older)	8.1	39.1	51.4	1.4

Source: Survey Documentation and Analysis, Computer-assisted Survey Methods Program, University of California, Berkeley, General Social Survey, 1972–2012 Cumulative Data Files, Internet site http://sda.berkeley.edu/cgi-bin/hsda?harcsda+gss12; calculations by New Strategist

Table 1.5 Human Evolution, 2012

"Human beings, as we know them today, developed from earlier species of animals. Is this true or false?"

(percent of people aged 18 or older responding by generation, 2012)

	true	false
Total people	**55.8%**	**44.2%**
Millennial (18 to 35)	61.0	39.0
Generation X (36 to 47)	58.7	41.3
Baby Boom (48 to 66)	55.7	44.3
Older Americans (67 or older)	38.0	62.0

Source: Survey Documentation and Analysis, Computer-assisted Survey Methods Program, University of California, Berkeley, General Social Survey, 1972–2012 Cumulative Data Files, Internet site http://sda.berkeley.edu/cgi-bin/hsda?harcsda+gss12; calculations by New Strategist

Religious Beliefs Shape the Perspectives of Older Americans

Younger generations are more secular in their outlook.

Technology is not the only thing that separates young from old. On religious issues, Millennials and Older Americans are often far apart. Only 32 percent of Millennials identify themselves as Protestant, for example, compared with 63 percent of Older Americans. Thirty percent of Millennials say they have no religious affiliation compared with just 10 percent of the older generation.

Fewer than half of Millennials believe in God without a doubt (48 percent). This is well below the figures for Gen Xers and Boomers (63 percent) and Older Americans (69 percent). Only 46 percent of Millenials say they are very or moderately religious compared with 59 percent of Gen Xers, 66 percent of Boomers, and 70 percent of Older Americans.

■ Millennials are ushering in a more secular society, but it will take many more decades for that to unfold.

Older Americans are the most religious

(percent of people aged 18 or older who say they are moderately or very religious, by generation, 2012)

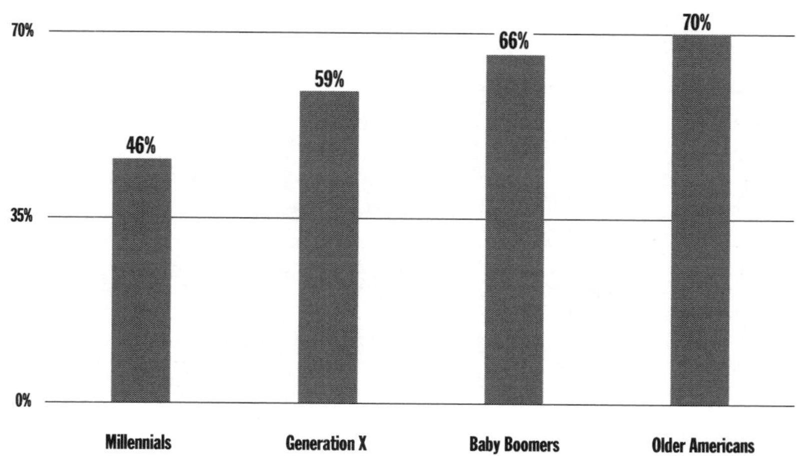

Table 1.6 Religious Preference, 2012

"What is your religious preference? "

(percent of people aged 18 or older responding by generation, 2012)

	Protestant	Catholic	none	Christian	Jewish	Moslem/ Islam	other
Total people	**44.3%**	**24.2%**	**19.7%**	**6.0%**	**1.5%**	**1.1%**	**3.2%**
Millennial (18 to 35)	31.9	24.4	29.5	7.4	0.8	0.7	5.3
Generation X (36 to 47)	42.5	24.7	18.4	7.4	2.7	2.2	2.1
Baby Boom (48 to 66)	50.5	24.7	15.1	5.1	0.9	1.0	2.7
Older Americans (67 or older)	62.9	21.5	9.7	2.5	2.6	0.3	0.5

Source: Survey Documentation and Analysis, Computer-assisted Survey Methods Program, University of California, Berkeley, General Social Survey, 1972–2012 Cumulative Data Files, Internet site http://sda.berkeley.edu/cgi-bin/hsda?harcsda+gss12; calculations by New Strategist

Table 1.7 Attendance at Religious Services, 2012

"How often do you attend religious services?"

(percent of people aged 18 or older responding by generation, 2012)

	more than once a week	every week	nearly every week	two or three times a month	once a month	several times a year	once a year	less than once a year	never
Total people	**6.5%**	**19.7%**	**4.0%**	**8.9%**	**6.8%**	**10.8%**	**13.0%**	**5.0%**	**25.3%**
Millennial (18 to 35)	4.4	13.7	2.2	8.2	8.9	10.4	16.4	5.7	30.1
Generation X (36 to 47)	6.5	21.3	5.0	8.5	6.7	12.1	13.0	3.8	23.2
Baby Boom (48 to 66)	6.5	22.1	4.3	10.8	5.9	10.1	12.2	5.0	23.3
Older Americans (67 or older)	11.6	26.1	5.9	6.7	4.2	11.6	7.2	4.7	22.0

Source: Survey Documentation and Analysis, Computer-assisted Survey Methods Program, University of California, Berkeley, General Social Survey, 1972–2012 Cumulative Data Files, Internet site http://sda.berkeley.edu/cgi-bin/hsda?harcsda+gss12; calculations by New Strategist

Table 1.8 Confidence in the Existence of God, 2012

"Which statement comes closest to expressing what you believe about God? 1) I don't believe in God. 2) I don't know whether there is a God and I don't believe there is any way to find out. 3) I don't believe in a personal God, but I do believe in a Higher Power of some kind. 4) I find myself believing in God some of the time, but not at others. 5) While I have doubts, I feel that I do believe in God. 6) I know God really exists and I have no doubts about it."

(percent of people aged 18 or older responding by generation, 2012)

	1 don't believe	2 no way to find out	3 higher power	4 believe sometimes	5 believe but doubts	6 know God exists
Total people	**3.1%**	**5.6%**	**11.6%**	**4.2%**	**16.5%**	**59.1%**
Millennial (18 to 35)	3.1	7.2	17.7	4.7	19.4	47.9
Generation X (36 to 47)	4.1	5.7	9.5	4.1	13.4	63.2
Baby Boom (48 to 66)	2.7	4.4	9.0	3.6	17.1	63.3
Older Americans (67 or older)	2.2	4.5	6.5	4.4	13.3	69.1

Source: Survey Documentation and Analysis, Computer-assisted Survey Methods Program, University of California, Berkeley, General Social Survey, 1972–2012 Cumulative Data Files, Internet site http://sda.berkeley.edu/cgi-bin/hsda?harcsda+gss12; calculations by New Strategist

Table 1.9 Degree of Religiosity, 2012

"To what extent do you consider yourself a religious person?"

(percent of people aged 18 or older responding by generation, 2012)

	very	moderately	slightly	not
Total people	**18.8%**	**39.5%**	**21.6%**	**20.1%**
Millennial (18 to 35)	11.2	34.5	26.2	28.1
Generation X (36 to 47)	20.3	38.3	20.1	21.3
Baby Boom (48 to 66)	25.0	40.7	18.6	15.7
Older Americans (67 or older)	20.0	50.1	20.5	9.4

Source: Survey Documentation and Analysis, Computer-assisted Survey Methods Program, University of California, Berkeley, General Social Survey, 1972–2012 Cumulative Data Files, Internet site http://sda.berkeley.edu/cgi-bin/hsda?harcsda+gss12; calculations by New Strategist

Table 1.10 Feelings about the Bible, 2012

"Which of these statements comes closes to describing your feelings about the Bible? 1) The Bible is the actual word of God and is to be taken literally. 2) The Bible is the inspired word of God but not everything in it should be taken literally, word for word. 3) The Bible is an ancient book of fables, legends, history, and moral precepts recorded by men."

(percent of people aged 18 or older responding by generation, 2012)

	word of God	inspired word	book of fables	other
Total people	**32.1%**	**44.6%**	**21.8%**	**1.5%**
Millennial (18 to 35)	25.9	45.1	27.8	1.3
Generation X (36 to 47)	33.5	44.7	21.4	0.4
Baby Boom (48 to 66)	33.8	45.1	18.3	2.8
Older Americans (67 or older)	41.2	41.4	16.6	0.8

Source: Survey Documentation and Analysis, Computer-assisted Survey Methods Program, University of California, Berkeley, General Social Survey, 1972–2012 Cumulative Data Files, Internet site http://sda.berkeley.edu/cgi-bin/hsda?harcsda+gss12; calculations by New Strategist

Younger Generations Support Gay Marriage

The majority of Millennials and Gen Xers think gays and lesbians should have the right to marry.

There is no longer any controversy about working women in our society. That's because most Americans were raised by a working mother. Regardless of age, the majority of the public now disagrees that "traditional" sex roles—where men go to work and women stay home—are best. The oldest generation is the only one in which the majority thinks there is something wrong with premarital sex.

Americans are still ambivalent about homosexuality, but less so with each passing year as more tolerant younger generations replace older people. The 55 percent majority of Millennials say there is nothing wrong with sexual relations between adults of the same sex. Sixty-two percent of Millennials believe gays and lesbians should have the right to marry, as do 51 percent of Gen Xers. Only 43 percent of Boomers and 30 percent of Older Americans support gay marriage.

■ Among Millennials, 6 percent identify as gay, lesbian, or bisexual—nearly four times the share among Older Americans.

Millennials and Gen Xers support gay marriage

(percent of people aged 18 or older who agree that gays and lesbians should have the right to marry, by generation, 2012)

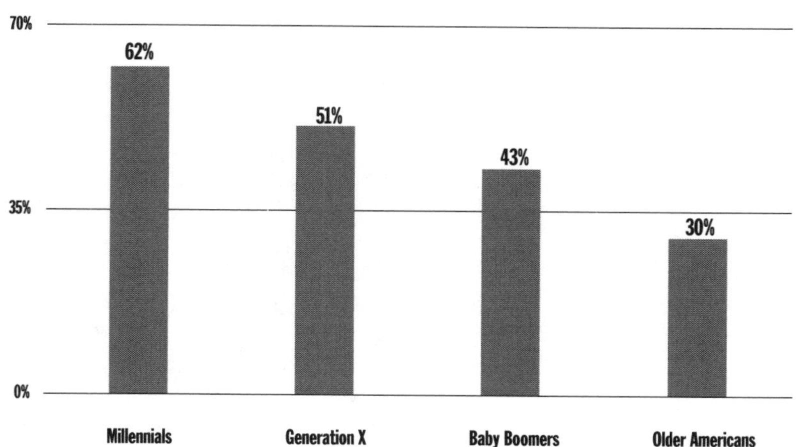

Table 1.11 Sex Roles, 2012

"It is much better for everyone involved if the man is the achiever outside the home and the woman takes care of the home and family. Do you agree or disagree?"

(percent of people aged 18 or older responding by generation, 2012)

	strongly agree	agree	disagree	strongly disagree
Total people	**6.5%**	**25.2%**	**48.3%**	**20.0%**
Millennial (18 to 35)	6.0	18.9	51.9	23.2
Generation X (36 to 47)	7.5	19.1	51.9	21.5
Baby Boom (48 to 66)	6.0	30.9	43.6	19.4
Older Americans (67 or older)	7.0	40.0	41.9	11.1

Source: Survey Documentation and Analysis, Computer-assisted Survey Methods Program, University of California, Berkeley, General Social Survey, 1972–2012 Cumulative Data Files, Internet site http://sda.berkeley.edu/cgi-bin/hsda?harcsda+gss12; calculations by New Strategist

Table 1.12 Mother Worked While You Were Growing Up, 2012

"Did your mother ever work for pay for as long as a year while you were growing up?"

(percent of people aged 18 or older responding by generation, 2012)

	yes	no
Total people	**72.5%**	**27.5%**
Millennial (18 to 35)	82.6	17.4
Generation X (36 to 47)	80.1	19.9
Baby Boom (48 to 66)	67.9	32.1
Older Americans (67 or older)	47.7	52.3

Source: Survey Documentation and Analysis, Computer-assisted Survey Methods Program, University of California, Berkeley, General Social Survey, 1972–2012 Cumulative Data Files, Internet site http://sda.berkeley.edu/cgi-bin/hsda?harcsda+gss12; calculations by New Strategist

Table 1.13 Premarital Sex, 2012

"If a man and a woman have sexual relations before marriage, do you think it is always wrong, almost always wrong, sometimes wrong, or not wrong at all?"

(percent of people aged 18 or older responding by generation, 2012)

	always wrong	almost always wrong	sometimes wrong	not wrong at all
Total people	**21.9%**	**5.1%**	**15.5%**	**57.5%**
Millennial (18 to 35)	13.7	4.0	16.6	65.7
Generation X (36 to 47)	24.2	4.5	13.1	58.2
Baby Boom (48 to 66)	23.0	5.7	13.8	57.5
Older Americans (67 or older)	37.0	8.0	20.2	34.8

Source: Survey Documentation and Analysis, Computer-assisted Survey Methods Program, University of California, Berkeley, General Social Survey, 1972–2012 Cumulative Data Files, Internet site http://sda.berkeley.edu/cgi-bin/hsda?harcsda+gss12; calculations by New Strategist

Table 1.14 Homosexuality, 2012

"What about sexual relations between two adults of the same sex—is it always wrong, almost always wrong, sometimes wrong, or not wrong at all?"

(percent of people aged 18 or older responding by generation, 2012)

	always wrong	almost always wrong	sometimes wrong	not wrong at all
Total people	**45.7%**	**2.9%**	**7.7%**	**43.8%**
Millennial (18 to 35)	32.3	2.7	10.2	54.8
Generation X (36 to 47)	46.8	3.4	5.7	44.0
Baby Boom (48 to 66)	48.7	2.8	8.2	40.3
Older Americans (67 or older)	69.9	2.6	3.7	23.8

Source: Survey Documentation and Analysis, Computer-assisted Survey Methods Program, University of California, Berkeley, General Social Survey, 1972–2012 Cumulative Data Files, Internet site http://sda.berkeley.edu/cgi-bin/hsda?harcsda+gss12; calculations by New Strategist

Table 1.15 Gay Marriage, 2012

"Homosexual couples should have the right to marry one another. Do you agree or disagree?"

(percent of people aged 18 or older responding by generation, 2012)

	agree	neither agree nor disagree	disagree
Total people	**48.9%**	**12.0%**	**39.1%**
Millennial (18 to 35)	62.3	13.0	24.7
Generation X (36 to 47)	50.7	9.9	39.4
Baby Boom (48 to 66)	42.6	13.8	43.6
Older Americans (67 or older)	29.8	9.1	61.2

Source: Survey Documentation and Analysis, Computer-assisted Survey Methods Program, University of California, Berkeley, General Social Survey, 1972–2012 Cumulative Data Files, Internet site http://sda.berkeley.edu/cgi-bin/hsda?harcsda+gss12; calculations by New Strategist

Table 1.16 Sexual Orientation, 2012

"Which of the following best describes you?"

(percent of people aged 18 or older responding by generation, 2012)

	gay, lesbian or homosexual	bisexual	heterosexual or straight
Total people	**1.5%**	**2.2%**	**96.3%**
Millennial (18 to 35)	1.8	4.0	94.2
Generation X (36 to 47)	2.1	2.4	95.4
Baby Boom (48 to 66)	1.0	0.7	98.3
Older Americans (67 or older)	0.6	0.9	98.5

Source: Survey Documentation and Analysis, Computer-assisted Survey Methods Program, University of California, Berkeley, General Social Survey, 1972–2012 Cumulative Data Files, Internet site http://sda.berkeley.edu/cgi-bin/hsda?harcsda+gss12; calculations by New Strategist

Most Americans Do Not Trust Others

Younger generations are less trusting than older ones.

When Americans are asked whether most people can be trusted, 64 percent say no. The percentage of people who say others cannot be trusted is as high as 75 percent among Millennials and as low as 56 to 57 percent among Boomers and Older Americans.

The 53 percent majority of the public says life is exciting, while 43 percent describe life as pretty routine. There are almost no differences in response to this question among Millennials, Gen Xers, or Boomers. Older Americans, however, are more likely to say life is pretty routine (54 percent) than exciting (43 percent).

■ Regardless of generation, about one-third of the population claims to be "very happy."

Younger generations are most likely to find life exciting

(percent of people aged 18 or older who say life is exciting, by generation, 2012)

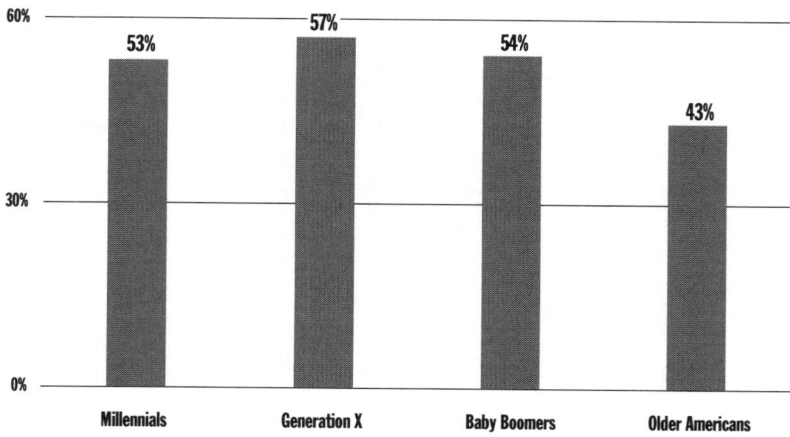

Table 1.17 Trust in Others, 2012

"Generally speaking, would you say that most people can be trusted or that you can't be too careful in life?"

(percent of people aged 18 or older responding by generation, 2012)

	can trust	cannot trust	depends
Total people	**32.2%**	**64.2%**	**3.7%**
Millennial (18 to 35)	21.2	75.2	3.6
Generation X (36 to 47)	32.5	64.6	2.9
Baby Boom (48 to 66)	39.9	56.5	3.6
Older Americans (67 or older)	38.0	56.8	5.2

Source: Survey Documentation and Analysis, Computer-assisted Survey Methods Program, University of California, Berkeley, General Social Survey, 1972–2012 Cumulative Data Files, Internet site http://sda.berkeley.edu/cgi-bin/hsda?harcsda+gss12; calculations by New Strategist

Table 1.18 Life Exciting or Dull, 2012

"In general, do you find life exciting, pretty routine, or dull?"

(percent of people aged 18 or older responding by generation, 2012)

	exciting	pretty routine	dull
Total people	**52.7%**	**42.6%**	**4.7%**
Millennial (18 to 35)	52.6	41.9	5.5
Generation X (36 to 47)	56.9	40.2	3.0
Baby Boom (48 to 66)	53.6	40.7	5.7
Older Americans (67 or older)	42.9	53.7	3.4

Source: Survey Documentation and Analysis, Computer-assisted Survey Methods Program, University of California, Berkeley, General Social Survey, 1972–2012 Cumulative Data Files, Internet site http://sda.berkeley.edu/cgi-bin/hsda?harcsda+gss12; calculations by New Strategist

Table 1.19 General Happiness, 2012

"Taken all together, how would you say things are these days—would you say that you are very happy, pretty happy, or not too happy?"

(percent of people aged 18 or older responding by generation, 2012)

	very happy	pretty happy	not too happy
Total people	**32.9%**	**54.2%**	**12.9%**
Millennial (18 to 35)	33.4	55.1	11.5
Generation X (36 to 47)	31.6	57.0	11.5
Baby Boom (48 to 66)	33.1	52.1	14.7
Older Americans (67 or older)	33.8	52.9	13.2

Source: Survey Documentation and Analysis, Computer-assisted Survey Methods Program, University of California, Berkeley, General Social Survey, 1972–2012 Cumulative Data Files, Internet site http://sda.berkeley.edu/cgi-bin/hsda?harcsda+gss12; calculations by New Strategist

Millennials Are Least Likely to Be Conservative

Older Americans are the most conservative.

There is a common misconception that people become increasingly conservative with age. In fact, political outlook develops in early adulthood and tends to remain stable throughout life. This stability in political leanings over the life course makes the current findings from the General Social Survey especially interesting. The 2012 results show Millennials to be the least conservative generation and the only one in which liberals are as numerous as conservatives. In 2012, 29 percent of Millennials identified themselves as liberal and 28 percent identified themselves as conservative. Among the oldest Americans, 42 percent are conservative and only 21 percent are liberal.

Millennials also are less likely than the older generations to identify themselves as Republican, with only 29 percent placing themselves on the Republican end of the scale. Among older generations, from 35 to 41 percent identify themselves as Republican at least somewhat.

■ Older Americans, who are protected by the government's Medicare health insurance program, are least likely to think the government should help people pay for medical care.

Millennials are most likely to think the government should help pay for medical care

(percent of people aged 18 or older who believe the federal government should help people pay for their medical care (a 1 or 2 on the scale), by generation, 2012)

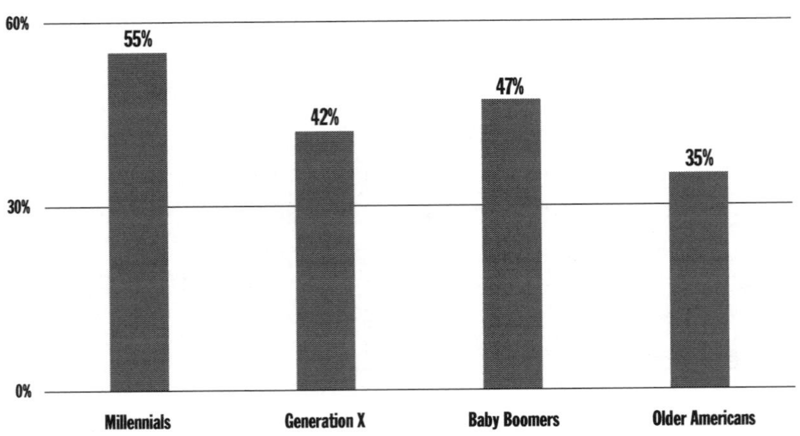

Table 1.20 Political Leanings, 2012

"We hear a lot of talk these days about liberals and conservatives. Where would you place yourself on a seven-point scale from extremely liberal (1) to extremely conservative (7)?"

(percent of people aged 18 or older responding by generation, 2012)

	liberal (1 to 3)	moderate (4)	conservative (5 to 7)
Total people	**27.0%**	**38.5%**	**34.6%**
Millennial (18 to 35)	29.0	42.7	28.2
Generation X (36 to 47)	30.4	35.4	34.3
Baby Boom (48 to 66)	24.9	37.6	37.7
Older Americans (67 or older)	21.4	36.1	42.4

Source: Survey Documentation and Analysis, Computer-assisted Survey Methods Program, University of California, Berkeley, General Social Survey, 1972–2012 Cumulative Data Files, Internet site http://sda.berkeley.edu/cgi-bin/hsda?harcsda+gss12; calculations by New Strategist

Table 1.21 Political Party Affiliation, 2012

"Generally speaking, do you usually think of yourself as a Republican, Democrat, Independent, or what?"

(percent of people aged 18 or older responding by generation, 2012)

	strong Democrat	not strong Democrat	independent, near Democrat	independent	independent, near Republican	not strong Republican	strong Republican	other party
Total people	**16.7%**	**17.0%**	**12.4%**	**19.8%**	**8.2%**	**13.7%**	**9.8%**	**2.3%**
Millennial (18 to 35)	13.5	17.9	13.6	26.2	6.9	14.7	5.2	2.1
Generation X (36 to 47)	13.5	17.3	14.1	20.4	10.3	15.3	7.0	2.1
Baby Boom (48 to 66)	20.1	14.9	12.0	16.7	7.8	11.6	13.9	3.0
Older Americans (67 or older)	21.2	18.9	8.2	10.5	9.4	13.8	16.0	2.0

Source: Survey Documentation and Analysis, Computer-assisted Survey Methods Program, University of California, Berkeley, General Social Survey, 1972–2012 Cumulative Data Files, Internet site http://sda.berkeley.edu/cgi-bin/hsda?harcsda+gss12; calculations by New Strategist

Table 1.22 Government Should Help Pay for Medical Care, 2012

"In general, some people think that it is the responsibility of the government in Washington to see to it that people have help in paying for doctors and hospital bills; they are at point 1. Others think that these matters are not the responsibility of the federal government and that people should take care of these things themselves; they are at point 5. Where would you place yourself on the scale?"

(percent of people aged 18 or older responding by generation, 2012)

	1 government should help	2	3 agree with both	4	5 people should help themselves
Total people	**28.4%**	**18.1%**	**31.4%**	**12.4%**	**9.7%**
Millennial (18 to 35)	29.4	25.2	26.9	13.8	4.6
Generation X (36 to 47)	24.3	17.7	36.3	12.6	9.2
Baby Boom (48 to 66)	31.3	15.3	29.3	11.8	12.3
Older Americans (67 or older)	25.4	9.7	38.7	10.4	15.7

Source: Survey Documentation and Analysis, Computer-assisted Survey Methods Program, University of California, Berkeley, General Social Survey, 1972–2012 Cumulative Data Files, Internet site http://sda.berkeley.edu/cgi-bin/hsda?harcsda+gss12; calculations by New Strategist

Many Think Their Income Is below Average

Fewer than half of Americans identify themselves as middle class.

Forty-six percent of Americans say their family income is average relative to others, while one-third says their income is below average. Only 44 percent identify themselves as middle class, while an equal proportion say they are working class. Among Older Americans, however, 60 percent say they are middle class.

Not surprisingly, as Millennials graduate from college and go to work, they are most likely to say their financial situation is improving. Thirty-nine percent of Millennials report that their finances have gotten better. Boomers are most likely to report worsening finances (38 percent).

When it comes to the American Dream, younger generations typically have the most optimistic outlook. Sixty-four percent of Millennials agree with the statement, "The way things are in America, people like me and my family have a good chance of improving our standard of living," a higher share than in any other generation. The figure is 56 percent among Gen Xers. In contrast, only 43 percent of Older Americans agree.

■ Older Americans are most likely to be satisfied with their financial situation.

Older Americans are most likely to identify themselves as middle class

(percent of people aged 18 or older who say they are middle class, by generation, 2012)

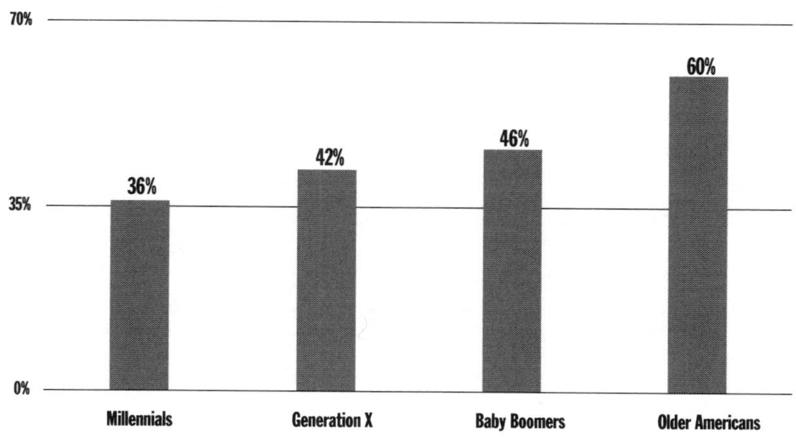

Table 1.23 Family Income Relative to Others, 2012

"Compared with American families in general, would you say your family income is far below average, below average, average, above average, or far above average?"

(percent of people aged 18 or older responding by generation, 2012)

	far below average	below average	average	above average	far above average
Total people	**6.8%**	**25.9%**	**45.5%**	**19.0%**	**2.7%**
Millennial (18 to 35)	5.7	27.7	49.9	15.3	1.4
Generation X (36 to 47)	7.7	22.3	40.5	25.3	4.3
Baby Boom (48 to 66)	8.3	24.9	43.6	19.9	3.2
Older Americans (67 or older)	4.6	29.8	48.1	15.0	2.4

Source: Survey Documentation and Analysis, Computer-assisted Survey Methods Program, University of California, Berkeley, General Social Survey, 1972–2012 Cumulative Data Files, Internet site http://sda.berkeley.edu/cgi-bin/hsda?harcsda+gss12; calculations by New Strategist

Table 1.24 Social Class Membership, 2012

"If you were asked to use one of four names for your social class, which would you say you belong in: the lower class, the working class, the middle class, or the upper class?"

(percent of people aged 18 or older responding by generation, 2012)

	lower	working	middle	upper
Total people	**8.4%**	**44.3%**	**43.7%**	**3.6%**
Millennial (18 to 35)	9.3	52.3	35.7	2.7
Generation X (36 to 47)	5.6	48.4	42.0	4.1
Baby Boom (48 to 66)	9.0	40.6	46.2	4.2
Older Americans (67 or older)	9.7	27.6	59.6	3.1

Source: Survey Documentation and Analysis, Computer-assisted Survey Methods Program, University of California, Berkeley, General Social Survey, 1972–2012 Cumulative Data Files, Internet site http://sda.berkeley.edu/cgi-bin/hsda?harcsda+gss12; calculations by New Strategist

Table 1.25 Change in Financial Situation, 2012

"During the last few years, has your financial situation been getting better, worse, or has it stayed the same?"

(percent of people aged 18 or older responding by generation, 2012)

	better	worse	stayed same
Total people	**28.2%**	**30.2%**	**41.6%**
Millennial (18 to 35)	39.1	22.7	38.1
Generation X (36 to 47)	29.3	28.9	41.8
Baby Boom (48 to 66)	23.2	38.0	38.8
Older Americans (67 or older)	12.5	32.0	55.5

Source: Survey Documentation and Analysis, Computer-assisted Survey Methods Program, University of California, Berkeley, General Social Survey, 1972–2012 Cumulative Data Files, Internet site http://sda.berkeley.edu/cgi-bin/hsda?harcsda+gss12; calculations by New Strategist

Table 1.26 Satisfaction with Financial Situation, 2012

"We are interested in how people are getting along financially these days. So far as you and your family are concerned, would you say that you are pretty well satisfied with your present financial situation, more or less satisfied, or not satisfied at all?"

(percent of people aged 18 or older responding by generation, 2012)

	satisfied	more or less satisfied	not at all satisfied
Total people	**27.0%**	**45.0%**	**28.0%**
Millennial (18 to 35)	22.4	48.7	28.9
Generation X (36 to 47)	25.2	46.3	28.5
Baby Boom (48 to 66)	27.2	41.9	30.9
Older Americans (67 or older)	39.9	41.2	18.9

Source: Survey Documentation and Analysis, Computer-assisted Survey Methods Program, University of California, Berkeley, General Social Survey, 1972–2012 Cumulative Data Files, Internet site http://sda.berkeley.edu/cgi-bin/hsda?harcsda+gss12; calculations by New Strategist

Table 1.27 Standard of Living Will Improve, 2012

"The way things are in America, people like me and my family have a good chance of improving our standard of living. Do you agree or disagree?"

(percent of people aged 18 or older responding by generation, 2012)

	agree	neither	disagree
Total people	**54.8%**	**17.9%**	**27.4%**
Millennial (18 to 35)	63.9	17.7	18.5
Generation X (36 to 47)	55.6	18.9	25.5
Baby Boom (48 to 66)	50.8	17.5	31.6
Older Americans (67 or older)	43.2	17.8	38.9

Source: Survey Documentation and Analysis, Computer-assisted Survey Methods Program, University of California, Berkeley, General Social Survey, 1972–2012 Cumulative Data Files, Internet site http://sda.berkeley.edu/cgi-bin/hsda?harcsda+gss12; calculations by New Strategist

Younger Generations See a Better Future

Fewer than half of Boomers and Older Americans think their children will be better off.

The 62 percent majority of Americans believe their standard of living is better than that of their parents' at the same age. The percentage who feel this way ranges from a low of 58 percent among Gen Xers to a high of 70 percent among Older Americans.

The public is not this positive about its children's standard of living, however. Overall, 57 percent of American parents think their children's standard of living will be better than their own. Among Millennials, 70 percent believe their children's standard of living will be better, as do 62 percent of Gen Xers. Among Boomers and Older Americans, however, fewer than half have a positive outlook on their children's future. Thirty percent of Boomers and 34 percent of Older Americans think their children's standard of living will be worse.

■ The percentage of parents who think their children's standard of living will be better than their own has fallen from 69 percent in 2000 to the 57 percent of 2012.

Optimism is greatest among younger adults

(percent of parents aged 18 or older who say their children's standard of living will be better than their own, by generation, 2012)

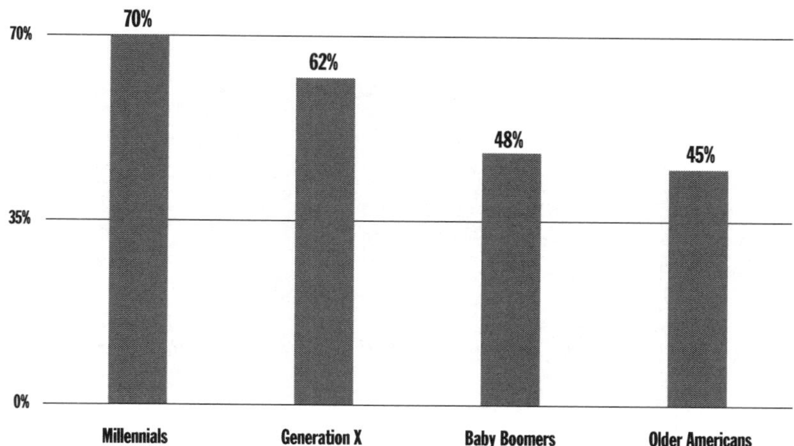

Table 1.28 Parents' Standard of Living, 2012

"Compared to your parents when they were the age you are now, do you think your own standard of living now is much better, somewhat better, about the same, somewhat worse, or much worse than theirs was?"

(percent of people aged 18 or older responding by generation, 2012)

	much better	somewhat better	about the same	somewhat worse	much worse
Total people	**33.5%**	**28.6%**	**21.2%**	**12.0%**	**4.6%**
Millennial (18 to 35)	33.0	30.5	22.2	10.2	4.1
Generation X (36 to 47)	32.1	25.6	21.5	14.6	6.3
Baby Boom (48 to 66)	33.1	27.2	20.5	13.6	5.7
Older Americans (67 or older)	37.7	32.1	20.5	8.6	1.1

Source: Survey Documentation and Analysis, Computer-assisted Survey Methods Program, University of California, Berkeley, General Social Survey, 1972–2012 Cumulative Data Files, Internet site http://sda.berkeley.edu/cgi-bin/hsda?harcsda+gss12; calculations by New Strategist

Table 1.29 Children's Standard of Living, 2012

"When your children are at the age you are now, do you think their standard of living will be much better, somewhat better, about the same, somewhat worse, or much worse than yours is now?"

(percent of people aged 18 or older with children responding by generation, 2012)

	much better	somewhat better	about the same	somewhat worse	much worse
Total people with children	**31.4%**	**25.6%**	**20.5%**	**16.3%**	**6.2%**
Millennial (18 to 35)	42.3	27.4	19.0	8.9	2.5
Generation X (36 to 47)	33.5	28.1	18.8	12.2	7.4
Baby Boom (48 to 66)	24.9	22.7	22.8	22.5	7.2
Older Americans (67 or older)	20.7	24.3	21.3	24.4	9.3

Source: Survey Documentation and Analysis, Computer-assisted Survey Methods Program, University of California, Berkeley, General Social Survey, 1972–2012 Cumulative Data Files, Internet site http://sda.berkeley.edu/cgi-bin/hsda?harcsda+gss12; calculations by New Strategist

Millennials Socialize the Most

Socializing with relatives is more common than socializing with friends.

Thirty-seven percent of Americans socialize with relatives at least weekly. Millennials are most likely to do so, with 46 percent spending a social evening with relatives at least weekly. Millennials are also most likely to socialize on a weekly basis with friends (36 percent). About one-third of Gen Xers and Boomers socialize with relatives on a weekly basis, but only 17 to 20 percent get together with friends that often. Older Americans are almost twice as likely to socialize with family (28 percent) than friends (15 percent) on a weekly basis.

A 34 percent minority of the public owns a gun, and the proportion rises with age. Among Older Americans, 46 percent have a gun in their home. Among Millennials, only 27 percent are gun owners.

■ Support is growing for the legalization of marijuana as Millennials replace older generations.

Millennials are most supportive of legalizing marijuana

(percent of people aged 18 or older who think marijuana should be made legal, by generation, 2012)

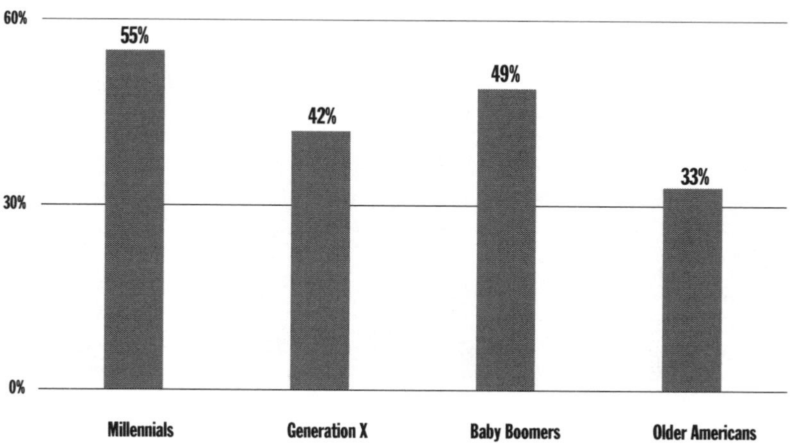

Table 1.30 Spend Evening with Relatives, 2012

"How often do you spend a social evening with relatives?"

(percent of people aged 18 or older responding by generation, 2012)

	almost daily	several times a week	several times a month	once a month	several times a year	once a year	never
Total people	**13.6%**	**23.5%**	**22.4%**	**13.6%**	**15.8%**	**6.7%**	**4.4%**
Millennial (18 to 35)	21.0	25.2	25.3	9.5	11.8	3.6	3.6
Generation X (36 to 47)	12.0	22.1	18.3	18.2	16.2	8.0	5.1
Baby Boom (48 to 66)	9.1	23.4	22.2	14.0	17.9	9.8	3.7
Older Americans (67 or older)	7.0	21.5	21.2	16.0	21.5	5.9	6.9

Source: Survey Documentation and Analysis, Computer-assisted Survey Methods Program, University of California, Berkeley, General Social Survey, 1972–2012 Cumulative Data Files, Internet site http://sda.berkeley.edu/cgi-bin/hsda?harcsda+gss12; calculations by New Strategist

Table 1.31 Spend Evening with Friends, 2012

"How often do you spend a social evening with friends who live outside the neighborhood?"

(percent of people aged 18 or older responding by generation, 2012)

	almost daily	several times a week	several times a month	once a month	several times a year	once a year	never
Total people	**4.5%**	**19.6%**	**21.0%**	**21.0%**	**16.2%**	**8.3%**	**9.5%**
Millennial (18 to 35)	9.1	26.6	27.7	13.9	12.1	5.7	5.0
Generation X (36 to 47)	2.6	14.7	21.9	27.0	17.2	7.1	9.5
Baby Boom (48 to 66)	2.2	17.3	16.6	25.9	18.4	10.7	8.9
Older Americans (67 or older)	0.7	14.4	11.1	18.4	20.7	12.0	22.8

Source: Survey Documentation and Analysis, Computer-assisted Survey Methods Program, University of California, Berkeley, General Social Survey, 1972–2012 Cumulative Data Files, Internet site http://sda.berkeley.edu/cgi-bin/hsda?harcsda+gss12; calculations by New Strategist

Table 1.32 Have Gun in Home, 2012

"Do you happen to have in your home (or garage) any guns or revolvers?"

(percent of people aged 18 or older responding by generation, 2012)

	yes	no	refused
Total people	**34.4%**	**63.6%**	**2.0%**
Millennial (18 to 35)	26.7	72.5	0.8
Generation X (36 to 47)	33.6	65.3	1.2
Baby Boom (48 to 66)	38.1	58.8	3.1
Older Americans (67 or older)	46.2	50.3	3.5

Source: Survey Documentation and Analysis, Computer-assisted Survey Methods Program, University of California, Berkeley, General Social Survey, 1972–2012 Cumulative Data Files, Internet site http://sda.berkeley.edu/cgi-bin/hsda?harcsda+gss12; calculations by New Strategist

Table 1.33 Should Marijuana Be Made Legal, 2012

"Do you think the use of marijuana should be made legal or not?"

(percent of people aged 18 or older responding by generation, 2012)

	legal	not legal
Total people	**46.9%**	**53.1%**
Millennial (18 to 35)	55.3	44.7
Generation X (36 to 47)	41.7	58.3
Baby Boom (48 to 66)	49.0	51.0
Older Americans (67 or older)	33.0	67.0

Source: Survey Documentation and Analysis, Computer-assisted Survey Methods Program, University of California, Berkeley, General Social Survey, 1972–2012 Cumulative Data Files, Internet site http://sda.berkeley.edu/cgi-bin/hsda?harcsda+gss12; calculations by New Strategist

CHAPTER

2

Education

■ The Millennial generation is better educated than any other. Nearly two-thirds of Millennials aged 25 or older have college experience and more than one-third has a bachelor's degree.

■ Among Millennials, women are much better educated than men. Thirty-nine percent of women aged 30 to 34 have a bachelor's degree compared with a smaller 32 percent of their male counterparts.

■ Among Millennials aged 25 or older, Asian women have the highest level of education and Hispanic men the lowest. Sixty-four percent of Asian women and only 13 percent of Hispanic men in the generation have a bachelor's degree.

■ The cost of college is driving down the enrollment rate. Sixty-six percent of 2012 high school graduates were enrolled in college by October, down from 70 percent in 2009.

■ Although Millennials account for the great majority of the nation's 20 million college students, only 27 percent of Millennials are enrolled in school.

Millennials Are the Best-Educated Generation

Generation X is close behind.

Among Millennials aged 25 to 36, more than one in three (34.9 percent) have a bachelor's degree. Millennials spanned the ages of 19 to 36 in 2013, but educational attainment traditionally is measured for those aged 25 or older because most have completed college by then. Gen Xers are not far behind Millennials in educational attainment, with 34.6 percent having a bachelor's degree.

Boomers were once the best-educated generation, but younger adults have surpassed them as the Great Recession kept them in school or drove them back into the classroom. Thirty-one percent of Boomers have a bachelor's degree. Among Americans aged 68 or older, only 24 percent are college graduates.

■ Among Millennials, women are better educated than men. This should boost women's earnings relative to men's in the years ahead.

Millennials are better educated than any other generation

(percent of people aged 25 or older with a bachelor's degree by generation, 2013)

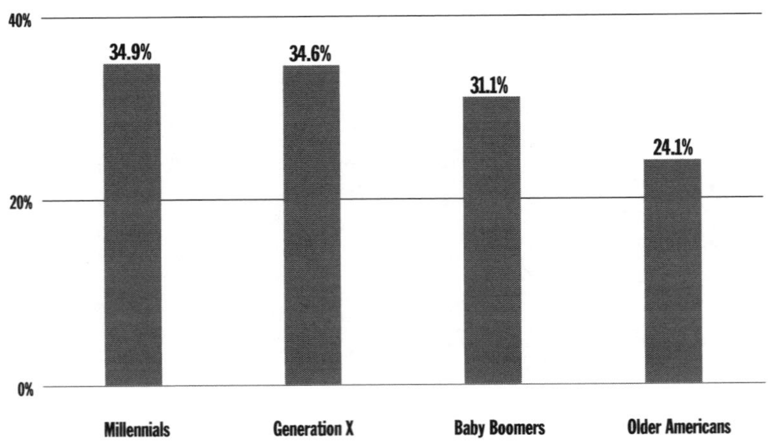

Table 2.1 Educational Attainment by Generation, 2013

(number and percent distribution of people aged 25 or older by highest level of education, by generation, 2013; numbers in thousands)

	total aged 25 or older	Millennials (aged 25 to 36)	Generation X (aged 37 to 48)	Boomers (aged 49 to 67)	Older Americans (aged 68 or older)
Total people	**206,899**	**49,485**	**49,038**	**73,751**	**34,624**
Not a high school graduate	24,517	5,279	5,108	7,680	6,450
High school graduate	61,704	12,902	13,453	22,997	12,350
Some college, no degree	34,805	9,010	8,146	12,516	5,133
Associate's degree	20,367	5,045	5,369	7,603	2,352
Bachelor's degree	41,575	12,084	10,832	13,880	4,778
Master's degree	17,395	3,929	4,558	6,472	2,435
Professional degree	3,066	611	766	1,220	470
Doctoral degree	3,470	627	803	1,384	656
High school graduate or more	182,382	44,208	43,927	66,072	28,173
Some college or more	120,678	31,306	30,474	43,075	15,823
Associate's degree or more	85,873	22,296	22,328	30,559	10,690
Bachelor's degree or more	65,506	17,251	16,959	22,956	8,338
PERCENT DISTRIBUTION					
Total people	**100.0%**	**100.0%**	**100.0%**	**100.0%**	**100.0%**
Not a high school graduate	11.8	10.7	10.4	10.4	18.6
High school graduate	29.8	26.1	27.4	31.2	35.7
Some college, no degree	16.8	18.2	16.6	17.0	14.8
Associate's degree	9.8	10.2	10.9	10.3	6.8
Bachelor's degree	20.1	24.4	22.1	18.8	13.8
Master's degree	8.4	7.9	9.3	8.8	7.0
Professional degree	1.5	1.2	1.6	1.7	1.4
Doctoral degree	1.7	1.3	1.6	1.9	1.9
High school graduate or more	88.2	89.3	89.6	89.6	81.4
Some college or more	58.3	63.3	62.1	58.4	45.7
Associate's degree or more	41.5	45.1	45.5	41.4	30.9
Bachelor's degree or more	31.7	34.9	34.6	31.1	24.1

Source: Bureau of the Census, Educational Attainment in the United States: 2013, detailed tables, Internet site http://www.census.gov/hhes/socdemo/education/data/cps/2013/tables.html; calculations by New Strategist

Among Millennials, Women Are Better Educated than Men

The best-educated Americans are women in their thirties.

Many Millennials are the children of the Baby-Boom generation, which was the first to make going to college the norm. Consequently, Millennials were encouraged by their Boomer parents to go to college. Overall, the 63 percent majority of Millennials aged 25 to 36 have at least some college education—18 percent have college experience but no degree, 10 percent have an associate's degree, 24 percent have a bachelor's degree, and 10 percent have a graduate degree.

Millennial women are more likely to have a college degree than any other segment of the United States population. Among women aged 30 to 34, nearly 39 percent have a bachelor's degree and more than half (51 percent) have at least an associate's degree. Among their male counterparts, 32 percent have a bachelor's degree and 42 percent have at least an associate's degree.

■ Many Millennials took out student loans to pay for college, a debt burden that is hampering their ability to buy cars, houses, or live independently.

More than 60 percent of Millennials have college experience

(percent distribution of people aged 25 to 36 by educational attainment, 2013)

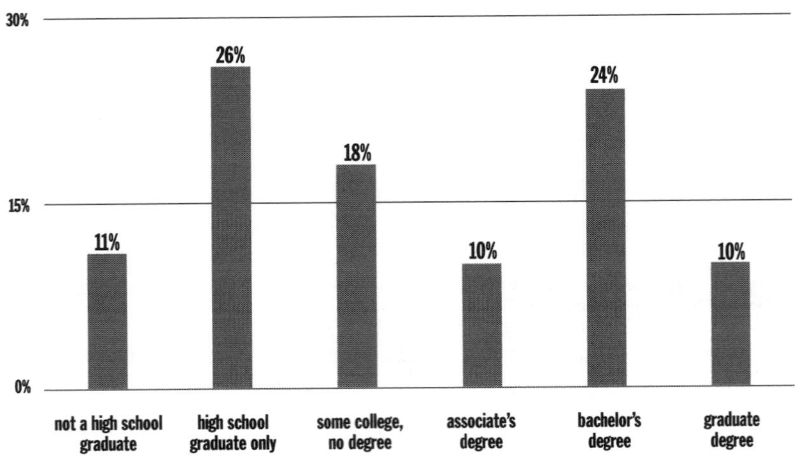

Table 2.2 Educational Attainment of Millennials, 2013

(number and percent distribution of people aged 25 or older, aged 25 to 36, and in five-year age groups that include Millennials, by educational attainment, 2013; numbers in thousands)

	total aged 25 or older	Millennials (aged 25 to 36)	25 to 29	30 to 34	35 to 39
Total people	**206,899**	**49,485**	**21,138**	**20,659**	**19,221**
Not a high school graduate	24,517	5,279	2,141	2,271	2,168
High school graduate	61,704	12,902	5,667	5,284	4,877
Some college, no degree	34,805	9,010	4,198	3,521	3,228
Associate's degree	20,367	5,045	2,033	2,203	2,022
Bachelor's degree	41,575	12,084	5,533	4,820	4,327
Master's degree	17,395	3,929	1,197	1,960	1,931
Professional degree	3,066	611	173	301	342
Doctoral degree	3,470	627	199	298	325
High school graduate or more	182,382	44,208	19,000	18,387	17,052
Some college or more	120,678	31,306	13,333	13,103	12,175
Associate's degree or more	85,873	22,296	9,135	9,582	8,947
Bachelor's degree or more	65,506	17,251	7,102	7,379	6,925
PERCENT DISTRIBUTION					
Total people	**100.0%**	**100.0%**	**100.0%**	**100.0%**	**100.0%**
Not a high school graduate	11.8	10.7	10.1	11.0	11.3
High school graduate	29.8	26.1	26.8	25.6	25.4
Some college, no degree	16.8	18.2	19.9	17.0	16.8
Associate's degree	9.8	10.2	9.6	10.7	10.5
Bachelor's degree	20.1	24.4	26.2	23.3	22.5
Master's degree	8.4	7.9	5.7	9.5	10.0
Professional degree	1.5	1.2	0.8	1.5	1.8
Doctoral degree	1.7	1.3	0.9	1.4	1.7
High school graduate or more	88.2	89.3	89.9	89.0	88.7
Some college or more	58.3	63.3	63.1	63.4	63.3
Associate's degree or more	41.5	45.1	43.2	46.4	46.5
Bachelor's degree or more	31.7	34.9	33.6	35.7	36.0

Source: Bureau of the Census, Educational Attainment in the United States: 2013, detailed tables, Internet site http://www.census .gov/hhes/socdemo/education/data/cps/2013/tables.html; calculations by New Strategist

Table 2.3 Educational Attainment of Millennial Men, 2013

(number and percent distribution of men aged 25 or older, aged 25 to 36, and in five-year age groups that include Millennials, by educational attainment, 2013; numbers in thousands)

	total aged 25 or older	Millennial men (aged 25 to 36)	25 to 29	30 to 34	35 to 39
Total men	**99,305**	**24,601**	**10,628**	**10,189**	**9,461**
Not a high school graduate	12,277	2,959	1,244	1,245	1,174
High school graduate	30,014	7,136	3,183	2,875	2,696
Some college, no degree	16,508	4,529	2,104	1,780	1,613
Associate's degree	8,773	2,199	890	975	836
Bachelor's degree	19,860	5,643	2,604	2,255	1,959
Master's degree	7,804	1,490	421	734	837
Professional degree	1,876	335	93	168	184
Doctoral degree	2,192	309	90	154	163
High school graduate or more	87,027	21,641	9,385	8,941	8,288
Some college or more	57,013	14,505	6,202	6,066	5,592
Associate's degree or more	40,505	9,976	4,098	4,286	3,979
Bachelor's degree or more	31,732	7,776	3,208	3,311	3,143
PERCENT DISTRIBUTION					
Total men	**100.0%**	**100.0%**	**100.0%**	**100.0%**	**100.0%**
Not a high school graduate	12.4	12.0	11.7	12.2	12.4
High school graduate	30.2	29.0	29.9	28.2	28.5
Some college, no degree	16.6	18.4	19.8	17.5	17.0
Associate's degree	8.8	8.9	8.4	9.6	8.8
Bachelor's degree	20.0	22.9	24.5	22.1	20.7
Master's degree	7.9	6.1	4.0	7.2	8.8
Professional degree	1.9	1.4	0.9	1.6	1.9
Doctoral degree	2.2	1.3	0.8	1.5	1.7
High school graduate or more	87.6	88.0	88.3	87.8	87.6
Some college or more	57.4	59.0	58.4	59.5	59.1
Associate's degree or more	40.8	40.5	38.6	42.1	42.1
Bachelor's degree or more	32.0	31.6	30.2	32.5	33.2

Source: Bureau of the Census, Educational Attainment in the United States: 2013, detailed tables, Internet site http://www.census.gov/hhes/socdemo/education/data/cps/2013/tables.html; calculations by New Strategist

Table 2.4 Educational Attainment of Millennial Women, 2013

(number and percent distribution of women aged 25 or older, aged 25 to 36, and in five-year age groups that include Millennials, by educational attainment, 2013; numbers in thousands)

	total aged 25 or older	Millennial women (aged 25 to 36)	25 to 29	30 to 34	35 to 39
Total women	**107,594**	**24,884**	**10,510**	**10,470**	**9,759**
Not a high school graduate	12,241	2,318	894	1,026	994
High school graduate	31,690	5,764	2484	2,408	2,181
Some college, no degree	18,298	4,480	2094	1,740	1,615
Associate's degree	11,592	2,844	1,143	1,227	1,186
Bachelor's degree	21,715	6,441	2929	2565	2,368
Master's degree	9,591	2,440	776	1226	1,094
Professional degree	1,191	276	80	132	159
Doctoral degree	1,278	319	109	145	162
High school graduate or more	95,355	22,564	9,615	9,443	8,765
Some college or more	63,665	16,800	7,131	7,035	6,584
Associate's degree or more	45,367	12,320	5,037	5,295	4,969
Bachelor's degree or more	33,775	9,475	3,894	4,068	3,783
PERCENT DISTRIBUTION					
Total women	**100.0%**	**100.0%**	**100.0%**	**100.0%**	**100.0%**
Not a high school graduate	11.4	9.3	8.5	9.8	10.2
High school graduate	29.5	23.2	23.6	23.0	22.3
Some college, no degree	17.0	18.0	19.9	16.6	16.5
Associate's degree	10.8	11.4	10.9	11.7	12.2
Bachelor's degree	20.2	25.9	27.9	24.5	24.3
Master's degree	8.9	9.8	7.4	11.7	11.2
Professional degree	1.1	1.1	0.8	1.3	1.6
Doctoral degree	1.2	1.3	1.0	1.4	1.7
High school graduate or more	88.6	90.7	91.5	90.2	89.8
Some college or more	59.2	67.5	67.8	67.2	67.5
Associate's degree or more	42.2	49.5	47.9	50.6	50.9
Bachelor's degree or more	31.4	38.1	37.1	38.9	38.8

Source: Bureau of the Census, Educational Attainment in the United States: 2013, detailed tables, Internet site http://www.census.gov/hhes/socdemo/education/data/cps/2013/tables.html; calculations by New Strategist

Asians Are the Best-Educated Millennials

Hispanics are the least educated.

Among Millennials aged 25 to 36, Asians have the highest level of education. Eighty-two percent of Asians in the age group have college experience and nearly 62 percent have a bachelor's degree.

Among Hispanics aged 25 to 36, only 38 percent have any college experience and just 15 percent have a bachelor's degree. Many Hispanics are immigrants who arrived in the United States with little formal schooling.

■ The gaps in educational attainment among Millennials by race and Hispanic origin will lead to a lifetime of occupational and earnings differences.

Asians are far better educated than others

(percent of people aged 25 to 36 with college experience, by sex, race, and Hispanic origin, 2013)

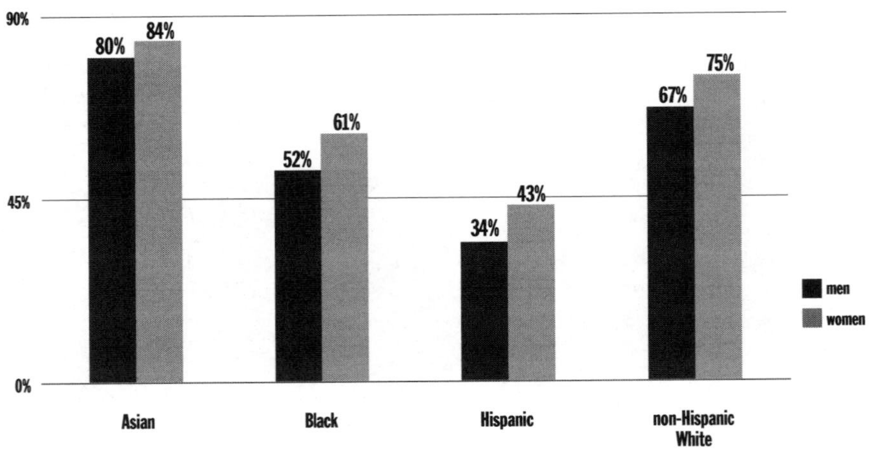

Table 2.5 Educational Attainment of Millennials by Race and Hispanic Origin, 2013

(number and percent distribution of people aged 25 to 36 by educational attainment, race, and Hispanic origin, 2013; numbers in thousands)

	total	Asian	Black	Hispanic	non-Hispanic White
Millennials (25 to 36)	**49,485**	**3,592**	**7,066**	**10,188**	**28,611**
Not a high school graduate	5,279	164	804	2,935	1,505
High school graduate	12,902	497	2,243	3,343	6,765
Some college, no degree	9,010	437	1,674	1,590	5,268
Associate's degree	5,045	271	712	748	3,307
Bachelor's degree	12,084	1,283	1,195	1,207	8,351
Master's degree	3,929	658	359	283	2,623
Professional degree	611	141	43	37	393
Doctoral degree	627	143	38	45	399
High school graduate or more	44,208	3,429	6,265	7,253	27,106
Some college or more	31,306	2,932	4,022	3,910	20,342
Associate's degree or more	22,296	2,495	2,348	2,320	15,073
Bachelor's degree or more	17,251	2,225	1,636	1,572	11,766
PERCENT DISTRIBUTION					
Millennials (25 to 36)	**100.0%**	**100.0%**	**100.0%**	**100.0%**	**100.0%**
Not a high school graduate	10.7	4.6	11.4	28.8	5.3
High school graduate	26.1	13.8	31.7	32.8	23.6
Some college, no degree	18.2	12.2	23.7	15.6	18.4
Associate's degree	10.2	7.5	10.1	7.3	11.6
Bachelor's degree	24.4	35.7	16.9	11.8	29.2
Master's degree	7.9	18.3	5.1	2.8	9.2
Professional degree	1.2	3.9	0.6	0.4	1.4
Doctoral degree	1.3	4.0	0.5	0.4	1.4
High school graduate or more	89.3	95.5	88.7	71.2	94.7
Some college or more	63.3	81.6	56.9	38.4	71.1
Associate's degree or more	45.1	69.5	33.2	22.8	52.7
Bachelor's degree or more	34.9	61.9	23.2	15.4	41.1

Note: Asians and Blacks are those who identify themselves as being of the race alone and those who identify themselves as being of the race in combination with other races. Non-Hispanic Whites are those who identify themselves as being White alone and not Hispanic. Numbers do not add to total because not all races are shown and Hispanics may be of any race.
Source: Bureau of the Census, Educational Attainment in the United States: 2013, detailed tables, Internet site http://www.census.gov/hhes/socdemo/education/data/cps/2013/tables.html; calculations by New Strategist

Table 2.6 Educational Attainment of Millennial Men by Race and Hispanic Origin, 2013

(number and percent distribution of men aged 25 to 36 by educational attainment, race, and Hispanic origin, 2013; numbers in thousands)

	total	Asian	Black	Hispanic	non-Hispanic White
Millennial men (25 to 36)	**24,601**	**1,724**	**3,242**	**5,304**	**14,328**
Not a high school graduate	2,959	87	436	1,671	848
High school graduate	7,136	267	1,133	1,837	3,869
Some college, no degree	4,529	217	757	780	2,770
Associate's degree	2,199	126	268	330	1,462
Bachelor's degree	5,643	552	504	539	4,020
Master's degree	1,490	320	116	107	945
Professional degree	335	77	12	18	230
Doctoral degree	309	79	18	24	190
High school graduate or more	21,641	1,638	2,807	3,633	13,485
Some college or more	14,505	1,372	1,674	1,797	9,616
Associate's degree or more	9,976	1,154	917	1,017	6,846
Bachelor's degree or more	7,776	1,028	650	687	5,384
PERCENT DISTRIBUTION					
Millennial men (25 to 36)	**100.0%**	**100.0%**	**100.0%**	**100.0%**	**100.0%**
Not a high school graduate	12.0	5.1	13.5	31.5	5.9
High school graduate	29.0	15.5	34.9	34.6	27.0
Some college, no degree	18.4	12.6	23.4	14.7	19.3
Associate's degree	8.9	7.3	8.3	6.2	10.2
Bachelor's degree	22.9	32.0	15.5	10.2	28.1
Master's degree	6.1	18.6	3.6	2.0	6.6
Professional degree	1.4	4.5	0.4	0.3	1.6
Doctoral degree	1.3	4.6	0.5	0.4	1.3
High school graduate or more	88.0	95.0	86.6	68.5	94.1
Some college or more	59.0	79.6	51.6	33.9	67.1
Associate's degree or more	40.5	67.0	28.3	19.2	47.8
Bachelor's degree or more	31.6	59.6	20.0	13.0	37.6

Note: Asians and Blacks are those who identify themselves as being of the race alone and those who identify themselves as being of the race in combination with other races. Non-Hispanic Whites are those who identify themselves as being White alone and not Hispanic. Numbers do not add to total because not all races are shown and Hispanics may be of any race.
Source: Bureau of the Census, Educational Attainment in the United States: 2013, detailed tables, Internet site http://www.census.gov/hhes/socdemo/education/data/cps/2013/tables.html; calculations by New Strategist

Table 2.7 Educational Attainment of Millennial Women by Race and Hispanic Origin, 2013

(number and percent distribution of women aged 25 to 36 by educational attainment, race, and Hispanic origin, 2013; numbers in thousands)

	total	Asian	Black	Hispanic	non-Hispanic White
Millennial women (25 to 36)	**24,884**	**1,869**	**3,823**	**4,883**	**14,283**
Not a high school graduate	2,318	75	366	1,261	660
High school graduate	5,764	231	1,109	1,507	2,895
Some college, no degree	4,480	219	918	810	2,500
Associate's degree	2,844	144	445	419	1,846
Bachelor's degree	6,441	731	691	668	4,331
Master's degree	2,440	340	244	177	1,678
Professional degree	276	63	31	19	163
Doctoral degree	319	64	21	22	209
High school graduate or more	22,564	1,792	3,459	3,621	13,624
Some college or more	16,800	1,560	2,349	2,115	10,728
Associate's degree or more	12,320	1,341	1,431	1,305	8,228
Bachelor's degree or more	9,475	1,198	986	885	6,382
PERCENT DISTRIBUTION					
Millennial women (25 to 36)	**100.0%**	**100.0%**	**100.0%**	**100.0%**	**100.0%**
Not a high school graduate	9.3	4.0	9.6	25.8	4.6
High school graduate	23.2	12.4	29.0	30.9	20.3
Some college, no degree	18.0	11.7	24.0	16.6	17.5
Associate's degree	11.4	7.7	11.6	8.6	12.9
Bachelor's degree	25.9	39.1	18.1	13.7	30.3
Master's degree	9.8	18.2	6.4	3.6	11.7
Professional degree	1.1	3.4	0.8	0.4	1.1
Doctoral degree	1.3	3.4	0.5	0.4	1.5
High school graduate or more	90.7	95.9	90.5	74.2	95.4
Some college or more	67.5	83.5	61.5	43.3	75.1
Associate's degree or more	49.5	71.8	37.4	26.7	57.6
Bachelor's degree or more	38.1	64.1	25.8	18.1	44.7

Note: Asians and Blacks are those who identify themselves as being of the race alone and those who identify themselves as being of the race in combination with other races. Non-Hispanic Whites are those who identify themselves as being White alone and not Hispanic. Numbers do not add to total because not all races are shown and Hispanics may be of any race.
Source: Bureau of the Census, Educational Attainment in the United States: 2013, detailed tables, Internet site http://www.census.gov/hhes/socdemo/education/data/cps/2013/tables.html; calculations by New Strategist

Many Millennials Are Students

More than one in four Millennials is still in school.

Among the nation's 71 million 18-to-34-year-olds (Millennials were aged 18 to 35 in 2012), a substantial 19 million were in school—27 percent of the age group. Most Millennials aged 18 to 21 are students, the proportion falling below 50 percent among 22-year-olds. Among Millennial students, women outnumber men at most ages.

Not surprisingly, most Millennial students are in college. Among 18-year-olds enrolled in school, 46 percent are in high school, 49 percent are in their first year of college, and 5 percent are in their second or higher year of college. Among students aged 30 to 34, 64 percent are undergraduates and 35 percent are in graduate school.

■ As the economy improves, the college enrollment rate has dropped among the youngest Millennials.

The school enrollment rate drops sharply among people in their early twenties

(percent of people aged 18 to 24 enrolled in school, by age, 2012)

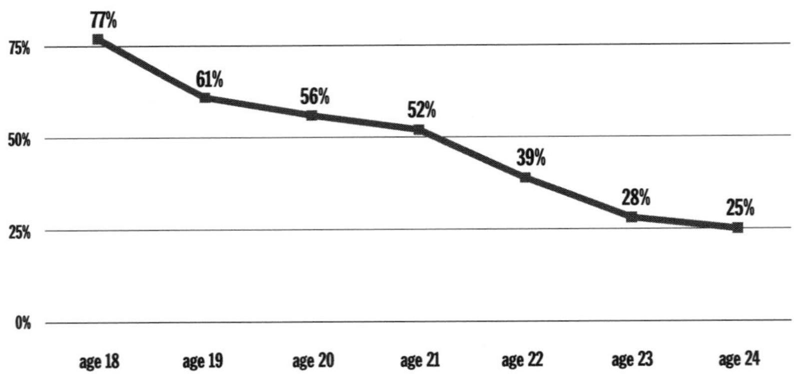

Table 2.8 School Enrollment Status by Age, 2012

(total number of people aged 18 or older and number and percent by school enrollment status, by age, 2012; numbers in thousands)

		enrolled in school		not enrolled in school	
	total	number	percent	number	percent
Total people	**235,561**	**22,106**	**9.4%**	**213,455**	**90.6%**
Aged 18 to 34	71,488	19,069	26.7	52,419	73.3
Aged 18	4,256	3,277	77.0	979	23.0
Aged 19	4,228	2,578	61.0	1,650	39.0
Aged 20	4,356	2,446	56.2	1,910	43.8
Aged 21	4,514	2,343	51.9	2,171	48.1
Aged 22	4,297	1,662	38.7	2,635	61.3
Aged 23	4,390	1,243	28.3	3,147	71.7
Aged 24	4,336	1,100	25.4	3,236	74.6
Aged 25 to 29	20,674	2,888	14.0	17,786	86.0
Aged 30 to 34	20,437	1,532	7.5	18,905	92.5
Aged 35 to 39	19,046	936	4.9	18,110	95.1
Aged 40 to 44	20,583	706	3.4	19,877	96.6
Aged 45 to 49	21,223	591	2.8	20,632	97.2
Aged 50 to 54	22,336	416	1.9	21,920	98.1
Aged 55 to 59	20,703	235	1.1	20,468	98.9
Aged 60 to 64	17,805	74	0.4	17,731	99.6
Aged 65 or older	42,377	79	0.2	42,298	99.8

Source: Bureau of the Census, School Enrollment—CPS October 2012 Detailed Tables, Internet site http://www.census.gov/hhes/school/data/cps/2012/tables.html; calculations by New Strategist

Table 2.9 School Enrollment by Age and Sex, 2012

(total number of people aged 18 or older enrolled in school, number enrolled by sex, and female share of total, by age, 2012; numbers in thousands)

			women	
	total	men	number	share of total
Total enrolled	**22,106**	**9,775**	**12,332**	**55.8%**
Aged 18 to 34	19,069	8,732	10,337	54.2
Aged 18	3,277	1,650	1,627	49.6
Aged 19	2,578	1,186	1,392	54.0
Aged 20	2,446	1,071	1,375	56.2
Aged 21	2,343	1,083	1,261	53.8
Aged 22	1,662	769	892	53.7
Aged 23	1,243	652	591	47.5
Aged 24	1,100	518	582	52.9
Aged 25 to 29	2,888	1,222	1,666	57.7
Aged 30 to 34	1,532	581	951	62.1
Aged 35 to 39	936	326	610	65.2
Aged 40 to 44	706	254	452	64.0
Aged 45 to 49	591	184	407	68.9
Aged 50 to 54	416	156	261	62.7
Aged 55 to 59	235	71	164	69.8
Aged 60 to 64	74	24	50	67.6
Aged 65 or older	79	28	51	64.6

Source: Bureau of the Census, School Enrollment—CPS October 2012 Detailed Tables, Internet site http://www.census.gov/hhes/school/data/cps/2012/tables.html; calculations by New Strategist

Table 2.10 Grade or College Level of Enrollment by Age, 2012

(number and percent distribution of students aged 18 to 34 by grade or college level of enrollment, by age, 2012; numbers in thousands)

	total enrolled	12th grade or less	undergraduate college					graduate school
			total	first year	second year	third year	fourth year	
Total aged 18 to 34	**19,069**	**2,280**	**14,231**	**4,150**	**4,299**	**3,283**	**2,499**	**2,559**
Aged 18	3,277	1,504	1,767	1,619	124	24	0	6
Aged 19	2,578	336	2,235	850	1,131	236	18	7
Aged 20	2,446	140	2,299	452	859	890	98	7
Aged 21	2,343	87	2,121	201	493	656	771	136
Aged 22	1,662	33	1,407	134	339	403	531	223
Aged 23	1,243	40	918	120	271	236	291	285
Aged 24	1,100	53	701	124	206	158	213	346
Aged 25 to 29	2,888	71	1,801	384	598	434	385	1,015
Aged 30 to 34	1,532	16	982	266	278	246	192	534
PERCENT DISTRIBUTION OF STUDENTS BY GRADE OR COLLEGE LEVEL								
Total aged 18 to 34	**100.0%**	**12.0%**	**74.6%**	**21.8%**	**22.5%**	**17.2%**	**13.1%**	**13.4%**
Aged 18	100.0	45.9	53.9	49.4	3.8	0.7	0.0	0.2
Aged 19	100.0	13.0	86.7	33.0	43.9	9.2	0.7	0.3
Aged 20	100.0	5.7	94.0	18.5	35.1	36.4	4.0	0.3
Aged 21	100.0	3.7	90.5	8.6	21.0	28.0	32.9	5.8
Aged 22	100.0	2.0	84.7	8.1	20.4	24.2	31.9	13.4
Aged 23	100.0	3.2	73.9	9.7	21.8	19.0	23.4	22.9
Aged 24	100.0	4.8	63.7	11.3	18.7	14.4	19.4	31.5
Aged 25 to 29	100.0	2.5	62.4	13.3	20.7	15.0	13.3	35.1
Aged 30 to 34	100.0	1.0	64.1	17.4	18.1	16.1	12.5	34.9

Source: Bureau of the Census, School Enrollment—CPS October 2012 Detailed Tables, Internet site http://www.census.gov/hhes/school/data/cps/2012/tables.html; calculations by New Strategist

Fewer Students Are Dropping Out of High School

The dropout rate remains in the double digits among Hispanics, however.

Among people aged 16 to 24, only 6.6 percent were neither high school graduates nor currently enrolled in school in 2012, down from 10.9 percent in 2000. Since 2000, dropout rates have fallen for both men and women and for every racial and ethnic group.

Dropout rates remain high for Hispanics, however. While just 4.3 percent of non-Hispanic Whites and 7.5 percent of Blacks aged 16 to 24 have dropped out of high school, a much larger 12.7 percent of Hispanics are high school dropouts. Among Hispanic men, the dropout rate was 13.9 percent in 2012, down considerably from the 31.8 percent in 2000 but still relatively high. Among Hispanic women aged 16 to 24, 11.3 percent were high school dropouts in 2012, down from 23.5 percent in 2000.

■ Many Hispanic Millennials did not drop out of an American high school, but came to the United States without a high school diploma.

Non-Hispanic Whites have the lowest dropout rate

(percent of people aged 16 to 24 who were neither enrolled in school nor high school graduates, by race and Hispanic origin, 2012)

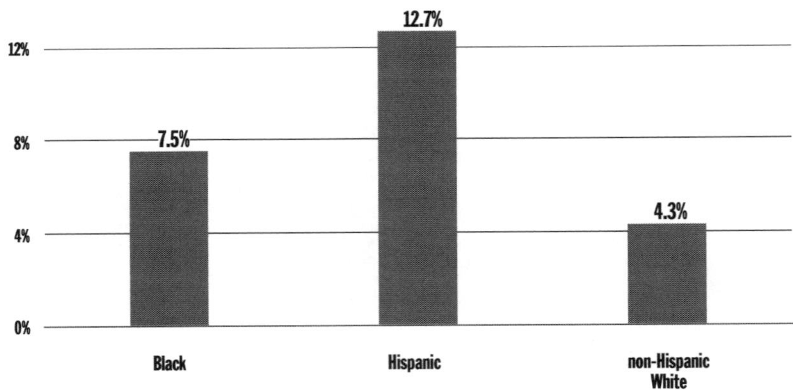

Table 2.11 High School Dropouts by Sex, Race, and Hispanic Origin, 2000 and 2012

(percentage of people aged 16 to 24 who were not enrolled in school and were not high school graduates by sex, race, and Hispanic origin, 2000 and 2012; percentage point change, 2000–12)

	2012	2000	percentage point change
Total people	**6.6%**	**10.9%**	**–4.3**
Black	7.5	13.1	–5.6
Hispanic	12.7	27.8	–15.1
Non-Hispanic White	4.3	6.9	–2.6
Total men	**7.3**	**12.0**	**–4.7**
Black	8.1	15.3	–7.2
Hispanic	13.9	31.8	–17.9
Non-Hispanic White	4.8	7.0	–2.2
Total women	**5.9**	**9.9**	**–4.0**
Black	7.0	11.1	–4.1
Hispanic	11.3	23.5	–12.2
Non-Hispanic White	3.8	6.9	–3.1

Note: Blacks are those who identify themselves as being of the race alone.
Source: National Center for Education Statistics, Digest of Education Statistics 2013, Internet site http://nces.ed.gov/programs/digest/2013menu_tables.asp; calculations by New Strategist

SAT Scores Vary by Income and Parent's Education

The more educated the parent, the higher the child's score.

SAT scores vary not only by sex, race, and Hispanic origin, but also by family income and parental education. Students with family incomes below $20,000 scored 461 on the math portion of the SAT in 2011–12, for example, compared with a score of 589 among students with family incomes of $200,000 or more. Reading scores ranged from a low of 433 among the lowest-income students to 567 for those with the highest incomes.

Parental education also has a big impact on test scores. Among students with a parent who did not graduate from high school, the average SAT math score was 450. Among those whose parent had a graduate degree, the average math score was 577. Reading scores ranged from a low of 420 for students with the least-educated parents to 560 for those with the best-educated parents.

■ Affluent, educated parents can afford SAT prep courses for their children, which can boost test scores.

A parent's education influences a child's test score

(average SAT mathematics score by highest level of parental education, 2011–12)

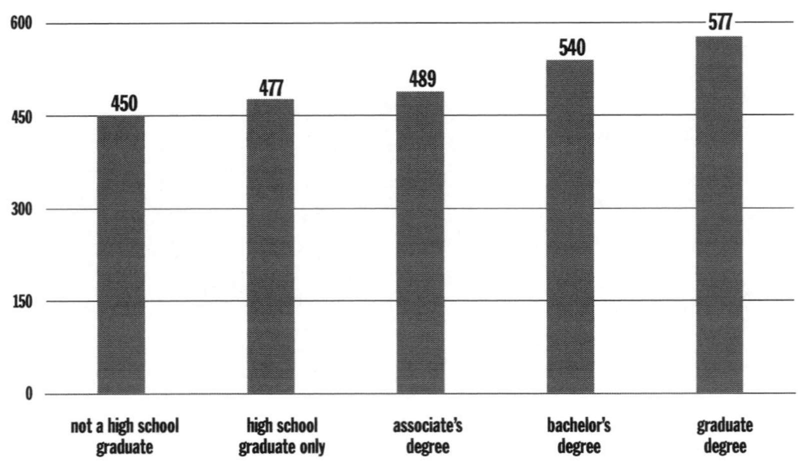

Table 2.12 SAT Scores by Selected Characteristics, 2011–12

(SAT scores of college-bound seniors by selected student and parent characteristics, 2011–12)

	critical reading	mathematics	writing
Total students	**496**	**514**	**488**
Sex			
Men	498	532	481
Women	493	499	494
Race and Hispanic origin			
American Indian or Alaska Native	482	489	462
Asian or Pacific Islander	518	595	528
Black	428	428	417
Mexican American	448	465	443
Puerto Rican	452	452	442
Other Hispanic	447	461	442
White	527	536	515
High school grade point average			
A+ (97 to 100)	593	620	593
A (93 to 96)	557	581	554
A– (90 to 92)	524	545	518
B (80 to 89)	466	478	455
C (70 to 79)	414	421	400
D or F (below 70)	411	429	399
Family income			
Less than $20,000	433	461	428
$20,000 to $39,999	463	481	453
$40,000 o $59,999	485	500	473
$60,000 to $79,999	499	512	486
$80,000 to $99,999	511	525	499
$100,000 to $119,999	523	539	512
$120,000 to $139,999	527	543	517
$140,000 to $159,999	534	551	525
$160,000 to $199,999	540	557	534
$200,000 or more	567	589	566
Highest level of parental education			
Not a high school graduate	420	450	418
High school graduate	463	477	452
Associate's degree	479	489	465
Bachelor's degree	522	540	513
Graduate degree	560	577	555

Source: National Center for Education Statistics, Digest of Education Statistics: 2012, Internet site http://nces.ed.gov/programs/digest/2012menu_tables.asp; calculations by New Strategist

College Enrollment Rates Are Below All-Time High

The cost of college may be taking a toll on enrollment rates.

The rate at which high school graduates enroll in college was lower in 2012 than in the peak year of 2009. Among men and women aged 16 to 24 who graduated from high school in 2012, two-thirds (66 percent) had enrolled in college (either a two-year or a four-year school) within 12 months. Among women, the rate was 71 percent in 2012, while among men it was a much lower 61 percent.

The college enrollment rate of Blacks was 13 percentage points lower in 2012 than in 2009. The enrollment rate of Asians fell 11 percentage points during those years, and the non-Hispanic White rate declined 6 percentage points. Among Hispanics, in contrast, the enrollment rate climbed 11 percentage points during those years.

Children from families with high incomes are much more likely than those from low- or middle-income families to attend college. In 2012, 81 percent of high school graduates from high-income families enrolled in college within 12 months compared with 65 percent from middle-income families and 51 percent from low-income families. Every income group had a lower enrollment rate in 2012 than in 2009.

■ Two-year schools saw their enrollment rate rise between 2009 and 2012, while four-year schools experienced a decline.

Enrollment rates are falling at four-year schools

(percent of people aged 16 to 24 who graduated from high school in the previous 12 months and were enrolled in college as of October, by sex and type of school, 2009 and 2012)

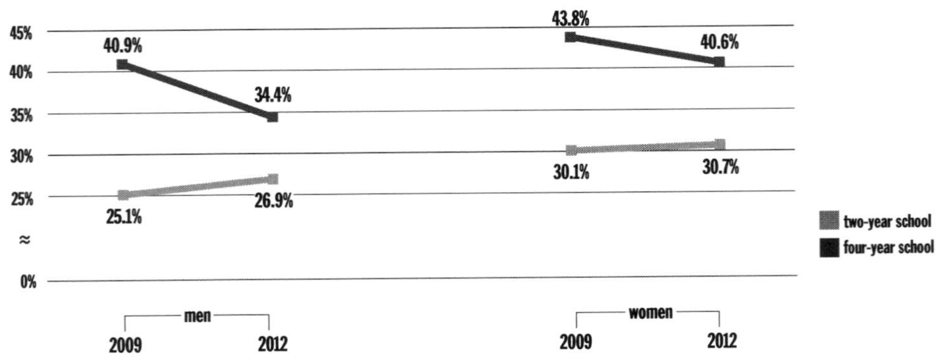

Table 2.13 College Enrollment Rate by Sex, 2000 to 2012

(percentage of people aged 16 to 24 who graduated from high school in the previous 12 months and were enrolled in college as of October, by sex, 2000 to 2012; percentage point change in enrollment rate for selected years)

	total	men	women
2012	66.2%	61.3%	71.3%
2011	68.2	64.7	72.2
2010	68.1	62.8	74.0
2009	70.1	66.0	73.8
2008	68.6	65.9	71.6
2007	67.2	66.1	68.3
2006	66.0	65.8	66.1
2005	68.6	66.5	70.4
2004	66.7	61.4	71.5
2003	63.9	61.2	66.5
2002	65.2	62.1	68.3
2001	61.7	59.7	63.6
2000	63.3	59.9	66.2
PERCENTAGE POINT CHANGE			
2009 to 2012	–3.9	–4.7	–2.5
2000 to 2009	6.8	6.1	7.6

Source: National Center for Education Statistics, Digest of Education Statistics 2013, Internet site http://nces.ed.gov/programs/digest/2013menu_tables.asp; calculations by New Strategist

Table 2.14 College Enrollment Rate by Race and Hispanic Origin, 2000 to 2012

(percentage of people aged 16 to 24 who graduated from high school in the previous 12 months and were enrolled in college as of October, by race and Hispanic origin, 2000 to 2012; percentage point change in enrollment rate for selected years)

	total	Asian	Black	Hispanic	non-Hispanic White
2012	66.2%	81.5%	56.4%	70.3%	65.7%
2011	68.2	86.1	67.1	66.6	68.3
2010	68.1	84.7	62.0	59.7	70.5
2009	70.1	92.1	69.5	59.3	71.3
2008	68.6	88.4	55.7	63.9	71.7
2007	67.2	88.8	55.7	64.0	69.5
2006	66.0	82.3	55.5	57.9	68.5
2005	68.6	86.7	55.7	54.0	73.2
2004	66.7	75.6	62.5	61.8	68.8
2003	63.9	84.1	57.5	58.6	66.2
2002	65.2	–	59.4	53.6	69.1
2001	61.7	–	55.0	51.7	64.3
2000	63.3	–	54.9	52.9	65.7
PERCENTAGE POINT CHANGE					
2009 to 2012	–3.9	–10.6	–13.1	11.0	–5.6
2000 to 2009	6.8	–	14.6	6.4	5.6

Note: "–" means data are not available.
Source: National Center for Education Statistics, Digest of Education Statistics 2013, Internet site http://nces.ed.gov/programs/digest/2013menu_tables.asp; calculations by New Strategist

Table 2.15 College Enrollment Rate by Family Income, 2000 to 2012

(percentage of people aged 16 to 24 who graduated from high school in the previous 12 months and were enrolled in college as of October, by family income level, 2000 to 2012; percentage point change in enrollment rate for selected years)

	total	family income level		
		low	middle	high
2012	66.2%	50.9%	64.7%	80.7%
2011	68.2	53.5	66.2	82.4
2010	68.1	50.7	66.7	82.2
2009	70.1	53.9	66.7	84.2
2008	68.6	55.9	65.2	81.9
2007	67.2	58.4	63.3	78.2
2006	66.0	50.9	61.4	80.7
2005	68.6	53.5	65.1	81.2
2004	66.7	47.8	63.3	80.1
2003	63.9	52.8	57.6	80.1
2002	65.2	56.3	60.9	78.2
2001	61.7	43.8	56.4	80.0
2000	63.3	49.7	59.5	76.9
PERCENTAGE POINT CHANGE				
2009 to 2012	–3.9	–3.0	–2.0	–3.5
2000 to 2009	6.8	4.2	7.2	7.3

Note: "Low" income refers to the bottom 20 percent of all family incomes, "high" income refers to the top 20 percent of all family incomes, and "middle" income refers to the 60 percent in between.
Source: National Center for Education Statistics, Digest of Education Statistics 2013, Internet site http://nces.ed.gov/programs/digest/2013menu_tables.asp; calculations by New Strategist

Table 2.16 College Enrollment Rate by Sex and Type of Institution, 2000 to 2012

(percentage of people aged 16 to 24 who graduated from high school in the previous 12 months and were enrolled in college as of October, by sex and type of institution, 2000 to 2012; percentage point change in enrollment rate for selected years)

	men			women		
	total	two-year	four-year	total	two-year	four-year
2012	61.3%	26.9%	34.4%	71.3%	30.7%	40.6%
2011	64.7	24.7	40.0	72.2	27.3	44.9
2010	62.8	28.5	34.3	74.0	24.6	49.5
2009	66.0	25.1	40.9	73.8	30.1	43.8
2008	65.9	24.9	41.0	71.6	30.6	40.9
2007	66.1	22.7	43.4	68.3	25.5	42.8
2006	65.8	24.9	40.9	66.1	24.5	41.7
2005	66.5	24.7	41.8	70.4	23.4	47.0
2004	61.4	21.8	39.6	71.5	23.1	48.5
2003	61.2	21.9	39.3	66.5	21.0	45.5
2002	62.1	20.5	41.7	68.3	23.0	45.3
2001	59.7	18.6	41.1	63.6	20.7	42.9
2000	59.9	23.1	36.8	66.2	20.0	46.2
PERCENTAGE POINT CHANGE						
2009 to 2012	–4.7	1.8	–6.5	–2.5	0.6	–3.2
2000 to 2009	6.1	2.0	4.1	7.6	10.1	–2.4

Source: National Center for Education Statistics, Digest of Education Statistics 2013, Internet site http://nces.ed.gov/programs/digest/2013menu_tables.asp; calculations by New Strategist

Most College Students Are Millennials

Women outnumber men on college campuses.

While older Millennials are well beyond traditional college age (Millennials spanned the ages of 18 to 35 in 2012), the generation accounts for the great majority of college students. In 2012, nearly 64 percent of the nation's 20 million college students were under age 25 and another 22 percent were aged 25 to 34. On college campuses, women outnumber men by a large margin.

Because the Millennial generation is so diverse, a large share of college students are Asian (8 percent), Black (17 percent), or Hispanic (17 percent). Non-Hispanic Whites account for only 58 percent of college students.

■ Among college students, just over half (52 percent) attend four-year schools. Another 29 percent are in two-year schools, and 19 percent are in graduate school.

Minorities are a large share of college students

(percent distribution of college students by race and Hispanic origin, 2012)

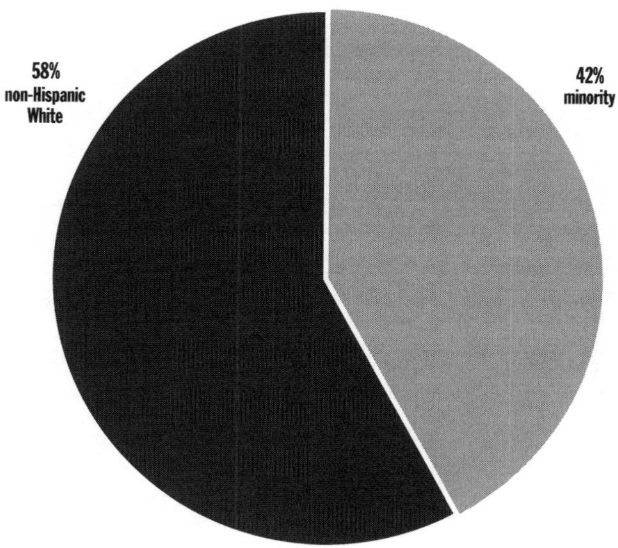

Table 2.17 College Students by Age and Sex, 2012

(number and percent distribution of people aged 15 or older enrolled in institutions of higher education, by age and sex, 2012; numbers in thousands)

	total	men	women
Total college students	**19,930**	**8,602**	**11,327**
Aged 15 to 19	4,284	1,933	2,351
Aged 20 to 21	4,562	2,049	2,513
Aged 22 to 24	3,879	1,878	2,001
Aged 25 to 29	2,817	1,194	1,623
Aged 30 to 34	1,516	576	940
Aged 35 or older	2,871	971	1,899
PERCENT DISTRIBUTION BY SEX			
Total college students	**100.0%**	**43.2%**	**56.8%**
Aged 15 to 19	100.0	45.1	54.9
Aged 20 to 21	100.0	44.9	55.1
Aged 22 to 24	100.0	48.4	51.6
Aged 25 to 29	100.0	42.4	57.6
Aged 30 to 34	100.0	38.0	62.0
Aged 35 or older	100.0	33.8	66.1
PERCENT DISTRIBUTION BY AGE			
Total college students	**100.0**	**100.0**	**100.0**
Aged 15 to 19	21.5	22.5	20.8
Aged 20 to 21	22.9	23.8	22.2
Aged 22 to 24	19.5	21.8	17.7
Aged 25 to 29	14.1	13.9	14.3
Aged 30 to 34	7.6	6.7	8.3
Aged 35 or older	14.4	11.3	16.8

Source: Bureau of the Census, School Enrollment, Historical Tables, Internet site http://www.census.gov/hhes/school/data/cps/historical/index.html; calculations by New Strategist

Table 2.18 College Students by Age, Race, and Hispanic Origin, 2012

(number and percent distribution of people aged 15 or older enrolled in institutions of higher education, by age, race, and Hispanic origin, 2012; numbers in thousands)

	total	Asian	Black	Hispanic	non-Hispanic White
Total college students	**19,930**	**1,617**	**3,335**	**3,400**	**11,650**
Aged 15 to 19	4,284	307	612	888	2,513
Aged 20 to 21	4,562	348	721	912	2,620
Aged 22 to 24	3,879	421	592	664	2,207
Aged 25 to 29	2,817	266	465	365	1,734
Aged 30 to 34	1,516	124	348	257	778
Aged 35 or older	2,871	151	598	313	1,799
PERCENT DISTRIBUTION BY RACE AND HISPANIC ORIGIN					
Total college students	**100.0%**	**8.1%**	**16.7%**	**17.1%**	**58.5%**
Aged 15 to 19	100.0	7.2	14.3	20.7	58.7
Aged 20 to 21	100.0	7.6	15.8	20.0	57.4
Aged 22 to 24	100.0	10.9	15.3	17.1	56.9
Aged 25 to 29	100.0	9.4	16.5	13.0	61.6
Aged 30 to 34	100.0	8.2	23.0	17.0	51.3
Aged 35 or older	100.0	5.3	20.8	10.9	62.7
PERCENT DISTRIBUTION BY AGE					
Total college students	**100.0**	**100.0**	**100.0**	**100.0**	**100.0**
Aged 15 to 19	21.5	19.0	18.4	26.1	21.6
Aged 20 to 21	22.9	21.5	21.6	26.8	22.5
Aged 22 to 24	19.5	26.0	17.8	19.5	18.9
Aged 25 to 29	14.1	16.5	13.9	10.7	14.9
Aged 30 to 34	7.6	7.7	10.4	7.6	6.7
Aged 35 or older	14.4	9.3	17.9	9.2	15.4

Note: Asians and Blacks are those who identify themselves as being of the race alone and those who identify themselves as being of the race in combination with other races. Non-Hispanic Whites are those who identify themselves as being White alone and not Hispanic.

Source: Bureau of the Census, School Enrollment, Historical Tables, Internet site http://www.census.gov/hhes/school/data/cps/historical/index.html; calculations by New Strategist

Table 2.19 College Students by Age and Type of School, 2012

(number and percent distribution of people aged 15 or older enrolled in institutions of higher education, by age and type of school, 2012; numbers in thousands)

	total	two-year college	four-year college	graduate school
Total college students	**19,930**	**5,830**	**10,340**	**3,760**
Aged 15 to 19	4,284	1,624	2,612	49
Aged 20 to 24	8,441	2,199	5,246	997
Aged 25 to 34	4,333	1,205	1,578	1,550
Aged 35 or older	2,872	802	904	1,165
PERCENT DISTRIBUTION BY TYPE OF SCHOOL				
Total college students	**100.0%**	**29.3%**	**51.9%**	**18.9%**
Aged 15 to 19	100.0	37.9	61.0	1.1
Aged 20 to 24	100.0	26.1	62.1	11.8
Aged 25 to 34	100.0	27.8	36.4	35.8
Aged 35 or older	100.0	27.9	31.5	40.6
PERCENT DISTRIBUTION BY AGE				
Total college students	**100.0**	**100.0**	**100.0**	**100.0**
Aged 15 to 19	21.5	27.9	25.3	1.3
Aged 20 to 24	42.4	37.7	50.7	26.5
Aged 25 to 34	21.7	20.7	15.3	41.2
Aged 35 or older	14.4	13.8	8.7	31.0

Source: Bureau of the Census, School Enrollment, CPS October 2012--Detailed Tables, Internet site http://www.census.gov/hhes/school/data/cps/2012/tables.html; calculations by New Strategist

Nearly Half of College Students Have Jobs

Among students at four-year schools, however, fewer than half are in the labor force.

Among the nation's 12.7 million college students under age 25, the 51 percent majority is in the labor force. Female college students are slightly more likely than their male counterparts to have a job—52 and 50 percent, respectively.

Among students enrolled in four-year colleges, most are not in the labor force. But a substantial 48 percent either have a job or are looking for one. Among two-year college students, 56 percent are in the labor force.

■ Not surprisingly, part-time students are much more likely than full-time students to be in the labor force (81 versus 46 percent).

Among college students, women are more likely than men to be in the labor force

(percent of college students under age 25 who are in the labor force, by sex, July 2012)

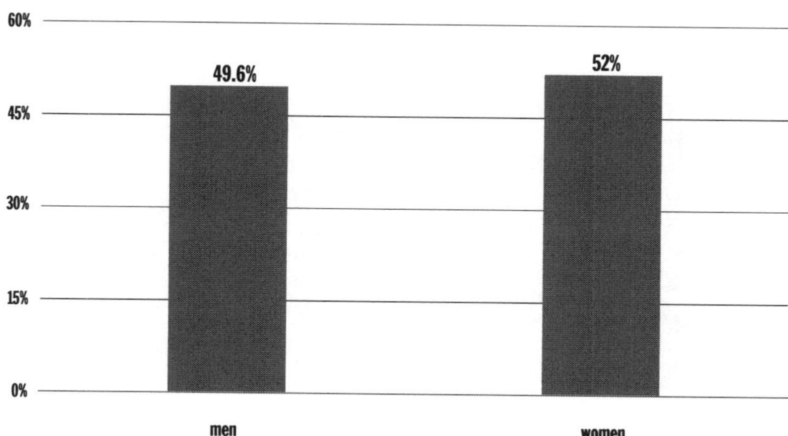

Table 2.20 Employment Status of College Students, 2012

(number and percent of college students under age 25 by selected characteristics and employment status, 2012; numbers in thousands)

		in labor force		not in labor force	
	total	number	percent	number	percent
Total under age 25 enrolled in college	**12,685**	**6,454**	**50.9%**	**6,231**	**49.1%**
Sex					
Men	5,842	2,897	49.6	2,945	50.4
Women	6,843	3,558	52.0	3,286	48.0
Type of college					
Enrolled in two-year college	3,956	2,234	56.5	1,722	43.5
Enrolled in four-year college	8,729	4,220	48.3	4,509	51.7
Enrollment status					
Full-time students	10,819	4,948	45.7	5,871	54.3
Part-time students	1,866	1,506	80.7	360	19.3

Source: Bureau of the Census, School Enrollment—CPS October 2012 Detailed Tables, Internet site http://www.census.gov/hhes/school/data/cps/2012/tables.html; calculations by New Strategist

Most Degrees Are Earned in a Few Fields

Business, social sciences, health, and education dominate the academic degrees awarded.

Nearly everyone earning a college degree these days is a member of the Millennial generation. Among the degrees Millennials earned in 2011–12, a few fields dominate.

At the associate's degree level, "liberal arts and sciences, general studies, and humanities" is the most popular field. One-third of associate's degrees awarded in 2011–12 were in this discipline. One in five associate's degrees was awarded in "health professions and related sciences," and 14 percent were in business.

At the bachelor's degree level, business was the preferred field in 2011–12, attracting 20 percent of graduates. The only other field in double digits was social sciences and history, in which 10 percent of all bachelor's degrees were awarded.

At the master's level, business was the field of choice for 25 percent, followed closely by education (24 percent). Together these two disciplines accounted for nearly half of all master's degrees awarded in 2011–12.

■ Women earned the majority of the associate's, bachelor's, master's, and doctoral degrees awarded in 2011–12. Among professional degrees, women earned 48 percent of medical degrees and 47 percent of law degrees.

One in five bachelor's degrees is in business

(percent of bachelor's degrees accounted for by the six most popular fields of study, 2011–12)

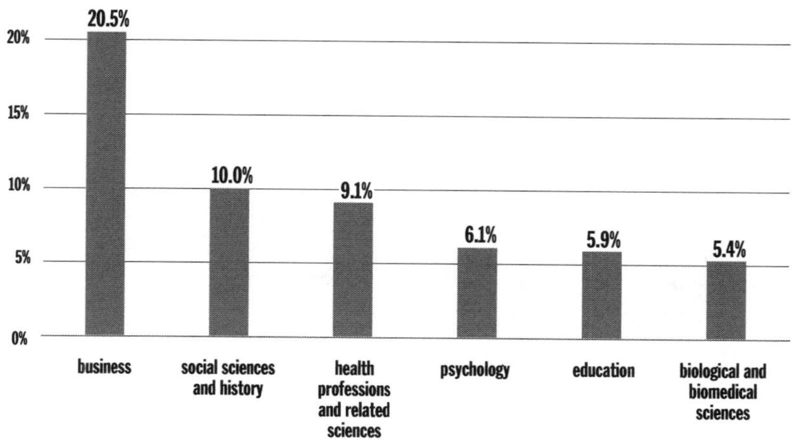

Table 2.21 Associate's Degrees Earned by Field of Study and Sex, 2011–12

(number and percent distribution of associate's degrees conferred by sex, and percent earned by women, by field of study, 2011–12)

	total		men		women		
	number	percent distribution	number	percent distribution	number	percent distribution	share of total
Total associate's degrees	**1,017,538**	**100.0%**	**391,990**	**100.0%**	**625,548**	**100.0%**	**61.5%**
Agriculture and natural resources	7,066	0.7	4,606	1.2	2,460	0.4	34.8
Architecture and related programs	593	0.1	332	0.1	261	0.0	44.0
Area, ethnic, cultural, and gender studies	194	0.0	62	0.0	132	0.0	68.0
Biological and biomedical sciences	3,834	0.4	1,280	0.3	2,554	0.4	66.6
Business	142,338	14.0	52,019	13.3	90,319	14.4	63.5
Communication, journalism, and related programs	3,495	0.3	1,625	0.4	1,870	0.3	53.5
Communications technologies	5,000	0.5	3,429	0.9	1,571	0.3	31.4
Computer and information sciences	41,161	4.0	32,290	8.2	8,871	1.4	21.6
Construction trades	5,752	0.6	5,483	1.4	269	0.0	4.7
Education	20,531	2.0	2,633	0.7	17,898	2.9	87.2
Engineering	3,382	0.3	2,931	0.7	451	0.1	13.3
Engineering technologies	36,510	3.6	32,224	8.2	4,286	0.7	11.7
English language and literature	2,137	0.2	708	0.2	1,429	0.2	66.9
Family and consumer sciences	9,503	0.9	369	0.1	9,134	1.5	96.1
Foreign languages and literatures	1,980	0.2	417	0.1	1,563	0.2	78.9
Health professions and related sciences	218,041	21.4	34,018	8.7	184,023	29.4	84.4
Homeland security, law enforcement, and firefighting	50,695	5.0	27,045	6.9	23,650	3.8	46.7
Legal professions and studies	12,182	1.2	1,679	0.4	10,503	1.7	86.2
Liberal arts and sciences, general studies, and humanities	336,554	33.1	129,179	33.0	207,375	33.2	61.6
Library science	159	0.0	19	0.0	140	0.0	88.1
Mathematics and statistics	1,529	0.2	1,050	0.3	479	0.1	31.3
Mechanic and repair technologies	20,714	2.0	19,709	5.0	1,005	0.2	4.9
Military technologies	986	0.1	770	0.2	216	0.0	21.9
Multi- and interdisciplinary studies	27,267	2.7	10,171	2.6	17,096	2.7	62.7
Parks, recreation, leisure, and fitness	3,123	0.3	1,998	0.5	1,125	0.2	36.0
Philosophy and religion	308	0.0	181	0.0	127	0.0	41.2
Physical sciences	5,824	0.6	3,404	0.9	2,420	0.4	41.6
Precision production	3,320	0.3	3,118	0.8	202	0.0	6.1
Psychology	4,717	0.5	1,093	0.3	3,624	0.6	76.8
Public administration and social services	9,143	0.9	1,382	0.4	7,761	1.2	84.9
Social sciences and history	14,132	1.4	5,139	1.3	8,993	1.4	63.6
Theology and religious vocations	839	0.1	423	0.1	416	0.1	49.6
Transportation and material moving	2,098	0.2	1,782	0.5	316	0.1	15.1
Visual and performing arts	22,431	2.2	9,422	2.4	13,009	2.1	58.0

Source: National Center for Education Statistics, Digest of Education Statistics 2013, Internet site http://nces.ed.gov/programs/digest/2013menu_tables.asp; calculations by New Strategist

Table 2.22 Bachelor's Degrees Earned by Field of Study and Sex, 2011–12

(number and percent distribution of bachelor's degrees conferred by sex, and percent earned by women, by field of study, 2011–12)

	total		men		women		
	number	percent distribution	number	percent distribution	number	percent distribution	share of total
Total bachelor's degrees	**1,791,046**	**100.0%**	**765,317**	**100.0%**	**1,025,729**	**100.0%**	**57.3%**
Agriculture and natural resources	30,929	1.7	15,453	2.0	15,476	1.5	50.0
Architecture and related programs	9,728	0.5	5,567	0.7	4,161	0.4	42.8
Area, ethnic, cultural, and gender studies	9,232	0.5	2,757	0.4	6,475	0.6	70.1
Biological and biomedical sciences	95,849	5.4	39,545	5.2	56,304	5.5	58.7
Business	366,815	20.5	190,082	24.8	176,733	17.2	48.2
Communication, journalism, and related programs	83,770	4.7	29,921	3.9	53,849	5.2	64.3
Communications technologies	4,982	0.3	3,604	0.5	1,378	0.1	27.7
Computer and information sciences	47,384	2.6	38,773	5.1	8,611	0.8	18.2
Construction trades	377	0.0	359	0.0	18	0.0	4.8
Education	105,785	5.9	21,757	2.8	84,028	8.2	79.4
Engineering	81,382	4.5	65,829	8.6	15,553	1.5	19.1
Engineering technologies	16,531	0.9	14,847	1.9	1,684	0.2	10.2
English language and literature	53,767	3.0	16,976	2.2	36,791	3.6	68.4
Family and consumer sciences	23,428	1.3	2,693	0.4	20,735	2.0	88.5
Foreign languages and literatures	21,764	1.2	6,630	0.9	15,134	1.5	69.5
Health professions and related sciences	163,440	9.1	24,868	3.2	138,572	13.5	84.8
Homeland security, law enforcement, and firefighting	53,767	3.0	27,740	3.6	26,027	2.5	48.4
Legal professions and studies	4,592	0.3	1,388	0.2	3,204	0.3	69.8
Liberal arts and sciences, general studies, and humanities	46,925	2.6	16,944	2.2	29,981	2.9	63.9
Library science	95	0.0	7	0.0	88	0.0	92.6
Mathematics and statistics	18,842	1.1	10,723	1.4	8,119	0.8	43.1
Mechanic and repair technologies	250	0.0	235	0.0	15	0.0	6.0
Military technologies	86	0.0	69	0.0	17	0.0	19.8
Multi- and interdisciplinary studies	45,716	2.6	14,594	1.9	31,122	3.0	68.1
Parks, recreation, leisure, and fitness	38,993	2.2	20,830	2.7	18,163	1.8	46.6
Philosophy and religion	12,651	0.7	7,963	1.0	4,688	0.5	37.1
Physical sciences	26,663	1.5	15,972	2.1	10,691	1.0	40.1
Precision production	37	0.0	28	0.0	9	0.0	24.3
Psychology	108,986	6.1	25,406	3.3	83,580	8.1	76.7
Public administration and social services	29,695	1.7	5,385	0.7	24,310	2.4	81.9
Social sciences and history	178,543	10.0	90,634	11.8	87,909	8.6	49.2
Theology and religious vocations	9,369	0.5	6,275	0.8	3,094	0.3	33.0
Transportation and material moving	4,876	0.3	4,305	0.6	571	0.1	11.7
Visual and performing arts	95,797	5.3	37,158	4.9	58,639	5.7	61.2

Source: National Center for Education Statistics, Digest of Education Statistics 2013, Internet site http://nces.ed.gov/programs/digest/2013menu_tables.asp; calculations by New Strategist

Table 2.23 Master's Degrees Earned by Field of Study and Sex, 2011–12

(number and percent distribution of master's degrees conferred by sex, and percent earned by women, by field of study, 2011–12)

	total		men		women		
	number	percent distribution	number	percent distribution	number	percent distribution	share of total
Total master's degrees	**754,329**	**100.0%**	**302,191**	**100.0%**	**452,038**	**100.0%**	**59.9%**
Agriculture and natural resources	6,391	0.8	3,026	1.0	3,364	0.7	52.6
Architecture and related programs	8,449	1.1	4,504	1.5	3,944	0.9	46.7
Area, ethnic, cultural, and gender studies	1,947	0.3	717	0.2	1,230	0.3	63.2
Biological and biomedical sciences	12,417	1.6	5,378	1.8	7,037	1.6	56.7
Business	191,605	25.4	103,253	34.2	88,318	19.5	46.1
Communication, journalism, and related programs	9,006	1.2	2,760	0.9	6,245	1.4	69.3
Communications technologies	491	0.1	305	0.1	186	0.0	37.9
Computer and information sciences	20,922	2.8	15,129	5.0	5,788	1.3	27.7
Construction trades	5	0.0	4	0.0	1	0.0	20.0
Education	178,076	23.6	41,180	13.6	136,882	30.3	76.9
Engineering	40,333	5.3	31,190	10.3	9,133	2.0	22.6
Engineering technologies	4,770	0.6	3,504	1.2	1,265	0.3	26.5
English language and literature	9,940	1.3	3,403	1.1	6,536	1.4	65.8
Family and consumer sciences	3,157	0.4	413	0.1	2,744	0.6	86.9
Foreign languages and literatures	3,827	0.5	1,280	0.4	2,547	0.6	66.5
Health professions and related sciences	83,898	11.1	15,625	5.2	68,268	15.1	81.4
Homeland security, law enforcement, and firefighting	8,403	1.1	3,947	1.3	4,455	1.0	53.0
Legal professions and studies	6,615	0.9	3,209	1.1	3,405	0.8	51.5
Liberal arts and sciences, general studies, and humanities	3,791	0.5	1,490	0.5	2,301	0.5	60.7
Library science	7,441	1.0	1,425	0.5	6,016	1.3	80.8
Mathematics and statistics	6,246	0.8	3,694	1.2	2,551	0.6	40.8
Military technologies	29	0.0	21	0.0	8	0.0	27.6
Multi- and interdisciplinary studies	7,746	1.0	2,988	1.0	4,757	1.1	61.4
Parks, recreation, leisure, and fitness	7,048	0.9	3,938	1.3	3,109	0.7	44.1
Philosophy and religion	2,003	0.3	1,253	0.4	750	0.2	37.4
Physical sciences	6,911	0.9	4,299	1.4	2,611	0.6	37.8
Precision production	11	0.0	9	0.0	2	0.0	18.2
Psychology	26,836	3.6	5,435	1.8	21,399	4.7	79.7
Public administration and social services	41,683	5.5	10,475	3.5	31,205	6.9	74.9
Social sciences and history	21,893	2.9	10,983	3.6	10,906	2.4	49.8
Theology and religious vocations	13,399	1.8	8,582	2.8	4,814	1.1	35.9
Transportation and material moving	1,702	0.2	1,441	0.5	261	0.1	15.3
Visual and performing arts	17,333	2.3	7,331	2.4	10,000	2.2	57.7

Source: National Center for Education Statistics, Digest of Education Statistics 2013, Internet site http://nces.ed.gov/programs/digest/2013menu_tables.asp; calculations by New Strategist

Table 2.24 Doctoral and Professional Degrees Earned by Field of Study and Sex, 2011–12

(number and percent distribution of doctoral and professional degrees conferred by sex, and percent earned by women, by field of study, 2011–12)

	total		men		women		
	number	percent distribution	number	percent distribution	number	percent distribution	share of total
Total doctoral and professional degrees	**170,162**	**100.0%**	**82,611**	**100.0%**	**87,451**	**100.0%**	**51.4%**
Agriculture and natural resources	1,334	0.8	721	0.9	612	0.7	45.9
Architecture and related programs	255	0.1	147	0.2	108	0.1	42.3
Area, ethnic, cultural, and gender studies	302	0.2	112	0.1	190	0.2	62.9
Biological and biomedical sciences	7,939	4.7	3,708	4.5	4,227	4.8	53.2
Business	2,533	1.5	1,460	1.8	1,071	1.2	42.3
Communication, journalism, and related programs	563	0.3	239	0.3	324	0.4	57.5
Communications technologies	4	0.0	3	0.0	1	0.0	25.0
Computer and information sciences	1,700	1.0	1,332	1.6	366	0.4	21.5
Education	9,994	5.9	3,215	3.9	6,775	7.7	67.8
Engineering	8,730	5.1	6,770	8.2	1,952	2.2	22.4
Engineering technologies	134	0.1	68	0.1	66	0.1	49.2
English language and literature	1,428	0.8	548	0.7	879	1.0	61.6
Family and consumer sciences	325	0.2	59	0.1	266	0.3	81.8
Foreign languages and literatures	1,232	0.7	497	0.6	734	0.8	59.6
Health professions and related sciences	62,122	36.5	26,074	31.6	36,016	41.2	58.0
Homeland security, law enforcement, and firefighting	117	0.1	63	0.1	54	0.1	46.1
Legal professions and studies	46,866	27.5	24,764	30.0	22,072	25.2	47.1
Liberal arts and sciences, general studies, and humanities	93	0.1	32	0.0	61	0.1	65.6
Library science	60	0.0	24	0.0	36	0.0	60.0
Mathematics and statistics	1,670	1.0	1,198	1.5	471	0.5	28.2
Multi- and interdisciplinary studies	727	0.4	297	0.4	430	0.5	59.1
Parks, recreation, leisure, and fitness	288	0.2	161	0.2	127	0.1	44.1
Philosophy and religion	779	0.5	542	0.7	236	0.3	30.3
Physical sciences	5,374	3.2	3,609	4.4	1,761	2.0	32.8
Psychology	5,930	3.5	1,519	1.8	4,409	5.0	74.4
Public administration and social services	884	0.5	338	0.4	546	0.6	61.7
Social sciences and history	4,600	2.7	2,464	3.0	2,133	2.4	46.4
Theology and religious vocations	2,449	1.4	1,857	2.2	590	0.7	24.1
Visual and performing arts	1,729	1.0	790	1.0	938	1.1	54.3

Source: National Center for Education Statistics, Digest of Education Statistics 2013, Internet site http://nces.ed.gov/programs/digest/2013menu_tables.asp; calculations by New Strategist

Table 2.25 Degrees Conferred in Selected Professional Fields by Sex, 2011–12

(number of degrees conferred in selected professional fields by sex, and percent earned by women, 2011–12)

			women	
	total	men	number	share of total
Dentistry (D.D.S. or D.M.D.)	5,109	2,748	2,361	46.2%
Medicine (M.D.)	16,927	8,809	8,118	48.0
Optometry (O.D.)	1,361	476	885	65.0
Osteopathic medicine (D.O.)	4,336	2,283	2,053	47.3
Pharmacy (Pharm.D.)	12,943	4,971	7,972	61.6
Podiatry (Pod.D. or D.P. or D.P.M.)	535	342	193	36.1
Veterinary medicine (D.V.M.)	2,616	588	2,028	77.5
Chiropractic (D.C. or D.C.M.)	2,496	1,538	958	38.4
Law (LL.B. or J.D.)	46,445	24,576	21,869	47.1
Theology (M. Div., M.H.L./Rav., B.D., or Ord.)	5,942	4,003	1,939	32.6

Source: National Center for Education Statistics, Digest of Education Statistics 2013, Internet site http://nces.ed.gov/programs/digest/2013menu_tables.asp; calculations by New Strategist

CHAPTER

3

Health

■ The 52 percent majority of Americans aged 18 or older is in very good or excellent health. The figure peaks at 63 percent in the 18-to-24 age group.

■ Americans have a weight problem, and young adults are no exception. The average man in his twenties weighs 184 pounds. The average woman in the age group weighs 162 pounds.

■ Men aged 30 to 34 have had a median of six opposite-sex partners in their lifetime. Women in the age group have had four partners.

■ Fully 85 percent of births in 2013 were to women in the Millennial generation.

■ Before the Affordable Care Act, the nation's 18-to-24-year-olds were most likely to lack health insurance. Now that distinction belongs to 25-to-34-year-olds—24 percent of whom did not have health insurance at any time in 2013.

■ More than one in four people aged 18 to 44 did not see a health care provider in the past 12 months. This age group visits a doctor less often than others in part because many in the cohort do not have health insurance.

■ Accidents are the leading cause of death among 25-to-44-year-olds, accounting for 26 percent of deaths. Suicide is the fourth leading cause of death, and homicide is fifth.

Most Young Adults Say Their Health Is Excellent or Very Good

The proportion in very good or excellent health declines with age.

Overall, the 52 percent majority of Americans aged 18 or older say their health is "very good" or "excellent." Not surprisingly, the percentage in very good or excellent health is higher among young adults than among middle-aged or older people. The figure peaks at 63 percent among 18-to-24-year-olds, then falls with age as chronic conditions become common.

Fewer than half of people aged 55 or older report their health as very good or excellent. Nevertheless, the proportion in poor health remains below 7 percent, regardless of age. Among people aged 65 or older, the proportion in very good or excellent health (41 percent) surpasses the proportion in fair or poor health (24 percent).

■ Medical advances allowing people to manage chronic conditions should boost the proportion of people reporting excellent or very good health in the years ahead.

Nearly two-thirds of 18-to-24-year-olds are in excellent or very good health

(percentage of people aged 18 or older in "excellent" or "very good" health, by age, 2013)

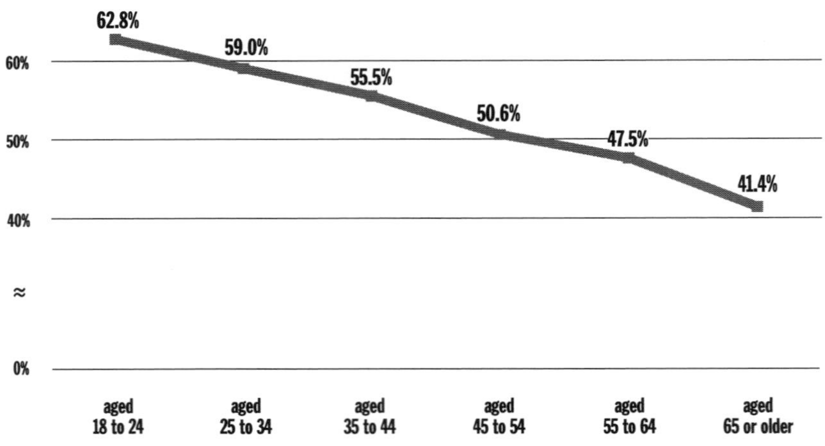

Table 3.1 Health Status by Age, 2013

(percent distribution of people aged 18 or older by self-reported health status, by age, 2013)

		excellent or very good				fair or poor		
	total	total	excellent	very good	good	total	fair	poor
Total people	**100.0%**	**52.2%**	**18.6%**	**33.6%**	**30.9%**	**16.7%**	**12.3%**	**4.4%**
Aged 18 to 24	100.0	62.8	24.9	37.9	28.9	8.6	7.5	1.1
Aged 25 to 34	100.0	59.0	23.0	36.0	30.1	10.5	8.5	2.0
Aged 35 to 44	100.0	55.5	20.6	34.9	30.8	13.6	10.5	3.1
Aged 45 to 54	100.0	50.6	18.0	32.6	30.1	18.3	12.6	5.7
Aged 55 to 64	100.0	47.5	15.3	32.2	31.0	21.1	14.4	6.7
Aged 65 or older	100.0	41.4	12.3	29.1	33.4	23.8	16.9	6.9

Source: Centers for Disease Control and Prevention, Behavioral Risk Factor Surveillance System, Prevalence Data, Internet site http://apps.nccd.cdc.gov/brfss/; calculations by New Strategist

Weight Problems are the Norm Even for Young Adults

Most young men and women are overweight.

Americans have a weight problem, and young adults are no exception. The average man in his twenties weighs 184 pounds. The average woman in the age group weighs 162 pounds. Fully 61 percent of men and 55 percent of women aged 20 to 34 are overweight, and more than one in four are obese.

Although many people say they exercise, only 20 percent of adults meet federal physical activity guidelines. The share of the public that meets both aerobic and muscle-strengthening guidelines is highest among 18-to-24-year-olds (30 percent) and falls with age to fewer than 12 percent of people aged 65 or older. The guidelines are demanding, however, which might explain why so few can meet them.

■ Most young adults lack the willpower to eat less or exercise more—fueling a diet and weight loss industry that never lacks for customers.

Most young adults weigh more than they should

(percent distribution of people aged 20 to 34 by weight status, by sex, 2009–12)

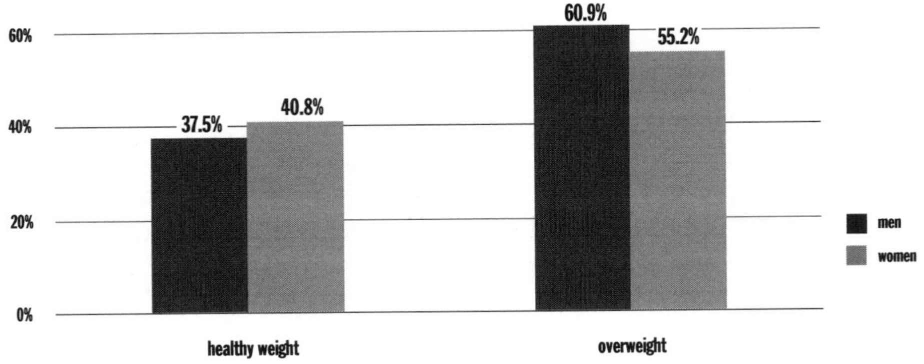

Table 3.2 Average Measured Weight by Age and Sex, 2007–10

(average weight in pounds of people aged 20 or older by age and sex, 2007–10)

	men	women
Total aged 20 or older	**195.5 lbs.**	**166.2 lbs.**
Aged 20 to 29	183.9	161.9
Aged 30 to 39	199.5	169.1
Aged 40 to 49	200.6	168.0
Aged 50 to 59	201.3	170.0
Aged 60 to 69	199.4	170.5
Aged 70 to 79	190.6	164.9
Aged 80 or older	174.9	143.1

Note: Data are based on measured weight of a sample of the civilian noninstitutionalized population.
Source: National Center for Health Statistics, Anthropometric Reference Data for Children and Adults: United States, 2007–2010, Vital Health Statistics, Series 11, No. 252, 2012, Internet site http://www.cdc.gov/nchs/products/series/series11.htm; calculations by New Strategist

Table 3.3 Weight Status by Sex and Age, 2009–12

(percent distribution of people aged 20 or older by weight status, sex, and age, 2009–12)

			overweight	
	total	healthy weight	total	obese
Total people	**100.0%**	**29.2%**	**69.1%**	**35.5%**
Total men	**100.0**	**26.2**	**72.9**	**34.6**
Aged 20 to 34	100.0	37.5	60.9	28.9
Aged 35 to 44	100.0	21.0	78.9	38.1
Aged 45 to 54	100.0	20.0	79.3	38.1
Aged 55 to 64	100.0	21.9	77.4	38.1
Aged 65 to 74	100.0	22.4	76.9	36.4
Aged 75 or older	100.0	28.2	70.4	27.4
Total women	**100.0**	**31.9**	**65.5**	**36.4**
Aged 20 to 34	100.0	40.8	55.2	30.0
Aged 35 to 44	100.0	35.2	62.4	36.0
Aged 45 to 54	100.0	27.3	70.5	38.3
Aged 55 to 64	100.0	23.8	75.1	42.9
Aged 65 to 74	100.0	23.5	73.8	44.2
Aged 75 or older	100.0	35.3	62.4	29.8

Note: Data are based on measured height and weight of a sample of the civilian noninstitutionalized population. "Overweight" is defined as a body mass index of 25 or higher. "Obese" is defined as a body mass index of 30 or higher. Body mass index is calculated by dividing weight in kilograms by height in meters squared. Percentages do not add to 100 because "underweight" is not shown.
Source: National Center for Health Statistics, Health, United States, 2013, Internet site http://www.cdc.gov/nchs/hus.htm

Table 3.4 Physical Activity Status of People Aged 18 or Older, 2012

(percent of people aged 18 or older by leisure-time aerobic and muscle-strengthening guideline activity status, by sex and age, 2012)

	met muscle-strengthening guideline	met aerobic activity guideline	met both guidelines	met neither guideline
Total people	**23.6%**	**49.6%**	**20.3%**	**47.1%**
Aged 18 to 24	32.1	59.6	29.7	37.9
Aged 25 to 44	27.2	54.9	24.2	42.2
Aged 45 to 54	21.4	48.5	18.2	48.3
Aged 55 to 64	19.8	45.0	16.0	51.2
Aged 65 or older	16.1	37.5	11.9	58.4
Total men	**28.4**	**54.0**	**24.6**	**42.2**
Aged 18 to 44	35.4	60.5	31.8	35.9
Aged 45 to 54	22.3	50.3	18.7	45.9
Aged 55 to 64	20.9	46.9	16.8	49.1
Aged 65 to 74	20.6	50.8	17.1	45.9
Aged 75 or older	15.4	33.8	10.5	61.3
Total women	**20.0**	**46.6**	**17.1**	**50.7**
Aged 18 to 44	21.9	51.9	19.8	46.0
Aged 45 to 54	20.5	46.7	17.7	50.5
Aged 55 to 64	18.8	43.3	15.3	53.2
Aged 65 to 74	17.1	39.1	12.8	56.7
Aged 75 or older	10.8	24.3	6.2	71.2

Note: Federal aerobic guideline recommends that adults perform at least 150 minutes per week of moderate-intensity or 75 minutes per week of vigorous-intensity aerobic physical activity or equivalent combination. Federal muscle-strengthening guideline recommends muscle-strengthening activities of moderate or high intensity involving all major muscle groups on two or more days per week.
Source: National Center for Health Statistics, Health, United States, 2013, Internet site http://www.cdc.gov/nchs/hus.htm

Americans Report on Their Sexual Behavior

Men aged 30 to 34 have had a median of six opposite-sex partners in their lifetime.

The federal government's National Survey of Family Growth examines the sexual behavior of Americans aged 15 to 44. Most people in the age group have had at least one opposite-sex partner in their lifetime. Even among 15-to-19-year-olds, 57 percent of men and 52 percent of women are sexually experienced. Overall, men aged 15 to 44 have had a median of 5.1 opposite-sex partners in their lifetime, and women have had a median of 3.2 partners.

Among 15-to-44-year-olds, 93.5 percent of men and 83.3 percent of women identify themselves as attracted only to the opposite sex. Just 2.8 percent of men and 4.6 percent of women identify themselves as homosexual or bisexual—a figure likely to be underreported.

■ The percentage of men who report any sexual activity with a same-sex partner rises from 2.5 percent among teenagers to 8.1 percent in the 40-to-44 age group.

Women are more likely than men to report some same-sex attraction

(percent distribution of men and women aged 15 to 44 by sexual attraction, 2006–08)

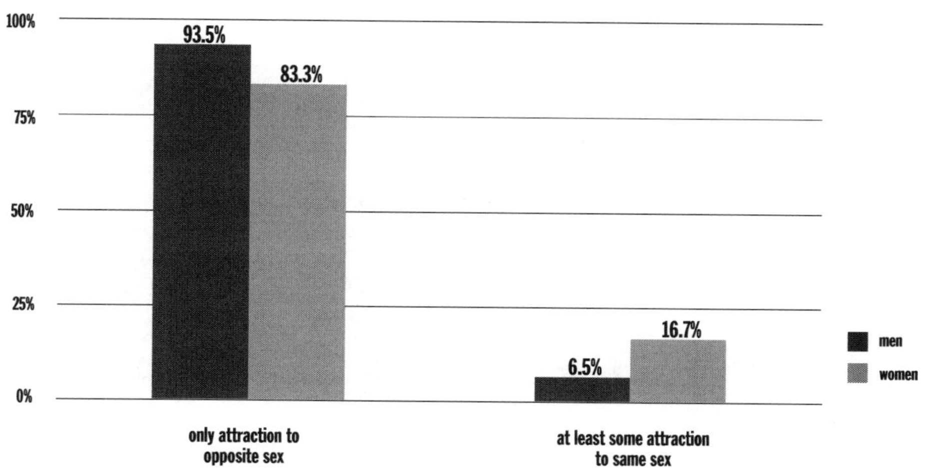

Table 3.5 Lifetime Sexual Activity of 15-to-44-Year-Olds by Sex, 2006–08

(number of people aged 15 to 44 and percent distribution by sexual experience with opposite-sex partners during lifetime, by sex and age, 2006–08; numbers in thousands)

	total		number of opposite-sex partners in lifetime							
	number	percent	0	1 or more	1	2	3 to 6	7 to 14	15 or more	median
Total men aged 15 to 44	**62,199**	**100.0%**	**11.4%**	**88.6%**	**15.0%**	**7.6%**	**26.5%**	**18.1%**	**21.4%**	**5.1**
Aged 15 to 19	10,777	100.0	43.3	56.7	21.2	9.4	17.6	5.4	3.1	1.8
Aged 20 to 24	10,404	100.0	14.4	85.5	19.1	8.0	26.1	18.1	14.2	4.1
Aged 25 to 29	10,431	100.0	3.8	96.2	11.8	8.9	29.5	22.9	23.1	5.7
Aged 30 to 34	9,575	100.0	3.1	96.9	14.2	6.1	26.6	21.7	28.3	6.4
Aged 35 to 39	10,318	100.0	1.4	98.8	13.3	5.6	29.7	19.6	30.6	6.2
Aged 40 to 44	10,695	100.0	1.3	98.8	10.3	7.2	29.7	21.6	30.0	6.4
Total women aged 15 to 44	**61,865**	**100.0**	**11.3**	**88.8**	**22.2**	**10.7**	**31.6**	**16.0**	**8.3**	**3.2**
Aged 15 to 19	10,431	100.0	48.1	51.8	22.7	8.2	15.7	4.1	1.1	1.4
Aged 20 to 24	10,140	100.0	12.6	87.5	24.5	12.5	31.6	11.7	7.2	2.6
Aged 25 to 29	10,250	100.0	3.4	96.6	20.0	12.4	31.0	20.4	12.8	3.6
Aged 30 to 34	9,587	100.0	1.9	98.1	20.9	10.6	31.9	21.3	13.4	4.2
Aged 35 to 39	10,475	100.0	0.9	99.1	22.2	9.9	38.3	20.8	7.9	3.5
Aged 40 to 44	10,982	100.0	0.4	99.7	22.4	10.8	40.5	18.0	8.0	3.4

Source: National Center for Health Statistics, Sexual Behavior, Sexual Attraction, and Sexual Identity in the United States: Data from the 2006–2008 National Survey of Family Growth, National Health Statistics Reports, No. 36, 2011, Internet site http://www.cdc.gov/nchs/nsfg/new_nsfg.htm; calculations by New Strategist

Table 3.6 Sexual Attraction among 18-to-44-Year-Olds, 2006–08

(number of people aged 18 to 44 and percent distribution by sexual attraction, by sex and age, 2006–08; numbers in thousands)

	total							
	number	percent	only opposite sex	mostly opposite sex	equally to both	mostly same sex	only same sex	not sure
Total men aged 18 to 44	**55,399**	**100.0%**	**93.5%**	**3.7%**	**0.5%**	**0.7%**	**1.2%**	**0.4%**
Aged 18 to 19	4,460	100.0	91.7	5.7	–	0.7	1.1	0.6
Aged 20 to 24	9,883	100.0	91.3	5.8	1.1	0.5	0.7	0.7
Aged 25 to 29	9,226	100.0	94.3	3.1	0.3	0.7	1.3	0.4
Aged 30 to 34	10,138	100.0	95.3	2.7	–	0.5	0.8	0.4
Aged 35 to 44	21,692	100.0	93.6	3.1	0.4	0.9	1.7	0.2
Total women aged 18 to 44	**56,032**	**100.0**	**83.3**	**11.9**	**2.8**	**0.6**	**0.8**	**0.7**
Aged 18 to 19	4,598	100.0	82.4	9.4	4.8	0.9	1.3	1.2
Aged 20 to 24	10,140	100.0	77.6	16.7	3.7	0.8	0.8	0.4
Aged 25 to 29	10,250	100.0	81.4	12.9	3.8	0.5	1.1	0.4
Aged 30 to 34	9,587	100.0	81.4	13.0	2.8	0.7	0.9	1.2
Aged 35 to 44	21,457	100.0	87.9	9.1	1.4	0.4	0.5	0.6

Note: "–" means sample is too small to make a reliable estimate.
Source: National Center for Health Statistics, Sexual Behavior, Sexual Attraction, and Sexual Identity in the United States: Data from the 2006–2008 National Survey of Family Growth, National Health Statistics Reports, No. 36, 2011, Internet site http://www.cdc.gov/nchs/nsfg/new_nsfg.htm; calculations by New Strategist

Table 3.7 Sexual Orientation of 18-to-44-Year-Olds, 2006–08

(number of people aged 18 to 44 and percent distribution by sexual orientation, by sex and age, 2006–08; numbers in thousands)

	total		heterosexual or straight	homosexual or gay	bisexual
	number	percent			
Total men aged 18 to 44	**55,399**	**100.0%**	**95.7%**	**1.7%**	**1.1%**
Aged 18 to 19	4,460	100.0	96.6	1.6	1.1
Aged 20 to 24	9,883	100.0	95.1	1.2	2.0
Aged 25 to 29	9,226	100.0	96.3	1.7	0.8
Aged 30 to 34	10,138	100.0	96.2	1.5	0.6
Aged 35 to 44	21,692	100.0	95.2	2.1	1.0
Total women aged 18 to 44	**56,032**	**100.0**	**93.7**	**1.1**	**3.5**
Aged 18 to 19	4,598	100.0	90.1	1.9	5.8
Aged 20 to 24	10,140	100.0	90.4	1.3	6.3
Aged 25 to 29	10,250	100.0	91.9	1.2	5.4
Aged 30 to 34	9,587	100.0	94.4	1.1	2.9
Aged 35 to 44	21,457	100.0	96.6	0.7	1.1

Note: Numbers do not add to 100 percent because "something else" and "not reported" are not shown.
Source: National Center for Health Statistics, Sexual Behavior, Sexual Attraction, and Sexual Identity in the United States: Data from the 2006–2008 National Survey of Family Growth, National Health Statistics Reports, No. 36, 2011, Internet site http://www.cdc.gov/nchs/nsfg/new_nsfg.htm; calculations by New Strategist

Table 3.8 Lifetime Same-Sex Sexual Activity of 15-to-44-Year-Olds, 2006–08

(percent of people aged 15 to 44 reporting any sexual activity with same-sex partners in their lifetime, by age and sex, 2006–08)

	men	women
Total aged 15 to 44	**5.2%**	**12.5%**
Aged 15 to 19	2.5	11.0
Aged 20 to 24	5.6	15.8
Aged 25 to 29	5.2	15.0
Aged 30 to 34	4.0	14.2
Aged 35 to 39	5.7	11.5
Aged 40 to 44	8.1	7.9

Source: National Center for Health Statistics, Sexual Behavior, Sexual Attraction, and Sexual Identity in the United States: Data from the 2006–2008 National Survey of Family Growth, National Health Statistics Reports, No. 36, 2011, Internet site http://www.cdc.gov/nchs/nsfg/new_nsfg.htm; calculations by New Strategist

Most Women of Childbearing Age Use Contraceptives

The pill and female sterilization are the most popular contraceptives.

Among the nation's women of childbearing age—defined as ages 15 to 44—the 62 percent majority uses contraceptives. The pill is most popular, with 17.1 percent of women using it, according to the federal government's National Survey of Family Growth. Female sterilization is the contraceptive choice of 16.5 percent of women, while condoms rank third at 10.2 percent. Use of the pill peaks at 27 percent among women aged 20 to 24, while women aged 30 or older are more likely to have been sterilized than to be on the pill.

Among women not using contraception, most are sexually inactive, pregnant, or postpartum. Only 8 percent of women aged 15 to 44 are not using contraceptives, able to become pregnant, and sexually active.

■ Contraception is a vital element of health care for American women.

The pill is popular among young women

(percent of women aged 15 to 44 who are using the contraceptive pill, 2006–10)

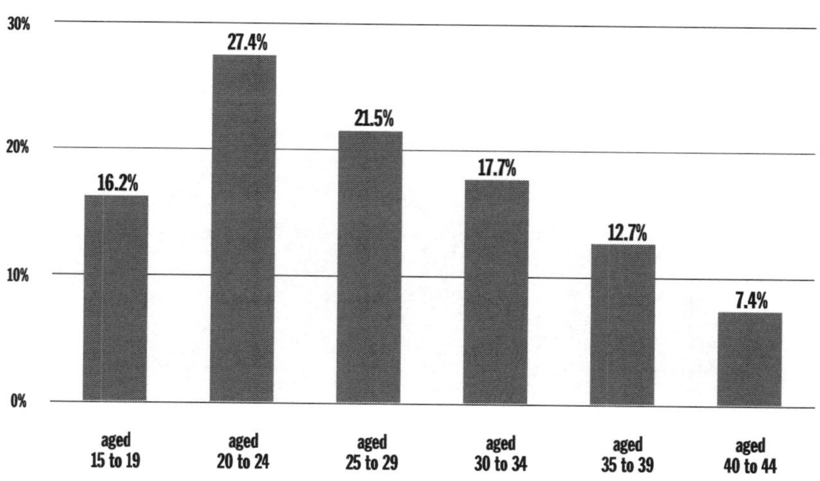

Table 3.9 Contraceptive Use by Age, 2006–10

(total number of women aged 15 to 44 and percent distribution by contraceptive status and age, 2006–10; numbers in thousands)

	total	15 to 19	20 to 24	25 to 29	30 to 34	35 to 39	40 to 44
Total women aged 15 to 44 (number)	**61,755**	**10,478**	**10,365**	**10,535**	**9,188**	**10,538**	**10,652**
Total women aged 15 to 44 (percent)	**100.0%**	**100.0%**	**100.0%**	**100.0%**	**100.0%**	**100.0%**	**100.0%**
USING CONTRACEPTION	**62.2**	**30.5**	**58.3**	**65.3**	**69.7**	**74.6**	**75.3**
Female sterilization	16.5	–	1.5	10.7	20.9	27.9	38.1
Male sterilization	6.2	–	0.5	2.7	6.6	12.4	15.1
Pill	17.1	16.2	27.4	21.5	17.7	12.7	7.4
Other hormonal methods	4.5	4.9	7.1	7.4	3.9	2.0	1.4
Implant, Lunelle, or Patch	0.9	0.7	1.1	1.5	0.9	0.5	–
Three-month injectable (Depo-Provera)	2.3	3.5	3.3	3.4	1.7	1.0	0.6
Contraceptive ring	1.3	0.7	2.7	2.4	1.4	0.5	0.4
Intrauterine device (IUD)	3.5	0.8	3.3	4.7	4.9	4.8	2.4
Condom	10.2	6.1	14.9	13.6	10.8	9.0	6.8
Periodic abstinence—calendar rhythm method	0.6	–	0.2	0.5	0.8	1.0	1.1
Periodic abstinence—natural family planning	0.1	0.0	0.0	0.0	0.4	–	–
Withdrawal	3.2	2.1	3.3	4.1	3.2	4.1	2.6
Other methods	0.3	0.2	–	0.3	0.5	0.6	0.4
NOT USING CONTRACEPTION	**37.8**	**69.5**	**41.7**	**34.7**	**30.3**	**25.4**	**24.7**
Surgically sterile, female (noncontraceptive)	0.4	–	–	0.2	–	0.4	1.5
Nonsurgically sterile, female or male	1.7	0.5	1.4	1.4	1.8	2.0	3.1
Pregnant or postpartum	5.0	3.2	8.1	8.4	7.2	2.3	1.4
Seeking pregnancy	4.0	0.6	4.0	6.3	6.0	4.8	2.4
Never had intercourse	11.8	51.4	11.6	3.1	1.9	1.1	0.6
No intercourse in past three months	7.3	7.1	7.9	7.0	6.6	6.5	8.6
Had intercourse during past three months	7.7	6.7	8.7	8.4	6.7	8.4	7.1

Note: "Other methods" includes diaphragm, emergency contraceptive, Today sponge, cervical cap, female condom, and other methods. "–" means sample is too small to make a reliable estimate.
Source: National Center for Health Statistics, Current Contraceptive Use in the United States, 2006–2010, and Changes in Patterns of Use since 1995, National Health Statistics Reports, No. 60, 2012, Internet site http://www.cdc.gov/nchs/nsfg.htm; calculations by New Strategist

Fertility Rate Is at a Record Low

The rate is rising among women aged 35 or older, however.

The women of the Millennial generation (aged 19 to 36 in 2013) are in their prime childbearing years. But many are delaying marriage and childbearing because of college attendance and the lingering effects of the Great Recession. The nation's overall fertility rate has dropped to a record low of 62.9 births per 1,000 women aged 15 to 44. As women reach their mid-thirties, however, they are having those postponed babies. The fertility rate of women aged 35 or older has increased since 2007, while the rate among women under age 35 has declined.

The delayed childbearing of Millennial women and the catch-up childbearing of Gen X women have upended a historic pattern. The fertility rate of women aged 20 to 24 has fallen below the rate of women aged 30 to 34—a pattern never seen before.

■ As millions of Millennial women reach their mid-thirties and begin to have children, the annual number of births may rise substantially.

Fertility rate peaks in the 25-to-29 age group

(births per 1,000 women in age group, 2013)

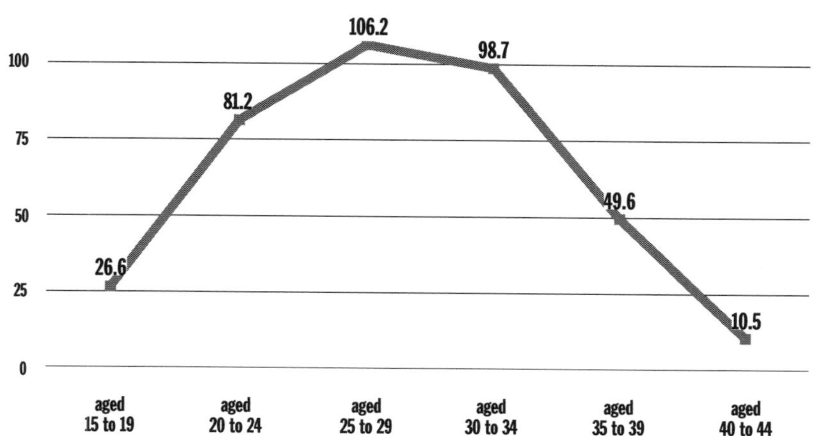

Table 3.10 Fertility Rate by Age, 2000 to 2013

(number of births per 1,000 women aged 15 to 44, and per 1,000 women in specified age group, 2000 to 2013; percent change for selected years)

	total	15 to 19	20 to 24	25 to 29	30 to 34	35 to 39	40 to 44	45 to 49
2013	62.9	26.6	81.2	106.2	98.7	49.6	10.5	0.8
2012	63.0	29.4	83.1	106.5	97.3	48.3	10.4	0.7
2011	63.2	31.3	85.3	107.2	96.5	47.2	10.3	0.7
2010	64.1	34.3	90.0	108.3	96.6	45.9	10.2	0.7
2009	66.2	37.9	96.2	111.5	97.5	46.1	10.0	0.7
2008	68.6	41.5	103.0	115.1	99.3	46.9	9.8	0.7
2007	69.5	42.5	106.3	117.5	99.9	47.5	9.5	0.6
2006	68.5	41.9	105.9	116.7	97.7	47.3	9.4	0.6
2005	66.7	40.4	102.2	115.6	95.9	46.3	9.1	0.6
2004	66.3	41.1	101.7	115.5	95.3	45.4	8.9	0.5
2003	66.1	41.6	102.6	115.6	95.1	43.8	8.7	0.5
2002	64.8	43.0	103.6	113.6	91.5	41.4	8.3	0.5
2001	65.3	45.3	106.2	113.4	91.9	40.6	8.1	0.5
2000	65.9	47.7	109.7	113.5	91.2	39.7	8.0	0.5
PERCENT CHANGE								
2007 to 2013	–9.5%	–37.4%	–23.6%	–9.6%	–1.2%	4.4%	10.5%	33.3%
2000 to 2013	–4.6	–44.2	–26.0	–6.4	8.2	24.9	31.3	60.0

Source: National Center for Health Statistics, Birth Data, Internet site http://www.cdc.gov/nchs/births.htm; calculations by New Strategist

Most Women Are Mothers by Age 30

Among women aged 35 to 50, more than 30 percent have had three or more children.

The proportion of women who have never had a child falls from 95 percent among 15-to-19-year-olds to a much smaller (but still substantial) 17 percent among women aged 45 to 50. Overall, 59 percent of women aged 15 to 50 have had at least one child. The largest share (23 percent) has had two.

Five percent of women aged 15 to 50 had a baby in the past year, according to the 2012 American Community Survey. Women aged 25 to 34 are most likely to have had a baby recently, with 10 percent having given birth in the past year. By race and Hispanic origin, Hispanics are most likely to have given birth in the past 12 months, at nearly 7 percent. By educational attainment, women with graduate degrees are most likely to have had a baby in the past year.

■ The two-child family has been the norm in the United States for several decades.

Most women aged 25 or older have had at least one child

(percent of women aged 15 to 50 who have had one or more children, by age, 2012)

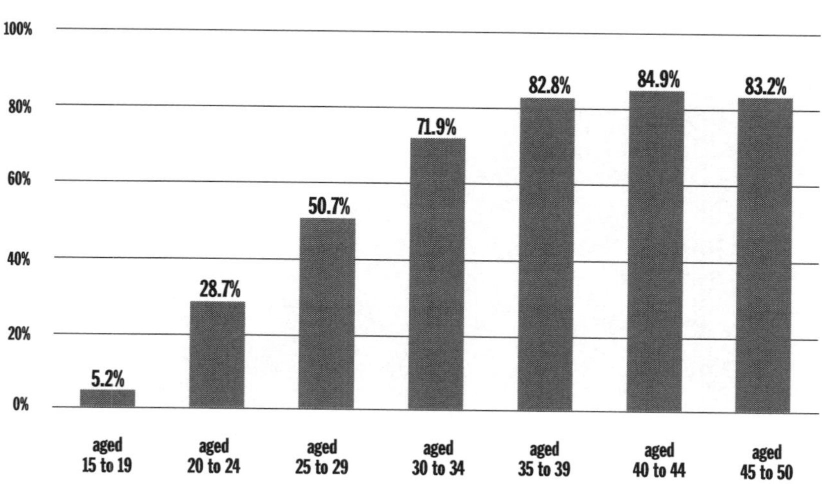

Table 3.11 Number of Children Born to Women Aged 15 to 50, 2012

(total number of women aged 15 to 50, and percent distribution by number of children ever born, by age, 2012; numbers in thousands)

	total			one or more			
	number	percent	none	total	one	two	three or more
Total aged 15 to 50	**75,392**	**100.0%**	**41.3%**	**58.8%**	**17.2%**	**23.1%**	**18.5%**
Aged 15 to 19	10,351	100.0	94.9	5.2	4.0	0.8	0.4
Aged 20 to 24	10,909	100.0	71.4	28.7	18.0	8.5	2.2
Aged 25 to 29	10,437	100.0	49.4	50.7	21.6	18.1	11.0
Aged 30 to 34	10,324	100.0	28.2	71.9	21.6	28.4	21.9
Aged 35 to 39	9,709	100.0	17.2	82.8	17.7	33.8	31.3
Aged 40 to 44	10,516	100.0	15.1	84.9	18.9	34.9	31.1
Aged 45 to 50	13,145	100.0	16.8	83.2	18.1	35.1	30.0

Note: Number of women aged 15 to 50 is based on Current Population Survey estimates.
Source: Bureau of the Census, Fertility of Women in the United States: 2012, Internet site http://www.census.gov/hhes/fertility/

Table 3.12 Women Having Given Birth in the Past Year, 2012

(total number of women aged 15 to 50 and number and percent who gave birth in the past year by selected characteristics, 2012; numbers in thousands)

		gave birth in past year	
	total	number	percent
Total aged 15 to 50	**76,187**	**4,125**	**5.4%**
Age			
Aged 15 to 19	10,504	225	2.1
Aged 20 to 24	10,964	867	7.9
Aged 25 to 29	10,487	1,083	10.3
Aged 30 to 34	10,402	1,073	10.3
Aged 35 to 39	9,813	584	6.0
Aged 40 to 44	10,617	200	1.9
Aged 45 to 50	13,400	93	0.7
Race and Hispanic origin			
Asian	4,544	259	5.7
Black	10,704	613	5.7
Hispanic	14,102	932	6.6
Non-Hispanic White	44,790	2,207	4.9
Nativity status			
Native born	63,537	3,266	5.1
Foreign born	12,651	859	6.8
Educational attainment			
Not a high school graduate	13,559	635	4.7
High school degree	16,492	951	5.8
Some college or associate's degree	25,636	1,322	5.2
Bachelor's degree	13,863	779	5.6
Graduate or professional degree	6,637	438	6.6

Note: Numbers by race and Hispanic origin do not add to total because Hispanics may be of any race and not all races are shown. Asians and Blacks are those who identify themselves as being of the race alone. Non-Hispanic Whites are those who identify themselves as being White alone and not Hispanic. Number of women aged 15 to 50 is based on American Community Survey estimates.

Source: Bureau of the Census, Fertility of Women in the United States: 2012, Internet site http://www.census.gov/hhes/fertility/

The Millennial Generation Dominates Births

More than 85 percent of births are to women in the Millennial generation.

Despite an increase in the number of older mothers during the past few decades, the 51 percent majority of women who gave birth in 2013 were in their twenties. Women aged 25 to 29 accounted for the single largest share of births—28 percent of the total. Because of the steep decline in the fertility rate of younger women, the 30-to-34 age group now accounts for a larger share of births (26 percent) than the 20-to-24 age group (23 percent).

The 54 percent majority of births in 2013 were to non-Hispanic Whites. Another 23 percent were to Hispanics, 15 percent to Blacks, and 7 percent to Asians. Among women aged 20 to 24 who gave birth in 2013, most were having their first child. Among women aged 25 to 34 who gave birth, most were having their second or higher-order birth.

■ The Millennial generation will dominate births for years to come.

Largest share of births is to women aged 25 to 29

(percent distribution of births by age of mother, 2013)

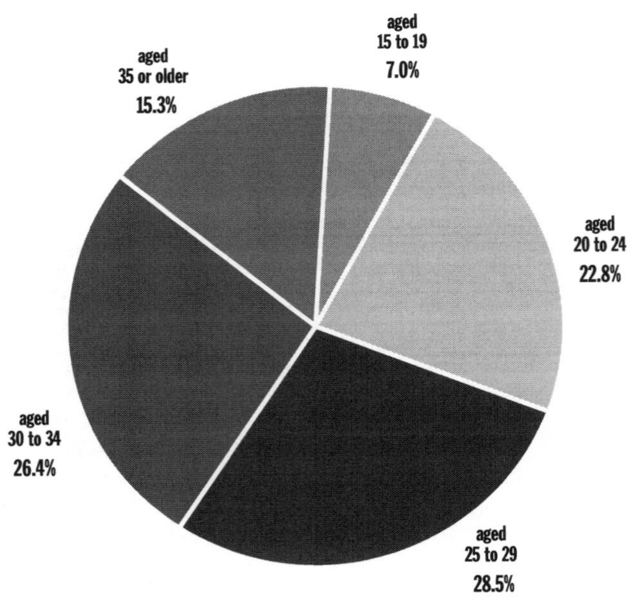

Table 3.13 Births by Age and Generation, 2013

(number and percent distribution of births by age and generation of mother, 2013)

	number	percent distribution
Total births	**3,957,577**	**100.0%**
Under age 15	3,108	0.1
Aged 15 to 17	75,234	1.9
Aged 18 to 19	199,407	5.0
Aged 20 to 24	902,146	22.8
Aged 25 to 29	1,127,561	28.5
Aged 30 to 34	1,044,029	26.4
Aged 35 to 39	487,476	12.3
Aged 40 to 44	110,332	2.8
Aged 45 to 54	8,284	0.2
Total births	**3,957,577**	**100.0**
iGeneration (under age 19)	178,046	4.5
Millennials (aged 19 to 36)	3,368,430	85.1
Gen X (aged 37 or older)	411,102	10.4

Source: National Center for Health Statistics, Births: Preliminary Data for 2013, National Vital Statistics Reports, Vol. 63, No. 2, 2014, Internet site http://www.cdc.gov/nchs/births.htm; calculations by New Strategist

Table 3.14 Births by Age, Race, and Hispanic Origin, 2013

(number and percent distribution of births by age, race, and Hispanic origin of mother, 2013)

	total	American Indian	Asian	Black, non-Hispanic	Hispanic	White, non-Hispanic
Total births	**3,957,577**	**46,167**	**268,559**	**587,612**	**907,859**	**2,140,273**
Under age 15	3,108	70	59	1,045	1,221	717
Aged 15 to 19	274,641	5,729	5,132	62,439	93,585	108,334
Aged 20 to 24	902,146	15,035	27,534	186,863	239,401	433,617
Aged 25 to 29	1,127,561	12,721	71,621	154,864	246,164	640,732
Aged 30 to 34	1,044,029	8,175	96,895	113,416	197,976	624,279
Aged 35 to 39	487,476	3,605	53,482	53,920	103,476	270,872
Aged 40 to 44	110,332	784	12,805	13,953	24,678	57,243
Aged 45 to 54	8,284	49	1,033	1,114	1,358	4,479
PERCENT DISTRIBUTION BY RACE AND HISPANIC ORIGIN						
Total births	**100.0%**	**1.2%**	**6.8%**	**14.8%**	**22.9%**	**54.1%**
Under age 15	100.0	2.3	1.9	33.6	39.3	23.1
Aged 15 to 19	100.0	2.1	1.9	22.7	34.1	39.4
Aged 20 to 24	100.0	1.7	3.1	20.7	26.5	48.1
Aged 25 to 29	100.0	1.1	6.4	13.7	21.8	56.8
Aged 30 to 34	100.0	0.8	9.3	10.9	19.0	59.8
Aged 35 to 39	100.0	0.7	11.0	11.1	21.2	55.6
Aged 40 to 44	100.0	0.7	11.6	12.6	22.4	51.9
Aged 45 to 54	100.0	0.6	12.5	13.4	16.4	54.1
PERCENT DISTRIBUTION BY AGE						
Total births	**100.0**	**100.0**	**100.0**	**100.0**	**100.0**	**100.0**
Under age 15	0.1	0.2	0.0	0.2	0.1	0.0
Aged 15 to 19	6.9	12.4	1.9	10.6	10.3	5.1
Aged 20 to 24	22.8	32.6	10.3	31.8	26.4	20.3
Aged 25 to 29	28.5	27.6	26.7	26.4	27.1	29.9
Aged 30 to 34	26.4	17.7	36.1	19.3	21.8	29.2
Aged 35 to 39	12.3	7.8	19.9	9.2	11.4	12.7
Aged 40 to 44	2.8	1.7	4.8	2.4	2.7	2.7
Aged 45 to 54	0.2	0.1	0.4	0.2	0.1	0.2

Note: Births by race and Hispanic origin do not add to total because Hispanics may be of any race and "not stated" is not shown.
Source: National Center for Health Statistics, Births: Preliminary Data for 2013, National Vital Statistics Reports, Vol. 63, No. 2, 2014, Internet site http://www.cdc.gov/nchs/births.htm; calculations by New Strategist

Table 3.15 Births by Age of Mother and Birth Order, 2013

(number and percent distribution of births by age of mother and birth order, 2013)

	total	first child	second child	third child	fourth or later child
Total births	**3,957,577**	**1,555,614**	**1,251,721**	**657,578**	**472,270**
Under age 15	3,108	3,038	50	3	1
Aged 15 to 19	274,641	226,650	40,478	5,567	753
Aged 20 to 24	902,146	456,161	293,099	108,760	39,641
Aged 25 to 29	1,127,561	421,982	371,466	203,371	125,021
Aged 30 to 34	1,044,029	311,003	356,382	207,433	163,724
Aged 35 to 39	487,476	110,071	157,067	108,664	108,974
Aged 40 to 44	110,332	24,320	31,056	22,503	31,736
Aged 45 to 54	8,284	2,390	2,124	1,277	2,420
PERCENT DISTRIBUTION BY BIRTH ORDER					
Total births	**100.0%**	**39.3%**	**31.6%**	**16.6%**	**11.9%**
Under age 15	100.0	97.7	1.6	0.1	0.0
Aged 15 to 19	100.0	82.5	14.7	2.0	0.3
Aged 20 to 24	100.0	50.6	32.5	12.1	4.4
Aged 25 to 29	100.0	37.4	32.9	18.0	11.1
Aged 30 to 34	100.0	29.8	34.1	19.9	15.7
Aged 35 to 39	100.0	22.6	32.2	22.3	22.4
Aged 40 to 44	100.0	22.0	28.1	20.4	28.8
Aged 45 to 54	100.0	28.9	25.6	15.4	29.2
PERCENT DISTRIBUTION BY AGE					
Total births	**100.0**	**100.0**	**100.0**	**100.0**	**100.0**
Under age 15	0.1	0.2	0.0	0.0	0.0
Aged 15 to 19	6.9	14.6	3.2	0.8	0.2
Aged 20 to 24	22.8	29.3	23.4	16.5	8.4
Aged 25 to 29	28.5	27.1	29.7	30.9	26.5
Aged 30 to 34	26.4	20.0	28.5	31.5	34.7
Aged 35 to 39	12.3	7.1	12.5	16.5	23.1
Aged 40 to 44	2.8	1.6	2.5	3.4	6.7
Aged 45 to 54	0.2	0.2	0.2	0.2	0.5

Note: Numbers do not add to total because "not stated" is not shown.
Source: National Center for Health Statistics, Births: Preliminary Data for 2013, National Vital Statistics Reports, Vol. 63, No. 2, 2014, Internet site http://www.cdc.gov/nchs/births.htm; calculations by New Strategist

Many Millennial Mothers Are Not Married

Out-of-wedlock births fall with age.

More than 40 percent of babies born in 2013 had a mother who was not married. There are big differences by age in the percentage of new mothers who are not married, however. The younger the woman, the more likely she is to give birth out of wedlock.

Among babies born to women under age 25 in 2013, most were born to single mothers. The figure falls to 36 percent in the 25-to-29 age group. Among babies born to women aged 30 or older, from 21 to 24 percent had a single mother.

■ Out-of-wedlock childbearing has increased greatly over the past few decades, and it has become common even among older mothers.

Sixty-five percent of births to women aged 20 to 24 are out of wedlock

(percent of babies born to unmarried women by age, 2013)

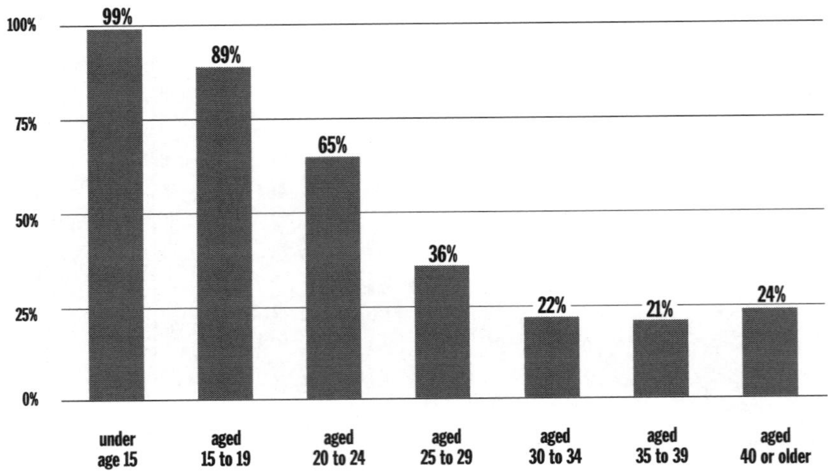

Table 3.16 Births to Unmarried Women by Age, 2013

(total number of births and number and percent to unmarried women, by age, 2013)

		unmarried women		
	total	number	percent distribution	percent of total
Total births	**3,957,577**	**1,605,643**	**100.0%**	**40.6%**
Under age 15	3,108	3,081	0.2	99.1
Aged 15 to 19	274,641	243,480	15.2	88.7
Aged 20 to 24	902,146	590,385	36.8	65.4
Aged 25 to 29	1,127,561	404,443	25.2	35.9
Aged 30 to 34	1,044,029	233,078	14.5	22.3
Aged 35 to 39	487,476	103,101	6.4	21.1
Aged 40 or older	118,616	28,075	1.7	23.7

Source: National Center for Health Statistics, Births: Preliminary Data for 2013, National Vital Statistics Reports, Vol. 63, No. 2, 2014, Internet site http://www.cdc.gov/nchs/births.htm; calculations by New Strategist

Caesarean Deliveries Are Common among Women of All Ages

The rate is highest among older women, however.

Delayed childbearing can have an unanticipated cost. The older a woman is when she has a child, the greater the likelihood of complications that necessitate Caesarean delivery.

Among babies born in 2012, nearly 33 percent were delivered by Caesarean section. The figure ranges from only 22 percent of babies born to women under age 20 to half of babies born to women aged 40 or older.

■ As women delay childbearing, the rate of Caesarean delivery increases.

Younger mothers are less likely to deliver by Caesarean

(percent of births delivered by Cesarean section, by age of mother, 2012)

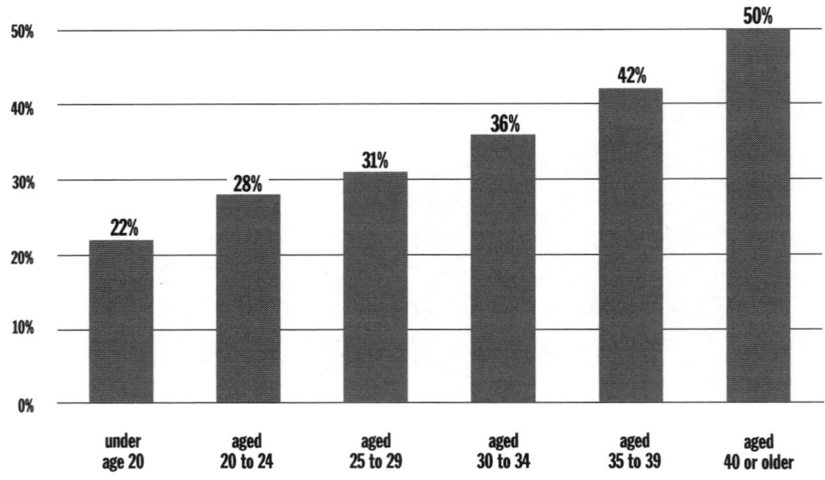

Table 3.17 Births by Age and Method of Delivery, 2012

(number and percent distribution of births by age and method of delivery, 2012)

	total births	vaginal	Caesarean
Total births	**3,952,841**	**2,650,744**	**1,296,070**
Under age 20	309,060	239,809	68,901
Aged 20 to 24	916,811	660,209	255,264
Aged 25 to 29	1,123,900	768,764	353,412
Aged 30 to 34	1,013,416	649,960	361,891
Aged 35 to 39	472,318	273,096	198,432
Aged 40 or older	117,336	58,906	58,170
PERCENT DISTRIBUTION BY METHOD OF DELIVERY			
Total births	**100.0%**	**67.1%**	**32.8%**
Under age 20	100.0	77.6	22.3
Aged 20 to 24	100.0	72.0	27.8
Aged 25 to 29	100.0	68.4	31.4
Aged 30 to 34	100.0	64.1	35.7
Aged 35 to 39	100.0	57.8	42.0
Aged 40 or older	100.0	50.2	49.6
PERCENT DISTRIBUTION BY AGE			
Total births	**100.0**	**100.0**	**100.0**
Under age 20	7.8	9.0	5.3
Aged 20 to 24	23.2	24.9	19.7
Aged 25 to 29	28.4	29.0	27.3
Aged 30 to 34	25.6	24.5	27.9
Aged 35 to 39	11.9	10.3	15.3
Aged 40 or older	3.0	2.2	4.5

Note: Numbers do not add to total because not stated is not shown.
Source: National Center for Health Statistics, Births: Final Data for 2012, National Vital Statistics Reports, Vol. 62, No. 9, 2013, Internet site http://www.cdc.gov/nchs/births.htm; calculations by New Strategist

Cigarette Smoking Is above Average among Millennials

Many young adults have smoked cigarettes in the past month.

Cigarette smoking among young adults remains stubbornly high. Overall, 22 percent of people aged 12 or older smoked a cigarette in the past month, according to a 2012 survey. The proportion surpasses the national average among 18-year-olds and rises as high as 35 percent among people in their twenties.

Another government survey shows that 21 to 27 percent of people ranging in age from 18 to 34 are current smokers. Among 18-to-24-year-olds, 72 percent say they have never smoked. The figure drops to just 55 percent in the 25-to-34 age group.

■ Although smoking is becoming less common, many young adults experiment with cigarettes and some will become lifelong smokers.

A large share of Millennials smoke cigarettes

(percent distribution of people aged 18 to 34 by cigarette smoking status, 2012)

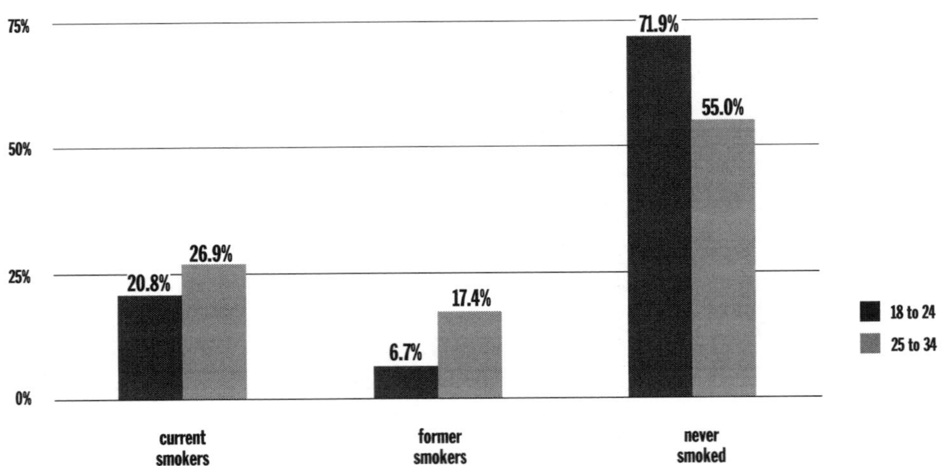

Table 3.18 Cigarette Smoking among People Aged 12 or Older, 2012

(percent of people aged 12 or older reporting any, past year, and past month use of cigarettes, 2012)

	ever smoked	smoked in past year	smoked in past month
Total people aged 12 or older	**61.9%**	**26.1%**	**22.1%**
Aged 12 to 17	17.4	11.8	6.6
Aged 18	47.3	36.1	25.1
Aged 19	50.3	37.3	27.7
Aged 20	58.3	42.8	32.1
Aged 21	60.8	43.3	33.4
Aged 22	63.2	44.4	35.1
Aged 23	62.9	40.9	33.0
Aged 24	66.5	42.5	35.4
Aged 25	68.9	41.2	33.6
Aged 26 to 29	68.8	40.0	33.4
Aged 30 to 34	69.2	36.7	31.9
Aged 35 to 39	67.9	31.0	26.7
Aged 40 to 44	67.1	27.2	24.3
Aged 45 to 49	66.6	28.2	26.0
Aged 50 to 54	68.7	26.4	24.5
Aged 55 to 59	69.8	23.4	21.5
Aged 60 to 64	66.7	19.0	16.9
Aged 65 or older	67.0	11.6	10.0

Source: SAMHSA, Office of Applied Studies, 2012 National Survey on Drug Use and Health, Detailed Tables, Internet site http://www.samhsa.gov/data/NSDUH/2012SummNatFindDetTables/Index.aspx

Table 3.19 Cigarette Smoking Status by Age, 2012

(percent distribution of people aged 18 or older by age and cigarette smoking status, 2012)

		all current smokers				
	total	total	smoke every day	smoke some days	former smoker	never smoked
Total people	**100.0 %**	**19.2%**	**13.5%**	**5.7%**	**25.2%**	**54.4%**
Aged 18 to 24	100.0	20.8	13.2	7.6	6.7	71.9
Aged 25 to 34	100.0	26.9	18.8	8.1	17.4	55.0
Aged 35 to 44	100.0	21.6	15.6	6.0	19.9	56.9
Aged 45 to 54	100.0	22.3	16.8	5.5	24.2	53.1
Aged 55 to 64	100.0	18.2	13.3	4.9	32.8	47.9
Aged 65 or older	100.0	8.8	6.4	2.4	43.1	47.0

Source: Centers for Disease Control and Prevention, Behavioral Risk Factor Surveillance System Prevalence Data, 2012, Internet site http://apps.nccd.cdc.gov/brfss/

Most Young Adults Have Had a Drink in the Past Month

Drinking peaks among 21-year-olds.

More than half of Americans aged 12 or older have had an alcoholic beverage in the past month. The figure peaks at 70 percent among 21- and 22-year-olds. Few young adults wait until their 21st birthday before they have a drink, however. The majority of 20-year-olds have had alcohol in the past month.

Many young adults take part in binge drinking, meaning they have had five or more drinks on one occasion in the past month. More than 40 percent of people ranging in age from 21 to 25 have participated in binge drinking during the past month. More than one in ten 19-to-25-year-olds have participated in heavy drinking—meaning they have binged at least five times during the month.

Another survey asks people aged 18 or older whether they have had a drink in the past 30 days, and 53 percent of 18-to-24-year-olds say yes. The figure rises to 64 percent in the 25-to-34 age group.

■ Among young adults, heavy drinking is a bigger problem than drug use.

Most young adults do not wait for legal drinking age

(percent of people aged 18 to 21 who have had an alcoholic drink in the past 30 days, by age, 2012)

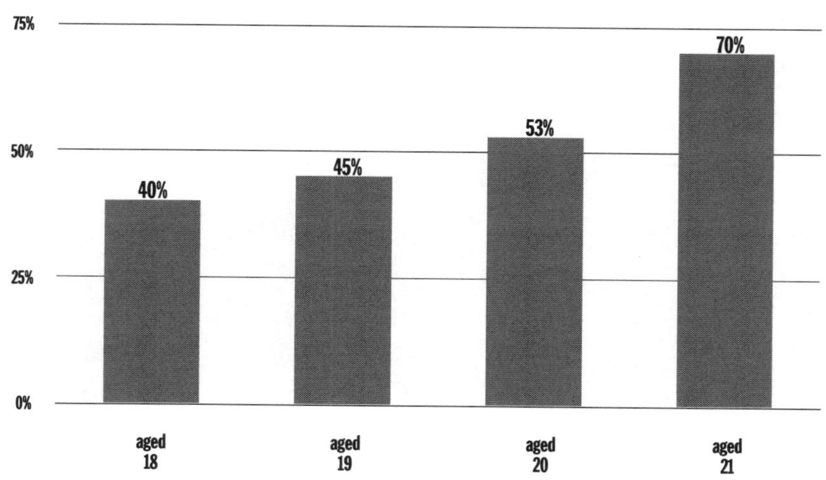

Table 3.20 Alcohol Use by People Aged 12 or Older, 2012

(percent of people aged 12 or older who drank alcoholic beverages during the past month, by level of alcohol use, 2012)

	drank at any time during past month	binge drinking during past month	heavy drinking during past month
Total people aged 12 or older	**52.1%**	**23.0%**	**6.5%**
Aged 12 to 17	12.9	7.2	1.3
Aged 18	39.9	26.0	6.6
Aged 19	44.7	30.7	11.1
Aged 20	53.3	35.3	12.6
Aged 21	69.7	47.4	16.2
Aged 22	69.6	46.3	14.8
Aged 23	68.6	44.1	13.8
Aged 24	69.2	44.3	12.6
Aged 25	68.9	43.0	14.2
Aged 26 to 29	67.0	37.7	9.9
Aged 30 to 34	62.2	33.7	8.9
Aged 35 to 39	62.3	28.9	8.2
Aged 40 to 44	60.1	27.4	8.0
Aged 45 to 49	59.0	25.0	7.1
Aged 50 to 54	58.5	22.7	6.6
Aged 55 to 59	53.2	16.7	5.0
Aged 60 to 64	53.1	14.3	4.3
Aged 65 or older	41.2	8.2	2.0

Note: "Binge drinking" is defined as having five or more drinks on the same occasion on at least one day in the 30 days prior to the survey. "Heavy drinking" is defined as having five or more drinks on the same occasion on each of five or more days in the 30 days prior to the survey.
Source: SAMHSA, Office of Applied Studies, 2012 National Survey on Drug Use and Health, Detailed Tables, Internet site http://www.samhsa.gov/data/NSDUH/2012SummNatFindDetTables/Index.aspx

Table 3.21 Alcohol Use by Age, 2012

(percent distribution of people aged 18 or older by whether they have had at least one drink of alcohol within the past 30 days, by age, 2012)

	total	yes	no
Total people	**100.0%**	**55.3%**	**44.7%**
Aged 18 to 24	100.0	52.6	47.4
Aged 25 to 34	100.0	64.3	35.7
Aged 35 to 44	100.0	59.1	40.9
Aged 45 to 54	100.0	57.3	42.7
Aged 55 to 64	100.0	53.1	46.9
Aged 65 or older	100.0	42.9	57.1

Source: Centers for Disease Control and Prevention, Behavioral Risk Factor Surveillance System Prevalence Data, 2012; Internet site http://apps.nccd.cdc.gov/brfss/v

Drug Use Is Prevalent among Young Adults

More than one in five 18-to-22-year-olds have used marijuana in the past month.

Among Americans aged 12 or older, only 9 percent have used an illicit drug in the past month. Young adults are much more likely than the average person to be a current drug user, with more than 20 percent having used an illicit drug in the past 30 days.

Marijuana is the drug of choice for many of the nation's young adults. The majority of people ranging in age from 20 to 59 (except for a slight dip below 50 percent among 35-to-44-year-olds) have used marijuana at some point in their lives. Among people aged 18 to 34, more than one in 10 have used marijuana in the past 30 days.

■ Support for legalizing marijuana is growing as Boomers and younger generations replace older Americans who are unfamiliar with the drug.

Many young adults use marijuana regularly

(percent of people aged 18 to 24 who have used marijuana in the past month, by age, 2012)

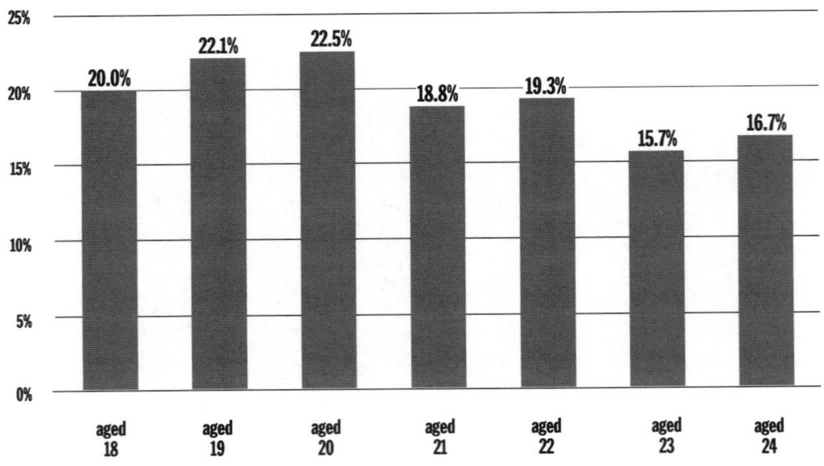

Table 3.22 Illicit Drug Use by People Aged 12 or Older, 2012

(percent of people aged 12 or older who ever used any illicit drug, who used an illicit drug in the past year, and who used an illicit drug in the past month, by age, 2012)

	ever used	used in past year	used in past month
Total people	**48.0%**	**16.0%**	**9.2%**
Aged 12 to 17	24.2	17.9	9.5
Aged 18	49.3	38.4	22.5
Aged 19	52.2	38.2	24.3
Aged 20	58.3	42.4	25.0
Aged 21	58.8	37.7	21.4
Aged 22	60.9	37.6	22.6
Aged 23	61.0	32.2	18.1
Aged 24	61.3	32.8	19.2
Aged 25	61.2	30.2	17.1
Aged 26 to 29	61.7	26.4	14.6
Aged 30 to 34	60.0	21.5	13.2
Aged 35 to 39	55.5	15.7	8.8
Aged 40 to 44	54.5	13.8	7.3
Aged 45 to 49	59.0	13.4	7.7
Aged 50 to 54	60.7	12.1	7.2
Aged 55 to 59	56.8	10.8	6.6
Aged 60 to 64	47.6	6.0	3.6
Aged 65 or older	19.3	2.3	1.3

Note: Illicit drugs include marijuana, hashish, cocaine (including crack), heroin, hallucinogens, inhalants, or any prescription-type psychotherapeutic used nonmedically.
Source: SAMHSA, Office of Applied Studies, 2012 National Survey on Drug Use and Health, Detailed Tables, Internet site http://www.samhsa.gov/data/NSDUH/2012SummNatFindDetTables/Index.aspx

Table 3.23 Marijuana Use by People Aged 12 or Older, 2012

(percent of people aged 12 or older who ever used marijuana, who used marijuana in the past year, and who used marijuana in the past month, by age, 2012)

	ever used	used in past year	used in past month
Total people	**42.8%**	**12.1%**	**7.3%**
Aged 12 to 17	17.0	13.5	7.2
Aged 18	43.3	34.2	20.0
Aged 19	46.1	34.4	22.1
Aged 20	53.4	37.3	22.5
Aged 21	52.9	33.2	18.8
Aged 22	55.7	32.1	19.3
Aged 23	55.8	27.7	15.7
Aged 24	55.9	27.6	16.7
Aged 25	55.4	24.3	14.5
Aged 26 to 29	56.2	20.1	11.9
Aged 30 to 34	54.3	16.5	10.8
Aged 35 to 39	49.6	10.8	6.6
Aged 40 to 44	47.8	9.1	5.1
Aged 45 to 49	53.7	9.4	5.2
Aged 50 to 54	56.7	8.0	5.1
Aged 55 to 59	53.0	7.4	4.8
Aged 60 to 64	44.4	4.4	2.4
Aged 65 or older	14.8	1.2	0.9

Source: SAMHSA, Office of Applied Studies, 2012 National Survey on Drug Use and Health, Detailed Tables, Internet site http://www.samhsa.gov/data/NSDUH/2012SummNatFindDetTables/Index.aspx

Millennials Are Most Likely to Lack Health Insurance

More than one in five have no insurance.

Before the Affordable Care Act allowed young adults under age 26 to remain on their parents' health insurance plan, the 18-to-24 age group was most likely to be without health insurance. Now that distinction belongs to people aged 25 to 34, 24 percent of whom were without health insurance at any time in 2013. The figure is a smaller (21 percent) among 18-to-24-year-olds.

Most Americans obtain health insurance coverage through an employer. But among 18-to-24-year-olds with health insurance, only 58 percent had employment-based coverage and just 15 percent had coverage through their own employer. Among those with health insurance in the 25-to-34 age group, a larger 73 have employment-based coverage and 54 percent have coverage through their own employer.

Three out of four Millennials had a health care expense in 2012, according to the Medical Expenditure Panel Survey, the median expense being $831. Millennials paid only 15 percent of that expense out-of-pocket, while private insurance paid 56.5 percent and Medicaid 16 percent.

■ The number of people in their twenties and thirties without health insurance is declining because of the Affordable Care Act.

Many Americans under age 65 are not covered by health insurance

(percent of people aged 18 or older not covered by health insurance at any time during the year, by age, 2013)

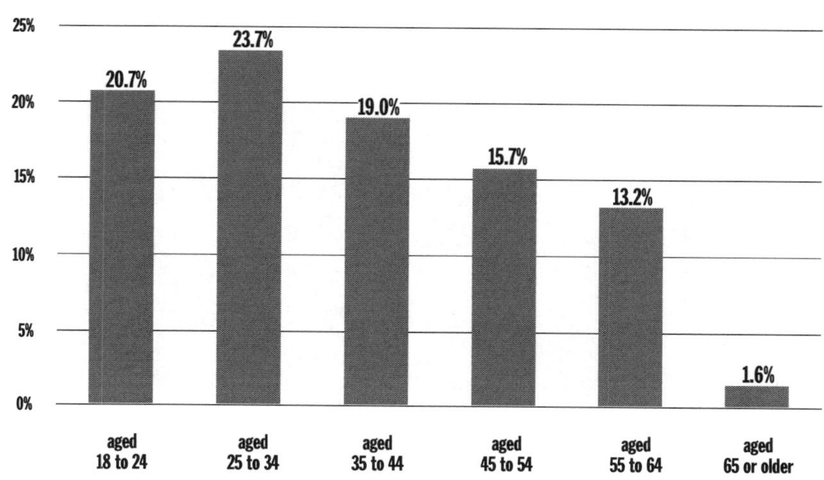

Table 3.24 Health Insurance Coverage by Age, 2013

(number and percent distribution of people by age and health insurance coverage status, 2013; numbers in thousands)

	total	covered by some type of health insurance during the year	not covered at any time during the year
Total people	**313,395**	**271,442**	**41,953**
Under age 65	268,888	227,627	41,260
Under age 18	74,055	68,613	5,441
Aged 18 to 24	30,054	23,846	6,208
Aged 25 to 34	42,466	32,397	10,069
Aged 35 to 44	39,789	32,233	7,556
Aged 45 to 54	42,898	36,159	6,739
Aged 55 to 64	39,626	34,380	5,247
Aged 65 or older	44,508	43,815	693
PERCENT DISTRIBUTION BY COVERAGE STATUS			
Total people	**100.0%**	**86.6%**	**13.4%**
Under age 65	100.0	84.7	15.3
Under age 18	100.0	92.7	7.3
Aged 18 to 24	100.0	79.3	20.7
Aged 25 to 34	100.0	76.3	23.7
Aged 35 to 44	100.0	81.0	19.0
Aged 45 to 54	100.0	84.3	15.7
Aged 55 to 64	100.0	86.8	13.2
Aged 65 or older	100.0	98.4	1.6
PERCENT DISTRIBUTION BY AGE			
Total people	**100.0**	**100.0**	**100.0**
Under age 65	85.8	83.9	98.3
Under age 18	23.6	25.3	13.0
Aged 18 to 24	9.6	8.8	14.8
Aged 25 to 34	13.6	11.9	24.0
Aged 35 to 44	12.7	11.9	18.0
Aged 45 to 54	13.7	13.3	16.1
Aged 55 to 64	12.6	12.7	12.5
Aged 65 or older	14.2	16.1	1.7

Source: Bureau of the Census, Health Insurance, Internet site http://www.census.gov/hhes/www/hlthins/; calculations by New Strategist

Table 3.25 Health Insurance Coverage by Age and Type of Coverage, 2013

(number and percent distribution of people with health insurance by age and type of coverage, 2013; numbers in thousands)

	total with coverage	total with private	employment based total	employment based own	direct purchase	total with government	Medicaid	Medicare	military
Total people	**271,442**	**201,064**	**169,015**	**87,097**	**34,531**	**107,581**	**54,081**	**48,977**	**14,147**
Under age 65	227,627	177,026	156,000	77,685	22,534	65,913	51,241	7,534	10,853
Under age 18	68,613	44,429	40,556	64	4,828	30,410	27,814	264	2,970
Aged 18 to 24	23,846	19,035	13,793	3,562	2,434	6,404	5,193	254	1,174
Aged 25 to 34	32,397	26,647	23,514	17,479	3,326	7,378	5,522	615	1,581
Aged 35 to 44	32,233	27,661	25,447	18,324	2,960	6,214	4,501	948	1,256
Aged 45 to 54	36,159	31,250	28,290	20,313	4,277	6,641	3,943	1,931	1,553
Aged 55 to 64	34,380	28,003	24,400	17,944	4,710	8,866	4,270	3,523	2,318
Aged 65 or older	43,815	24,039	13,015	9,413	11,996	41,668	2,840	41,442	3,294
PERCENT DISTRIBUTION BY TYPE OF COVERAGE									
Total people	**100.0%**	**74.1%**	**62.3%**	**32.1%**	**12.7%**	**39.6%**	**19.9%**	**18.0%**	**5.2%**
Under age 65	100.0	77.8	68.5	34.1	9.9	29.0	22.5	3.3	4.8
Under age 18	100.0	64.8	59.1	0.1	7.0	44.3	40.5	0.4	4.3
Aged 18 to 24	100.0	79.8	57.8	14.9	10.2	26.9	21.8	1.1	4.9
Aged 25 to 34	100.0	82.3	72.6	54.0	10.3	22.8	17.0	1.9	4.9
Aged 35 to 44	100.0	85.8	78.9	56.8	9.2	19.3	14.0	2.9	3.9
Aged 45 to 54	100.0	86.4	78.2	56.2	11.8	18.4	10.9	5.3	4.3
Aged 55 to 64	100.0	81.5	71.0	52.2	13.7	25.8	12.4	10.2	6.7
Aged 65 or older	100.0	54.9	29.7	21.5	27.4	95.1	6.5	94.6	7.5
PERCENT DISTRIBUTION BY AGE									
Total people	**100.0**	**100.0**	**100.0**	**100.0**	**100.0**	**100.0**	**100.0**	**100.0**	**100.0**
Under age 65	83.9	88.0	92.3	89.2	65.3	61.3	94.7	15.4	76.7
Under age 18	25.3	22.1	24.0	0.1	14.0	28.3	51.4	0.5	21.0
Aged 18 to 24	8.8	9.5	8.2	4.1	7.0	6.0	9.6	0.5	8.3
Aged 25 to 34	11.9	13.3	13.9	20.1	9.6	6.9	10.2	1.3	11.2
Aged 35 to 44	11.9	13.8	15.1	21.0	8.6	5.8	8.3	1.9	8.9
Aged 45 to 54	13.3	15.5	16.7	23.3	12.4	6.2	7.3	3.9	11.0
Aged 55 to 64	12.7	13.9	14.4	20.6	13.6	8.2	7.9	7.2	16.4
Aged 65 or older	16.1	12.0	7.7	10.8	34.7	38.7	5.3	84.6	23.3

Note: Numbers do not add to total because some people are covered by more than one type of health insurance.
Source: Bureau of the Census, Health Insurance, Internet site http://www.census.gov/hhes/www/hlthins/; calculations by New Strategist

Table 3.26 Spending on Health Care by Age, 2012

(percent of people with health care expense, median expense per person, total expenses, and percent distribution of total expenses by source of payment, by age, 2012)

	total (thousands)	percent with expense	median expense per person	total expenses: amount (millions)	total expenses: percent distribution
Total people	**313,490**	**84.7%**	**$1,286**	**$1,350,721**	**100.0%**
Under age 18	73,913	86.7	541	133,951	9.9
Aged 18 to 25	35,050	71.0	681	68,081	5.0
Aged 26 to 34	37,139	74.9	947	112,697	8.3
Aged 35 to 44	39,769	80.1	1,098	116,212	8.6
Aged 45 to 54	43,598	85.8	1,539	215,894	16.0
Aged 55 to 64	38,751	92.3	2,509	281,776	20.9
Aged 65 or older	45,271	96.3	4,292	422,109	31.3

	percent distribution by source of payment: total	out of pocket	private insurance	Medicare	Medicaid
Total people	**100.0%**	**14.1%**	**42.5%**	**24.5%**	**10.5%**
Under age 18	100.0	15.0	50.6	1.3	27.5
Aged 18 to 25	100.0	15.3	56.3	1.7	18.9
Aged 26 to 34	100.0	14.9	55.9	2.8	15.0
Aged 35 to 44	100.0	16.6	55.9	7.6	11.7
Aged 45 to 54	100.0	14.4	55.7	9.5	11.6
Aged 55 to 64	100.0	13.9	54.7	13.1	6.9
Aged 65 or older	100.0	12.8	15.5	61.3	4.1

Note: Source of payment does not sum to 100 because "other" is not shown.
Source: Agency for Healthcare Research and Quality, Medical Expenditure Panel Survey, 2012, Internet site http://meps.ahrq.gov/mepsweb/survey_comp/household.jsp; calculations by New Strategist

Table 3.27 Spending on Health Care by Generation, 2012

(percent of people with health care expense, median expense per person, total expenses, and percent distribution of total expenses by source of payment, by generation, 2012)

	total (thousands)	percent with expense	median expense per person	total expenses amount (millions)	total expenses percent distribution
Total people	**313,490**	**84.7%**	**$1,286**	**$1,350,721**	**100.0%**
iGeneration (under age 18)	73,913	86.7	541	133,951	9.9
Millennials (aged 18 to 35)	76,263	73.4	831	193,924	14.4
Generation X (aged 36 to 47)	47,418	81.1	1,143	149,346	11.1
Baby Boomers (aged 48 to 66)	77,615	90.1	2,202	503,104	37.2
Older Americans (aged 67 or older)	38,281	96.7	4,481	370,397	27.4

	percent distribution by source of payment				
	total	out of pocket	private insurance	Medicare	Medicaid
Total people	**100.0%**	**14.1%**	**42.5%**	**24.5%**	**10.5%**
iGeneration (under age 18)	100.0	15.0	50.6	1.3	27.5
Millennials (aged 18 to 35)	100.0	14.9	56.5	2.9	16.0
Generation X (aged 36 to 47)	100.0	16.5	56.8	7.1	11.4
Baby Boomers (aged 48 to 66)	100.0	13.9	52.0	15.5	8.1
Older Americans (aged 67 or older)	100.0	12.8	13.5	63.5	4.4

Note: Source of payment does not sum to 100 because "other" is not shown.
Source: Agency for Healthcare Research and Quality, Medical Expenditure Panel Survey, 2012, Internet site http://meps.ahrq.gov/mepsweb/survey_comp/household.jsp; calculations by New Strategist

Health Problems Are Few in the 18-to-44 Age Group

Lower back pain is by far the most common health condition in the age group.

Twenty-four percent of Americans aged 18 to 44 have experienced lower back pain for at least one full day in the past three months, according to a 2012 National Center for Health Statistics survey, making it the most common health condition in the age group (Millennials were aged 18 to 35 in 2012). Migraines or severe headaches are second, with 17 percent having them. Chronic joint symptoms are third, with 15 percent reporting the problem.

The 18-to-44 age group accounts for more than half of those who have ever had asthma, and they are nearly half of those who still have asthma. They account for 58 percent of those with migraines or severe headaches.

■ As the Millennial generation ages into its thirties and forties, the percentage with health problems will rise.

Headaches are the second most common health problem among 18-to-44-year-olds

(percent of people aged 18 to 44 with health condition, 2012)

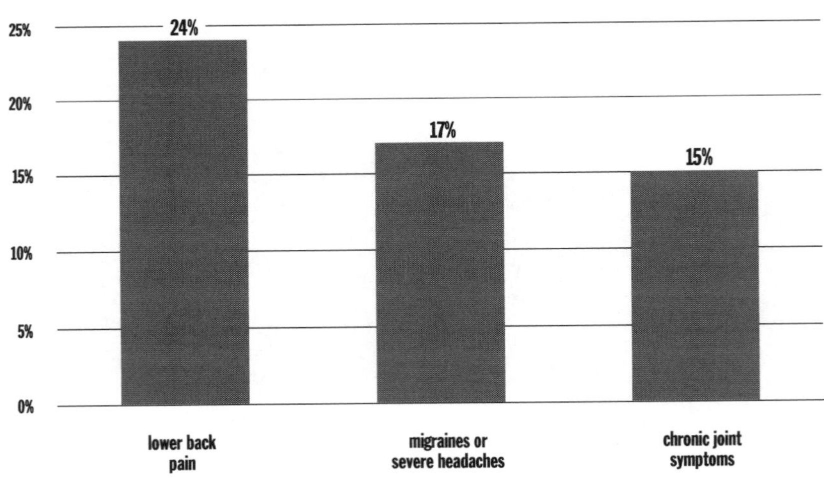

Table 3.28 Health Conditions among People Aged 18 to 44, 2012

(number of people aged 18 or older and aged 18 to 44 with selected health conditions, percent of 18-to-44-year-olds with condition and 18-to-44 share of total, by type of condition, 2012; numbers in thousands)

		aged 18 to 44		
	total	total	percent with condition	share of total
Total people aged 18 or older	**234,921**	**111,034**	**100.0%**	**47.3%**
Selected circulatory diseases				
Heart disease, all types	26,561	4,168	3.8	15.7
Coronary	15,281	980	0.9	6.4
Hypertension	59,830	9,187	8.3	15.4
Stroke	6,370	635	0.6	10.0
Selected respiratory conditions				
Emphysema	4,108	292	0.3	7.1
Asthma, ever	29,660	14,929	13.4	50.3
Asthma, still	18,719	8,943	8.1	47.8
Hay fever	17,596	6,774	6.1	38.5
Sinusitis	28,504	10,889	9.8	38.2
Chronic bronchitis	8,658	2,721	2.5	31.4
Chronic obstructive pulmonary disease	6,790	512	0.5	7.5
Selected types of cancer				
Any cancer	20,073	2,265	2.0	11.3
Breast cancer	3,312	171	0.2	5.2
Cervical cancer	1,330	524	0.9	39.4
Prostate cancer	2,453	–	–	–
Other selected diseases and conditions				
Diabetes	21,319	2,673	2.4	12.5
Ulcers	15,435	4,555	4.1	29.5
Kidney disease	3,882	633	0.6	16.3
Liver disease	3,034	688	0.6	22.7
Arthritis	51,830	7,582	6.8	14.6
Chronic joint symptoms	63,085	16,734	15.1	26.5
Migraines or severe headaches	32,453	18,920	17.1	58.3
Pain in neck	33,515	12,528	11.3	37.4
Pain in lower back	65,823	26,611	24.0	40.4
Pain in face or jaw	11,326	5,457	4.9	48.2
Selected sensory problems				
Hearing	37,567	6,830	6.2	18.2
Vision	20,609	6,014	5.4	29.2
Absence of all natural teeth	17,952	2,785	2.5	15.5

Note: The conditions shown are those that have ever been diagnosed by a doctor, except as noted. Hay fever, sinusitis, chronic bronchitis, and chronic obstructive pulmonary disease have been diagnosed in the past 12 months. Kidney and liver diseases have been diagnosed in the past 12 months and exclude kidney stones, bladder infections, and incontinence. Chronic joint symptoms are shown if respondent had pain, aching, or stiffness in or around a joint (excluding back and neck) and the condition began more than three months ago. Migraines and pain in neck, lower back, face, or jaw are shown only if pain lasted a whole day or more. "–" means sample is too small to make a reliable estimate.

Source: National Center for Health Statistics, Summary Health Statistics for U.S. Adults: National Health Interview Survey, 2012, Vital and Health Statistics, Series 10, No. 260, 2014, Internet site http://www.cdc.gov/nchs/nhis.htm

More than 1 Million Americans Have Been Diagnosed with AIDS

For most, the diagnosis occurred when they were aged 30 or older.

As of 2011, more than 1 million people had been diagnosed with AIDS in the United States. Only 17 percent were diagnosed before the age of 30, 40 percent when they were in their thirties, and 43 percent at age 40 or older.

Although new drug treatments have lowered mortality rates from AIDS, the cost of treatment can be prohibitive.

■ The threat of AIDS has boosted condom use among young adults.

Few are diagnosed with AIDS before age 30

(percent distribution of cumulative number of AIDS cases by age at diagnosis, through 2011)

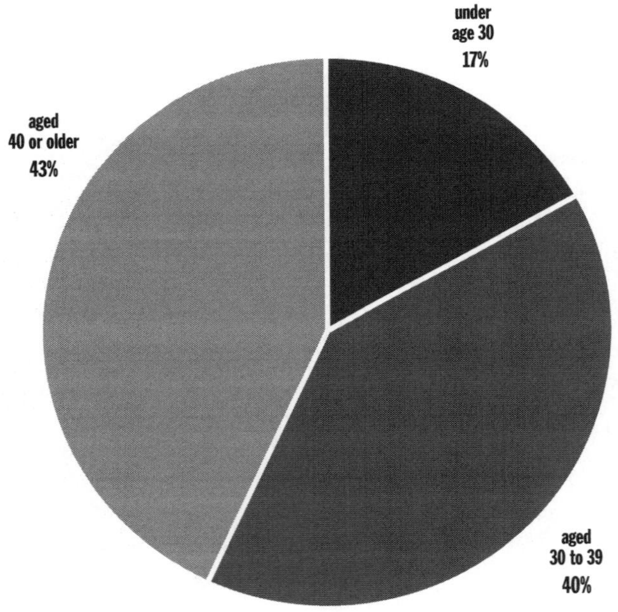

Table 3.29 AIDS Cases by Age, through 2011

(cumulative number and percent distribution of AIDS cases by age at diagnosis, 2011)

	number	percent distribution
Total cases	**1,155,792**	**100.0%**
Under age 13	9,521	0.8
Aged 13 to 14	1,452	0.1
Aged 15 to 19	8,129	0.7
Aged 20 to 24	46,957	4.1
Aged 25 to 29	135,135	11.7
Aged 30 to 34	219,784	19.0
Aged 35 to 39	239,749	20.7
Aged 40 to 44	199,727	17.3
Aged 45 to 49	133,612	11.6
Aged 50 to 54	77,843	6.7
Aged 55 to 59	42,372	3.7
Aged 60 to 64	22,369	1.9
Aged 65 or older	19,143	1.7

Source: Centers for Disease Control and Prevention, Diagnoses of HIV Infection in the United States and Dependent Areas, 2011, Internet site http://www.cdc.gov/hiv/surveillance/resources/reports/2011report/index.htm; calculations by New Strategist

Most Millennials Have Seen a Health Care Provider in the Past Year

Most also have a usual place of care.

Nearly 80 percent of adults visited a health care provider at least once in 2012. Among 18-to-44-year-olds, the figure is 71 percent (Millennials were aged 18 to 35 in 2012). Most of the adult population also has a usual place of care, and for the majority that place is a doctor's office or HMO.

When adults who visited a doctor or health care clinic are asked to rate the care they received, only half give it the highest rating (a 9 or 10 on a scale of 0 to 10). Among Millennials and Generation Xers, only 43 to 44 percent give their health care the highest rating. The figure peaks at 63 percent among Older Americans, almost all of them on Medicare.

■ Many Millennials struggle to get health insurance coverage, a factor that contributes to their jaded view of the quality of care they receive.

Fewer than half of Millennials give their health care the highest rating

(percent of people aged 18 or older who visited a health care provider in the past year who rated the health care they received a 9 or 10 on a scale from 0 (worst) to 10 (best), by generation, 2012)

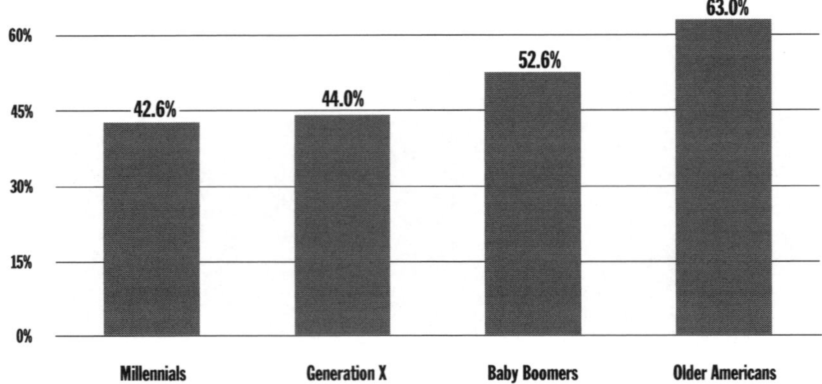

Table 3.30 Health Care Office Visits by Age, 2012

(number of people aged 18 or older and percent distribution by number of office visits to a health care provider in past 12 months, by selected characteristics, 2012; numbers in thousands)

			one or more visits				
	total	no visits	total	one	two to three	four to nine	10 or more
Total people	**234,921**	**45,321**	**184,823**	**41,398**	**59,307**	**53,239**	**30,879**
Aged 18 to 44	111,034	29,657	79,328	22,923	26,482	18,419	11,504
Aged 45 to 64	82,038	12,900	67,495	14,058	22,149	20,126	11,162
Aged 65 to 74	23,760	1,759	21,542	2,925	6,428	7,930	4,259
Aged 75 or older	18,089	1,005	16,458	1,492	4,249	6,764	3,953
PERCENT DISTRIBUTION							
Total people	**100.0%**	**19.3%**	**78.7%**	**17.6%**	**25.2%**	**22.7%**	**13.1%**
Aged 18 to 44	100.0	26.7	71.4	20.6	23.9	16.6	10.4
Aged 45 to 64	100.0	15.7	82.3	17.1	27.0	24.5	13.6
Aged 65 to 74	100.0	7.4	90.7	12.3	27.1	33.4	17.9
Aged 75 or older	100.0	5.6	91.0	8.2	23.5	37.4	21.9

Note: Health care visits exclude overnight hospitalizations, visits to emergency rooms, home visits, dental visits, and telephone calls. Numbers do not add to total because "unknown" is not shown.
Source: National Center for Health Statistics, Summary Health Statistics for U.S. Adults: National Health Interview Survey, 2012, Vital and Health Statistics, Series 10, No. 260, 2014, Internet site http://www.cdc.gov/nchs/products/series/series10.htm; calculations by New Strategist

Table 3.31 Usual Place of Health Care for Adults, 2012

(number and percent distribution of people aged 18 or older by usual place of care status and type of place, by age, 2012; numbers in thousands)

			with a usual place of care				
	number	without a usual place of care	total	doctor's office or HMO	clinic or health center	hospital emergency room or outpatient department	some other place
Total people	**234,921**	**37,458**	**194,933**	**145,366**	**40,518**	**5,463**	**2,049**
Aged 18 to 44	111,034	26,361	83,537	57,795	20,597	2,974	1,108
Aged 45 to 64	82,038	9,733	71,466	54,716	13,821	1,860	694
Aged 65 to 74	23,760	869	22,633	18,386	3,698	369	139
Aged 75 or older	18,089	495	17,298	14,469	2,403	261	108
PERCENT DISTRIBUTION							
Total people	**100.0%**	**15.9%**	**83.0%**	**61.9%**	**17.2%**	**2.3%**	**0.9%**
Aged 18 to 44	100.0	23.7	75.2	52.1	18.6	2.7	1.0
Aged 45 to 64	100.0	11.9	87.1	66.7	16.8	2.3	0.8
Aged 65 to 74	100.0	3.7	95.3	77.4	15.6	1.6	0.6
Aged 75 or older	100.0	2.7	95.6	80.0	13.3	1.4	0.6

Source: National Center for Health Statistics, Summary Health Statistics for U.S. Adults: National Health Interview Survey, 2012, Vital and Health Statistics, Series 10, No. 260, 2014, Internet site http://www.cdc.gov/nchs/products/series/series10.htm; calculations by New Strategist

Table 3.32 Rating of Health Care Received from Doctor's Office or Clinic by Age, 2012

(number of people aged 18 or older visiting a doctor or health care clinic in past 12 months, and percent distribution by rating for health care received on a scale from 0 (worst) to 10 (best), by age, 2012; people in thousands)

	with health care visit		rating		
	number	percent	9 to 10	7 to 8	0 to 6
Total adults	**159,173**	**100.0%**	**50.6%**	**36.1%**	**12.2%**
Aged 18 to 25	17,745	100.0	45.7	39.0	14.7
Aged 26 to 34	20,172	100.0	39.7	45.0	14.5
Aged 35 to 44	24,353	100.0	43.0	41.2	14.7
Aged 45 to 54	28,240	100.0	47.1	38.4	13.6
Aged 55 to 64	30,738	100.0	55.3	32.5	10.9
Aged 65 or older	37,925	100.0	62.2	28.1	8.2

Source: Agency for Healthcare Research and Quality, Medical Expenditure Panel Survey, 2012; Internet site http://meps.ahrq.gov/mepsweb/survey_comp/household.jsp; calculations by New Strategist

Table 3.33 Rating of Health Care Received from Doctor's Office or Clinic by Generation, 2012

(number of people aged 18 or older visiting a doctor or health care clinic in past 12 months, and percent distribution by rating for health care received on a scale from 0 (worst) to 10 (best), by generation, 2012; people in thousands)

	with health care visit		rating		
	number	percent	9 to 10	7 to 8	0 to 6
Total adults	**159,173**	**100.0%**	**50.6%**	**36.1%**	**12.2%**
Millennials (aged 18 to 35)	40,331	100.0	42.6	42.3	14.4
Generation X (aged 36 to 47)	29,748	100.0	44.0	40.4	14.4
Baby Boomers (aged 48 to 66)	57,110	100.0	52.6	34.5	11.8
Older Americans (aged 67 or older)	31,983	100.0	63.0	27.4	8.2

Source: Agency for Healthcare Research and Quality, Medical Expenditure Panel Survey, 2012; Internet site http://meps.ahrq.gov/mepsweb/survey_comp/household.jsp; calculations by New Strategist

Most Deaths among Young Adults Are Preventable

Accidents are the leading killers of 15-to-44-year-olds.

The deaths of young adults are often preventable. Accidents are the leading cause of death among 15-to-44-year-olds, accounting for 41 percent of deaths in the 15-to-24 age group and 26 percent of deaths in the 25-to-44 age group in 2011 (Millennials were aged 17 to 34 in 2011). Suicide ranks second among 15-to-24-year-olds, and homicide is third. Among 25-to-44-year-olds, suicide is fourth and homicide is fifth. HIV infection ranks eighth as a cause of death among 25-to-44-year-olds. Pregnancy and childbirth rank ninth as a cause of death among 15-to-24-year-olds.

Although more could be done to reduce deaths among young adults, some progress has been made. The life expectancy of Americans continues to rise. At birth, Americans can expect to live 78.7 years. At age 25, life expectancy is another 54.8 years.

■ As Millennials age, heart disease and cancer will become increasingly important causes of death.

Accidents are the most important cause of death among people aged 15 to 44

(percent of deaths due to accidents, homicide, and suicide among people aged 15 to 44, 2011)

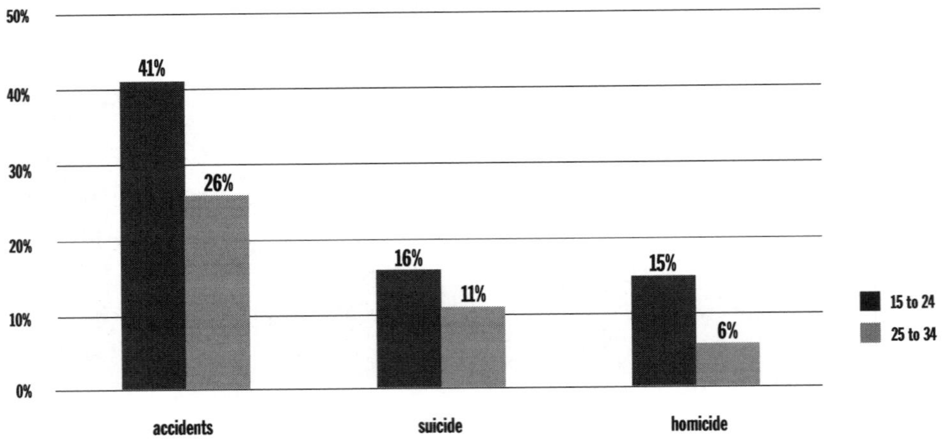

Table 3.34 Leading Causes of Death for People Aged 15 to 24, 2011

(number and percent distribution of deaths accounted for by the 10 leading causes of death for people aged 15 to 24, 2011)

	number	percent
All causes	**29,605**	**100.0%**
1. Accidents (5)	12,032	40.6
2. Suicide (10)	4,688	15.8
3. Homicide	4,508	15.2
4. Malignant neoplasms (cancer) (2)	1,609	5.4
5. Diseases of the heart (1)	948	3.2
6. Congenital malformations	429	1.4
7. Influenza and pneumonia (8)	213	0.7
8. Cerebrovascular diseases (4)	186	0.6
9. Pregnancy, childbirth, and the puerperium	166	0.6
10. Chronic lower respiratory diseases (3)	160	0.5
All other causes	4,666	15.8

Note: Number in parentheses shows rank for all Americans if the cause of death is in top 10.
Source: National Center for Health Statistics, Deaths: Preliminary Data for 2011, National Vital Statistics Report, Vol. 61, No. 6, 2012, Internet site http://www.cdc.gov/nchs/deaths.htm; calculations by New Strategist

Table 3.35 Leading Causes of Death for People Aged 25 to 44, 2011

(number and percent distribution of deaths accounted for by the 10 leading causes of death for people aged 25 to 44, 2011)

	number	percent
All causes	**113,341**	**100.0%**
1. Accidents (5)	29,424	26.0
2. Malignant neoplasms (cancer) (2)	15,210	13.4
3. Diseases of the heart (1)	13,479	11.9
4. Suicide (10)	12,269	10.8
5. Homicide	6,639	5.9
6. Chronic liver disease and cirrhosis	2,919	2.6
7. Diabetes mellitus (7)	2,474	2.2
8. Human immunodeficiency virus infection	2,262	2.0
9. Cerebrovascular diseases (4)	2,245	2.0
10. Influenza and pneumonia (8)	1,341	1.2
All other causes	25,079	22.1

Note: Number in parentheses shows rank for all Americans if the cause of death is in top 10.
Source: National Center for Health Statistics, Deaths: Preliminary Data for 2011, National Vital Statistics Report, Vol. 61, No. 6, 2012, Internet site http://www.cdc.gov/nchs/deaths.htm; calculations by New Strategist

Table 3.36 Life Expectancy by Age and Sex, 2011

(average years of life remaining at selected ages, by sex, 2011)

	total	females	males
At birth	78.7 yrs.	81.1 yrs.	76.3 yrs.
Aged 1	78.2	80.5	75.8
Aged 5	74.3	76.6	71.9
Aged 10	69.3	71.6	66.9
Aged 15	64.4	66.7	62.0
Aged 20	59.5	61.8	57.2
Aged 25	54.8	56.9	52.5
Aged 30	50.0	52.0	47.9
Aged 35	45.3	47.2	43.2
Aged 40	40.6	42.5	38.6
Aged 45	36.0	37.8	34.0
Aged 50	31.5	33.2	29.6
Aged 55	27.2	28.8	25.5
Aged 60	23.1	24.5	21.5
Aged 65	19.2	20.4	17.8
Aged 70	15.5	16.5	14.3
Aged 75	12.1	12.9	11.0
Aged 80	9.1	9.7	8.2
Aged 85	6.5	6.9	5.9
Aged 90	4.6	4.8	4.1
Aged 95	3.2	3.3	2.9
Aged 100	2.3	2.3	2.1

Source: National Center for Health Statistics, Deaths: Preliminary Data for 2011, National Vital Statistics Report, Vol. 61, No. 6, 2012, Internet site http://www.cdc.gov/nchs/deaths.htm

CHAPTER

4

Housing

■ The homeownership rate in the United States reached a peak of 69.0 percent in 2004. By 2013, the rate had fallen 3.9 percentage points to 65.1 percent. The homeownership rate fell the most among 30-to-39-year-olds during those years—a 9 to 10 percentage point decline.

■ Only 39 percent of Millennials own their home. Millennials accounts for 15 percent of the nation's homeowners and 43 percent of all renters.

■ Among Millennials, non-Hispanic Whites are most likely to own a home (42 percent). The rate is 19 percent among Black, 27 percent among Hispanic, and 30 percent among Asian Millennials.

■ The majority of American households (69 percent) live in a single-family home. Among householders under age 35, however, only 49 percent live in a single-family home and almost as many (46 percent) live in a multi-unit building.

■ Young adults are most likely to move. Overall, just 11.7 percent of Americans moved from one house to another between March 2012 and March 2013. Among Millennials, the mobility rate was a much higher 20.4 percent.

Homeownership Rate Has Declined

Rate has fallen the most among 35-to-39-year-olds.

The homeownership rate in the United States reached a peak of 69.0 percent in 2004. Then the Great Recession set in and the housing market collapsed. The overall homeownership rate fell 3.9 percentage points between 2004 and 2013, to 65.1 percent. The 2013 rate is 2.4 percentage points below the rate of 2000.

Since the peak of 2004, the homeownership rate has fallen the most among households headed by 30-to-39-year-olds. This drop occurred primarily as younger renters aged into their thirties and found themselves unable or unwilling to buy a home. In 2013, the homeownership rate of householders aged 35 to 39 was more than 10 percentage points below the rate for that age group in 2004. Among householders aged 30 to 34, the homeownership rate fell 9 percentage points during those years. Householders aged 75 or older were the only ones more likely to be homeowners in 2013 than in 2004.

■ The homeownership rate is falling the most among householders in their thirties because younger adults are unable or unwilling to buy.

After peaking in 2004, the homeownership rate fell sharply among adults in their thirties

(percentage point change in homeownership rate for householders under age 40, by age, 2004 and 2013)

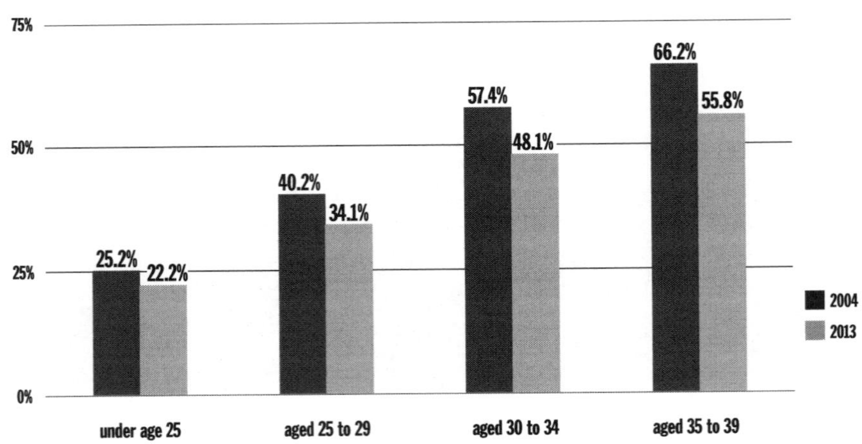

Table 4.1 Homeownership Rate by Age of Householder, 2000 to 2013

(percentage of householders who own their home by age of householder, 2000 to 2013; percentage point change for selected years)

					percentage point change	
	2013	2010	2004	2000	2004–13	2000–13
Total households	**65.1%**	**66.8%**	**69.0%**	**67.5%**	**–3.9**	**–2.4**
Under age 25	22.2	22.8	25.2	21.8	–3.0	0.4
Aged 25 to 29	34.1	36.8	40.2	37.8	–6.1	–3.7
Aged 30 to 34	48.1	51.6	57.4	54.5	–9.3	–6.4
Aged 35 to 39	55.8	61.9	66.2	65.2	–10.4	–9.4
Aged 40 to 44	65.0	67.8	71.9	70.6	–6.9	–5.6
Aged 45 to 49	69.6	72.0	76.3	75.0	–6.7	–5.4
Aged 50 to 54	72.6	75.0	78.3	78.7	–5.7	–6.1
Aged 55 to 59	75.8	77.7	81.2	79.8	–5.4	–4.0
Aged 60 to 64	77.6	80.4	82.4	80.6	–4.8	–3.0
Aged 65 to 69	80.5	81.6	83.2	83.4	–2.7	–2.9
Aged 70 to 74	82.8	82.4	83.4	81.6	–0.6	1.2
Aged 75 or older	80.0	78.9	78.8	78.2	1.2	1.8
Total households	**65.1**	**66.8**	**69.0**	**67.5**	**–3.9**	**–2.4**
Under age 35	36.8	39.0	43.1	40.7	–6.3	–3.9
Aged 35 to 44	60.6	65.0	69.2	68.0	–8.6	–7.4
Aged 45 to 54	71.2	73.5	77.2	76.8	–6.0	–5.6
Aged 55 to 64	76.6	79.0	81.7	80.2	–5.1	–3.6
Aged 65 or older	80.8	80.5	81.1	80.5	–0.3	0.3

Source: Bureau of the Census, Housing Vacancies and Homeownership, Internet site http://www.census.gov/housing/hvs/; calculations by New Strategist

Homeownership Rises with Age

Fewer than 40 percent of Millennials own their home.

For decades, homeownership became the norm in the 30-to-34 age group, until the Great Recession set in. With young adults financially strained and postponing marriage, homeownership now becomes the norm in the 35-to-39 age group—the one now filling with the Millennial generation. In 2013, only 48.1 percent of householders aged 30 to 34 owned their home. The figure rises to the 55.8 percent majority among householders aged 35 to 39.

Young adults are least likely to own a home because they have not yet accumulated the savings for a down payment and are not yet earning enough to qualify for a mortgage. Only 39 percent of Millennial households own their home. The homeownership rate is 76 percent among Boomers and peaks at 81 percent among older Americans.

■ Although homeownership rates are down from their peak, the pattern of homeownership—with rates rising as people age—is unchanged.

Homeownership varies greatly by generation

(percent of households that own their home by generation, 2013)

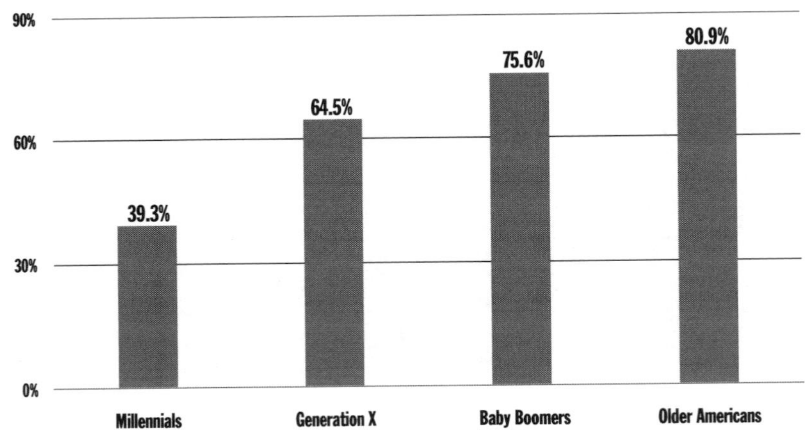

Table 4.2 Owners and Renters by Generation of Householder, 2013

(number and percent distribution of householders by homeownership status, by generation of householder, 2013; numbers in thousands)

	total	owners	renters
Total households	**114,673**	**74,668**	**40,005**
Millennials (under age 37)	28,619	11,251	17,368
Generation Xers (aged 37 to 48)	24,617	15,875	8,742
Baby Boomers (aged 49 to 67)	40,241	30,402	9,839
Older Americans (aged 68 or older)	21,197	17,141	4,056
PERCENT DISTRIBUTION BY HOMEOWNERSHIP STATUS			
Total households	**100.0%**	**65.1%**	**34.9%**
Millennials (under age 37)	100.0	39.3	60.7
Generation Xers (aged 37 to 48)	100.0	64.5	35.5
Baby Boomers (aged 49 to 67)	100.0	75.6	24.4
Older Americans (aged 68 or older)	100.0	80.9	19.1
PERCENT DISTRIBUTION BY AGE OF HOUSEHOLDER			
Total households	**100.0**	**100.0**	**100.0**
Millennials (under age 37)	25.0	15.1	43.4
Generation Xers (aged 37 to 48)	21.5	21.3	21.9
Baby Boomers (aged 49 to 67)	35.1	40.7	24.6
Older Americans (aged 68 or older)	18.5	23.0	10.1

Source: Bureau of the Census, Housing Vacancies and Homeownership, Internet site http://www.census.gov/housing/hvs/; calculations by New Strategist

Table 4.3 Households by Homeownership Status, Generation, and Age Group, 2013

(number and percent distribution of total households, households headed by people under age 37, and households in age groups that include Millennials, by homeownership status, 2013; numbers in thousands)

	total	owners	renters
Total households	**114,673**	**74,668**	**40,005**
Millennials (under age 37)	**28,619**	**11,251**	**17,368**
Under age 25	6,126	1,361	4,765
Aged 25 to 29	8,729	2,977	5,752
Aged 30 to 34	9,963	4,792	5,171
Aged 35 to 39	9,502	5,302	4,200
PERCENT DISTRIBUTION BY HOMEOWNERSHIP STATUS			
Total households	**100.0%**	**65.1%**	**34.9%**
Millennials (under age 37)	**100.0**	**39.3**	**60.7**
Under age 25	100.0	22.2	77.8
Aged 25 to 29	100.0	34.1	65.9
Aged 30 to 34	100.0	48.1	51.9
Aged 35 to 39	100.0	55.8	44.2

Source: Bureau of the Census, Housing Vacancies and Homeownership, Internet site http://www.census.gov/housing/hvs/; calculations by New Strategist

Married Couples Are Most Likely to Be Homeowners

Homeownership rate is highest in the Midwest.

The homeownership rate among married couples was 80.7 percent in 2013, much higher than the 65.1 percent for all households. Among married couples, the homeownership rate surpasses 50 percent in the youthful 25-to-29 age group. For other types of households, the homeownership rate does not surpass 50 percent until older age groups. Male-headed families cross the 50-percent threshold in the 40-to-44 age group, female-headed families and men who live alone in the 45-to-49 age group, and women who live alone in the 50-to-54 age group.

In 2013, the homeownership rate was highest in the Midwest (69.7 percent) and lowest in the West (59.4 percent). Homeownership becomes the norm in the 30-to-34 age group in the Midwest, in the 35-to-39 age group in the Northeast and South, and in the 40-to-44 age group in the West. Homeownership peaks at 86.9 percent among householders aged 70 to 74 in the Midwest.

■ The collapse of the housing market and the decline in homeownership did not eliminate differences in homeownership rate by household type.

Most married couples under age 35 own their home

(percent of married-couple householders who own their home, by age, 2013)

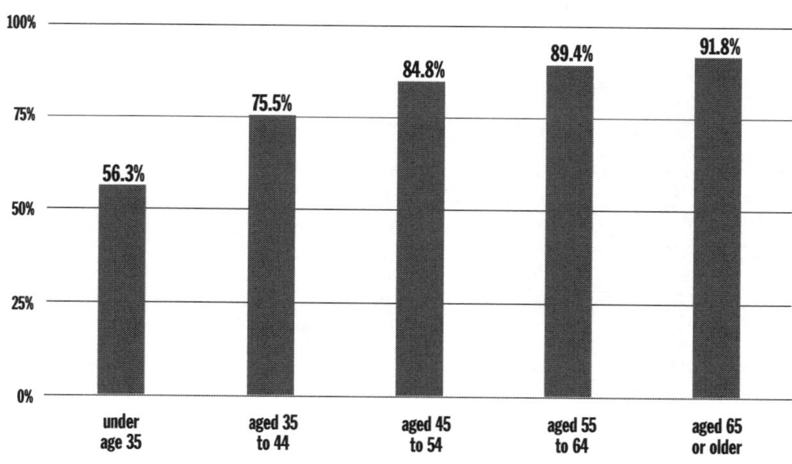

Table 4.4 Homeownership Rate by Age of Householder and Type of Household, 2013

(percent of households owning their home, by age of householder and type of household, 2013)

	total	married couples	female family householder, no spouse present	male family householder, no spouse present	people living alone	
					females	males
Total households	**65.1%**	**80.7%**	**46.7%**	**55.3%**	**57.2%**	**49.8%**
Under age 25	22.2	31.7	25.9	41.9	10.8	13.3
Aged 25 to 29	34.1	51.5	22.0	37.8	20.1	26.4
Aged 30 to 34	48.1	63.9	28.8	42.4	29.3	32.3
Aged 35 to 39	55.8	70.8	33.7	46.6	37.1	39.7
Aged 40 to 44	65.0	79.6	43.6	54.7	43.1	45.1
Aged 45 to 49	69.6	83.4	50.6	62.9	48.8	50.2
Aged 50 to 54	72.6	86.1	58.6	67.9	53.7	51.7
Aged 55 to 59	75.8	88.6	65.0	70.7	59.3	55.6
Aged 60 to 64	77.6	90.4	66.9	69.5	63.3	58.1
Aged 65 to 69	80.5	91.8	72.0	80.1	66.6	62.5
Aged 70 to 74	82.8	92.7	78.5	78.4	71.9	69.4
Aged 75 or older	80.0	91.0	86.1	87.1	71.4	73.0
Total households	**65.1**	**80.7**	**46.7**	**55.3**	**57.2**	**49.8**
Under age 35	36.8	56.3	25.7	40.7	20.3	25.5
Aged 35 to 44	60.6	75.5	38.6	50.8	40.3	42.6
Aged 45 to 54	71.2	84.8	54.5	65.4	51.7	51.0
Aged 55 to 64	76.6	89.4	65.8	70.2	61.4	56.8
Aged 65 or older	80.8	91.8	80.4	83.1	70.4	69.0

Source: Bureau of the Census, Housing Vacancies and Homeownership, Internet site http://www.census.gov/housing/hvs/; calculations by New Strategist

Table 4.5 Homeownership Rate by Age of Householder and Region, 2013

(percent of households owning their home, by age of householder and region, 2013)

	total	Northeast	Midwest	South	West
Total households	**65.1%**	**63.0%**	**69.7%**	**66.7%**	**59.4%**
Under age 25	22.2	22.8	20.1	24.3	20.1
Aged 25 to 29	34.1	30.0	41.5	34.7	28.8
Aged 30 to 34	48.1	42.1	57.9	49.8	40.6
Aged 35 to 39	55.8	53.9	63.4	56.6	48.7
Aged 40 to 44	65.0	64.4	70.7	66.1	58.2
Aged 45 to 49	69.6	67.8	75.4	70.5	63.7
Aged 50 to 54	72.6	71.1	77.6	74.4	66.0
Aged 55 to 59	75.8	72.9	79.2	77.6	71.4
Aged 60 to 64	77.6	74.6	79.6	79.6	74.6
Aged 65 to 69	80.5	75.7	83.6	83.7	75.9
Aged 70 to 74	82.8	75.2	86.9	86.3	78.5
Aged 75 or older	80.0	73.6	79.7	85.4	77.2
Total households	**65.1**	**63.0**	**69.7**	**66.7**	**59.4**
Under age 35	36.8	33.5	42.6	37.9	31.6
Aged 35 to 44	60.6	59.5	67.2	61.6	53.6
Aged 45 to 54	71.2	69.6	76.6	72.5	64.9
Aged 55 to 64	76.6	73.7	79.4	78.5	72.9
Aged 65 or older	80.8	74.6	82.5	85.1	77.1

Source: Bureau of the Census, Housing Vacancies and Homeownership, Internet site http://www.census.gov/housing/hvs/; calculations by New Strategist

Non-Hispanic Whites Are Most Likely to Be Homeowners

Among non-Hispanic Whites, the homeownership rate reaches 50 percent in the 25-to-34 age group.

Households headed by Asians, Blacks, and Hispanics are less likely than the average household to own a home. The homeownership rate was 65.1 percent for all households in 2010, according to the census. By race and Hispanic origin the rate was 58 percent among Asians, 44 percent among Blacks, and 47 percent among Hispanics. Non-Hispanic Whites are the only race-and-Hispanic-origin group that has an above-average homeownership rate, at 72 percent in 2010.

Overall, just under 36 percent of Millennials owned a home in 2010. By race and Hispanic origin, the homeownership rate of Millennials was 30 percent among Asians, 19 percent among Blacks, 27 percent among Hispanics, and 42 percent among non-Hispanic Whites.

■ Non-Hispanic Whites account for three out of four Millennial homeowners.

More than 40 percent of non-Hispanic White Millennials own their home

(homeownership rate of householders under age 34, by race and Hispanic origin, 2010)

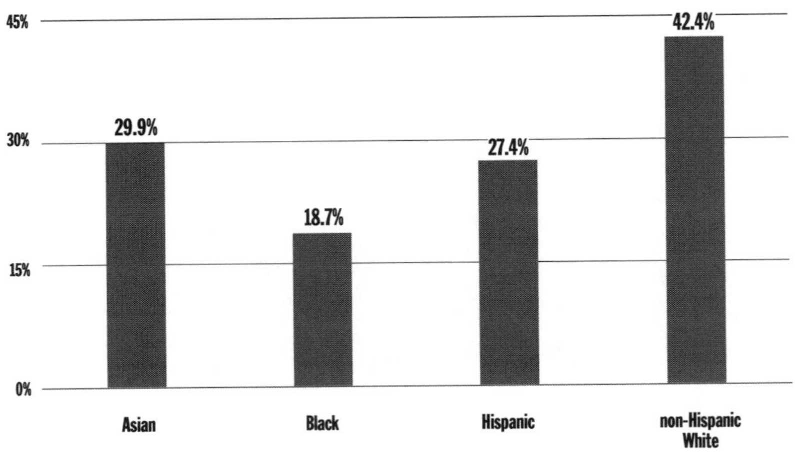

Table 4.6 Homeownership by Generation, Race, and Hispanic Origin, 2010

(number and percent of households that own their home, by generation, race, and Hispanic origin of householder, 2010; numbers in thousands)

	total	Asian	Black	Hispanic	non-Hispanic White
Total households	**116,716**	**4,632**	**14,130**	**13,461**	**82,333**
Millennials (under age 34)	21,562	1,049	3,022	3,695	13,235
Generation Xers (aged 34 to 45)	25,577	1,337	3,456	4,050	16,206
Baby Boomers (aged 46 to 64)	43,757	1,623	5,322	4,220	31,823
Older Americans (aged 65 or older)	25,820	624	2,331	1,496	21,069
HOMEOWNERS					
Total households	**75,986**	**2,689**	**6,261**	**6,368**	**59,484**
Millennials (under age 34)	7,662	313	564	1,012	5,607
Generation Xers (aged 34 to 45)	15,791	808	1,405	1,918	11,375
Baby Boomers (aged 46 to 64)	32,526	1,161	2,832	2,498	25,525
Older Americans (aged 65 or older)	20,007	407	1,460	941	16,977
HOMEOWNERSHIP RATE					
Total households	**65.1%**	**58.0%**	**44.3%**	**47.3%**	**72.2%**
Millennials (under age 34)	35.5	29.9	18.7	27.4	42.4
Generation Xers (aged 34 to 45)	61.7	60.4	40.7	47.4	70.2
Baby Boomers (aged 46 to 64)	74.3	71.5	53.2	59.2	80.2
Older Americans (aged 65 or older)	77.5	65.2	62.6	62.9	80.6

Note: Asians and Blacks are those who identify themselves as being of the race alone. Hispanics may be of any race. Non-Hispanic Whites are those who identify themselves as being White alone and not Hispanic.
Source: Bureau of the Census, 2010 Census, American Factfinder, Internet site http://factfinder2.census.gov/faces/nav/jsf/pages/index.xhtml; calculations by New Strategist

Table 4.7 Homeownership by Age, Race, and Hispanic Origin, 2010

(number and percent of households that own their home, by age, race, and Hispanic origin of householder, 2010; numbers in thousands)

	total	Asian	Black	Hispanic	non-Hispanic White
Total households	**116,716**	**4,632**	**14,130**	**13,461**	**82,333**
Under age 25	5,401	217	802	885	3,333
Aged 25 to 34	17,957	924	2,466	3,122	11,003
Aged 35 to 44	21,291	1,145	2,890	3,457	13,362
Aged 45 to 54	24,907	1,002	3,190	2,808	17,438
Aged 55 to 64	21,340	720	2,450	1,693	16,129
Aged 65 or older	25,820	624	2,331	1,496	21,069
HOMEOWNERS					
Total households	**75,986**	**2,689**	**6,261**	**6,368**	**59,484**
Under age 25	870	26	63	133	622
Aged 25 to 34	7,547	319	557	976	5,538
Aged 35 to 44	13,256	706	1,190	1,659	9,461
Aged 45 to 54	17,804	701	1,594	1,611	13,601
Aged 55 to 64	16,503	530	1,398	1,048	13,285
Aged 65 or older	20,007	407	1,460	941	16,977
HOMEOWNERSHIP RATE					
Total households	**65.1%**	**58.0%**	**44.3%**	**47.3%**	**72.2%**
Under age 25	16.1	12.1	7.8	15.1	18.7
Aged 25 to 34	42.0	34.5	22.6	31.3	50.3
Aged 35 to 44	62.3	61.7	41.2	48.0	70.8
Aged 45 to 54	71.5	69.9	50.0	57.4	78.0
Aged 55 to 64	77.3	73.6	57.0	61.9	82.4
Aged 65 or older	77.5	65.2	62.6	62.9	80.6

Note: Asians and Blacks are those who identify themselves as being of the race alone. Hispanics may be of any race. Non-Hispanic Whites are those who identify themselves as being White alone and not Hispanic.
Source: Bureau of the Census, 2010 Census, American Factfinder, Internet site http://factfinder2.census.gov/faces/nav/jsf/pages/index.xhtml; calculations by New Strategist

Many Millennials Live in a Multi-Unit Building

Fewer than half of householders under age 35 live in a single-family home.

The majority of American households (69 percent) live in a single-family home. Among adults under age 35, the age group now filled with the Millennial generation, only 49 percent live in this traditional type of home. Almost as many Millennials (46 percent) live in a multi-unit building.

Among the nation's homeowners, 88 percent live in a single-family home with little variation by age. Only 5 percent of homeowners are in a multi-unit building. They are outnumbered by the 7 percent who live in a mobile home, boat, or RV.

Among renters, there is more variation in type of structure by age. Sixty-four percent of renters under age 35 live in a multi-unit building. This is greater than the 55 percent among renters aged 35 to 64, but less than the 70 percent among renters aged 65 or older.

■ Despite the collapse of the housing market in the wake of the Great Recession, the percentage of Americans who live in a single-family house has barely changed over the years.

Millennials are less likely than older Americans to live in a single-family home

(percent of households living in a single-family house, by age of householder, 2012)

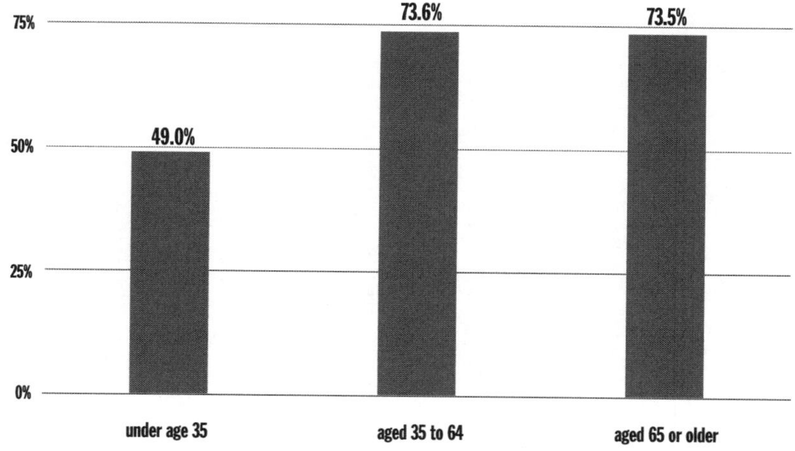

Table 4.8 Number of Units in Structure by Age of Householder, 2012: Total Occupied Units

(number and percent distribution of households by age of householder and number of units in structure, 2012; numbers in thousands)

	total	one detached or attached	multi-unit building: total	2 to 4	5 to 19	20 to 49	50 or more	mobile home, boat, RV, etc.
Total households	**115,970**	**79,800**	**29,269**	**9,195**	**10,342**	**4,012**	**5,719**	**6,901**
Under age 35	22,404	10,981	10,219	3,052	4,232	1,412	1,523	1,205
Aged 35 to 64	67,038	49,320	13,735	4,788	4,872	1,765	2,310	3,984
Aged 65 or older	26,527	19,500	5,315	1,356	1,237	835	1,887	1,712
PERCENT DISTRIBUTION OF HOUSEHOLDS BY UNITS IN STRUCTURE								
Total households	**100.0%**	**68.8%**	**25.2%**	**7.9%**	**8.9%**	**3.5%**	**4.9%**	**6.0%**
Under age 35	100.0	49.0	45.6	13.6	18.9	6.3	6.8	5.4
Aged 35 to 64	100.0	73.6	20.5	7.1	7.3	2.6	3.4	5.9
Aged 65 or older	100.0	73.5	20.0	5.1	4.7	3.1	7.1	6.5
PERCENT DISTRIBUTION OF HOUSEHOLDS BY AGE OF HOUSEHOLDER								
Total households	**100.0**	**100.0**	**100.0**	**100.0**	**100.0**	**100.0**	**100.0**	**100.0**
Under age 35	19.3	13.8	34.9	33.2	40.9	35.2	26.6	17.5
Aged 35 to 64	57.8	61.8	46.9	52.1	47.1	44.0	40.4	57.7
Aged 65 or older	22.9	24.4	18.2	14.7	12.0	20.8	33.0	24.8

Source: Bureau of the Census, 2012 American Community Survey, Internet site http://factfinder2.census.gov/faces/nav/jsf/pages/index.xhtml; calculations by New Strategist

Table 4.9 Number of Units in Structure by Age of Householder, 2012: Owner-Occupied Units

(number and percent distribution of homeowners by age of householder and number of units in structure, 2012; numbers in thousands)

	total	one detached or attached	multi-unit building: total	2 to 4	5 to 19	20 to 49	50 or more	mobile home, boat, RV, etc.
Total homeowners	**74,119**	**65,249**	**3,914**	**1,537**	**1,009**	**490**	**877**	**4,956**
Under age 35	7,304	6,239	509	161	169	68	112	556
Aged 35 to 64	45,946	40,988	2,058	876	529	232	421	2,899
Aged 65 or older	20,869	18,021	1,347	500	312	190	345	1,501
PERCENT DISTRIBUTION OF HOMEOWNERS BY UNITS IN STRUCTURE								
Total homeowners	**100.0%**	**88.0%**	**5.3%**	**2.1%**	**1.4%**	**0.7%**	**1.2%**	**6.7%**
Under age 35	100.0	85.4	7.0	2.2	2.3	0.9	1.5	7.6
Aged 35 to 64	100.0	89.2	4.5	1.9	1.2	0.5	0.9	6.3
Aged 65 or older	100.0	86.4	6.5	2.4	1.5	0.9	1.7	7.2
PERCENT DISTRIBUTION OF HOMEOWNERS BY AGE OF HOUSEHOLDER								
Total homeowners	**100.0**	**100.0**	**100.0**	**100.0**	**100.0**	**100.0**	**100.0**	**100.0**
Under age 35	9.9	9.6	13.0	10.5	16.7	13.9	12.7	11.2
Aged 35 to 64	62.0	62.8	52.6	57.0	52.4	47.3	48.0	58.5
Aged 65 or older	28.2	27.6	34.4	32.5	30.9	38.8	39.3	30.3

Source: Bureau of the Census, 2012 American Community Survey, Internet site http://factfinder2.census.gov/faces/nav/jsf/pages/index.xhtml; calculations by New Strategist

Table 4.10 Number of Units in Structure by Age of Householder, 2012: Renter-Occupied Units

(number and percent distribution of renters by age of householder and number of units in structure, 2012; numbers in thousands)

			multi-unit building					
	total	one detached or attached	total	2 to 4	5 to 19	20 to 49	50 or more	mobile home, boat, RV, etc.
Total renters	**41,850**	**14,551**	**25,355**	**7,659**	**9,333**	**3,522**	**4,842**	**1,945**
Under age 35	15,100	4,741	9,710	2,891	4,064	1,344	1,411	649
Aged 35 to 64	21,092	8,331	11,677	3,912	4,344	1,533	1,888	1,084
Aged 65 or older	5,658	1,478	3,969	856	925	645	1,542	211
PERCENT DISTRIBUTION OF RENTERS BY UNITS IN STRUCTURE								
Total renters	**100.0%**	**34.8%**	**60.6%**	**18.3%**	**22.3%**	**8.4%**	**11.6%**	**4.6%**
Under age 35	100.0	31.4	64.3	19.1	26.9	8.9	9.3	4.3
Aged 35 to 64	100.0	39.5	55.4	18.5	20.6	7.3	9.0	5.1
Aged 65 or older	100.0	26.1	70.1	15.1	16.4	11.4	27.3	3.7
PERCENT DISTRIBUTION OF RENTERS BY AGE OF HOUSEHOLDER								
Total renters	**100.0**	**100.0**	**100.0**	**100.0**	**100.0**	**100.0**	**100.0**	**100.0**
Under age 35	36.1	32.6	38.3	37.7	43.5	38.2	29.1	33.4
Aged 35 to 64	50.4	57.3	46.1	51.1	46.5	43.5	39.0	55.8
Aged 65 or older	13.5	10.2	15.7	11.2	9.9	18.3	31.9	10.9

Source: Bureau of the Census, 2012 American Community Survey, Internet site http://factfinder2.census.gov/faces/nav/jsf/pages/index.xhtml; calculations by New Strategist

Millennials Are Most Likely to Move

More than 20 percent move from one house to another during a year's time.

Young adults are most likely to move. Overall, just 11.7 percent of Americans moved from one house to another between March 2012 and March 2013. Among people aged 20 to 24, the mobility rate was a much higher 24.4 percent. In the 25-to-29 age group, the rate was 23.2 percent. The mobility rate falls with age to just 3.7 percent among people aged 68 or older.

Most movers stay within the same county. Only 13 percent cross state lines. Among 20-to-29-year-olds who moved between 2012 and 2013, the single biggest reason given for the move was to establish their own household, cited by 14 to 16 percent of movers in the age group.

■ Mobility has been declining in the United States for decades, and the Great Recession lowered the mobility rate even further among young adults.

Millennials have a higher mobility rate than any other generation

(percent of people who moved between March 2012 and March 2013, by generation)

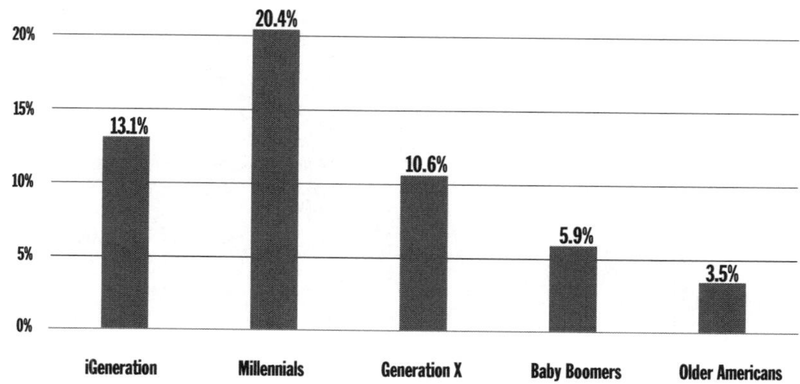

Table 4.11 Geographic Mobility by Generation and Type of Move, 2012–13

(total number of people aged 1 or older, and number and percent who moved between March 2012 and March 2013, by generation and type of move; numbers in thousands)

					different state			
	total	total movers	same county	different county, same state	total	same region	different region	movers from abroad
Total, aged 1 or older	**307,243**	**35,918**	**23,150**	**6,961**	**4,770**	**2,323**	**2,447**	**1,036**
iGeneration (under age 19)	74,252	9,735	6,627	1,677	1,167	598	570	263
Millennials (aged 19 to 36)	75,576	15,432	9,839	3,008	2,105	956	1,149	479
Generation Xers (aged 37 to 48)	49,038	5,213	3,355	1,031	660	348	312	167
Baby Boomers (aged 49 to 67)	73,751	4,315	2,634	937	647	336	311	103
Older Americans (aged 68 or older)	34,625	1,222	698	307	193	86	107	24
PERCENT DISTRIBUTION BY MOBILITY STATUS								
Total, aged 1 or older	**100.0%**	**11.7%**	**7.5%**	**2.3%**	**1.6%**	**0.8%**	**0.8%**	**0.3%**
iGeneration (under age 19)	100.0	13.1	8.9	2.3	1.6	0.8	0.8	0.4
Millennials (aged 19 to 36)	100.0	20.4	13.0	4.0	2.8	1.3	1.5	0.6
Generation Xers (aged 37 to 48)	100.0	10.6	6.8	2.1	1.3	0.7	0.6	0.3
Baby Boomers (aged 49 to 67)	100.0	5.9	3.6	1.3	0.9	0.5	0.4	0.1
Older Americans (aged 68 or older)	100.0	3.5	2.0	0.9	0.6	0.2	0.3	0.1
PERCENT DISTRIBUTION OF MOVERS BY TYPE OF MOVE								
Total, aged 1 or older	–	**100.0**	**64.5**	**19.4**	**13.3**	**6.5**	**6.8**	**2.9**
iGeneration (under age 19)	–	100.0	68.1	17.2	12.0	6.1	5.9	2.7
Millennials (aged 19 to 36)	–	100.0	63.8	19.5	13.6	6.2	7.4	3.1
Generation Xers (aged 37 to 48)	–	100.0	64.4	19.8	12.7	6.7	6.0	3.2
Baby Boomers (aged 49 to 67)	–	100.0	61.0	21.7	15.0	7.8	7.2	2.4
Older Americans (aged 68 or older)	–	100.0	57.1	25.1	15.8	7.0	8.8	2.0

Note: "–" means not applicable.
Source: Bureau of the Census, Geographic Mobility: 2012 to 2013, Internet site http://www.census.gov/hhes/migration/data/cps/cps2013.html; calculations by New Strategist

Table 4.12 Geographic Mobility by Generation, Age, and Type of Move, 2012–13

(number and percent distribution of people aged 1 or older, aged 19 to 36, and in age groups that include the Millennial generation, by mobility status between March 2012 and March 2013; numbers in thousands)

	total	total movers	same county	different county, same state	different state: total	different state: same region	different state: different region	movers from abroad
Total, aged 1 or older	**307,243**	**35,918**	**23,150**	**6,961**	**4,770**	**2,323**	**2,447**	**1,036**
Millennials (aged 19 to 36)	**75,576**	**15,432**	**9,839**	**3,008**	**2,105**	**956**	**1,149**	**479**
Aged 18 to 19	7,876	1,081	726	202	118	61	57	36
Aged 20 to 24	22,153	5,416	3,514	1,087	676	318	358	140
Aged 25 to 29	21,138	4,914	3,054	985	714	299	415	161
Aged 30 to 34	20,659	3,510	2,268	626	498	231	267	117
Aged 35 to 39	19,221	2,628	1,600	523	396	194	202	108
PERCENT DISTRIBUTION BY MOBILITY STATUS								
Total, aged 1 or older	**100.0%**	**11.7%**	**7.5%**	**2.3%**	**1.6%**	**0.8%**	**0.8%**	**0.3%**
Millennials (aged 19 to 36)	**100.0**	**20.4**	**13.0**	**4.0**	**2.8**	**1.3**	**1.5**	**0.6**
Aged 18 to 19	100.0	13.7	9.2	2.6	1.5	0.8	0.7	0.5
Aged 20 to 24	100.0	24.4	15.9	4.9	3.1	1.4	1.6	0.6
Aged 25 to 29	100.0	23.2	14.4	4.7	3.4	1.4	2.0	0.8
Aged 30 to 34	100.0	17.0	11.0	3.0	2.4	1.1	1.3	0.6
Aged 35 to 39	100.0	13.7	8.3	2.7	2.1	1.0	1.1	0.6

Source: Bureau of the Census, Geographic Mobility: 2012 to 2013, Internet site http://www.census.gov/hhes/migration/data/cps/cps2013.html; calculations by New Strategist

Table 4.13 Movers by Generation, Age, and Type of Move, 2012–13

(number and percent distribution of people aged 1 or older, aged 19 to 36, and in age groups that include Millennials who moved between March 2012 and March 2013, by type of move; numbers in thousands)

	total movers	same county	different county, same state	different state: total	different state: same region	different state: different region	movers from abroad
Total movers aged 1 or older	**35,918**	**23,150**	**6,961**	**4,770**	**2,323**	**2,447**	**1,036**
Millennials (aged 19 to 37)	**15,432**	**9,839**	**3,008**	**2,105**	**956**	**1,149**	**479**
Aged 18 to 19	1,081	726	202	118	61	57	36
Aged 20 to 24	5,416	3,514	1,087	676	318	358	140
Aged 25 to 29	4,914	3,054	985	714	299	415	161
Aged 30 to 34	3,510	2,268	626	498	231	267	117
Aged 35 to 39	2,628	1,600	523	396	194	202	108
PERCENT DISTRIBUTION BY MOBILITY STATUS							
Total movers aged 1 or older	**100.0%**	**64.5%**	**19.4%**	**13.3%**	**6.5%**	**6.8%**	**2.9%**
Millennials (aged 19 to 37)	**100.0**	**63.8**	**19.5**	**13.6**	**6.2**	**7.4**	**3.1**
Aged 18 to 19	100.0	67.2	18.7	10.9	5.6	5.3	3.3
Aged 20 to 24	100.0	64.9	20.1	12.5	5.9	6.6	2.6
Aged 25 to 29	100.0	62.1	20.0	14.5	6.1	8.4	3.3
Aged 30 to 34	100.0	64.6	17.8	14.2	6.6	7.6	3.3
Aged 35 to 39	100.0	60.9	19.9	15.1	7.4	7.7	4.1

Source: Bureau of the Census, Geographic Mobility: 2012 to 2013, Internet site http://www.census.gov/hhes/migration/data/cps/cps2013.html; calculations by New Strategist

Table 4.14 Reason for Moving among People Aged 20 to 24, 2012–13

(number and percent distribution of movers aged 20 to 24 by primary reason for move and share of total movers between March 2012 and March 2013, by age; numbers in thousands)

		movers aged 20 to 24		
	total movers	number	percent distribution	share of total
Total movers	**35,918**	**5,416**	**100.0%**	**15.1%**
Family reasons	10,871	1,695	31.3	15.6
Change in marital status	1,817	198	3.7	10.9
To establish own household	3,753	893	16.5	23.8
Other family reasons	5,301	604	11.2	11.4
Employment reasons	6,979	1,057	19.5	15.1
New job or job transfer	3,242	511	9.4	15.8
To look for work or lost job	750	125	2.3	16.7
To be closer to work/easier commute	1,941	334	6.2	17.2
Retired	237	0	0.0	0.0
Other job-related reason	809	87	1.6	10.8
Housing reasons	17,225	2,477	45.7	14.4
Wanted own home, not rent	2,099	178	3.3	8.5
Wanted better home/apartment	5,332	778	14.4	14.6
Wanted better neighborhood/less crime	1,135	107	2.0	9.4
Wanted cheaper housing	2,989	474	8.8	15.9
Foreclosure/eviction	654	59	1.1	9.0
Other housing reasons	5,016	881	16.3	17.6
Other reasons	844	188	3.5	22.3
To attend or leave college	215	95	1.8	44.2
Change of climate	20	0	0.0	0.0
Health reasons	136	6	0.1	4.4
Natural disaster	11	0	0.0	0.0
Other reasons	462	87	1.6	18.8

Source: Bureau of the Census, Geographic Mobility: 2012 to 2013, Internet site http://www.census.gov/hhes/migration/data/cps/cps2013.html; calculations by New Strategist

Table 4.15 Reason for Moving among People Aged 25 to 29, 2012–13

(number and percent distribution of movers aged 25 to 29 by primary reason for move and share of total movers between March 2012 and March 2013, by age; numbers in thousands)

		movers aged 25 to 29		
	total movers	number	percent distribution	share of total
Total movers	**35,918**	**4,915**	**100.0%**	**13.7%**
Family reasons	10,871	1,526	31.0	14.0
Change in marital status	1,817	180	3.7	9.9
To establish own household	3,753	697	14.2	18.6
Other family reasons	5,301	649	13.2	12.2
Employment reasons	6,979	1,162	23.6	16.6
New job or job transfer	3,242	541	11.0	16.7
To look for work or lost job	750	132	2.7	17.6
To be closer to work/easier commute	1,941	367	7.5	18.9
Retired	237	0	0.0	0.0
Other job-related reason	809	122	2.5	15.1
Housing reasons	17,225	2,087	42.5	12.1
Wanted own home, not rent	2,099	258	5.2	12.3
Wanted better home/apartment	5,332	681	13.9	12.8
Wanted better neighborhood/less crime	1,135	148	3.0	13.0
Wanted cheaper housing	2,989	322	6.6	10.8
Foreclosure/eviction	654	51	1.0	7.8
Other housing reasons	5,016	627	12.8	12.5
Other reasons	844	140	2.8	16.6
To attend or leave college	215	67	1.4	31.2
Change of climate	20	3	0.1	15.0
Health reasons	136	3	0.1	2.2
Natural disaster	11	0	0.0	0.0
Other reasons	462	67	1.4	14.5

Source: Bureau of the Census, Geographic Mobility: 2012 to 2013, Internet site http://www.census.gov/hhes/migration/data/cps/cps2013.html; calculations by New Strategist

Table 4.16 Reason for Moving among People Aged 30 to 44, 2012–13

(number and percent distribution of movers aged 30 to 44 by primary reason for move and share of total movers between March 2012 and March 2013; numbers in thousands)

		movers aged 30 to 44		
	total movers	number	percent distribution	share of total
Total movers	**35,918**	**5,416**	**100.0%**	**15.1%**
Family reasons	10,871	2,289	27.6	21.1
Change in marital status	1,817	561	6.8	30.9
To establish own household	3,753	756	9.1	20.1
Other family reasons	5,301	972	11.7	18.3
Employment reasons	6,979	1,878	22.7	26.9
New job or job transfer	3,242	952	11.5	29.4
To look for work or lost job	750	156	1.9	20.8
To be closer to work/easier commute	1,941	495	6.0	25.5
Retired	237	16	0.2	6.8
Other job-related reason	809	259	3.1	32.0
Housing reasons	17,225	4,006	48.3	23.3
Wanted own home, not rent	2,099	654	7.9	31.2
Wanted better home/apartment	5,332	1,251	15.1	23.5
Wanted better neighborhood/less crime	1,135	306	3.7	27.0
Wanted cheaper housing	2,989	674	8.1	22.5
Foreclosure/eviction	654	117	1.4	17.9
Other housing reasons	5,016	1,004	12.1	20.0
Other reasons	844	115	1.4	13.6
To attend or leave college	215	11	0.1	5.1
Change of climate	20	6	0.1	30.0
Health reasons	136	13	0.2	9.6
Natural disaster	11	0	0.0	0.0
Other reasons	462	85	1.0	18.4

Source: Bureau of the Census, Geographic Mobility: 2012 to 2013, Internet site http://www.census.gov/hhes/migration/data/cps/cps2013.html; calculations by New Strategist

CHAPTER

5

Income

■ Millennials are struggling to recover from the Great Recession. In 2013, the median income of households headed by people under age 25 was 8.9 percent below the median income of their counterparts in 2000, after adjusting for inflation.

■ Households headed by people aged 25 to 34 saw their median income fall by 12.3 percent between 2000 and 2013, after adjusting for inflation. (Millennials were aged 19 to 36 in 2013.)

■ Householders under age 25 had a median income of $34,311 in 2013, well below the $51,939 overall median. Those aged 25 to 34 had a median income of $52,702, slightly above average.

■ Between 2000 and 2013, men aged 25 to 34 saw their median income fall by an enormous 16.5 percent, after adjusting for inflation. Women of the same age experienced a 7.4 percent decline.

■ While 14.5 percent of Americans were poor in 2013, the poverty rate among 18-to-24-year-olds was a much larger 19.4 percent. The poverty rate of 25-to-34-year-olds was an above-average 15.8 percent.

Incomes of Millennials Have Declined

Households headed by people ranging in age from 25 to 44 experienced double-digit percentage declines in median household income.

Nationally, median household income fell 8.6 percent between 2000 and 2013, after adjusting for inflation. Among households headed by people under age 25, the decline was a similar 8.9 percent. (Millennials were aged 19 to 36 in 2013.)

Households headed by people aged 25 to 34 saw their median income fall by a larger 12.3 percent between 2000 and 2013, after adjusting for inflation. In 2000, the median household income of this age group was 6 percent greater than the national median. By 2013, it was only 1 percent higher.

Households headed by people aged 35 to 44, the age group now filling with Millennials, saw their median household income fall 10.7 percent between 2000 and 2013, after adjusting for inflation. Their median income was 25 percent above the national median in 2013, down from a 28 percent margin in 2000.

■ The median income of households headed by people under age 25 is only 66 percent of the national median because many are in college rather than the labor force.

Household incomes began to decline before the Great Recession

(median income of households headed by people aged 15 to 44, 2000 to 2013; in 2013 dollars)

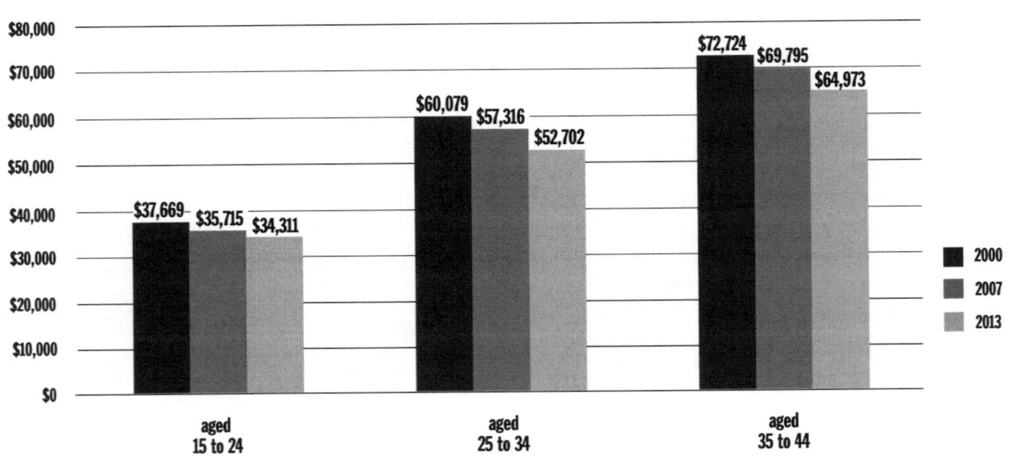

Table 5.1 Median Income of Households Headed by People under Age 45, 2000 to 2013

(median income of total households and households headed by people aged 15 to 44, and index of age group to total, 2000 to 2013; percent change for selected years; in 2013 dollars)

	total households	15 to 24	25 to 34	35 to 44
2013	$51,939	$34,311	$52,702	$64,973
2012	51,758	31,049	52,128	64,554
2011	51,842	31,548	52,588	64,128
2010	52,646	30,154	53,288	65,619
2009	54,059	33,377	54,518	66,338
2008	54,423	34,913	55,610	68,111
2007	56,436	35,715	57,316	69,795
2006	55,689	35,743	56,802	69,789
2005	55,278	34,329	56,534	69,308
2004	54,674	34,007	56,069	69,902
2003	54,865	34,264	56,716	69,717
2002	54,913	36,033	58,696	69,302
2001	55,562	37,099	59,315	70,157
2000	56,800	37,669	60,079	72,724
PERCENT CHANGE				
2007 to 2013	–8.0%	–3.9%	–8.1%	–6.9%
2000 to 2013	–8.6	–8.9	–12.3	–10.7
INDEX				
2013	100	66	101	125
2012	100	60	101	125
2011	100	61	101	124
2010	100	57	101	125
2009	100	62	101	123
2008	100	64	102	125
2007	100	63	102	124
2006	100	64	102	125
2005	100	62	102	125
2004	100	62	103	128
2003	100	62	103	127
2002	100	66	107	126
2001	100	67	107	126
2000	100	66	106	128

Note: The index is calculated by dividing the median income of the age group by the national median and multiplying by 100.
Source: Bureau of the Census, Historical Income Data, Internet site http://www.census.gov/hhes/www/income/data/historical/index .html; calculations by New Strategist

Millennial Household Incomes Rise with Age

Despite the decline in median income, some Millennials are doing well and many have household incomes of $100,000 or more.

Household income typically rises to a peak in middle age. The Millennial generation, aged 19 to 36 in 2013, is now approaching middle age as the oldest enter their late thirties. The median household income of Millennials ranges from a low of $34,311 for the youngest householders, those under age 25, to a high of $61,383 for the oldest householders, those in the 35-to-39 age group.

Median household income surpasses the overall median in the 30-to-34 age group. Twenty-three percent of households headed by people aged 30 to 34 have incomes of $100,000 or more, almost identical to the national figure. In the 35-to-39 age group, a larger 28 percent have incomes of $100,000 or more.

■ Household income shows more variation by age in the Millennial generation than in any other because the youngest are still teenagers and the oldest are almost 40.

Median household income rises as householders approach their forties

(median income of households by age of householder, 2013)

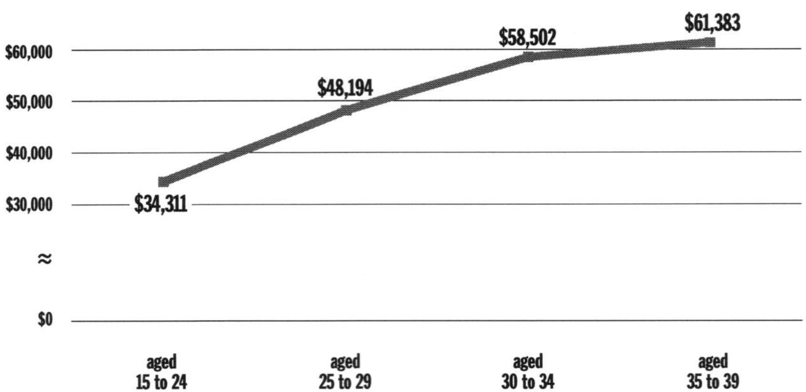

Table 5.2 Income of Households Headed by People under Age 40, 2013: Total Households

(number and percent distribution of total households and households headed by people under age 40, by household income, 2013; households in thousands as of 2014)

			aged 25 to 34			
	total	15 to 24	total	25 to 29	30 to 34	35 to 39
Total households	**122,952**	**6,323**	**20,008**	**9,344**	**10,664**	**10,322**
Under $10,000	8,939	875	1,521	785	736	525
$10,000 to $19,999	14,014	912	1,703	843	860	821
$20,000 to $29,999	12,879	967	1,980	973	1,008	878
$30,000 to $39,999	12,281	839	2,154	1,125	1,029	922
$40,000 to $49,999	10,850	710	1,964	1,069	895	970
$50,000 to $59,999	9,547	453	1,736	834	902	891
$60,000 to $69,999	8,240	377	1,533	722	810	778
$70,000 to $79,999	7,574	261	1,505	698	807	709
$80,000 to $89,999	6,006	190	1,181	473	708	492
$90,000 to $99,999	4,980	178	856	355	501	477
$100,000 or more	27,641	562	3,876	1,467	2,409	2,859
$100,000 to $124,999	9,459	286	1,623	640	983	1,063
$125,000 to $149,999	5,806	105	865	355	510	565
$150,000 to $174,999	4,175	77	567	210	357	437
$175,000 to $199,999	2,288	23	306	91	215	213
$200,000 or more	5,913	71	515	171	344	582
Median income	**$51,939**	**$34,311**	**$52,702**	**$48,194**	**$58,502**	**$61,383**
Total households	**100.0%**	**100.0%**	**100.0%**	**100.0%**	**100.0%**	**100.0%**
Under $10,000	7.3	13.8	7.6	8.4	6.9	5.1
$10,000 to $19,999	11.4	14.4	8.5	9.0	8.1	8.0
$20,000 to $29,999	10.5	15.3	9.9	10.4	9.5	8.5
$30,000 to $39,999	10.0	13.3	10.8	12.0	9.6	8.9
$40,000 to $49,999	8.8	11.2	9.8	11.4	8.4	9.4
$50,000 to $59,999	7.8	7.2	8.7	8.9	8.5	8.6
$60,000 to $69,999	6.7	6.0	7.7	7.7	7.6	7.5
$70,000 to $79,999	6.2	4.1	7.5	7.5	7.6	6.9
$80,000 to $89,999	4.9	3.0	5.9	5.1	6.6	4.8
$90,000 to $99,999	4.1	2.8	4.3	3.8	4.7	4.6
$100,000 or more	22.5	8.9	19.4	15.7	22.6	27.7
$100,000 to $124,999	7.7	4.5	8.1	6.9	9.2	10.3
$125,000 to $149,999	4.7	1.7	4.3	3.8	4.8	5.5
$150,000 to $174,999	3.4	1.2	2.8	2.2	3.3	4.2
$175,000 to $199,999	1.9	0.4	1.5	1.0	2.0	2.1
$200,000 or more	4.8	1.1	2.6	1.8	3.2	5.6

Source: Bureau of the Census, 2014 Current Population Survey, Internet site http://www.census.gov/hhes/www/income/data/index.html; calculations by New Strategist

Household Incomes Differ by Race and Hispanic Origin

Asians have higher incomes than non-Hispanic Whites.

Typically, household income rises with age as young adults finish their education, embark on a career, and marry. Median household income in 2013 was just $34,311 among householders under age 25, exceeded $50,000 as householders aged from their late twenties into their early thirties, and reached $61,383 among householders aged 35 to 39. (The Millennial generation was aged 19 to 36 in 2013.)

The pattern is the same regardless of race or Hispanic origin, but the household income figures are higher for Asians and non-Hispanic Whites than for Blacks or Hispanics. Black incomes are lower because married couples head few Black households. Hispanic incomes are lower because many Hispanics have little education or earning power.

■ Differences in household income by race and Hispanic origin are due to differences in household composition, educational attainment, and employment opportunities.

Hispanic household incomes vary the least by age

(median income of households headed by people aged 15 to 39, by race and Hispanic origin, 2013)

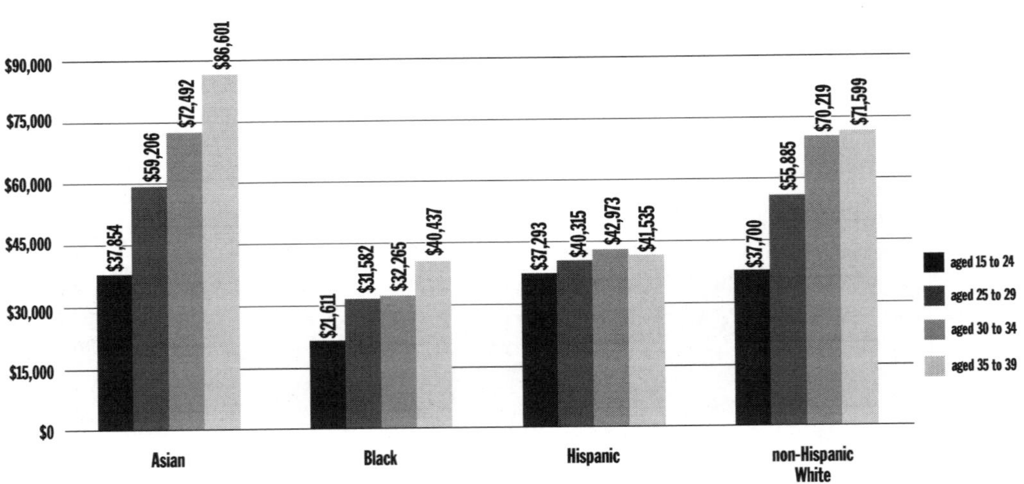

Table 5.3 Income of Households Headed by People under Age 40, 2013: Asian Households

(number and percent distribution of total Asian households and households headed by Asians under age 40, by income, 2013; households in thousands as of 2014)

			aged 25 to 34			
	total	15 to 24	total	25 to 29	30 to 34	35 to 39
Total Asian households	**6,111**	**340**	**1,398**	**621**	**778**	**663**
Under $10,000	459	65	135	74	61	23
$10,000 to $19,999	417	44	67	24	43	22
$20,000 to $29,999	480	36	111	60	51	37
$30,000 to $39,999	448	32	93	44	49	28
$40,000 to $49,999	503	54	107	56	51	59
$50,000 to $59,999	404	21	100	60	40	58
$60,000 to $69,999	431	23	111	46	64	31
$70,000 to $79,999	385	3	112	50	62	50
$80,000 to $89,999	286	17	74	33	41	31
$90,000 to $99,999	226	9	72	31	41	18
$100,000 or more	2,072	36	416	142	274	305
$100,000 to $124,999	647	21	152	53	99	107
$125,000 to $149,999	365	11	74	29	45	44
$150,000 to $174,999	339	4	66	24	42	42
$175,000 to $199,999	198	0	39	12	28	29
$200,000 or more	522	0	85	24	60	82
Median income	**$67,366**	**$37,854**	**$67,127**	**$59,206**	**$72,492**	**$86,601**
Total Asian households	**100.0%**	**100.0%**	**100.0%**	**100.0%**	**100.0%**	**100.0%**
Under $10,000	7.5	19.2	9.7	11.9	7.9	3.5
$10,000 to $19,999	6.8	13.0	4.8	3.8	5.6	3.4
$20,000 to $29,999	7.8	10.7	7.9	9.7	6.5	5.6
$30,000 to $39,999	7.3	9.3	6.6	7.0	6.3	4.1
$40,000 to $49,999	8.2	15.8	7.6	9.1	6.5	9.0
$50,000 to $59,999	6.6	6.3	7.1	9.6	5.2	8.8
$60,000 to $69,999	7.1	6.7	7.9	7.4	8.3	4.7
$70,000 to $79,999	6.3	1.0	8.0	8.1	8.0	7.6
$80,000 to $89,999	4.7	4.9	5.3	5.4	5.3	4.6
$90,000 to $99,999	3.7	2.6	5.2	5.0	5.3	2.7
$100,000 or more	33.9	10.6	29.7	22.9	35.2	46.0
$100,000 to $124,999	10.6	6.3	10.9	8.5	12.8	16.1
$125,000 to $149,999	6.0	3.1	5.3	4.7	5.7	6.7
$150,000 to $174,999	5.5	1.2	4.7	3.9	5.3	6.4
$175,000 to $199,999	3.2	0.0	2.8	1.9	3.6	4.4
$200,000 or more	8.5	0.0	6.1	3.9	7.8	12.4

Note: Asians are those who identify themselves as being of the race alone and those who identify themselves as being of the race in combination with other races.
Source: Bureau of the Census, 2014 Current Population Survey, Internet site http://www.census.gov/hhes/www/income/data/index.html; calculations by New Strategist

Table 5.4 Income of Households Headed by People under Age 40, 2013: Black Households

(number and percent distribution of total Black households and households headed by Blacks under age 40, by income, 2013; households in thousands as of 2014)

			aged 25 to 34			
	total	15 to 24	total	25 to 29	30 to 34	35 to 39
Total Black households	**16,855**	**1,153**	**3,062**	**1,446**	**1,616**	**1,606**
Under $10,000	2,385	283	461	194	268	186
$10,000 to $19,999	2,830	248	487	230	257	189
$20,000 to $29,999	2,164	172	460	250	210	199
$30,000 to $39,999	2,006	131	439	233	207	219
$40,000 to $49,999	1,578	113	300	172	128	151
$50,000 to $59,999	1,217	57	224	109	115	148
$60,000 to $69,999	904	46	164	51	114	90
$70,000 to $79,999	723	18	125	48	76	93
$80,000 to $89,999	558	13	84	22	62	39
$90,000 to $99,999	470	18	60	19	41	52
$100,000 or more	2,018	54	257	118	139	240
$100,000 to $124,999	870	31	124	55	70	120
$125,000 to $149,999	443	5	67	38	29	53
$150,000 to $174,999	278	11	26	11	15	33
$175,000 to $199,999	136	4	14	9	5	13
$200,000 or more	291	2	25	5	20	20
Median income	**$34,775**	**$21,611**	**$31,930**	**$31,582**	**$32,265**	**$40,437**
Total Black households	**100.0%**	**100.0%**	**100.0%**	**100.0%**	**100.0%**	**100.0%**
Under $10,000	14.2	24.5	15.1	13.4	16.6	11.6
$10,000 to $19,999	16.8	21.5	15.9	15.9	15.9	11.7
$20,000 to $29,999	12.8	14.9	15.0	17.3	13.0	12.4
$30,000 to $39,999	11.9	11.4	14.3	16.1	12.8	13.6
$40,000 to $49,999	9.4	9.8	9.8	11.9	7.9	9.4
$50,000 to $59,999	7.2	4.9	7.3	7.5	7.1	9.2
$60,000 to $69,999	5.4	4.0	5.4	3.5	7.0	5.6
$70,000 to $79,999	4.3	1.6	4.1	3.3	4.7	5.8
$80,000 to $89,999	3.3	1.2	2.8	1.5	3.8	2.4
$90,000 to $99,999	2.8	1.6	2.0	1.3	2.5	3.3
$100,000 or more	12.0	4.7	8.4	8.2	8.6	15.0
$100,000 to $124,999	5.2	2.7	4.1	3.8	4.3	7.5
$125,000 to $149,999	2.6	0.4	2.2	2.7	1.8	3.3
$150,000 to $174,999	1.6	1.0	0.9	0.8	0.9	2.1
$175,000 to $199,999	0.8	0.4	0.5	0.6	0.3	0.8
$200,000 or more	1.7	0.2	0.8	0.4	1.3	1.3

Note: Blacks are those who identify themselves as being of the race alone and those who identify themselves as being of the race in combination with other races.
Source: Bureau of the Census, 2014 Current Population Survey, Internet site http://www.census.gov/hhes/www/income/data/index .html; calculations by New Strategist

Table 5.5 Income of Households Headed by People under Age 40, 2013: Hispanic Households

(number and percent distribution of total Hispanic households and households headed by Hispanics under age 40, by income, 2013; households in thousands as of 2014)

	total	15 to 24	aged 25 to 34 total	aged 25 to 34: 25 to 29	aged 25 to 34: 30 to 34	35 to 39
Total Hispanic households	**15,811**	**1,314**	**3,625**	**1,674**	**1,951**	**1,906**
Under $10,000	1,467	131	293	146	146	128
$10,000 to $19,999	2,127	169	457	211	246	201
$20,000 to $29,999	2,142	242	490	212	278	280
$30,000 to $39,999	1,968	146	486	259	228	313
$40,000 to $49,999	1,664	187	476	223	253	170
$50,000 to $59,999	1,288	116	334	150	183	151
$60,000 to $69,999	959	70	220	98	123	129
$70,000 to $79,999	923	88	221	102	119	104
$80,000 to $89,999	586	37	136	59	76	65
$90,000 to $99,999	609	26	134	68	66	86
$100,000 or more	2,077	104	379	146	233	280
$100,000 to $124,999	895	39	187	72	115	121
$125,000 to $149,999	461	23	77	33	44	65
$150,000 to $174,999	298	16	60	22	38	34
$175,000 to $199,999	136	14	19	9	10	16
$200,000 or more	287	13	36	10	26	43
Median income	**$40,963**	**$37,293**	**$41,526**	**$40,315**	**$42,973**	**$41,535**
Total Hispanic households	**100.0%**	**100.0%**	**100.0%**	**100.0%**	**100.0%**	**100.0%**
Under $10,000	9.3	9.9	8.1	8.7	7.5	6.7
$10,000 to $19,999	13.5	12.9	12.6	12.6	12.6	10.5
$20,000 to $29,999	13.5	18.4	13.5	12.7	14.2	14.7
$30,000 to $39,999	12.4	11.1	13.4	15.5	11.7	16.4
$40,000 to $49,999	10.5	14.3	13.1	13.3	13.0	8.9
$50,000 to $59,999	8.1	8.8	9.2	9.0	9.4	7.9
$60,000 to $69,999	6.1	5.3	6.1	5.8	6.3	6.7
$70,000 to $79,999	5.8	6.7	6.1	6.1	6.1	5.4
$80,000 to $89,999	3.7	2.8	3.7	3.6	3.9	3.4
$90,000 to $99,999	3.9	2.0	3.7	4.1	3.4	4.5
$100,000 or more	13.1	7.9	10.4	8.7	11.9	14.7
$100,000 to $124,999	5.7	2.9	5.2	4.3	5.9	6.3
$125,000 to $149,999	2.9	1.7	2.1	2.0	2.3	3.4
$150,000 to $174,999	1.9	1.2	1.6	1.3	1.9	1.8
$175,000 to $199,999	0.9	1.0	0.5	0.5	0.5	0.8
$200,000 or more	1.8	1.0	1.0	0.6	1.3	2.3

Source: Bureau of the Census, 2014 Current Population Survey, Internet site http://www.census.gov/hhes/www/income/data/index.html; calculations by New Strategist

Table 5.6 Income of Households Headed by People under Age 40, 2013: Non-Hispanic White Households

(number and percent distribution of total non-Hispanic White households and households headed by non-Hispanic Whites under age 40, by income, 2013; households in thousands as of 2014)

			aged 25 to 34			
	total	15 to 24	total	25 to 29	30 to 34	35 to 39
Total non-Hispanic White households	**83,641**	**3,491**	**11,972**	**5,648**	**6,324**	**6,172**
Under $10,000	4,569	383	628	362	267	191
$10,000 to $19,999	8,577	452	708	375	333	407
$20,000 to $29,999	7,996	513	927	461	466	355
$30,000 to $39,999	7,871	525	1,164	623	541	393
$40,000 to $49,999	7,070	355	1,094	627	467	583
$50,000 to $59,999	6,592	253	1,089	531	559	531
$60,000 to $69,999	5,892	247	1,026	511	515	531
$70,000 to $79,999	5,469	148	1,041	497	544	461
$80,000 to $89,999	4,570	130	889	354	535	353
$90,000 to $99,999	3,660	121	604	242	361	321
$100,000 or more	21,375	364	2,802	1,064	1,738	2,047
$100,000 to $124,999	7,032	196	1,153	461	693	728
$125,000 to $149,999	4,509	63	645	261	384	397
$150,000 to $174,999	3,242	43	407	150	257	330
$175,000 to $199,999	1,808	7	230	62	167	155
$200,000 or more	4,784	55	368	131	237	438
Median income	**$58,270**	**$37,700**	**$62,363**	**$55,885**	**$70,219**	**$71,599**
Total non-Hispanic White households	**100.0%**	**100.0%**	**100.0%**	**100.0%**	**100.0%**	**100.0%**
Under $10,000	5.5	11.0	5.2	6.4	4.2	3.1
$10,000 to $19,999	10.3	12.9	5.9	6.6	5.3	6.6
$20,000 to $29,999	9.6	14.7	7.7	8.2	7.4	5.8
$30,000 to $39,999	9.4	15.0	9.7	11.0	8.6	6.4
$40,000 to $49,999	8.5	10.2	9.1	11.1	7.4	9.4
$50,000 to $59,999	7.9	7.3	9.1	9.4	8.8	8.6
$60,000 to $69,999	7.0	7.1	8.6	9.0	8.1	8.6
$70,000 to $79,999	6.5	4.2	8.7	8.8	8.6	7.5
$80,000 to $89,999	5.5	3.7	7.4	6.3	8.5	5.7
$90,000 to $99,999	4.4	3.5	5.0	4.3	5.7	5.2
$100,000 or more	25.6	10.4	23.4	18.8	27.5	33.2
$100,000 to $124,999	8.4	5.6	9.6	8.2	11.0	11.8
$125,000 to $149,999	5.4	1.8	5.4	4.6	6.1	6.4
$150,000 to $174,999	3.9	1.2	3.4	2.7	4.1	5.4
$175,000 to $199,999	2.2	0.2	1.9	1.1	2.6	2.5
$200,000 or more	5.7	1.6	3.1	2.3	3.7	7.1

Note: Non-Hispanic Whites are those who identify themselves as being White alone and not Hispanic.
Source: Bureau of the Census, 2014 Current Population Survey, Internet site http://www.census.gov/hhes/www/income/data/index .html; calculations by New Strategist

Married Couples Have Above-Average Incomes

Among householders under age 25, the median income of male-headed families is higher than that of married couples, however.

In most age groups married couples are the most affluent household type. Among households headed by people under age 25, however, the $50,604 median income of male-headed families is higher than the $41,360 median of married couples. Female-headed families in the age group had a median income of just $30,826, while men who live alone had the lowest incomes—a median of just $18,472.

Male-headed families often have more than one working adult in the household, which boosts income. Although most married couples also have more than one earner in the household, many young couples have preschoolers and the wife is caring for kids rather than working outside the home.

In the 25-to-34 age group, the incomes of married couples soar as dual earners become more common. The median income of married couples aged 25 to 34 stood at $72,107 in 2013. Among households headed by people aged 35 to 39, the median income of married couples was an even higher $83,609.

■ Households headed by people under age 25 are diverse, many having at most one earner, which limits their income.

Among households headed by 25-to-34-year-olds, female-headed families have the lowest median income

(median income of households headed by people aged 25 to 34, by household type, 2013)

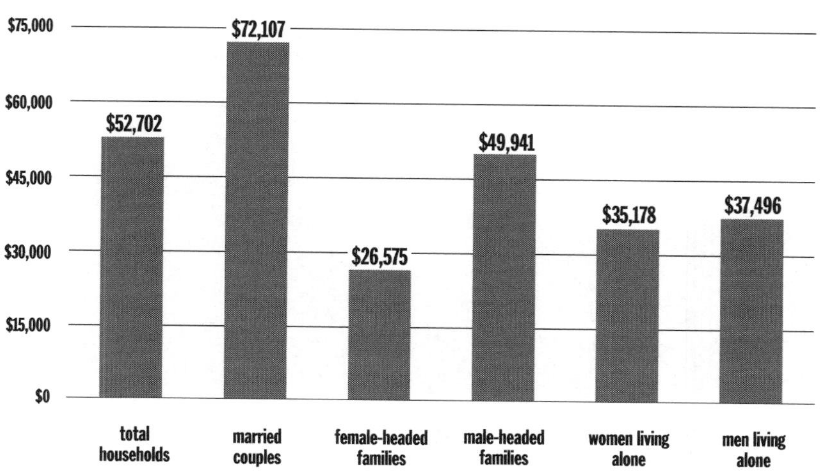

Table 5.7 Income of Households by Household Type, 2013: Aged 15 to 24

(number and percent distribution of households headed by people aged 15 to 24, by household income and household type, 2013; households in thousands as of 2014)

		family households			nonfamily households			
					female householder		male householder	
	total	married couples	female householder, no spouse present	male householder, no spouse present	total	living alone	total	living alone
Total households headed by 15-to-24-year-olds	**6,323**	**1,057**	**1,309**	**920**	**1,496**	**781**	**1,541**	**720**
Under $10,000	875	39	279	61	221	198	275	192
$10,000 to $19,999	912	86	174	85	288	212	280	212
$20,000 to $29,999	967	229	182	92	270	177	193	115
$30,000 to $39,999	839	149	170	107	233	118	181	60
$40,000 to $49,999	710	164	141	109	138	34	158	56
$50,000 to $59,999	453	96	65	88	90	14	114	37
$60,000 to $69,999	377	84	86	74	64	22	68	19
$70,000 to $79,999	261	61	53	39	50	0	59	14
$80,000 to $89,999	190	36	14	68	25	0	46	3
$90,000 to $99,999	178	28	20	64	41	4	26	5
$100,000 or more	562	86	128	133	77	1	138	7
$100,000 to $124,999	286	71	53	55	38	0	69	7
$125,000 to $149,999	105	7	27	26	10	0	34	0
$150,000 to $174,999	77	7	22	29	13	1	7	0
$175,000 to $199,999	23	1	14	5	0	0	2	0
$200,000 or more	71	0	11	18	15	0	26	0
Median income	**$34,311**	**$41,360**	**$30,826**	**$50,604**	**$28,813**	**$18,885**	**$30,814**	**$18,472**
Total households headed by 15-to-24-year-olds	**100.0%**	**100.0%**	**100.0%**	**100.0%**	**100.0%**	**100.0%**	**100.0%**	**100.0%**
Under $10,000	13.8	3.7	21.3	6.7	14.8	25.3	17.9	26.6
$10,000 to $19,999	14.4	8.1	13.3	9.2	19.3	27.2	18.2	29.4
$20,000 to $29,999	15.3	21.7	13.9	10.0	18.1	22.7	12.6	16.0
$30,000 to $39,999	13.3	14.1	13.0	11.6	15.6	15.1	11.7	8.4
$40,000 to $49,999	11.2	15.5	10.7	11.9	9.2	4.4	10.3	7.7
$50,000 to $59,999	7.2	9.1	4.9	9.6	6.0	1.8	7.4	5.2
$60,000 to $69,999	6.0	8.0	6.5	8.1	4.3	2.9	4.4	2.7
$70,000 to $79,999	4.1	5.7	4.0	4.2	3.3	0.0	3.9	1.9
$80,000 to $89,999	3.0	3.4	1.1	7.4	1.7	0.0	3.0	0.4
$90,000 to $99,999	2.8	2.6	1.5	6.9	2.7	0.5	1.7	0.7
$100,000 or more	8.9	8.1	9.7	14.5	5.1	0.1	9.0	1.0
$100,000 to $124,999	4.5	6.7	4.0	6.0	2.6	0.0	4.5	1.0
$125,000 to $149,999	1.7	0.7	2.1	2.8	0.7	0.0	2.2	0.0
$150,000 to $174,999	1.2	0.6	1.7	3.1	0.8	0.1	0.5	0.0
$175,000 to $199,999	0.4	0.1	1.1	0.6	0.0	0.0	0.1	0.0
$200,000 or more	1.1	0.0	0.9	2.0	1.0	0.0	1.7	0.0

Source: Bureau of the Census, 2014 Current Population Survey, Internet site http://www.census.gov/hhes/www/income/data/index .html; calculations by New Strategist

Table 5.8 Income of Households by Household Type, 2013: Aged 25 to 34

(number and percent distribution of households headed by people aged 25 to 34, by income and household type, 2013; households in thousands as of 2014)

		family households			nonfamily households			
					female householder		male householder	
	total	married couples	female householder, no spouse present	male householder, no spouse present	total	living alone	total	living alone
Total households headed by 25-to-34-year-olds	**20,008**	**8,462**	**3,387**	**1,454**	**2,707**	**1,729**	**3,998**	**2,388**
Under $10,000	1,521	186	606	65	316	273	348	308
$10,000 to $19,999	1,703	352	676	107	255	216	313	242
$20,000 to $29,999	1,980	499	621	176	292	251	392	313
$30,000 to $39,999	2,154	727	412	184	314	261	516	389
$40,000 to $49,999	1,964	764	282	196	309	206	413	270
$50,000 to $59,999	1,736	708	237	137	234	164	420	238
$60,000 to $69,999	1,533	773	125	112	215	130	307	157
$70,000 to $79,999	1,505	755	139	124	172	98	315	173
$80,000 to $89,999	1,181	725	51	64	105	50	236	84
$90,000 to $99,999	856	567	48	42	73	15	127	52
$100,000 or more	3,876	2,406	192	247	421	63	610	161
$100,000 to $124,999	1,623	1,026	90	83	161	35	263	84
$125,000 to $149,999	865	555	34	83	73	7	119	26
$150,000 to $174,999	567	344	31	13	91	9	88	14
$175,000 to $199,999	306	208	4	29	22	0	45	13
$200,000 or more	515	272	33	39	75	13	95	24
Median income	**$52,702**	**$72,107**	**$26,575**	**$49,941**	**$45,459**	**$35,178**	**$50,229**	**$37,496**
Total households headed by 25-to-34-year-olds	**100.0%**	**100.0%**	**100.0%**	**100.0%**	**100.0%**	**100.0%**	**100.0%**	**100.0%**
Under $10,000	7.6	2.2	17.9	4.4	11.7	15.8	8.7	12.9
$10,000 to $19,999	8.5	4.2	20.0	7.4	9.4	12.5	7.8	10.1
$20,000 to $29,999	9.9	5.9	18.3	12.1	10.8	14.5	9.8	13.1
$30,000 to $39,999	10.8	8.6	12.2	12.7	11.6	15.1	12.9	16.3
$40,000 to $49,999	9.8	9.0	8.3	13.5	11.4	11.9	10.3	11.3
$50,000 to $59,999	8.7	8.4	7.0	9.4	8.6	9.5	10.5	10.0
$60,000 to $69,999	7.7	9.1	3.7	7.7	8.0	7.5	7.7	6.6
$70,000 to $79,999	7.5	8.9	4.1	8.5	6.3	5.7	7.9	7.3
$80,000 to $89,999	5.9	8.6	1.5	4.4	3.9	2.9	5.9	3.5
$90,000 to $99,999	4.3	6.7	1.4	2.9	2.7	0.9	3.2	2.2
$100,000 or more	19.4	28.4	5.7	17.0	15.5	3.7	15.3	6.7
$100,000 to $124,999	8.1	12.1	2.7	5.7	5.9	2.0	6.6	3.5
$125,000 to $149,999	4.3	6.6	1.0	5.7	2.7	0.4	3.0	1.1
$150,000 to $174,999	2.8	4.1	0.9	0.9	3.4	0.5	2.2	0.6
$175,000 to $199,999	1.5	2.5	0.1	2.0	0.8	0.0	1.1	0.5
$200,000 or more	2.6	3.2	1.0	2.7	2.8	0.7	2.4	1.0

Source: Bureau of the Census, 2014 Current Population Survey, Internet site http://www.census.gov/hhes/www/income/data/index.html; calculations by New Strategist

Table 5.9 Income of Households by Household Type, 2013: Aged 25 to 29

(number and percent distribution of households headed by people aged 25 to 29, by income and household type, 2013; households in thousands as of 2014)

		family households			nonfamily households			
					female householder		male householder	
	total	married couples	female householder, no spouse present	male householder, no spouse present	total	living alone	total	living alone
Total households headed by 25-to-29-year-olds	**9,344**	**3,025**	**1,607**	**798**	**1,634**	**982**	**2,280**	**1,233**
Under $10,000	785	88	286	32	186	156	193	165
$10,000 to $19,999	843	143	334	54	172	145	140	98
$20,000 to $29,999	973	196	299	100	165	138	212	159
$30,000 to $39,999	1,125	331	190	81	197	158	327	239
$40,000 to $49,999	1,069	364	139	113	207	123	246	144
$50,000 to $59,999	834	276	107	66	151	97	234	119
$60,000 to $69,999	722	306	39	61	133	70	183	94
$70,000 to $79,999	698	249	77	83	109	57	180	85
$80,000 to $89,999	473	232	22	32	56	22	131	43
$90,000 to $99,999	355	208	15	22	28	0	82	22
$100,000 or more	1,467	632	99	154	231	15	352	64
$100,000 to $124,999	640	312	40	45	90	15	153	36
$125,000 to $149,999	355	155	25	65	39	0	71	11
$150,000 to $174,999	210	88	15	3	51	0	53	3
$175,000 to $199,999	91	39	3	16	14	0	19	2
$200,000 or more	171	38	17	25	36	0	55	12
Median income	**$48,194**	**$62,801**	**$25,828**	**$51,972**	**$43,386**	**$34,406**	**$50,595**	**$36,905**
Total households headed by 25-to-29-year-olds	**100.0%**	**100.0%**	**100.0%**	**100.0%**	**100.0%**	**100.0%**	**100.0%**	**100.0%**
Under $10,000	8.4	2.9	17.8	4.0	11.4	15.9	8.5	13.4
$10,000 to $19,999	9.0	4.7	20.8	6.8	10.5	14.8	6.1	8.0
$20,000 to $29,999	10.4	6.5	18.6	12.5	10.1	14.0	9.3	12.9
$30,000 to $39,999	12.0	10.9	11.8	10.2	12.0	16.1	14.3	19.4
$40,000 to $49,999	11.4	12.0	8.6	14.2	12.7	12.5	10.8	11.7
$50,000 to $59,999	8.9	9.1	6.6	8.3	9.3	9.9	10.3	9.6
$60,000 to $69,999	7.7	10.1	2.4	7.7	8.1	7.1	8.0	7.6
$70,000 to $79,999	7.5	8.2	4.8	10.3	6.7	5.8	7.9	6.9
$80,000 to $89,999	5.1	7.7	1.4	4.0	3.4	2.2	5.7	3.5
$90,000 to $99,999	3.8	6.9	0.9	2.7	1.7	0.0	3.6	1.8
$100,000 or more	15.7	20.9	6.2	19.3	14.1	1.6	15.4	5.2
$100,000 to $124,999	6.9	10.3	2.5	5.6	5.5	1.5	6.7	2.9
$125,000 to $149,999	3.8	5.1	1.5	8.1	2.4	0.0	3.1	0.9
$150,000 to $174,999	2.2	2.9	0.9	0.4	3.1	0.0	2.3	0.2
$175,000 to $199,999	1.0	1.3	0.2	2.0	0.8	0.0	0.8	0.2
$200,000 or more	1.8	1.2	1.0	3.2	2.2	0.0	2.4	1.0

Source: Bureau of the Census, 2014 Current Population Survey, Internet site http://www.census.gov/hhes/www/income/data/index .html; calculations by New Strategist

Table 5.10 Income of Households by Household Type, 2013: Aged 30 to 34

(number and percent distribution of households headed by people aged 30 to 34, by income and household type, 2013; households in thousands as of 2014)

		family households			nonfamily households			
					female householder		male householder	
	total	married couples	female householder, no spouse present	male householder, no spouse present	total	living alone	total	living alone
Total households headed by 30-to-34-year-olds	**10,664**	**5,437**	**1,780**	**657**	**1,073**	**747**	**1,718**	**1,155**
Under $10,000	736	98	319	33	130	117	155	143
$10,000 to $19,999	860	209	342	53	83	71	173	144
$20,000 to $29,999	1,008	303	322	76	126	114	181	154
$30,000 to $39,999	1,029	396	222	103	118	104	190	150
$40,000 to $49,999	895	400	143	83	102	83	167	126
$50,000 to $59,999	902	432	130	70	83	67	186	119
$60,000 to $69,999	810	467	86	51	82	60	124	63
$70,000 to $79,999	807	506	62	41	63	41	135	89
$80,000 to $89,999	708	493	29	32	49	29	105	40
$90,000 to $99,999	501	359	33	20	45	15	44	31
$100,000 or more	2,409	1,774	93	94	190	48	258	96
$100,000 to $124,999	983	715	50	39	70	20	109	48
$125,000 to $149,999	510	400	9	18	34	7	48	15
$150,000 to $174,999	357	256	16	10	39	9	35	11
$175,000 to $199,999	215	168	1	13	8	0	25	10
$200,000 or more	344	235	16	14	39	13	40	12
Median income	**$58,502**	**$77,181**	**$27,438**	**$47,980**	**$47,160**	**$35,908**	**$49,345**	**$38,821**
Total households headed by 30-to-34-year-olds	**100.0%**	**100.0%**	**100.0%**	**100.0%**	**100.0%**	**100.0%**	**100.0%**	**100.0%**
Under $10,000	6.9	1.8	17.9	5.0	12.2	15.7	9.0	12.4
$10,000 to $19,999	8.1	3.8	19.2	8.0	7.7	9.5	10.1	12.5
$20,000 to $29,999	9.5	5.6	18.1	11.6	11.8	15.2	10.5	13.3
$30,000 to $39,999	9.6	7.3	12.5	15.7	11.0	13.9	11.0	13.0
$40,000 to $49,999	8.4	7.4	8.0	12.6	9.5	11.1	9.7	10.9
$50,000 to $59,999	8.5	8.0	7.3	10.7	7.7	9.0	10.8	10.3
$60,000 to $69,999	7.6	8.6	4.8	7.8	7.7	8.0	7.2	5.5
$70,000 to $79,999	7.6	9.3	3.5	6.3	5.9	5.5	7.8	7.7
$80,000 to $89,999	6.6	9.1	1.6	4.9	4.6	3.8	6.1	3.5
$90,000 to $99,999	4.7	6.6	1.8	3.0	4.2	2.0	2.6	2.6
$100,000 or more	22.6	32.6	5.2	14.3	17.7	6.4	15.0	8.3
$100,000 to $124,999	9.2	13.1	2.8	5.9	6.6	2.6	6.4	4.1
$125,000 to $149,999	4.8	7.4	0.5	2.7	3.2	0.9	2.8	1.3
$150,000 to $174,999	3.3	4.7	0.9	1.6	3.7	1.2	2.0	1.0
$175,000 to $199,999	2.0	3.1	0.0	1.9	0.7	0.0	1.5	0.9
$200,000 or more	3.2	4.3	0.9	2.1	3.6	1.7	2.3	1.0

Source: Bureau of the Census, 2014 Current Population Survey, Internet site http://www.census.gov/hhes/www/income/data/index .html; calculations by New Strategist

Table 5.11 Income of Households by Household Type, 2013: Aged 35 to 39

(number and percent distribution of households headed by people aged 35 to 39, by income and household type, 2013; households in thousands as of 2014)

		family households			nonfamily households			
					female householder		male householder	
	total	married couples	female householder, no spouse present	male householder, no spouse present	total	living alone	total	living alone
Total households headed by 35-to-39-year-olds	**10,322**	**5,536**	**1,735**	**694**	**808**	**599**	**1,550**	**1,186**
Under $10,000	525	60	214	28	73	64	150	138
$10,000 to $19,999	821	170	265	71	125	99	191	173
$20,000 to $29,999	878	274	270	75	71	62	187	160
$30,000 to $39,999	922	326	240	81	101	80	174	146
$40,000 to $49,999	970	425	165	69	118	103	192	143
$50,000 to $59,999	891	496	153	71	66	56	105	92
$60,000 to $69,999	778	432	108	53	44	17	141	95
$70,000 to $79,999	709	460	85	34	47	33	83	47
$80,000 to $89,999	492	290	40	54	42	33	65	38
$90,000 to $99,999	477	340	58	27	23	4	30	12
$100,000 or more	2,859	2,263	137	131	98	48	231	143
$100,000 to $124,999	1,063	780	69	76	56	33	82	69
$125,000 to $149,999	565	479	21	16	18	6	32	13
$150,000 to $174,999	437	350	24	14	4	0	45	33
$175,000 to $199,999	213	161	13	13	6	0	19	11
$200,000 or more	582	493	10	12	14	8	52	17
Median income	**$61,383**	**$83,609**	**$35,061**	**$53,164**	**$42,142**	**$38,910**	**$43,115**	**$37,276**
Total households headed by 35-to-39-year-olds	**100.0%**	**100.0%**	**100.0%**	**100.0%**	**100.0%**	**100.0%**	**100.0%**	**100.0%**
Under $10,000	5.1	1.1	12.3	4.1	9.0	10.7	9.7	11.6
$10,000 to $19,999	8.0	3.1	15.3	10.2	15.4	16.6	12.3	14.6
$20,000 to $29,999	8.5	5.0	15.6	10.8	8.8	10.3	12.1	13.5
$30,000 to $39,999	8.9	5.9	13.9	11.7	12.5	13.3	11.3	12.3
$40,000 to $49,999	9.4	7.7	9.5	10.0	14.6	17.2	12.4	12.0
$50,000 to $59,999	8.6	9.0	8.8	10.2	8.2	9.3	6.8	7.8
$60,000 to $69,999	7.5	7.8	6.2	7.6	5.5	2.9	9.1	8.0
$70,000 to $79,999	6.9	8.3	4.9	4.9	5.9	5.5	5.4	4.0
$80,000 to $89,999	4.8	5.2	2.3	7.9	5.2	5.5	4.2	3.2
$90,000 to $99,999	4.6	6.1	3.3	3.8	2.8	0.6	1.9	1.0
$100,000 or more	27.7	40.9	7.9	18.9	12.1	8.1	14.9	12.0
$100,000 to $124,999	10.3	14.1	4.0	11.0	6.9	5.6	5.3	5.8
$125,000 to $149,999	5.5	8.6	1.2	2.2	2.2	1.1	2.0	1.1
$150,000 to $174,999	4.2	6.3	1.4	2.1	0.5	0.1	2.9	2.8
$175,000 to $199,999	2.1	2.9	0.7	1.8	0.8	0.0	1.3	0.9
$200,000 or more	5.6	8.9	0.6	1.7	1.8	1.4	3.3	1.5

Source: Bureau of the Census, 2014 Current Population Survey, Internet site http://www.census.gov/hhes/www/income/data/index .html; calculations by New Strategist

Men and Women under Age 45 Have Lost Ground

They had lower incomes in 2013 than in 2007.

The Great Recession and subsequent slow recovery has been hard on the Millennial generation (aged 19 to 36 in 2013). Between 2007 and 2013, the median income of men under age 45 fell by 7 to 10 percent, after adjusting for inflation. The median income of women aged 25 to 34 fell by a substantial 9 percent, while women aged 35 to 44 experienced a smaller 2 percent loss. Women under age 25, however, saw their median income rise slightly during those years.

Men's woes did not begin with the Great Recession. Their incomes were declining well before 2007. Between 2000 and 2013, the median income of men under age 45 declined by double-digit percentages, after adjusting for inflation. Among women under age 45, only those in the 25-to-34 age group had a lower median income in 2013 than in 2000.

■ Many young adults have student loans to pay off even as their incomes decline.

Men under age 45 have experienced double-digit percentage losses since 2000

(percent change in median income of total men and men under age 45, 2000 to 2013; in 2013 dollars)

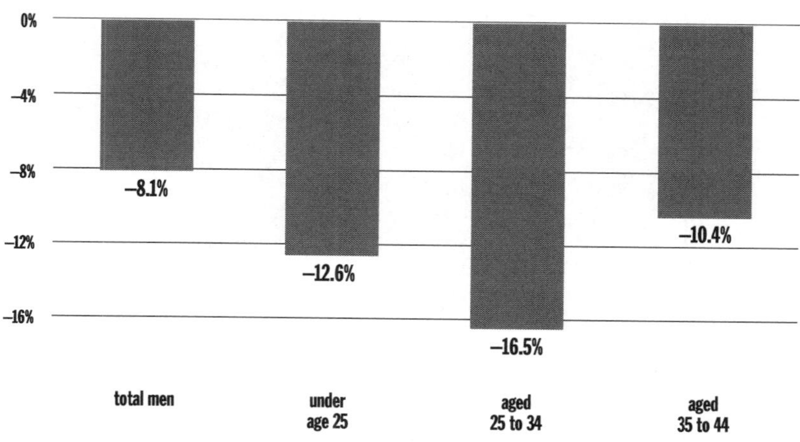

Table 5.12 Median Income of Men under Age 45, 2000 to 2013

(median income of men aged 15 or older and aged 15 to 44, and index of age group to total, 2000 to 2013; percent change for selected years; in 2013 dollars)

	total men	15 to 24	25 to 34	35 to 44
2013	$35,228	$11,288	$34,170	$45,942
2012	34,397	11,027	34,609	45,881
2011	34,164	10,894	33,745	45,538
2010	34,408	10,585	34,126	45,120
2009	34,953	10,899	34,660	45,857
2008	35,877	11,661	36,152	47,809
2007	37,295	12,593	36,934	50,577
2006	37,277	12,667	37,123	49,261
2005	37,318	12,492	37,182	48,880
2004	37,633	12,433	38,220	49,988
2003	37,910	12,616	38,709	49,643
2002	37,859	12,485	39,722	49,065
2001	38,290	12,238	40,144	50,447
2000	38,340	12,913	40,925	51,297
PERCENT CHANGE				
2007 to 2013	–5.5%	–10.4%	–7.5%	–9.2%
2000 to 2013	–8.1	–12.6	–16.5	–10.4
INDEX				
2013	100	32	97	130
2012	100	32	101	133
2011	100	32	99	133
2010	100	31	99	131
2009	100	31	99	131
2008	100	33	101	133
2007	100	34	99	136
2006	100	34	100	132
2005	100	33	100	131
2004	100	33	102	133
2003	100	33	102	131
2002	100	33	105	130
2001	100	32	105	132
2000	100	34	107	134

Note: The index is calculated by dividing the median income of the age group by the national median and multiplying by 100.
Source: Bureau of the Census, Historical Income Data, Internet site http://www.census.gov/hhes/www/income/data/historical/index.html; calculations by New Strategist

Table 5.13 Median Income of Women under Age 45, 2000 to 2013

(median income of women aged 15 or older and aged 15 to 44, and index of age group to total, 2000 to 2013; percent change for selected years; in 2013 dollars)

	total women	15 to 24	25 to 34	35 to 44
2013	$22,063	$10,175	$26,375	$30,571
2012	21,833	9,720	26,553	30,498
2011	21,856	9,432	26,642	30,134
2010	22,196	9,292	27,310	31,274
2009	22,760	9,720	27,407	30,294
2008	22,576	9,630	27,646	29,613
2007	23,505	10,065	29,080	31,123
2006	23,123	9,997	27,935	30,464
2005	22,166	9,808	27,224	30,350
2004	21,788	9,500	27,214	30,093
2003	21,860	9,417	27,854	29,729
2002	21,769	9,818	28,032	28,904
2001	21,860	9,825	28,254	29,567
2000	21,729	9,956	28,473	29,864
PERCENT CHANGE				
2007 to 2013	–6.1%	1.1%	–9.3%	–1.8%
2000 to 2013	1.5	2.2	–7.4	2.4
INDEX				
2013	100	46	120	139
2012	100	45	122	140
2011	100	43	122	138
2010	100	42	123	141
2009	100	43	120	133
2008	100	43	122	131
2007	100	43	124	132
2006	100	43	121	132
2005	100	44	123	137
2004	100	44	125	138
2003	100	43	127	136
2002	100	45	129	133
2001	100	45	129	135
2000	100	46	131	137

Note: The index is calculated by dividing the median income of the age group by the national median and multiplying by 100.
Source: Bureau of the Census, Historical Income Data, Internet site http://www.census.gov/hhes/www/income/data/historical/index.html; calculations by New Strategist

By Age 30 to 34, Men's Incomes Are above Average

The incomes of men under age 25 are low because few work full-time.

The median income of men under age 25 was a meager $11,288 in 2013. Among men aged 25 to 34, median income was a much larger $34,170, and those aged 35 to 39 had a median income of $43,645. (Millennials were aged 19 to 36 in 2013.) Behind the low figure for the youngest age group is the fact that few men under age 25 work full-time—only 19 percent in 2013. In the 25-to-34 age group, 65 percent of men work full-time, hence their higher incomes. An even larger 73 percent of men aged 35 to 39 are full-time workers.

Among men under age 25, Hispanics have the highest median income ($12,336) because they are most likely to work full-time. In the 25-to-34 age group, things change. Among full-time workers, the median income of Hispanic men is lower than that of Asians, Blacks, or non-Hispanic Whites because Hispanics are the least educated. This pattern continues in the 35-to-39 age group, with the median income of full-time workers ranging from a low of $35,027 for Hispanics to a high of $75,843 for Asians.

■ Men's incomes rise as they commit themselves to a career.

Among men aged 25 to 34, Hispanics have the lowest median income

(median income of men aged 25 to 34 who work full-time, by race and Hispanic origin, 2013)

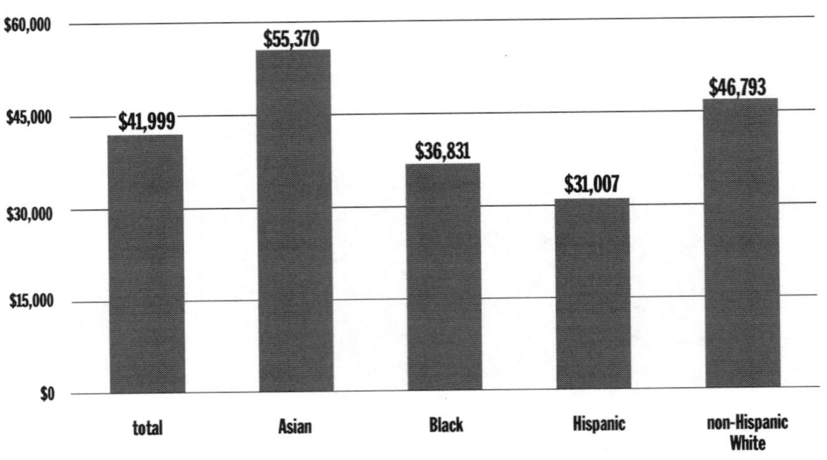

Table 5.14 Income of Men under Age 40, 2013: Total Men

(number and percent distribution of men aged 15 or older and aged 15 to 39 by income and age, 2013; median income of men with income and of men working full-time, year-round; percent working full-time, year-round; men in thousands as of 2014)

	total	15 to 24	aged 25 to 34 total	aged 25 to 34: 25 to 29	aged 25 to 34: 30 to 34	35 to 39
TOTAL MEN	**122,414**	**21,822**	**21,217**	**10,831**	**10,386**	**9,562**
Without income	**13,707**	**8,368**	**1,613**	**942**	**671**	**549**
With income	**108,706**	**13,454**	**19,604**	**9,889**	**9,715**	**9,014**
Under $5,000	7,073	3,865	947	601	346	216
$5,000 to $9,999	7,227	2,344	1,230	719	512	398
$10,000 to $14,999	7,751	1,512	1,144	660	484	437
$15,000 to $19,999	8,834	1,364	1,586	839	747	576
$20,000 to $24,999	8,947	1,329	1,802	993	809	712
$25,000 to $29,999	7,106	730	1,500	907	593	513
$30,000 to $34,999	7,054	562	1,735	929	806	546
$35,000 to $39,999	6,027	375	1,213	657	556	620
$40,000 to $44,999	6,034	391	1,344	639	705	566
$45,000 to $49,999	4,608	148	925	440	485	482
$50,000 to $54,999	5,239	202	1,127	525	602	500
$55,000 to $59,999	2,987	127	577	255	322	287
$60,000 to $64,999	3,837	107	773	324	450	367
$65,000 to $69,999	2,653	66	520	206	314	294
$70,000 to $74,999	2,639	49	524	248	276	276
$75,000 to $79,999	2,339	52	439	120	319	277
$80,000 to $84,999	2,208	41	418	220	198	281
$85,000 to $89,999	1,451	42	225	78	147	136
$90,000 to $94,999	1,605	38	210	78	133	166
$95,000 to $99,999	1,084	12	188	64	124	124
$100,000 or more	12,003	99	1,176	388	788	1,239
MEDIAN INCOME						
Men with income	$35,228	$11,288	$34,170	$30,808	$40,023	$43,645
Working full-time	50,943	26,117	41,999	38,329	46,880	51,139
Percent full-time	49.7%	18.6%	64.9%	61.4%	68.7%	73.4%
PERCENT DISTRIBUTION						
TOTAL MEN	**100.0%**	**100.0%**	**100.0%**	**100.0%**	**100.0%**	**100.0%**
Without income	**11.2**	**38.3**	**7.6**	**8.7**	**6.5**	**5.7**
With income	**88.8**	**61.7**	**92.4**	**91.3**	**93.5**	**94.3**
Under $15,000	18.0	35.4	15.7	18.3	12.9	11.0
$15,000 to $24,999	14.5	12.3	16.0	16.9	15.0	13.5
$25,000 to $34,999	11.6	5.9	15.2	17.0	13.5	11.1
$35,000 to $49,999	13.6	4.2	16.4	16.0	16.8	17.4
$50,000 to $74,999	14.2	2.5	16.6	14.4	18.9	18.0
$75,000 to $99,999	7.1	0.8	7.0	5.2	8.9	10.3
$100,000 or more	9.8	0.5	5.5	3.6	7.6	13.0

Source: Bureau of the Census, 2014 Current Population Survey, Internet site http://www.census.gov/hhes/www/income/data/index.html; calculations by New Strategist

Table 5.15 Income of Men under Age 40, 2013: Asian Men

(number and percent distribution of Asian men aged 15 or older and aged 15 to 39 by income and age, 2013; median income of men with income and of men working full-time, year-round; percent working full-time, year-round; men in thousands as of 2014)

	total	15 to 24	aged 25 to 34 total	aged 25 to 34: 25 to 29	aged 25 to 34: 30 to 34	35 to 39
ASIAN MEN	**7,135**	**1,329**	**1,505**	**752**	**752**	**678**
Without income	**973**	**572**	**124**	**69**	**55**	**32**
With income	**6,162**	**757**	**1,381**	**683**	**697**	**645**
Under $5,000	433	214	63	32	31	18
$5,000 to $9,999	450	156	73	40	33	7
$10,000 to $14,999	451	108	81	50	31	25
$15,000 to $19,999	463	93	89	39	50	9
$20,000 to $24,999	384	64	97	69	28	35
$25,000 to $29,999	357	31	90	60	29	21
$30,000 to $34,999	307	21	83	41	43	19
$35,000 to $39,999	261	2	47	37	11	53
$40,000 to $44,999	316	12	87	37	50	12
$45,000 to $49,999	209	3	55	21	34	34
$50,000 to $54,999	259	21	75	55	20	35
$55,000 to $59,999	186	0	60	35	25	21
$60,000 to $64,999	207	7	70	25	44	23
$65,000 to $69,999	176	6	38	14	24	21
$70,000 to $74,999	196	6	67	16	51	21
$75,000 to $79,999	131	3	31	17	13	31
$80,000 to $84,999	137	0	44	27	17	16
$85,000 to $89,999	75	3	10	5	5	9
$90,000 to $94,999	133	2	40	24	16	25
$95,000 to $99,999	63	1	27	5	23	0
$100,000 or more	966	4	151	33	118	207
MEDIAN INCOME						
Men with income	$39,204	$10,427	$41,910	$36,050	$51,106	$66,283
Working full-time	60,191	22,445	55,370	50,282	61,735	75,843
Percent full-time	52.6%	10.4%	61.1%	55.5%	66.6%	81.5%
PERCENT DISTRIBUTION						
ASIAN MEN	**100.0%**	**100.0%**	**100.0%**	**100.0%**	**100.0%**	**100.0%**
Without income	**13.6**	**43.0**	**8.2**	**9.2**	**7.3**	**4.8**
With income	**86.4**	**57.0**	**91.8**	**90.8**	**92.7**	**95.2**
Under $15,000	18.7	36.0	14.4	16.3	12.6	7.3
$15,000 to $24,999	11.9	11.8	12.4	14.4	10.4	6.5
$25,000 to $34,999	9.3	4.0	11.5	13.4	9.6	5.9
$35,000 to $49,999	11.0	1.2	12.6	12.6	12.6	14.8
$50,000 to $74,999	14.4	3.0	20.6	19.3	21.9	17.8
$75,000 to $99,999	7.6	0.7	10.2	10.5	9.9	12.2
$100,000 or more	13.5	0.3	10.1	4.4	15.7	30.6

Note: Asians are those who identify themselves as being of the race alone and those who identify themselves as being of the race in combination with other races.
Source: Bureau of the Census, 2014 Current Population Survey, Internet site http://www.census.gov/hhes/www/income/data/index .html; calculations by New Strategist

Table 5.16 Income of Men under Age 40, 2013: Black Men

(number and percent distribution of Black men aged 15 or older and aged 15 to 39 by income and age, 2013; median income of men with income and of men working full-time, year-round; percent working full-time, year-round; men in thousands as of 2014)

			aged 25 to 34			
	total	15 to 24	total	25 to 29	30 to 34	35 to 39
BLACK MEN	**15,188**	**3,546**	**2,908**	**1,556**	**1,352**	**1,211**
Without income	**2,876**	**1,708**	**439**	**282**	**157**	**163**
With income	**12,311**	**1,838**	**2,469**	**1,274**	**1,195**	**1,048**
Under $5,000	1,059	591	170	79	92	29
$5,000 to $9,999	1,533	411	278	159	119	142
$10,000 to $14,999	1,224	201	238	134	104	66
$15,000 to $19,999	1,269	226	314	160	154	57
$20,000 to $24,999	1,130	126	232	117	115	113
$25,000 to $29,999	888	91	183	115	68	75
$30,000 to $34,999	736	47	181	92	89	70
$35,000 to $39,999	596	40	150	81	70	77
$40,000 to $44,999	574	20	136	52	84	41
$45,000 to $49,999	508	17	130	70	60	39
$50,000 to $54,999	468	11	99	56	43	61
$55,000 to $59,999	269	10	38	24	14	43
$60,000 to $64,999	344	4	71	24	46	39
$65,000 to $69,999	213	12	37	16	21	25
$70,000 to $74,999	221	11	48	28	20	26
$75,000 to $79,999	211	2	36	6	30	34
$80,000 to $84,999	190	1	25	13	12	31
$85,000 to $89,999	92	6	15	5	10	4
$90,000 to $94,999	97	2	13	7	6	6
$95,000 to $99,999	73	0	6	3	4	5
$100,000 or more	617	10	66	32	34	65
MEDIAN INCOME						
Men with income	$24,643	$9,066	$25,021	$24,345	$25,693	$32,339
Working full-time	41,555	21,332	36,831	35,855	38,274	42,333
Percent full-time	40.2%	13.2%	51.1	47.8	54.9	60.0
PERCENT DISTRIBUTION						
BLACK MEN	**100.0%**	**100.0%**	**100.0%**	**100.0%**	**100.0%**	**100.0%**
Without income	**18.9**	**48.2**	**15.1**	**18.1**	**11.6**	**13.4**
With income	**81.1**	**51.8**	**84.9**	**81.9**	**88.4**	**86.6**
Under $15,000	25.1	33.9	23.6	23.9	23.3	19.6
$15,000 to $24,999	15.8	9.9	18.8	17.9	19.9	14.1
$25,000 to $34,999	10.7	3.9	12.5	13.3	11.6	12.0
$35,000 to $49,999	11.0	2.2	14.3	13.0	15.8	13.0
$50,000 to $74,999	10.0	1.3	10.1	9.5	10.7	16.0
$75,000 to $99,999	4.4	0.3	3.3	2.1	4.6	6.6
$100,000 or more	4.1	0.3	2.3	2.1	2.5	5.4

Note: Blacks are those who identify themselves as being of the race alone and those who identify themselves as being of the race in combination with other races.
Source: Bureau of the Census, 2014 Current Population Survey, Internet site http://www.census.gov/hhes/www/income/data/index.html; calculations by New Strategist

Table 5.17 Income of Men under Age 40, 2013: Hispanic Men

(number and percent distribution of Hispanic men aged 15 or older and aged 15 to 39 by income and age, 2013; median income of men with income and of men working full-time, year-round; percent working full-time, year-round; men in thousands as of 2014)

	total	15 to 24	aged 25 to 34: total	aged 25 to 34: 25 to 29	aged 25 to 34: 30 to 34	35 to 39
HISPANIC MEN	**19,683**	**4,764**	**4,572**	**2,369**	**2,203**	**2,017**
Without income	**3,199**	**2,079**	**399**	**243**	**156**	**141**
With income	**16,484**	**2,686**	**4,173**	**2,126**	**2,047**	**1,875**
Under $5,000	1,077	567	208	153	55	53
$5,000 to $9,999	1,524	525	301	182	118	116
$10,000 to $14,999	1,598	360	357	200	157	146
$15,000 to $19,999	1,877	336	536	272	263	212
$20,000 to $24,999	2,005	310	552	273	279	247
$25,000 to $29,999	1,431	158	425	220	205	173
$30,000 to $34,999	1,299	116	428	206	222	169
$35,000 to $39,999	928	51	228	115	113	137
$40,000 to $44,999	962	88	228	106	122	122
$45,000 to $49,999	555	45	172	76	97	73
$50,000 to $54,999	579	20	178	90	88	59
$55,000 to $59,999	317	40	77	29	48	35
$60,000 to $64,999	425	6	118	66	52	70
$65,000 to $69,999	244	5	78	31	46	17
$70,000 to $74,999	224	7	41	19	22	31
$75,000 to $79,999	210	14	47	23	24	34
$80,000 to $84,999	213	12	42	16	26	33
$85,000 to $89,999	119	2	22	5	17	14
$90,000 to $94,999	131	1	29	16	13	15
$95,000 to $99,999	96	2	15	2	12	15
$100,000 or more	671	21	92	26	66	103
MEDIAN INCOME						
Men with income	$25,411	$12,336	$26,243	$24,560	$28,236	$29,621
Working full-time	32,949	23,535	31,007	29,837	32,057	35,027
Percent full-time	50.9%	21.4%	64.0%	61.1%	67.1%	67.7%
PERCENT DISTRIBUTION						
HISPANIC MEN	**100.0%**	**100.0%**	**100.0%**	**100.0%**	**100.0%**	**100.0%**
Without income	**16.3**	**43.6**	**8.7**	**10.2**	**7.1**	**7.0**
With income	**83.7**	**56.4**	**91.3**	**89.8**	**92.9**	**93.0**
Under $15,000	21.3	30.5	18.9	22.6	15.0	15.6
$15,000 to $24,999	19.7	13.6	23.8	23.0	24.6	22.8
$25,000 to $34,999	13.9	5.7	18.7	18.0	19.4	16.9
$35,000 to $49,999	12.4	3.9	13.8	12.5	15.1	16.4
$50,000 to $74,999	9.1	1.6	10.8	9.9	11.7	10.6
$75,000 to $99,999	3.9	0.6	3.4	2.6	4.2	5.6
$100,000 or more	3.4	0.4	2.0	1.1	3.0	5.1

Source: Bureau of the Census, 2014 Current Population Survey, Internet site http://www.census.gov/hhes/www/income/data/index .html; calculations by New Strategist

Table 5.18 Income of Men under Age 40, 2013: Non-Hispanic White Men

(number and percent distribution of non-Hispanic White men aged 15 or older and aged 15 to 39 by income and age, 2013; median income of men with income and of men working full-time, year-round; percent working full-time, year-round; men in thousands as of 2014)

			aged 25 to 34			
	total	15 to 24	total	25 to 29	30 to 34	35 to 39
NON-HISPANIC WHITE MEN	**80,003**	**12,164**	**12,313**	**6,247**	**6,066**	**5,642**
Without income	**6,669**	**4,032**	**660**	**378**	**282**	**203**
With income	**73,333**	**8,132**	**11,653**	**5,869**	**5,784**	**5,440**
Under $5,000	4,477	2,491	507	344	163	112
$5,000 to $9,999	3,724	1,264	581	334	247	146
$10,000 to $14,999	4,412	838	504	308	196	190
$15,000 to $19,999	5,227	699	676	399	277	299
$20,000 to $24,999	5,383	790	933	534	399	323
$25,000 to $29,999	4,416	449	815	522	292	236
$30,000 to $34,999	4,688	378	1,037	583	454	289
$35,000 to $39,999	4,199	279	789	419	370	349
$40,000 to $44,999	4,146	272	886	443	443	394
$45,000 to $49,999	3,338	76	583	277	306	330
$50,000 to $54,999	3,930	150	764	323	441	343
$55,000 to $59,999	2,204	85	397	164	233	187
$60,000 to $64,999	2,872	93	524	211	313	239
$65,000 to $69,999	2,017	47	376	148	228	230
$70,000 to $74,999	1,987	25	371	190	181	197
$75,000 to $79,999	1,747	31	303	61	243	180
$80,000 to $84,999	1,673	29	311	168	143	207
$85,000 to $89,999	1,145	31	175	60	115	108
$90,000 to $94,999	1,227	34	131	36	96	121
$95,000 to $99,999	851	9	139	54	85	102
$100,000 or more	9,669	64	852	293	559	857
MEDIAN INCOME						
Men with income	$40,122	$11,402	$39,844	$33,695	$45,558	$50,451
Working full-time	56,456	28,549	46,793	41,220	51,617	57,060
Percent full-time	50.9%	19.8%	68.8%	65.0%	72.8%	77.4%
PERCENT DISTRIBUTION						
NON-HISPANIC WHITE MEN	**100.0%**	**100.0%**	**100.0%**	**100.0%**	**100.0%**	**100.0%**
Without income	**8.3**	**33.2**	**5.4**	**6.1**	**4.7**	**3.6**
With income	**91.7**	**66.8**	**94.6**	**93.9**	**95.3**	**96.4**
Under $15,000	15.8	37.8	12.9	15.8	10.0	7.9
$15,000 to $24,999	13.3	12.2	13.1	14.9	11.2	11.0
$25,000 to $34,999	11.4	6.8	15.0	17.7	12.3	9.3
$35,000 to $49,999	14.6	5.2	18.3	18.2	18.5	19.0
$50,000 to $74,999	16.3	3.3	19.7	16.6	23.0	21.2
$75,000 to $99,999	8.3	1.1	8.6	6.0	11.2	12.7
$100,000 or more	12.1	0.5	6.9	4.7	9.2	15.2

Note: Non-Hispanic Whites are those who identify themselves as being White alone and not Hispanic.
Source: Bureau of the Census, 2014 Current Population Survey, Internet site http://www.census.gov/hhes/www/income/data/index.html; calculations by New Strategist

Women's Incomes Are above Average by Age 25 to 29

The incomes of women under age 25 are low because few work full-time.

The median income of women under age 25 was just $10,175 in 2013. Among women aged 25 to 34, median income was a larger $26,375, and women aged 35 to 39 had a median income of $30,411. (Millennials were aged 19 to 36 in 2013.) Behind the low figure for the youngest age group is the fact that few women under age 25 work full-time—only 14 percent in 2013. In the 25-to-34 age group, 47 percent of women work full-time, hence their higher incomes. In the 35-to-39 age group an even larger 49 percent are full-time workers.

Among full-time workers aged 25 to 34, the median income of Hispanic women is lower than that of Asians, Blacks, or non-Hispanic Whites because Hispanics are the least educated. The median income of full-time workers in the age group ranges from a low of $30,741 for Hispanics to a high of $48,386 for Asians. The pattern is the same for women in the 35-to-39 age group: the median income of full-time workers ranges from a low of $34,031 for Hispanics to a high of $51,453 for Asians.

■ Women's median income remains flat with age, hovering at around $30,000 from the 35-to-39 to the 60-to-64 age group.

Among women aged 25 to 34, Hispanics have the lowest median income

(median income of women aged 25 to 34 who work full-time, by race and Hispanic origin, 2013)

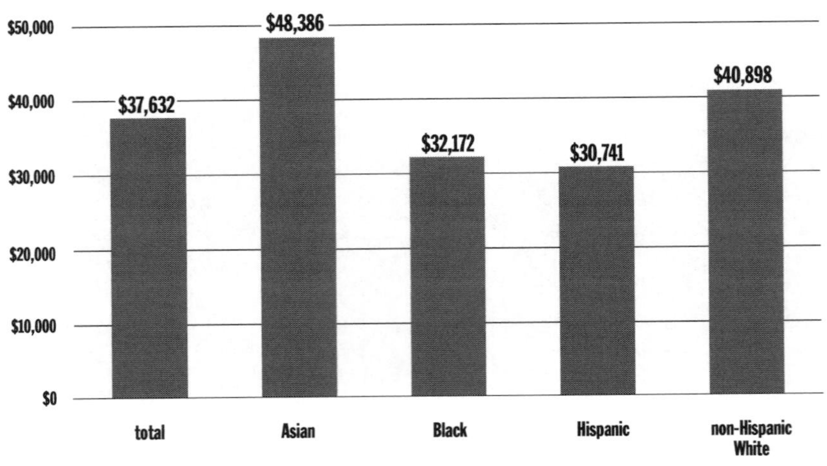

Table 5.19 Income of Women under Age 40, 2013: Total Women

(number and percent distribution of women aged 15 or older and aged 15 to 39 by income and age, 2013; median income of women with income and of women working full-time, year-round; percent working full-time, year-round; women in thousands as of 2014)

			aged 25 to 34			
	total	15 to 24	total	25 to 29	30 to 34	35 to 39
TOTAL WOMEN	**129,930**	**21,235**	**21,248**	**10,655**	**10,594**	**9,848**
Without income	**19,975**	**8,195**	**3,302**	**1,591**	**1,711**	**1,487**
With income	**109,956**	**13,041**	**17,946**	**9,064**	**8,883**	**8,361**
Under $5,000	11,888	3,874	1,906	994	912	822
$5,000 to $9,999	13,431	2,562	1,637	954	683	589
$10,000 to $14,999	13,771	1,815	1,594	869	725	759
$15,000 to $19,999	11,145	1,476	1,628	918	710	685
$20,000 to $24,999	9,350	1,083	1,704	885	819	691
$25,000 to $29,999	7,492	704	1,398	737	661	564
$30,000 to $34,999	6,989	526	1,452	772	681	590
$35,000 to $39,999	5,478	318	1,145	584	561	548
$40,000 to $44,999	5,150	183	1,115	534	582	485
$45,000 to $49,999	3,947	128	921	447	474	382
$50,000 to $54,999	3,800	110	716	282	434	446
$55,000 to $59,999	2,267	60	432	174	259	237
$60,000 to $64,999	2,643	60	450	189	261	316
$65,000 to $69,999	1,737	27	367	158	209	137
$70,000 to $74,999	1,810	15	342	194	148	207
$75,000 to $79,999	1,441	25	273	93	180	167
$80,000 to $84,999	1,301	0	169	67	102	88
$85,000 to $89,999	740	12	80	24	57	77
$90,000 to $94,999	664	10	97	33	64	64
$95,000 to $99,999	468	12	32	7	25	42
$100,000 or more	4,442	42	487	151	336	464
MEDIAN INCOME						
Women with income	$22,063	$10,175	$26,375	$24,317	$29,251	$30,411
Working full-time	40,597	24,633	37,632	35,578	40,832	41,931
Percent full-time	34.7%	14.4%	46.9%	45.8%	48.0%	49.0%
PERCENT DISTRIBUTION						
TOTAL WOMEN	**100.0%**	**100.0%**	**100.0%**	**100.0%**	**100.0%**	**100.0%**
Without income	**15.4**	**38.6**	**15.5**	**14.9**	**16.2**	**15.1**
With income	**84.6**	**61.4**	**84.5**	**85.1**	**83.8**	**84.9**
Under $15,000	30.1	38.9	24.2	26.4	21.9	22.0
$15,000 to $24,999	15.8	12.0	15.7	16.9	14.4	14.0
$25,000 to $34,999	11.1	5.8	13.4	14.2	12.7	11.7
$35,000 to $49,999	11.2	3.0	15.0	14.7	15.3	14.4
$50,000 to $74,999	9.4	1.3	10.9	9.4	12.4	13.6
$75,000 to $99,999	3.6	0.3	3.1	2.1	4.0	4.4
$100,000 or more	3.4	0.2	2.3	1.4	3.2	4.7

Source: Bureau of the Census, 2014 Current Population Survey, Internet site http://www.census.gov/hhes/www/income/data/index.html; calculations by New Strategist

Table 5.20 Income of Women under Age 40, 2013: Asian Women

(number and percent distribution of Asian women aged 15 or older and aged 15 to 39 by income and age, 2013; median income of women with income and of women working full-time, year-round; percent working full-time, year-round; women in thousands as of 2014)

	total	15 to 24	aged 25 to 34			35 to 39
			total	25 to 29	30 to 34	
ASIAN WOMEN	**7,877**	**1,283**	**1,640**	**790**	**849**	**796**
Without income	**1,834**	**551**	**427**	**198**	**229**	**202**
With income	**6,043**	**732**	**1,213**	**592**	**621**	**595**
Under $5,000	827	253	134	80	55	68
$5,000 to $9,999	745	181	89	48	40	37
$10,000 to $14,999	586	103	72	43	29	27
$15,000 to $19,999	447	50	78	52	27	41
$20,000 to $24,999	433	24	81	46	34	52
$25,000 to $29,999	379	35	69	25	43	26
$30,000 to $34,999	364	16	105	50	55	42
$35,000 to $39,999	253	9	71	33	38	24
$40,000 to $44,999	282	13	72	38	34	19
$45,000 to $49,999	239	24	57	39	17	35
$50,000 to $54,999	185	7	42	12	30	28
$55,000 to $59,999	111	6	24	9	15	7
$60,000 to $64,999	209	1	72	25	46	32
$65,000 to $69,999	81	0	15	5	11	7
$70,000 to $74,999	121	0	32	21	11	24
$75,000 to $79,999	100	7	27	7	20	17
$80,000 to $84,999	95	0	31	20	11	23
$85,000 to $89,999	45	0	10	6	5	5
$90,000 to $94,999	56	0	22	13	10	7
$95,000 to $99,999	27	0	6	1	5	3
$100,000 or more	459	3	103	19	83	68
MEDIAN INCOME						
Women with income	$24,734	$7,269	$32,665	$30,110	$38,016	$35,909
Working full-time	45,335	26,071	48,386	45,707	52,231	51,453
Percent full-time	35.5%	6.5%	42.6%	39.0%	46.0%	45.1%
PERCENT DISTRIBUTION						
ASIAN WOMEN	**100.0%**	**100.0%**	**100.0%**	**100.0%**	**100.0%**	**100.0%**
Without income	**23.3**	**43.0**	**26.0**	**25.1**	**26.9**	**25.3**
With income	**76.7**	**57.0**	**74.0**	**74.9**	**73.1**	**74.7**
Under $15,000	27.4	41.8	18.0	21.6	14.7	16.7
$15,000 to $24,999	11.2	5.7	9.7	12.4	7.2	11.7
$25,000 to $34,999	9.4	4.0	10.6	9.6	11.5	8.5
$35,000 to $49,999	9.8	3.6	12.2	14.0	10.5	9.8
$50,000 to $74,999	9.0	1.1	11.3	9.1	13.4	12.5
$75,000 to $99,999	4.1	0.6	5.9	5.8	5.9	6.9
$100,000 or more	5.8	0.3	6.3	2.4	9.8	8.6

Note: Asians are those who identify themselves as being of the race alone and those who identify themselves as being of the race in combination with other races.
Source: Bureau of the Census, 2014 Current Population Survey, Internet site http://www.census.gov/hhes/www/income/data/index.html; calculations by New Strategist

Table 5.21 Income of Women under Age 40, 2013: Black Women

(number and percent distribution of Black women aged 15 or older and aged 15 to 39 by income and age, 2013; median income of women with income and of women working full-time, year-round; percent working full-time, year-round; women in thousands as of 2014)

			aged 25 to 34			
	total	15 to 24	total	25 to 29	30 to 34	35 to 39
BLACK WOMEN	**18,038**	**3,742**	**3,291**	**1,698**	**1,594**	**1,486**
Without income	**2,999**	**1,593**	**363**	**181**	**182**	**189**
With income	**15,038**	**2,149**	**2,928**	**1,517**	**1,412**	**1,298**
Under $5,000	1,590	558	350	200	149	95
$5,000 to $9,999	2,234	525	391	217	174	105
$10,000 to $14,999	2,063	276	293	153	139	117
$15,000 to $19,999	1,643	320	312	178	135	121
$20,000 to $24,999	1,336	211	304	184	120	118
$25,000 to $29,999	1,037	82	251	144	106	105
$30,000 to $34,999	1,009	72	244	124	120	92
$35,000 to $39,999	792	32	162	68	94	126
$40,000 to $44,999	610	14	136	61	75	74
$45,000 to $49,999	544	17	117	55	62	65
$50,000 to $54,999	450	12	98	31	67	49
$55,000 to $59,999	259	2	34	13	21	42
$60,000 to $64,999	294	2	40	24	16	34
$65,000 to $69,999	186	4	48	12	36	15
$70,000 to $74,999	218	0	35	18	17	31
$75,000 to $79,999	163	0	33	7	26	18
$80,000 to $84,999	108	0	19	1	17	7
$85,000 to $89,999	80	4	14	7	8	9
$90,000 to $94,999	60	2	12	10	2	11
$95,000 to $99,999	52	5	4	0	4	9
$100,000 or more	309	12	32	9	23	55
MEDIAN INCOME						
Women with income	$19,955	$9,915	$21,556	$20,200	$24,502	$29,023
Working full-time	35,460	21,260	32,172	30,298	35,911	37,516
Percent full-time	37.0%	14.3%	46.3%	44.4%	48.4%	56.6%
PERCENT DISTRIBUTION						
BLACK WOMEN	**100.0%**	**100.0%**	**100.0%**	**100.0%**	**100.0%**	**100.0%**
Without income	**16.6**	**42.6**	**11.0**	**10.7**	**11.4**	**12.7**
With income	**83.4**	**57.4**	**89.0**	**89.3**	**88.6**	**87.3**
Under $15,000	32.6	36.3	31.4	33.6	29.0	21.3
$15,000 to $24,999	16.5	14.2	18.7	21.3	16.0	16.1
$25,000 to $34,999	11.3	4.1	15.0	15.8	14.2	13.2
$35,000 to $49,999	10.8	1.7	12.6	10.9	14.5	17.9
$50,000 to $74,999	7.8	0.5	7.7	5.8	9.9	11.5
$75,000 to $99,999	2.6	0.3	2.5	1.5	3.6	3.6
$100,000 or more	1.7	0.3	1.0	0.5	1.5	3.7

Note: Blacks are those who identify themselves as being of the race alone and those who identify themselves as being of the race in combination with other races.

Source: Bureau of the Census, 2014 Current Population Survey, Internet site http://www.census.gov/hhes/www/income/data/index.html; calculations by New Strategist

Table 5.22 Income of Women under Age 40, 2013: Hispanic Women

(number and percent distribution of Hispanic women aged 15 or older and aged 15 to 39 by income and age, 2013; median income of women with income and of women working full-time, year-round; percent working full-time, year-round; women in thousands as of 2014)

	total	15 to 24	aged 25 to 34 total	aged 25 to 34: 25 to 29	aged 25 to 34: 30 to 34	35 to 39
HISPANIC WOMEN	**19,476**	**4,476**	**4,138**	**2,060**	**2,078**	**1,967**
Without income	**5,442**	**2,159**	**1,050**	**504**	**546**	**477**
With income	**14,034**	**2,317**	**3,088**	**1,556**	**1,532**	**1,490**
Under $5,000	1,766	624	366	195	171	134
$5,000 to $9,999	2,211	480	340	207	133	135
$10,000 to $14,999	2,015	328	357	211	146	192
$15,000 to $19,999	1,643	268	369	206	164	156
$20,000 to $24,999	1,408	238	355	163	192	143
$25,000 to $29,999	1,050	130	259	120	139	148
$30,000 to $34,999	862	109	231	126	106	113
$35,000 to $39,999	655	55	187	67	119	127
$40,000 to $44,999	526	36	161	71	90	70
$45,000 to $49,999	367	17	126	63	63	41
$50,000 to $54,999	351	13	75	33	41	47
$55,000 to $59,999	177	5	49	14	35	31
$60,000 to $64,999	225	8	48	12	36	51
$65,000 to $69,999	117	1	24	5	19	15
$70,000 to $74,999	143	1	34	23	11	16
$75,000 to $79,999	105	0	29	12	17	10
$80,000 to $84,999	72	0	23	10	12	5
$85,000 to $89,999	46	2	10	4	7	6
$90,000 to $94,999	31	0	8	5	3	6
$95,000 to $99,999	25	0	0	0	0	6
$100,000 or more	239	2	37	9	29	37
MEDIAN INCOME						
Women with income	$17,762	$10,560	$21,221	$18,767	$23,631	$24,237
Working full-time	30,799	23,050	30,741	28,745	32,087	34,031
Percent full-time	31.7%	13.2%	40.6%	38.0%	43.1%	43.8%
PERCENT DISTRIBUTION						
HISPANIC WOMEN	**100.0%**	**100.0%**	**100.0%**	**100.0%**	**100.0%**	**100.0%**
Without income	**27.9**	**48.2**	**25.4**	**24.5**	**26.3**	**24.2**
With income	**72.1**	**51.8**	**74.6**	**75.5**	**73.7**	**75.8**
Under $15,000	30.8	32.0	25.7	29.8	21.7	23.4
$15,000 to $24,999	15.7	11.3	17.5	17.9	17.1	15.2
$25,000 to $34,999	9.8	5.3	11.8	11.9	11.8	13.3
$35,000 to $49,999	8.0	2.4	11.5	9.8	13.1	12.1
$50,000 to $74,999	5.2	0.6	5.5	4.2	6.8	8.2
$75,000 to $99,999	1.4	0.0	1.7	1.5	1.9	1.7
$100,000 or more	1.2	0.0	0.9	0.4	1.4	1.9

Source: Bureau of the Census, 2014 Current Population Survey, Internet site http://www.census.gov/hhes/www/income/data/index .html; calculations by New Strategist

Table 5.23 Income of Women under Age 40, 2013: Non-Hispanic White Women

(number and percent distribution of non-Hispanic White women aged 15 or older and aged 15 to 39 by income and age, 2013; median income of women with income and of women working full-time, year-round; percent working full-time, year-round; women in thousands as of 2014)

	total	15 to 24	aged 25 to 34 total	aged 25 to 34 25 to 29	aged 25 to 34 30 to 34	35 to 39
NON-HISPANIC WHITE WOMEN	**84,038**	**11,753**	**12,168**	**6,110**	**6,058**	**5,606**
Without income	**9,656**	**3,923**	**1,444**	**702**	**742**	**626**
With income	**74,382**	**7,829**	**10,725**	**5,408**	**5,316**	**4,980**
Under $5,000	7,662	2,409	1,059	538	522	515
$5,000 to $9,999	8,189	1,404	822	483	339	308
$10,000 to $14,999	9,052	1,102	862	461	401	423
$15,000 to $19,999	7,370	850	860	466	394	360
$20,000 to $24,999	6,114	605	967	492	475	374
$25,000 to $29,999	4,972	445	805	439	365	279
$30,000 to $34,999	4,746	329	889	487	402	344
$35,000 to $39,999	3,767	218	731	412	320	298
$40,000 to $44,999	3,690	120	740	363	377	326
$45,000 to $49,999	2,761	74	616	282	334	238
$50,000 to $54,999	2,805	78	512	204	308	315
$55,000 to $59,999	1,719	46	327	142	185	156
$60,000 to $64,999	1,912	50	291	132	159	209
$65,000 to $69,999	1,354	22	274	136	138	101
$70,000 to $74,999	1,328	14	246	139	107	136
$75,000 to $79,999	1,065	18	181	64	117	122
$80,000 to $84,999	1,007	0	94	32	62	54
$85,000 to $89,999	561	6	45	8	37	54
$90,000 to $94,999	517	8	59	9	50	40
$95,000 to $99,999	365	8	22	5	16	22
$100,000 or more	3,426	26	321	114	207	309
MEDIAN INCOME						
Women with income	$23,780	$10,356	$29,883	$27,377	$31,608	$32,540
Working full-time	42,784	26,058	40,898	37,278	42,957	45,809
Percent full-time	34.9%	15.6%	49.9%	49.8%	50.0%	49.9%
PERCENT DISTRIBUTION						
NON-HISPANIC WHITE WOMEN	**100.0%**	**100.0%**	**100.0%**	**100.0%**	**100.0%**	**100.0%**
Without income	**11.5**	**33.4**	**11.9**	**11.5**	**12.2**	**11.2**
With income	**88.5**	**66.6**	**88.1**	**88.5**	**87.8**	**88.8**
Under $15,000	29.6	41.8	22.5	24.2	20.8	22.2
$15,000 to $24,999	16.0	12.4	15.0	15.7	14.3	13.1
$25,000 to $34,999	11.6	6.6	13.9	15.2	12.7	11.1
$35,000 to $49,999	12.2	3.5	17.2	17.3	17.0	15.4
$50,000 to $74,999	10.9	1.8	13.6	12.3	14.8	16.3
$75,000 to $99,999	4.2	0.3	3.3	1.9	4.7	5.2
$100,000 or more	4.1	0.2	2.6	1.9	3.4	5.5

Note: Non-Hispanic Whites are those who identify themselves as being White alone and not Hispanic.
Source: Bureau of the Census, 2014 Current Population Survey, Internet site http://www.census.gov/hhes/www/income/data/index.html; calculations by New Strategist

Earnings Rise with Education

The highest earners are men and women with a graduate degree.

For many years, a college degree has been well worth the cost. Even among young adults, the higher their education the greater are their earnings. Among people aged 25 to 34 who work full-time, men with a graduate degree and women with a doctoral or professional degree earned about $70,000 in 2013. Among full-time workers aged 35 to 44, the earnings of men with a professional or doctoral degree were above $100,000.

Among men aged 25 to 34 who went no further than high school, full-time workers earned only $32,129 in 2013. For their counterparts with at least a bachelor's degree, median earnings were $57,757. The pattern is the same for women. Among women aged 25 to 34 who went no further than high school, full-time workers earned only $26,000 in 2013. Among women in the age group with a bachelor's degree, median earnings were above $47,000.

■ Rising college costs may reduce the financial return of a bachelor's degree.

The college bonus still exists for Millennial men and women

(median earnings of people aged 25 to 34 by sex and educational attainment, 2013)

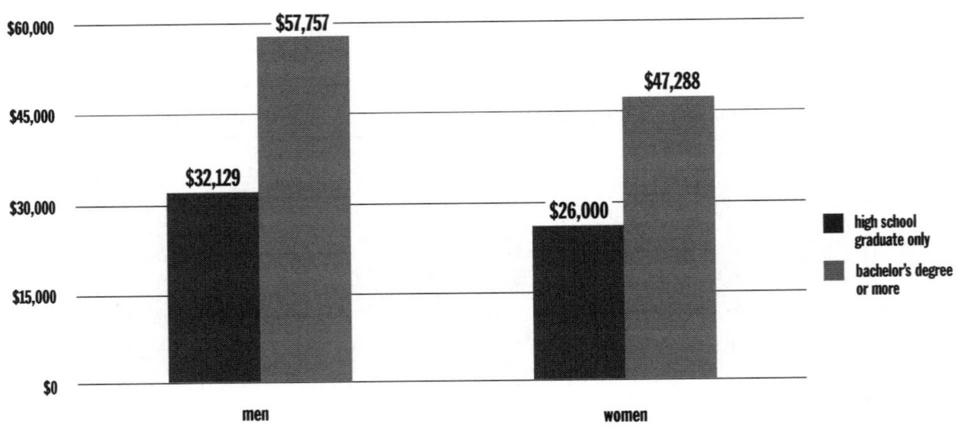

Table 5.24 Earnings of Men by Education, 2013: Aged 25 to 34

(number and percent distribution of men aged 25 to 34 who work full-time, year-round, by earnings and educational attainment, 2013; median earnings of men with earnings; men in thousands as of 2014)

							bachelor's degree or more				
	total	less than 9th grade	9th to 12th grade, no degree	high school graduate	some college	associate's degree	total	bachelor's degree	master's degree	professional degree	doctoral degree
Men aged 25 to 34 who work full-time	**13,779**	**382**	**805**	**3,866**	**2,307**	**1,436**	**4,983**	**3,622**	**998**	**188**	**174**
Under $5,000	54	1	3	28	11	2	9	5	4	0	0
$5,000 to $9,999	128	22	14	65	13	5	10	6	4	0	0
$10,000 to $14,999	390	21	74	170	51	50	25	22	4	0	0
$15,000 to $19,999	837	99	116	311	159	41	111	104	7	0	0
$20,000 to $24,999	1,200	57	140	499	214	128	162	127	31	4	0
$25,000 to $29,999	1,143	52	110	455	231	99	195	176	19	0	0
$30,000 to $34,999	1,449	41	92	600	271	143	301	248	50	0	3
$35,000 to $39,999	1,024	17	47	310	209	97	345	302	31	6	5
$40,000 to $44,999	1,238	24	74	352	230	188	370	316	45	0	9
$45,000 to $49,999	865	13	25	187	162	124	354	251	72	20	11
$50,000 to $54,999	958	9	22	249	178	105	396	323	43	17	13
$55,000 to $59,999	543	7	12	142	60	74	248	172	50	8	17
$60,000 to $64,999	718	6	26	139	125	84	339	224	80	22	12
$65,000 to $69,999	457	5	8	68	66	80	230	144	54	19	13
$70,000 to $74,999	459	2	4	63	66	39	284	216	49	9	10
$75,000 to $79,999	373	1	3	61	33	17	258	172	68	5	12
$80,000 to $84,999	379	2	9	48	51	38	231	150	71	5	5
$85,000 to $89,999	199	0	0	19	42	28	110	68	28	9	5
$90,000 to $94,999	207	0	6	22	16	15	148	109	37	2	0
$95,000 to $99,999	147	1	1	10	15	17	104	78	19	3	5
$100,000 or more	1,011	3	20	67	106	61	753	407	233	60	53
Median earnings	**$41,634**	**$22,982**	**$26,658**	**$32,129**	**$39,796**	**$42,350**	**$57,757**	**$52,454**	**$70,410**	**$69,435**	**$71,115**
PERCENT DISTRIBUTION											
Men aged 25 to 34 who work full-time	**100.0%**	**100.0%**	**100.0%**	**100.0%**	**100.0%**	**100.0%**	**100.0%**	**100.0%**	**100.0%**	**100.0%**	**100.0%**
Under $15,000	4.2	11.4	11.2	6.8	3.2	3.9	0.9	0.9	1.2	0.0	0.0
$15,000 to $24,999	14.8	40.8	31.7	21.0	16.2	11.8	5.5	6.4	3.8	1.9	0.0
$25,000 to $34,999	18.8	24.4	25.1	27.3	21.8	16.9	10.0	11.7	6.9	0.0	1.7
$35,000 to $49,999	22.7	14.1	18.1	21.9	26.0	28.6	21.5	24.0	14.8	13.8	15.1
$50,000 to $74,999	22.8	7.6	8.9	17.1	21.4	26.6	30.0	29.8	27.7	39.8	37.4
$75,000 to $99,999	9.5	0.8	2.4	4.1	6.8	8.0	17.1	15.9	22.3	12.4	15.6
$100,000 or more	7.3	0.9	2.5	1.7	4.6	4.3	15.1	11.2	23.3	32.1	30.2

Note: Earnings include wages and salary only.
Source: Bureau of the Census, 2014 Current Population Survey, Internet site http://www.census.gov/hhes/www/income/data/index.html; calculations by New Strategist

Table 5.25 Earnings of Men by Education, 2013: Aged 35 to 44

(number and percent distribution of men aged 35 to 44 who work full-time, year-round, by earnings and educational attainment, 2013; median earnings of men with earnings; men in thousands as of 2014)

							bachelor's degree or more				
	total	less than 9th grade	9th to 12th grade, no degree	high school graduate	some college	associate's degree	total	bachelor's degree	master's degree	professional degree	doctoral degree
Men aged 35 to 44 who work full-time	**14,332**	**610**	**744**	**3,833**	**2,239**	**1,486**	**5,420**	**3,354**	**1,412**	**301**	**352**
Under $5,000	42	0	1	22	6	1	12	9	1	0	3
$5,000 to $9,999	90	15	7	57	3	0	8	6	2	0	0
$10,000 to $14,999	236	44	35	95	26	8	28	28	0	0	0
$15,000 to $19,999	634	105	85	241	92	62	48	41	5	2	0
$20,000 to $24,999	895	149	151	360	99	64	71	68	3	0	0
$25,000 to $29,999	841	57	101	295	172	68	149	131	16	0	2
$30,000 to $34,999	935	81	63	376	163	114	138	111	14	10	4
$35,000 to $39,999	946	38	61	371	203	95	179	139	34	0	6
$40,000 to $44,999	977	19	73	362	165	136	223	173	43	5	2
$45,000 to $49,999	923	17	29	285	214	119	258	182	51	11	13
$50,000 to $54,999	898	17	18	288	184	95	297	211	68	6	12
$55,000 to $59,999	596	19	18	172	124	101	162	113	43	2	4
$60,000 to $64,999	775	19	26	197	118	112	303	211	63	11	18
$65,000 to $69,999	507	5	10	125	100	76	191	120	54	10	6
$70,000 to $74,999	555	5	24	64	91	70	302	198	85	13	6
$75,000 to $79,999	543	6	4	96	115	38	283	173	81	6	23
$80,000 to $84,999	587	8	15	98	63	99	304	185	89	18	12
$85,000 to $89,999	279	0	4	38	40	29	168	97	45	16	9
$90,000 to $94,999	327	2	4	28	47	14	232	140	63	4	26
$95,000 to $99,999	226	0	5	34	30	27	128	81	38	5	5
$100,000 or more	2,520	4	9	228	184	158	1,936	937	616	183	201
Median earnings	**$52,054**	**$24,365**	**$29,097**	**$40,802**	**$49,369**	**$52,090**	**$80,591**	**$71,864**	**$90,422**	**$120,534**	**$107,575**
PERCENT DISTRIBUTION											
Men aged 35 to 44 who work full-time	**100.0%**	**100.0%**	**100.0%**	**100.0%**	**100.0%**	**100.0%**	**100.0%**	**100.0%**	**100.0%**	**100.0%**	**100.0%**
Under $15,000	2.6	9.7	5.9	4.5	1.6	0.6	0.9	1.3	0.2	0.0	0.7
$15,000 to $24,999	10.7	41.7	31.7	15.7	8.5	8.5	2.2	3.2	0.6	0.7	0.0
$25,000 to $34,999	12.4	22.5	22.1	17.5	15.0	12.2	5.3	7.2	2.1	3.2	1.5
$35,000 to $49,999	19.9	12.2	22.0	26.5	26.0	23.6	12.2	14.8	9.1	5.1	6.1
$50,000 to $74,999	23.2	10.6	12.9	22.1	27.5	30.5	23.2	25.4	22.2	14.0	13.1
$75,000 to $99,999	13.7	2.7	4.3	7.7	13.2	14.0	20.6	20.1	22.3	16.2	21.4
$100,000 or more	17.6	0.7	1.2	6.0	8.2	10.6	35.7	27.9	43.6	60.7	57.2

Note: Earnings include wages and salary only.
Source: Bureau of the Census, 2014 Current Population Survey, Internet site http://www.census.gov/hhes/www/income/data/index .html; calculations by New Strategist

Table 5.26 Earnings of Women by Education, 2013: Aged 25 to 34

(number and percent distribution of women aged 25 to 34 who work full-time, year-round, by earnings and educational attainment, 2013; median earnings of women with earnings; women in thousands as of 2014)

	total	less than 9th grade	9th to 12th grade, no degree	high school graduate	some college	associate's degree	bachelor's degree or more: total	bachelor's degree	master's degree	professional degree	doctoral degree
Women aged 25 to 34 who work full-time	**9,956**	**128**	**295**	**1,680**	**1,636**	**1,257**	**4,960**	**3,358**	**1,252**	**201**	**149**
Under $5,000	44	0	3	3	11	12	14	3	11	0	0
$5,000 to $9,999	126	15	13	32	15	28	23	19	4	0	0
$10,000 to $14,999	330	32	36	139	61	22	39	35	4	0	0
$15,000 to $19,999	684	25	76	206	165	88	124	90	34	0	0
$20,000 to $24,999	1,141	24	60	394	266	162	235	198	30	0	7
$25,000 to $29,999	984	9	34	241	228	180	292	244	41	5	2
$30,000 to $34,999	1,157	13	21	219	270	209	426	326	86	7	7
$35,000 to $39,999	865	4	18	130	177	116	419	317	92	10	1
$40,000 to $44,999	980	0	17	127	158	124	553	398	144	7	4
$45,000 to $49,999	763	0	7	69	74	116	496	343	130	16	6
$50,000 to $54,999	600	2	3	26	46	66	458	304	134	17	3
$55,000 to $59,999	346	0	0	29	22	29	266	143	105	8	9
$60,000 to $64,999	378	0	2	10	39	29	298	179	82	18	20
$65,000 to $69,999	308	1	1	20	17	29	241	163	54	11	13
$70,000 to $74,999	308	0	0	8	36	19	246	177	59	2	9
$75,000 to $79,999	220	0	0	2	8	9	201	125	56	15	5
$80,000 to $84,999	149	3	3	1	20	0	123	51	49	16	6
$85,000 to $89,999	75	0	0	0	0	3	72	34	28	10	0
$90,000 to $94,999	67	0	0	0	6	3	59	37	18	3	1
$95,000 to $99,999	33	0	0	0	1	0	32	19	8	2	3
$100,000 or more	398	0	0	24	15	15	344	155	83	52	53
Median earnings	**$36,976**	**$17,894**	**$21,205**	**$26,000**	**$30,820**	**$32,407**	**$47,288**	**$45,496**	**$51,183**	**$70,634**	**$70,643**
PERCENT DISTRIBUTION											
Women aged 25 to 34 who work full-time	**100.0%**	**100.0%**	**100.0%**	**100.0%**	**100.0%**	**100.0%**	**100.0%**	**100.0%**	**100.0%**	**100.0%**	**100.0%**
Under $15,000	5.0	36.6	17.8	10.4	5.3	5.0	1.5	1.7	1.5	0.0	0.0
$15,000 to $24,999	18.3	38.3	46.1	35.7	26.4	19.9	7.2	8.5	5.1	0.0	4.7
$25,000 to $34,999	21.5	17.2	18.5	27.4	30.5	30.9	14.5	17.0	10.2	6.1	5.6
$35,000 to $49,999	26.2	3.8	14.7	19.4	25.0	28.3	29.6	31.5	29.2	16.9	7.8
$50,000 to $74,999	19.5	2.1	2.1	5.5	9.8	13.6	30.4	28.7	34.7	27.7	36.3
$75,000 to $99,999	5.5	2.0	0.9	0.2	2.1	1.2	9.8	7.9	12.7	23.3	9.9
$100,000 or more	4.0	0.0	0.0	1.4	0.9	1.2	6.9	4.6	6.6	26.0	35.6

Note: Earnings include wages and salary only.
Source: Bureau of the Census, 2014 Current Population Survey, Internet site http://www.census.gov/hhes/www/income/data/index.html; calculations by New Strategist

Table 5.27 Earnings of Women by Education, 2013: Aged 35 to 44

(number and percent distribution of women aged 35 to 44 who work full-time, year-round, by earnings and educational attainment, 2013; median earnings of women with earnings; women in thousands as of 2014)

							bachelor's degree or more				
	total	less than 9th grade	9th to 12th grade, no degree	high school graduate	some college	associate's degree	total	bachelor's degree	master's degree	professional degree	doctoral degree
Women aged 35 to 44 who work full-time	**10,111**	**186**	**339**	**2,111**	**1,601**	**1,353**	**4,522**	**2,691**	**1,412**	**209**	**210**
Under $5,000	46	2	7	13	3	2	19	19	0	0	0
$5,000 to $9,999	85	4	9	23	11	16	23	20	3	0	0
$10,000 to $14,999	305	42	61	86	50	27	40	26	12	2	0
$15,000 to $19,999	690	55	74	259	133	95	75	67	5	3	0
$20,000 to $24,999	953	33	42	435	173	142	128	99	21	2	6
$25,000 to $29,999	869	27	37	276	231	147	152	118	30	0	4
$30,000 to $34,999	881	12	58	244	197	120	250	218	31	0	1
$35,000 to $39,999	787	5	9	172	166	167	267	195	65	1	6
$40,000 to $44,999	901	2	14	186	108	143	448	284	140	21	2
$45,000 to $49,999	603	0	1	112	131	105	254	148	96	2	8
$50,000 to $54,999	726	2	1	116	147	97	364	205	142	12	5
$55,000 to $59,999	391	0	2	39	61	56	234	144	79	0	10
$60,000 to $64,999	532	0	6	70	64	66	327	169	122	10	27
$65,000 to $69,999	278	0	0	10	18	30	220	115	77	12	15
$70,000 to $74,999	398	3	13	11	23	40	307	167	100	21	20
$75,000 to $79,999	286	0	0	17	18	38	213	103	93	10	7
$80,000 to $84,999	222	0	0	7	13	15	186	96	75	10	5
$85,000 to $89,999	124	0	0	6	9	13	96	57	32	0	7
$90,000 to $94,999	100	0	1	4	3	3	90	45	38	0	6
$95,000 to $99,999	100	0	0	2	5	4	89	32	34	8	14
$100,000 or more	836	0	6	22	39	27	741	363	217	94	68
Median earnings	**$41,535**	**$19,260**	**$21,706**	**$29,021**	**$35,065**	**$38,022**	**$60,080**	**$52,325**	**$62,245**	**$82,413**	**$75,949**
PERCENT DISTRIBUTION											
Women aged 35 to 44 who work full-time	**100.0%**	**100.0%**	**100.0%**	**100.0%**	**100.0%**	**100.0%**	**100.0%**	**100.0%**	**100.0%**	**100.0%**	**100.0%**
Under $15,000	4.3	25.8	22.6	5.7	4.0	3.3	1.8	2.4	1.1	0.8	0.0
$15,000 to $24,999	16.2	47.1	34.1	32.9	19.1	17.5	4.5	6.2	1.8	2.5	2.7
$25,000 to $34,999	17.3	21.1	27.9	24.6	26.7	19.7	8.9	12.5	4.3	0.0	2.5
$35,000 to $49,999	22.7	3.6	6.9	22.3	25.3	30.7	21.4	23.3	21.4	11.5	7.4
$50,000 to $74,999	23.0	2.5	6.4	11.7	19.5	21.3	32.1	29.7	36.9	26.2	36.5
$75,000 to $99,999	8.2	0.0	0.3	1.7	2.9	5.4	14.9	12.4	19.3	14.0	18.4
$100,000 or more	8.3	0.0	1.7	1.0	2.5	2.0	16.4	13.5	15.3	44.9	32.5

Note: Earnings include wages and salary only.
Source: Bureau of the Census, 2014 Current Population Survey, Internet site http://www.census.gov/hhes/www/income/data/index .html; calculations by New Strategist

Many Young Adults Are Poor

The Millennial generation accounts for more than one in four of the poor.

Young adults are much more likely to be poor than the middle aged or elderly. The poverty rate of people aged 18 to 24 was 19.4 percent in 2013—much higher than the 14.5 percent overall poverty rate. Among people aged 25 to 34, the poverty rate was an above-average 15.8 percent. (The Millennial generation ranged in age from 19 to 36 in 2013.)

The poverty rate among Millennials varies by race and Hispanic origin. In the 18-to-24 age group, the rate ranges from a low of 15.6 percent among non-Hispanic Whites to a high of 31.3 percent among Blacks. In the 25-to-34 age group, the rate ranges from a low of 11.7 percent among non-Hispanic Whites to a high of 25.8 percent among Blacks.

■ Poverty rates for Millennials are above average because many live in female-headed families—the poorest household type.

Among Millennials, Asians and non-Hispanic Whites are least likely to be poor

(percent of people aged 25 to 34 living below poverty level, by race and Hispanic origin, 2013)

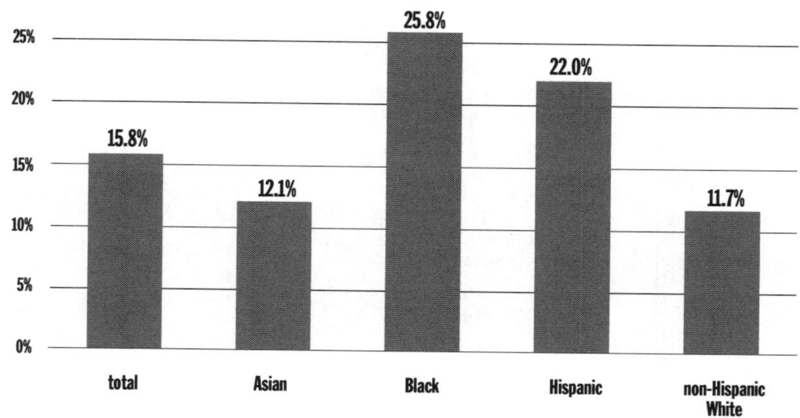

Table 5.28 People below Poverty Level by Age, Race, and Hispanic Origin, 2013

(number, percent, and percent distribution of people below poverty level by age, race, and Hispanic origin, 2013; people in thousands as of 2014)

NUMBER IN POVERTY	total	Asian	Black	Hispanic	non-Hispanic White
Total people	**45,318**	**1,974**	**11,959**	**12,744**	**18,796**
Under age 18	14,659	457	4,838	5,415	4,094
Aged 18 to 24	5,819	309	1,585	1,358	2,595
Aged 25 to 34	6,694	379	1,601	1,918	2,857
Aged 35 to 44	4,871	231	1,170	1,548	1,926
Aged 45 to 54	4,533	169	1,021	1,076	2,242
Aged 55 to 59	2,476	74	611	427	1,346
Aged 60 to 64	2,036	96	422	327	1,168
Aged 65 or older	4,231	259	712	676	2,569
PERCENT IN POVERTY					
Total people	**14.5%**	**10.4%**	**27.1%**	**23.5%**	**9.6%**
Under age 18	19.9	9.6	36.9	30.4	10.7
Aged 18 to 24	19.4	16.4	31.3	21.3	15.6
Aged 25 to 34	15.8	12.1	25.8	22.0	11.7
Aged 35 to 44	12.2	7.9	21.5	20.0	8.2
Aged 45 to 54	10.6	6.8	18.7	17.5	7.8
Aged 55 to 59	11.7	7.3	23.7	19.6	8.8
Aged 60 to 64	11.0	10.5	19.4	18.8	8.6
Aged 65 or older	9.5	13.6	17.4	19.8	7.4
PERCENT DISTRIBUTION OF POOR BY AGE					
Total in poverty	**100.0**	**100.0**	**100.0**	**100.0**	**100.0**
Under age 18	32.3	23.2	40.5	42.5	21.8
Aged 18 to 24	12.8	15.7	13.3	10.7	13.8
Aged 25 to 34	14.8	19.2	13.4	15.1	15.2
Aged 35 to 44	10.7	11.7	9.8	12.1	10.2
Aged 45 to 54	10.0	8.6	8.5	8.4	11.9
Aged 55 to 59	5.5	3.7	5.1	3.4	7.2
Aged 60 to 64	4.5	4.9	3.5	2.6	6.2
Aged 65 or older	9.3	13.1	6.0	5.3	13.7
PERCENT DISTRIBUTION OF POOR BY RACE AND HISPANIC ORIGIN					
Total in poverty	**100.0**	**4.4**	**26.4**	**28.1**	**41.5**
Under age 18	100.0	3.1	33.0	36.9	27.9
Aged 18 to 24	100.0	5.3	27.2	23.3	44.6
Aged 25 to 34	100.0	5.7	23.9	28.7	42.7
Aged 35 to 44	100.0	4.7	24.0	31.8	39.5
Aged 45 to 54	100.0	3.7	22.5	23.7	49.5
Aged 55 to 59	100.0	3.0	24.7	17.2	54.4
Aged 60 to 64	100.0	4.7	20.7	16.1	57.4
Aged 65 or older	100.0	6.1	16.8	16.0	60.7

Note: Numbers do not add to total because Asians and Blacks are those who identify themselves as being of the race alone and those who identify themselves as being of the race in combination with other races. Non-Hispanic Whites are those who identify themselves as being White alone and not Hispanic. Hispanics may be of any race.
Source: Bureau of the Census, Poverty, Internet site http://www.census.gov/hhes/www/cpstables/032014/pov/toc.htm; calculations by New Strategist

CHAPTER

6

Labor Force

■ The percentage of younger adults in the labor force fell sharply between 2000 and 2013. The decline was in the double digits for adults under age 20.

■ The Millennial generation (aged 19 to 36 in 2013) accounts for a substantial 37 percent of the labor force, a larger share than any other generation.

■ Among the youngest Millennial men, Asians have the lowest labor force participation rate because most are in college.

■ Workers under age 25 account for nearly half of waiters and waitresses, cashiers, and food prep workers. Workers aged 25 to 44 are more than half of software developers, police, social workers, and teachers.

■ Among the nation's 3.3 million minimum wage workers in 2013, nearly two out of three were under age 30.

■ Between 2012 and 2022, the Millennial generation will age into its forties. The number of workers aged 25 to 44 will expand by more than 5 million.

Fewer Young Adults Have Jobs

The labor force participation rate has fallen sharply among adults under age 25.

The labor force participation rate of young adults has plummeted. Among 18-to-19-year-old males (in 2013, 19-year-olds were the youngest members of the Millennial generation), the labor force participation rate fell by 16.7 percentage points between 2000 and 2013—from 65.0 to 48.3. Among their female counterparts, labor force participation fell from 61.3 to 47.6 percent during those years—a 13.7 percentage point decline. Labor force participation also slipped substantially among men and women in their twenties and thirties.

The weak economy is one factor behind the declining labor force participation rate. Among 18-to-24-year-olds, college attendance has also dampened labor force participation.

■ Young adults must compete with older adults for hard-to-find jobs, an effort that discourages some from entering the labor force at all.

Fewer young men are in the labor force

(percentage of men aged 18 to 29 in the labor force, 2000 and 2013)

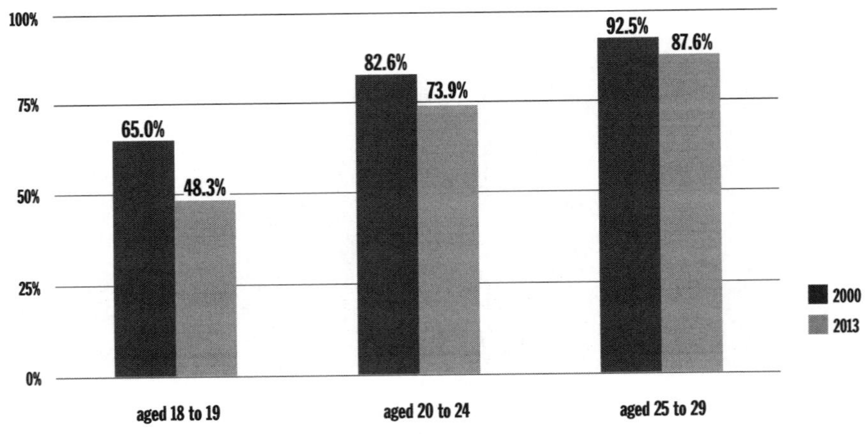

Table 6.1 Labor Force Participation Rate by Sex and Age, 2000 to 2013

(civilian labor force participation rate of people aged 16 or older, by sex and age, 2000 to 2013; percentage point change, 2010–13 and 2000–13)

	2013	2010	2000	percentage point change 2010–13	percentage point change 2000–13
Men aged 16 or older	**69.7%**	**71.2%**	**74.8%**	**–1.5**	**–5.1**
Aged 16 to 17	21.8	21.8	40.9	0.0	–19.1
Aged 18 to 19	48.3	49.6	65.0	–1.3	–16.7
Aged 20 to 24	73.9	74.5	82.6	–0.6	–8.7
Aged 25 to 29	87.6	88.4	92.5	–0.8	–4.9
Aged 30 to 34	90.7	91.1	94.2	–0.4	–3.5
Aged 35 to 39	90.9	92.2	93.2	–1.3	–2.3
Aged 40 to 44	90.6	90.7	92.1	–0.1	–1.5
Aged 45 to 49	87.3	88.5	90.2	–1.2	–2.9
Aged 50 to 54	83.9	85.1	86.8	–1.2	–2.9
Aged 55 to 59	78.0	78.5	77.0	–0.5	1.0
Aged 60 to 64	60.5	60.0	54.9	0.5	5.6
Aged 65 or older	23.5	22.1	17.7	1.4	5.8
Women aged 16 or older	**57.2**	**58.6**	**59.9**	**–1.4**	**–2.7**
Aged 16 to 17	23.5	23.0	40.8	0.5	–17.3
Aged 18 to 19	47.6	48.6	61.3	–1.0	–13.7
Aged 20 to 24	67.5	68.3	73.1	–0.8	–5.6
Aged 25 to 29	73.7	75.6	76.7	–1.9	–3.0
Aged 30 to 34	73.3	73.8	75.5	–0.5	–2.2
Aged 35 to 39	73.8	74.1	75.7	–0.3	–1.9
Aged 40 to 44	74.2	76.2	78.7	–2.0	–4.5
Aged 45 to 49	75.3	76.8	79.1	–1.5	–3.8
Aged 50 to 54	73.0	74.6	74.1	–1.6	–1.1
Aged 55 to 59	67.2	68.4	61.4	–1.2	5.8
Aged 60 to 64	50.0	50.7	40.2	–0.7	9.8
Aged 65 or older	14.9	13.8	9.4	1.1	5.5

Source: Bureau of Labor Statistics, Labor Force Statistics from the Current Population Survey, Internet site http://www.bls.gov/cps/tables.htm#empstat; calculations by New Strategist

Most Millennials Are in the Labor Force

The Millennial generation accounts for the largest share of the labor force.

Young men join the labor force at a slower rate than they once did. The labor force participation rate of men aged 18-to-19 in 2013 (19-year-olds were the youngest Millennials in 2013) was just 48 percent. Participation rises to 74 percent among men aged 20 to 24, climbs to 88 percent in the 25-to-29 age group, and reaches 91 percent among men in their thirties. The labor force participation rate of women follows a similar pattern with a slow start among young adults. The rate climbs as high as 73 to 74 percent among women in their late twenties and thirties.

The Millennial generation accounts for a substantial 37 percent of the labor force, a larger share than any other generation. Millennials in the labor force outnumber Boomers by more than 8 million.

■ The Millennial generation accounts for 46 percent of the nation's unemployed workers.

More than one-third of American workers are Millennials

(percent distribution of the labor force by generation, 2013)

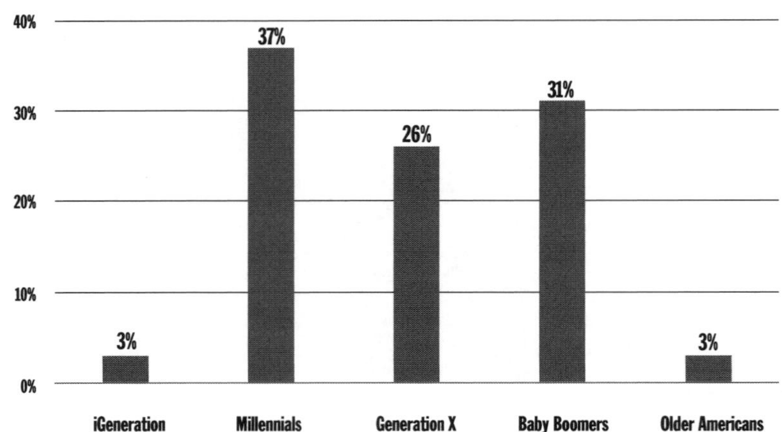

Table 6.2 Employment Status by Sex and Generation, 2013

(number and percent of people aged 16 or older in the civilian labor force by sex and generation, 2013; numbers in thousands)

	civilian noninstitutional population	civilian labor force: total	civilian labor force: percent of population	civilian labor force: employed	unemployed: number	unemployed: percent of labor force	not in labor force: number	not in labor force: percent of population
Total aged 16 or older	**245,679**	**155,389**	**63.2%**	**143,929**	**11,460**	**7.4%**	**90,290**	**36.8%**
iGeneration (aged 16 to 18)	12,590	4,339	34.5	3,344	995	22.9	8,252	65.5
Millennials (aged 19 to 36)	75,456	57,080	75.6	51,857	5,224	9.2	18,375	24.4
Generation Xers (aged 37 to 48)	48,677	39,842	81.9	37,552	2,290	5.7	8,834	18.1
Baby Boomers (aged 49 to 67)	74,209	48,798	65.8	46,124	2,676	5.5	25,410	34.2
Older Americans (aged 68 or older)	34,748	5,330	15.3	5,054	277	5.2	29,417	84.7
Men aged 16 or older	**118,555**	**82,667**	**69.7**	**76,353**	**6,314**	**7.6**	**35,889**	**30.3**
iGeneration (aged 16 to 18)	6,404	2,192	34.2	1,633	560	25.5	4,211	65.8
Millennials (aged 19 to 36)	37,437	30,585	81.7	27,669	2,915	9.5	6,852	18.3
Generation Xers (aged 37 to 48)	23,837	21,338	89.5	20,121	1,217	5.7	2,499	10.5
Baby Boomers (aged 49 to 67)	35,780	25,568	71.5	24,105	1,463	5.7	10,212	28.5
Older Americans (aged 68 or older)	15,098	2,983	19.8	2,824	159.4	5.3	12,114	80.2
Women aged 16 or older	**127,124**	**72,722**	**57.2**	**67,577**	**5,146**	**7.1**	**54,401**	**42.8**
iGeneration (aged 16 to 18)	6,187	2,147	34.7	1,711	436	20.3	4,040	65.3
Millennials (aged 19 to 36)	38,020	26,497	69.7	24,186	2,309	8.7	11,523	30.3
Generation Xers (aged 37 to 48)	24,839	18,502	74.5	17,429	1,074	5.8	6,335	25.5
Baby Boomers (aged 49 to 67)	38,427	23,230	60.5	22,018	1,211	5.2	15,198	39.6
Older Americans (aged 68 or older)	19,651	2,347	11.9	2,231	116	5.0	17,304	88.1

Source: Bureau of Labor Statistics, Labor Force Statistics from the Current Population Survey, Internet site http://www.bls.gov/cps/tables.htm#empstat; calculations by New Strategist

Table 6.3 Employment Status of the Millennial Generation by Sex, 2013

(number and percent of people aged 16 or older, aged 19 to 36, and in age groups that include Millennials, by sex and employment status, 2013; numbers in thousands)

		civilian labor force					not in labor force	
					unemployed			
	civilian noninstitutional population	total	percent of population	employed	number	percent of labor force	number	percent of population
Total, aged 16 or older	**245,679**	**155,389**	**63.2%**	**143,929**	**11,460**	**7.4%**	**90,290**	**36.8%**
Millennials (aged 19 to 36)	**75,456**	**57,080**	**75.6**	**51,857**	**5,224**	**9.2**	**18,375**	**24.4**
Aged 18 to 19	7,845	3,762	48.0	2,971	791	21.0	4,082	52.0
Aged 20 to 24	22,052	15,595	70.7	13,599	1,997	12.8	6,456	29.3
Aged 25 to 29	20,876	16,821	80.6	15,457	1,364	8.1	4,055	19.4
Aged 30 to 34	20,672	16,926	81.9	15,786	1,140	6.7	3,746	18.1
Aged 35 to 39	19,149	15,730	82.1	14,752	977	6.2	3,419	17.9
Men aged 16 or older	**118,555**	**82,667**	**69.7**	**76,353**	**6,314**	**7.6**	**35,889**	**30.3**
Millennials (aged 19 to 36)	**37,437**	**30,585**	**81.7**	**27,669**	**2,915**	**9.5**	**6,852**	**18.3**
Aged 18 to 19	4,006	1,936	48.3	1,477	459	23.7	2,071	51.7
Aged 20 to 24	11,038	8,156	73.9	7,013	1,143	14.0	2,882	26.1
Aged 25 to 29	10,341	9,062	87.6	8,283	778	8.6	1,279	12.4
Aged 30 to 34	10,170	9,226	90.7	8,623	603	6.5	944	9.3
Aged 35 to 39	9,383	8,525	90.9	8,014	511	6.0	858	9.1
Women aged 16 or older	**127,124**	**72,722**	**57.2**	**67,577**	**5,146**	**7.1**	**54,401**	**42.8**
Millennials (aged 19 to 36)	**38,020**	**26,497**	**69.7**	**24,186**	**2,309**	**8.7**	**11,523**	**30.3**
Aged 18 to 19	3,838	1,826	47.6	1,494	332	18.2	2,012	52.4
Aged 20 to 24	11,014	7,440	67.5	6,586	854	11.5	3,574	32.4
Aged 25 to 29	10,535	7,759	73.7	7,173	586	7.5	2,776	26.4
Aged 30 to 34	10,502	7,700	73.3	7,162	537	7.0	2,802	26.7
Aged 35 to 39	9,766	7,205	73.8	6,738	467	6.5	2,561	26.2

Source: Bureau of Labor Statistics, Labor Force Statistics from the Current Population Survey, Internet site http://www.bls.gov/cps/tables.htm#empstat; calculations by New Strategist

Table 6.4 Labor Force Status by Generation, 2013

(number and percent distribution of people aged 16 or older by labor force status and by generation, 2013; numbers in thousands)

	in labor force	employed	unemployed	not in labor force
Total aged 16 or older	**155,389**	**143,929**	**11,460**	**90,290**
iGeneration (aged 16 to 18)	4,339	3,344	995	8,252
Millennials (aged 19 to 36)	57,080	51,857	5,224	18,375
Generation Xers (aged 37 to 48)	39,842	37,552	2,290	8,834
Baby Boomers (aged 49 to 67)	48,798	46,124	2,676	25,410
Older Americans (aged 68 or older)	5,330	5,054	277	29,417
PERCENT DISTRIBUTION BY GENERATION				
Total aged 16 or older	**100.0%**	**100.0%**	**100.0%**	**100.0%**
iGeneration (aged 16 to 18)	2.8	2.3	8.7	9.1
Millennials (aged 19 to 36)	36.7	36.0	45.6	20.4
Generation Xers (aged 37 to 48)	25.6	26.1	20.0	9.8
Baby Boomers (aged 49 to 67)	31.4	32.0	23.3	28.1
Older Americans (aged 68 or older)	3.4	3.5	2.4	32.6

Source: Bureau of Labor Statistics, Labor Force Statistics from the Current Population Survey, Internet site http://www.bls.gov/cps/tables.htm#empstat; calculations by New Strategist

Among Millennial Men, Hispanics Have Highest Labor Force Participation Rate

College attendance lowers the labor force participation rate of Asian men.

Among men aged 19 to 36 in 2013 (the Millennial generation), more than 80 percent were in the labor force. The labor force includes both the employed and the unemployed. Among Millennial men, the labor force participation rate varies significantly by race and Hispanic origin. Behind the variation is college attendance. Among 20-to-24-year-old men, for example, only 57 percent of Asians are in the labor force compared with 79 percent of Hispanics. Behind this disparity is the greater college attendance of Asian men in the age group.

The unemployment rate is much higher for Black and Hispanic men than for Asians or non-Hispanic Whites. Asian Millennial men had the lowest unemployment rate, at 6.5 percent in 2013. Non-Hispanic White Millennials had an unemployment rate of 7.8 percent, while the figure was 9.5 percent among Hispanic Millennials and a much higher 17.9 percent among Black Millennials.

■ Among Millennial men in the labor force, only 56 percent are non-Hispanic White.

Millennial labor force participation rate varies by race and Hispanic origin

(percentage of men aged 19 to 36 in the labor force by race and Hispanic origin, 2013)

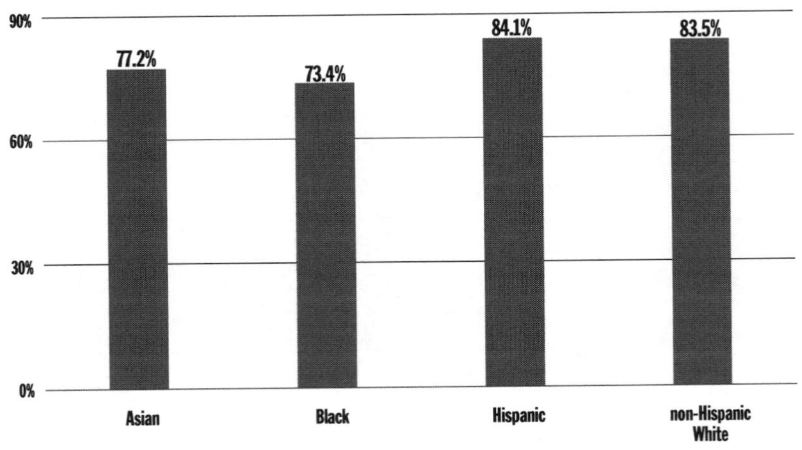

Table 6.5 Employment Status of Millennial Men by Race, Hispanic Origin, and Age, 2013

(number and percent of men aged 16 or older, aged 19 to 36, and in age groups that include Millennials, by race, Hispanic origin, and employment status, 2013; numbers in thousands)

		civilian labor force					not in labor force	
					unemployed			
	civilian noninstitutional population	total	percent of population	employed	number	percent of labor force	number	percent of population
Asian men aged 16 or older	**6,225**	**4,547**	**73.0%**	**4,294**	**253**	**5.6%**	**1,678**	**27.0%**
Asian Millennials (aged 19 to 36)	**2,287**	**1,766**	**77.2**	**1,652**	**115**	**6.5**	**522**	**22.8**
Aged 18 to 19	219	75	34.3	60	15	20.3	144	65.8
Aged 20 to 24	618	352	57.0	309	44	12.4	266	43.0
Aged 25 to 29	654	551	84.3	516	35	6.4	103	15.7
Aged 30 to 34	660	599	90.7	576	23	3.8	61	9.2
Aged 35 to 39	632	601	95.0	581	20	3.3	32	5.1
Black men aged 16 or older	**13,747**	**8,733**	**63.5**	**7,497**	**1,236**	**14.2**	**5,014**	**36.5**
Black Millennials (aged 19 to 36)	**4,950**	**3,635**	**73.4**	**2,982**	**652**	**17.9**	**1,315**	**26.6**
Aged 18 to 19	591	242	40.9	141	101	41.6	349	59.1
Aged 20 to 24	1,647	1,091	66.2	818	273	25.1	556	33.8
Aged 25 to 29	1,307	1,068	81.7	897	171	16.0	239	18.3
Aged 30 to 34	1,230	1,013	82.4	885	128	12.6	217	17.6
Aged 35 to 39	1,117	941	84.2	836	104	11.1	176	15.8
Hispanic men aged 16 or older	**18,798**	**14,341**	**76.3**	**13,078**	**1,263**	**8.8**	**4,457**	**23.7**
Hispanic Millennials (aged 19 to 36)	**8,092**	**6,806**	**84.1**	**6,161**	**645**	**9.5**	**1,286**	**15.9**
Aged 18 to 19	882	444	50.4	329	115	25.8	438	49.7
Aged 20 to 24	2,364	1,857	78.6	1,609	248	13.4	507	21.4
Aged 25 to 29	2,246	2,003	89.2	1,839	164	8.2	243	10.8
Aged 30 to 34	2,207	2,050	92.9	1,909	141	6.9	157	7.1
Aged 35 to 39	2,019	1,858	92.0	1,736	122	6.6	161	8.0
Non-Hispanic White men aged 16 or older	**76,067**	**52,501**	**69.0**	**49,244**	**3,257**	**6.2**	**23,567**	**31.0**
Non-Hispanic White Millennials (aged 19 to 36)	**20,503**	**17,128**	**83.5**	**15,796**	**1,331**	**7.8**	**3,376**	**16.5**
Aged 18 to 19	2,096	1,072	51.1	874	198	18.5	1,025	48.9
Aged 20 to 24	5,892	4,496	76.3	3,988	508	11.3	1,396	23.7
Aged 25 to 29	5,696	5,059	88.8	4,699	360	7.1	637	11.2
Aged 30 to 34	5,675	5,213	91.9	4,934	278	5.3	463	8.2
Aged 35 to 39	5,274	4,822	91.4	4,581	242	5.0	451	8.6

Note: Race is shown only for those who identify themselves as being of the race alone. People who selected more than one race are not included. Hispanics may be of any race. Non-Hispanic Whites are estimated by subtracting Hispanics from Whites.
Source: Bureau of Labor Statistics, Labor Force Statistics from the Current Population Survey, Internet site http://www.bls.gov/cps/tables.htm#empstat; calculations by New Strategist

Among Millennial Women, Non-Hispanic Whites Have Highest Labor Force Participation Rate

College attendance lowers the labor force participation rate of Asian women.

Among women aged 19 to 36 in 2013 (the Millennial generation), nearly 70 percent were in the labor force. The labor force includes both the employed and the unemployed. Among Millennial women, the labor force participation rate varies significantly by race and Hispanic origin. Behind the variation is college attendance. Among 20-to-24-year-old women, for example, only 54 percent of Asians are in the labor force compared with 71 percent of non-Hispanic Whites. Behind this disparity is the greater college attendance of Asian women in the age group.

The unemployment rate is much higher for Black and Hispanic women than for Asians or non-Hispanic Whites. Asian Millennial women had the lowest unemployment rate, at 5.4 percent in 2013. Non-Hispanic White Millennials had an unemployment rate of 6.5 percent, while the figure was 10.5 percent among Hispanic Millennials and 15.5 percent among Black Millennials.

■ Among Millennial women in the labor force, only 57 percent are non-Hispanic White.

Millennial labor force participation rate varies by race and Hispanic origin

(percentage of women aged 19 to 36 in the labor force by race and Hispanic origin, 2013)

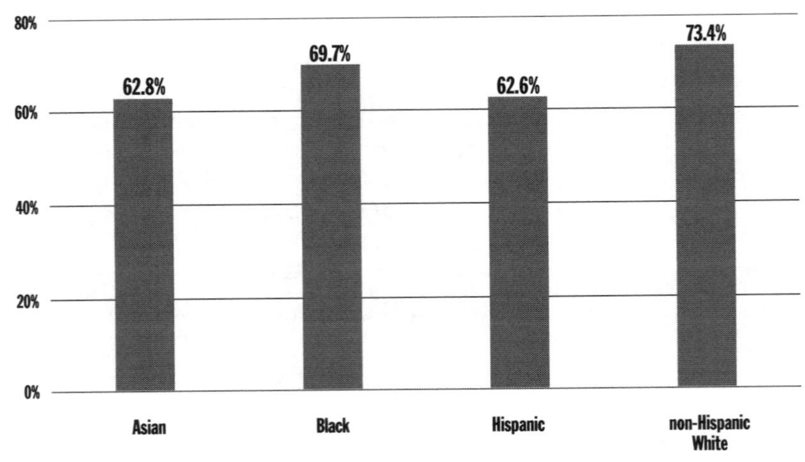

Table 6.6 Employment Status of Millennial Women by Race, Hispanic Origin, and Age, 2013

(number and percent of women aged 16 or older, aged 19 to 36, and in age groups that include Millennials, by race, Hispanic origin, and employment status, 2013; numbers in thousands)

		civilian labor force					not in labor force	
					unemployed			
	civilian noninstitutional population	total	percent of population	employed	number	percent of labor force	number	percent of population
Asian women aged 16 or older	**7,071**	**4,037**	**57.1%**	**3,842**	**195**	**4.8%**	**3,034**	**42.9%**
Asian Millennials (aged 19 to 36)	**2,445**	**1,535**	**62.8**	**1,452**	**84**	**5.4**	**909**	**37.2**
Aged 18 to 19	181	55	30.2	44	11	19.3	127	70.2
Aged 20 to 24	599	324	54.1	300	24	7.4	275	45.9
Aged 25 to 29	720	486	67.6	461	26	5.2	233	32.4
Aged 30 to 34	728	497	68.3	476	21	4.1	231	31.7
Aged 35 to 39	739	517	70.0	495	22	4.3	222	30.0
Black women aged 16 or older	**16,629**	**9,846**	**59.2**	**8,654**	**1,192**	**12.1**	**6,783**	**40.8**
Black Millennials (aged 19 to 36)	**5,703**	**3,976**	**69.7**	**3,359**	**616**	**15.5**	**1,726**	**30.3**
Aged 18 to 19	630	257	40.8	180	77	29.8	373	59.2
Aged 20 to 24	1,778	1,145	64.4	909	235	20.6	633	35.6
Aged 25 to 29	1,539	1,142	74.2	978	164	14.4	397	25.8
Aged 30 to 34	1,509	1,161	76.9	1,020	141	12.1	348	23.1
Aged 35 to 39	1,386	1,089	78.6	976	113	10.4	296	21.4
Hispanic women aged 16 or older	**18,719**	**10,430**	**55.7**	**9,437**	**994**	**9.5**	**8,289**	**44.3**
Hispanic Millennials (aged 19 to 36)	**7,544**	**4,723**	**62.6**	**4,227**	**496**	**10.5**	**2,822**	**37.4**
Aged 18 to 19	858	361	42.0	274	86	23.9	497	57.9
Aged 20 to 24	2,208	1,419	64.3	1,249	170	12.0	789	35.7
Aged 25 to 29	2,042	1,332	65.2	1,214	118	8.8	710	34.8
Aged 30 to 34	2,068	1,321	63.8	1,195	126	9.5	748	36.2
Aged 35 to 39	1,952	1,302	66.7	1,184	118	9.0	650	33.3
Non-Hispanic White women aged 16 or older	**80,748**	**46,141**	**57.1**	**43,620**	**2,519**	**5.5**	**34,608**	**42.9**
Non-Hispanic White Millennials (aged 19 to 36)	**20,668**	**15,176**	**73.4**	**14,194**	**981**	**6.5**	**5,491**	**26.6**
Aged 18 to 19	1,972	1,062	53.9	921	142	13.4	910	46.1
Aged 20 to 24	5,893	4,190	71.1	3,817	373	8.9	1,703	28.9
Aged 25 to 29	5,800	4,507	77.7	4,268	239	5.3	1,293	22.3
Aged 30 to 34	5,754	4,413	76.7	4,189	224	5.1	1,340	23.3
Aged 35 to 39	5,349	4,070	76.1	3,876	193	4.7	1,279	23.9

Note: Race is shown only for those who identify themselves as being of the race alone. People who selected more than one race are not included. Hispanics may be of any race. Non-Hispanic Whites are estimated by subtracting Hispanics from Whites.
Source: Bureau of Labor Statistics, Labor Force Statistics from the Current Population Survey, Internet site http://www.bls.gov/cps/tables.htm#empstat; calculations by New Strategist

Most Millennial Couples Are Dual Earners

The husband is the sole support of only 30 percent of young couples.

Dual incomes are by far the norm among married couples. Both husband and wife are in the labor force in 52 percent of the nation's couples. In another 23 percent, the husband is the only worker. Not far behind are the 18 percent of couples in which neither spouse is in the labor force. The wife is the sole worker in 8 percent of couples.

Sixty-four percent of Millennial couples are dual earners. The proportion is just 51 percent among the few couples under age 25, but is a larger 62 to 67 percent among those aged 25 to 39.

■ The proportion of couples in which the husband is the sole earner is highest among the youngest adults because many wives are at home with newborns.

Few Millennial couples are supported solely by the husband

(percent distribution of married couples under age 37 by labor force status of husband and wife, 2013)

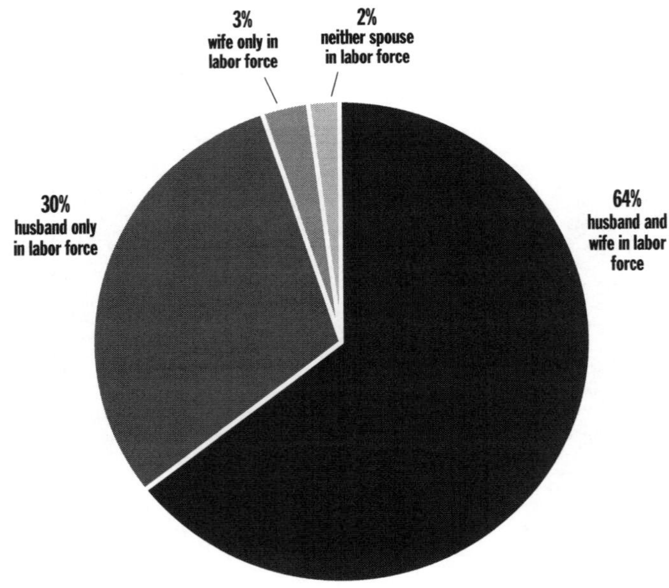

Table 6.7 Labor Force Status of Married-Couple Family Groups by Generation, 2013

(number and percent distribution of married-couple family groups by generation of reference person and labor force status of husband and wife, 2013; numbers in thousands)

	total	husband and wife in labor force	husband only in labor force	wife only in labor force	neither husband nor wife in labor force
Total married-couple family groups	**61,295**	**31,673**	**13,901**	**4,656**	**11,065**
Millennials (under age 37)	13,604	8,693	4,083	468	340
Generation Xers (aged 37 to 48)	14,367	9,699	3,558	680	428
Baby Boomers (aged 49 to 67)	23,112	12,161	4,929	2,458	3,562
Older Americans (aged 68 or older)	10,213	1,099	1,330	1,049	6,736
PERCENT DISTRIBUTION BY LABOR FORCE STATUS					
Total married-couple family groups	**100.0%**	**51.7%**	**22.7%**	**7.6%**	**18.1%**
Millennials (under age 37)	100.0	63.9	30.0	3.4	2.5
Generation Xers (aged 37 to 48)	100.0	67.5	24.8	4.7	3.0
Baby Boomers (aged 49 to 67)	100.0	52.6	21.3	10.6	15.4
Older Americans (aged 68 or older)	100.0	10.8	13.0	10.3	66.0
PERCENT DISTRIBUTION BY GENERATION					
Total married-couple family groups	**100.0**	**100.0**	**100.0**	**100.0**	**100.0**
Millennials (under age 37)	22.2	27.4	29.4	10.1	3.1
Generation Xers (aged 37 to 48)	23.4	30.6	25.6	14.6	3.9
Baby Boomers (aged 49 to 67)	37.7	38.4	35.5	52.8	32.2
Older Americans (aged 68 or older)	16.7	3.5	9.6	22.5	60.9

Source: Bureau of the Census, America's Families and Living Arrangements: 2013, Internet site http://www.census.gov/hhes/families/data/cps2013.html; calculations by New Strategist

Table 6.8 Labor Force Status of Married-Couple Family Groups in the Millennial Generation, 2013

(number and percent distribution of total married-couple family groups, married-couple family groups headed by people under age 37, and married-couple family groups in age groups that include Millennials, by labor force status of husband and wife, 2013; numbers in thousands)

	total	husband and wife in labor force	husband only in labor force	wife only in labor force	neither husband nor wife in labor force
Total married-couple family groups	**61,295**	**31,673**	**13,901**	**4,656**	**11,065**
Millennials (under age 37)	**13,604**	**8,693**	**4,083**	**468**	**340**
Under age 25	1,173	601	456	51	64
Aged 25 to 29	3,457	2,151	1,097	130	80
Aged 30 to 34	5,525	3,720	1,536	148	120
Aged 35 to 39	5,749	3,734	1,656	232	126
PERCENT DISTRIBUTION BY LABOR FORCE STATUS					
Total married-couple family groups	**100.0%**	**51.7%**	**22.7%**	**7.6%**	**18.1%**
Millennials (under age 37)	**100.0**	**63.9**	**30.0**	**3.4**	**2.5**
Under age 25	100.0	51.2	38.9	4.3	5.5
Aged 25 to 29	100.0	62.2	31.7	3.8	2.3
Aged 30 to 34	100.0	67.3	27.8	2.7	2.2
Aged 35 to 39	100.0	65.0	28.8	4.0	2.2
PERCENT DISTRIBUTION BY GENERATION					
Total married-couple family groups	**100.0**	**100.0**	**100.0**	**100.0**	**100.0**
Millennials (under age 37)	**22.2**	**27.4**	**29.4**	**10.1**	**3.1**
Under age 25	1.9	1.9	3.3	1.1	0.6
Aged 25 to 29	5.6	6.8	7.9	2.8	0.7
Aged 30 to 34	9.0	11.7	11.0	3.2	1.1
Aged 35 to 39	9.4	11.8	11.9	5.0	1.1

Source: Bureau of the Census, America's Families and Living Arrangements: 2013, Internet site http://www.census.gov/hhes/families/data/cps2013.html; calculations by New Strategist

Younger Workers Dominate Most Occupations

Workers under age 45 account for only 28 percent of CEOs, however.

Among the 144 million employed Americans in 2013, 80 million were under age 45—or 56 percent of the total. In some occupations, however, workers under age 45 account for less than 50 percent of the total. Workers under age 45 are only 44 percent of the nation's managers, 47 percent of physicians, and 45 percent of lawyers.

The youngest workers, under age 25, account for nearly half of waiters and waitresses, cashiers, and food prep workers. More than one in four employed 16-to-19-year-olds works in a food preparation and serving occupation. People aged 25 to 44 account for more than half of software developers, police, marketing managers, social workers, and teachers.

■ By age 25 to 34, the largest share of workers (39 percent) is employed in a managerial or professional occupation.

The youngest adults account for nearly half of workers in some occupations

(share of workers under age 25 by occupation, 2013)

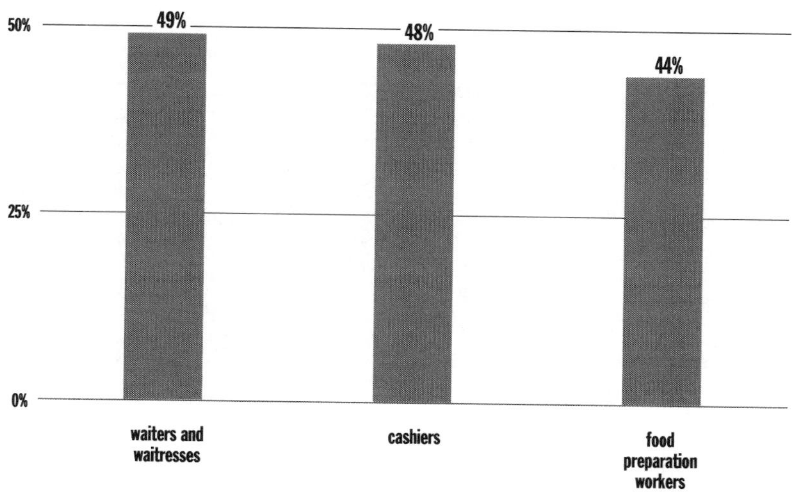

Table 6.9 Occupations of Workers under Age 45, 2013

(number of employed workers aged 16 or older, median age of workers, and number of workers under age 45, by occupation, 2013; numbers in thousands)

			under age 45				
	total	median age	total	16 to 19	20 to 24	25 to 34	35 to 44
TOTAL WORKERS	**143,929**	**42.4 yrs.**	**79,949**	**4,458**	**13,599**	**31,242**	**30,650**
Management and professional occupations	**54,712**	**44.4**	**28,180**	**326**	**2,777**	**12,084**	**12,993**
Management, business and financial operations	22,794	46.4	10,574	71	840	4,321	5,342
Management	16,037	47.5	6,978	51	463	2,702	3,762
Business and financial operations	6,757	43.6	3,597	20	377	1,620	1,580
Professional and related occupations	31,917	43.1	17,604	255	1,936	7,762	7,651
Computer and mathematical	3,980	41.1	2,460	20	235	1,062	1,143
Architecture and engineering	2,806	44.3	1,451	11	163	672	605
Life, physical, and social sciences	1,307	42.8	739	5	79	330	325
Community and social services	2,332	43.9	1,238	24	117	551	546
Legal	1,809	46.0	848	6	56	367	419
Education, training, and library	8,623	43.3	4,706	90	579	2,029	2,008
Arts, design, entertainment, sports, and media	2,879	40.5	1,723	77	300	752	594
Health care practitioner and technician	8,182	43.7	4,440	22	408	2,000	2,010
Service occupations	**25,929**	**37.9**	**16,566**	**1,897**	**3,939**	**5,774**	**4,956**
Health care support	3,537	39.1	2,229	74	529	900	726
Protective service	3,130	40.8	1,907	108	246	746	807
Food preparation and serving	8,209	29.4	6,315	1,210	1,971	1,946	1,188
Building and grounds cleaning and maintenance	5,661	44.1	2,911	207	457	1,027	1,220
Personal care and service	5,392	40.0	3,204	298	736	1,155	1,015
Sales and office occupations	**33,246**	**41.7**	**18,608**	**1,500**	**4,081**	**6,891**	**6,136**
Sales and related occupations	15,444	39.9	9,113	1,012	2,216	3,147	2,738
Office and administrative support	17,802	43.1	9,493	488	1,864	3,743	3,398
Natural resources, construction, and maintenance occupations	**13,058**	**41.9**	**7,499**	**295**	**1,138**	**3,052**	**3,014**
Farming, fishing, and forestry	964	37.2	641	89	138	225	189
Construction and extraction	7,130	41.6	4,192	139	582	1,755	1,716
Installation, maintenance, and repair	4,964	43.0	2,667	67	419	1,072	1,109
Production, transportation and material moving occupations	**16,984**	**43.1**	**9,098**	**441**	**1,664**	**3,442**	**3,551**
Production	8,275	43.0	4,439	144	767	1,745	1,783
Transportation and material moving	8,709	43.1	4,659	297	897	1,697	1,768

Source: Bureau of Labor Statistics, unpublished data from the 2013 Current Population Survey; calculations by New Strategist

Table 6.10 Share of Workers under Age 45 by Occupation, 2013

(percent of employed people under age 45 by occupation, 2013)

		under age 45				
	total	total	16 to 19	20 to 24	25 to 34	35 to 44
TOTAL WORKERS	100.0%	55.5%	3.1%	9.4%	21.7%	21.3%
Management and professional occupations	**100.0**	**51.5**	**0.6**	**5.1**	**22.1**	**23.7**
Management, business and financial operations	100.0	46.4	0.3	3.7	19.0	23.4
Management	100.0	43.5	0.3	2.9	16.8	23.5
Business and financial operations	100.0	53.2	0.3	5.6	24.0	23.4
Professional and related occupations	100.0	55.2	0.8	6.1	24.3	24.0
Computer and mathematical	100.0	61.8	0.5	5.9	26.7	28.7
Architecture and engineering	100.0	51.7	0.4	5.8	23.9	21.6
Life, physical, and social sciences	100.0	56.5	0.4	6.0	25.2	24.9
Community and social services	100.0	53.1	1.0	5.0	23.6	23.4
Legal	100.0	46.9	0.3	3.1	20.3	23.2
Education, training, and library	100.0	54.6	1.0	6.7	23.5	23.3
Arts, design, entertainment, sports, and media	100.0	59.8	2.7	10.4	26.1	20.6
Health care practitioner and technician	100.0	54.3	0.3	5.0	24.4	24.6
Service occupations	**100.0**	**63.9**	**7.3**	**15.2**	**22.3**	**19.1**
Health care support	100.0	63.0	2.1	15.0	25.4	20.5
Protective service	100.0	60.9	3.5	7.9	23.8	25.8
Food preparation and serving	100.0	76.9	14.7	24.0	23.7	14.5
Building and grounds cleaning and maintenance	100.0	51.4	3.7	8.1	18.1	21.6
Personal care and service	100.0	59.4	5.5	13.6	21.4	18.8
Sales and office occupations	**100.0**	**56.0**	**4.5**	**12.3**	**20.7**	**18.5**
Sales and related occupations	100.0	59.0	6.6	14.3	20.4	17.7
Office and administrative support	100.0	53.3	2.7	10.5	21.0	19.1
Natural resources, construction, and maintenance occupations	**100.0**	**57.4**	**2.3**	**8.7**	**23.4**	**23.1**
Farming, fishing, and forestry	100.0	66.5	9.2	14.3	23.3	19.6
Construction and extraction	100.0	58.8	1.9	8.2	24.6	24.1
Installation, maintenance, and repair	100.0	53.7	1.3	8.4	21.6	22.3
Production, transportation and material moving occupations	**100.0**	**53.6**	**2.6**	**9.8**	**20.3**	**20.9**
Production	100.0	53.6	1.7	9.3	21.1	21.5
Transportation and material moving	100.0	53.5	3.4	10.3	19.5	20.3

Source: Bureau of Labor Statistics, unpublished data from the 2013 Current Population Survey; calculations by New Strategist

Table 6.11 Share of Workers under Age 45 by Occupation, 2013

(percent distribution of employed people aged 16 or older and under age 45 by occupation, 2013)

		under age 45				
	total	total	16 to 19	20 to 24	25 to 34	35 to 44
TOTAL WORKERS	100.0%	100.0%	100.0%	100.0%	100.0%	100.0%
Management and professional occupations	**38.0**	**35.2**	**7.3**	**20.4**	**38.7**	**42.4**
Management, business and financial operations	15.8	13.2	1.6	6.2	13.8	17.4
Management	11.1	8.7	1.1	3.4	8.6	12.3
Business and financial operations	4.7	4.5	0.4	2.8	5.2	5.2
Professional and related occupations	22.2	22.0	5.7	14.2	24.8	25.0
Computer and mathematical	2.8	3.1	0.4	1.7	3.4	3.7
Architecture and engineering	1.9	1.8	0.2	1.2	2.2	2.0
Life, physical, and social sciences	0.9	0.9	0.1	0.6	1.1	1.1
Community and social services	1.6	1.5	0.5	0.9	1.8	1.8
Legal	1.3	1.1	0.1	0.4	1.2	1.4
Education, training, and library	6.0	5.9	2.0	4.3	6.5	6.6
Arts, design, entertainment, sports, and media	2.0	2.2	1.7	2.2	2.4	1.9
Health care practitioner and technician	5.7	5.6	0.5	3.0	6.4	6.6
Service occupations	**18.0**	**20.7**	**42.6**	**29.0**	**18.5**	**16.2**
Health care support	2.5	2.8	1.7	3.9	2.9	2.4
Protective service	2.2	2.4	2.4	1.8	2.4	2.6
Food preparation and serving	5.7	7.9	27.1	14.5	6.2	3.9
Building and grounds cleaning and maintenance	3.9	3.6	4.6	3.4	3.3	4.0
Personal care and service	3.7	4.0	6.7	5.4	3.7	3.3
Sales and office occupations	**23.1**	**23.3**	**33.6**	**30.0**	**22.1**	**20.0**
Sales and related occupations	10.7	11.4	22.7	16.3	10.1	8.9
Office and administrative support	12.4	11.9	10.9	13.7	12.0	11.1
Natural resources, construction, and maintenance occupations	**9.1**	**9.4**	**6.6**	**8.4**	**9.8**	**9.8**
Farming, fishing, and forestry	0.7	0.8	2.0	1.0	0.7	0.6
Construction and extraction	5.0	5.2	3.1	4.3	5.6	5.6
Installation, maintenance, and repair	3.4	3.3	1.5	3.1	3.4	3.6
Production, transportation and material moving occupations	**11.8**	**11.4**	**9.9**	**12.2**	**11.0**	**11.6**
Production	5.7	5.6	3.2	5.6	5.6	5.8
Transportation and material moving	6.1	5.8	6.7	6.6	5.4	5.8

Source: Bureau of Labor Statistics, unpublished data from the 2013 Current Population Survey; calculations by New Strategist

Table 6.12 Workers under Age 45 by Detailed Occupation, 2013

(number of employed workers aged 16 or older, median age, and number under age 45 by detailed occupations with at least 500,000 workers, 2013; numbers in thousands)

	total	median age	under age 45				
			total	16 to 19	20 to 24	25 to 34	35 to 44
TOTAL WORKERS	**143,929**	**42.4 yrs.**	**79,949**	**4,458**	**13,599**	**31,242**	**30,650**
Chief executives	1,520	52.5	428	0	9	107	312
General and operations managers	1,075	45.6	507	0	22	202	283
Marketing and sales managers	907	42.8	509	5	30	225	249
Computer and information systems managers	602	44.3	319	–	12	108	199
Financial managers	1,218	43.8	640	4	41	299	296
Farmers, ranchers, and other agricultural managers	929	56.1	241	8	27	95	111
Construction managers	821	46.9	363	1	20	151	191
Education administrators	804	48.1	326	0	17	112	197
Food service managers	1,077	40.0	667	22	127	269	249
Medical and health services managers	585	48.3	244	1	13	83	147
Property, real estate, and community association managers	654	50.8	239	0	15	96	128
Human resources workers	584	42.2	343	1	34	150	158
Management analysts	811	47.2	359	1	34	156	168
Accountants and auditors	1,814	43.2	984	4	87	451	442
Computer systems analysts	534	41.6	321	1	36	132	152
Software developers, applications and systems software	1,103	40.6	707	6	49	332	320
Computer support specialists	517	40.1	326	5	46	150	125
Counselors	727	43.2	398	11	35	181	171
Social workers	727	41.4	435	1	36	203	195
Lawyers	1,092	47.1	489	1	4	205	279
Postsecondary teachers	1,313	45.7	645	5	100	285	255
Preschool and kindergarten teachers	695	39.6	438	8	75	195	160
Elementary and middle school teachers	3,038	43.0	1,719	6	132	743	838
Secondary school teachers	1,063	42.5	608	2	45	303	258
Teacher assistants	918	44.8	448	26	80	164	178
Designers	784	41.0	462	5	64	214	179
Physicians and surgeons	934	46.8	440	–	5	192	243
Registered nurses	2,892	44.2	1,524	2	127	685	710
Health practitioner support technologists and technicians	554	36.1	384	11	91	172	110
Licensed practical and licensed vocational nurses	558	43.8	295	2	35	115	143
Nursing, psychiatric, and home health aides	2,134	40.4	1,271	43	300	495	433
Police and sheriff's patrol officers	697	40.0	475	2	26	212	235
Security guards and gaming surveillance officers	858	41.0	488	13	115	218	142
First-line supervisors of food preparation and serving workers	581	33.8	409	27	123	153	106
Cooks	1,988	33.4	1,425	197	371	502	355
Food preparation workers	885	27.8	688	175	216	183	114
Waiters and waitresses	2,124	26.2	1,805	323	708	524	250
Janitors and building cleaners	2,275	46.8	1,038	83	181	364	410
Maids and housekeeping cleaners	1,401	44.3	717	38	96	241	342
Grounds maintenance workers	1,327	38.5	861	84	161	312	304
Hairdressers, hairstylists, and cosmetologists	786	40.3	479	10	77	217	175
Childcare workers	1,230	37.7	759	122	211	226	200
Personal care aides	1,242	44.2	623	31	148	232	212
First-line supervisors of retail sales workers	3,223	43.0	1,750	25	262	750	713

	total	median age	under age 45 total	16 to 19	20 to 24	25 to 34	35 to 44
First-line supervisors of nonretail sales workers	1,188	46.4 yrs.	529	2	35	206	286
Cashiers	3,254	26.7	2,498	664	887	592	355
Retail salespersons	3,230	34.7	2,089	260	739	644	446
Insurance sales agents	602	45.6	296	4	36	148	108
Sales representatives, wholesale and manufacturing	1,319	44.9	661	8	63	258	332
Real estate brokers and sales agents	769	50.7	270	3	22	105	140
First-line supervisors of office and administrative support workers	1,363	45.7	656	2	54	262	338
Bookkeeping, accounting, and auditing clerks	1,241	50.0	487	5	59	187	236
Customer service representatives	2,069	36.7	1,369	109	306	566	388
Receptionists and information clerks	1,326	37.6	823	63	243	311	206
Shipping, receiving, and traffic clerks	563	41.1	318	10	81	120	107
Stock clerks and order fillers	1,508	35.2	1,003	121	303	353	226
Secretaries and administrative assistants	2,922	48.5	1,210	28	135	504	543
Office clerks, general	1,184	42.7	640	41	135	237	227
Miscellaneous agricultural workers	679	33.7	492	79	112	179	122
First-line supervisors of construction trades and extraction workers	631	46.2	292	0	18	119	155
Carpenters	1,164	42.2	666	16	84	292	274
Construction laborers	1,536	38.8	992	55	175	416	346
Electricians	730	42.8	408	8	48	161	191
Painters, construction and maintenance	517	41.5	305	12	45	123	125
Pipelayers, plumbers, pipefitters, and steamfitters	553	41.6	322	5	46	141	130
Automotive service technicians and mechanics	863	39.4	522	16	117	195	194
First-line supervisors of production and operating workers	731	47.2	313	1	17	124	171
Miscellaneous assemblers and fabricators	1,013	41.6	590	21	120	214	235
Welding, soldering, and brazing workers	575	39.2	369	8	67	162	132
Inspectors, testers, sorters, samplers, and weighers	686	43.8	363	8	58	153	144
Bus drivers	582	52.7	174	1	21	53	99
Driver/sales workers and truck drivers	3,252	46.0	1,524	39	199	545	741
Industrial truck and tractor operators	557	40.0	342	7	54	163	118
Laborers and freight, stock, and material movers, hand	1,752	35.8	1,193	123	315	420	335

Note: "–" means sample is too small to make a reliable estimate.
Source: Bureau of Labor Statistics, unpublished tables from the 2013 Current Population Survey; calculations by New Strategist

Table 6.13 Workers under Age 45 by Detailed Occupation, 2013

(percent distribution of employed people aged 16 or older and under age 45 by occupation, 2013)

	total workers	under age 45				
		total	16 to 19	20 to 24	25 to 34	35 to 44
TOTAL WORKERS	**100.0%**	**55.5%**	**3.1%**	**9.4%**	**21.7%**	**21.3%**
Chief executives	100.0	28.2	0.0	0.6	7.0	20.5
General and operations managers	100.0	47.2	0.0	2.0	18.8	26.3
Marketing and sales managers	100.0	56.1	0.6	3.3	24.8	27.5
Computer and information systems managers	100.0	53.0	–	2.0	17.9	33.1
Financial managers	100.0	52.5	0.3	3.4	24.5	24.3
Farmers, ranchers, and other agricultural managers	100.0	25.9	0.9	2.9	10.2	11.9
Construction managers	100.0	44.2	0.1	2.4	18.4	23.3
Education administrators	100.0	40.5	0.0	2.1	13.9	24.5
Food service managers	100.0	61.9	2.0	11.8	25.0	23.1
Medical and health services managers	100.0	41.7	0.2	2.2	14.2	25.1
Property, real estate, and community association managers	100.0	36.5	0.0	2.3	14.7	19.6
Human resources workers	100.0	58.7	0.2	5.8	25.7	27.1
Management analysts	100.0	44.3	0.1	4.2	19.2	20.7
Accountants and auditors	100.0	54.2	0.2	4.8	24.9	24.4
Computer systems analysts	100.0	60.1	0.2	6.7	24.7	28.5
Software developers, applications and systems software	100.0	64.1	0.5	4.4	30.1	29.0
Computer support specialists	100.0	63.1	1.0	8.9	29.0	24.2
Counselors	100.0	54.7	1.5	4.8	24.9	23.5
Social workers	100.0	59.8	0.1	5.0	27.9	26.8
Lawyers	100.0	44.8	0.1	0.4	18.8	25.5
Postsecondary teachers	100.0	49.1	0.4	7.6	21.7	19.4
Preschool and kindergarten teachers	100.0	63.0	1.2	10.8	28.1	23.0
Elementary and middle school teachers	100.0	56.6	0.2	4.3	24.5	27.6
Secondary school teachers	100.0	57.2	0.2	4.2	28.5	24.3
Teacher assistants	100.0	48.8	2.8	8.7	17.9	19.4
Designers	100.0	58.9	0.6	8.2	27.3	22.8
Physicians and surgeons	100.0	47.1	–	0.5	20.6	26.0
Registered nurses	100.0	52.7	0.1	4.4	23.7	24.6
Health practitioner support technologists and technicians	100.0	69.3	2.0	16.4	31.0	19.9
Licensed practical and licensed vocational nurses	100.0	52.9	0.4	6.3	20.6	25.6
Nursing, psychiatric, and home health aides	100.0	59.6	2.0	14.1	23.2	20.3
Police and sheriff's patrol officers	100.0	68.1	0.3	3.7	30.4	33.7
Security guards and gaming surveillance officers	100.0	56.9	1.5	13.4	25.4	16.6
First-line supervisors of food preparation and serving workers	100.0	70.4	4.6	21.2	26.3	18.2
Cooks	100.0	71.7	9.9	18.7	25.3	17.9
Food preparation workers	100.0	77.7	19.8	24.4	20.7	12.9
Waiters and waitresses	100.0	85.0	15.2	33.3	24.7	11.8
Janitors and building cleaners	100.0	45.6	3.6	8.0	16.0	18.0
Maids and housekeeping cleaners	100.0	51.2	2.7	6.9	17.2	24.4
Grounds maintenance workers	100.0	64.9	6.3	12.1	23.5	22.9
Hairdressers, hairstylists, and cosmetologists	100.0	60.9	1.3	9.8	27.6	22.3
Childcare workers	100.0	61.7	9.9	17.2	18.4	16.3
Personal care aides	100.0	50.2	2.5	11.9	18.7	17.1
First-line supervisors of retail sales workers	100.0	54.3	0.8	8.1	23.3	22.1

	total workers	under age 45				
		total	16 to 19	20 to 24	25 to 34	35 to 44
First-line supervisors of nonretail sales workers	100.0%	44.5%	0.2%	2.9%	17.3%	24.1%
Cashiers	100.0	76.8	20.4	27.3	18.2	10.9
Retail salespersons	100.0	64.7	8.0	22.9	19.9	13.8
Insurance sales agents	100.0	49.2	0.7	6.0	24.6	17.9
Sales representatives, wholesale and manufacturing	100.0	50.1	0.6	4.8	19.6	25.2
Real estate brokers and sales agents	100.0	35.1	0.4	2.9	13.7	18.2
First-line supervisors of office and administrative support workers	100.0	48.1	0.1	4.0	19.2	24.8
Bookkeeping, accounting, and auditing clerks	100.0	39.2	0.4	4.8	15.1	19.0
Customer service representatives	100.0	66.2	5.3	14.8	27.4	18.8
Receptionists and information clerks	100.0	62.1	4.8	18.3	23.5	15.5
Shipping, receiving, and traffic clerks	100.0	56.5	1.8	14.4	21.3	19.0
Stock clerks and order fillers	100.0	66.5	8.0	20.1	23.4	15.0
Secretaries and administrative assistants	100.0	41.4	1.0	4.6	17.2	18.6
Office clerks, general	100.0	54.1	3.5	11.4	20.0	19.2
Miscellaneous agricultural workers	100.0	72.5	11.6	16.5	26.4	18.0
First-line supervisors of construction trades and extraction workers	100.0	46.3	0.0	2.9	18.9	24.6
Carpenters	100.0	57.2	1.4	7.2	25.1	23.5
Construction laborers	100.0	64.6	3.6	11.4	27.1	22.5
Electricians	100.0	55.9	1.1	6.6	22.1	26.2
Painters, construction and maintenance	100.0	59.0	2.3	8.7	23.8	24.2
Pipelayers, plumbers, pipefitters, and steamfitters	100.0	58.2	0.9	8.3	25.5	23.5
Automotive service technicians and mechanics	100.0	60.5	1.9	13.6	22.6	22.5
First-line supervisors of production and operating workers	100.0	42.8	0.1	2.3	17.0	23.4
Miscellaneous assemblers and fabricators	100.0	58.2	2.1	11.8	21.1	23.2
Welding, soldering, and brazing workers	100.0	64.2	1.4	11.7	28.2	23.0
Inspectors, testers, sorters, samplers, and weighers	100.0	52.9	1.2	8.5	22.3	21.0
Bus drivers	100.0	29.9	0.2	3.6	9.1	17.0
Driver/sales workers and truck drivers	100.0	46.9	1.2	6.1	16.8	22.8
Industrial truck and tractor operators	100.0	61.4	1.3	9.7	29.3	21.2
Laborers and freight, stock, and material movers, hand	100.0	68.1	7.0	18.0	24.0	19.1

Note: "–" means sample is too small to make a reliable estimate.
Source: Bureau of Labor Statistics, unpublished tables from the 2013 Current Population Survey; calculations by New Strategist

Many Workers Have a Part-Time Job

The youngest workers are most likely to work part-time.

Nearly one in four American workers has a part-time job. The figure is as high as 75 percent among workers aged 16 to 19, falls to 41 percent among workers aged 20 to 24, and bottoms out at 18 percent among workers in the broad 25-to-54 age group. Women are more likely than men to work part-time.

Among workers holding a part-time job, many would prefer full-time employment. Among men aged 20 to 24, for example, a substantial 35 percent work part-time. Of those who do, 31 percent work part-time for economic reasons—meaning they want a full-time job. Among women in the age group, 47 percent work part-time and 25 percent of the part-timers want a full-time position.

■ The percentage of workers holding a part-time job because they could not find full-time employment grew during the Great Recession.

Many part-time workers want full-time jobs

(percentage of employed men who work part-time but would prefer a full-time job, by age, 2013)

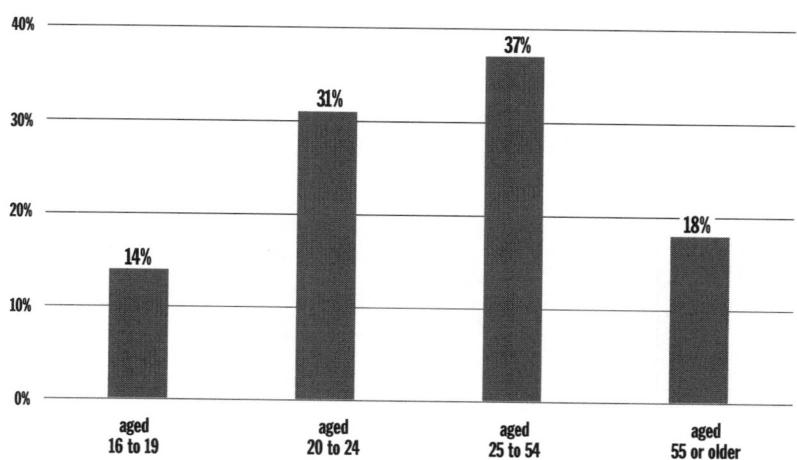

Table 6.14 Full-Time and Part-Time Workers by Age and Sex, 2013

(number and percent distribution of people aged 16 or older at work in nonagricultural industries by age, employment status, and sex, 2013; numbers in thousands)

	total			men			women		
	total	full-time	part-time	total	full-time	part-time	total	full-time	part-time
Total at work	**136,891**	**103,607**	**33,284**	**72,604**	**59,338**	**13,266**	**64,287**	**44,269**	**20,017**
Aged 16 to 19	4,209	1,048	3,161	2,028	602	1,426	2,181	446	1,735
Aged 20 to 24	13,103	7,751	5,352	6,746	4,363	2,383	6,357	3,388	2,969
Aged 25 to 54	90,260	73,589	16,672	48,422	42,348	6,075	41,838	31,241	10,597
Aged 55 or older	29,318	21,220	8,099	15,408	12,025	3,382	13,911	9,194	4,716
PERCENT DISTRIBUTION BY EMPLOYMENT STATUS									
Total at work	**100.0%**	**75.7%**	**24.3%**	**100.0%**	**81.7%**	**18.3%**	**100.0%**	**68.9%**	**31.1%**
Aged 16 to 19	100.0	24.9	75.1	100.0	29.7	70.3	100.0	20.4	79.6
Aged 20 to 24	100.0	59.2	40.8	100.0	64.7	35.3	100.0	53.3	46.7
Aged 25 to 54	100.0	81.5	18.5	100.0	87.5	12.5	100.0	74.7	25.3
Aged 55 or older	100.0	72.4	27.6	100.0	78.0	21.9	100.0	66.1	33.9
PERCENT DISTRIBUTION BY AGE									
Total at work	**100.0**	**100.0**	**100.0**	**100.0**	**100.0**	**100.0**	**100.0**	**100.0**	**100.0**
Aged 16 to 19	3.1	1.0	9.5	2.8	1.0	10.7	3.4	1.0	8.7
Aged 20 to 24	9.6	7.5	16.1	9.3	7.4	18.0	9.9	7.7	14.8
Aged 25 to 54	65.9	71.0	50.1	66.7	71.4	45.8	65.1	70.6	52.9
Aged 55 or older	21.4	20.5	24.3	21.2	20.3	25.5	21.6	20.8	23.6

Note: Part-time work is less than 35 hours per week. Part-time workers exclude those who worked less than 35 hours in the previous week because of vacation, holidays, child care problems, weather issues, and other temporary, noneconomic reasons. "Economic reasons" means a worker's hours have been reduced or worker cannot find full-time employment.
Source: Bureau of Labor Statistics, Labor Force Statistics from the Current Population Survey, Internet site http://www.bls.gov/cps/tables.htm#empstat; calculations by New Strategist

Table 6.15 Part-Time Workers by Sex, Age, and Reason, 2013

(total number of people aged 16 or older who work in nonagricultural industries part-time, and number and percent working part-time for economic reasons, by sex and age, 2013; numbers in thousands)

		working part-time for economic reasons	
	total	number	share of total
Men working part-time	**13,266**	**3,825**	**28.8%**
Aged 16 to 19	1,426	203	14.2
Aged 20 to 24	2,383	745	31.3
Aged 25 to 54	6,075	2,251	37.1
Aged 55 or older	3,382	625	18.5
Women working part-time	**20,017**	**3,998**	**20.0%**
Aged 16 to 19	1,735	204	11.8
Aged 20 to 24	2,969	748	25.2
Aged 25 to 54	10,597	2,378	22.4
Aged 55 or older	4,716	667	14.1

Note: Part-time work is less than 35 hours per week. Part-time workers exclude those who worked less than 35 hours in the previous week because of vacation, holidays, child care problems, weather issues, and other temporary, noneconomic reasons. "Economic reasons" means a worker's hours have been reduced or worker cannot find full-time employment.
Source: Bureau of Labor Statistics, Labor Force Statistics from the Current Population Survey, Internet site http://www.bls.gov/cps/tables.htm#empstat; calculations by New Strategist

Few Millennials Are Self-Employed

Self-employment rises with age and experience.

Although many young adults dream of being their own boss, few are able to do so. Among the nation's 144 million employed workers, only 6.5 percent are self-employed. Among workers under age 35, the figure is only 2 to 4 percent.

As people age, self-employment increases, peaking at 17 percent among workers aged 65 or older. Self-employment increases with age because it takes years of experience to gain marketable skills.

■ Self-employment is relatively rare in the United States because health insurance has been difficult to obtain or afford for those under age 65. The Affordable Care Act may boost self-employment among younger Americans.

Self-employment rises with age

(percent of workers who are self-employed, by age, 2013)

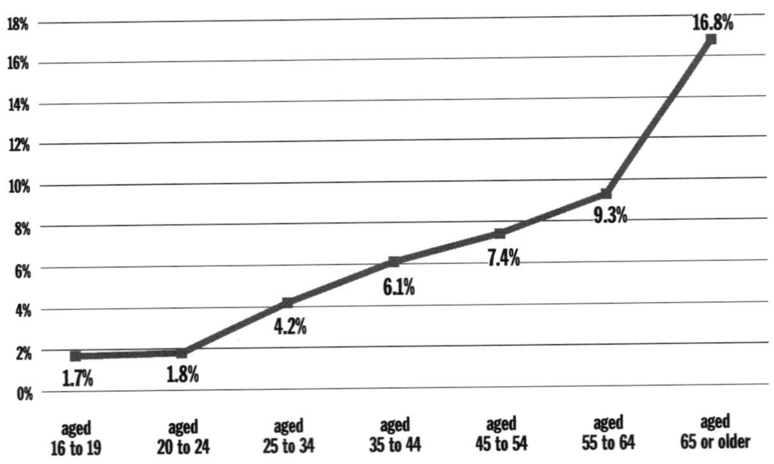

Table 6.16 Self-Employed Workers by Sex and Age, 2013

(number of employed workers aged 16 or older, number and percent who are self-employed, and percent distribution of self-employed, by age, 2013; numbers in thousands)

		self-employed		percent distribution of self-employed
	total	number	percent	by age
Total aged 16 or older	**143,929**	**9,408**	**6.5%**	**100.0%**
Aged 16 to 19	4,458	78	1.7	0.8
Aged 20 to 24	13,599	242	1.8	2.6
Aged 25 to 34	31,242	1,318	4.2	14.0
Aged 35 to 44	30,650	1,861	6.1	19.8
Aged 45 to 54	32,522	2,412	7.4	25.6
Aged 55 to 64	23,777	2,205	9.3	23.4
Aged 65 or older	7,681	1,292	16.8	13.7
Total men	**76,353**	**5,682**	**7.4**	**100.0**
Aged 16 to 19	2,177	53	2.4	0.9
Aged 20 to 24	7,013	157	2.2	2.8
Aged 25 to 34	16,907	776	4.6	13.7
Aged 35 to 44	16,590	1,092	6.6	19.2
Aged 45 to 54	17,033	1,445	8.5	25.4
Aged 55 to 64	12,376	1,346	10.9	23.7
Aged 65 or older	4,257	814	19.1	14.3
Total women	**67,577**	**3,726**	**5.5**	**100.0**
Aged 16 to 19	2,281	26	1.1	0.7
Aged 20 to 24	6,585	84	1.3	2.3
Aged 25 to 34	14,336	542	3.8	14.5
Aged 35 to 44	14,060	769	5.5	20.6
Aged 45 to 54	15,490	968	6.2	26.0
Aged 55 to 64	11,400	859	7.5	23.1
Aged 65 or older	3,424	477	13.9	12.8

Source: Bureau of Labor Statistics, Labor Force Statistics from the Current Population Survey, Internet site http://www.bls.gov/cps/tables.htm#empstat; calculations by New Strategist

Job Tenure Has Been Stable for Younger Workers

Long-term employment has fallen among younger men, however.

Job tenure (the median number of years a worker has been with his current employer) has been stable among younger men and women over the past 12 years. The average male worker aged 25 to 34 had been with his current employer for 2.7 years in 2000 and for a slightly longer 3.2 years in 2012. Among women in the age group, tenure grew during the time period from 2.5 to 3.1 years.

Not surprisingly, long-term employment is uncommon among younger workers and it is becoming even less common among men. The percentage of men in their thirties who have worked for their current employer for 10 or more years fell by 2 to 4 percentage points between 2000 and 2012. In contrast, long-term employment increased by 2 percentage points among women in their late thirties.

■ The decline in long-term employment among young men is due to greater college attendance and job cuts during the Great Recession.

Fewer men aged 25 to 39 have long-term jobs

(percent of men aged 25 to 39 who have worked for their current employer for 10 or more years, 2000 and 2012)

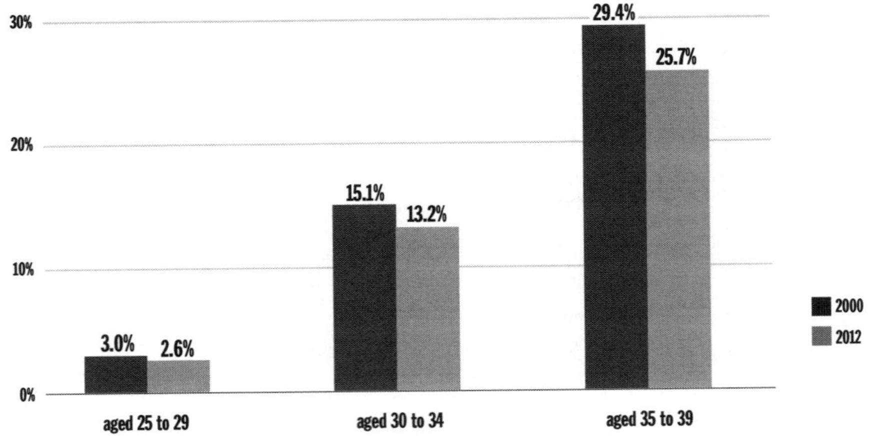

Table 6.17 Job Tenure by Sex and Age, 2000 to 2012

(median number of years workers aged 16 or older have been with their current employer by sex and age, 2000 to 2012; change in years, 2000–12)

	2012	2010	2000	change in years 2000–12
Total employed men	**4.7 yrs.**	**4.6 yrs.**	**3.8 yrs.**	**0.9 yrs.**
Aged 16 to 17	0.6	0.7	0.6	0.0
Aged 18 to 19	0.8	1.0	0.7	0.1
Aged 20 to 24	1.4	1.6	1.2	0.2
Aged 25 to 34	3.2	3.2	2.7	0.5
Aged 35 to 44	5.4	5.3	5.3	0.1
Aged 45 to 54	8.5	8.5	9.5	–1.0
Aged 55 to 64	10.7	10.4	10.2	0.5
Aged 65 or older	10.2	9.7	9.0	1.2
Total employed women	**4.6**	**4.2**	**3.3**	**1.3**
Aged 16 to 17	0.7	0.7	0.6	0.1
Aged 18 to 19	0.8	1.0	0.7	0.1
Aged 20 to 24	1.3	1.5	1.0	0.3
Aged 25 to 34	3.1	3.0	2.5	0.6
Aged 35 to 44	5.2	4.9	4.3	0.9
Aged 45 to 54	7.3	7.1	7.3	0.0
Aged 55 to 64	10.0	9.7	9.9	0.1
Aged 65 or older	10.5	10.1	9.7	0.8

Source: Bureau of Labor Statistics, Employee Tenure, Internet site http://www.bls.gov/news.release/tenure.toc.htm; calculations by New Strategist

Table 6.18 Long-Term Employment by Sex and Age, 2000 to 2012

(percent of employed wage and salary workers aged 25 or older who have been with their current employer for 10 or more years, by sex and age, 2000 to 2012; percentage point change in share, 2000–12)

	2012	2010	2000	percentage point change 2000–12
Total employed men	**34.6%**	**34.3%**	**33.4%**	**1.2**
Aged 25 to 29	2.6	3.1	3.0	–0.4
Aged 30 to 34	13.2	14.3	15.1	–1.9
Aged 35 to 39	25.7	27.2	29.4	–3.7
Aged 40 to 44	36.9	37.5	40.2	–3.3
Aged 45 to 49	44.8	43.7	49.0	–4.2
Aged 50 to 54	51.4	51.3	51.6	–0.2
Aged 55 to 59	55.7	53.6	53.7	2.0
Aged 60 to 64	56.2	56.8	52.4	3.8
Aged 65 or older	55.5	51.9	48.6	6.9
Total employed women	**32.8**	**31.9**	**29.5**	**3.3**
Aged 25 to 29	2.3	1.6	1.9	0.4
Aged 30 to 34	11.8	11.1	12.5	–0.7
Aged 35 to 39	24.7	24.0	22.3	2.4
Aged 40 to 44	33.2	32.9	31.2	2.0
Aged 45 to 49	38.3	38.0	41.4	–3.1
Aged 50 to 54	45.5	46.5	45.8	–0.3
Aged 55 to 59	52.6	51.2	52.5	0.1
Aged 60 to 64	54.0	52.2	53.6	0.4
Aged 65 or older	55.6	54.3	51.0	4.6

Source: Bureau of Labor Statistics, Employee Tenure, Internet site http://www.bls.gov/news.release/tenure.toc.htm; calculations by New Strategist

Most Minimum-Wage Workers Are under Age 25

Nearly two-thirds are under age 30.

Among the nation's 76 million workers who were paid hourly rates in 2013, only 3.3 million (4 percent) made minimum wage or less, according to the Bureau of Labor Statistics. Of those workers, half are under age 25.

Twenty-four percent of minimum wage workers are aged 16 to 19, and another 26 percent are aged 20 to 24. Among workers paid hourly rates in the 16-to-19 age group, 19 percent earn minimum wage or less. In the 20-to-24 age group, 8 percent earn minimum wage or less.

■ Younger workers are most likely to earn minimum wage or less because many are in entry-level jobs.

Younger adults account for the majority of minimum wage workers

(percent distribution of workers making minimum wage or less by age, 2013)

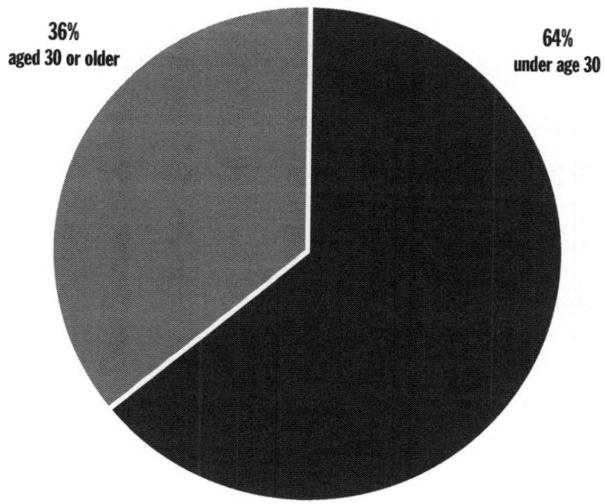

Table 6.19 Minimum-Wage Workers, 2013

(number and percent distribution of total workers paid hourly rates and those paid at or below the prevailing federal minimum wage, by age, 2013; numbers in thousands)

	total paid hourly rates	at or below minimum wage
Total aged 16 or older	**75,948**	**3,300**
Aged 16 to 19	4,089	797
Aged 20 to 24	11,021	866
Aged 25 to 29	9,430	436
Aged 30 to 34	8,177	267
Aged 35 to 44	14,195	354
Aged 45 to 54	15,097	314
Aged 55 to 64	10,713	154
Aged 65 or older	3,227	111
PERCENT DISTRIBUTION BY WAGE STATUS		
Total aged 16 or older	**100.0%**	**4.3%**
Aged 16 to 19	100.0	19.5
Aged 20 to 24	100.0	7.9
Aged 25 to 29	100.0	4.6
Aged 30 to 34	100.0	3.3
Aged 35 to 44	100.0	2.5
Aged 45 to 54	100.0	2.1
Aged 55 to 64	100.0	1.4
Aged 65 or older	100.0	3.4
PERCENT DISTRIBUTION BY AGE		
Total aged 16 or older	**100.0**	**100.0**
Aged 16 to 19	5.4	24.2
Aged 20 to 24	14.5	26.2
Aged 25 to 29	12.4	13.2
Aged 30 to 34	10.8	8.1
Aged 35 to 44	18.7	10.7
Aged 45 to 54	19.9	9.5
Aged 55 to 64	14.1	4.7
Aged 65 or older	4.2	3.4

Source: Bureau of Labor Statistics, Characteristics of Minimum Wage Workers: 2013, Internet site http://www.bls.gov/cps/minwage2013tbls.htm; calculations by New Strategist

Few of Today's Workers Are Represented by a Union

Millennials are least likely to be represented by a union.

Union representation has fallen sharply over the past few decades. In 2013, unions represented only 12 percent of wage and salary workers.

The percentage of workers who are represented by a union peaks in the 55-to-64 age group at 16 percent. Among 25-to-34-year-olds, unions represented a smaller 11 percent (Millennials were aged 19 to 36 in 2013). One reason for the decline in labor union representation is the shift from manufacturing to service jobs, with fewer service workers being unionized.

■ Union representation could rise among service workers as they demand better pay and benefits.

Few workers are represented by a union

(percentage of employed wage and salary workers who are represented by a union, by age, 2013)

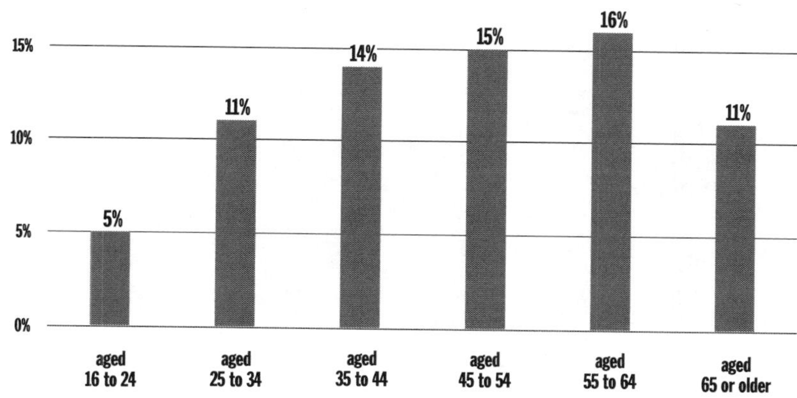

Table 6.20 Union Representation by Age, 2013

(number and percent of employed wage and salary workers aged 16 or older by age and union representation status, 2013; numbers in thousands)

	total employed	represented by a union	
		number	percent
Total aged 16 or older	**129,110**	**16,028**	**12.4%**
Aged 16 to 24	17,647	854	4.8
Aged 25 to 34	29,404	3,228	11.0
Aged 35 to 44	27,631	3,790	13.7
Aged 45 to 54	28,498	4,377	15.4
Aged 55 to 64	20,207	3,176	15.7
Aged 65 or older	5,723	603	10.5

Note: Workers represented by unions are either members of a labor union or similar employee association or workers who report no union affiliation but whose jobs are covered by a union or an employee association contract.
Source: Bureau of Labor Statistics, Labor Force Statistics from the Current Population Survey, Internet site http://www.bls.gov/cps/tables.htm#empstat; calculations by New Strategist

Millennial Generation Will Expand the Labor Force

The number of workers aged 25 to 44 will increase during the coming decade.

Between 2012 and 2022, the Millennial generation will age into its forties (the oldest Millennials turn 45 in 2022). The number of workers aged 25 to 34 will expand by 10 percent between 2012 and 2022, a gain of more than 3 million. The number of workers aged 35 to 44 will grow by 2 million for a gain of 6 percent.

The number of older workers is projected to soar during the coming decade as Boomers age into their late sixties and early seventies. Between 2012 and 2022, the Bureau of Labor Statistics projects a 66 percent increase in the number of male workers and an even larger 86 percent increase in the number of female workers aged 65 or older.

■ As Boomers retire, Millennials may find plenty of job opportunities.

Number of workers aged 25 to 44 will increase

(percent change in number of workers aged 25 to 54, by sex and age, 2012–22)

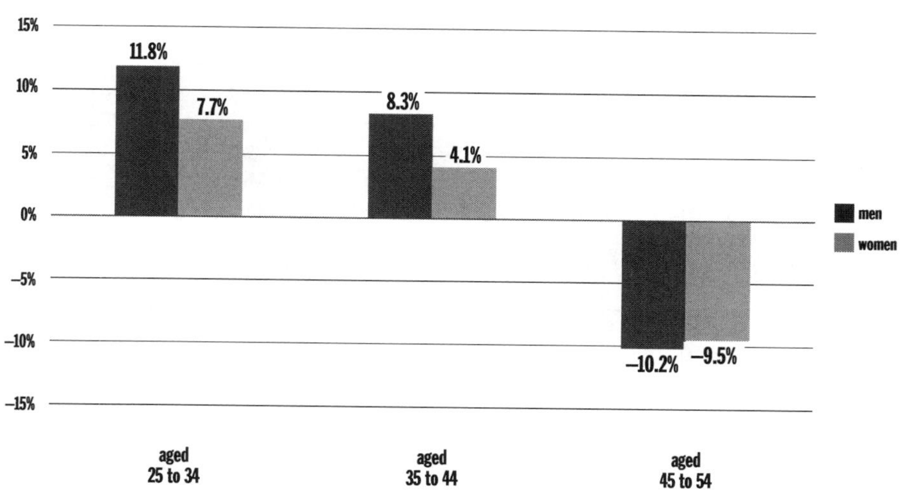

Table 6.21 Projections of the Labor Force by Sex and Age, 2012 and 2022

(number of people aged 16 or older in the civilian labor force by sex and age, 2012 and 2022; percent change, 2012–22; numbers in thousands)

	2012	2022	percent change
Total labor force	**154,975**	**163,450**	**5.5%**
Aged 16 to 19	5,823	4,473	–23.2
Aged 20 to 24	15,462	13,989	–9.5
Aged 25 to 34	33,465	36,786	9.9
Aged 35 to 44	32,734	34,810	6.3
Aged 45 to 54	35,054	31,600	–9.9
Aged 55 to 64	24,710	28,317	14.6
Aged 65 or older	7,727	13,476	74.4
Total men in labor force	**82,327**	**86,913**	**5.6**
Aged 16 to 19	2,940	2,316	–21.2
Aged 20 to 24	8,110	7,266	–10.4
Aged 25 to 34	18,083	20,212	11.8
Aged 35 to 44	17,607	19,061	8.3
Aged 45 to 54	18,363	16,495	–10.2
Aged 55 to 64	12,879	14,370	11.6
Aged 65 or older	4,345	7,193	65.56
Total women in labor force	**72,648**	**76,537**	**5.4**
Aged 16 to 19	2,883	2,156	–25.2
Aged 20 to 24	7,352	6,724	–8.5
Aged 25 to 34	15,382	16,574	7.7
Aged 35 to 44	15,127	15,749	4.1
Aged 45 to 54	16,692	15,104	–9.5
Aged 55 to 64	11,830	13,947	17.9
Aged 65 or older	3,382	6,284	85.8

Source: Bureau of Labor Statistics, Labor Force Projections to 2022: The Labor Force Participation Rate Continues to Fall, Monthly Labor Review, December 2013, Internet site http://www.bls.gov/opub/mlr/2013/article/labor-force-projections-to-2022-the-labor-force-participation-rate-continues-to-fall.htm; calculations by New Strategist

Table 6.22 Projections of Labor Force Participation by Sex and Age, 2012 and 2022

(percent of people aged 16 or older in the civilian labor force by sex and age, 2012 and 2022; percentage point change, 2012–22)

	2012	2022	percentage point change
Total labor force participation rate	**63.7%**	**61.6%**	**–2.1**
Men in labor force	**70.2**	**67.6**	**–2.6**
Aged 16 to 19	34.0	27.8	–6.2
Aged 20 to 24	74.5	69.9	–4.6
Aged 25 to 34	89.5	88.8	–0.7
Aged 35 to 44	90.7	90.4	–0.3
Aged 45 to 54	86.1	85.1	–1.0
Aged 55 to 59	78.0	77.8	–0.2
Aged 60 to 64	60.5	64.3	3.8
Aged 65 or older	23.6	27.2	3.6
Women in labor force	**57.7**	**56.0**	**–1.7**
Aged 16 to 19	34.6	26.7	–7.9
Aged 20 to 24	67.4	64.7	–2.7
Aged 25 to 34	74.1	73.4	–0.7
Aged 35 to 44	74.8	73.3	–1.5
Aged 45 to 54	74.7	74.9	0.2
Aged 55 to 59	67.3	73.3	6.0
Aged 60 to 64	50.4	55.6	5.2
Aged 65 or older	14.4	19.5	5.1

Source: Bureau of Labor Statistics, Labor Force Projections to 2022: The Labor Force Participation Rate Continues to Fall, Monthly Labor Review, December 2013, Internet site http://www.bls.gov/opub/mlr/2013/article/labor-force-projections-to-2022-the-labor-force-participation-rate-continues-to-fall.htm; calculations by New Strategist

CHAPTER

7

Living Arrangements

■ The Millennial generation accounted for 25 percent of the nation's 122 million households in 2013. (Millennials were aged 19 to 36 in that year.)

■ Regardless of race or Hispanic origin, married couples head fewer than half of Millennial households.

■ Only 46 percent of households headed by Millennials include children under age 18. The figure varies from just 31 percent of households headed by Asians to 59 percent of those headed by Hispanics.

■ The Millennial generation accounts for the majority of households with children under age 12 (51 percent), preschoolers (67 percent), and infants (80 percent).

■ Among Millennials, a substantial 29 percent of men and 23 percent of women still live with their parents.

■ The majority of Millennials have not yet married. But counting cohabitation, most Millennials aged 25 or older are in some sort of union.

Millennial Generation Heads One in Four Households

Millennials are a smaller share of married-couple households, however.

The Millennial generation heads 25 percent of the nation's 122 million households. (Millennials were aged 19 to 36 in 2013.) Young adults have been slow to establish their own households because high unemployment, low wages, and outstanding student loans are forcing many to live with their parents and postpone marriage and childbearing.

Households headed by Millennials are diverse. Married couples account for the 39 percent plurality of their households, but this figure ranges from a low of 15 percent among the youngest in their early twenties to a high of 55 percent among the oldest in their late thirties. Twenty-one percent of Millennial households are people who live alone, while another 18 percent are female-headed families. Fourteen percent of Millennial householders live with people to whom they are not related. The Millennial generation accounts for the 52 percent majority of this household type.

■ The diversity of Millennial living arrangements makes it difficult for marketers, politicians, and community organizations to reach them.

Married couples become the majority of households in the 35-to-39 age group

(percent of households headed by married couples, by age of householder, 2013)

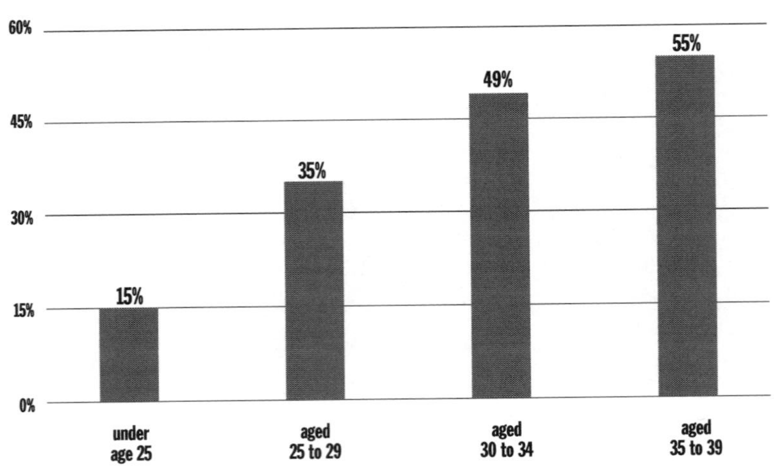

Table 7.1 Households by Generation and Household Type, 2013

(number and percent distribution of households by household type and generation, 2013; numbers in thousands)

	total	Millennials (under age 37)	Generation Xers (aged 37 to 48)	Baby Boomers (aged 49 to 67)	Older Americans (aged 68 or older)
Total households	**122,459**	**30,378**	**26,514**	**43,003**	**22,565**
Married couples	59,204	11,755	14,879	23,036	9,533
Female-headed family, no spouse present	15,469	5,485	4,179	4,152	1,653
Male-headed family, no spouse present	6,229	2,588	1,506	1,626	510
Living alone	33,570	6,430	4,675	12,158	10,305
Living with nonrelatives	7,987	4,121	1,273	2,032	564
PERCENT DISTRIBUTION BY HOUSEHOLD TYPE					
Total households	**100.0%**	**100.0%**	**100.0%**	**100.0%**	**100.0%**
Married couples	48.3	38.7	56.1	53.6	42.2
Female-headed family, no spouse present	12.6	18.1	15.8	9.7	7.3
Male-headed family, no spouse present	5.1	8.5	5.7	3.8	2.3
Living alone	27.4	21.2	17.6	28.3	45.7
Living with nonrelatives	6.5	13.6	4.8	4.7	2.5
PERCENT DISTRIBUTION BY AGE OF HOUSEHOLDER					
Total households	**100.0**	**24.8**	**21.7**	**35.1**	**18.4**
Married couples	100.0	19.9	25.1	38.9	16.1
Female-headed family, no spouse present	100.0	35.5	27.0	26.8	10.7
Male-headed family, no spouse present	100.0	41.5	24.2	26.1	8.2
Living alone	100.0	19.2	13.9	36.2	30.7
Living with nonrelatives	100.0	51.6	15.9	25.4	7.1

Source: Bureau of the Census, 2013 Current Population Survey, Internet site http://www.census.gov/hhes/www/cpstables/032013/hhinc/toc.html; calculations by New Strategist

Table 7.2 Millennial Households by Age and Household Type, 2013

(number and percent distribution of total households, households headed by people under age 37, and households in age groups that include Millennials, by household type, 2013; numbers in thousands)

		family households				
	total	married couple	female-headed	male-headed	living alone	living with nonrelatives
Total households	**122,459**	**59,204**	**15,469**	**6,229**	**33,570**	**7,987**
Millennials (under age 37)	**30,378**	**11,755**	**5,485**	**2,588**	**6,430**	**4,121**
Under age 25	6,314	970	1,394	921	1,548	1,482
Aged 25 to 29	9,251	3,235	1,640	736	2,098	1,541
Aged 30 to 34	10,767	5,316	1,733	680	2,152	886
Aged 35 to 39	10,116	5,588	1,795	627	1,587	519
PERCENT DISTRIBUTION BY HOUSEHOLD TYPE						
Total households	**100.0%**	**48.3%**	**12.6%**	**5.1%**	**27.4%**	**6.5%**
Millennials (under age 37)	**100.0**	**38.7**	**18.1**	**8.5**	**21.2**	**13.6**
Under age 25	100.0	15.4	22.1	14.6	24.5	23.5
Aged 25 to 29	100.0	35.0	17.7	8.0	22.7	16.7
Aged 30 to 34	100.0	49.4	16.1	6.3	20.0	8.2
Aged 35 to 39	100.0	55.2	17.7	6.2	15.7	5.1

Source: Bureau of the Census, 2013 Current Population Survey, Internet site http://www.census.gov/hhes/www/cpstables/032013/hhinc/toc.html; calculations by New Strategist

Millennial Households Differ by Race and Hispanic Origin

A large share of the nation's Millennial households are headed by Hispanics.

Non-Hispanic Whites account for the 58 percent majority of Millennial households (the generation was aged 19 to 36 in 2013). Hispanics head a substantial 19 percent of Millennial households, and the figure climbs as high as 31 percent among male-headed families. Blacks head 16 percent of Millennial households, the figure peaking at 34 percent among female-headed families. Asians head only 6 percent of Millennial households.

The largest share of Asian, Hispanic, and non-Hispanic White Millennial households are headed by married couples (41 to 43 percent). Among Black Millennials, female-headed families account for the 37 percent plurality of households and married couples for only 18 percent. Many Asian, Black, and non-Hispanic White Millennial households are people who live alone, ranging from 22 to 26 percent of the total. Only 12 percent of Hispanic Millennial households are people who live alone.

■ Young adults have different wants and needs depending on their living arrangements.

People who live alone head many Millennial households

(percent of Millennial households headed by people who live alone, by race and Hispanic origin, 2013)

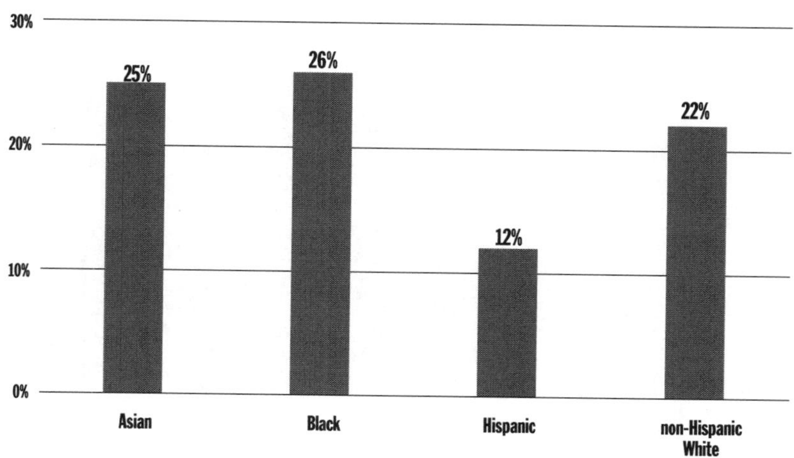

Table 7.3 Households Headed by Millennials by Household Type, Race, and Hispanic Origin, 2013

(number and percent distribution of households headed by people under age 37, by household type, race, and Hispanic origin, 2013; numbers in thousands)

	total	Asian	Black	Hispanic	non-Hispanic White
Total Millennial households	**30,378**	**1,943**	**5,003**	**5,775**	**17,606**
Married couples	11,755	809	913	2,394	7,610
Female-headed family, no spouse present	5,485	192	1,842	1,385	2,093
Male-headed family, no spouse present	2,588	175	504	798	1,137
Living alone	6,430	485	1,304	665	3,945
Living with nonrelatives	4,121	282	440	532	2,822
PERCENT DISTRIBUTION BY RACE AND HISPANIC ORIGIN					
Total Millennial households	**100.0%**	**6.4%**	**16.5%**	**19.0%**	**58.0%**
Married couples	100.0	6.9	7.8	20.4	64.7
Female-headed family, no spouse present	100.0	3.5	33.6	25.3	38.2
Male-headed family, no spouse present	100.0	6.8	19.5	30.8	43.9
Living alone	100.0	7.5	20.3	10.3	61.3
Living with nonrelatives	100.0	6.8	10.7	12.9	68.5

Note: Numbers do not add to total because Asians and Blacks are those who identify themselves as being of the race alone and those who identify themselves as being of the race in combination with other races. Hispanics may be of any race. Non-Hispanic Whites are those who identify themselves as being White alone and not Hispanic.
Source: Bureau of the Census, 2013 Current Population Survey, Internet site http://www.census.gov/hhes/www/cpstables/032013/hhinc/toc.html; calculations by New Strategist

Table 7.4 Asian Households by Generation and Age Group, 2013

(number and percent distribution of total Asian households, households headed by Asians under age 37, and Asian households in age groups that include Millennials, by household type, 2013; numbers in thousands)

		family households				
	total	married couple	female-headed	male-headed	living alone	living with nonrelatives
Total Asian households	**5,872**	**3,409**	**565**	**346**	**1,149**	**403**
Millennials (under age 37)	**1,943**	**809**	**192**	**175**	**485**	**282**
Under age 25	363	27	62	61	115	97
Aged 25 to 29	594	203	62	50	168	110
Aged 30 to 34	694	381	43	51	162	58
Aged 35 to 39	731	496	61	33	101	41
PERCENT DISTRIBUTION BY HOUSEHOLD TYPE						
Total Asian households	**100.0%**	**58.1%**	**9.6%**	**5.9%**	**19.6%**	**6.9%**
Millennials (under age 37)	**100.0**	**41.6**	**9.9**	**9.0**	**25.0**	**14.5**
Under age 25	100.0	7.5	17.1	16.8	31.7	26.8
Aged 25 to 29	100.0	34.3	10.5	8.4	28.3	18.5
Aged 30 to 34	100.0	54.8	6.3	7.3	23.3	8.3
Aged 35 to 39	100.0	67.8	8.4	4.5	13.8	5.5

Note: Asians are those who identify themselves as being of the race alone and those who identify themselves as being of the race in combination with other races.
Source: Bureau of the Census, 2013 Current Population Survey, Internet site http://www.census.gov/hhes/www/cpstables/032013/hhinc/toc.html; calculations by New Strategist

Table 7.5 Black Households by Generation and Age Group, 2013

(number and percent distribution of total Black households, households headed by Blacks under age 37, and Black households in age groups that include Millennials, by household type, 2013; numbers in thousands)

		family households				
	total	married couple	female-headed	male-headed	living alone	living with nonrelatives
Total Black households	**16,559**	**4,700**	**4,473**	**1,105**	**5,412**	**869**
Millennials (under age 37)	**5,003**	**913**	**1,842**	**504**	**1,304**	**440**
Under age 25	1,217	68	445	176	343	185
Aged 25 to 29	1,500	245	540	145	421	149
Aged 30 to 34	1,663	417	613	135	414	84
Aged 35 to 39	1,559	458	611	121	314	55
PERCENT DISTRIBUTION BY HOUSEHOLD TYPE						
Total Black households	**100.0%**	**28.4%**	**27.0%**	**6.7%**	**32.7%**	**5.2%**
Millennials (under age 37)	**100.0**	**18.3**	**36.8**	**10.1**	**26.1**	**8.8**
Under age 25	100.0	5.6	36.6	14.4	28.2	15.2
Aged 25 to 29	100.0	16.4	36.0	9.7	28.1	9.9
Aged 30 to 34	100.0	25.1	36.9	8.1	24.9	5.1
Aged 35 to 39	100.0	29.4	39.2	7.7	20.1	3.6

Note: Blacks are those who identify themselves as being of the race alone and those who identify themselves as being of the race in combination with other races.
Source: Bureau of the Census, 2013 Current Population Survey, Internet site http://www.census.gov/hhes/www/cpstables/032013/hhinc/toc.html; calculations by New Strategist

Table 7.6 Hispanic Households by Generation and Age Group, 2013

(number and percent distribution of total Hispanic households, households headed by Hispanics under age 37, and Hispanic households in age groups that include Millennials, by household type, 2013; numbers in thousands)

		family households				
	total	married couple	female-headed	male-headed	living alone	living with nonrelatives
Total Hispanic households	**15,589**	**7,455**	**3,106**	**1,391**	**2,711**	**926**
Millennials (under age 37)	**5,775**	**2,394**	**1,385**	**798**	**665**	**532**
Under age 25	1,363	310	384	335	146	188
Aged 25 to 29	1,657	657	405	194	219	182
Aged 30 to 34	1,985	1,020	415	210	223	117
Aged 35 to 39	1,925	1,017	452	147	195	113
PERCENT DISTRIBUTION BY HOUSEHOLD TYPE						
Total Hispanic households	**100.0%**	**47.8%**	**19.9%**	**8.9%**	**17.4%**	**5.9%**
Millennials (under age 37)	**100.0**	**41.5**	**24.0**	**13.8**	**11.5**	**9.2**
Under age 25	100.0	22.7	28.2	24.6	10.7	13.8
Aged 25 to 29	100.0	39.7	24.4	11.7	13.2	11.0
Aged 30 to 34	100.0	51.4	20.9	10.6	11.2	5.9
Aged 35 to 39	100.0	52.8	23.5	7.6	10.2	5.9

Source: Bureau of the Census, 2013 Current Population Survey, Internet site http://www.census.gov/hhes/www/cpstables/032013/hhinc/toc.html; calculations by New Strategist

Table 7.7 Non-Hispanic White Households by Generation and Age Group, 2013

(number and percent distribution of total non-Hispanic White households, households headed by non-Hispanic Whites under age 37, and non-Hispanic White households in age groups that include Millennials, by household type, 2013; numbers in thousands)

		family households				
	total	married couple	female-headed	male-headed	living alone	living with nonrelatives
Total non-Hispanic White households	**83,792**	**43,299**	**7,317**	**3,388**	**24,085**	**5,702**
Millennials (under age 37)	**17,606**	**7,610**	**2,093**	**1,137**	**3,945**	**2,822**
Under age 25	3,346	550	513	357	933	994
Aged 25 to 29	5,488	2,115	632	352	1,295	1,094
Aged 30 to 34	6,400	3,501	667	294	1,328	610
Aged 35 to 39	5,928	3,610	700	333	972	313
PERCENT DISTRIBUTION BY HOUSEHOLD TYPE						
Total non-Hispanic White households	**100.0%**	**51.7%**	**8.7%**	**4.0%**	**28.7%**	**6.8%**
Millennials (under age 37)	**100.0**	**43.2**	**11.9**	**6.5**	**22.4**	**16.0**
Under age 25	100.0	16.4	15.3	10.7	27.9	29.7
Aged 25 to 29	100.0	38.5	11.5	6.4	23.6	19.9
Aged 30 to 34	100.0	54.7	10.4	4.6	20.8	9.5
Aged 35 to 39	100.0	60.9	11.8	5.6	16.4	5.3

Note: Non-Hispanic Whites are those who identify themselves as being White alone and not Hispanic.
Source: Bureau of the Census, 2013 Current Population Survey, Internet site http://www.census.gov/hhes/www/cpstables/032013/hhinc/toc.html; calculations by New Strategist

Households of Young Adults Vary in Size

Household size rises well above three in the 35-to-39 age group.

Households headed by younger adults (the Millennial generation was aged 19 to 36 in 2013) vary in size. At one extreme are the 3.05 people who live in households headed by the youngest adults (under age 20). At the other extreme are the 2.41 people in households headed by 20-to-24-year-olds.

Overall, household size grows as householders age through their thirties. It peaks among householders aged 35 to 39—at 3.39 people—because this age group is most likely to be raising children. As householders age into their forties and fifties, the nest empties and household size shrinks.

■ As Millennials marry and have children, the nest will become increasingly crowded.

Among householders in their twenties, average household size is less than three

(average household size by selected age of householder, 2013)

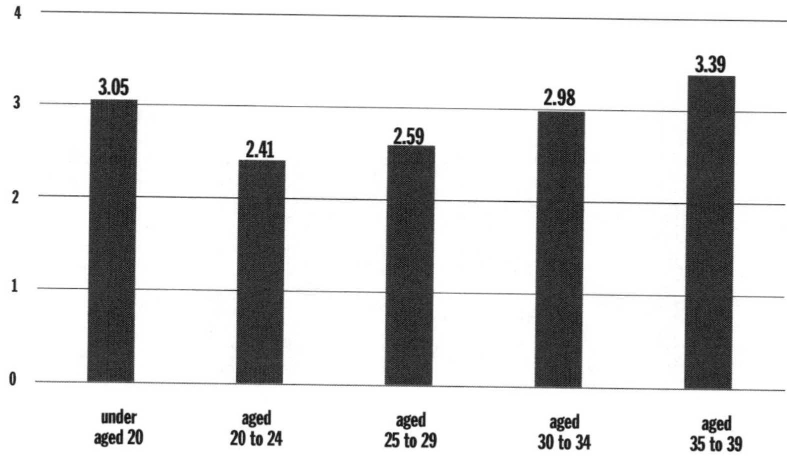

Table 7.8 Average Size of Household by Age of Householder, 2013

(number of households, average number of people per household, and average number of people under age 18 per household, by age of householder, 2013; number of households in thousands)

	number	average number of people	average number of people under age 18
Total households	**122,459**	**2.54**	**0.61**
Under age 20	740	3.05	0.90
Aged 20 to 24	5,574	2.41	0.48
Aged 25 to 29	9,251	2.59	0.76
Aged 30 to 34	10,767	2.98	1.17
Aged 35 to 39	10,116	3.39	1.50
Aged 40 to 44	11,218	3.32	1.29
Aged 45 to 49	11,533	3.01	0.85
Aged 50 to 54	12,535	2.66	0.45
Aged 55 to 59	12,217	2.30	0.23
Aged 60 to 64	10,585	2.06	0.14
Aged 65 to 74	15,349	1.91	0.09
Aged 75 or older	12,575	1.61	0.04

Source: Bureau of the Census, America's Families and Living Arrangements: 2013, Internet site http://www.census.gov/hhes/families/data/cps2013.html; calculations by New Strategist

Fewer than Half of Millennial Households Include Children

Most Hispanic Millennials are raising children, however.

Forty-six percent of households headed by Millennials (aged 19 to 36 in 2013) include children under age 18. Among householders under age 25, only 26 percent are raising children. The figure rises above 50 percent in the 30-to-34 age group and peaks at 67 percent among householders aged 35 to 39.

The percentage of households with children under age 18 varies greatly by race and Hispanic origin. Fifty-nine percent of Millennial households headed by Hispanics include children under age 18, as do 50 percent of those headed by Blacks. This compares with a smaller 43 percent of non-Hispanic White and 31 percent of Asian Millennial households.

■ The lifestyles of young adults are diverse, ranging from students with class schedules to parents with family and work schedules.

Asian Millennials are least likely to have children under age 18 at home

(percent of households headed by people under age 37 with children under age 18, by race and Hispanic origin, 2013)

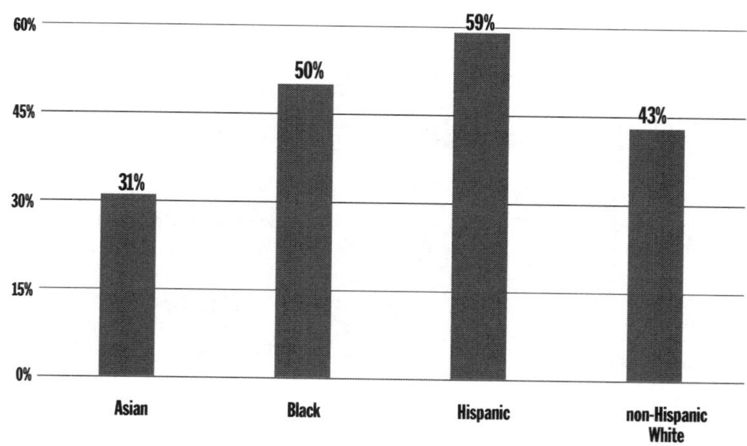

Table 7.9 Households by Generation, Age of Householder, and Presence of Children, 2013

(total number of households and number and percent with own children under age 18 or children of any age at home, by generation and age of householder, 2013; numbers in thousands)

		with own children under age 18		with own children, any age	
	total	number	percent	number	percent
Total households	**122,459**	**35,058**	**28.6%**	**48,105**	**39.3%**
Millennials (under age 37)	30,378	14,013	46.1	14,190	46.7
Generation Xers (aged 37 to 48)	26,514	15,158	57.2	17,312	65.3
Baby Boomers (aged 49 to 67)	42,249	5,645	13.4	13,691	32.4
Older Americans (aged 68 or older)	23,319	242	1.0	2,912	12.5
Total households	**122,459**	**35,058**	**28.6**	**48,105**	**39.3**
Under age 25	6,314	1,629	25.8	1,642	26.0
Aged 25 to 29	9,251	3,734	40.4	3,776	40.8
Aged 30 to 34	10,767	5,953	55.3	6,012	55.8
Aged 35 to 39	10,116	6,743	66.7	6,900	68.2
Aged 40 to 44	11,218	6,911	61.6	7,624	68.0
Aged 45 to 49	11,533	5,252	45.5	6,935	60.1
Aged 50 to 54	12,535	2,955	23.6	5,645	45.0
Aged 55 to 64	22,802	1,576	6.9	6,035	26.5
Aged 65 to 74	15,349	211	1.4	2,079	13.5
Aged 75 or older	12,575	94	0.7	1,457	11.6

Source: Bureau of the Census, America's Families and Living Arrangements: 2013, Internet site http://www.census.gov/hhes/families/data/cps2013.html; calculations by New Strategist

Table 7.10 Millennial Households with Children under Age 18 by Race and Hispanic Origin of Householder, 2013

(total number of households headed by people under age 37 and number and percent with own children under age 18, by race and Hispanic origin of householder, 2013; numbers in thousands)

		with own children under age 18	
	total	number	percent
Millennial households	**30,378**	**14,013**	**46.1%**
Asians	1,943	595	30.6
Blacks	5,003	2,523	50.4
Hispanics	5,775	3,386	58.6
Non-Hispanic Whites	17,606	7,512	42.7

Note: Numbers do not add to total because Asians and Blacks are those who identify themselves as being of the race alone and those who identify themselves as being of the race in combination with other races. Hispanics may be of any race. Non-Hispanic Whites are those who identify themselves as being White alone and not Hispanic.
Source: Bureau of the Census, America's Families and Living Arrangements: 2013, Internet site http://www.census.gov/hhes/families/data/cps2013.html; calculations by New Strategist

Table 7.11 Asian Households by Generation, Age of Householder, and Presence of Children, 2013

(total number of Asian households and number and percent with own children under age 18 or children of any age at home, by generation and age of householder, 2013; numbers in thousands)

		with own children under age 18		with own children, any age	
	total	number	percent	number	percent
Total Asian households	**5,872**	**2,076**	**35.4%**	**2,808**	**47.8%**
Millennials (under age 37)	1,943	595	30.6	604	31.1
Generation Xers (aged 37 to 48)	1,620	1,079	66.6	1,164	71.9
Baby Boomers (aged 49 to 67)	1,645	392	23.8	889	54.0
Older Americans (aged 68 or older)	662	11	1.7	152	23.0
Total Asian households	**5,872**	**2,076**	**35.4**	**2,808**	**47.8**
Under age 25	363	20	5.5	20	5.5
Aged 25 to 29	594	110	18.5	112	18.9
Aged 30 to 34	694	277	39.9	281	40.5
Aged 35 to 39	731	471	64.4	477	65.3
Aged 40 to 44	708	509	71.9	530	74.9
Aged 45 to 49	592	359	60.6	435	73.5
Aged 50 to 54	541	227	42.0	358	66.2
Aged 55 to 64	839	92	11.0	404	48.2
Aged 65 to 74	488	3	0.6	133	27.3
Aged 75 or older	320	9	2.8	59	18.4

Note: Asians are those who identify themselves as being of the race alone and those who identify themselves as being of the race in combination with other races.
Source: Bureau of the Census, America's Families and Living Arrangements: 2013, Internet site http://www.census.gov/hhes/families/data/cps2013.html; calculations by New Strategist

Table 7.12 Black Households by Generation, Age of Householder, and Presence of Children, 2013

(total number of Black households and number and percent with own children under age 18 or children of any age at home, by generation and age of householder, 2013; numbers in thousands)

		with own children under age 18		with own children, any age	
	total	number	percent	number	percent
Total Black households	**16,559**	**5,256**	**31.7%**	**7,269**	**43.9%**
Millennials (under age 37)	5,003	2,523	50.4	2,561	51.2
Generation Xers (aged 37 to 48)	3,949	2,009	50.9	2,441	61.8
Baby Boomers (aged 49 to 67)	5,365	680	12.7	1,814	33.8
Older Americans (aged 68 or older)	2,242	46	2.0	453	20.2
Total Black households	**16,559**	**5,256**	**31.7**	**7,269**	**43.9**
Under age 25	1,217	398	32.7	400	32.9
Aged 25 to 29	1,500	729	48.6	738	49.2
Aged 30 to 34	1,663	982	59.1	997	60.0
Aged 35 to 39	1,559	1,036	66.5	1,065	68.3
Aged 40 to 44	1,654	906	54.8	1,080	65.3
Aged 45 to 49	1,701	602	35.4	902	53.0
Aged 50 to 54	1,705	349	20.5	718	42.1
Aged 55 to 64	2,825	199	7.0	810	28.7
Aged 65 to 74	1,650	38	2.3	352	21.3
Aged 75 or older	1,087	19	1.7	207	19.0

Note: Blacks are those who identify themselves as being of the race alone and those who identify themselves as being of the race in combination with other races.
Source: Bureau of the Census, America's Families and Living Arrangements: 2013, Internet site http://www.census.gov/hhes/families/data/cps2013.html; calculations by New Strategist

Table 7.13 Hispanic Households by Generation, Age of Householder, and Presence of Children, 2013

(total number of Hispanic households and number and percent with own children under age 18 or children of any age at home, by generation and age of householder, 2013; numbers in thousands)

		with own children under age 18		with own children, any age	
	total	number	percent	number	percent
Total Hispanic households	**15,589**	**6,953**	**44.6%**	**8,760**	**56.2%**
Millennials (under age 37)	5,775	3,386	58.6	3,421	59.2
Generation Xers (aged 37 to 48)	4,253	2,699	63.4	3,083	72.5
Baby Boomers (aged 49 to 67)	4,096	833	20.3	1,942	47.4
Older Americans (aged 68 or older)	1,465	34	2.3	314	21.4
Total Hispanic households	**15,589**	**6,953**	**44.6**	**8,760**	**56.2**
Under age 25	1,363	542	39.8	545	40.0
Aged 25 to 29	1,657	912	55.1	925	55.8
Aged 30 to 34	1,985	1,376	69.3	1,383	69.7
Aged 35 to 39	1,925	1,391	72.3	1,419	73.7
Aged 40 to 44	1,836	1,228	66.9	1,375	74.9
Aged 45 to 49	1,578	795	50.4	1,071	67.9
Aged 50 to 54	1,401	428	30.6	841	60.0
Aged 55 to 64	2,057	236	11.5	811	39.4
Aged 65 to 74	1,075	32	3.0	254	23.6
Aged 75 or older	712	12	1.7	136	19.1

Source: Bureau of the Census, America's Families and Living Arrangements: 2013, Internet site http://www.census.gov/hhes/families/data/cps2013.html; calculations by New Strategist

Table 7.14 Non-Hispanic White Households by Generation, Age of Householder, and Presence of Children, 2013

(total number of non-Hispanic White households and number and percent with own children under age 18 or children of any age at home, by generation and age of householder, 2013; numbers in thousands)

		with own children under age 18		with own children, any age	
	total	number	percent	number	percent
Total non-Hispanic White households	**83,792**	**20,730**	**24.7%**	**29,107**	**34.7%**
Millennials (under age 37)	17,606	7,512	42.7	7,606	43.2
Generation Xers (aged 37 to 48)	16,680	9,380	56.2	10,622	63.7
Baby Boomers (aged 49 to 67)	30,712	3,687	12.0	8,915	29.0
Older Americans (aged 68 or older)	18,794	150	0.8	1,964	10.4
Total non-Hispanic White households	**83,792**	**20,730**	**24.7**	**29,107**	**34.7**
Under age 25	3,346	670	20.0	677	20.2
Aged 25 to 29	5,488	1,960	35.7	1,979	36.1
Aged 30 to 34	6,400	3,332	52.1	3,364	52.6
Aged 35 to 39	5,928	3,876	65.4	3,966	66.9
Aged 40 to 44	7,015	4,261	60.7	4,637	66.1
Aged 45 to 49	7,635	3,492	45.7	4,507	59.0
Aged 50 to 54	8,702	1,909	21.9	3,662	42.1
Aged 55 to 64	16,882	1,038	6.1	3,954	23.4
Aged 65 to 74	12,001	139	1.2	1,324	11.0
Aged 75 or older	10,393	53	0.5	1,037	10.0

Note: Non-Hispanic Whites are those who identify themselves as being White alone and not Hispanic.
Source: Bureau of the Census, America's Families and Living Arrangements: 2013, Internet site http://www.census.gov/hhes/families/data/cps2013.html; calculations by New Strategist

One-Third of Millennial Households Include Preschoolers

Millennials head the majority of households with infants and preschoolers.

Most young adults go to college after high school, postponing marriage and family formation until their late twenties or early thirties. Consequently, the proportion of households headed by young adults that include children under age 18 rises from a low of 26 percent among householders under age 25 to the 67 percent majority among householders aged 35 to 39.

While 12 percent of all households include children under age 6, the proportion is a much larger 33 percent among Millennials. Similarly, while only 2 percent of all households include infants under age 1, the figure is 7 percent among Millennials. The Millennial generation now heads the majority of households with preschoolers (67 percent) and infants (80 percent).

■ While most young adults postpone childbearing, others establish independent households because they have children.

Millennials are the majority of parents with preschoolers

(percent of households with children that are headed by people under age 37, by age of child, 2013)

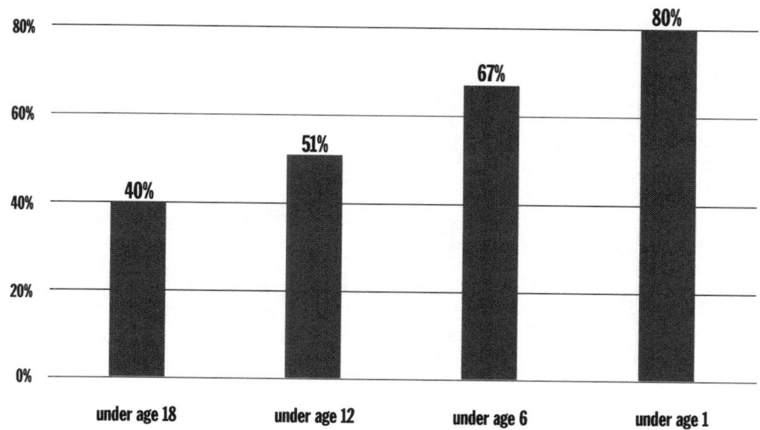

Table 7.15 Millennial Households by Presence and Age of Children, 2013

(number and percent distribution of total households, households headed by people under age 37, and in age groups that include Millennials, by presence and age of own children at home, by age of children, 2013; numbers in thousands)

	total	Millennials (under age 37)	under 25	25 to 29	30 to 34	35 to 39
Total households	**122,459**	**30,378**	**6,314**	**9,251**	**10,767**	**10,116**
With children of any age	**48,105**	**14,190**	**1,642**	**3,776**	**6,012**	**6,900**
Under age 25	41,660	14,133	1,638	3,753	5,986	6,890
Under age 18	35,058	14,013	1,629	3,734	5,953	6,743
Under age 12	25,623	13,171	1,611	3,676	5,633	5,628
Under age 6	15,046	10,026	1,540	3,114	4,038	3,334
Under age 1	2,743	2,192	421	754	833	460
Aged 12 to 17	16,708	3,061	35	236	1,567	3,058
PERCENT DISTRIBUTION BY AGE OF CHILD						
Total households	**100.0%**	**100.0%**	**100.0%**	**100.0%**	**100.0%**	**100.0%**
With children of any age	**39.3**	**46.7**	**26.0**	**40.8**	**55.8**	**68.2**
Under age 25	34.0	46.5	25.9	40.6	55.6	68.1
Under age 18	28.6	46.1	25.8	40.4	55.3	66.7
Under age 12	20.9	43.4	25.5	39.7	52.3	55.6
Under age 6	12.3	33.0	24.4	33.7	37.5	33.0
Under age 1	2.2	7.2	6.7	8.2	7.7	4.5
Aged 12 to 17	13.6	10.1	0.6	2.6	14.6	30.2
PERCENT DISTRIBUTION BY AGE OF HOUSEHOLDER						
Total households	**100.0**	**24.8**	**5.2**	**7.6**	**8.8**	**8.3**
With children of any age	**100.0**	**29.5**	**3.4**	**7.8**	**12.5**	**14.3**
Under age 25	100.0	33.9	3.9	9.0	14.4	16.5
Under age 18	100.0	40.0	4.6	10.7	17.0	19.2
Under age 12	100.0	51.4	6.3	14.3	22.0	22.0
Under age 6	100.0	66.6	10.2	20.7	26.8	22.2
Under age 1	100.0	79.9	15.3	27.5	30.4	16.8
Aged 12 to 17	100.0	18.3	0.2	1.4	9.4	18.3

Source: Bureau of the Census, America's Families and Living Arrangements: 2013, Internet site http://www.census.gov/hhes/families/data/cps2013.html; calculations by New Strategist

Table 7.16 Millennial Households by Number of Children under Age 18, 2013

(number and percent distribution of total households, households headed by people under age 37, and in age groups that include Millennials, by number of own children under age 18 at home, 2013; numbers in thousands)

	total	Millennials (under age 37)	under 25	25 to 29	30 to 34	35 to 39
Total households	**122,459**	**30,378**	**6,314**	**9,251**	**10,767**	**10,116**
With children under age 18	**35,058**	**14,013**	**1,629**	**3,734**	**5,953**	**6,743**
One child	14,784	5,453	1,027	1,649	1,993	1,959
Two children	13,187	5,321	470	1,390	2,304	2,893
Three children	5,086	2,253	84	507	1,123	1,348
Four or more children	2,001	985	48	187	533	542
PERCENT DISTRIBUTION BY NUMBER OF CHILDREN						
Total households	**100.0%**	**100.0%**	**100.0%**	**100.0%**	**100.0%**	**100.0%**
With children under age 18	**28.6**	**46.1**	**25.8**	**40.4**	**55.3**	**66.7**
One child	12.1	17.9	16.3	17.8	18.5	19.4
Two children	10.8	17.5	7.4	15.0	21.4	28.6
Three children	4.2	7.4	1.3	5.5	10.4	13.3
Four or more children	1.6	3.2	0.8	2.0	5.0	5.4
PERCENT DISTRIBUTION BY AGE OF HOUSEHOLDER						
Total households	**100.0**	**24.8**	**5.2**	**7.6**	**8.8**	**8.3**
With children under age 18	**100.0**	**40.0**	**4.6**	**10.7**	**17.0**	**19.2**
One child	100.0	36.9	6.9	11.2	13.5	13.3
Two children	100.0	40.4	3.6	10.5	17.5	21.9
Three children	100.0	44.3	1.7	10.0	22.1	26.5
Four or more children	100.0	49.2	2.4	9.3	26.6	27.1

Source: Bureau of the Census, America's Families and Living Arrangements: 2013, Internet site http://www.census.gov/hhes/families/data/cps2013.html; calculations by New Strategist

Many Millennials Still Live with Their Parents

Few live by themselves.

Among Millennials (aged 19 to 36 in 2013), a substantial 26 percent live with their parents. These figures include college students in dormitories because they are considered dependents. Not surprisingly, the proportion of young adults who live with their parents falls with age from 77 percent among 18-to-19-year-olds to a still substantial 19 percent among 25-to-29-year-olds. Fewer than 10 percent of Millennials in their thirties still live with mom and dad.

Few younger adults live by themselves. In 2013, only 8 percent of Millennials lived alone. The figure exceeds 10 percent among 30-to-34-year-olds, however. Because Millennials have been slow to form independent households, those who live by themselves account for a substantial share (21 percent) of total Millennial households.

■ With more young adults going to college and job hunting in the midst of the struggling economy, the dependency of childhood has stretched well into the twenties.

Many young adults live with their parents

(percent of people aged 18 to 39 who live with their parents, by age, 2013)

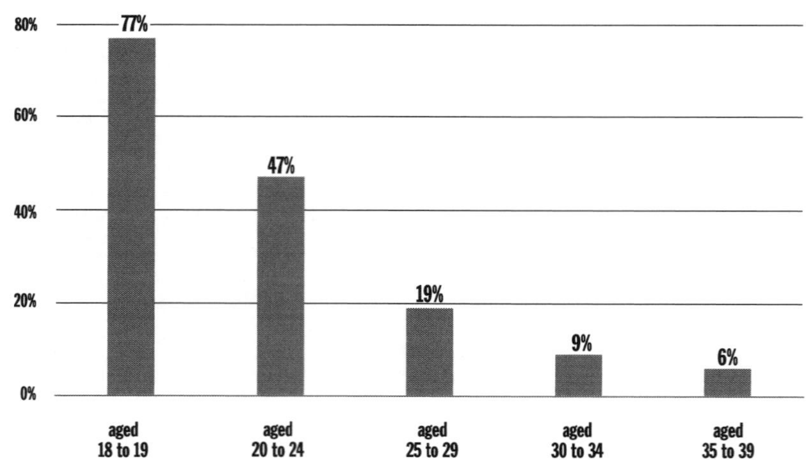

Table 7.17 Millennials Who Live with Their Parents, 2013

(number and percent of people aged 15 or older, people aged 19 to 36 and in age groups that include Millenials, who are children of the householder, 2013; numbers in thousands)

		child of householder	
	total	number	percent
Total aged 15 or older	**249,893**	**38,229**	**15.3%**
Millennials (19 to 36)	**75,520**	**19,839**	**26.3**
Aged 18 to 19	7,869	6,084	77.3
Aged 20 to 24	22,135	10,514	47.5
Aged 25 to 29	21,123	3,973	18.8
Aged 30 to 34	20,646	1,840	8.9
Aged 35 to 39	19,204	1,175	6.1

Note: College students who live in dormitories are classified as living with their parents.
Source: Bureau of the Census, America's Families and Living Arrangements: 2013, Internet site http://www.census.gov/hhes/families/data/cps2013.html; calculations by New Strategist

Table 7.18 People Who Live Alone by Generation and Age, 2013

(number of people aged 15 or older and number, percent, and percent distribution of people who live alone by generation and age, 2013; numbers in thousands)

		living alone		
	total	number	percent	percent distribution
Total people	**250,023**	**33,570**	**13.4%**	**100.0%**
Millennials (aged 19 to 36)	75,520	6,375	8.4	19.0
Generation Xers (aged 37 to 48)	49,037	4,676	9.5	13.9
Baby Boomers (aged 49 to 67)	73,752	12,158	16.5	36.2
Older Americans (aged 68 or older)	34,625	10,304	29.8	30.7
Total people	**250,023**	**33,570**	**13.4**	**100.0**
Aged 15 to 24	43,124	1,548	3.6	4.6
Aged 25 to 29	21,138	2,098	9.9	6.3
Aged 30 to 34	20,659	2,152	10.4	6.4
Aged 35 to 39	19,221	1,587	8.3	4.7
Aged 40 to 44	20,657	1,871	9.1	5.6
Aged 45 to 49	21,060	2,317	11.0	6.9
Aged 50 to 54	22,386	2,995	13.4	8.9
Aged 55 to 59	20,880	3,424	16.4	10.2
Aged 60 to 64	17,611	3,491	19.8	10.4
Aged 65 to 69	14,437	2,972	20.6	8.9
Aged 70 to 74	10,264	2,450	23.9	7.3
Aged 75 or older	18,585	6,665	35.9	19.9

Source: Bureau of the Census, 2013 Current Population Survey, Internet site http://www.census.gov/hhes/www/cpstables/032013/hhinc/toc.html; calculations by New Strategist

Living Arrangements Differ by Generation

Only 29 percent of Millennial men are a married-couple householder or spouse.

The living arrangements of generations differ depending on their lifestage. Many Millennials still live with their parents (29 percent of Millennial men and 23 percent of Millennial women). Among Generation Xers and Boomers, most men and women are married-couple householders or spouses. Among Older Americans, a substantial 37 percent of women live alone and only 42 percent are a married-couple householder or spouse.

Women marry at a younger age than men, and they are more likely than men to be widowed and live alone in old age. Among Millennials, women are more likely than men to be a married-couple householder or spouse (35 versus 29 percent). Millennial women are more likely to be married than living with their parents. Millennial men, however, are as likely to be living with their parents as they are to be married.

■ As Millennials age, the great majority will become a married-couple householder or spouse.

Millennial women are more likely than their male counterparts to be a married-couple householder or spouse

(percent of Americans who are married and living with their spouse, by generation and sex, 2013)

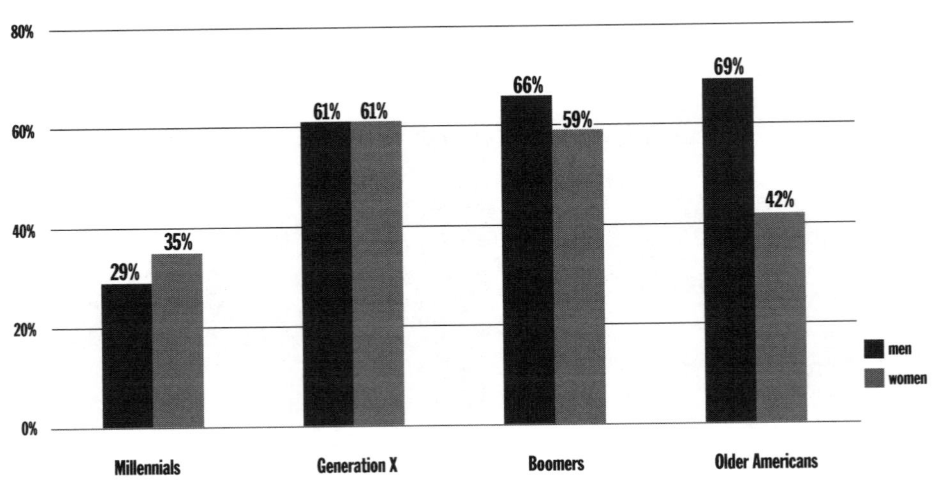

Table 7.19 Men by Living Arrangement and Generation, 2013

(number and percent distribution of men aged 15 or older by living arrangement and generation, 2013; numbers in thousands)

	total	iGeneration (under age 19)	Millennials (aged 19 to 36)	Generation X (aged 37 to 48)	Baby Boom (aged 49 to 67)	Older Americans (68 or older)
Total men	**121,067**	**8,668**	**37,719**	**24,087**	**34,781**	**15,812**
Householder	85,180	221	19,248	19,881	31,030	14,801
Married-couple householder or spouse	59,203	19	10,793	14,733	22,815	10,843
Other family householder	6,231	145	2,442	1,506	1,609	530
Living alone	15,001	25	3,561	2,814	5,509	3,092
Living with nonrelatives	4,745	33	2,451	828	1,096	337
Not a householder	35,885	8,448	18,472	4,204	3,750	1,011
Child of householder	20,834	7,535	11,061	1,452	755	31
Other relative of householder	6,667	696	2,698	1,036	1,522	715
In nonfamily household	8,384	217	4,713	1,716	1,473	265
PERCENT DISTRIBUTION BY LIVING ARRANGEMENT						
Total men	**100.0%**	**100.0%**	**100.0%**	**100.0%**	**100.0%**	**100.0%**
Householder	70.4	2.5	51.0	82.5	89.2	93.6
Married-couple householder or spouse	48.9	0.2	28.6	61.2	65.6	68.6
Other family householder	5.1	1.7	6.5	6.3	4.6	3.4
Living alone	12.4	0.3	9.4	11.7	15.8	19.6
Living with nonrelatives	3.9	0.4	6.5	3.4	3.2	2.1
Not a householder	29.6	97.5	49.0	17.5	10.8	6.4
Child of householder	17.2	86.9	29.3	6.0	2.2	0.2
Other relative of householder	5.5	8.0	7.2	4.3	4.4	4.5
In nonfamily household	6.9	2.5	12.5	7.1	4.2	1.7

Source: Bureau of the Census, America's Families and Living Arrangements: 2013, Internet site http://www.census.gov/hhes/families/data/cps2013.html; calculations by New Strategist

Table 7.20 Women by Living Arrangement and Generation, 2013

(number and percent distribution of women aged 15 or older by living arrangement and generation, 2013; numbers in thousands)

	total	iGeneration (under age 19)	Millennials (aged 19 to 36)	Generation X (aged 37 to 48)	Baby Boom (aged 49 to 67)	Older Americans (68 or older)
Total women	**128,827**	**8,351**	**37,803**	**24,932**	**37,695**	**20,047**
Householder	96,479	269	22,945	21,819	33,732	17,714
Married-couple householder or spouse	59,203	38	13,214	15,333	22,259	8,359
Other family householder	15,469	164	5,320	4,179	4,101	1,704
Living alone	18,566	33	2,812	1,862	6,492	7,369
Living with nonrelatives	3,241	34	1,599	445	880	283
Not a householder	32,339	8,081	14,854	3,111	3,962	2,331
Child of householder	17,394	7,095	8,777	936	554	33
Other relative of householder	7,891	737	1,886	988	2,238	2,043
In nonfamily household	7,054	250	4,191	1,188	1,170	255
PERCENT DISTRIBUTION BY LIVING ARRANGEMENT						
Total women	**100.0%**	**100.0%**	**100.0%**	**100.0%**	**100.0%**	**100.0%**
Householder	74.9	3.2	60.7	87.5	89.5	88.4
Married-couple householder or spouse	46.0	0.5	35.0	61.5	59.1	41.7
Other family householder	12.0	2.0	14.1	16.8	10.9	8.5
Living alone	14.4	0.4	7.4	7.5	17.2	36.8
Living with nonrelatives	2.5	0.4	4.2	1.8	2.3	1.4
Not a householder	25.1	96.8	39.3	12.5	10.5	11.6
Child of householder	13.5	85.0	23.2	3.8	1.5	0.2
Other relative of householder	6.1	8.8	5.0	4.0	5.9	10.2
In nonfamily household	5.5	3.0	11.1	4.8	3.1	1.3

Source: Bureau of the Census, America's Families and Living Arrangements: 2013, Internet site http://www.census.gov/hhes/families/data/cps2013.html; calculations by New Strategist

Few Millennials Are Married

The median age at first marriage is at a record high.

Overall, only 35 percent of Millennials (aged 19 to 36 in 2013) are married. The 58 percent majority of Millennials have not yet married. The generation has postponed marriage longer than any other in part because of the Great Recession and also because of greater college attendance. The median age at first marriage is at a record high of 29.0 years for men and 26.6 years for women.

Although fewer than half of Millennials are married, many are cohabiting. In fact, among Millennials aged 25 to 29, most are either married or cohabiting. Among women in the age group, fully 61 percent are in a union (42 percent are in their first marriage, 2 percent are in their second or higher marriage, and 17 percent are cohabiting). Among men in the age group, the 54 percent majority is in some type of union.

■ Cohabitation is a common living arrangement for Millennials.

For Millennials, relationships are complex

(percent distribution of people aged 25 to 29 by current marital/union status, by sex, 2006–2010)

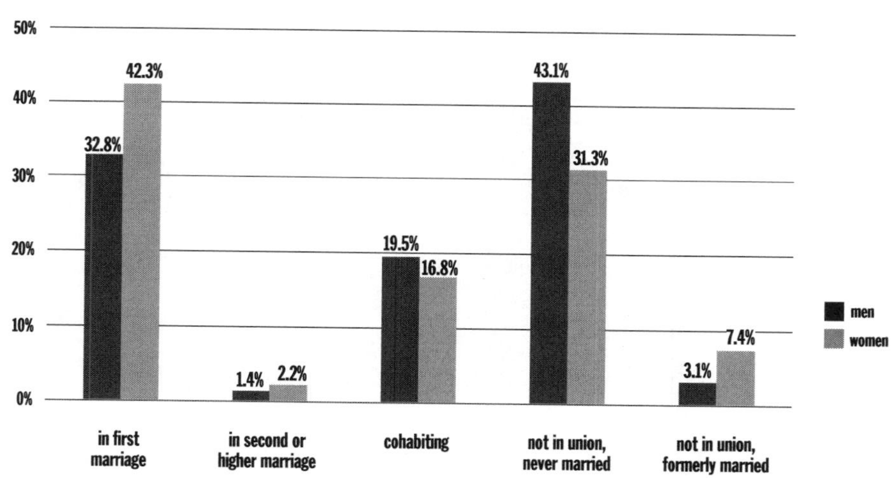

Table 7.21 Median Age at First Marriage by Sex, 1950 to 2013

(median age at first marriage by sex, 1950 to 2013; change in age for selected years)

	men	women
2013	29.0 yrs.	26.6 yrs.
2012	28.6	26.6
2011	28.4	26.4
2010	28.2	26.1
2009	28.1	25.9
2008	27.6	25.9
2007	27.5	25.6
2006	27.5	25.5
2005	27.1	25.3
2004	27.4	25.3
2003	27.1	25.3
2002	26.9	25.3
2001	26.9	25.1
2000	26.8	25.1
1990	26.1	23.9
1980	24.7	22.0
1970	23.2	20.8
1960	22.8	20.3
1950	22.8	20.3
CHANGE IN YEARS		
2000 to 2013	2.2	1.5
1950 to 2013	6.2	6.3

Source: Bureau of the Census, Families and Living Arrangements, Historical Tables—Households, Internet site http://www.census .gov/hhes/families/data/children.html; calculations by New Strategist

Table 7.22 Marital Status by Generation and Age, 2013

(number and percent distribution of people aged 15 or older by current marital status, by generation and age groups that include Gen Xers, 2013; numbers in thousands)

	total	never married	married	separated	divorced	widowed
Total people	**249,893**	**78,499**	**126,055**	**5,600**	**25,388**	**14,349**
Millennials (aged 19 to 36)	75,520	44,172	26,275	1,633	3,214	227
Generation Xers (aged 37 to 48)	49,018	8,657	31,856	1,634	6,365	507
Baby Boomers (aged 49 to 67)	72,476	7,411	47,599	1,851	12,011	3,603
Older Americans (aged 68 or older)	35,859	1,540	20,189	368	3,762	10,002
PERCENT DISTRIBUTION BY MARITAL STATUS AND GENERATION						
Total people	**100.0%**	**31.4%**	**50.4%**	**2.2%**	**10.2%**	**5.7%**
Millennials (under age 37)	100.0	58.5	34.8	2.2	4.3	0.3
Generation Xers (aged 37 to 48)	100.0	17.7	65.0	3.3	13.0	1.0
Baby Boomers (aged 49 to 67)	100.0	10.2	65.7	2.6	16.6	5.0
Older Americans (aged 68 or older)	100.0	4.3	56.3	1.0	10.5	27.9
PERCENT DISTRIBUTION BY MARITAL STATUS AND AGE						
Total people	**100.0**	**31.4**	**50.5**	**2.2**	**10.2**	**5.7**
Millennials (aged 19 to 36)	**100.0**	**58.5**	**34.8**	**2.2**	**4.3**	**0.3**
Aged 18 to 19	100.0	96.6	2.1	0.9	0.4	0.1
Aged 20 to 24	100.0	86.3	11.1	1.4	1.1	0.2
Aged 25 to 29	100.0	58.7	35.3	2.2	3.5	0.3
Aged 30 to 34	100.0	34.3	55.5	2.8	7.1	0.3
Aged 35 to 39	100.0	23.4	62.8	3.3	9.8	0.6

Source: Bureau of the Census, America's Families and Living Arrangements: 2013, Internet site http://www.census.gov/hhes/families/data/cps2013.html; calculations by New Strategist

Table 7.23 Marital Status of Men by Generation and Age, 2013

(number and percent distribution of men aged 15 or older by current marital status, by generation and age groups that include Gen Xers, 2013; numbers in thousands)

	total	never married	married	separated	divorced	widowed
Total men	**121,067**	**41,620**	**62,934**	**2,435**	**10,954**	**3,124**
Millennials (aged 19 to 36)	37,719	23,766	11,846	677	1,371	60
Generation Xers (aged 37 to 48)	24,087	4,742	15,619	707	2,881	136
Baby Boomers (aged 49 to 67)	34,781	3,881	24,034	830	5,228	807
Older Americans (aged 68 or older)	15,812	701	11,387	159	1,454	2,111
PERCENT DISTRIBUTION BY MARITAL STATUS AND GENERATION						
Total men	**100.0%**	**34.4%**	**52.0%**	**2.0%**	**9.0%**	**2.6%**
Millennials (aged 19 to 36)	100.0	63.0	31.4	1.8	3.6	0.2
Generation Xers (aged 37 to 48)	100.0	19.7	64.8	2.9	12.0	0.6
Baby Boomers (aged 49 to 67)	100.0	11.2	69.1	2.4	15.0	2.3
Older Americans (aged 68 or older)	100.0	4.4	72.0	1.0	9.2	13.4
PERCENT DISTRIBUTION BY MARITAL STATUS AND AGE						
Total men	**100.0**	**34.4**	**52.0**	**2.0**	**9.0**	**2.6**
Millennials (aged 19 to 36)	**100.0**	**63.0**	**31.4**	**1.8**	**3.6**	**0.2**
Aged 18 to 19	100.0	97.4	1.6	0.8	0.1	0.1
Aged 20 to 24	100.0	89.5	8.3	1.3	0.8	0.1
Aged 25 to 29	100.0	65.7	29.5	1.8	2.8	0.2
Aged 30 to 34	100.0	38.2	53.1	2.2	6.4	0.1
Aged 35 to 39	100.0	25.9	62.4	2.7	8.7	0.3

Source: Bureau of the Census, America's Families and Living Arrangements: 2013, Internet site http://www.census.gov/hhes/families/data/cps2013.html; calculations by New Strategist

Table 7.24 Marital Status of Women by Generation and Age, 2013

(number and percent distribution of women aged 15 or older by current marital status, by generation and age groups that include Gen Xers, 2013; numbers in thousands)

	total	never married	married	separated	divorced	widowed
Total women	**128,826**	**36,879**	**63,122**	**3,165**	**14,434**	**11,225**
Millennials (aged 19 to 36)	37,803	20,407	14,430	957	1,842	167
Generation Xers (aged 37 to 48)	24,932	3,916	16,238	927	3,482	369
Baby Boomers (aged 49 to 67)	37,695	3,532	23,565	1,021	6,783	2,795
Older Americans (aged 68 or older)	20,047	838	8,802	209	2,307	7,891
PERCENT DISTRIBUTION BY MARITAL STATUS AND GENERATION						
Total women	**100.0%**	**28.6%**	**49.0%**	**2.5%**	**11.2%**	**8.7%**
Millennials (aged 19 to 36)	100.0	54.0	38.2	2.5	4.9	0.4
Generation Xers (aged 37 to 48)	100.0	15.7	65.1	3.7	14.0	1.5
Baby Boomers (aged 49 to 67)	100.0	9.4	62.5	2.7	18.0	7.4
Older Americans (aged 68 or older)	100.0	4.2	43.9	1.0	11.5	39.4
PERCENT DISTRIBUTION BY MARITAL STATUS AND AGE						
Total women	**100.0**	**28.6**	**49.0**	**2.5**	**11.2**	**8.7**
Millennials (aged 19 to 36)	**100.0**	**54.0**	**38.2**	**2.5**	**4.9**	**0.4**
Aged 18 to 19	100.0	95.8	2.6	0.9	0.6	0.1
Aged 20 to 24	100.0	82.9	13.9	1.5	1.4	0.3
Aged 25 to 29	100.0	51.5	41.3	2.6	4.2	0.4
Aged 30 to 34	100.0	30.5	57.9	3.4	7.8	0.5
Aged 35 to 39	100.0	21.1	63.2	3.8	10.9	0.9

Source: Bureau of the Census, America's Families and Living Arrangements: 2013, Internet site http://www.census.gov/hhes/families/data/cps2013.html; calculations by New Strategist

Table 7.25 Current Marital Status of Men, 2006–2010

(total number of men aged 15 to 44, and percent distribution by current marital status, by selected characteristics, 2006–2010; numbers in thousands)

	total		in a union				not in a union	
	number	percent	total	first marriage	second or higher marriage	cohabiting	never married	formerly married
Total men aged 15 to 44	**62,128**	**100.0%**	**49.8%**	**32.8%**	**4.8%**	**12.2%**	**45.0%**	**5.2%**
Aged 15 to 19	10,816	100.0	2.6	0.3	0.0	2.3	97.3	–
Aged 20 to 24	10,394	100.0	26.3	11.3	–	15.0	72.6	0.8
Aged 25 to 29	10,758	100.0	53.7	32.8	1.4	19.5	43.1	3.1
Aged 30 to 34	9,228	100.0	71.1	50.9	5.2	15.0	22.0	7.0
Aged 35 to 39	10,405	100.0	74.3	54.1	7.9	12.3	16.0	9.7
Aged 40 to 44	10,526	100.0	74.2	50.2	14.6	9.4	14.8	11.1
Number of biologial children								
None	34,307	100.0	23.5	13.3	0.8	9.4	74.1	2.4
One or more children	27,821	100.0	82.1	56.7	9.8	15.6	9.1	8.7
Race and Hispanic origin								
Asian	2,406	100.0	50.0	44.7	1.9	3.4	49.4	0.7
Black	7,341	100.0	39.7	24.2	2.7	12.8	55.1	5.2
Hispanic	11,847	100.0	52.5	31.7	3.2	17.6	42.0	5.4
Non-Hispanic White	37,283	100.0	50.5	34.3	5.9	10.3	44.0	5.6
Education								
Not a high school graduate	9,004	100.0	70.1	37.7	5.8	26.6	23.3	6.7
High school graduate or GED	12,068	100.0	61.5	40.6	8.3	12.6	28.6	9.9
Some college, no degree	13,206	100.0	59.1	37.8	7.2	14.1	34.7	6.3
Bachelor's degree	8,924	100.0	62.3	48.6	4.1	9.6	32.9	4.7
Master's degree or more	3,857	100.0	74.9	65.7	4.2	5.0	20.7	4.3

Note: Asians and Blacks are those who identify themselves as being of the race alone. Education categories include only people aged 22 to 44. "–" means sample is too small to make a reliable estimate.
Source: National Center for Health Statistics, First Marriages in the United States: Data from the 2006–2010 National Survey of Family Growth, National Health Statistics Reports, No. 49, 2012; Internet site http://www.cdc.gov/nchs/nsfg.htm

Table 7.26 Current Marital Status of Women, 2006–2010

(total number of women aged 15 to 44, and percent distribution by current marital status, by selected characteristics, 2006–2010; numbers in thousands)

	total		in a union				not in a union	
	number	percent	total	first marriage	second or higher marriage	cohabiting	never married	formerly married
Total women aged 15 to 44	**61,755**	**100.0 %**	**52.7%**	**36.4%**	**5.1%**	**11.2%**	**38.2%**	**9.2%**
Aged 15 to 19	10,478	100.0	5.9	1.1	0.0	4.8	94.1	0.0
Aged 20 to 24	10,365	100.0	36.0	17.3	–	18.7	60.8	2.9
Aged 25 to 29	10,535	100.0	61.3	42.3	2.2	16.8	31.3	7.4
Aged 30 to 34	9,188	100.0	71.4	53.7	5.6	12.1	18.1	10.5
Aged 35 to 39	10,538	100.0	72.4	55.9	8.7	7.8	13.0	14.6
Aged 40 to 44	10,652	100.0	70.4	49.6	13.6	7.2	10.2	19.4
Number of biologial children								
None	27,401	100.0	27.6	17.0	1.3	9.3	69.1	3.2
One or more births	34,353	100.0	72.6	51.8	8.1	12.7	13.5	13.9
Race and Hispanic origin								
Asian	2,456	100.0	56.2	48.5	4.2	3.5	38.7	5.2
Black	8,451	100.0	33.3	21.3	2.7	9.3	55.1	11.6
Hispanic	10,474	100.0	55.2	35.9	4.2	15.1	35.5	9.3
Non-Hispanic White	37,384	100.0	56.8	40.2	5.9	10.7	34.3	8.9
Education								
Not a high school graduate	6,844	100.0	64.5	36.6	7.7	20.2	19.1	16.5
High school graduate or GED	11,578	100.0	64.2	39.5	9.2	15.5	20.3	15.6
Some college, no degree	13,702	100.0	61.1	42.1	7.4	11.6	26.4	12.6
Bachelor's degree	11,024	100.0	68.4	58.3	3.3	6.8	25.5	6.1
Master's degree or more	4,059	100.0	72.9	63.0	4.4	5.5	20.1	7.0

Note: Asians and Blacks are those who identify themselves as being of the race alone. Education categories include only people aged 22 to 44. "–" means sample is too small to make a reliable estimate.
Source: National Center for Health Statistics, First Marriages in the United States: Data from the 2006–2010 National Survey of Family Growth, National Health Statistics Reports, No. 49, 2012; Internet site http://www.cdc.gov/nchs/nsfg.htm

CHAPTER

8

Population

■ The Millennial generation numbers 78 million, a figure that includes everyone born between 1977 and 1994 (aged 19 to 36 in 2013). Millennials account for 25 percent of the total population, larger than the Boomer share.

■ Millennials are much more diverse than middle-aged or older people. Non-Hispanic Whites account for only 57 percent of Millennials and for a much larger 72 percent of Boomers.

■ Millennials account for a large share of immigrants. Nearly one-third of immigrants admitted to the United States in 2013 were aged 20 to 34.

■ By state, Millennials range from a low of 21 percent of the population of Maine to a high of 28 percent of the populations of Alaska, North Dakota, and Utah.

Millennials Are the Largest Generation

They reinvigorated the youth market.

The Millennial generation numbers 78 million, a figure that includes everyone born between 1977 and 1994 (aged 19 to 36 in 2013). Millennials account for 25 percent of the total population, making them the largest generation. Boomers, many of whom are the parents of Millennials, are in second place. They numbered 76 million in 2013 and accounted for 24 percent of the population.

During the past few years, Millennials have boosted the number of young adults. Members of the large generation have been competing against one another to get into college and now they are battling for jobs. Competitive positioning is the defining characteristic of large generations, and it continues throughout life.

■ Millennials are bringing renewed attention to the youth market because of their numbers and the devotion of their Boomer parents.

The Millennial generation is bigger than the Baby-Boom generation

(number of people by generation, 2013)

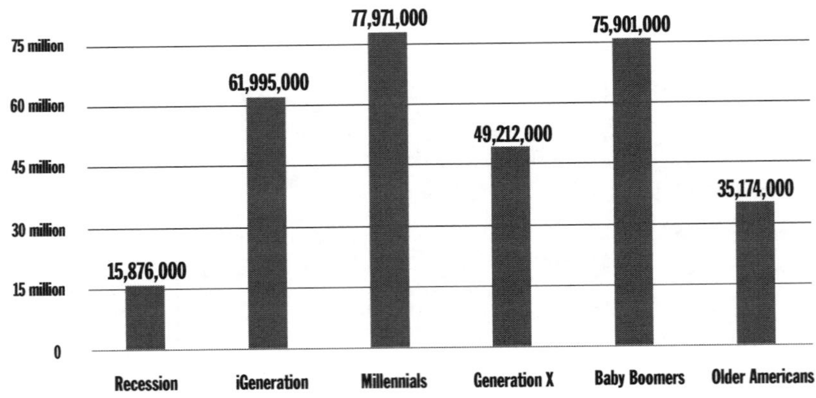

Table 8.1 Population by Age and Generation, 2013

(number and percent distribution of people by age and generation, 2013; numbers in thousands)

	number	percent distribution
Total people	**316,129**	**100.0%**
Under age 5	19,868	6.3
Aged 5 to 9	20,571	6.5
Aged 10 to 14	20,650	6.5
Aged 15 to 19	21,159	6.7
Aged 20 to 24	22,795	7.2
Aged 25 to 29	21,580	6.8
Aged 30 to 34	21,264	6.7
Aged 35 to 39	19,604	6.2
Aged 40 to 44	20,849	6.6
Aged 45 to 49	21,208	6.7
Aged 50 to 54	22,559	7.1
Aged 55 to 59	21,194	6.7
Aged 60 to 64	18,122	5.7
Aged 65 to 69	14,609	4.6
Aged 70 to 74	10,608	3.4
Aged 75 to 79	7,678	2.4
Aged 80 to 84	5,769	1.8
Aged 85 or older	6,041	1.9
Total people	**316,129**	**100.0**
Recession (aged 0 to 3)	15,876	5.0
iGeneration (aged 4 to 18)	61,995	19.6
Millennial (aged 19 to 36)	77,971	24.7
Generation X (aged 37 to 48)	49,212	15.6
Baby Boom (aged 49 to 67)	75,901	24.0
Older Americans (aged 68 or older)	35,174	11.1

Source: Bureau of the Census, Population Estimates, Internet site http://www.census.gov/popest/; calculations by New Strategist

Table 8.2 Population by Age, Generation, and Sex, 2013

(number of people by age, generation, and sex, and sex ratio by age and generation, 2013; numbers in thousands)

	total	female	male	sex ratio
Total people	**316,129**	**160,477**	**155,652**	**97**
Under age 5	19,868	9,716	10,152	104
Aged 5 to 9	20,571	10,062	10,509	104
Aged 10 to 14	20,650	10,098	10,553	105
Aged 15 to 19	21,159	10,313	10,846	105
Aged 20 to 24	22,795	11,116	11,679	105
Aged 25 to 29	21,580	10,620	10,960	103
Aged 30 to 34	21,264	10,583	10,682	101
Aged 35 to 39	19,604	9,819	9,785	100
Aged 40 to 44	20,849	10,489	10,360	99
Aged 45 to 49	21,208	10,710	10,498	98
Aged 50 to 54	22,559	11,488	11,071	96
Aged 55 to 59	21,194	10,912	10,282	94
Aged 60 to 64	18,122	9,448	8,674	92
Aged 65 to 69	14,609	7,696	6,913	90
Aged 70 to 74	10,608	5,724	4,884	85
Aged 75 to 79	7,678	4,288	3,390	79
Aged 80 to 84	5,769	3,398	2,370	70
Aged 85 or older	6,041	3,999	2,042	51
Total people	**316,129**	**160,477**	**155,652**	**97**
Recession (aged 0 to 3)	15,876	7,761	8,116	105
iGeneration (aged 4 to 18)	61,995	30,300	31,695	105
Millennial (aged 19 to 36)	77,971	38,427	39,544	103
Generation X (aged 37 to 48)	49,212	24,758	24,453	99
Baby Boom (aged 49 to 67)	75,901	39,127	36,774	94
Older Americans (aged 68 or older)	35,174	20,105	15,069	75

Note: The sex ratio is the number of males per 100 females.
Source: Bureau of the Census, Population Estimates, Internet site http://www.census.gov/popest/; calculations by New Strategist

Table 8.3 Millennial Generation by Single Year of Age, 2013

(number of people aged 19 to 36 by single year of age and sex, and sex ratio by age, 2013; numbers in thousands)

	total	female	male	sex ratio
Total Millennials	**77,971**	**38,427**	**39,544**	**103**
Aged 19	4,377	2,127	2,249	106
Aged 20	4,446	2,156	2,290	106
Aged 21	4,569	2,221	2,348	106
Aged 22	4,656	2,274	2,382	105
Aged 23	4,653	2,276	2,376	104
Aged 24	4,473	2,189	2,284	104
Aged 25	4,372	2,143	2,229	104
Aged 26	4,301	2,110	2,191	104
Aged 27	4,322	2,124	2,198	103
Aged 28	4,360	2,150	2,210	103
Aged 29	4,225	2,093	2,132	102
Aged 30	4,295	2,132	2,162	101
Aged 31	4,297	2,139	2,159	101
Aged 32	4,254	2,121	2,133	101
Aged 33	4,343	2,157	2,186	101
Aged 34	4,075	2,034	2,041	100
Aged 35	3,997	1,997	2,000	100
Aged 36	3,958	1,983	1,974	100

Note: The sex ratio is the number of males per 100 females.
Source: Bureau of the Census, Population Estimates, Internet site http://www.census.gov/popest/; calculations by New Strategist

Table 8.4 Population by Age, 2010 and 2013

(number of people by age, 2010 and 2013; percent change, 2010–13; numbers in thousands)

	2013	2010	percent change 2010–13
Total people	**316,129**	**309,326**	**2.2%**
Under age 5	19,868	20,189	–1.6
Aged 5 to 9	20,571	20,332	1.2
Aged 10 to 14	20,650	20,680	–0.1
Aged 15 to 19	21,159	21,979	–3.7
Aged 20 to 24	22,795	21,702	5.0
Aged 25 to 29	21,580	21,144	2.1
Aged 30 to 34	21,264	20,068	6.0
Aged 35 to 39	19,604	20,078	–2.4
Aged 40 to 44	20,849	20,904	–0.3
Aged 45 to 49	21,208	22,636	–6.3
Aged 50 to 54	22,559	22,353	0.9
Aged 55 to 59	21,194	19,795	7.1
Aged 60 to 64	18,122	16,990	6.7
Aged 65 to 69	14,609	12,521	16.7
Aged 70 to 74	10,608	9,336	13.6
Aged 75 to 79	7,678	7,319	4.9
Aged 80 to 84	5,769	5,759	0.2
Aged 85 or older	6,041	5,543	9.0
Aged 18 to 24	31,458	30,762	2.3
Aged 18 or older	242,543	235,206	3.1
Aged 65 or older	44,704	40,477	10.4

Source: Bureau of the Census, Population Estimates, Internet site http://www.census.gov/popest/; calculations by New Strategist

The Nation's Young Adults Are Diverse

Hispanics outnumber Blacks among Millennials.

America's young adults are much more diverse than middle-aged or older people. While non-Hispanic Whites account for 63 percent of all Americans, their share is a smaller 57 percent among Millennials, aged 19 to 36 in 2013. Among the iGeneration (aged 4 to 18), non-Hispanic Whites account for only 53 percent of the population.

Hispanics are a larger share of the Millennial generation than Blacks—21 percent are Hispanic and 16 percent are Black. In the iGeneration, Hispanics outnumber Blacks by an even larger margin—24 to 17 percent. Among Asians, Hispanics, and Blacks, Millennials are the largest generation, outnumbering Boomers. Among non-Hispanic Whites, Boomers outnumber Millennials.

■ Racial and ethnic differences between young and old may lead to political tension in the years ahead.

Minorities account for a large share of young adults

(minority share of population by generation, 2013)

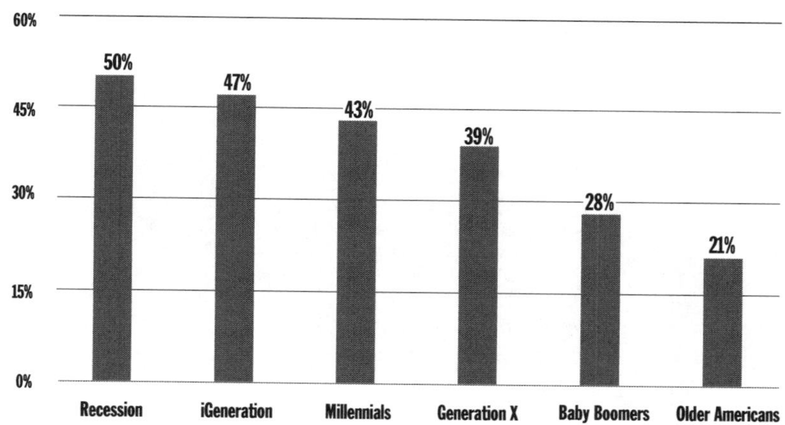

Table 8.5 Population by Generation, Race, and Hispanic Origin, 2013

(number and percent distribution of people by generation, race, and Hispanic origin, 2013; numbers in thousands)

	total	Asian	Black	Hispanic	non-Hispanic White
Total people	**316,129**	**19,437**	**45,004**	**54,071**	**197,836**
Recession (aged 0 to 3)	15,876	1,139	2,928	4,101	7,926
iGeneration (aged 4 to 18)	61,995	4,048	10,825	14,575	32,987
Millennial (aged 19 to 36)	77,971	5,564	12,258	16,020	44,314
Generation X (aged 37 to 48)	49,212	3,446	6,806	8,798	30,117
Baby Boom (aged 49 to 67)	75,901	3,811	9,074	8,011	54,592
Older Americans (aged 68 or older)	35,174	1,429	3,112	2,567	27,900
PERCENT DISTRIBUTION BY RACE AND HISPANIC ORIGIN					
Total people	**100.0%**	**6.1%**	**14.2%**	**17.1%**	**62.6%**
Recession (aged 0 to 3)	100.0	7.2	18.4	25.8	49.9
iGeneration (aged 4 to 18)	100.0	6.5	17.5	23.5	53.2
Millennial (aged 19 to 36)	100.0	7.1	15.7	20.5	56.8
Generation X (aged 37 to 48)	100.0	7.0	13.8	17.9	61.2
Baby Boom (aged 49 to 67)	100.0	5.0	12.0	10.6	71.9
Older Americans (aged 68 or older)	100.0	4.1	8.8	7.3	79.3
PERCENT DISTRIBUTION BY GENERATION					
Total people	**100.0**	**100.0**	**100.0**	**100.0**	**100.0**
Recession (aged 0 to 3)	5.0	5.9	6.5	7.6	4.0
iGeneration (aged 4 to 18)	19.6	20.8	24.1	27.0	16.7
Millennial (aged 19 to 36)	24.7	28.6	27.2	29.6	22.4
Generation X (aged 37 to 48)	15.6	17.7	15.1	16.3	15.2
Baby Boom (aged 49 to 67)	24.0	19.6	20.2	14.8	27.6
Older Americans (aged 68 or older)	11.1	7.4	6.9	4.7	14.1

Note: Asians and Blacks are those who identify themselves as being of the race alone and those who identify themselves as being of the race in combination with other races. Non-Hispanic Whites are those who identify themselves as being White alone and not Hispanic. Numbers do not add to total because not all races are shown and Hispanics may be of any race.
Source: Bureau of the Census, Population Estimates, Internet site http://www.census.gov/popest/; calculations by New Strategist

Table 8.6 Population by Age, Race, and Hispanic Origin, 2013

(number of people by age, race, and Hispanic origin, 2013; numbers in thousands)

	total	Asian	Black	Hispanic	non-Hispanic White
Total people	**316,129**	**19,437**	**45,004**	**54,071**	**197,836**
Under age 5	19,868	1,420	3,659	5,119	9,937
Aged 5 to 9	20,571	1,419	3,635	5,126	10,594
Aged 10 to 14	20,650	1,324	3,566	4,767	11,118
Aged 15 to 19	21,159	1,287	3,668	4,599	11,678
Aged 20 to 24	22,795	1,489	3,948	4,676	12,736
Aged 25 to 29	21,580	1,592	3,275	4,396	12,369
Aged 30 to 34	21,264	1,616	3,112	4,366	12,223
Aged 35 to 39	19,604	1,524	2,792	4,044	11,276
Aged 40 to 44	20,849	1,500	2,877	3,746	12,708
Aged 45 to 49	21,208	1,285	2,880	3,285	13,699
Aged 50 to 54	22,559	1,186	2,914	2,797	15,552
Aged 55 to 59	21,194	1,061	2,591	2,196	15,226
Aged 60 to 64	18,122	882	2,035	1,623	13,474
Aged 65 to 69	14,609	654	1,436	1,177	11,254
Aged 70 to 74	10,608	458	996	810	8,285
Aged 75 to 79	7,678	324	701	583	6,033
Aged 80 to 84	5,769	218	467	403	4,659
Aged 85 or older	6,041	200	450	357	5,015
PERCENT DISTRIBUTION BY RACE AND HISPANIC ORIGIN					
Total people	**100.0%**	**6.1%**	**14.2%**	**17.1%**	**62.6%**
Under age 5	100.0	7.1	18.4	25.8	50.0
Aged 5 to 9	100.0	6.9	17.7	24.9	51.5
Aged 10 to 14	100.0	6.4	17.3	23.1	53.8
Aged 15 to 19	100.0	6.1	17.3	21.7	55.2
Aged 20 to 24	100.0	6.5	17.3	20.5	55.9
Aged 25 to 29	100.0	7.4	15.2	20.4	57.3
Aged 30 to 34	100.0	7.6	14.6	20.5	57.5
Aged 35 to 39	100.0	7.8	14.2	20.6	57.5
Aged 40 to 44	100.0	7.2	13.8	18.0	61.0
Aged 45 to 49	100.0	6.1	13.6	15.5	64.6
Aged 50 to 54	100.0	5.3	12.9	12.4	68.9
Aged 55 to 59	100.0	5.0	12.2	10.4	71.8
Aged 60 to 64	100.0	4.9	11.2	9.0	74.4
Aged 65 to 69	100.0	4.5	9.8	8.1	77.0
Aged 70 to 74	100.0	4.3	9.4	7.6	78.1
Aged 75 to 79	100.0	4.2	9.1	7.6	78.6
Aged 80 to 84	100.0	3.8	8.1	7.0	80.8
Aged 85 or older	100.0	3.3	7.5	5.9	83.0

Note: Asians and Blacks are those who identify themselves as being of the race alone and those who identify themselves as being of the race in combination with other races. Non-Hispanic Whites are those who identify themselves as being White alone and not Hispanic. Numbers do not add to total because not all races are shown and Hispanics may be of any race.
Source: Bureau of the Census, Population Estimates, Internet site http://www.census.gov/popest/; calculations by New Strategist

Table 8.7 Millennial Generation by Single Year of Age, Race, and Hispanic Origin, 2013

(number and percent distribution of people aged 19 to 36 by single year of age, race, and Hispanic origin, 2013; numbers in thousands)

	total	Asian	Black	Hispanic	non-Hispanic White
Total Millennials	**77,971**	**5,564**	**12,258**	**16,020**	**44,314**
Aged 19	4,377	264	776	935	2,413
Aged 20	4,446	268	793	940	2,453
Aged 21	4,569	283	807	957	2,531
Aged 22	4,656	305	812	949	2,603
Aged 23	4,653	315	795	938	2,617
Aged 24	4,473	319	741	892	2,532
Aged 25	4,372	315	694	886	2,488
Aged 26	4,301	312	665	875	2,460
Aged 27	4,322	316	652	882	2,482
Aged 28	4,360	325	647	889	2,510
Aged 29	4,225	325	618	863	2,429
Aged 30	4,295	329	625	880	2,470
Aged 31	4,297	330	624	884	2,470
Aged 32	4,254	320	619	873	2,453
Aged 33	4,343	327	644	899	2,484
Aged 34	4,075	310	600	830	2,345
Aged 35	3,997	302	578	827	2,299
Aged 36	3,958	302	570	819	2,274
PERCENT DISTRIBUTION BY RACE AND HISPANIC ORIGIN					
Total Millennials	**100.0%**	**7.1%**	**15.7%**	**20.5%**	**56.8%**
Aged 19	100.0	6.0	17.7	21.4	55.1
Aged 20	100.0	6.0	17.8	21.2	55.2
Aged 21	100.0	6.2	17.7	20.9	55.4
Aged 22	100.0	6.5	17.4	20.4	55.9
Aged 23	100.0	6.8	17.1	20.2	56.2
Aged 24	100.0	7.1	16.6	19.9	56.6
Aged 25	100.0	7.2	15.9	20.3	56.9
Aged 26	100.0	7.2	15.5	20.3	57.2
Aged 27	100.0	7.3	15.1	20.4	57.4
Aged 28	100.0	7.4	14.8	20.4	57.6
Aged 29	100.0	7.7	14.6	20.4	57.5
Aged 30	100.0	7.7	14.6	20.5	57.5
Aged 31	100.0	7.7	14.5	20.6	57.5
Aged 32	100.0	7.5	14.6	20.5	57.7
Aged 33	100.0	7.5	14.8	20.7	57.2
Aged 34	100.0	7.6	14.7	20.4	57.5
Aged 35	100.0	7.6	14.5	20.7	57.5
Aged 36	100.0	7.6	14.4	20.7	57.5

Note: Asians and Blacks are those who identify themselves as being of the race alone and those who identify themselves as being of the race in combination with other races. Non-Hispanic Whites are those who identify themselves as being White alone and not Hispanic. Numbers do not add to total because not all races are shown and Hispanics may be of any race.
Source: Bureau of the Census, Population Estimates, Internet site http://www.census.gov/popest/; calculations by New Strategist

Rapid Growth Is Projected for the Older Population

Some age groups will shrink during the coming decades.

As large and small generations grow older, age groups expand and contract. Between 2012 and 2050, the largest expansion will be among people aged 65 or older, according to Census Bureau population projections. The number of people aged 65 or older will climb from 43 million in 2012 to 84 million in 2050. In that distant year, Millennials will be 56-to-73-years-old.

Several age groups will shrink during the decades to come as they fill with the small Generation X. The number of 45-to-54-year-olds is projected to decline between 2012 and 2020, and the number of 55-to-64-year-olds will decline between 2020 and 2030.

■ Not evident in these projections is the baby bust emerging from the Great Recession, which occurred too recently to be included in the Census Bureau's fertility assumptions.

Number of Americans aged 65 or older will nearly double in the next few decades

(number of people aged 65 or older, 2012 and 2050)

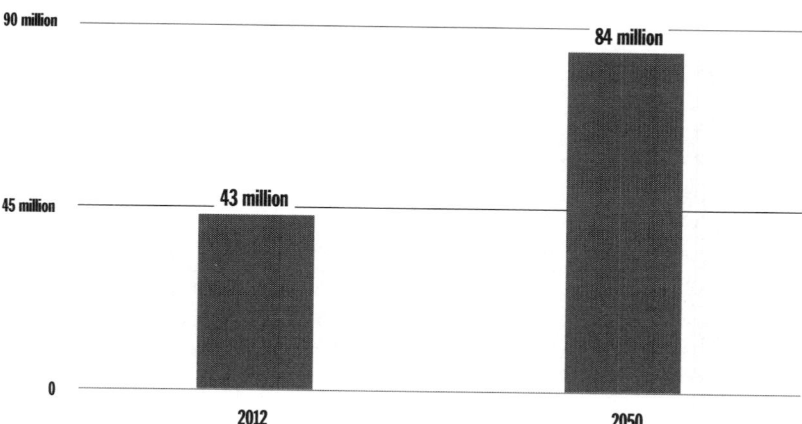

Table 8.8 Population Projections by Age, 2012 to 2050

(projected number of people by age, 2012 to 2050; percent change for selected years; numbers in thousands)

	2012	2020	2030	2040	2050
Total people	**314,004**	**333,896**	**358,471**	**380,016**	**399,803**
Under age 5	20,274	21,808	22,252	23,004	24,115
Aged 5 to 9	20,457	21,307	22,451	22,886	23,983
Aged 10 to 14	20,639	20,616	22,365	22,893	23,682
Aged 15 to 19	21,326	20,806	21,946	23,174	23,642
Aged 20 to 24	22,554	21,651	21,940	23,863	24,463
Aged 25 to 29	21,375	23,366	22,712	24,151	25,493
Aged 30 to 34	20,901	22,906	23,340	23,924	25,949
Aged 35 to 39	19,479	21,869	24,423	24,002	25,513
Aged 40 to 44	21,017	20,361	23,403	24,000	24,655
Aged 45 to 49	21,678	20,008	21,935	24,595	24,262
Aged 50 to 54	22,572	20,467	20,083	23,176	23,866
Aged 55 to 59	20,769	21,747	19,393	21,384	24,094
Aged 60 to 64	17,808	21,017	19,454	19,242	22,348
Aged 65 or older	43,155	55,969	72,774	79,719	83,739
PERCENT CHANGE	**2012–20**	**2020–30**	**2030–40**	**2040–50**	**2012–2050**
Total people	**6.3%**	**7.4%**	**6.0%**	**5.2%**	**27.3%**
Under age 5	7.6	2.0	3.4	4.8	18.9
Aged 5 to 9	4.2	5.4	1.9	4.8	17.2
Aged 10 to 14	–0.1	8.5	2.4	3.4	14.7
Aged 15 to 19	–2.4	5.5	5.6	2.0	10.9
Aged 20 to 24	–4.0	1.3	8.8	2.5	8.5
Aged 25 to 29	9.3	–2.8	6.3	5.6	19.3
Aged 30 to 34	9.6	1.9	2.5	8.5	24.1
Aged 35 to 39	12.3	11.7	–1.7	6.3	31.0
Aged 40 to 44	–3.1	14.9	2.6	2.7	17.3
Aged 45 to 49	–7.7	9.6	12.1	–1.4	11.9
Aged 50 to 54	–9.3	–1.9	15.4	3.0	5.7
Aged 55 to 59	4.7	–10.8	10.3	12.7	16.0
Aged 60 to 64	18.0	–7.4	–1.1	16.1	25.5
Aged 65 or older	29.7	30.0	9.5	5.0	94.0

Note: Numbers are for July 1 of each year.
Source: Bureau of the Census, Population Projections, Internet site http://www.census.gov/population/projections/; calculations by New Strategist

Minorities Are Close to Becoming the Majority

Minorities may account for well over half of children under age 5 by 2020.

Children are far more diverse than older Americans, and this diversity will intensify over the next decade. In 2020, fewer than half of children under age 5 will be non-Hispanic White, according to Census Bureau projections. More than one in four will be Hispanic. In contrast, 76 percent of people aged 65 or older will be non-Hispanic White and only 9 percent will be Hispanic.

The number of Hispanics will more than double between 2012 and 2050. Asians are also projected to more than double during those years, and Blacks will grow 56 percent. Meanwhile, the number of non-Hispanic Whites will shrink by 6 percent. Between 2040 and 2050, non-Hispanic Whites will fall below 50 percent of the population and the nation's minorities will become the majority.

■ By 2030, minorities will account for the majority of Americans under age 30.

The generation gap will be a racial and ethnic divide

(minority share of selected age groups, 2030)

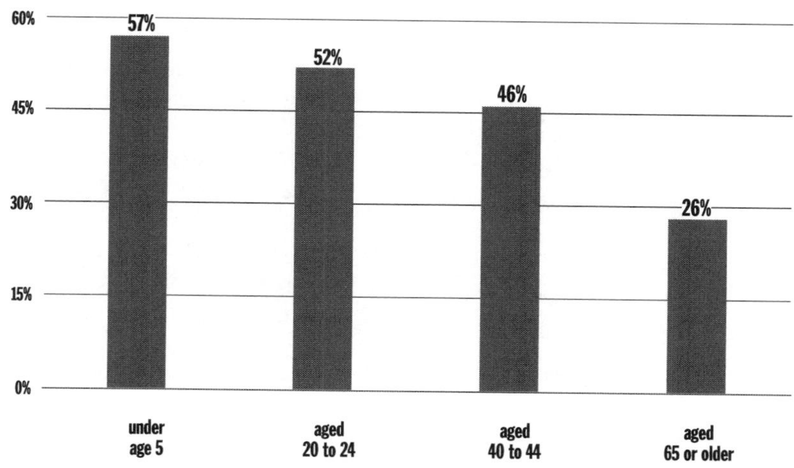

Table 8.9 Minority Population, 2012 to 2050

(projected number of minorities by age, and minority share of total population, 2012 to 2050, percent and percentage point change for selected years; numbers in thousands)

	2012	2020	2030	2040	2050	percent change 2012–50
Total minorities	**116,242**	**134,583**	**159,654**	**186,129**	**213,469**	**83.6%**
Under age 5	10,160	11,517	12,725	14,253	15,805	55.6
Aged 5 to 9	9,781	10,993	12,391	13,742	15,386	57.3
Aged 10 to 14	9,424	10,292	11,986	13,261	14,819	57.3
Aged 15 to 19	9,486	9,904	11,550	13,019	14,397	51.8
Aged 20 to 24	9,825	10,111	11,444	13,286	14,620	48.8
Aged 25 to 29	9,059	10,879	11,560	13,457	15,021	65.8
Aged 30 to 34	8,862	10,266	11,577	13,151	15,076	70.1
Aged 35 to 39	8,232	9,524	11,809	12,668	14,617	77.6
Aged 40 to 44	8,020	8,807	10,744	12,167	13,784	71.9
Aged 45 to 49	7,460	8,263	9,686	12,034	12,938	73.4
Aged 50 to 54	6,835	7,585	8,750	10,702	12,167	78.0
Aged 55 to 59	5,731	7,086	8,038	9,465	11,814	106.2
Aged 60 to 64	4,457	6,147	7,213	8,383	10,319	131.5
Aged 65 or older	8,913	13,207	20,181	26,540	32,706	267.0

MINORITY SHARE OF TOTAL POPULATION	2012	2020	2030	2040	2050	percentage point change 2012–50
Total minorities	**37.0%**	**40.3%**	**44.5%**	**49.0%**	**53.4%**	**16.4**
Under age 5	50.1	52.8	57.2	62.0	65.5	15.4
Aged 5 to 9	47.8	51.6	55.2	60.0	64.2	16.3
Aged 10 to 14	45.7	49.9	53.6	57.9	62.6	16.9
Aged 15 to 19	44.5	47.6	52.6	56.2	60.9	16.4
Aged 20 to 24	43.6	46.7	52.2	55.7	59.8	16.2
Aged 25 to 29	42.4	46.6	50.9	55.7	58.9	16.5
Aged 30 to 34	42.4	44.8	49.6	55.0	58.1	15.7
Aged 35 to 39	42.3	43.6	48.4	52.8	57.3	15.0
Aged 40 to 44	38.2	43.3	45.9	50.7	55.9	17.8
Aged 45 to 49	34.4	41.3	44.2	48.9	53.3	18.9
Aged 50 to 54	30.3	37.1	43.6	46.2	51.0	20.7
Aged 55 to 59	27.6	32.6	41.4	44.3	49.0	21.4
Aged 60 to 64	25.0	29.2	37.1	43.6	46.2	21.1
Aged 65 or older	20.7	23.6	27.7	33.3	39.1	18.4

Note: Minorities are calculated by subtracting non-Hispanic Whites from the total population.
Source: Bureau of the Census, Population Projections, Internet site http://www.census.gov/population/projections/; calculations by New Strategist

Table 8.10 Asian Population Projections, 2012 to 2050

(projected number of Asians by age, and Asian share of total population, 2012 to 2050, percent and percentage point change, 2012–50; numbers in thousands)

	2012	2020	2030	2040	2050	percent change 2012–50
Total Asians	**18,647**	**22,384**	**27,482**	**32,876**	**38,407**	**106.0%**
Under age 5	1,414	1,664	1,912	2,238	2,558	80.9
Aged 5 to 9	1,378	1,602	1,878	2,169	2,505	81.7
Aged 10 to 14	1,270	1,489	1,817	2,079	2,409	89.8
Aged 15 to 19	1,247	1,447	1,750	2,036	2,329	86.8
Aged 20 to 24	1,430	1,474	1,788	2,136	2,403	68.0
Aged 25 to 29	1,514	1,689	1,964	2,309	2,604	72.0
Aged 30 to 34	1,535	1,825	2,009	2,367	2,725	77.6
Aged 35 to 39	1,493	1,779	2,053	2,359	2,710	81.5
Aged 40 to 44	1,436	1,627	2,036	2,241	2,601	81.2
Aged 45 to 49	1,252	1,571	1,893	2,181	2,487	98.7
Aged 50 to 54	1,137	1,360	1,676	2,088	2,295	101.9
Aged 55 to 59	1,012	1,221	1,575	1,897	2,187	116.0
Aged 60 to 64	836	1,086	1,339	1,649	2,055	145.9
Aged 65 or older	1,694	2,550	3,792	5,126	6,539	286.0

ASIAN SHARE OF TOTAL POPULATION	2012	2020	2030	2040	2050	percentage point change 2012–50
Total Asians	**5.9%**	**6.7%**	**7.7%**	**8.7%**	**9.6%**	**3.7**
Under age 5	7.0	7.6	8.6	9.7	10.6	3.6
Aged 5 to 9	6.7	7.5	8.4	9.5	10.4	3.7
Aged 10 to 14	6.2	7.2	8.1	9.1	10.2	4.0
Aged 15 to 19	5.8	7.0	8.0	8.8	9.9	4.0
Aged 20 to 24	6.3	6.8	8.2	9.0	9.8	3.5
Aged 25 to 29	7.1	7.2	8.6	9.6	10.2	3.1
Aged 30 to 34	7.3	8.0	8.6	9.9	10.5	3.2
Aged 35 to 39	7.7	8.1	8.4	9.8	10.6	3.0
Aged 40 to 44	6.8	8.0	8.7	9.3	10.5	3.7
Aged 45 to 49	5.8	7.9	8.6	8.9	10.3	4.5
Aged 50 to 54	5.0	6.6	8.3	9.0	9.6	4.6
Aged 55 to 59	4.9	5.6	8.1	8.9	9.1	4.2
Aged 60 to 64	4.7	5.2	6.9	8.6	9.2	4.5
Aged 65 or older	3.9	4.6	5.2	6.4	7.8	3.9

Note: Asians are those who identify themselves as being of the race alone and those who identify themselves as being of the race in combination with other races.
Source: Bureau of the Census, Population Projections, Internet site http://www.census.gov/population/projections/; calculations by New Strategist

Table 8.11 Black Population Projections, 2012 to 2050

(projected number of Blacks by age, and Black share of total population, 2012 to 2050, percent and percentage point change, 2012–50; numbers in thousands)

	2012	2020	2030	2040	2050	percent change 2012–50
Total Blacks	**44,462**	**49,338**	**55,727**	**62,350**	**69,525**	**56.4%**
Under age 5	3,748	4,179	4,408	4,809	5,321	42.0
Aged 5 to 9	3,559	3,990	4,348	4,625	5,147	44.6
Aged 10 to 14	3,574	3,719	4,252	4,503	4,923	37.8
Aged 15 to 19	3,718	3,547	4,067	4,446	4,740	27.5
Aged 20 to 24	3,830	3,666	3,866	4,439	4,723	23.3
Aged 25 to 29	3,192	4,024	3,766	4,350	4,782	49.8
Aged 30 to 34	3,049	3,631	3,870	4,138	4,763	56.2
Aged 35 to 39	2,760	3,172	4,150	3,951	4,575	65.8
Aged 40 to 44	2,877	2,935	3,687	3,966	4,266	48.3
Aged 45 to 49	2,919	2,787	3,171	4,165	4,002	37.1
Aged 50 to 54	2,893	2,754	2,878	3,639	3,942	36.3
Aged 55 to 59	2,505	2,809	2,666	3,068	4,056	61.9
Aged 60 to 64	1,966	2,584	2,558	2,717	3,471	76.5
Aged 65 or older	3,871	5,541	8,039	9,534	10,814	179.3

BLACK SHARE OF TOTAL POPULATION	2012	2020	2030	2040	2050	percentage point change 2012–50
Total Blacks	**14.2%**	**14.8%**	**15.5%**	**16.4%**	**17.4%**	**3.2**
Under age 5	18.5	19.2	19.8	20.9	22.1	3.6
Aged 5 to 9	17.4	18.7	19.4	20.2	21.5	4.1
Aged 10 to 14	17.3	18.0	19.0	19.7	20.8	3.5
Aged 15 to 19	17.4	17.0	18.5	19.2	20.0	2.6
Aged 20 to 24	17.0	16.9	17.6	18.6	19.3	2.3
Aged 25 to 29	14.9	17.2	16.6	18.0	18.8	3.8
Aged 30 to 34	14.6	15.9	16.6	17.3	18.4	3.8
Aged 35 to 39	14.2	14.5	17.0	16.5	17.9	3.8
Aged 40 to 44	13.7	14.4	15.8	16.5	17.3	3.6
Aged 45 to 49	13.5	13.9	14.5	16.9	16.5	3.0
Aged 50 to 54	12.8	13.5	14.3	15.7	16.5	3.7
Aged 55 to 59	12.1	12.9	13.7	14.3	16.8	4.8
Aged 60 to 64	11.0	12.3	13.1	14.1	15.5	4.5
Aged 65 or older	9.0	9.9	11.0	12.0	12.9	3.9

Note: Blacks are those who identify themselves as being of the race alone and those who identify themselves as being of the race in combination with other races.
Source: Bureau of the Census, Population Projections, Internet site http://www.census.gov/population/projections/; calculations by New Strategist

Table 8.12 Hispanic Population Projections, 2012 to 2050

(projected number of Hispanics by age, and Hispanic share of total population, 2012 to 2050, percent and percentage point change, 2012–50; numbers in thousands)

	2012	2020	2030	2040	2050	percent change 2012–50
Total Hispanics	**53,274**	**63,784**	**78,655**	**94,876**	**111,732**	**109.7%**
Under age 5	5,267	6,035	6,924	7,970	8,930	69.5
Aged 5 to 9	5,026	5,715	6,597	7,591	8,628	71.7
Aged 10 to 14	4,689	5,329	6,289	7,211	8,264	76.2
Aged 15 to 19	4,579	5,069	6,063	6,987	7,988	74.4
Aged 20 to 24	4,616	5,079	6,065	7,117	8,061	74.6
Aged 25 to 29	4,401	5,239	6,027	7,173	8,130	84.7
Aged 30 to 34	4,326	4,878	5,837	6,958	8,031	85.6
Aged 35 to 39	4,001	4,633	5,701	6,579	7,731	93.2
Aged 40 to 44	3,680	4,295	5,100	6,112	7,241	96.8
Aged 45 to 49	3,215	3,910	4,687	5,788	6,675	107.6
Aged 50 to 54	2,688	3,434	4,249	5,057	6,083	126.3
Aged 55 to 59	2,093	2,968	3,805	4,566	5,673	171.0
Aged 60 to 64	1,548	2,370	3,288	4,072	4,876	214.9
Aged 65 or older	3,142	4,831	8,023	11,695	15,421	390.8

HISPANIC SHARE OF TOTAL POPULATION	2012	2020	2030	2040	2050	percentage point change 2012–50
Total Hispanics	**17.0%**	**19.1%**	**21.9%**	**25.0%**	**27.9%**	**11.0**
Under age 5	26.0	27.7	31.1	34.6	37.0	11.0
Aged 5 to 9	24.6	26.8	29.4	33.2	36.0	11.4
Aged 10 to 14	22.7	25.8	28.1	31.5	34.9	12.2
Aged 15 to 19	21.5	24.4	27.6	30.1	33.8	12.3
Aged 20 to 24	20.5	23.5	27.6	29.8	33.0	12.5
Aged 25 to 29	20.6	22.4	26.5	29.7	31.9	11.3
Aged 30 to 34	20.7	21.3	25.0	29.1	30.9	10.2
Aged 35 to 39	20.5	21.2	23.3	27.4	30.3	9.8
Aged 40 to 44	17.5	21.1	21.8	25.5	29.4	11.9
Aged 45 to 49	14.8	19.5	21.4	23.5	27.5	12.7
Aged 50 to 54	11.9	16.8	21.2	21.8	25.5	13.6
Aged 55 to 59	10.1	13.6	19.6	21.3	23.5	13.5
Aged 60 to 64	8.7	11.3	16.9	21.2	21.8	13.1
Aged 65 or older	7.3	8.6	11.0	14.7	18.4	11.1

Source: Bureau of the Census, Population Projections, Internet site http://www.census.gov/population/projections/; calculations by New Strategist

Table 8.13 Non-Hispanic White Population, 2012 to 2050

(projected number of non-Hispanic Whites by age, and non-Hispanic White share of total population, 2012 to 2050, percent and percentage point change, 2012–50; numbers in thousands)

	2012	2020	2030	2040	2050	percent change 2012–50
Total non-Hispanic Whites	**197,762**	**199,313**	**198,817**	**193,887**	**186,334**	**–5.8%**
Under age 5	10,114	10,291	9,527	8,751	8,311	–17.8
Aged 5 to 9	10,676	10,314	10,060	9,144	8,597	–19.5
Aged 10 to 14	11,215	10,324	10,379	9,631	8,863	–21.0
Aged 15 to 19	11,840	10,902	10,396	10,155	9,245	–21.9
Aged 20 to 24	12,729	11,539	10,496	10,577	9,843	–22.7
Aged 25 to 29	12,315	12,486	11,153	10,694	10,472	–15.0
Aged 30 to 34	12,040	12,639	11,763	10,773	10,873	–9.7
Aged 35 to 39	11,248	12,344	12,613	11,334	10,896	–3.1
Aged 40 to 44	12,998	11,554	12,659	11,833	10,870	–16.4
Aged 45 to 49	14,219	11,745	12,249	12,562	11,324	–20.4
Aged 50 to 54	15,737	12,882	11,333	12,474	11,700	–25.7
Aged 55 to 59	15,038	14,661	11,356	11,920	12,279	–18.3
Aged 60 to 64	13,351	14,870	12,241	10,860	12,029	–9.9
Aged 65 or older	34,243	42,761	52,594	53,180	51,033	49.0

NON-HISPANIC WHITE SHARE OF TOTAL POPULATION	2012	2020	2030	2040	2050	percentage point change 2012–50
Total non-Hispanic Whites	**63.0%**	**59.7%**	**55.5%**	**51.0%**	**46.6%**	**–16.4**
Under age 5	49.9	47.2	42.8	38.0	34.5	–15.4
Aged 5 to 9	52.2	48.4	44.8	40.0	35.8	–16.3
Aged 10 to 14	54.3	50.1	46.4	42.1	37.4	–16.9
Aged 15 to 19	55.5	52.4	47.4	43.8	39.1	–16.4
Aged 20 to 24	56.4	53.3	47.8	44.3	40.2	–16.2
Aged 25 to 29	57.6	53.4	49.1	44.3	41.1	–16.5
Aged 30 to 34	57.6	55.2	50.4	45.0	41.9	–15.7
Aged 35 to 39	57.7	56.4	51.6	47.2	42.7	–15.0
Aged 40 to 44	61.8	56.7	54.1	49.3	44.1	–17.8
Aged 45 to 49	65.6	58.7	55.8	51.1	46.7	–18.9
Aged 50 to 54	69.7	62.9	56.4	53.8	49.0	–20.7
Aged 55 to 59	72.4	67.4	58.6	55.7	51.0	–21.4
Aged 60 to 64	75.0	70.8	62.9	56.4	53.8	–21.1
Aged 65 or older	79.3	76.4	72.3	66.7	60.9	–18.4

Note: Non-Hispanic Whites are those who identify themselves as being White alone and not Hispanic.
Source: Bureau of the Census, Population Projections, Internet site http://www.census.gov/population/projections/; calculations by New Strategist

Most Millennials Live in Their State of Birth

Among 25-to-34-year-olds, nearly one in five is foreign-born.

According to the 2012 American Community Survey, most Americans live in the state in which they were born. In the Millennial age groups, the share who live in their state of birth is 65 percent among 18-to-24-year-olds and 54 percent among 25-to-34-year-olds. About one-quarter of 18-to-34-year-olds were born in the United States but live in a state other than the one in which they were born. Only 10 percent of 18-to-24-year-olds are foreign-born, but the figure rises to 18 percent among 25-to-34-year-olds.

In 2013, nearly 1 million legal immigrants were admitted to the United States. Nearly one-third were aged 20 to 34, adding to the Millennial population.

Sixty-two million residents of the United States speak a language other than English at home, according to the Census Bureau's 2012 American Community Survey—21 percent of the population aged 5 or older. Among working-age adults (aged 18 to 64), 22 percent do not speak English at home. Most of those who do not speak English at home speak Spanish.

■ Among people aged 18 to 64 who speak Spanish at home, most also speak English "very well."

Many Millennials were born in another country

(percent distribution of people aged 25 to 34 by place of birth, 2012)

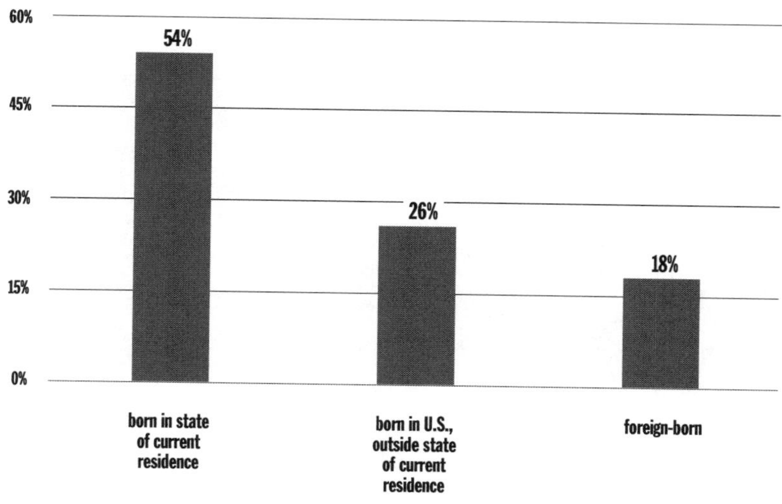

Table 8.14 Population by Age and Place of Birth, 2012

(number and percent distribution of people by age and place of birth, 2012; numbers in thousands)

		born in United States			
	total	in state of current residence	outside state of current residence	citizen born outside United States	foreign-born
Total people	**313,914**	**184,556**	**84,147**	**4,386**	**40,825**
Under age 5	19,910	17,835	1,711	129	236
Aged 5 to 17	53,800	42,565	8,315	592	2,328
Aged 18 to 24	31,472	20,472	7,335	459	3,207
Aged 25 to 34	42,101	22,560	11,080	693	7,769
Aged 35 to 44	40,698	19,467	11,571	720	8,939
Aged 45 to 54	44,205	21,881	14,039	755	7,529
Aged 55 to 59	20,622	10,371	7,014	308	2,930
Aged 60 to 61	7,539	3,756	2,673	93	1,018
Aged 62 to 64	10,426	5,103	3,805	140	1,378
Aged 65 to 74	24,005	11,260	9,297	296	3,151
Aged 75 or older	19,136	9,287	7,308	200	2,340
PERCENT DISTRIBUTION BY PLACE OF BIRTH					
Total people	**100.0%**	**58.8%**	**26.8%**	**1.4%**	**13.0%**
Under age 5	100.0	89.6	8.6	0.6	1.2
Aged 5 to 17	100.0	79.1	15.5	1.1	4.3
Aged 18 to 24	100.0	65.0	23.3	1.5	10.2
Aged 25 to 34	100.0	53.6	26.3	1.6	18.5
Aged 35 to 44	100.0	47.8	28.4	1.8	22.0
Aged 45 to 54	100.0	49.5	31.8	1.7	17.0
Aged 55 to 59	100.0	50.3	34.0	1.5	14.2
Aged 60 to 61	100.0	49.8	35.5	1.2	13.5
Aged 62 to 64	100.0	48.9	36.5	1.3	13.2
Aged 65 to 74	100.0	46.9	38.7	1.2	13.1
Aged 75 or older	100.0	48.5	38.2	1.0	12.2

Source: Bureau of the Census, 2012 American Community Survey, Internet site http://factfinder2.census.gov/faces/nav/jsf/pages/index.xhtml; calculations by New Strategist

Table 8.15 Immigrants by Age, 2013

(number and percent distribution of immigrants by age, 2013)

	number	percent distribution
Total immigrants	**990,553**	**100.0%**
Under age 1	3,507	0.4
Aged 1 to 4	30,243	3.1
Aged 5 to 9	46,203	4.7
Aged 10 to 14	56,988	5.8
Aged 15 to 19	75,497	7.6
Aged 20 to 24	90,396	9.1
Aged 25 to 29	112,244	11.3
Aged 30 to 34	122,446	12.4
Aged 35 to 39	104,210	10.5
Aged 40 to 44	81,892	8.3
Aged 45 to 49	63,818	6.4
Aged 50 to 54	50,001	5.0
Aged 55 to 59	40,195	4.1
Aged 60 to 64	31,529	3.2
Aged 65 to 74	36,117	3.6
Aged 75 or older	12,758	1.3

Note: Immigrants are those granted legal permanent residence in the United States. They either arrive in the United States with immigrant visas issued abroad or adjust their status in the United States from temporary to permanent residence. Numbers may not sum to total because "age not stated" is not shown.
Source: Department of Homeland Security, 2013 Yearbook of Immigration Statistics, Internet site http://www.dhs.gov/yearbook-immigration-statistics-2013-lawful-permanent-residents

Table 8.16 Language Spoken at Home by People Aged 18 to 64, 2012

(number and percent distribution of people aged 5 or older and aged 18 to 64 who speak a language other than English at home by language spoken at home and ability to speak English "very well," 2012; numbers in thousands)

	total		aged 18 to 64	
	number	percent distribution	number	percent distribution
Total, aged 5 or older	**294,004**	**100.0%**	**197,063**	**100.0%**
Speak only English at home	232,126	79.0	153,444	77.9
Speak a language other than English at home	61,877	21.0	43,619	22.1
Speak English less than "very well"	25,088	8.5	18,908	9.6
Total who speak a language other than English at home	**61,877**	**100.0**	**43,619**	**100.0**
Speak Spanish at home	38,325	61.9	26,861	61.6
Speak other Indo-European language at home	11,035	17.8	7,517	17.2
Speak Asian or Pacific Island language at home	9,752	15.8	7,224	16.6
Speak other language at home	2,765	4.5	2,017	4.6
Speak Spanish at home	38,325	100.0	26,861	100.0
Speak English less than "very well"	16,149	42.1	12,566	46.8
Speak other Indo-European language at home	11,035	100.0	7,517	100.0
Speak English less than "very well"	3,462	31.4	2,296	30.5
Speak Asian or Pacific Island language at home	9,752	100.0	7,224	100.0
Speak English less than "very well"	4,618	47.4	3,406	47.1
Speak other language at home	2,765	100.0	2,017	100.0
Speak English less than "very well"	859	31.1	640	31.7

Source: Bureau of the Census, 2012 American Community Survey, Internet site http://factfinder2.census.gov/faces/nav/jsf/pages/index.xhtml; calculations by New Strategist

Largest Share of Millennials Lives in the South

Millennials outnumber Boomers in 26 states.

The South is home to the largest share of the population, and consequently to the largest share of Millennials. Thirty-seven percent of Millennials live in the South, according to Census Bureau estimates for 2013, where they account for 25 percent of the population.

By state, Millennials range from a low of 21 percent of the population of Maine to a high of 28 percent of the populations of Alaska, North Dakota, and Utah. Millennials outnumber Boomers in 26 states and the District of Columbia.

■ Millennials will outnumber Boomers in a growing number of states as the Boomer population shrinks with age.

The Northeast is home to just 17 percent of Millennials

(percent distribution of people aged 19 to 36 by region, 2013)

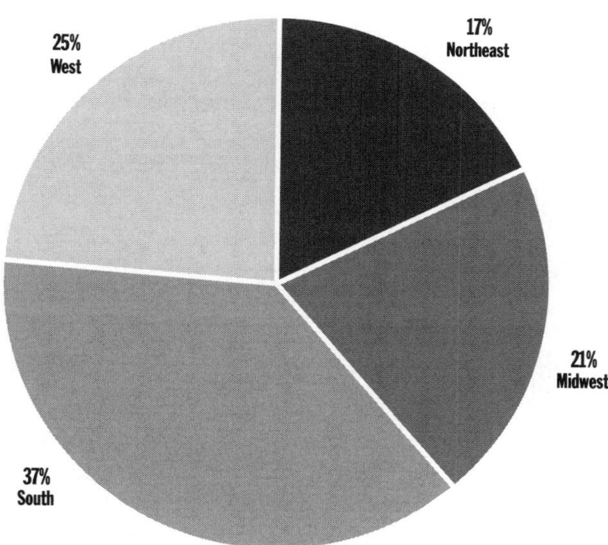

Table 8.17 Population by Generation and Region, 2013

(number and percent distribution of people by generation and region, 2013; numbers in thousands)

	total	Northeast	Midwest	South	West
Total people	**316,129**	**55,943**	**67,548**	**118,383**	**74,254**
Recession (aged 0 to 3)	15,876	2,557	3,349	6,085	3,903
iGeneration (aged 4 to 18)	61,995	10,306	13,380	23,486	14,949
Millennial (aged 19 to 36)	77,971	13,398	16,121	29,085	19,108
Generation X (aged 37 to 48)	49,212	8,897	10,300	18,689	11,692
Baby Boom (aged 49 to 67)	75,901	13,934	16,466	27,656	16,826
Older Americans (aged 68 or older)	35,174	6,850	7,931	13,382	7,776
PERCENT DISTRIBUTION BY GENERATION					
Total people	**100.0%**	**100.0%**	**100.0%**	**100.0%**	**100.0%**
Recession (aged 0 to 3)	5.0	4.6	5.0	5.1	5.3
iGeneration (aged 4 to 18)	19.6	18.4	19.8	19.8	20.1
Millennial (aged 19 to 36)	24.7	24.0	23.9	24.6	25.7
Generation X (aged 37 to 48)	15.6	15.9	15.2	15.8	15.7
Baby Boom (aged 49 to 67)	24.0	24.9	24.4	23.4	22.7
Older Americans (aged 68 or older)	11.1	12.2	11.7	11.3	10.5
PERCENT DISTRIBUTION BY REGION					
Total people	**100.0**	**17.7**	**21.4**	**37.4**	**23.5**
Recession (aged 0 to 3)	100.0	16.1	21.1	38.3	24.6
iGeneration (aged 4 to 18)	100.0	16.6	21.6	37.9	24.1
Millennial (aged 19 to 36)	100.0	17.2	20.7	37.3	24.5
Generation X (aged 37 to 48)	100.0	18.1	20.9	38.0	23.8
Baby Boom (aged 49 to 67)	100.0	18.4	21.7	36.4	22.2
Older Americans (aged 68 or older)	100.0	19.5	22.5	38.0	22.1

Source: Bureau of the Census, State Population Estimates, Internet site http://www.census.gov/popest/data/state/asrh/2013/index .html; calculations by New Strategist

Table 8.18 Population by Age and Region, 2013

(number and percent distribution of people by age and region, 2013; numbers in thousands)

	total	Northeast	Midwest	South	West
Total people	**316,129**	**55,943**	**67,548**	**118,383**	**74,254**
Under age 5	19,868	3,196	4,186	7,607	4,879
Aged 5 to 9	20,571	3,287	4,405	7,855	5,023
Aged 10 to 14	20,650	3,410	4,468	7,840	4,932
Aged 15 to 19	21,159	3,713	4,588	7,837	5,022
Aged 20 to 24	22,795	3,900	4,810	8,551	5,534
Aged 25 to 29	21,580	3,796	4,377	8,044	5,363
Aged 30 to 34	21,264	3,621	4,407	7,956	5,280
Aged 35 to 39	19,604	3,345	4,024	7,417	4,818
Aged 40 to 44	20,849	3,696	4,304	7,905	4,944
Aged 45 to 49	21,208	3,993	4,477	7,917	4,822
Aged 50 to 54	22,559	4,237	4,959	8,308	5,055
Aged 55 to 59	21,194	3,968	4,737	7,736	4,754
Aged 60 to 64	18,122	3,335	4,014	6,683	4,090
Aged 65 to 69	14,609	2,660	3,101	5,575	3,273
Aged 70 to 74	10,608	1,924	2,284	4,082	2,317
Aged 75 to 79	7,678	1,425	1,683	2,922	1,649
Aged 80 to 84	5,769	1,145	1,303	2,101	1,219
Aged 85 or older	6,041	1,292	1,420	2,047	1,282
PERCENT DISTRIBUTION BY REGION					
Total people	**100.0%**	**17.7%**	**21.4%**	**37.4%**	**23.5%**
Under age 5	100.0	16.1	21.1	38.3	24.6
Aged 5 to 9	100.0	16.0	21.4	38.2	24.4
Aged 10 to 14	100.0	16.5	21.6	38.0	23.9
Aged 15 to 19	100.0	17.5	21.7	37.0	23.7
Aged 20 to 24	100.0	17.1	21.1	37.5	24.3
Aged 25 to 29	100.0	17.6	20.3	37.3	24.9
Aged 30 to 34	100.0	17.0	20.7	37.4	24.8
Aged 35 to 39	100.0	17.1	20.5	37.8	24.6
Aged 40 to 44	100.0	17.7	20.6	37.9	23.7
Aged 45 to 49	100.0	18.8	21.1	37.3	22.7
Aged 50 to 54	100.0	18.8	22.0	36.8	22.4
Aged 55 to 59	100.0	18.7	22.3	36.5	22.4
Aged 60 to 64	100.0	18.4	22.2	36.9	22.6
Aged 65 to 69	100.0	18.2	21.2	38.2	22.4
Aged 70 to 74	100.0	18.1	21.5	38.5	21.8
Aged 75 to 79	100.0	18.6	21.9	38.1	21.5
Aged 80 to 84	100.0	19.8	22.6	36.4	21.1
Aged 85 or older	100.0	21.4	23.5	33.9	21.2

Source: Bureau of the Census, State Population Estimates, Internet site http://www.census.gov/popest/data/state/asrh/2013/index.html; calculations by New Strategist

Table 8.19 Population by State and Generation, 2013

(number of people by state and generation, 2013; numbers in thousands)

	total population	Recession (0 to 3)	iGeneration (4 to 18)	Millennial (19 to 36)	Generation X (37 to 48)	Baby Boom (49 to 67)	Older Americans (68 or older)
United States	**316,129**	**15,876**	**61,995**	**77,971**	**49,212**	**75,901**	**35,174**
Alabama	4,834	238	940	1,157	745	1,177	577
Alaska	735	44	153	206	110	172	50
Arizona	6,627	345	1,363	1,620	992	1,488	819
Arkansas	2,959	154	593	706	443	697	365
California	38,333	2,006	7,719	10,061	6,204	8,496	3,847
Colorado	5,268	268	1,042	1,363	849	1,237	509
Connecticut	3,596	154	689	809	581	921	442
Delaware	926	45	173	219	140	231	118
District of Columbia	646	33	93	231	101	129	59
Florida	19,553	863	3,398	4,460	3,006	4,841	2,985
Georgia	9,992	535	2,099	2,501	1,668	2,251	938
Hawaii	1,404	73	251	361	210	333	176
Idaho	1,612	91	358	387	233	366	178
Illinois	12,882	639	2,562	3,196	2,050	3,025	1,409
Indiana	6,571	337	1,344	1,575	1,013	1,565	737
Iowa	3,090	156	616	731	445	747	395
Kansas	2,894	160	606	714	416	668	330
Kentucky	4,395	220	851	1,043	695	1,080	506
Louisiana	4,625	247	926	1,187	689	1,087	490
Maine	1,328	52	227	275	206	380	188
Maryland	5,929	294	1,133	1,446	970	1,452	634
Massachusetts	6,693	292	1,217	1,647	1,073	1,664	799
Michigan	9,896	458	1,929	2,274	1,520	2,517	1,198
Minnesota	5,420	278	1,075	1,306	828	1,320	613
Mississippi	2,991	159	623	732	449	695	333
Missouri	6,044	301	1,178	1,453	902	1,475	735
Montana	1,015	49	189	237	140	269	132
Nebraska	1,869	104	388	458	269	433	216
Nevada	2,790	143	550	695	457	647	298
New Hampshire	1,323	53	239	287	215	369	161
New Jersey	8,899	427	1,705	2,047	1,488	2,193	1,040
New Mexico	2,085	111	426	508	297	500	244
New York	19,651	939	3,587	4,989	3,133	4,707	2,296
North Carolina	9,848	490	1,939	2,366	1,599	2,337	1,118
North Dakota	723	39	137	199	97	166	85
Ohio	11,571	553	2,257	2,670	1,768	2,904	1,420
Oklahoma	3,851	212	788	960	561	888	442
Oregon	3,930	184	723	955	606	979	483
Pennsylvania	12,774	573	2,339	2,947	1,946	3,260	1,709
Rhode Island	1,052	44	191	256	163	265	132
South Carolina	4,775	234	916	1,146	734	1,172	574
South Dakota	845	48	173	203	116	202	104

	total population	Recession (0 to 3)	iGeneration (4 to 18)	Millennial (19 to 36)	Generation X (37 to 48)	Baby Boom (49 to 67)	Older Americans (68 or older)
Tennessee	6,496	320	1,256	1,553	1,032	1,579	757
Texas	26,448	1,553	5,857	6,886	4,227	5,573	2,353
Utah	2,901	203	735	812	412	512	227
Vermont	627	24	111	140	94	176	81
Virginia	8,260	410	1,575	2,080	1,344	1,974	878
Washington	6,971	356	1,325	1,757	1,100	1,683	752
West Virginia	1,854	82	324	412	285	495	257
Wisconsin	5,743	275	1,115	1,343	875	1,445	690
Wyoming	583	31	115	146	83	145	63

Source: Bureau of the Census, State Population Estimates, Internet site http://www.census.gov/popest/data/state/asrh/2013/index .html; calculations by New Strategist

Table 8.20 Distribution of State Population by Generation, 2013

(percent distribution of people by state and generation, 2013)

	total population	Recession (0 to 3)	iGeneration (4 to 18)	Millennial (19 to 36)	Generation X (37 to 48)	Baby Boom (49 to 67)	Older Americans (68 or older)
United States	**100.0%**	**5.0%**	**19.6%**	**24.7%**	**15.6%**	**24.0%**	**11.1%**
Alabama	100.0	4.9	19.4	23.9	15.4	24.3	11.9
Alaska	100.0	6.0	20.8	28.0	14.9	23.4	6.8
Arizona	100.0	5.2	20.6	24.4	15.0	22.5	12.4
Arkansas	100.0	5.2	20.1	23.9	15.0	23.6	12.3
California	100.0	5.2	20.1	26.2	16.2	22.2	10.0
Colorado	100.0	5.1	19.8	25.9	16.1	23.5	9.7
Connecticut	100.0	4.3	19.2	22.5	16.2	25.6	12.3
Delaware	100.0	4.9	18.7	23.6	15.2	25.0	12.7
District of Columbia	100.0	5.1	14.4	35.8	15.6	19.9	9.1
Florida	100.0	4.4	17.4	22.8	15.4	24.8	15.3
Georgia	100.0	5.4	21.0	25.0	16.7	22.5	9.4
Hawaii	100.0	5.2	17.9	25.7	15.0	23.7	12.6
Idaho	100.0	5.6	22.2	24.0	14.5	22.7	11.0
Illinois	100.0	5.0	19.9	24.8	15.9	23.5	10.9
Indiana	100.0	5.1	20.5	24.0	15.4	23.8	11.2
Iowa	100.0	5.0	19.9	23.7	14.4	24.2	12.8
Kansas	100.0	5.5	20.9	24.7	14.4	23.1	11.4
Kentucky	100.0	5.0	19.4	23.7	15.8	24.6	11.5
Louisiana	100.0	5.3	20.0	25.7	14.9	23.5	10.6
Maine	100.0	3.9	17.1	20.7	15.5	28.6	14.2
Maryland	100.0	5.0	19.1	24.4	16.4	24.5	10.7
Massachusetts	100.0	4.4	18.2	24.6	16.0	24.9	11.9
Michigan	100.0	4.6	19.5	23.0	15.4	25.4	12.1
Minnesota	100.0	5.1	19.8	24.1	15.3	24.4	11.3
Mississippi	100.0	5.3	20.8	24.5	15.0	23.2	11.1
Missouri	100.0	5.0	19.5	24.0	14.9	24.4	12.2
Montana	100.0	4.8	18.6	23.3	13.8	26.5	13.0
Nebraska	100.0	5.6	20.8	24.5	14.4	23.1	11.6
Nevada	100.0	5.1	19.7	24.9	16.4	23.2	10.7
New Hampshire	100.0	4.0	18.1	21.7	16.2	27.9	12.2
New Jersey	100.0	4.8	19.2	23.0	16.7	24.6	11.7
New Mexico	100.0	5.3	20.4	24.4	14.2	24.0	11.7
New York	100.0	4.8	18.3	25.4	15.9	24.0	11.7
North Carolina	100.0	5.0	19.7	24.0	16.2	23.7	11.3
North Dakota	100.0	5.4	19.0	27.6	13.4	23.0	11.7
Ohio	100.0	4.8	19.5	23.1	15.3	25.1	12.3
Oklahoma	100.0	5.5	20.5	24.9	14.6	23.1	11.5
Oregon	100.0	4.7	18.4	24.3	15.4	24.9	12.3
Pennsylvania	100.0	4.5	18.3	23.1	15.2	25.5	13.4
Rhode Island	100.0	4.2	18.2	24.4	15.5	25.2	12.6
South Carolina	100.0	4.9	19.2	24.0	15.4	24.5	12.0
South Dakota	100.0	5.7	20.4	24.0	13.7	23.9	12.3

	total population	Recession (0 to 3)	iGeneration (4 to 18)	Millennial (19 to 36)	Generation X (37 to 48)	Baby Boom (49 to 67)	Older Americans (68 or older)
Tennessee	100.0%	4.9%	19.3%	23.9%	15.9%	24.3%	11.7%
Texas	100.0	5.9	22.1	26.0	16.0	21.1	8.9
Utah	100.0	7.0	25.3	28.0	14.2	17.7	7.8
Vermont	100.0	3.9	17.7	22.3	15.1	28.0	13.0
Virginia	100.0	5.0	19.1	25.2	16.3	23.9	10.6
Washington	100.0	5.1	19.0	25.2	15.8	24.1	10.8
West Virginia	100.0	4.4	17.5	22.2	15.4	26.7	13.8
Wisconsin	100.0	4.8	19.4	23.4	15.2	25.2	12.0
Wyoming	100.0	5.3	19.7	25.1	14.2	24.9	10.7

Source: Bureau of the Census, State Population Estimates, Internet site http://www.census.gov/popest/data/state/asrh/2013/index .html; calculations by New Strategist

Table 8.21 Millennial Generation by State, 2013

(number of total people, people aged 19 to 36, and in age groups that include Millennials, by state, 2013; numbers in thousands)

	total population	Millennials (19 to 36)	15 to 19	20 to 24	25 to 29	30 to 34	35 to 39
Total population	**316,129**	**77,971**	**21,159**	**22,795**	**21,580**	**21,264**	**19,604**
Alabama	4,834	1,157	321	355	312	309	292
Alaska	735	206	49	63	61	54	45
Arizona	6,627	1,620	451	485	441	440	409
Arkansas	2,959	706	196	211	191	193	179
California	38,333	10,061	2,659	2,927	2,841	2,751	2,526
Colorado	5,268	1,363	340	375	391	388	352
Connecticut	3,596	809	254	236	222	217	207
Delaware	926	219	60	66	62	58	52
District of Columbia	646	231	38	59	77	69	48
Florida	19,553	4,460	1,171	1,314	1,255	1,202	1,140
Georgia	9,992	2,501	695	734	680	685	657
Hawaii	1,404	361	80	105	107	99	87
Idaho	1,612	387	114	112	105	107	99
Illinois	12,882	3,196	877	906	888	897	825
Indiana	6,571	1,575	456	481	418	425	400
Iowa	3,090	731	213	227	191	199	178
Kansas	2,894	714	201	218	193	194	171
Kentucky	4,395	1,043	283	314	277	287	273
Louisiana	4,625	1,187	302	353	337	325	279
Maine	1,328	275	83	79	76	74	72
Maryland	5,929	1,446	390	404	414	404	367
Massachusetts	6,693	1,647	457	484	475	438	398
Michigan	9,896	2,274	685	726	595	592	563
Minnesota	5,420	1,306	359	361	366	377	327
Mississippi	2,991	732	208	228	194	196	181
Missouri	6,044	1,453	398	434	398	399	355
Montana	1,015	237	64	74	63	64	57
Nebraska	1,869	458	127	135	125	128	112
Nevada	2,790	695	177	189	198	199	184
New Hampshire	1,323	287	91	88	77	75	72
New Jersey	8,899	2,047	582	566	565	575	562
New Mexico	2,085	508	140	153	141	137	121
New York	19,651	4,989	1,280	1,441	1,446	1,358	1,223
North Carolina	9,848	2,366	651	712	639	635	623
North Dakota	723	199	49	70	54	50	41
Ohio	11,571	2,670	780	793	732	720	671
Oklahoma	3,851	960	256	289	263	264	232
Oregon	3,930	955	246	268	262	274	254
Pennsylvania	12,774	2,947	847	879	829	783	717
Rhode Island	1,052	256	75	82	70	65	59
South Carolina	4,775	1,146	311	355	311	304	284
South Dakota	845	203	57	61	56	55	47

	total population	Millennials (19 to 36)	15 to 19	20 to 24	25 to 29	30 to 34	35 to 39
Tennessee	6,496	1,553	419	462	421	425	402
Texas	26,448	6,886	1,887	1,968	1,920	1,912	1,771
Utah	2,901	812	224	246	213	228	201
Vermont	627	140	45	45	36	36	34
Virginia	8,260	2,080	537	602	585	576	525
Washington	6,971	1,757	439	494	499	497	448
West Virginia	1,854	412	112	125	106	113	111
Wisconsin	5,743	1,343	385	399	361	372	335
Wyoming	583	146	38	43	41	41	35

Source: Bureau of the Census, State Population Estimates, Internet site http://www.census.gov/popest/data/state/asrh/2013/index .html; calculations by New Strategist

Table 8.22 Millennial Share of State Populations, 2013

(percent of population aged 19 to 36 and in age groups that include Millennials, by state, 2013)

	total population	Millennials (19 to 36)	15 to 19	20 to 24	25 to 29	30 to 34	35 to 39
United States	**100.0%**	**24.7%**	**6.7%**	**7.2%**	**6.8%**	**6.7%**	**6.2%**
Alabama	100.0	23.9	6.6	7.4	6.4	6.4	6.0
Alaska	100.0	28.0	6.7	8.6	8.3	7.3	6.1
Arizona	100.0	24.4	6.8	7.3	6.7	6.6	6.2
Arkansas	100.0	23.9	6.6	7.1	6.5	6.5	6.0
California	100.0	26.2	6.9	7.6	7.4	7.2	6.6
Colorado	100.0	25.9	6.4	7.1	7.4	7.4	6.7
Connecticut	100.0	22.5	7.1	6.6	6.2	6.0	5.8
Delaware	100.0	23.6	6.5	7.1	6.6	6.3	5.7
District of Columbia	100.0	35.8	5.8	9.1	11.9	10.6	7.4
Florida	100.0	22.8	6.0	6.7	6.4	6.1	5.8
Georgia	100.0	25.0	7.0	7.3	6.8	6.9	6.6
Hawaii	100.0	25.7	5.7	7.5	7.6	7.0	6.2
Idaho	100.0	24.0	7.0	6.9	6.5	6.7	6.1
Illinois	100.0	24.8	6.8	7.0	6.9	7.0	6.4
Indiana	100.0	24.0	6.9	7.3	6.4	6.5	6.1
Iowa	100.0	23.7	6.9	7.3	6.2	6.4	5.8
Kansas	100.0	24.7	6.9	7.5	6.7	6.7	5.9
Kentucky	100.0	23.7	6.4	7.1	6.3	6.5	6.2
Louisiana	100.0	25.7	6.5	7.6	7.3	7.0	6.0
Maine	100.0	20.7	6.2	6.0	5.7	5.6	5.4
Maryland	100.0	24.4	6.6	6.8	7.0	6.8	6.2
Massachusetts	100.0	24.6	6.8	7.2	7.1	6.5	6.0
Michigan	100.0	23.0	6.9	7.3	6.0	6.0	5.7
Minnesota	100.0	24.1	6.6	6.7	6.7	7.0	6.0
Mississippi	100.0	24.5	7.0	7.6	6.5	6.6	6.0
Missouri	100.0	24.0	6.6	7.2	6.6	6.6	5.9
Montana	100.0	23.3	6.3	7.3	6.2	6.3	5.6
Nebraska	100.0	24.5	6.8	7.2	6.7	6.8	6.0
Nevada	100.0	24.9	6.3	6.8	7.1	7.1	6.6
New Hampshire	100.0	21.7	6.9	6.7	5.8	5.7	5.5
New Jersey	100.0	23.0	6.5	6.4	6.3	6.5	6.3
New Mexico	100.0	24.4	6.7	7.4	6.8	6.6	5.8
New York	100.0	25.4	6.5	7.3	7.4	6.9	6.2
North Carolina	100.0	24.0	6.6	7.2	6.5	6.4	6.3
North Dakota	100.0	27.6	6.8	9.6	7.5	6.9	5.6
Ohio	100.0	23.1	6.7	6.9	6.3	6.2	5.8
Oklahoma	100.0	24.9	6.7	7.5	6.8	6.9	6.0
Oregon	100.0	24.3	6.3	6.8	6.7	7.0	6.5
Pennsylvania	100.0	23.1	6.6	6.9	6.5	6.1	5.6
Rhode Island	100.0	24.4	7.1	7.8	6.7	6.2	5.6
South Carolina	100.0	24.0	6.5	7.4	6.5	6.4	6.0
South Dakota	100.0	24.0	6.8	7.2	6.6	6.6	5.6

	total population	Millennials (19 to 36)	15 to 19	20 to 24	25 to 29	30 to 34	35 to 39
Tennessee	100.0%	23.9%	6.5%	7.1%	6.5%	6.5%	6.2%
Texas	100.0	26.0	7.1	7.4	7.3	7.2	6.7
Utah	100.0	28.0	7.7	8.5	7.3	7.9	6.9
Vermont	100.0	22.3	7.1	7.2	5.7	5.7	5.4
Virginia	100.0	25.2	6.5	7.3	7.1	7.0	6.4
Washington	100.0	25.2	6.3	7.1	7.2	7.1	6.4
West Virginia	100.0	22.2	6.1	6.8	5.7	6.1	6.0
Wisconsin	100.0	23.4	6.7	7.0	6.3	6.5	5.8
Wyoming	100.0	25.1	6.5	7.4	7.0	7.0	6.0

Source: Bureau of the Census, State Population Estimates, Internet site http://www.census.gov/popest/data/state/asrh/2013/index .html; calculations by New Strategist

Young Adults Are Least Likely to Vote

People aged 65 or older are most likely to vote.

The older people are, the more likely they are to vote. This has long been true, but the gap between young and old has widened over the years. In the 1972 presidential election (the first in which 18-to-20-year-olds could vote), 63.5 percent of people aged 65 or older reported voting compared with 49.6 percent of those aged 18 to 24 (a 13.9 percentage point difference). In the 2012 election, 72.0 percent of citizens aged 65 or older voted versus only 41.2 percent of citizens aged 18 to 24 (a 30.8 percentage point difference). (The voting rates of citizens by age are not available before 2004.)

Despite the excitement generated by Barack Obama during the 2008 presidential campaign, the overall voting rate fell slightly between 2004 and 2008. Young adults were the only ones who boosted their voting rate, the percentage of 18-to-24-year-olds who voted rising from 46.7 to 48.5 percent. In the 2012 presidential election, however, the voting rate of young adults fell by more than 7 percentage points to 41.2 percent. Voting rates also fell among citizens ranging in age from 25 to 64, but the rate increased among citizens aged 65 or older.

■ Non-Hispanic Whites aged 45 or older accounted for only 48 percent of voters in the 2012 presidential election.

Less than half of young adults vote

(percent of citizens aged 18 or older voting in the 2012 presidential election, by age)

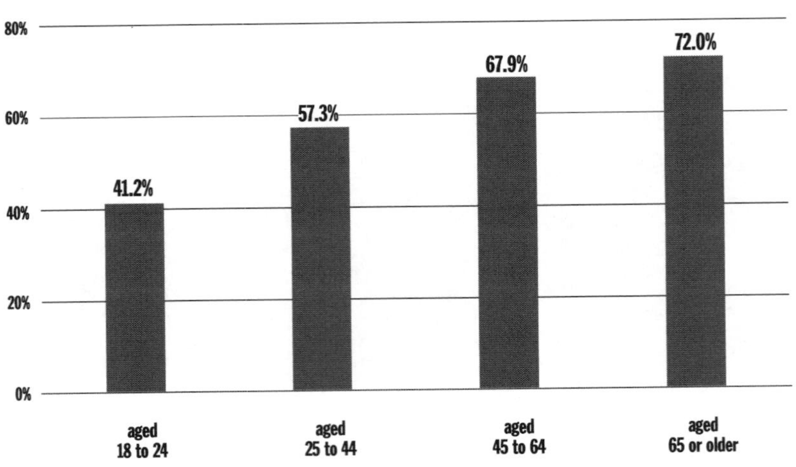

Table 8.23 Voting Rate in Presidential Elections by Age, 1972 to 2012

(percent of people aged 18 or older who reported voting in presidential elections by age, and index of age group to total, 1972 to 2012)

	total people of voting age	18 to 24	25 to 44	45 to 64	65 or older
Citizen population					
2012	61.8%	41.2%	57.3%	67.9%	72.0%
2008	63.6	48.5	60.0	69.2	70.3
2004	63.8	46.7	60.1	70.4	71.0
Total population					
2000	54.7	32.3	49.8	64.1	67.6
1996	54.2	32.4	49.2	64.4	67.0
1992	61.3	42.8	58.3	70.0	70.1
1988	57.4	36.2	54.0	67.9	68.8
1984	59.9	40.8	58.4	69.8	67.7
1980	59.3	39.9	58.7	69.3	65.1
1976	59.2	42.2	58.7	68.7	62.2
1972	63.0	49.6	62.7	70.8	63.5
INDEX OF AGE GROUP TO TOTAL					
Citizen population					
2012	100	67	93	110	117
2008	100	76	94	109	111
2004	100	73	94	110	111
Total population					
2000	100	59	91	117	124
1996	100	60	91	119	124
1992	100	70	95	114	114
1988	100	63	94	118	120
1984	100	68	97	117	113
1980	100	67	99	117	110
1976	100	71	99	116	105
1972	100	79	100	112	101

Note: Voting rates of citizens by age are not available before 2004. The index is calculated by dividing the voting rate of each age group by the total voting rate and multiplying by 100.
Source: Bureau of the Census, Voting and Registration, Internet site http://www.census.gov/hhes/www/socdemo/voting/index.html; calculations by New Strategist

Table 8.24 Voters by Age, Race, and Hispanic Origin, 2012

(number, percent distribution, and share of people who reported voting in the presidential election by age, race, and Hispanic origin, 2012; numbers in thousands)

	total	Asian	Black	Hispanic	non-Hispanic White
Total voters	**132,948**	**4,331**	**18,558**	**11,188**	**98,041**
Aged 18 to 24	11,353	408	2,306	1,677	6,933
Aged 25 to 44	39,942	1,652	6,595	4,365	27,216
Aged 45 to 64	52,013	1,522	6,890	3,609	39,507
Aged 65 or older	29,641	748	2,767	1,537	24,385
PERCENT DISTRIBUTION OF VOTERS BY RACE AND HISPANIC ORIGIN					
Total voters	**100.0%**	**3.3%**	**14.0%**	**8.4%**	**73.7%**
Aged 18 to 24	100.0	3.6	20.3	14.8	61.1
Aged 25 to 44	100.0	4.1	16.5	10.9	68.1
Aged 45 to 64	100.0	2.9	13.2	6.9	76.0
Aged 65 or older	100.0	2.5	9.3	5.2	82.3
SHARE OF VOTERS BY AGE GROUP, RACE, AND HISPANIC ORIGIN					
Under age 45	38.6	1.5	6.7	4.5	25.7
Aged 45 or older	61.4	1.7	7.3	3.9	48.1

Note: Asians and Blacks are those who identify themselves as being of the race alone and those who identify themselves as being of the race in combination with other races. Non-Hispanic Whites are those who identify themselves as being White alone and not Hispanic.
Source: Bureau of the Census, Voting and Registration, Internet site http://www.census.gov/hhes/www/socdemo/voting/index.html; calculations by New Strategist

CHAPTER

9

Spending

■ The Great Recession was a setback for young adults. Households headed by people under age 25 cut their spending by 7 percent between 2006 and 2013, after adjusting for inflation. Since 2010, however, their spending has begun to grow again.

■ Households headed by people ranging in age from 25 to 44 (the Millennial generation was aged 19 to 36 in 2013) cut their spending by 11 to 13 percent between 2006 and 2013, after adjusting for inflation. Their spending continued to decline in the more recent 2010-to-2013 time period. In 2013, these households spent less than their counterparts did in 2000.

■ Many Millennials are adults living at home with their parents. Couples with adult children at home spent $76,085 in 2013—6 percent less than they spent in 2006, after adjusting for inflation. But during the 2010-to-2013 time period, the spending of this household type began to grow again.

Spending Has Dropped among Young Adults

Their spending began to recover in the 2010-to-2013 time period, however.

Households headed by people under age 25 cut their spending by 7 percent between 2006 and 2013, after adjusting for inflation. Between 2010 and 2013, however, their spending grew 3 percent. In contrast, spending continued to decline for the average household during those years, falling by 0.6 percent.

Householders under age 25 reduced their spending on many discretionary items between 2006 and 2013. Their spending on food away from home fell 8 percent, after adjusting for inflation. Spending on alcoholic beverages declined by an even larger 31 percent. Spending on new cars and trucks fell 26 percent. Since 2010, however, spending has begun to increase in some categories. Most notably, householders under age 25 spent 92 percent more on new cars and trucks in 2013 than they did in 2010. Their spending on food away from home climbed 5 percent during those years.

Many householders under age 25 are in college, and their spending on education climbed 41 percent between 2006 and 2013, after adjusting for inflation. Between 2010 and 2013, however, they brought this spending spree to a halt, registering only a small 0.9 percent increase in spending on education.

■ The Great Recession was a major setback for young adults, but they appear to be regaining stability and their spending is beginning to recover.

Young adults are spending more on some items

(percent change in spending by householders under age 25, 2010 to 2013; in 2013 dollars)

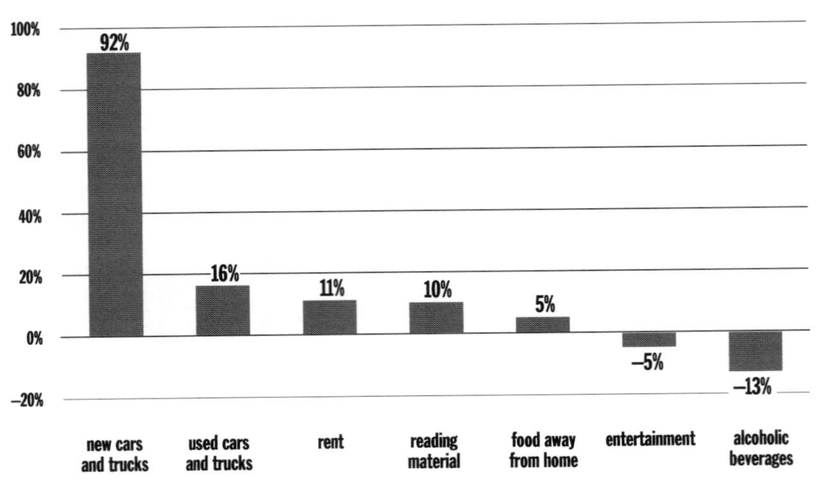

Table 9.1 Average Household Spending, 2000 to 2013

(average annual spending of consumer units on products and services, 2000 to 2013; percent change for selected years; in 2013 dollars)

	average spending				percent change		
	2013	2010	2006	2000	2010–13	2006–13	2000–06
Number of consumer units (in 000s)	**125,670**	**121,107**	**118,843**	**109,367**	**3.8%**	**5.7%**	**8.7%**
Average annual spending of consumer units	**$51,100**	**$51,397**	**$55,926**	**$51,468**	**–0.6**	**–8.6**	**8.7**
FOOD	**6,602**	**6,548**	**7,062**	**6,978**	**0.8**	**–6.5**	**1.2**
Food at home	**3,977**	**3,872**	**3,948**	**4,087**	**2.7**	**0.7**	**–3.4**
Cereals and bakery products	544	536	515	613	1.4	5.6	–15.9
Cereals and cereal products	185	176	165	211	4.9	12.0	–21.7
Bakery products	359	360	351	402	–0.3	2.2	–12.6
Meats, poultry, fish, and eggs	856	838	921	1,075	2.2	–7.1	–14.4
Beef	219	232	273	322	–5.5	–19.7	–15.3
Pork	170	159	181	226	6.8	–6.3	–19.7
Other meats	119	125	121	137	–4.8	–1.9	–11.2
Poultry	170	147	163	196	15.3	4.3	–16.9
Fish and seafood	122	125	141	149	–2.4	–13.5	–5.3
Eggs	56	49	43	46	14.0	31.0	–7.0
Dairy products	414	406	425	440	2.0	–2.6	–3.3
Fresh milk and cream	152	151	162	177	0.9	–6.0	–8.7
Other dairy products	262	256	263	261	2.2	–0.6	0.9
Fruits and vegetables	751	725	684	705	3.5	9.8	–2.9
Fresh fruits	270	248	225	221	8.9	19.8	2.2
Fresh vegetables	236	224	223	215	5.2	5.8	3.7
Processed fruits	115	121	126	156	–4.7	–8.7	–19.0
Processed vegetables	130	132	110	114	–1.9	18.4	–3.4
Other food at home	1,412	1,365	1,401	1,254	3.4	0.8	11.7
Sugar and other sweets	143	141	144	158	1.4	–1.0	–8.7
Fats and oils	117	110	99	112	6.3	17.7	–11.5
Miscellaneous foods	728	713	725	591	2.2	0.5	22.6
Nonalcoholic beverages	384	356	384	338	7.9	0.1	13.4
Food prepared by consumer unit on trips	42	46	50	54	–8.6	–15.5	–8.2
Food away from home	**2,625**	**2,676**	**3,113**	**2,891**	**–1.9**	**–15.7**	**7.7**
ALCOHOLIC BEVERAGES	**445**	**440**	**574**	**503**	**1.1**	**–22.5**	**14.1**
HOUSING	**17,148**	**17,688**	**18,912**	**16,665**	**–3.1**	**–9.3**	**13.5**
Shelter	**10,080**	**10,483**	**11,178**	**9,624**	**–3.8**	**–9.8**	**16.1**
Owned dwellings	6,108	6,706	7,530	6,226	–8.9	–18.9	20.9
Mortgage interest and charges	3,078	3,580	4,337	3,570	–14.0	–29.0	21.5
Property taxes	1,848	1,938	1,905	1,541	–4.6	–3.0	23.7
Maintenance, repair, insurance, other expenses	1,182	1,188	1,288	1,116	–0.5	–8.3	15.4
Rented dwellings	3,324	3,098	2,993	2,752	7.3	11.1	8.8
Other lodging	649	678	655	647	–4.3	–0.9	1.3

	average spending				percent change		
	2013	2010	2006	2000	2010–13	2006–13	2000–06
Utilities, fuels, and public services	**$3,737**	**$3,910**	**$3,925**	**$3,367**	**–4.4%**	**–4.8%**	**16.6%**
Natural gas	393	470	588	415	–16.4	–33.2	41.6
Electricity	1,422	1,510	1,463	1,232	–5.8	–2.8	18.7
Fuel oil and other fuels	142	150	159	131	–5.1	–11.0	21.5
Telephone services	1,271	1,258	1,256	1,186	1.0	1.2	5.9
Residential telephone, VOIP, and phone cards	358	447	651	1,025	–19.8	–45.0	–36.6
Cellular phone service	913	812	606	161	12.5	50.8	276.1
Water and other public services	509	522	459	400	–2.6	11.0	14.6
Household services	**1,144**	**1,076**	**1,095**	**925**	**6.3**	**4.4**	**18.4**
Personal services	368	363	454	441	1.3	–19.0	3.0
Other household services	776	713	641	484	8.9	21.0	32.4
Housekeeping supplies	**645**	**654**	**740**	**652**	**–1.3**	**–12.8**	**13.4**
Laundry and cleaning supplies	154	160	174	177	–3.9	–11.7	–1.5
Other household products	350	351	381	306	–0.4	–8.2	24.7
Postage and stationery	140	141	184	170	–0.7	–23.8	7.8
Household furnishings and equipment	**1,542**	**1,567**	**1,974**	**2,096**	**–1.6**	**–21.9**	**–5.8**
Household textiles	97	109	178	143	–11.0	–45.5	24.1
Furniture	382	379	535	529	0.7	–28.6	1.1
Floor coverings	20	38	55	60	–48.0	–63.9	–6.8
Major appliances	214	223	278	256	–4.2	–23.2	8.9
Small appliances and miscellaneous housewares	100	114	126	118	–12.5	–20.6	7.0
Miscellaneous household equipment	727	702	801	989	3.6	–9.2	–19.0
APPAREL AND RELATED SERVICES	**1,604**	**1,816**	**2,165**	**2,511**	**–11.7**	**–25.9**	**–13.8**
Men and boys	**374**	**408**	**513**	**595**	**–8.4**	**–27.1**	**–13.8**
Men, aged 16 or older	304	325	408	465	–6.4	–25.5	–12.3
Boys, aged 2 to 15	70	83	105	130	–16.0	–33.4	–19.0
Women and girls	**636**	**708**	**868**	**981**	**–10.2**	**–26.7**	**–11.5**
Women, aged 16 or older	527	600	727	821	–12.2	–27.5	–11.5
Girls, aged 2 to 15	109	108	141	160	1.0	–22.7	–11.7
Children under age 2	**75**	**97**	**111**	**111**	**–22.9**	**–32.4**	**0.0**
Footwear	**307**	**324**	**351**	**464**	**–5.2**	**–12.6**	**–24.3**
Other apparel products and services	**211**	**279**	**324**	**360**	**–24.3**	**–34.8**	**–10.1**
TRANSPORTATION	**9,004**	**8,202**	**9,831**	**10,034**	**9.8**	**–8.4**	**–2.0**
Vehicle purchases	**3,271**	**2,765**	**3,953**	**4,624**	**18.3**	**–17.3**	**–14.5**
Cars and trucks, new	1,563	1,302	2,078	2,171	20.0	–24.8	–4.3
Cars and trucks, used	1,669	1,408	1,812	2,395	18.5	–7.9	–24.3
Gasoline and motor oil	**2,611**	**2,278**	**2,573**	**1,747**	**14.6**	**1.5**	**47.3**
Other vehicle expenses	**2,584**	**2,632**	**2,721**	**3,086**	**–1.8**	**–5.0**	**–11.8**
Vehicle finance charges	204	260	344	444	–21.4	–40.8	–22.4
Maintenance and repairs	835	841	795	844	–0.7	5.0	–5.8
Vehicle insurance	1,013	1,079	1,024	1,053	–6.1	–1.1	–2.7
Vehicle rentals, leases, licenses, other charges	533	452	557	745	17.9	–4.3	–25.3
Public transportation	**537**	**527**	**584**	**578**	**2.0**	**–8.0**	**1.0**

	average spending				percent change		
	2013	2010	2006	2000	2010–13	2006–13	2000–06
HEALTH CARE	**$3,631**	**$3,373**	**$3,196**	**$2,795**	**7.7%**	**13.6%**	**14.4%**
Health insurance	2,229	1,956	1,693	1,330	13.9	31.7	27.3
Medical services	796	771	774	768	3.2	2.8	0.8
Drugs	470	518	594	563	–9.3	–20.9	5.5
Medical supplies	135	127	135	134	6.2	–0.1	0.9
ENTERTAINMENT	**2,482**	**2,675**	**2,746**	**2,520**	**–7.2**	**–9.6**	**8.9**
Fees and admissions	569	621	700	697	–8.3	–18.7	0.5
Audio and visual equipment and services	964	1,019	1,047	841	–5.4	–7.9	24.4
Pets, toys, and playground equipment	596	647	476	452	–7.9	25.2	5.4
Pets	460	513	365	283	–10.3	26.0	29.1
Toys, hobbies, and playground equipment	136	134	111	169	1.8	22.6	–34.4
Other entertainment products and services	353	389	521	532	–9.2	–32.3	–2.0
PERSONAL CARE PRODUCTS AND SERVICES	**608**	**622**	**676**	**763**	**–2.2**	**–10.1**	**–11.4**
READING	**102**	**107**	**135**	**198**	**–4.5**	**–24.6**	**–31.5**
EDUCATION	**1,138**	**1,147**	**1,026**	**855**	**–0.8**	**10.9**	**20.0**
TOBACCO PRODUCTS AND SMOKING SUPPLIES	**330**	**387**	**378**	**432**	**–14.7**	**–12.7**	**–12.4**
MISCELLANEOUS	**645**	**907**	**978**	**1,050**	**–28.9**	**–34.0**	**–6.9**
CASH CONTRIBUTIONS	**1,834**	**1,745**	**2,160**	**1,613**	**5.1**	**–15.1**	**33.9**
PERSONAL INSURANCE AND PENSIONS	**5,528**	**5,740**	**6,090**	**4,552**	**–3.7**	**–9.2**	**33.8**
Life and other personal insurance	319	340	372	540	–6.1	–14.3	–31.1
Pensions and Social Security*	5,209	5,399	5,718	4,012	–3.5	–8.9	*
GIFTS FOR PEOPLE IN OTHER HOUSEHOLDS	**1,078**	**1,099**	**1,333**	**1,465**	**–1.9**	**–19.2**	**–9.0**

**Recent spending on pensions and Social Security is not comparable with 2000 because of changes in methodology.*
Note: The Bureau of Labor Statistics uses consumer unit rather than household as the sampling unit in the Consumer Expenditure Survey. For the definition of consumer unit, see the glossary. Spending on gifts is also included in the preceding product and service categories.
Source: Bureau of Labor Statistics, 2000, 2006, 2010, and 2013 Consumer Expenditure Surveys, Internet site http://www.bls.gov/cex/; calculations by New Strategist

Table 9.2 Average Spending of Householders under Age 25, 2000 to 2013

(average annual spending of consumer units headed by people under age 25 on products and services, 2000 to 2013; percent change for selected years; in 2013 dollars)

	average spending				percent change		
	2013	**2010**	**2006**	**2000**	**2010–13**	**2006–13**	**2000–06**
Number of consumer units under age 25 (in 000s)	**8,275**	**8,034**	**8,167**	**8,306**	**3.0%**	**1.3%**	**–1.7%**
Average annual spending of consumer units	**$30,373**	**$29,361**	**$32,564**	**$30,497**	**3.4**	**–6.7**	**6.8**
FOOD	**4,698**	**4,351**	**4,529**	**4,347**	**8.0**	**3.7**	**4.2**
Food at home	**2,602**	**2,347**	**2,249**	**2,223**	**10.9**	**15.7**	**1.2**
Cereals and bakery products	363	333	277	322	8.9	30.9	–13.9
Cereals and cereal products	130	110	109	122	18.1	19.7	–10.8
Bakery products	233	223	169	200	4.4	38.1	–15.7
Meats, poultry, fish, and eggs	580	478	502	591	21.5	15.7	–15.2
Beef	141	145	149	183	–3.0	–5.4	–18.4
Pork	105	89	103	120	18.4	2.1	–14.6
Other meats	75	74	68	74	1.7	10.0	–8.4
Poultry	126	90	92	116	40.4	36.3	–20.5
Fish and seafood	93	48	61	70	93.4	51.9	–12.9
Eggs	40	33	27	28	20.8	50.5	–6.4
Dairy products	274	233	253	237	17.6	8.3	6.9
Fresh milk and cream	109	94	106	99	15.9	2.5	7.6
Other dairy products	165	139	147	137	18.8	12.4	7.4
Fruits and vegetables	448	422	369	342	6.2	21.5	7.7
Fresh fruits	147	127	114	104	15.6	28.5	9.8
Fresh vegetables	137	140	114	100	–2.1	19.8	14.3
Processed fruits	79	73	79	84	8.7	0.5	–6.3
Processed vegetables	85	82	61	55	3.3	38.8	10.4
Other food at home	936	882	848	732	6.1	10.4	15.9
Sugar and other sweets	89	67	80	81	32.2	11.6	–1.8
Fats and oils	73	68	54	57	6.8	34.4	–4.4
Miscellaneous foods	486	495	463	367	–1.7	4.9	26.4
Nonalcoholic beverages	276	238	231	199	15.9	19.4	16.2
Food prepared by consumer unit on trips	13	14	18	26	–6.4	–29.7	–28.1
Food away from home	**2,096**	**2,004**	**2,280**	**2,123**	**4.6**	**–8.1**	**7.4**
ALCOHOLIC BEVERAGES	**379**	**434**	**547**	**530**	**–12.6**	**–30.7**	**3.1**
HOUSING	**10,379**	**10,206**	**10,810**	**9,617**	**1.7**	**–4.0**	**12.4**
Shelter	**6,944**	**6,587**	**6,844**	**6,188**	**5.4**	**1.5**	**10.6**
Owned dwellings	1,003	1,200	1,624	858	–16.4	–38.2	89.3
Mortgage interest and charges	449	733	1,052	522	–38.7	–57.3	101.4
Property taxes	403	269	414	238	49.7	–2.6	73.7
Maintenance, repair, insurance, other expenses	151	198	158	97	–23.6	–4.6	62.5
Rented dwellings	5,728	5,142	4,986	4,895	11.4	14.9	1.9
Other lodging	213	247	235	436	–13.7	–9.2	–46.2

	average spending				percent change		
	2013	2010	2006	2000	2010–13	2006–13	2000–06
Utilities, fuels, and public services	**$1,842**	**$1,942**	**$2,058**	**$1,688**	**–5.2%**	**–10.5%**	**21.9%**
Natural gas	163	199	215	138	–18.0	–24.2	55.8
Electricity	728	765	801	601	–4.8	–9.1	33.3
Fuel oil and other fuels	30	21	35	28	40.4	–13.5	22.0
Telephone services	737	762	834	797	–3.2	–11.7	4.7
Residential telephone, VOIP, and phone cards	87	104	255	683	–16.6	–65.9	–62.6
Cellular phone service	651	657	579	115	–1.0	12.4	405.6
Water and other public services	184	197	173	123	–6.4	6.2	40.8
Household services	**428**	**444**	**432**	**306**	**–3.7**	**–1.0**	**41.4**
Personal services	134	165	246	208	–18.6	–45.6	18.1
Other household services	293	279	186	97	5.1	57.5	91.0
Housekeeping supplies	**323**	**298**	**341**	**262**	**8.4**	**–5.2**	**29.9**
Laundry and cleaning supplies	93	96	96	74	–3.3	–3.0	28.9
Other household products	193	166	172	120	16.6	12.1	43.0
Postage and stationery	38	36	74	68	4.6	–48.6	9.3
Household furnishings and equipment	**842**	**934**	**1,135**	**1,173**	**–9.8**	**–25.8**	**–3.3**
Household textiles	56	57	65	47	–1.1	–13.5	36.7
Furniture	258	286	404	365	–9.9	–36.2	10.7
Floor coverings	6	9	28	8	–29.8	–78.4	241.7
Major appliances	95	98	120	104	–3.3	–20.9	15.4
Small appliances and miscellaneous housewares	85	48	60	68	76.8	41.5	–11.2
Miscellaneous household equipment	343	437	458	580	–21.5	–25.0	–21.2
APPAREL AND RELATED SERVICES	**1,513**	**1,666**	**1,692**	**1,921**	**–9.2**	**–10.6**	**–11.9**
Men and boys	**316**	**278**	**340**	**433**	**13.8**	**–7.0**	**–21.5**
Men, aged 16 or older	285	234	315	398	21.8	–9.7	–20.7
Boys, aged 2 to 15	31	44	24	35	–29.2	27.7	–31.0
Women and girls	**516**	**716**	**640**	**588**	**–27.9**	**–19.4**	**8.8**
Women, aged 16 or older	441	671	601	548	–34.3	–26.6	9.7
Girls, aged 2 to 15	75	45	38	42	67.1	96.7	–9.1
Children under age 2	**152**	**156**	**150**	**137**	**–2.5**	**1.2**	**9.9**
Footwear	**333**	**326**	**290**	**491**	**2.2**	**14.8**	**–40.9**
Other apparel products and services	**197**	**189**	**270**	**272**	**4.2**	**–27.1**	**–0.6**
TRANSPORTATION	**5,672**	**5,013**	**6,548**	**7,020**	**13.2**	**–13.4**	**–6.7**
Vehicle purchases	**2,262**	**1,700**	**2,769**	**3,555**	**33.1**	**–18.3**	**–22.1**
Cars and trucks, new	805	420	1,090	1,435	91.7	–26.1	–24.1
Cars and trucks, used	1,371	1,183	1,625	2,093	15.9	–15.6	–22.4
Gasoline and motor oil	**1,717**	**1,595**	**1,892**	**1,281**	**7.6**	**–9.2**	**47.7**
Other vehicle expenses	**1,444**	**1,424**	**1,633**	**1,890**	**1.4**	**–11.6**	**–13.6**
Vehicle finance charges	108	146	230	308	–26.2	–53.0	–25.4
Maintenance and repairs	491	513	462	598	–4.3	6.2	–22.7
Vehicle insurance	616	532	633	607	15.8	–2.7	4.3
Vehicle rentals, leases, licenses, other charges	229	232	307	376	–1.2	–25.5	–18.3
Public transportation	**249**	**294**	**255**	**292**	**–15.2**	**–2.5**	**–12.6**

	average spending				percent change		
	2013	2010	2006	2000	2010–13	2006–13	2000–06
HEALTH CARE	**$943**	**$828**	**$816**	**$682**	**13.9%**	**15.6%**	**19.7%**
Health insurance	526	433	424	285	21.6	24.0	48.6
Medical services	272	252	223	241	7.9	22.0	–7.4
Drugs	103	109	112	110	–5.5	–8.1	2.3
Medical supplies	42	34	57	46	22.9	–25.8	23.1
ENTERTAINMENT	**1,243**	**1,304**	**1,558**	**1,476**	**–4.7**	**–20.2**	**5.5**
Fees and admissions	245	251	324	367	–2.4	–24.3	–11.7
Audio and visual equipment and services	576	636	777	640	–9.4	–25.8	21.4
Pets, toys, and playground equipment	243	248	242	234	–2.0	0.6	3.2
Pets	177	182	162	133	–2.6	9.2	21.4
Toys, hobbies, and playground equipment	66	66	80	101	–0.1	–17.1	–20.9
Other entertainment products and services	179	169	216	237	6.0	–17.2	–8.7
PERSONAL CARE PRODUCTS AND SERVICES	**342**	**371**	**402**	**467**	**–7.7**	**–15.0**	**–13.8**
READING	**46**	**42**	**53**	**77**	**10.4**	**–13.5**	**–31.1**
EDUCATION	**2,055**	**2,036**	**1,455**	**1,701**	**0.9**	**41.3**	**–14.4**
TOBACCO PRODUCTS AND SMOKING SUPPLIES	**219**	**302**	**330**	**321**	**–27.6**	**–33.7**	**3.1**
MISCELLANEOUS	**207**	**296**	**448**	**436**	**–30.1**	**–53.8**	**2.9**
CASH CONTRIBUTIONS	**473**	**335**	**730**	**256**	**41.0**	**–35.2**	**185.6**
PERSONAL INSURANCE AND PENSIONS	**2,203**	**2,175**	**2,647**	**1,645**	**1.3**	**–16.8**	**60.9**
Life and other personal insurance	50	24	49	73	112.7	3.0	–33.6
Pensions and Social Security	2,153	2,151	2,599	1,572	0.1	–17.2	65.3
GIFTS FOR PEOPLE IN OTHER HOUSEHOLDS	**271**	**452**	**454**	**808**	**–40.0**	**–40.3**	**–43.8**

Note: The Bureau of Labor Statistics uses consumer unit rather than household as the sampling unit in the Consumer Expenditure Survey. For the definition of consumer unit, see the glossary. Spending on gifts is also included in the preceding product and service categories.
Source: Bureau of Labor Statistics, 2000, 2006, 2010, and 2013 Consumer Expenditure Surveys, Internet site http://www.bls.gov/cex/; calculations by New Strategist

Household Spending Has Dropped Sharply among Millennials

Householders aged 25 to 34 spent much less in 2013 than in 2006.

Households headed by people aged 25 to 34 (Millennials were aged 19 to 36 in 2013) cut their spending by 13 percent between 2006 and 2013, after adjusting for inflation. Their spending in 2013 was 9 percent below what their counterparts spent in 2000.

Households headed by people aged 25 to 34 reduced their spending on many discretionary items in the 2006-to-2013 time period, after adjusting for inflation. Their spending on food away from home fell 22 percent. Spending on alcoholic beverages declined by an even larger 36 percent. Average household spending on new cars and trucks fell 43 percent. Mortgage interest spending declined 42 percent as some in the age group lost their home during the Great Recession and others were unable or unwilling to buy. The age group's spending on entertainment fell 14 percent between 2006 and 2013.

Households headed by people aged 35 to 44 did not fare much better. Their spending fell by 11 percent between 2006 and 2013, after adjusting for inflation. Spending continued to decline in the 2010-to-2013 time period for householders aged 25 to 34 as well as those aged 35 to 44.

■ The widespread unemployment of the Great Recession and the slow recovery have been a setback for householders under age 45.

Householders aged 25 to 44 spent less in 2013 than their counterparts did in 2000

(average annual spending of households headed by people aged 25 to 44, 2000 and 2013; in 2013 dollars)

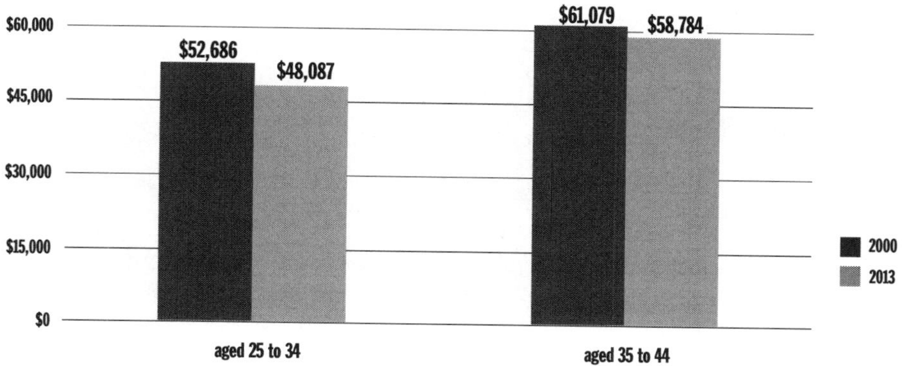

Table 9.3 Average Spending of Householders Aged 25 to 34, 2000 to 2013

(average annual spending of consumer units headed by people aged 25 to 34, 2000 to 2013; percent change for selected years; in 2013 dollars)

	average spending				percent change		
	2013	2010	2006	2000	2010–13	2006–13	2000–06
Number of consumer units aged 25 to 34 (in 000s)	**20,707**	**20,166**	**20,071**	**18,887**	**2.7%**	**3.2%**	**6.3%**
Average annual spending of consumer units	**$48,087**	**$49,803**	**$54,983**	**$52,686**	**–3.4**	**–12.5**	**4.4**
FOOD	**6,197**	**6,507**	**7,053**	**7,116**	**–4.8**	**–12.1**	**–0.9**
Food at home	**3,559**	**3,566**	**3,682**	**3,992**	**–0.2**	**–3.3**	**–7.8**
Cereals and bakery products	467	471	469	580	–0.9	–0.5	–19.2
Cereals and cereal products	174	163	165	226	6.5	5.3	–26.9
Bakery products	292	308	304	356	–5.1	–3.9	–14.6
Meats, poultry, fish, and eggs	775	762	862	1,042	1.7	–10.1	–17.2
Beef	185	194	265	323	–4.9	–30.1	–18.2
Pork	146	132	163	210	10.2	–10.4	–22.3
Other meats	101	112	106	133	–10.0	–5.0	–19.8
Poultry	175	162	165	196	7.8	5.9	–15.8
Fish and seafood	113	111	125	138	1.7	–9.5	–9.6
Eggs	54	49	39	41	9.9	37.4	–3.2
Dairy products	383	377	407	429	1.6	–5.8	–5.2
Fresh milk and cream	144	144	164	181	–0.2	–12.2	–9.5
Other dairy products	240	233	243	248	3.0	–1.1	–2.0
Fruits and vegetables	689	656	621	660	5.0	11.0	–6.0
Fresh fruits	253	224	191	198	12.8	32.7	–3.5
Fresh vegetables	222	203	206	200	9.4	7.9	2.7
Processed fruits	101	109	126	153	–7.3	–19.8	–17.6
Processed vegetables	112	121	99	111	–7.2	12.7	–10.4
Other food at home	1,245	1,300	1,322	1,280	–4.2	–5.8	3.3
Sugar and other sweets	115	119	110	142	–3.0	4.8	–22.7
Fats and oils	105	92	88	104	14.3	19.6	–15.7
Miscellaneous foods	653	731	720	656	–10.6	–9.3	9.7
Nonalcoholic beverages	343	332	364	334	3.2	–5.8	8.9
Food prepared by consumer unit on trips	29	27	40	42	8.6	–28.3	–3.6
Food away from home	**2,639**	**2,941**	**3,372**	**3,124**	**–10.3**	**–21.7**	**7.9**
ALCOHOLIC BEVERAGES	**489**	**505**	**759**	**583**	**–3.2**	**–35.6**	**30.2**
HOUSING	**17,207**	**17,996**	**19,805**	**17,654**	**–4.4**	**–13.1**	**12.2**
Shelter	**10,712**	**11,165**	**12,393**	**10,694**	**–4.1**	**–13.6**	**15.9**
Owned dwellings	4,560	5,476	7,086	5,603	–16.7	–35.6	26.5
Mortgage interest and charges	2,862	3,648	4,948	3,907	–21.6	–42.2	26.6
Property taxes	1,023	1,184	1,376	1,021	–13.6	–25.7	34.7
Maintenance, repair, insurance, other expenses	675	643	763	675	5.0	–11.5	13.0
Rented dwellings	5,881	5,330	4,953	4,754	10.3	18.7	4.2
Other lodging	271	359	355	336	–24.5	–23.6	5.7

	average spending				percent change		
	2013	2010	2006	2000	2010–13	2006–13	2000–06
Utilities, fuels, and public services	**$3,186**	**$3,449**	**$3,574**	**$3,167**	**–7.6%**	**–10.9%**	**12.9%**
Natural gas	297	379	486	369	–21.7	–38.9	31.7
Electricity	1,233	1,339	1,309	1,117	–7.9	–5.8	17.2
Fuel oil and other fuels	59	75	84	78	–21.1	–30.1	7.5
Telephone services	1,202	1,239	1,305	1,285	–3.0	–7.9	1.5
Residential telephone, VOIP, and phone cards	156	259	544	1,098	–39.8	–71.3	–50.4
Cellular phone service	1,046	980	760	186	6.7	37.7	307.8
Water and other public services	396	417	389	317	–5.0	1.7	23.0
Household services	**1,404**	**1,329**	**1,306**	**1,178**	**5.6**	**7.5**	**10.8**
Personal services	826	809	816	867	2.1	1.2	–5.9
Other household services	578	520	490	311	11.1	18.0	57.5
Housekeeping supplies	**497**	**497**	**614**	**591**	**0.0**	**–19.0**	**3.8**
Laundry and cleaning supplies	133	135	179	169	–1.2	–25.7	5.9
Other household products	262	262	307	272	0.1	–14.8	13.0
Postage and stationery	102	99	128	152	2.7	–20.5	–15.3
Household furnishings and equipment	**1,408**	**1,558**	**1,918**	**2,022**	**–9.6**	**–26.6**	**–5.2**
Household textiles	68	84	143	162	–19.4	–52.5	–11.7
Furniture	421	458	589	618	–8.1	–28.6	–4.7
Floor coverings	22	47	40	57	–53.2	–45.6	–28.8
Major appliances	166	171	224	245	–2.9	–26.0	–8.4
Small appliances and miscellaneous housewares	86	104	126	106	–17.0	–31.7	19.4
Miscellaneous household equipment	645	694	794	835	–7.1	–18.8	–4.9
APPAREL AND RELATED SERVICES	**1,832**	**2,230**	**2,487**	**2,785**	**–17.8**	**–26.3**	**–10.7**
Men and boys	**437**	**458**	**629**	**691**	**–4.7**	**–30.5**	**–9.1**
Men, aged 16 or older	337	347	473	498	–2.9	–28.7	–5.1
Boys, aged 2 to 15	100	111	156	193	–10.0	–35.9	–19.4
Women and girls	**651**	**721**	**852**	**952**	**–9.7**	**–23.6**	**–10.6**
Women, aged 16 or older	515	588	669	759	–12.4	–23.0	–11.8
Girls, aged 2 to 15	135	134	183	195	1.1	–26.1	–6.3
Children under age 2	**158**	**208**	**216**	**223**	**–24.2**	**–26.9**	**–3.2**
Footwear	**335**	**334**	**429**	**533**	**0.2**	**–21.9**	**–19.6**
Other apparel products and services	**251**	**507**	**362**	**386**	**–50.5**	**–30.6**	**–6.2**
TRANSPORTATION	**9,183**	**8,793**	**10,454**	**11,306**	**4.4**	**–12.2**	**–7.5**
Vehicle purchases	**3,641**	**3,648**	**4,520**	**5,599**	**–0.2**	**–19.5**	**–19.3**
Cars and trucks, new	1,296	1,584	2,265	2,496	–18.2	–42.8	–9.3
Cars and trucks, used	2,323	2,023	2,174	2,999	14.8	6.9	–27.5
Gasoline and motor oil	**2,676**	**2,359**	**2,711**	**1,814**	**13.4**	**–1.3**	**49.4**
Other vehicle expenses	**2,416**	**2,323**	**2,706**	**3,358**	**4.0**	**–10.7**	**–19.4**
Vehicle finance charges	261	324	463	590	–19.4	–43.7	–21.4
Maintenance and repairs	681	753	721	771	–9.6	–5.6	–6.5
Vehicle insurance	880	792	950	1,047	11.2	–7.4	–9.3
Vehicle rentals, leases, licenses, other charges	594	453	572	948	31.1	3.8	–39.7
Public transportation	**450**	**464**	**518**	**534**	**–2.9**	**–13.1**	**–3.1**

	average spending				percent change		
	2013	2010	2006	2000	2010–13	2006–13	2000–06
HEALTH CARE	**$2,189**	**$1,923**	**$1,909**	**$1,699**	**13.8%**	**14.7%**	**12.3%**
Health insurance	1,334	1,160	1,020	866	15.0	30.7	17.8
Medical services	580	473	542	496	22.6	7.0	9.2
Drugs	197	214	281	245	–7.8	–29.8	14.7
Medical supplies	77	76	67	93	1.5	14.9	–28.2
ENTERTAINMENT	**2,214**	**2,405**	**2,585**	**2,538**	**–7.9**	**–14.4**	**1.9**
Fees and admissions	498	491	549	622	1.3	–9.3	–11.8
Audio and visual equipment and services	899	1,031	1,120	920	–12.8	–19.7	21.7
Pets, toys, and playground equipment	533	513	471	475	3.9	13.1	–0.7
Pets	371	385	298	232	–3.8	24.6	28.6
Toys, hobbies, and playground equipment	162	127	173	243	27.2	–6.4	–28.9
Other entertainment products and services	284	370	445	521	–23.2	–36.2	–14.6
PERSONAL CARE PRODUCTS AND SERVICES	**538**	**552**	**632**	**779**	**–2.6**	**–14.9**	**–18.9**
READING	**60**	**65**	**95**	**160**	**–7.9**	**–36.7**	**–40.6**
EDUCATION	**1,019**	**896**	**820**	**791**	**13.7**	**24.2**	**3.7**
TOBACCO PRODUCTS AND SMOKING SUPPLIES	**309**	**387**	**367**	**419**	**–20.1**	**–15.9**	**–12.4**
MISCELLANEOUS	**577**	**714**	**711**	**1,088**	**–19.1**	**–18.8**	**–34.7**
CASH CONTRIBUTIONS	**970**	**1,147**	**1,236**	**877**	**–15.5**	**–21.5**	**41.0**
PERSONAL INSURANCE AND PENSIONS	**5,304**	**5,681**	**6,069**	**4,889**	**–6.6**	**–12.6**	**24.1**
Life and other personal insurance	125	178	199	327	–29.9	–37.1	–39.3
Pensions and Social Security	5,178	5,503	5,869	4,563	–5.9	–11.8	28.6
GIFTS FOR PEOPLE IN OTHER HOUSEHOLDS	**474**	**578**	**1,073**	**969**	**–18.0**	**–55.8**	**10.8**

Note: The Bureau of Labor Statistics uses consumer unit rather than household as the sampling unit in the Consumer Expenditure Survey. For the definition of consumer unit, see the glossary. Spending on gifts is also included in the preceding product and service categories.
Source: Bureau of Labor Statistics, 2000, 2006, 2010, and 2013 Consumer Expenditure Surveys, Internet site http://www.bls.gov/cex/; calculations by New Strategist

Table 9.4 Average Spending of Householders Aged 35 to 44, 2000 to 2013

(average annual spending of consumer units headed by people aged 35 to 44, 2000 to 2013; percent change for selected years; in 2013 dollars)

	average spending				percent change		
	2013	2010	2006	2000	2010–13	2006–13	2000–06
Number of consumer units aged 35 to 44 (in 000s)	**21,257**	**21,912**	**23,950**	**23,983**	**–3.0%**	**–11.2%**	**–0.1%**
Average annual spending of consumer units	**$58,784**	**$59,769**	**$66,416**	**$61,079**	**–1.6**	**–11.5**	**8.7**
FOOD	**7,920**	**7,994**	**8,471**	**8,241**	**–0.9**	**–6.5**	**2.8**
Food at home	**4,641**	**4,546**	**4,770**	**4,713**	**2.1**	**–2.7**	**1.2**
Cereals and bakery products	646	648	639	718	–0.4	1.1	–11.0
Cereals and cereal products	233	226	214	257	2.9	9.0	–16.8
Bakery products	412	422	426	461	–2.4	–3.4	–7.6
Meats, poultry, fish, and eggs	993	957	1,112	1,242	3.7	–10.7	–10.5
Beef	276	246	314	365	12.3	–12.2	–14.0
Pork	184	184	215	252	0.1	–14.4	–14.6
Other meats	138	150	151	162	–7.7	–8.8	–6.8
Poultry	215	179	214	241	19.8	0.6	–11.2
Fish and seafood	119	141	165	170	–15.6	–28.0	–3.1
Eggs	61	58	52	50	5.7	17.3	3.9
Dairy products	495	489	522	518	1.2	–5.2	0.8
Fresh milk and cream	196	189	207	212	3.7	–5.2	–2.6
Other dairy products	299	300	315	306	–0.4	–5.2	3.2
Fruits and vegetables	866	841	775	747	3.0	11.7	3.8
Fresh fruits	312	292	253	229	7.0	23.3	10.7
Fresh vegetables	259	249	239	222	4.0	8.3	7.8
Processed fruits	136	143	151	169	–5.0	–10.2	–10.5
Processed vegetables	158	156	132	124	1.3	19.9	5.8
Other food at home	1,641	1,611	1,722	1,489	1.9	–4.7	15.6
Sugar and other sweets	157	165	168	199	–4.6	–6.3	–15.7
Fats and oils	128	127	112	122	0.7	14.2	–7.9
Miscellaneous foods	881	853	916	701	3.3	–3.9	30.8
Nonalcoholic beverages	435	410	473	406	6.0	–8.0	16.5
Food prepared by consumer unit on trips	41	57	52	62	–27.6	–21.2	–16.4
Food away from home	**3,280**	**3,448**	**3,701**	**3,527**	**–4.9**	**–11.4**	**4.9**
ALCOHOLIC BEVERAGES	**443**	**531**	**573**	**568**	**–16.6**	**–22.7**	**0.9**
HOUSING	**20,619**	**21,411**	**23,461**	**20,443**	**–3.7**	**–12.1**	**14.8**
Shelter	**12,271**	**12,969**	**14,381**	**12,081**	**–5.4**	**–14.7**	**19.0**
Owned dwellings	7,981	8,706	10,359	8,703	–8.3	–23.0	19.0
Mortgage interest and charges	5,078	5,551	6,834	5,820	–8.5	–25.7	17.4
Property taxes	1,964	2,110	2,238	1,686	–6.9	–12.3	32.8
Maintenance, repair, insurance, other expenses	939	1,045	1,287	1,196	–10.1	–27.1	7.6
Rented dwellings	3,834	3,712	3,395	2,796	3.3	12.9	21.4
Other lodging	455	550	625	582	–17.3	–27.2	7.5

	average spending				percent change		
	2013	2010	2006	2000	2010–13	2006–13	2000–06
Utilities, fuels, and public services	**$4,299**	**$4,356**	**$4,453**	**$3,801**	**–1.3%**	**–3.5%**	**17.2%**
Natural gas	445	531	646	473	–16.2	–31.1	36.4
Electricity	1,635	1,674	1,640	1,365	–2.3	–0.3	20.1
Fuel oil and other fuels	121	112	181	131	7.9	–33.3	38.3
Telephone services	1,508	1,457	1,469	1,377	3.5	2.7	6.6
Residential telephone, VOIP, and phone cards	298	431	718	1,164	–30.9	–58.5	–38.3
Cellular phone service	1,209	1,026	750	213	17.9	61.2	251.4
Water and other public services	590	581	519	455	1.5	13.7	14.1
Household services	**1,612**	**1,511**	**1,595**	**1,212**	**6.7**	**1.1**	**31.6**
Personal services	825	785	937	733	5.1	–12.0	27.8
Other household services	787	725	658	479	8.5	19.7	37.3
Housekeeping supplies	**674**	**708**	**879**	**771**	**–4.8**	**–23.4**	**14.0**
Laundry and cleaning supplies	170	197	218	212	–13.5	–22.2	2.8
Other household products	368	355	477	379	3.8	–22.9	26.0
Postage and stationery	136	158	184	180	–14.0	–26.0	2.1
Household furnishings and equipment	**1,763**	**1,867**	**2,154**	**2,578**	**–5.6**	**–18.1**	**–16.5**
Household textiles	108	119	162	168	–8.9	–33.2	–3.6
Furniture	449	478	619	675	–6.0	–27.5	–8.2
Floor coverings	17	45	46	72	–62.1	–63.2	–35.5
Major appliances	268	280	314	287	–4.3	–14.7	9.6
Small appliances and miscellaneous housewares	102	112	131	126	–9.1	–21.9	3.8
Miscellaneous household equipment	819	833	881	1,253	–1.7	–7.0	–29.7
APPAREL AND RELATED SERVICES	**1,960**	**2,179**	**2,736**	**3,143**	**–10.1**	**–28.4**	**–12.9**
Men and boys	**533**	**520**	**664**	**745**	**2.4**	**–19.8**	**–10.9**
Men, aged 16 or older	378	342	466	496	10.6	–18.8	–6.2
Boys, aged 2 to 15	154	177	199	249	–13.2	–22.5	–20.2
Women and girls	**718**	**817**	**1,065**	**1,265**	**–12.1**	**–32.6**	**–15.8**
Women, aged 16 or older	513	593	775	936	–13.5	–33.8	–17.2
Girls, aged 2 to 15	205	224	290	327	–8.6	–29.3	–11.4
Children under age 2	**109**	**125**	**148**	**142**	**–12.8**	**–26.3**	**4.1**
Footwear	**398**	**442**	**467**	**542**	**–10.0**	**–14.7**	**–13.9**
Other apparel products and services	**202**	**276**	**391**	**448**	**–26.7**	**–48.3**	**–12.8**
TRANSPORTATION	**10,519**	**9,362**	**11,529**	**11,772**	**12.4**	**–8.8**	**–2.1**
Vehicle purchases	**4,010**	**3,104**	**4,688**	**5,406**	**29.2**	**–14.5**	**–13.3**
Cars and trucks, new	1,774	1,433	2,310	2,332	23.8	–23.2	–1.0
Cars and trucks, used	2,218	1,579	2,280	2,974	40.5	–2.7	–23.3
Gasoline and motor oil	**3,218**	**2,710**	**3,046**	**2,133**	**18.7**	**5.6**	**42.8**
Other vehicle expenses	**2,740**	**2,966**	**3,149**	**3,622**	**–7.6**	**–13.0**	**–13.1**
Vehicle finance charges	288	331	432	549	–13.0	–33.4	–21.3
Maintenance and repairs	841	950	860	958	–11.5	–2.2	–10.2
Vehicle insurance	1,019	1,147	1,128	1,196	–11.2	–9.6	–5.7
Vehicle rentals, leases, licenses, other charges	592	537	729	920	10.2	–18.8	–20.7
Public transportation	**552**	**582**	**646**	**610**	**–5.2**	**–14.5**	**5.9**

	average spending				percent change		
	2013	2010	2006	2000	2010–13	2006–13	2000–06
HEALTH CARE	**$3,188**	**$2,760**	**$2,639**	**$2,400**	**15.5%**	**20.8%**	**10.0%**
Health insurance	1,944	1,552	1,403	1,150	25.2	38.6	22.0
Medical services	786	728	733	751	8.0	7.3	–2.4
Drugs	343	363	399	384	–5.6	–14.0	3.8
Medical supplies	116	116	104	115	–0.4	11.5	–9.6
ENTERTAINMENT	**2,958**	**3,267**	**3,427**	**3,333**	**–9.5**	**–13.7**	**2.8**
Fees and admissions	736	907	969	967	–18.9	–24.1	0.2
Audio and visual equipment and services	1,139	1,152	1,216	1,067	–1.1	–6.3	13.9
Pets, toys, and playground equipment	638	765	574	610	–16.6	11.1	–5.9
Pets	473	570	423	357	–17.1	11.8	18.4
Toys, hobbies, and playground equipment	165	195	151	253	–15.3	9.0	–40.1
Other entertainment products and services	446	442	668	689	0.8	–33.2	–3.0
PERSONAL CARE PRODUCTS AND SERVICES	**672**	**729**	**795**	**871**	**–7.8**	**–15.5**	**–8.7**
READING	**105**	**85**	**129**	**204**	**22.9**	**–18.9**	**–36.6**
EDUCATION	**903**	**1,029**	**990**	**832**	**–12.2**	**–8.8**	**19.0**
TOBACCO PRODUCTS AND SMOKING SUPPLIES	**331**	**382**	**409**	**578**	**–13.5**	**–19.1**	**–29.2**
MISCELLANEOUS	**643**	**985**	**1,090**	**1,153**	**–34.7**	**–41.0**	**–5.5**
CASH CONTRIBUTIONS	**1,440**	**1,637**	**1,973**	**1,357**	**–12.0**	**–27.0**	**45.4**
PERSONAL INSURANCE AND PENSIONS	**7,081**	**7,419**	**8,193**	**6,182**	**–4.5**	**–13.6**	**32.5**
Life and other personal insurance	290	299	421	557	–3.1	–31.1	–24.5
Pensions and Social Security	6,791	7,119	7,772	5,625	–4.6	–12.6	38.2
GIFTS FOR PEOPLE IN OTHER HOUSEHOLDS	**604**	**782**	**896**	**1,354**	**–22.8**	**–32.6**	**–33.9**

Note: The Bureau of Labor Statistics uses consumer unit rather than household as the sampling unit in the Consumer Expenditure Survey. For the definition of consumer unit, see the glossary. Spending on gifts is also included in the preceding product and service categories.

Source: Bureau of Labor Statistics, 2000, 2006, 2010, and 2013 Consumer Expenditure Surveys, Internet site http://www.bls.gov/cex/; calculations by New Strategist

Householders under Age 25 Spend Less than Average

Households headed by people aged 25 to 34 spend close to the average on most things.

The incomes of householders under age 25 are well below average, and so is their spending. On some things, however, this age group spends more. Not surprisingly, they spend 72 percent more than average on rent. Because some young adults are new parents, they spend twice as much as the average household on clothes for children under age 2. Households headed by people under age 25 spend 81 percent more than average on education.

Households headed by people aged 25 to 34 spend close to the average on most things. But they spend more than twice the average on household personal services (mostly daycare). They also spend more than average on alcoholic beverages (with an index of 110) and used cars and trucks (139). They spend 77 percent more than average on rent. As Millennials (aged 19 to 36 in 2013) fill the 35-to-44 age group in the next few years, their spending on many categories will rise above average.

■ As the large Millennial generation boosts the number of households headed by people aged 35 to 44, their greater spending could stimulate the economy.

Millennials are now filling the 35-to-44 age group, in which spending rises above average

(indexed spending of households by age of householder, 2013; 100 is the index for the average household)

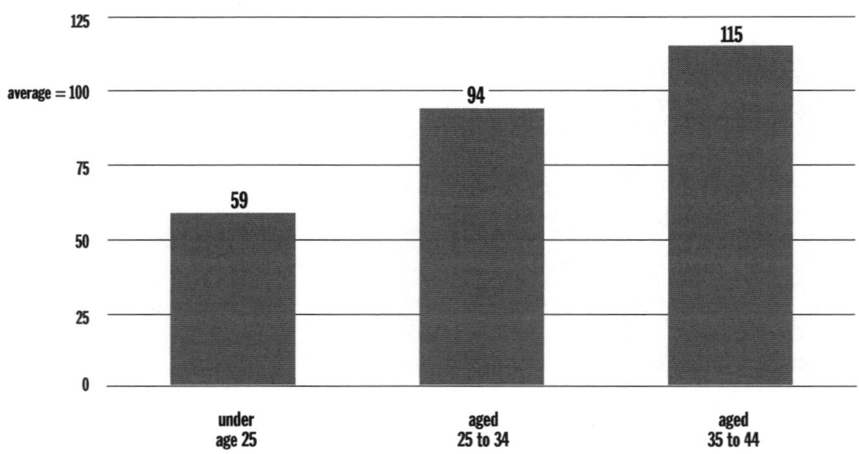

Table 9.5 Average, Indexed, and Market Share of Spending by Householders under Age 25, 2013

(average annual spending of total consumer units and average annual, indexed, and market share of spending by consumer units headed by people under age 25, 2013)

		consumer units headed by people under age 25		
	total consumer units	average spending	indexed spending	market share
Number of consumer units (in 000s)	**125,670**	**8,275**	**–**	**6.6%**
Average annual spending	**$51,100**	**$30,373**	**59**	**3.9**
FOOD	**6,602**	**4,698**	**71**	**4.7**
Food at home	**3,977**	**2,602**	**65**	**4.3**
Cereals and bakery products	544	363	67	4.4
Cereals and cereal products	185	130	70	4.6
Bakery products	359	233	65	4.3
Meats, poultry, fish, and eggs	856	580	68	4.5
Beef	219	141	64	4.2
Pork	170	105	62	4.1
Other meats	119	75	63	4.2
Poultry	170	126	74	4.9
Fish and seafood	122	93	76	5.0
Eggs	56	40	71	4.7
Dairy products	414	274	66	4.4
Fresh milk and cream	152	109	72	4.7
Other dairy products	262	165	63	4.1
Fruits and vegetables	751	448	60	3.9
Fresh fruits	270	147	54	3.6
Fresh vegetables	236	137	58	3.8
Processed fruits	115	79	69	4.5
Processed vegetables	130	85	65	4.3
Other food at home	1,412	936	66	4.4
Sugar and other sweets	143	89	62	4.1
Fats and oils	117	73	62	4.1
Miscellaneous foods	728	486	67	4.4
Nonalcoholic beverages	384	276	72	4.7
Food prepared by consumer unit on trips	42	13	31	2.0
Food away from home	**2,625**	**2,096**	**80**	**5.3**
ALCOHOLIC BEVERAGES	**445**	**379**	**85**	**5.6**
HOUSING	**17,148**	**10,379**	**61**	**4.0**
Shelter	**10,080**	**6,944**	**69**	**4.5**
Owned dwellings	6,108	1,003	16	1.1
Mortgage interest and charges	3,078	449	15	1.0
Property taxes	1,848	403	22	1.4
Maintenance, repair, insurance, other expenses	1,182	151	13	0.8
Rented dwellings	3,324	5,728	172	11.3
Other lodging	649	213	33	2.2

	total consumer units	consumer units headed by people under age 25		
		average spending	indexed spending	market share
Utilities, fuels, and public services	**$3,737**	**$1,842**	**49**	**3.2%**
Natural gas	393	163	41	2.7
Electricity	1,422	728	51	3.4
Fuel oil and other fuels	142	30	21	1.4
Telephone services	1,271	737	58	3.8
Residential telephone, VOIP, and phone cards	358	87	24	1.6
Cellular phone service	913	651	71	4.7
Water and other public services	509	184	36	2.4
Household services	**1,144**	**428**	**37**	**2.5**
Personal services	368	134	36	2.4
Other household services	776	293	38	2.5
Housekeeping supplies	**645**	**323**	**50**	**3.3**
Laundry and cleaning supplies	154	93	60	4.0
Other household products	350	193	55	3.6
Postage and stationery	140	38	27	1.8
Household furnishings and equipment	**1,542**	**842**	**55**	**3.6**
Household textiles	97	56	58	3.8
Furniture	382	258	68	4.4
Floor coverings	20	6	30	2.0
Major appliances	214	95	44	2.9
Small appliances and miscellaneous housewares	100	85	85	5.6
Miscellaneous household equipment	727	343	47	3.1
APPAREL AND RELATED SERVICES	**1,604**	**1,513**	**94**	**6.2**
Men and boys	**374**	**316**	**84**	**5.6**
Men, aged 16 or older	304	285	94	6.2
Boys, aged 2 to 15	70	31	44	2.9
Women and girls	**636**	**516**	**81**	**5.3**
Women, aged 16 or older	527	441	84	5.5
Girls, aged 2 to 15	109	75	69	4.5
Children under age 2	**75**	**152**	**203**	**13.3**
Footwear	**307**	**333**	**108**	**7.1**
Other apparel products and services	**211**	**197**	**93**	**6.1**
TRANSPORTATION	**9,004**	**5,672**	**63**	**4.1**
Vehicle purchases	**3,271**	**2,262**	**69**	**4.6**
Cars and trucks, new	1,563	805	52	3.4
Cars and trucks, used	1,669	1,371	82	5.4
Gasoline and motor oil	**2,611**	**1,717**	**66**	**4.3**
Other vehicle expenses	**2,584**	**1,444**	**56**	**3.7**
Vehicle finance charges	204	108	53	3.5
Maintenance and repairs	835	491	59	3.9
Vehicle insurance	1,013	616	61	4.0
Vehicle rentals, leases, licenses, other charges	533	229	43	2.8
Public transportation	**537**	**249**	**46**	**3.1**

	total consumer units	consumer units headed by people under age 25		
		average spending	indexed spending	market share
HEALTH CARE	**$3,631**	**$943**	**26**	**1.7%**
Health insurance	2,229	526	24	1.6
Medical services	796	272	34	2.3
Drugs	470	103	22	1.4
Medical supplies	135	42	31	2.0
ENTERTAINMENT	**2,482**	**1,243**	**50**	**3.3**
Fees and admissions	569	245	43	2.8
Audio and visual equipment and services	964	576	60	3.9
Pets, toys, and playground equipment	596	243	41	2.7
Pets	460	177	38	2.5
Toys, hobbies, and playground equipment	136	66	49	3.2
Other entertainment products and services	353	179	51	3.3
PERSONAL CARE PRODUCTS AND SERVICES	**608**	**342**	**56**	**3.7**
READING	**102**	**46**	**45**	**3.0**
EDUCATION	**1,138**	**2,055**	**181**	**11.9**
TOBACCO PRODUCTS AND SMOKING SUPPLIES	**330**	**219**	**66**	**4.4**
MISCELLANEOUS	**645**	**207**	**32**	**2.1**
CASH CONTRIBUTIONS	**1,834**	**473**	**26**	**1.7**
PERSONAL INSURANCE AND PENSIONS	**5,528**	**2,203**	**40**	**2.6**
Life and other personal insurance	319	50	16	1.0
Pensions and Social Security	5,209	2,153	41	2.7
GIFTS FOR PEOPLE IN OTHER HOUSEHOLDS	**1,078**	**271**	**25**	**1.7**

Note: The Bureau of Labor Statistics uses consumer unit rather than household as the sampling unit in the Consumer Expenditure Survey. For the definition of consumer unit, see the glossary. Spending on gifts is also included in the preceding product and service categories. "–" means not applicable.
Source: Bureau of Labor Statistics, 2013 Consumer Expenditure Survey, Internet site http://www.bls.gov/cex/; calculations by New Strategist

Table 9.6 Average, Indexed, and Market Share of Spending by Householders Aged 25 to 34, 2013

(average annual spending of total consumer units and average annual, indexed, and market share of spending by consumer units headed by people aged 25 to 34, 2013)

		consumer units headed by people aged 25 to 34		
	total consumer units	**average spending**	**indexed spending**	**market share**
Number of consumer units (in 000s)	**125,670**	**20,707**	–	**16.5%**
Average annual spending	**$51,100**	**$48,087**	**94**	**15.5**
FOOD	**6,602**	**6,197**	**94**	**15.5**
Food at home	**3,977**	**3,559**	**89**	**14.7**
Cereals and bakery products	544	467	86	14.1
Cereals and cereal products	185	174	94	15.5
Bakery products	359	292	81	13.4
Meats, poultry, fish, and eggs	856	775	91	14.9
Beef	219	185	84	13.9
Pork	170	146	86	14.2
Other meats	119	101	85	14.0
Poultry	170	175	103	17.0
Fish and seafood	122	113	93	15.3
Eggs	56	54	96	15.9
Dairy products	414	383	93	15.2
Fresh milk and cream	152	144	95	15.6
Other dairy products	262	240	92	15.1
Fruits and vegetables	751	689	92	15.1
Fresh fruits	270	253	94	15.4
Fresh vegetables	236	222	94	15.5
Processed fruits	115	101	88	14.5
Processed vegetables	130	112	86	14.2
Other food at home	1,412	1,245	88	14.5
Sugar and other sweets	143	115	80	13.3
Fats and oils	117	105	90	14.8
Miscellaneous foods	728	653	90	14.8
Nonalcoholic beverages	384	343	89	14.7
Food prepared by consumer unit on trips	42	29	69	11.4
Food away from home	**2,625**	**2,639**	**101**	**16.6**
ALCOHOLIC BEVERAGES	**445**	**489**	**110**	**18.1**
HOUSING	**17,148**	**17,207**	**100**	**16.5**
Shelter	**10,080**	**10,712**	**106**	**17.5**
Owned dwellings	6,108	4,560	75	12.3
Mortgage interest and charges	3,078	2,862	93	15.3
Property taxes	1,848	1,023	55	9.1
Maintenance, repair, insurance, other expenses	1,182	675	57	9.4
Rented dwellings	3,324	5,881	177	29.2
Other lodging	649	271	42	6.9

	total consumer units	consumer units headed by people aged 25 to 34 average spending	indexed spending	market share
Utilities, fuels, and public services	**$3,737**	**$3,186**	**85**	**14.0%**
Natural gas	393	297	76	12.5
Electricity	1,422	1,233	87	14.3
Fuel oil and other fuels	142	59	42	6.8
Telephone services	1,271	1,202	95	15.6
Residential telephone, VOIP, and phone cards	358	156	44	7.2
Cellular phone service	913	1,046	115	18.9
Water and other public services	509	396	78	12.8
Household services	**1,144**	**1,404**	**123**	**20.2**
Personal services	368	826	224	37.0
Other household services	776	578	74	12.3
Housekeeping supplies	**645**	**497**	**77**	**12.7**
Laundry and cleaning supplies	154	133	86	14.2
Other household products	350	262	75	12.3
Postage and stationery	140	102	73	12.0
Household furnishings and equipment	**1,542**	**1,408**	**91**	**15.0**
Household textiles	97	68	70	11.6
Furniture	382	421	110	18.2
Floor coverings	20	22	110	18.1
Major appliances	214	166	78	12.8
Small appliances and miscellaneous housewares	100	86	86	14.2
Miscellaneous household equipment	727	645	89	14.6
APPAREL AND RELATED SERVICES	**1,604**	**1,832**	**114**	**18.8**
Men and boys	**374**	**437**	**117**	**19.3**
Men, aged 16 or older	304	337	111	18.3
Boys, aged 2 to 15	70	100	143	23.5
Women and girls	**636**	**651**	**102**	**16.9**
Women, aged 16 or older	527	515	98	16.1
Girls, aged 2 to 15	109	135	124	20.4
Children under age 2	**75**	**158**	**211**	**34.7**
Footwear	**307**	**335**	**109**	**18.0**
Other apparel products and services	**211**	**251**	**119**	**19.6**
TRANSPORTATION	**9,004**	**9,183**	**102**	**16.8**
Vehicle purchases	**3,271**	**3,641**	**111**	**18.3**
Cars and trucks, new	1,563	1,296	83	13.7
Cars and trucks, used	1,669	2,323	139	22.9
Gasoline and motor oil	**2,611**	**2,676**	**102**	**16.9**
Other vehicle expenses	**2,584**	**2,416**	**93**	**15.4**
Vehicle finance charges	204	261	128	21.1
Maintenance and repairs	835	681	82	13.4
Vehicle insurance	1,013	880	87	14.3
Vehicle rentals, leases, licenses, other charges	533	594	111	18.4
Public transportation	**537**	**450**	**84**	**13.8**

	total consumer units	consumer units headed by people aged 25 to 34		
		average spending	indexed spending	market share
HEALTH CARE	**$3,631**	**$2,189**	**60**	**9.9%**
Health insurance	2,229	1,334	60	9.9
Medical services	796	580	73	12.0
Drugs	470	197	42	6.9
Medical supplies	135	77	57	9.4
ENTERTAINMENT	**2,482**	**2,214**	**89**	**14.7**
Fees and admissions	569	498	88	14.4
Audio and visual equipment and services	964	899	93	15.4
Pets, toys, and playground equipment	596	533	89	14.7
Pets	460	371	81	13.3
Toys, hobbies, and playground equipment	136	162	119	19.6
Other entertainment products and services	353	284	80	13.3
PERSONAL CARE PRODUCTS AND SERVICES	**608**	**538**	**88**	**14.6**
READING	**102**	**60**	**59**	**9.7**
EDUCATION	**1,138**	**1,019**	**90**	**14.8**
TOBACCO PRODUCTS AND SMOKING SUPPLIES	**330**	**309**	**94**	**15.4**
MISCELLANEOUS	**645**	**577**	**89**	**14.7**
CASH CONTRIBUTIONS	**1,834**	**970**	**53**	**8.7**
PERSONAL INSURANCE AND PENSIONS	**5,528**	**5,304**	**96**	**15.8**
Life and other personal insurance	319	125	39	6.5
Pensions and Social Security	5,209	5,178	99	16.4
GIFTS FOR PEOPLE IN OTHER HOUSEHOLDS	**1,078**	**474**	**44**	**7.2**

Note: The Bureau of Labor Statistics uses consumer unit rather than household as the sampling unit in the Consumer Expenditure Survey. For the definition of consumer unit, see the glossary. Spending on gifts is also included in the preceding product and service categories. "–" means not applicable.
Source: Bureau of Labor Statistics, 2013 Consumer Expenditure Survey, Internet site http://www.bls.gov/cex/; calculations by New Strategist

Table 9.7 Average, Indexed, and Market Share of Spending by Householders Aged 35 to 44, 2013

(average annual spending of total consumer units and average annual, indexed, and market share of spending by consumer units headed by people aged 35 to 44, 2013)

	total consumer units	consumer units headed by 35-to-44-year-olds average spending	indexed spending	market share
Number of consumer units (in 000s)	**125,670**	**21,257**	–	**16.9%**
Average annual spending	**$51,100**	**$58,784**	**115**	**19.5**
FOOD	**6,602**	**7,920**	**120**	**20.3**
Food at home	**3,977**	**4,641**	**117**	**19.7**
Cereals and bakery products	544	646	119	20.1
Cereals and cereal products	185	233	126	21.3
Bakery products	359	412	115	19.4
Meats, poultry, fish, and eggs	856	993	116	19.6
Beef	219	276	126	21.3
Pork	170	184	108	18.3
Other meats	119	138	116	19.6
Poultry	170	215	126	21.4
Fish and seafood	122	119	98	16.5
Eggs	56	61	109	18.4
Dairy products	414	495	120	20.2
Fresh milk and cream	152	196	129	21.8
Other dairy products	262	299	114	19.3
Fruits and vegetables	751	866	115	19.5
Fresh fruits	270	312	116	19.5
Fresh vegetables	236	259	110	18.6
Processed fruits	115	136	118	20.0
Processed vegetables	130	158	122	20.6
Other food at home	1,412	1,641	116	19.7
Sugar and other sweets	143	157	110	18.6
Fats and oils	117	128	109	18.5
Miscellaneous foods	728	881	121	20.5
Nonalcoholic beverages	384	435	113	19.2
Food prepared by consumer unit on trips	42	41	98	16.5
Food away from home	**2,625**	**3,280**	**125**	**21.1**
ALCOHOLIC BEVERAGES	**445**	**443**	**100**	**16.8**
HOUSING	**17,148**	**20,619**	**120**	**20.3**
Shelter	**10,080**	**12,271**	**122**	**20.6**
Owned dwellings	6,108	7,981	131	22.1
Mortgage interest and charges	3,078	5,078	165	27.9
Property taxes	1,848	1,964	106	18.0
Maintenance, repair, insurance, other expenses	1,182	939	79	13.4
Rented dwellings	3,324	3,834	115	19.5
Other lodging	649	455	70	11.9

	total consumer units	consumer units headed by 35-to-44-year-olds average spending	indexed spending	market share
Utilities, fuels, and public services	**$3,737**	**$4,299**	**115**	**19.5%**
Natural gas	393	445	113	19.2
Electricity	1,422	1,635	115	19.4
Fuel oil and other fuels	142	121	85	14.4
Telephone services	1,271	1,508	119	20.1
Residential telephone, VOIP, and phone cards	358	298	83	14.1
Cellular phone service	913	1,209	132	22.4
Water and other public services	509	590	116	19.6
Household services	**1,144**	**1,612**	**141**	**23.8**
Personal services	368	825	224	37.9
Other household services	776	787	101	17.2
Housekeeping supplies	**645**	**674**	**104**	**17.7**
Laundry and cleaning supplies	154	170	110	18.7
Other household products	350	368	105	17.8
Postage and stationery	140	136	97	16.4
Household furnishings and equipment	**1,542**	**1,763**	**114**	**19.3**
Household textiles	97	108	111	18.8
Furniture	382	449	118	19.9
Floor coverings	20	17	85	14.4
Major appliances	214	268	125	21.2
Small appliances and miscellaneous housewares	100	102	102	17.3
Miscellaneous household equipment	727	819	113	19.1
APPAREL AND RELATED SERVICES	**1,604**	**1,960**	**122**	**20.7**
Men and boys	**374**	**533**	**143**	**24.1**
Men, aged 16 or older	304	378	124	21.0
Boys, aged 2 to 15	70	154	220	37.2
Women and girls	**636**	**718**	**113**	**19.1**
Women, aged 16 or older	527	513	97	16.5
Girls, aged 2 to 15	109	205	188	31.8
Children under age 2	**75**	**109**	**145**	**24.6**
Footwear	**307**	**398**	**130**	**21.9**
Other apparel products and services	**211**	**202**	**96**	**16.2**
TRANSPORTATION	**9,004**	**10,519**	**117**	**19.8**
Vehicle purchases	**3,271**	**4,010**	**123**	**20.7**
Cars and trucks, new	1,563	1,774	113	19.2
Cars and trucks, used	1,669	2,218	133	22.5
Gasoline and motor oil	**2,611**	**3,218**	**123**	**20.8**
Other vehicle expenses	**2,584**	**2,740**	**106**	**17.9**
Vehicle finance charges	204	288	141	23.9
Maintenance and repairs	835	841	101	17.0
Vehicle insurance	1,013	1,019	101	17.0
Vehicle rentals, leases, licenses, other charges	533	592	111	18.8
Public transportation	**537**	**552**	**103**	**17.4**

	total consumer units	consumer units headed by 35-to-44-year-olds		
		average spending	indexed spending	market share
HEALTH CARE	**$3,631**	**$3,188**	**88**	**14.9%**
Health insurance	2,229	1,944	87	14.8
Medical services	796	786	99	16.7
Drugs	470	343	73	12.3
Medical supplies	135	116	86	14.5
ENTERTAINMENT	**2,482**	**2,958**	**119**	**20.2**
Fees and admissions	569	736	129	21.9
Audio and visual equipment and services	964	1,139	118	20.0
Pets, toys, and playground equipment	596	638	107	18.1
Pets	460	473	103	17.4
Toys, hobbies, and playground equipment	136	165	121	20.5
Other entertainment products and services	353	446	126	21.4
PERSONAL CARE PRODUCTS AND SERVICES	**608**	**672**	**111**	**18.7**
READING	**102**	**105**	**103**	**17.4**
EDUCATION	**1,138**	**903**	**79**	**13.4**
TOBACCO PRODUCTS AND SMOKING SUPPLIES	**330**	**331**	**100**	**17.0**
MISCELLANEOUS	**645**	**643**	**100**	**16.9**
CASH CONTRIBUTIONS	**1,834**	**1,440**	**79**	**13.3**
PERSONAL INSURANCE AND PENSIONS	**5,528**	**7,081**	**128**	**21.7**
Life and other personal insurance	319	290	91	15.4
Pensions and Social Security	5,209	6,791	130	22.1
GIFTS FOR PEOPLE IN OTHER HOUSEHOLDS	**1,078**	**604**	**56**	**9.5**

Note: The Bureau of Labor Statistics uses consumer unit rather than household as the sampling unit in the Consumer Expenditure Survey. For the definition of consumer unit, see the glossary. Spending on gifts is also included in the preceding product and service categories. "–" means not applicable.
Source: Bureau of Labor Statistics, 2013 Consumer Expenditure Survey, Internet site http://www.bls.gov/cex/; calculations by New Strategist

Couples with Adult Children at Home Are Beginning to Spend More

New cars and trucks are among the items on which these households have boosted their spending.

Many members of the Millennial generation are adults living at home with their parents. Married couples with grown children (aged 18 or older) at home rank among the most affluent households because they have more earners—2.5 versus 1.6 earners in the average household. Couples with adult children at home cut their spending by 12 percent between 2006 and 2010, then boosted their spending by 6 percent between 2010 and 2013, after adjusting for inflation.

The spending of married couples with adult children at home did an about-face in the 2010-to-2013 time period in a variety of categories such as food away from home, alcoholic beverages, and furniture. Perhaps the biggest reversal was in spending on new cars and trucks. Couples with adult children at home cut their spending on this category by an enormous 55 percent between 2006 and 2010, then boosted their spending by 50 percent between 2010 and 2013, after adjusting for inflation. Despite this increase, the average spending of these households on new vehicles in 2013 remained well below the 2006 level.

Some categories saw spending declines throughout the 2006-to-2013 time period, after adjusting for inflation. Spending on mortgage interest fell 22 percent during those years as some couples lost their home when the housing market collapsed and others chose to rent rather than buy. Spending on education, which had grown 36 percent between 2000 and 2006, fell by 0.9 percent between 2006 and 2013.

■ Many couples with adult children at home postponed buying new vehicles in the aftermath of the Great Recession. Pent-up demand is driving recent spending in this category.

For couples with adult children at home, spending is growing again in some categories

(percent change in spending by married couples with children aged 18 or older at home, 2010 to 2013; in 2013 dollars)

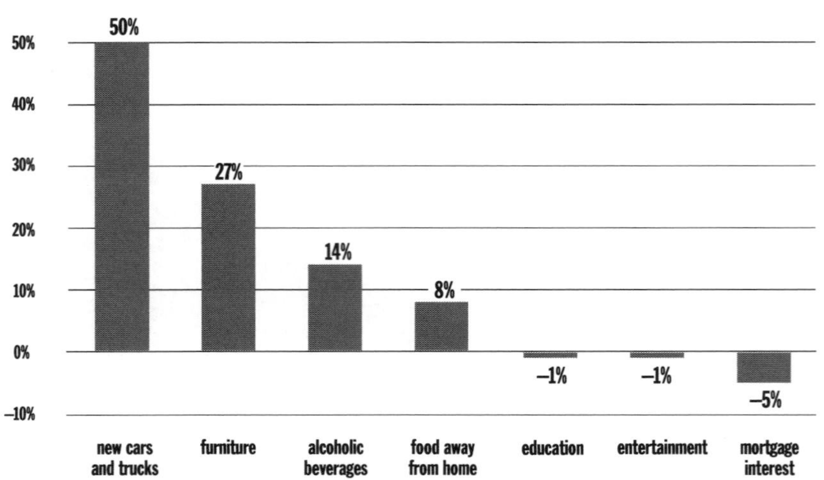

Table 9.8 Average Spending of Married Couples with Oldest Child Aged 18 or Older, 2000 to 2013

(average annual spending of married-couple consumer units with oldest child aged 18 or older at home, 2000 to 2013; percent change for selected years; in 2013 dollars)

	average spending				percent change		
	2013	2010	2006	2000	2010–13	2006–13	2000–06
Number of consumer units (in 000s)	**9,042**	**8,745**	**8,452**	**8,090**	**3.4%**	**7.0%**	**4.5%**
Average annual spending	**$76,085**	**$71,639**	**$81,158**	**$73,797**	**6.2**	**–6.3**	**10.0**
FOOD	**10,026**	**9,673**	**10,811**	**10,631**	**3.7**	**–7.3**	**1.7**
Food at home	**6,015**	**5,969**	**6,446**	**6,391**	**0.8**	**–6.7**	**0.9**
Cereals and bakery products	854	834	826	1,013	2.4	3.4	–18.5
Cereals and cereal products	280	272	272	340	2.8	3.1	–20.0
Bakery products	573	563	555	672	1.8	3.3	–17.5
Meats, poultry, fish, and eggs	1,327	1,332	1,619	1,719	–0.4	–18.0	–5.8
Beef	354	397	481	529	–10.9	–26.4	–9.1
Pork	287	245	321	363	17.3	–10.7	–11.4
Other meats	190	197	222	230	–3.3	–14.4	–3.5
Poultry	258	225	289	311	14.5	–10.7	–7.2
Fish and seafood	163	197	244	211	–17.1	–33.1	15.5
Eggs	74	71	62	76	4.9	18.6	–17.6
Dairy products	585	630	633	683	–7.2	–7.6	–7.3
Fresh milk and cream	202	234	230	279	–13.7	–12.2	–17.5
Other dairy products	383	396	403	404	–3.4	–5.0	–0.3
Fruits and vegetables	1,082	1,097	1,106	1,043	–1.4	–2.2	6.0
Fresh fruits	364	365	361	326	–0.4	1.0	10.6
Fresh vegetables	334	334	398	310	–0.1	–16.0	28.3
Processed fruits	178	184	190	221	–3.1	–6.1	–14.1
Processed vegetables	206	214	158	187	–3.6	30.1	–15.2
Other food at home	2,167	2,074	2,261	1,932	4.5	–4.2	17.1
Sugar and other sweets	220	218	231	273	0.9	–4.8	–15.4
Fats and oils	188	175	170	183	7.3	10.7	–7.0
Miscellaneous foods	1,122	1,075	1,168	850	4.4	–4.0	37.5
Nonalcoholic beverages	573	544	619	559	5.4	–7.5	10.9
Food prepared by consumer unit on trips	65	63	73	68	3.1	–10.7	7.6
Food away from home	**4,011**	**3,704**	**4,364**	**4,240**	**8.3**	**–8.1**	**2.9**
ALCOHOLIC BEVERAGES	**511**	**449**	**580**	**645**	**13.9**	**–11.9**	**–10.1**
HOUSING	**22,412**	**21,858**	**23,714**	**21,019**	**2.5**	**–5.5**	**12.8**
Shelter	**12,447**	**12,314**	**12,966**	**11,609**	**1.1**	**–4.0**	**11.7**
Owned dwellings	9,757	9,575	10,334	9,122	1.9	–5.6	13.3
Mortgage interest and charges	4,775	5,048	6,109	5,327	–5.4	–21.8	14.7
Property taxes	3,123	2,989	2,562	2,326	4.5	21.9	10.2
Maintenance, repair, insurance, other expenses	1,859	1,539	1,662	1,469	20.8	11.9	13.1
Rented dwellings	1,587	1,729	1,480	1,343	–8.2	7.2	10.2
Other lodging	1,103	1,009	1,152	1,143	9.4	–4.3	0.8

	average spending				percent change		
	2013	2010	2006	2000	2010–13	2006–13	2000–06
Utilities, fuels, and public services	**$5,747**	**$5,487**	**$5,559**	**$4,601**	**4.7%**	**3.4%**	**20.8%**
Natural gas	596	658	797	565	–9.4	–25.2	41.0
Electricity	2,022	2,055	2,028	1,728	–1.6	–0.3	17.4
Fuel oil and other fuels	297	210	207	176	41.1	43.6	17.6
Telephone services	2,026	1,856	1,880	1,533	9.2	7.8	22.7
Residential telephone, VOIP, and phone cards	540	625	876	1,291	–13.6	–38.3	–32.1
Cellular phone service	1,487	1,231	1,004	242	20.8	48.1	314.7
Water and other public services	805	708	646	599	13.7	24.6	7.8
Household services	**1,042**	**965**	**1,171**	**722**	**8.0**	**–11.0**	**62.0**
Personal services	94	129	474	145	–27.3	–80.2	227.3
Other household services	949	835	697	578	13.6	36.2	20.6
Housekeeping supplies	**887**	**896**	**1,168**	**988**	**–1.0**	**–24.1**	**18.3**
Laundry and cleaning supplies	258	228	292	271	13.4	–11.8	8.1
Other household products	471	466	632	478	1.1	–25.5	32.4
Postage and stationery	158	203	243	239	–22.2	–34.9	1.3
Household furnishings and equipment	**2,289**	**2,198**	**2,850**	**3,099**	**4.2**	**–19.7**	**–8.1**
Household textiles	184	165	321	221	11.8	–42.7	45.7
Furniture	571	451	611	655	26.7	–6.6	–6.6
Floor coverings	18	31	74	146	–41.9	–75.7	–49.4
Major appliances	345	337	503	463	2.5	–31.4	8.6
Small appliances and miscellaneous housewares	148	203	213	168	–27.1	–30.4	26.7
Miscellaneous household equipment	1,023	1,012	1,128	1,449	1.1	–9.3	–22.2
APPAREL AND RELATED SERVICES	**2,310**	**2,365**	**3,268**	**3,650**	**–2.3**	**–29.3**	**–10.5**
Men and boys	**637**	**656**	**872**	**984**	**–2.9**	**–27.0**	**–11.3**
Men, aged 16 or older	569	561	782	839	1.4	–27.3	–6.7
Boys, aged 2 to 15	68	95	90	145	–28.5	–24.6	–37.7
Women and girls	**899**	**917**	**1,412**	**1,610**	**–1.9**	**–36.3**	**–12.3**
Women, aged 16 or older	739	813	1,246	1,460	–9.1	–40.7	–14.7
Girls, aged 2 to 15	160	104	166	150	54.4	–3.8	10.8
Children under age 2	**77**	**73**	**82**	**85**	**6.0**	**–6.1**	**–3.7**
Footwear	**460**	**444**	**545**	**524**	**3.5**	**–15.7**	**4.2**
Other apparel products and services	**237**	**276**	**357**	**448**	**–14.0**	**–33.6**	**–20.3**
TRANSPORTATION	**14,464**	**12,360**	**16,072**	**16,448**	**17.0**	**–10.0**	**–2.3**
Vehicle purchases	**5,339**	**3,908**	**6,615**	**7,733**	**36.6**	**–19.3**	**–14.4**
Cars and trucks, new	2,145	1,432	3,164	3,462	49.8	–32.2	–8.6
Cars and trucks, used	3,175	2,369	3,323	4,219	34.1	–4.5	–21.2
Gasoline and motor oil	**4,252**	**3,612**	**4,252**	**2,830**	**17.7**	**0.0**	**50.3**
Other vehicle expenses	**4,110**	**4,172**	**4,391**	**5,131**	**–1.5**	**–6.4**	**–14.4**
Vehicle finance charges	283	403	562	752	–29.7	–49.6	–25.3
Maintenance and repairs	1,364	1,312	1,273	1,337	4.0	7.1	–4.7
Vehicle insurance	1,697	1,732	1,856	1,905	–2.0	–8.6	–2.6
Vehicle rentals, leases, licenses, other charges	765	725	699	1,138	5.5	9.4	–38.6
Public transportation	**763**	**667**	**815**	**755**	**14.5**	**–6.3**	**7.9**

	average spending				percent change		
	2013	2010	2006	2000	2010–13	2006–13	2000–06
HEALTH CARE	**$5,153**	**$4,582**	**$4,140**	**$3,627**	**12.5%**	**24.5%**	**14.2%**
Health insurance	2,929	2,573	2,125	1,763	13.9	37.8	20.6
Medical services	1,387	1,086	1,033	990	27.7	34.3	4.3
Drugs	631	729	785	689	–13.4	–19.6	13.9
Medical supplies	206	194	198	187	5.9	4.3	5.8
ENTERTAINMENT	**3,356**	**3,404**	**3,541**	**3,498**	**–1.4**	**–5.2**	**1.2**
Fees and admissions	799	870	921	958	–8.1	–13.2	–3.8
Audio and visual equipment and services	1,225	1,230	1,370	1,116	–0.4	–10.6	22.8
Pets, toys, and playground equipment	694	863	637	572	–19.6	9.0	11.3
Pets	579	695	555	429	–16.7	4.4	29.3
Toys, hobbies, and playground equipment	114	168	82	143	–32.0	39.0	–42.8
Other entertainment products and services	639	442	614	851	44.5	4.1	–27.9
PERSONAL CARE PRODUCTS AND SERVICES	**872**	**897**	**1,064**	**1,143**	**–2.8**	**–18.1**	**–6.9**
READING	**130**	**131**	**169**	**245**	**–1.1**	**–22.9**	**–31.1**
EDUCATION	**3,235**	**3,278**	**3,266**	**2,393**	**–1.3**	**–0.9**	**36.5**
TOBACCO PRODUCTS AND SMOKING SUPPLIES	**399**	**458**	**417**	**616**	**–12.9**	**–4.4**	**–32.2**
MISCELLANEOUS	**1,019**	**1,095**	**1,186**	**1,230**	**–6.9**	**–14.1**	**–3.6**
CASH CONTRIBUTIONS	**2,363**	**2,092**	**2,918**	**1,853**	**13.0**	**–19.0**	**57.4**
PERSONAL INSURANCE AND PENSIONS	**9,834**	**8,998**	**10,014**	**6,801**	**9.3**	**–1.8**	**47.2**
Life and other personal insurance	558	616	644	950	–9.5	–13.3	–32.2
Pensions and Social Security	9,276	8,380	9,370	5,851	10.7	–1.0	60.1
GIFTS FOR PEOPLE IN OTHER HOUSEHOLDS	**1,776**	**1,263**	**1,487**	**2,338**	**40.6**	**19.4**	**–36.4**

Note: The Bureau of Labor Statistics uses consumer unit rather than household as the sampling unit in the Consumer Expenditure Survey. For the definition of consumer unit, see the glossary. Spending on gifts is also included in the preceding product and service categories.
Source: Bureau of Labor Statistics, 2000, 2006, 2010, and 2013 Consumer Expenditure Surveys, Internet site http://www.bls.gov/cex/; calculations by New Strategist

Table 9.9 Average, Indexed, and Market Share of Spending by Married Couples with Oldest Child Aged 18 or Older, 2013

(average annual spending of total consumer units, and average annual, indexed, and market share of spending by married-couple consumer units with children aged 18 or older at home, 2013)

	total consumer units	consumer units headed by married couples with children aged 18 or older at home: average spending	indexed spending	market share
Number of consumer units (in 000s)	**125,670**	**9,042**	–	**7.2%**
Average annual spending	**$51,100**	**$76,085**	**149**	**10.7**
FOOD	**6,602**	**10,026**	**152**	**10.9**
Food at home	**3,977**	**6,015**	**151**	**10.9**
Cereals and bakery products	544	854	157	11.3
Cereals and cereal products	185	280	151	10.9
Bakery products	359	573	160	11.5
Meats, poultry, fish, and eggs	856	1,327	155	11.2
Beef	219	354	162	11.6
Pork	170	287	169	12.1
Other meats	119	190	160	11.5
Poultry	170	258	152	10.9
Fish and seafood	122	163	134	9.6
Eggs	56	74	132	9.5
Dairy products	414	585	141	10.2
Fresh milk and cream	152	202	133	9.6
Other dairy products	262	383	146	10.5
Fruits and vegetables	751	1,082	144	10.4
Fresh fruits	270	364	135	9.7
Fresh vegetables	236	334	142	10.2
Processed fruits	115	178	155	11.1
Processed vegetables	130	206	158	11.4
Other food at home	1,412	2,167	153	11.0
Sugar and other sweets	143	220	154	11.1
Fats and oils	117	188	161	11.6
Miscellaneous foods	728	1,122	154	11.1
Nonalcoholic beverages	384	573	149	10.7
Food prepared by consumer unit on trips	42	65	155	11.1
Food away from home	**2,625**	**4,011**	**153**	**11.0**
ALCOHOLIC BEVERAGES	**445**	**511**	**115**	**8.3**
HOUSING	**17,148**	**22,412**	**131**	**9.4**
Shelter	**10,080**	**12,447**	**123**	**8.9**
Owned dwellings	6,108	9,757	160	11.5
Mortgage interest and charges	3,078	4,775	155	11.2
Property taxes	1,848	3,123	169	12.2
Maintenance, repair, insurance, other expenses	1,182	1,859	157	11.3
Rented dwellings	3,324	1,587	48	3.4
Other lodging	649	1,103	170	12.2

	total consumer units	consumer units headed by married couples with children aged 18 or older at home		
		average spending	indexed spending	market share
Utilities, fuels, and public services	**$3,737**	**$5,747**	**154**	**11.1%**
Natural gas	393	596	152	10.9
Electricity	1,422	2,022	142	10.2
Fuel oil and other fuels	142	297	209	15.0
Telephone services	1,271	2,026	159	11.5
Residential telephone, VOIP, and phone cards	358	540	151	10.9
Cellular phone service	913	1,487	163	11.7
Water and other public services	509	805	158	11.4
Household services	**1,144**	**1,042**	**91**	**6.6**
Personal services	368	94	26	1.8
Other household services	776	949	122	8.8
Housekeeping supplies	**645**	**887**	**138**	**9.9**
Laundry and cleaning supplies	154	258	168	12.1
Other household products	350	471	135	9.7
Postage and stationery	140	158	113	8.1
Household furnishings and equipment	**1,542**	**2,289**	**148**	**10.7**
Household textiles	97	184	190	13.6
Furniture	382	571	149	10.8
Floor coverings	20	18	90	6.5
Major appliances	214	345	161	11.6
Small appliances and miscellaneous housewares	100	148	148	10.6
Miscellaneous household equipment	727	1,023	141	10.1
APPAREL AND RELATED SERVICES	**1,604**	**2,310**	**144**	**10.4**
Men and boys	**374**	**637**	**170**	**12.3**
Men, aged 16 or older	304	569	187	13.5
Boys, aged 2 to 15	70	68	97	7.0
Women and girls	**636**	**899**	**141**	**10.2**
Women, aged 16 or older	527	739	140	10.1
Girls, aged 2 to 15	109	160	147	10.6
Children under age 2	**75**	**77**	**103**	**7.4**
Footwear	**307**	**460**	**150**	**10.8**
Other apparel products and services	**211**	**237**	**112**	**8.1**
TRANSPORTATION	**9,004**	**14,464**	**161**	**11.6**
Vehicle purchases	**3,271**	**5,339**	**163**	**11.7**
Cars and trucks, new	1,563	2,145	137	9.9
Cars and trucks, used	1,669	3,175	190	13.7
Gasoline and motor oil	**2,611**	**4,252**	**163**	**11.7**
Other vehicle expenses	**2,584**	**4,110**	**159**	**11.4**
Vehicle finance charges	204	283	139	10.0
Maintenance and repairs	835	1,364	163	11.8
Vehicle insurance	1,013	1,697	168	12.1
Vehicle rentals, leases, licenses, other charges	533	765	144	10.3
Public transportation	**537**	**763**	**142**	**10.2**

	total consumer units	consumer units headed by married couples with children aged 18 or older at home average spending	indexed spending	market share
HEALTH CARE	**$3,631**	**$5,153**	**142**	**10.2%**
Health insurance	2,229	2,929	131	9.5
Medical services	796	1,387	174	12.5
Drugs	470	631	134	9.7
Medical supplies	135	206	153	11.0
ENTERTAINMENT	**2,482**	**3,356**	**135**	**9.7**
Fees and admissions	569	799	140	10.1
Audio and visual equipment and services	964	1,225	127	9.1
Pets, toys, and playground equipment	596	694	116	8.4
Pets	460	579	126	9.1
Toys, hobbies, and playground equipment	136	114	84	6.0
Other entertainment products and services	353	639	181	13.0
PERSONAL CARE PRODUCTS AND SERVICES	**608**	**872**	**143**	**10.3**
READING	**102**	**130**	**127**	**9.2**
EDUCATION	**1,138**	**3,235**	**284**	**20.5**
TOBACCO PRODUCTS AND SMOKING SUPPLIES	**330**	**399**	**121**	**8.7**
MISCELLANEOUS	**645**	**1,019**	**158**	**11.4**
CASH CONTRIBUTIONS	**1,834**	**2,363**	**129**	**9.3**
PERSONAL INSURANCE AND PENSIONS	**5,528**	**9,834**	**178**	**12.8**
Life and other personal insurance	319	558	175	12.6
Pensions and Social Security	5,209	9,276	178	12.8
GIFTS FOR PEOPLE IN OTHER HOUSEHOLDS	**1,078**	**1776**	**165**	**11.9**

Note: The Bureau of Labor Statistics uses consumer unit rather than household as the sampling unit in the Consumer Expenditure Survey. For the definition of consumer unit, see the glossary. Spending on gifts is also included in the preceding product and service categories. "–" means not applicable.
Source: Bureau of Labor Statistics, 2013 Consumer Expenditure Survey, Internet site http://www.bls.gov/cex/; calculations by New Strategist

CHAPTER

10

Time Use

■ The time use of the youngest Millennials, aged 20 to 24, differs from that of older Millennials aged 25 to 34. The younger adults are more likely to spend time taking classes, looking for a job, and socializing.

■ People aged 25-to-34 spend more time working or in work-related activities on an average day (4.29 hours) than they do at leisure (3.80), a situation that will continue until they reach the 55-to-64-age group.

■ Men aged 25 to 34 have less leisure time than the average man, and they spend more time caring for children and working.

■ Women aged 25 to 34 spend more than twice as much time working or in work-related activities as the average woman caring for household children.

Time Use Changes as Young Adults Take on Work and Family Responsibilities

Adults aged 20 to 24 have much more leisure time.

The Millennial generation is segmented by lifestage. Many younger Millennials are in college and busy socializing. Many older Millennials, in their late twenties and early thirties, have a career and family. Consequently, the priorities of those aged 20 to 24 differ greatly from those aged 25 to 34.

On an average day, only 47 percent of 20-to-24-year-olds spend time working or in work-related activities, while the figure is a larger 56 percent among 25-to-34-year-olds. But 20-to-24-year-olds are much more likely to be in class on an average day (11 percent) than those aged 25 to 34 (4 percent). Only 14 percent of 20-to-24-year-olds care for household children on an average day versus 39 percent of 25-to-34-year-olds. As people age from their early twenties into their late twenties and thirties, leisure time shrinks. People aged 25 to 34 spend more time working on an average day (4.29 hours) than they do at leisure (3.80), a situation that will continue for many years—until they reach the 55-to-64-age group.

■ Women aged 25 to 34 spend more than twice as much time as the average woman caring for household children.

Leisure time falls to a low point in middle age

(average number of hours per day of leisure time, by age, 2013)

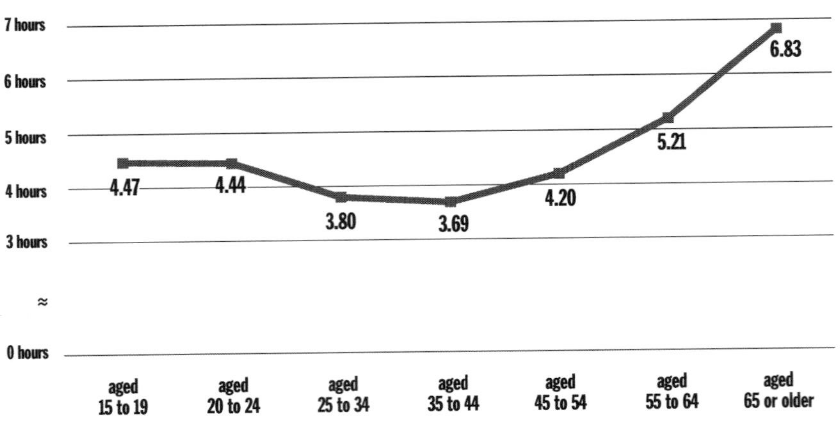

Table 10.1 Detailed Time Use of People Aged 20 to 24, 2013

(hours per day spent in primary activities by total people aged 15 or older and people aged 20 to 24, index of age group to total, and number and percent of people aged 20 to 24 participating in activity on an average day, 2013)

	average hours per day for total people	average hours per day for people aged 20 to 24	index, 20 to 24 to total	people aged 20 to 24 participating in activity	
				number (in 000s)	percent
Total, all activities	**24.00 hrs.**	**24.00 hrs.**	**100**	**22,052**	**100.0%**
Personal care activities	9.53	9.90	104	22,045	100.0
Sleeping	8.74	9.13	104	22,016	99.8
Grooming	0.70	0.74	106	18,144	82.3
Health-related self-care	0.09	–	–	258	1.2
Household activities	1.78	0.92	52	13,752	62.4
Housework	0.57	0.32	56	5,036	22.8
Food preparation and cleanup	0.57	0.31	54	8,933	40.5
Lawn, garden, and houseplants	0.18	0.06	33	601	2.7
Animals and pets	0.10	0.05	50	1,865	8.5
Vehicles	0.04	0.05	125	474	2.1
Household management	0.18	0.09	50	3,730	16.9
Financial management	0.03	–	–	222	1.0
Household and personal organization and planning	0.10	0.07	70	2,803	12.7
Household and personal mail and messages (except email)	0.01	–	–	433	2.0
Household and personal email and messages	0.03	0.01	33	590	2.7
Caring for and helping household members	0.44	0.36	82	4,290	19.5
Caring for and helping household children	0.36	0.32	89	3,087	14.0
Caring for household adults	0.02	–	–	295	1.3
Helping household adults	0.01	0.02	200	1,115	5.1
Caring for and helping people in other households	0.14	0.12	86	2,726	12.4
Caring for and helping children in other households	0.07	0.03	43	913	4.1
Caring for adults in other households	0.01	–	–	174	0.8
Helping adults in other households	0.05	0.08	160	1,915	8.7
Working and work-related activities	3.20	3.41	107	10,378	47.1
Working	3.14	3.24	103	9,635	43.7
Job search and interviewing	0.04	0.12	300	502	2.3
Educational activities	0.45	0.97	216	4,083	18.5
Taking class	0.26	0.33	127	2,382	10.8
Homework and research	0.18	–	–	–	–
Consumer purchases	0.37	0.35	95	9,439	42.8
Grocery shopping	0.11	0.05	45	1,862	8.4
Shopping (except groceries, food, and gas)	0.24	0.25	104	4,232	19.2
Professional and personal care services	0.08	0.04	50	1,450	6.6
Medical and care services	0.05	–	–	425	1.9

	average hours per day for total people	average hours per day for people aged 20 to 24	index, 20 to 24 to total	people aged 20 to 24 participating in activity	
				number (in 000s)	percent
Eating and drinking	1.11 hrs.	1.06 hrs.	95	21,156	95.9%
Socializing, relaxing, and leisure	4.71	4.44	94	20,898	94.8
Socializing and communicating	0.65	0.83	128	8,965	40.7
Attending or hosting social events	0.07	0.06	86	548	2.5
Relaxing and leisure	3.91	3.49	89	19,543	88.6
Television and movies	2.77	2.18	79	16,535	75.0
Playing games	0.22	0.47	214	2,918	13.2
Computer use for leisure (except games)	0.21	0.25	119	3,443	15.6
Reading for personal interest	0.32	0.23	72	2,861	13.0
Arts and entertainment (other than sports)	0.08	0.06	75	497	2.3
Attending movies	0.03	0.04	133	300	1.4
Sports, exercise, and recreation	0.32	0.49	153	4,816	21.8
Participating in sports, exercise, and recreation	0.30	0.44	147	4,488	20.4
Attending sporting or recreational events	0.03	–	–	356	1.6
Religious and spiritual activities	0.14	0.11	79	1,469	6.7
Volunteer activities	0.14	0.08	57	644	2.9
Telephone calls	0.10	0.08	80	2,445	11.1
Traveling	1.18	1.26	107	19,651	89.1

Note: Primary activities are those respondents identified as their main activity. Other activities done simultaneously are not included. Travel related to activities is reported separately. Numbers do not sum to total because not all activities are shown. The index is calculated by dividing time spent by age group by time spent by the average person and multiplying by 100. "–" means sample is too small to make a reliable estimate.
Source: Bureau of Labor Statistics, unpublished tables from the 2013 American Time Use Survey, Internet site http://www.bls .gov/tus/home.htm; calculations by New Strategist

Table 10.2 Detailed Time Use of Men Aged 20 to 24, 2013

(hours per day spent in primary activities by total men aged 15 or older and men aged 20 to 24, index of age group to total, and number and percent of men aged 20 to 24 participating in activity on an average day, 2013)

	average hours per day for total men	average hours per day for men aged 20 to 24	index, 20 to 24 to total	men aged 20 to 24 participating in activity: number (in 000s)	percent
Total, all activities	**24.00 hrs.**	**24.00 hrs.**	**100**	**21,124**	**100.0%**
Personal care activities	9.29	9.06	98	21,124	100.0
Sleeping	8.65	8.40	97	21,109	99.9
Grooming	0.57	0.56	98	16,285	77.1
Health-related self-care	0.60	0.10	17	1,481	7.0
Household activities	1.34	1.43	107	14,957	70.8
Housework	0.25	0.32	128	4,763	22.5
Food preparation and cleanup	0.33	0.35	106	9,321	44.1
Lawn, garden, and houseplants	0.25	0.26	104	2,445	11.6
Animals and pets	0.09	0.11	122	3,271	15.5
Vehicles	0.08	0.08	100	1,011	4.8
Household management	0.14	0.13	93	4,095	19.4
Financial management	0.02	0.01	50	463	2.2
Household and personal organization and planning	0.08	0.08	100	2,356	11.2
Household and personal mail and messages (except email)	0.01	0.01	100	818	3.9
Household and personal email and messages	0.03	0.02	67	988	4.7
Caring for and helping household members	0.30	0.30	100	4,517	21.4
Caring for and helping household children	0.24	0.20	83	3,476	16.5
Caring for household adults	0.01	0.03	300	399	1.9
Helping household adults	0.01	0.01	100	915	4.3
Caring for and helping people in other households	0.12	0.12	100	1,903	9.0
Caring for and helping children in other households	0.05	0.02	40	529	2.5
Caring for adults in other households	0.01	–	–	91	0.4
Helping adults in other households	0.06	0.09	150	1,394	6.6
Working and work-related activities	3.88	4.92	127	13,086	61.9
Working	3.80	4.85	128	12,768	60.4
Job search and interviewing	0.05	0.03	60	245	1.2
Educational activities	0.45	0.05	11	389	1.8
Taking class	0.27	–	–	35	0.2
Homework and research	0.17	0.04	24	307	1.5
Consumer purchases	0.29	0.29	100	7,135	33.8
Grocery shopping	0.07	0.08	114	2,565	12.1
Shopping (except groceries, food, and gas)	0.19	0.18	95	3,622	17.1
Professional and personal care services	0.06	0.06	100	1,150	5.4
Medical and care services	0.04	0.04	100	456	2.2

	average hours per day for total men	average hours per day for men aged 20 to 24	index, 20 to 24 to total	men aged 20 to 24 participating in activity	
				number (in 000s)	percent
Eating and drinking	1.14 hrs.	1.09 hrs.	96	20,296	96.1%
Socializing, relaxing, and leisure	4.94	4.49	91	19,747	93.5
Socializing and communicating	0.60	0.57	95	7,131	33.8
Attending or hosting social events	0.06	0.05	83	284	1.3
Relaxing and leisure	4.20	3.80	90	19,145	90.6
Television and movies	2.98	2.97	100	16,955	80.3
Playing games	0.32	0.07	22	860	4.1
Computer use for leisure (except games)	0.22	0.21	95	2,639	12.5
Reading for personal interest	0.26	0.18	69	2,986	14.1
Arts and entertainment (other than sports)	0.08	0.07	88	386	1.8
Attending movies	0.03	0.02	67	162	0.8
Sports, exercise, and recreation	0.42	0.29	69	3,891	18.4
Participating in sports, exercise, and recreation	0.40	0.26	65	3,663	17.3
Attending sporting or recreational events	0.02	0.03	150	271	1.3
Religious and spiritual activities	0.12	0.11	92	1,473	7.0
Volunteer activities	0.13	0.15	115	1,200	5.7
Telephone calls	0.06	0.05	83	1,632	7.7
Traveling	1.21	1.33	110	18,670	88.4

Note: Primary activities are those respondents identified as their main activity. Other activities done simultaneously are not included. Travel related to activities is reported separately. Numbers do not sum to total because not all activities are shown. The index is calculated by dividing time spent by age group by time spent by the average man and multiplying by 100. "–" means sample is too small to make a reliable estimate.
Source: Bureau of Labor Statistics, unpublished tables from the 2013 American Time Use Survey, Internet site http://www.bls .gov/tus/home.htm; calculations by New Strategist

Table 10.3 Detailed Time Use of Women Aged 20 to 24, 2013

(hours per day spent in primary activities by total women aged 15 or older and women aged 20 to 24, index of age group to total, and number and percent of women aged 20 to 24 participating in activity on an average day, 2013)

	average hours per day for total women	average hours per day for women aged 20 to 24	index, 20 to 24 to total	women aged 20 to 24 participating in activity	
				number (in 000s)	percent
Total, all activities	**24.00 hrs.**	**24.00 hrs.**	**100**	**11,014**	**100.0%**
Personal care activities	9.75	10.33	106	11,014	100.0
Sleeping	8.82	9.41	107	10,985	99.7
Grooming	0.82	0.86	105	9,379	85.2
Health-related self-care	0.11	–	–	208	1.9
Household activities	2.20	1.20	55	8,001	72.6
Housework	0.87	0.51	59	3,624	32.9
Food preparation and cleanup	0.80	0.40	50	5,741	52.1
Lawn, garden, and houseplants	0.12	–	–	346	3.1
Animals and pets	0.11	0.06	55	1,215	11.0
Vehicles	0.01	–	–	16	0.1
Household management	0.21	0.11	52	2,092	19.0
Financial management	0.04	–	–	129	1.2
Household and personal organization and planning	0.12	0.09	75	1,575	14.3
Household and personal mail and messages (except email)	0.02	–	–	249	2.3
Household and personal email and messages	0.04	0.01	25	411	3.7
Caring for and helping household members	0.58	0.63	109	3,392	30.8
Caring for and helping household children	0.47	0.57	121	2,518	22.9
Caring for household adults	0.03	–	–	255	2.3
Helping household adults	0.01	0.03	300	811	7.4
Caring for and helping people in other households	0.16	0.11	69	1,704	15.5
Caring for and helping children in other households	0.10	0.02	20	651	5.9
Caring for adults in other households	0.01	–	–	174	1.6
Helping adults in other households	0.05	0.06	120	1,109	10.1
Working and work-related activities	2.57	2.68	104	4,400	39.9
Working	2.52	2.59	103	4,161	37.8
Job search and interviewing	0.03	–	–	135	1.2
Educational activities	0.45	0.91	202	2,065	18.7
Taking class	0.25	–	–	1,021	9.3
Homework and research	0.19	–	–	–	–
Consumer purchases	0.45	0.52	116	5,486	49.8
Grocery shopping	0.14	0.06	43	779	7.1
Shopping (except groceries, food, and gas)	0.28	0.41	146	3,295	29.9
Professional and personal care services	0.10	0.05	50	700	6.4
Medical and care services	0.07	–	–	281	2.6

	average hours per day for total women	average hours per day for women aged 20 to 24	index, 20 to 24 to total	women aged 20 to 24 participating in activity	
				number (in 000s)	percent
Eating and drinking	1.09 hrs.	1.05 hrs.	96	10,515	95.5%
Socializing, relaxing, and leisure	4.50	4.33	96	10,522	95.5
Socializing and communicating	0.70	0.96	137	4,986	45.3
Attending or hosting social events	0.08	0.11	138	461	4.2
Relaxing and leisure	3.63	3.22	89	9,699	88.1
Television and movies	2.56	2.27	89	8,102	73.6
Playing games	0.13	–	–	290	2.6
Computer use for leisure (except games)	0.20	0.20	100	1,501	13.6
Reading for personal interest	0.38	–	–	1,911	17.4
Arts and entertainment (other than sports)	0.09	–	–	222	2.0
Attending movies	0.03	–	–	159	1.4
Sports, exercise, and recreation	0.23	0.24	104	2,041	18.5
Participating in sports, exercise, and recreation	0.20	0.19	95	1,896	17.2
Attending sporting or recreational events	0.03	–	–	173	1.6
Religious and spiritual activities	0.17	0.09	53	713	6.5
Volunteer activities	0.15	–	–	392	3.6
Telephone calls	0.14	0.08	57	1,434	13.0
Traveling	1.16	1.27	109	9,709	88.2

Note: Primary activities are those respondents identified as their main activity. Other activities done simultaneously are not included. Travel related to activities is reported separately. Numbers do not sum to total because not all activities are shown. The index is calculated by dividing time spent by age group by time spent by the average woman and multiplying by 100. "–" means sample is too small to make a reliable estimate.
Source: Bureau of Labor Statistics, unpublished tables from the 2013 American Time Use Survey, Internet site http://www.bls.gov/tus/home.htm; calculations by New Strategist

Table 10.4 Detailed Time Use of People Aged 25 to 34, 2013

(hours per day spent in primary activities by total people aged 15 or older and people aged 25 to 34, index of age group to total, and number and percent of people aged 25 to 34 participating in activity on an average day, 2013)

	average hours per day for total people	average hours per day for people aged 25 to 34	index, 25 to 34 to total	people aged 25 to 34 participating in activity	
				number (in 000s)	percent
Total, all activities	**24.00 hrs.**	**24.00 hrs.**	**100**	**41,550**	**100.0%**
Personal care activities	9.53	9.38	98	41,540	100.0
Sleeping	8.74	8.65	99	41,485	99.8
Grooming	0.70	0.69	99	34,296	82.5
Health-related self-care	0.09	0.03	33	935	2.3
Household activities	1.78	1.51	85	30,614	73.7
Housework	0.57	0.52	91	13,357	32.1
Food preparation and cleanup	0.57	0.57	100	22,957	55.3
Lawn, garden, and houseplants	0.18	0.09	50	2,061	5.0
Animals and pets	0.10	0.06	60	4,656	11.2
Vehicles	0.04	0.04	100	926	2.2
Household management	0.18	0.11	61	8,109	19.5
Financial management	0.03	0.02	67	949	2.3
Household and personal organization and planning	0.10	0.08	80	5,491	13.2
Household and personal mail and messages (except email)	0.01	–	–	780	1.9
Household and personal email and messages	0.03	0.02	67	1,568	3.8
Caring for and helping household members	0.44	0.92	209	17,584	42.3
Caring for and helping household children	0.36	0.85	236	16,083	38.7
Caring for household adults	0.02	–	–	566	1.4
Helping household adults	0.01	0.01	100	1,958	4.7
Caring for and helping people in other households	0.14	0.09	64	3,719	9.0
Caring for and helping children in other households	0.07	0.03	43	874	2.1
Caring for adults in other households	0.01	–	–	206	0.5
Helping adults in other households	0.05	0.05	100	2,836	6.8
Working and work-related activities	3.20	4.29	134	23,458	56.5
Working	3.14	4.23	135	22,745	54.7
Job search and interviewing	0.04	0.03	75	549	1.3
Educational activities	0.45	0.39	87	3,101	7.5
Taking class	0.26	0.16	62	1,622	3.9
Homework and research	0.18	0.21	117	2,318	5.6
Consumer purchases	0.37	0.39	105	17,966	43.2
Grocery shopping	0.11	0.10	91	5,887	14.2
Shopping (except groceries, food, and gas)	0.24	0.25	104	9,315	22.4
Professional and personal care services	0.08	0.08	100	2,355	5.7
Medical and care services	0.05	0.04	80	842	2.0

	average hours per day for total people	average hours per day for people aged 25 to 34	index, 25 to 34 to total	people aged 25 to 34 participating in activity	
				number (in 000s)	percent
Eating and drinking	1.11 hrs.	1.11 hrs.	100	39,914	96.1%
Socializing, relaxing, and leisure	4.71	3.80	81	37,806	91.0
Socializing and communicating	0.65	0.68	105	13,524	32.5
Attending or hosting social events	0.07	0.09	129	1,099	2.6
Relaxing and leisure	3.91	2.93	75	35,738	86.0
Television and movies	2.77	2.14	77	30,751	74.0
Playing games	0.22	0.22	100	4,184	10.1
Computer use for leisure (except games)	0.21	0.19	90	5,209	12.5
Reading for personal interest	0.32	0.11	34	3,878	9.3
Arts and entertainment (other than sports)	0.08	0.10	125	1,356	3.3
Attending movies	0.03	0.04	133	688	1.7
Sports, exercise, and recreation	0.32	0.29	91	8,252	19.9
Participating in sports, exercise, and recreation	0.30	0.27	90	8,062	19.4
Attending sporting or recreational events	0.03	0.01	33	273	0.7
Religious and spiritual activities	0.14	0.09	64	2,504	6.0
Volunteer activities	0.14	0.09	64	1,990	4.8
Telephone calls	0.10	0.07	70	3,492	8.4
Traveling	1.18	1.26	107	38,109	91.7

Note: Primary activities are those respondents identified as their main activity. Other activities done simultaneously are not included. Travel related to activities is reported separately. Numbers do not sum to total because not all activities are shown. The index is calculated by dividing time spent by age group by time spent by the average person and multiplying by 100. "–" means sample is too small to make a reliable estimate.
Source: Bureau of Labor Statistics, unpublished tables from the 2013 American Time Use Survey, Internet site http://www.bls.gov/tus/home.htm; calculations by New Strategist

Table 10.5 Detailed Time Use of Men Aged 25 to 34, 2013

(hours per day spent in primary activities by total men aged 15 or older and men aged 25 to 34, index of age group to total, and number and percent of men aged 25 to 34 participating in activity on an average day, 2013)

	average hours per day for total men	average hours per day for men aged 25 to 34	index, 25 to 34 to total	men aged 25 to 34 participating in activity	
				number (in 000s)	percent
Total, all activities	**24.00 hrs.**	**24.00 hrs.**	**100**	**20,536**	**100.0%**
Personal care activities	9.29	9.06	98	20,527	100.0
Sleeping	8.65	8.45	98	20,527	100.0
Grooming	0.57	0.59	104	16,825	81.9
Health-related self-care	0.60	0.01	2	286	1.4
Household activities	1.34	1.06	79	13,434	65.4
Housework	0.25	0.21	84	3,444	16.8
Food preparation and cleanup	0.33	0.31	94	8,760	42.7
Lawn, garden, and houseplants	0.25	0.15	60	1,406	6.8
Animals and pets	0.09	0.06	67	2,080	10.1
Vehicles	0.08	0.07	88	814	4.0
Household management	0.14	0.12	86	3,524	17.2
Financial management	0.02	0.02	100	478	2.3
Household and personal organization and planning	0.08	0.08	100	2,343	11.4
Household and personal mail and messages (except email)	0.01	–	–	354	1.7
Household and personal email and messages	0.03	0.01	33	559	2.7
Caring for and helping household members	0.30	0.49	163	6,097	29.7
Caring for and helping household children	0.24	0.46	192	5,091	24.8
Caring for household adults	0.01	–	–	225	1.1
Helping household adults	0.01	0.01	100	1,071	5.2
Caring for and helping people in other households	0.12	0.08	67	1,800	8.8
Caring for and helping children in other households	0.05	0.02	40	277	1.3
Caring for adults in other households	0.01	–	–	83	0.4
Helping adults in other households	0.06	0.06	100	1,523	7.4
Working and work-related activities	3.88	5.10	131	13,258	64.6
Working	3.80	5.03	132	12,857	62.6
Job search and interviewing	0.05	0.05	100	321	1.6
Educational activities	0.45	–	–	1,380	6.7
Taking class	0.27	–	–	777	3.8
Homework and research	0.17	0.23	135	1,194	5.8
Consumer purchases	0.29	0.32	110	8,209	40.0
Grocery shopping	0.07	0.07	100	2,216	10.8
Shopping (except groceries, food, and gas)	0.19	0.22	116	4,218	20.5
Professional and personal care services	0.06	0.05	83	770	3.7
Medical and care services	0.04	–	–	106	0.5

	average hours per day for total men	average hours per day for men aged 25 to 34	index, 25 to 34 to total	men aged 25 to 34 participating in activity	
				number (in 000s)	percent
Eating and drinking	1.14 hrs.	1.15 hrs.	101	19,820	96.5%
Socializing, relaxing, and leisure	4.94	4.27	86	18,759	91.3
Socializing and communicating	0.60	0.72	120	6,798	33.1
Attending or hosting social events	0.06	0.09	150	515	2.5
Relaxing and leisure	4.20	3.37	80	17,928	87.3
Television and movies	2.98	2.43	82	15,768	76.8
Playing games	0.32	0.38	119	3,158	15.4
Computer use for leisure (except games)	0.22	0.20	91	2,441	11.9
Reading for personal interest	0.26	0.10	38	1,598	7.8
Arts and entertainment (other than sports)	0.08	0.10	125	692	3.4
Attending movies	0.03	0.04	133	406	2.0
Sports, exercise, and recreation	0.42	0.33	79	4,295	20.9
Participating in sports, exercise, and recreation	0.40	0.31	78	4,223	20.6
Attending sporting or recreational events	0.02	–	–	135	0.7
Religious and spiritual activities	0.12	0.09	75	1,199	5.8
Volunteer activities	0.13	0.07	54	656	3.2
Telephone calls	0.06	0.04	67	1,066	5.2
Traveling	1.21	1.28	106	19,178	93.4

Note: Primary activities are those respondents identified as their main activity. Other activities done simultaneously are not included. Travel related to activities is reported separately. Numbers do not sum to total because not all activities are shown. The index is calculated by dividing time spent by age group by time spent by the average man and multiplying by 100. "–" means sample is too small to make a reliable estimate.
Source: Bureau of Labor Statistics, unpublished tables from the 2013 American Time Use Survey, Internet site http://www.bls.gov/tus/home.htm; calculations by New Strategist

Table 10.6 Detailed Time Use of Women Aged 25 to 34, 2013

(hours per day spent in primary activities by total women aged 15 or older and women aged 25 to 34, index of age group to total, and number and percent of women aged 25 to 34 participating in activity on an average day, 2013)

	average hours per day for total women	average hours per day for women aged 25 to 34	index, 25 to 34 to total	women aged 25 to 34 participating in activity	
				number (in 000s)	percent
Total, all activities	**24.00 hrs.**	**24.00 hrs.**	**100**	**21,013**	**100.0%**
Personal care activities	9.75	9.70	99	21,013	100.0
Sleeping	8.82	8.85	100	20,957	99.7
Grooming	0.82	0.80	98	17,470	83.1
Health-related self-care	0.11	0.05	45	649	3.1
Household activities	2.20	1.95	89	17,180	81.8
Housework	0.87	0.83	95	9,912	47.2
Food preparation and cleanup	0.80	0.81	101	14,197	67.6
Lawn, garden, and houseplants	0.12	0.04	33	655	3.1
Animals and pets	0.11	0.07	64	2,576	12.3
Vehicles	0.01	–	–	112	0.5
Household management	0.21	0.11	52	4,586	21.8
Financial management	0.04	0.01	25	471	2.2
Household and personal organization and planning	0.12	0.08	67	3,148	15.0
Household and personal mail and messages (except email)	0.02	–	–	425	2.0
Household and personal email and messages	0.04	0.02	50	1,009	4.8
Caring for and helping household members	0.58	1.35	233	11,487	54.7
Caring for and helping household children	0.47	1.23	262	10,993	52.3
Caring for household adults	0.03	0.01	33	341	1.6
Helping household adults	0.01	0.01	100	887	4.2
Caring for and helping people in other households	0.16	0.10	63	1,919	9.1
Caring for and helping children in other households	0.10	0.04	40	596	2.8
Caring for adults in other households	0.01	–	–	123	0.6
Helping adults in other households	0.05	0.05	100	1,314	6.3
Working and work-related activities	2.57	3.49	136	10,200	48.5
Working	2.52	3.46	137	9,887	47.1
Job search and interviewing	0.03	0.02	67	227	1.1
Educational activities	0.45	0.32	71	1,721	8.2
Taking class	0.25	0.10	40	846	4.0
Homework and research	0.19	0.20	105	1,124	5.3
Consumer purchases	0.45	0.45	100	9,757	46.4
Grocery shopping	0.14	0.14	100	3,671	17.5
Shopping (except groceries, food, and gas)	0.28	0.28	100	5,097	24.3
Professional and personal care services	0.10	0.10	100	1,584	7.5
Medical and care services	0.07	0.07	100	736	3.5

	average hours per day for total women	average hours per day for women aged 25 to 34	index, 25 to 34 to total	women aged 25 to 34 participating in activity	
				number (in 000s)	percent
Eating and drinking	1.09 hrs.	1.07 hrs.	98	20,094	95.6%
Socializing, relaxing, and leisure	4.50	3.33	74	19,047	90.6
Socializing and communicating	0.70	0.63	90	6,726	32.0
Attending or hosting social events	0.08	0.10	125	585	2.8
Relaxing and leisure	3.63	2.50	69	17,809	84.8
Television and movies	2.56	1.86	73	14,984	71.3
Playing games	0.13	0.07	54	1,026	4.9
Computer use for leisure (except games)	0.20	0.17	85	2,768	13.2
Reading for personal interest	0.38	0.12	32	2,280	10.9
Arts and entertainment (other than sports)	0.09	0.10	111	664	3.2
Attending movies	0.03	0.03	100	282	1.3
Sports, exercise, and recreation	0.23	0.25	109	3,957	18.8
Participating in sports, exercise, and recreation	0.20	0.23	115	3,840	18.3
Attending sporting or recreational events	0.03	0.02	67	138	0.7
Religious and spiritual activities	0.17	0.09	53	1,305	6.2
Volunteer activities	0.15	0.11	73	1,334	6.3
Telephone calls	0.14	0.10	71	2,427	11.5
Traveling	1.15	1.24	108	18,931	90.1

Note: Primary activities are those respondents identified as their main activity. Other activities done simultaneously are not included. Travel related to activities is reported separately. Numbers do not sum to total because not all activities are shown. The index is calculated by dividing time spent by age group by time spent by the average woman and multiplying by 100. "–" means sample is too small to make a reliable estimate.
Source: Bureau of Labor Statistics, unpublished tables from the 2013 American Time Use Survey, Internet site http://www.bls .gov/tus/home.htm; calculations by New Strategist

CHAPTER

11

Wealth

■ The net worth of households headed by people under age 35 (the Millennial generation was aged 19 to 36 in 2013) fell 21 percent between 2007 and 2013—to $10,400, after adjusting for inflation. That decline was dwarfed by the 42 to 53 percent drop in net worth experienced by householders aged 35 to 64.

■ The median value of the financial assets owned by householders under age 35 fell 24 percent between 2007 and 2013, after adjusting for inflation. In 2013, this age group had a median of only $5,800 in financial assets.

■ Householders under age 35 saw the median value of their nonfinancial assets plummet by 40 percent between 2010 and 2013, after adjusting for inflation. Behind the decline were two factors: less homeownership and the fall in housing values.

■ The debt of householders under age 35 fell 27 percent between 2010 and 2013, after adjusting for inflation. Behind the decline was the drop in the percentage with mortgage debt, the figure falling from 34 to 29 percent during those years.

■ A substantial 42 percent of householders under age 35 had education loans in 2013, greater than the 35 percent with vehicle loans. They owe a median of $17,200 in education debt, greater than the $11,000 they owe for vehicle debt.

Net Worth Continues to Decline

Several age groups experienced double-digit percentage declines in net worth between 2010 and 2013.

Net worth is what remains when a household's debts are subtracted from its assets. During and after the Great Recession, the value of houses, stocks, and retirement accounts fell sharply. At the same time, debt increased. Consequently, median net worth fell 39 percent between 2007 and 2010, after adjusting for inflation. Between 2010 and 2013, median household net worth fell by another 2 percent, with double-digit percentage declines experienced by householders ranging in age from 45 to 64 and by householders aged 75 or older.

Some age groups made gains in the 2010-to-2013 time period. Householders under age 45 saw their net worth rise 3 to 4 percent, and the net worth of householders aged 65 to 74 gained 5 percent, after adjusting for inflation. But for households in every age group, 2013 net worth was far below net worth in 2007. Householders aged 65 to 74 experienced the smallest decline: their 2013 net worth was 14 percent below what it was in 2007. Householders aged 35 to 44 experienced the biggest decline—a stunning 53 percent drop during those years.

■ Net worth rises with age as people pay off their debt. In 2013, net worth peaked in the 65-to-74 age group at $232,100.

Net worth peaks among householders aged 65 to 74

(median household net worth by age of householder, 2013)

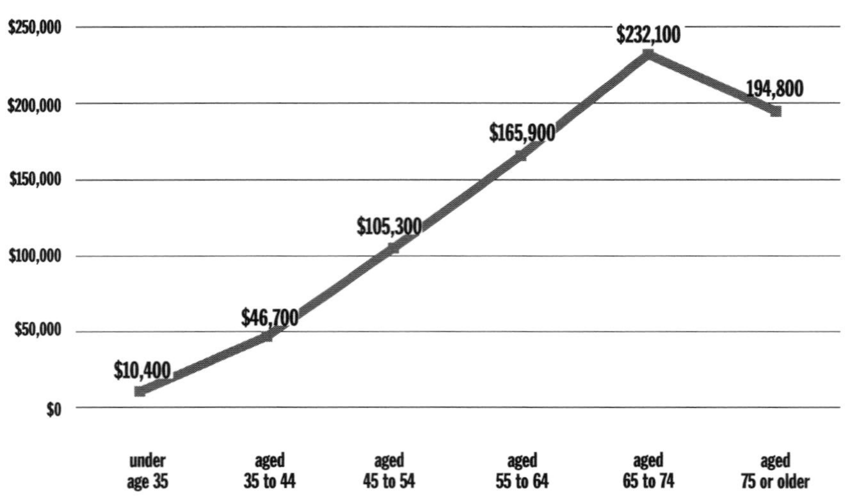

Table 11.1 Net Worth of Households, 2007 to 2013

(median net worth of households by age of householder, 2007 to 2013; percent change, 2007–13; in 2013 dollars)

	2013	2010	2007	percent change 2010–13	percent change 2007–13
Total households	**$81,200**	**$82,800**	**$135,400**	**–1.9%**	**–40.0%**
Under age 35	10,400	10,000	13,200	4.0	–21.2
Aged 35 to 44	46,700	45,200	99,100	3.3	–52.9
Aged 45 to 54	105,300	126,300	207,600	–16.6	–49.3
Aged 55 to 64	165,900	192,300	285,300	–13.7	–41.9
Aged 65 to 74	232,100	221,500	268,800	4.8	–13.7
Aged 75 or older	194,800	232,300	239,700	–16.1	–18.7

Source: Federal Reserve Board, Survey of Consumer Finances, Internet site http://www.federalreserve.gov/econresdata/scf/scfindex .html; calculations by New Strategist

Financial Asset Value Has Declined in Every Age Group

Some households made gains between 2010 and 2013, however.

Most households own financial assets, which range from transaction accounts (checking and saving) to stocks, mutual funds, retirement accounts, and life insurance. The median value of the financial assets owned by the average household stood at $21,200 in 2013. This was 35 percent below the median in 2007, after adjusting for inflation. Householders aged 35 to 44 and aged 65 to 74 were the only ones who made financial asset gains between 2010 and 2013.

Transaction accounts, the most commonly owned financial asset, are held by 93 percent of households. Their median value was just $4,100 in 2013—slightly lower than the $4,500 of 2007, after adjusting for inflation. Retirement accounts are the second most commonly owned financial asset, with 49 percent of households owning them. In 2007, a larger 53 percent of households owned retirement accounts. Most retirement accounts are modest, with an overall median value of just $59,000 in 2013.

Only 14 percent of households owned stock directly in 2013 (outside of a retirement account or mutual fund). The median value of stock owned by stockholding households was $27,000 in 2013, a substantial 41 percent greater than the value in 2007 after adjusting for inflation.

■ Financial asset value peaks in the 65-to-74 age group, at $72,000.

The value of retirement accounts peaks in the 65-to-74 age group

(median value of retirement accounts owned by households, by age of householder, 2013)

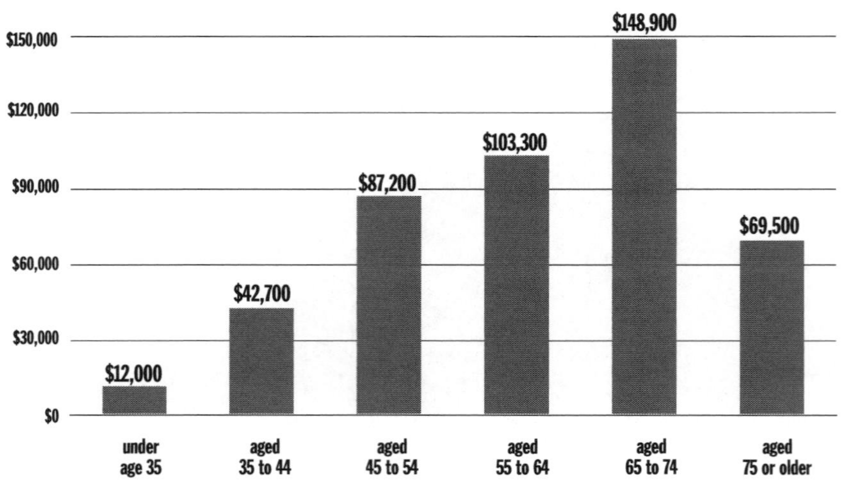

Table 11.2 Ownership and Value of Financial Assets, 2007 to 2013

(percentage of households owning any financial asset and median value for owners, by age of householder, 2007 to 2013; percentage point change in ownership and percent change in value, 2010–13 and 2007–13; in 2013 dollars)

				percentage point change	
PERCENT OWNING FINANCIAL ASSETS	**2013**	**2010**	**2007**	**2010–13**	**2007–13**
Total households	**94.5%**	**94.0%**	**93.9%**	**0.5**	**0.6**
Under age 35	92.5	91.3	89.2	1.2	3.3
Aged 35 to 44	93.1	92.7	93.1	0.4	0.0
Aged 45 to 54	93.3	94.2	93.3	–0.9	0.0
Aged 55 to 64	95.7	95.8	97.8	–0.1	–2.1
Aged 65 to 74	97.4	96.2	96.1	1.2	1.3
Aged 75 or older	96.9	96.4	97.4	0.5	–0.5

				percent change	
MEDIAN VALUE OF FINANCIAL ASSETS	**2013**	**2010**	**2007**	**2010–13**	**2007–13**
Total households	**$21,200**	**$23,000**	**$32,400**	**–7.8%**	**–34.6%**
Under age 35	5,800	5,900	7,600	–1.7	–23.7
Aged 35 to 44	20,400	15,500	29,200	31.6	–30.1
Aged 45 to 54	31,500	36,100	61,000	–12.7	–48.4
Aged 55 to 64	52,100	59,800	82,800	–12.9	–37.1
Aged 65 to 74	72,000	48,400	76,400	48.8	–5.8
Aged 75 or older	28,000	46,900	46,600	–40.3	–39.9

Source: Federal Reserve Board, Survey of Consumer Finances, Internet site http://www.federalreserve.gov/econresdata/scf/scfindex .html; calculations by New Strategist

Table 11.3 Ownership and Value of Transaction Accounts, 2007 to 2013

(percentage of households owning transactions accounts and median value for owners, by age of householder, 2007 to 2013; percentage point change in ownership and percent change in value, 2010–13 and 2007–13; in 2013 dollars)

				percentage point change	
PERCENT OWNING TRANSACTION ACCOUNTS	**2013**	**2010**	**2007**	**2010–13**	**2007–13**
Total households	**93.2%**	**92.5%**	**92.1%**	**0.7**	**1.1**
Under age 35	90.2	89.0	87.3	1.2	2.9
Aged 35 to 44	91.8	90.6	91.2	1.2	0.6
Aged 45 to 54	91.8	92.5	91.7	–0.7	0.1
Aged 55 to 64	94.6	94.2	96.4	0.4	–1.8
Aged 65 to 74	97.1	95.8	94.6	1.3	2.5
Aged 75 or older	96.7	96.4	95.3	0.3	1.4

				percent change	
MEDIAN VALUE OF TRANSACTION ACCOUNTS	**2013**	**2010**	**2007**	**2010–13**	**2007–13**
Total households	**$4,100**	**$3,800**	**$4,500**	**7.9%**	**–8.9%**
Under age 35	2,200	2,200	2,700	0.0	–18.5
Aged 35 to 44	3,800	2,700	3,900	40.7	–2.6
Aged 45 to 54	4,000	3,800	5,600	5.3	–28.6
Aged 55 to 64	5,000	5,400	5,800	–7.4	–13.8
Aged 65 to 74	7,000	6,100	8,600	14.8	–18.6
Aged 75 or older	7,000	7,700	6,800	–9.1	2.9

Source: Federal Reserve Board, Survey of Consumer Finances, Internet site http://www.federalreserve.gov/econresdata/scf/scfindex.html; calculations by New Strategist

Table 11.4 Ownership and Value of Cash Value Life Insurance, 2007 to 2013

(percentage of households owning cash value life insurance and median value for owners, by age of householder, 2007 to 2013; percentage point change in ownership and percent change in value, 2010–13 and 2007–13; in 2013 dollars)

				percentage point change	
PERCENT OWNING CASH VALUE LIFE INSURANCE	**2013**	**2010**	**2007**	**2010–13**	**2007–13**
Total households	**19.2%**	**19.7%**	**23.0%**	**–0.5**	**–3.8**
Under age 35	9.2	9.6	11.4	–0.4	–2.2
Aged 35 to 44	13.3	12.3	17.5	1.0	–4.2
Aged 45 to 54	17.1	19.8	22.3	–2.7	–5.2
Aged 55 to 64	24.4	25.7	35.2	–1.3	–10.8
Aged 65 to 74	29.4	28.4	34.4	1.0	–5.0
Aged 75 or older	30.4	32.4	27.6	–2.0	2.8

				percent change	
MEDIAN VALUE OF CASH VALUE LIFE INSURANCE	**2013**	**2010**	**2007**	**2010–13**	**2007–13**
Total households	**$8,000**	**$7,800**	**$9,000**	**2.6%**	**–11.1%**
Under age 35	2,500	2,300	3,100	8.7	–19.4
Aged 35 to 44	7,000	5,400	9,300	29.6	–24.7
Aged 45 to 54	8,000	10,700	11,200	–25.2	–28.6
Aged 55 to 64	9,800	10,000	11,200	–2.0	–12.5
Aged 65 to 74	9,800	10,700	11,200	–8.4	–12.5
Aged 75 or older	8,000	7,500	5,600	6.7	42.9

Source: Federal Reserve Board, Survey of Consumer Finances, Internet site http://www.federalreserve.gov/econresdata/scf/scfindex .html; calculations by New Strategist

Table 11.5 Ownership and Value of Certificates of Deposit, 2007 to 2013

(percentage of households owning certificates of deposit and median value for owners, by age of householder, 2007 to 2013; percentage point change in ownership and percent change in value, 2010–13 and 2007–13; in 2013 dollars)

				percentage point change	
PERCENT OWNING CERTIFICATES OF DEPOSIT	2013	2010	2007	2010–13	2007–13
Total households	**7.8%**	**12.2%**	**16.1%**	**–4.4**	**–8.3**
Under age 35	5.2	5.7	6.7	–0.5	–1.5
Aged 35 to 44	4.4	5.7	9.0	–1.3	–4.6
Aged 45 to 54	6.7	10.0	14.3	–3.3	–7.6
Aged 55 to 64	5.8	14.6	20.5	–8.8	–14.7
Aged 65 to 74	11.7	20.6	24.2	–8.9	–12.5
Aged 75 or older	18.8	27.2	37.0	–8.4	–18.2

				percent change	
MEDIAN VALUE OF CERTIFICATES OF DEPOSIT	2013	2010	2007	2010–13	2007–13
Total households	**$16,000**	**$21,400**	**$22,500**	**–25.2%**	**–28.9%**
Under age 35	4,000	5,600	5,600	–28.6	–28.6
Aged 35 to 44	6,300	7,500	5,600	–16.0	12.5
Aged 45 to 54	10,000	17,100	16,800	–41.5	–40.5
Aged 55 to 64	25,000	21,400	25,800	16.8	–3.1
Aged 65 to 74	31,000	26,800	26,100	15.7	18.8
Aged 75 or older	22,000	34,500	33,700	–36.2	–34.7

Source: Federal Reserve Board, Survey of Consumer Finances, Internet site http://www.federalreserve.gov/econresdata/scf/scfindex .html; calculations by New Strategist

Table 11.6 Ownership and Value of Stock, 2007 to 2013

(percentage of households owning stock and median value for owners, by age of householder, 2007 to 2013; percentage point change in ownership and percent change in value, 2010–13 and 2007–13; in 2013 dollars)

				percentage point change	
PERCENT OWNING STOCK	**2013**	**2010**	**2007**	**2010–13**	**2007–13**
Total households	**13.8%**	**15.1%**	**17.9%**	**–1.3**	**–4.1**
Under age 35	7.2	10.1	13.7	–2.9	–6.5
Aged 35 to 44	14.3	12.1	17.0	2.2	–2.7
Aged 45 to 54	14.7	16.0	18.7	–1.3	–4.0
Aged 55 to 64	15.5	19.5	21.3	–4.0	–5.8
Aged 65 to 74	18.4	16.1	19.1	2.3	–0.7
Aged 75 or older	15.3	20.1	20.2	–4.8	–4.9

				percent change	
MEDIAN VALUE OF STOCK	**2013**	**2010**	**2007**	**2010–13**	**2007–13**
Total households	**$27,000**	**$21,400**	**$19,100**	**26.2%**	**41.4%**
Under age 35	6,600	5,800	3,400	13.8	94.1
Aged 35 to 44	20,000	10,700	16,800	86.9	19.0
Aged 45 to 54	16,000	32,200	20,200	–50.3	–20.8
Aged 55 to 64	30,000	37,500	26,900	–20.0	11.5
Aged 65 to 74	50,000	51,400	42,700	–2.7	17.1
Aged 75 or older	76,400	48,200	44,900	58.5	70.2

Note: Stock ownership is defined as direct ownership outside of a retirement account or mutual fund.
Source: Federal Reserve Board, Survey of Consumer Finances, Internet site http://www.federalreserve.gov/econresdata/scf/scfindex .html; calculations by New Strategist

Table 11.7 Ownership and Value of Retirement Accounts, 2007 to 2013

(percentage of households owning retirement accounts and median value for owners, by age of householder, 2007 to 2013; percentage point change in ownership and percent change in value, 2010–13 and 2007–13; in 2013 dollars)

				percentage point change	
PERCENT OWNING RETIREMENT ACCOUNTS	2013	2010	2007	2010–13	2007–13
Total households	**49.2%**	**50.4%**	**53.0%**	**–1.2**	**–3.8**
Under age 35	39.3	41.1	42.1	–1.8	–2.8
Aged 35 to 44	55.4	52.2	57.8	3.2	–2.4
Aged 45 to 54	56.5	60.0	65.4	–3.5	–8.9
Aged 55 to 64	59.3	59.8	61.2	–0.5	–1.9
Aged 65 to 74	48.0	49.0	51.7	–1.0	–3.7
Aged 75 or older	29.0	32.8	30.0	–3.8	–1.0

				percent change	
MEDIAN VALUE OF RETIREMENT ACCOUNTS	2013	2010	2007	2010–13	2007–13
Total households	**$59,000**	**$47,200**	**$50,500**	**25.0%**	**16.8%**
Under age 35	12,000	11,300	10,700	6.2	12.1
Aged 35 to 44	42,700	33,400	41,500	27.8	2.9
Aged 45 to 54	87,200	64,300	70,700	35.6	23.3
Aged 55 to 64	103,300	107,200	112,300	–3.6	–8.0
Aged 65 to 74	148,900	107,200	86,500	38.9	72.1
Aged 75 or older	69,500	57,900	39,300	20.0	76.8

Source: Federal Reserve Board, Survey of Consumer Finances, Internet site http://www.federalreserve.gov/econresdata/scf/scfindex .html; calculations by New Strategist

Table 11.8 Ownership and Value of Pooled Investment Funds, 2007 to 2013

(percentage of households owning pooled investment funds and median value for owners, by age of householder, 2007 to 2013; percentage point change in ownership and percent change in value, 2010–13 and 2007–13; in 2013 dollars)

				percentage point change	
PERCENT OWNING POOLED INVESTMENT FUNDS	2013	2010	2007	2010–13	2007–13
Total households	**8.2%**	**8.7%**	**11.4%**	**–0.5**	**–3.2**
Under age 35	4.2	3.6	5.3	0.6	–1.1
Aged 35 to 44	6.3	7.7	11.6	–1.4	–5.3
Aged 45 to 54	8.2	9.6	12.6	–1.4	–4.4
Aged 55 to 64	10.6	11.3	14.3	–0.7	–3.7
Aged 65 to 74	11.7	11.1	14.6	0.6	–2.9
Aged 75 or older	10.3	11.9	13.2	–1.6	–2.9

				percent change	
MEDIAN VALUE OF POOLED INVESTMENT FUNDS	2013	2010	2007	2010–13	2007–13
Total households	**$80,000**	**$85,700**	**$62,900**	**–6.7%**	**27.2%**
Under age 35	10,300	9,100	20,200	13.2	–49.0
Aged 35 to 44	48,000	43,900	25,300	9.3	89.7
Aged 45 to 54	53,000	117,900	56,100	–55.0	–5.5
Aged 55 to 64	143,000	117,900	125,800	21.3	13.7
Aged 65 to 74	155,000	123,200	96,600	25.8	60.5
Aged 75 or older	145,000	128,600	84,200	12.8	72.2

Note: Pooled investment funds exclude money market funds and indirectly held mutual funds. They include open-end and closed-end mutual funds, real estate investment trusts, and hedge funds.
Source: Federal Reserve Board, Survey of Consumer Finances, Internet site http://www.federalreserve.gov/econresdata/scf/scfindex.html; calculations by New Strategist

Nonfinancial Assets Are the Basis of Household Wealth

The average household saw the value of its nonfinancial assets fall steeply between 2007 and 2013.

The median value of the nonfinancial assets owned by the average American household stood at $148,400 in 2013, far surpassing the $21,200 median value of the average household's financial assets. Between 2007 and 2010, the value of the nonfinancial assets owned by the average household fell 17 percent, after adjusting for inflation. Between 2010 and 2013, the median fell by another 10 percent. Every age group saw its nonfinancial assets lose value in both time periods, primarily because of the decline in housing values.

Eighty-six percent of households own a vehicle, the most commonly held nonfinancial asset. The median value of vehicles owned by the average household fell 9 percent between 2007 and 2013, after adjusting for inflation. Behind the decline was vehicle depreciation because of Americans' reluctance to buy new vehicles during and after the Great Recession.

The second most commonly owned nonfinancial asset is a home, owned by 65 percent of households. Homes are by far the most valuable asset owned by Americans, and they account for the largest share of net worth. In 2013, the median value of the average owned home was $170,000, a hefty 24 percent below the $224,600 median of 2007 (in 2013 dollars).

■ Housing has a bigger impact on household net worth than any other asset.

Median housing value peaks in the 55-to-64 age group

(median value of the primary residence among homeowners, by age of householder, 2013)

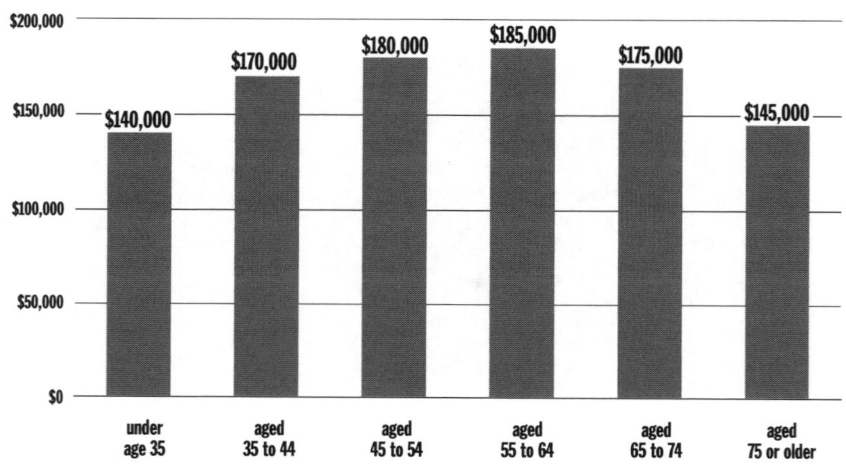

Table 11.9 Ownership and Value of Nonfinancial Assets, 2007 to 2013

(percentage of households owning any nonfinancial asset and median value for owners, by age of householder, 2007 to 2013; percentage point change in ownership and percent change in value, 2010–13 and 2007–13; in 2013 dollars)

				percentage point change	
PERCENT OWNING NONFINANCIAL ASSETS	**2013**	**2010**	**2007**	**2010–13**	**2007–13**
Total households	**91.0%**	**91.3%**	**92.0%**	**–0.3**	**–1.0**
Under age 35	84.9	82.8	88.2	2.1	–3.3
Aged 35 to 44	92.8	92.7	91.3	0.1	1.5
Aged 45 to 54	91.8	94.7	95.0	–2.9	–3.2
Aged 55 to 64	92.9	94.4	95.6	–1.5	–2.7
Aged 65 to 74	95.9	92.6	94.5	3.3	1.4
Aged 75 or older	89.6	93.0	87.3	–3.4	2.3

				percent change	
MEDIAN VALUE OF NONFINANCIAL ASSETS	**2013**	**2010**	**2007**	**2010–13**	**2007–13**
Total households	**$148,400**	**$165,600**	**$199,200**	**–10.4%**	**–25.5%**
Under age 35	22,000	36,700	34,700	–40.1	–36.6
Aged 35 to 44	135,800	153,000	205,000	–11.2	–33.8
Aged 45 to 54	174,900	205,100	252,500	–14.7	–30.7
Aged 55 to 64	189,600	221,400	261,700	–14.4	–27.6
Aged 65 to 74	206,800	214,200	238,300	–3.5	–13.2
Aged 75 or older	158,100	180,300	176,300	–12.3	–10.3

Source: Federal Reserve Board, Survey of Consumer Finances, Internet site http://www.federalreserve.gov/econresdata/scf/scfindex.html; calculations by New Strategist

Table 11.10 Ownership and Value of Primary Residence, 2007 to 2013

(percentage of households owning their primary residence and median value for owners, by age of householder, 2007 to 2013; percentage point change in ownership and percent change in value, 2010–13 and 2007–13; in 2013 dollars)

				percentage point change	
PERCENT OWNING PRIMARY RESIDENCE	2013	2010	2007	2010–13	2007–13
Total households	**65.2%**	**67.3%**	**68.6%**	**–2.1**	**–3.4**
Under age 35	35.6	37.5	40.6	–1.9	–5.0
Aged 35 to 44	61.7	63.8	66.1	–2.1	–4.4
Aged 45 to 54	69.1	75.2	77.3	–6.1	–8.2
Aged 55 to 64	74.2	78.1	81.0	–3.9	–6.8
Aged 65 to 74	85.8	82.6	85.5	3.2	0.3
Aged 75 or older	80.2	81.9	77.0	–1.7	3.2

				percent change	
MEDIAN VALUE OF PRIMARY RESIDENCE	2013	2010	2007	2010–13	2007–13
Total households	**$170,000**	**$182,200**	**$224,600**	**–6.7%**	**–24.3%**
Under age 35	140,000	150,000	196,500	–6.7	–28.8
Aged 35 to 44	170,000	182,200	230,200	–6.7	–26.2
Aged 45 to 54	180,000	214,300	258,200	–16.0	–30.3
Aged 55 to 64	185,000	198,300	235,800	–6.7	–21.5
Aged 65 to 74	175,000	176,800	224,600	–1.0	–22.1
Aged 75 or older	145,000	160,800	168,400	–9.8	–13.9

Source: Federal Reserve Board, Survey of Consumer Finances, Internet site http://www.federalreserve.gov/econresdata/scf/scfindex .html; calculations by New Strategist

Table 11.11 Ownership and Value of Other Residential Property, 2007 to 2013

(percentage of households owning other residential property and median value for owners, by age of householder, 2007 to 2013; percentage point change in ownership and percent change in value, 2010–13 and 2007–13; in 2013 dollars)

				percentage point change	
PERCENT OWNING OTHER RESIDENTIAL PROPERTY	2013	2010	2007	2010–13	2007–13
Total households	**13.2%**	**14.3%**	**13.8%**	**–1.1**	**–0.6**
Under age 35	4.7	4.5	5.6	0.2	–0.9
Aged 35 to 44	9.2	9.7	12.0	–0.5	–2.8
Aged 45 to 54	15.8	17.0	15.7	–1.2	0.1
Aged 55 to 64	18.4	22.1	20.9	–3.7	–2.5
Aged 65 to 74	21.3	22.8	18.9	–1.5	2.4
Aged 75 or older	12.8	14.6	13.4	–1.8	–0.6

				percent change	
MEDIAN VALUE OF OTHER RESIDENTIAL PROPERTY	2013	2010	2007	2010–13	2007–13
Total households	**$123,800**	**$128,600**	**$165,100**	**–3.7%**	**–25.0%**
Under age 35	102,500	77,200	95,400	32.8	7.4
Aged 35 to 44	107,000	80,400	168,400	33.1	–36.5
Aged 45 to 54	100,000	110,900	168,400	–9.8	–40.6
Aged 55 to 64	150,000	176,800	176,300	–15.2	–14.9
Aged 65 to 74	137,000	134,000	168,400	2.2	–18.6
Aged 75 or older	120,000	134,000	112,300	–10.4	6.9

Source: Federal Reserve Board, Survey of Consumer Finances, Internet site http://www.federalreserve.gov/econresdata/scf/scfindex .html; calculations by New Strategist

Table 11.12 Ownership and Value of Nonresidential Property, 2007 to 2013

(percentage of households owning nonresidential property and median value for owners, by age of householder, 2007 to 2013; percentage point change in ownership and percent change in value, 2010–13 and 2007–13; in 2013 dollars)

				percentage point change	
PERCENT OWNING NONRESIDENTIAL PROPERTY	2013	2010	2007	2010–13	2007–13
Total households	**7.2%**	**7.7%**	**8.1%**	**–0.5**	**–0.9**
Under age 35	1.8	2.3	3.2	–0.5	–1.4
Aged 35 to 44	5.7	3.9	7.5	1.8	–1.8
Aged 45 to 54	7.0	7.5	9.5	–0.5	–2.5
Aged 55 to 64	8.9	12.6	11.5	–3.7	–2.6
Aged 65 to 74	14.1	11.0	12.3	3.1	1.8
Aged 75 or older	8.9	13.4	6.8	–4.5	2.1

				percent change	
MEDIAN VALUE OF NONRESIDENTIAL PROPERTY	2013	2010	2007	2010–13	2007–13
Total households	**$60,000**	**$69,700**	**$84,200**	**–13.9%**	**–28.7%**
Under age 35	45,000	25,700	56,100	75.1	–19.8
Aged 35 to 44	54,200	53,600	56,100	1.1	–3.4
Aged 45 to 54	37,000	53,600	89,800	–31.0	–58.8
Aged 55 to 64	96,000	109,300	101,100	–12.2	–5.0
Aged 65 to 74	96,500	64,300	84,200	50.1	14.6
Aged 75 or older	55,000	69,700	123,500	–21.1	–55.5

Source: Federal Reserve Board, Survey of Consumer Finances, Internet site http://www.federalreserve.gov/econresdata/scf/scfindex.html; calculations by New Strategist

Table 11.13 Ownership and Value of Vehicles, 2007 to 2013

(percentage of households owning vehicles and median value for owners, by age of householder, 2007 to 2013; percentage point change in ownership and percent change in value, 2010–13 and 2007–13; in 2013 dollars)

				percentage point change	
PERCENT OWNING VEHICLES	**2013**	**2010**	**2007**	**2010–13**	**2007–13**
Total households	**86.3%**	**86.7%**	**87.0%**	**–0.4**	**–0.7**
Under age 35	82.7	79.4	85.4	3.3	–2.7
Aged 35 to 44	89.9	88.9	87.5	1.0	2.4
Aged 45 to 54	87.7	91.0	90.3	–3.3	–2.6
Aged 55 to 64	89.2	90.3	92.2	–1.1	–3.0
Aged 65 to 74	89.4	86.5	90.6	2.9	–1.2
Aged 75 or older	76.0	83.4	71.5	–7.4	4.5

				percent change	
MEDIAN VALUE OF VEHICLES	**2013**	**2010**	**2007**	**2010–13**	**2007–13**
Total households	**$15,800**	**$16,300**	**$17,300**	**–3.1%**	**–8.7%**
Under age 35	12,500	13,200	15,000	–5.3	–16.7
Aged 35 to 44	16,800	17,700	19,600	–5.1	–14.3
Aged 45 to 54	19,200	19,700	21,000	–2.5	–8.6
Aged 55 to 64	17,100	19,000	19,500	–10.0	–12.3
Aged 65 to 74	16,400	17,200	16,400	–4.7	0.0
Aged 75 or older	10,500	11,400	10,600	–7.9	–0.9

Source: Federal Reserve Board, Survey of Consumer Finances, Internet site http://www.federalreserve.gov/econresdata/scf/scfindex.html; calculations by New Strategist

Table 11.14 Ownership and Value of Business Equity, 2007 to 2013

(percentage of households owning business equity and median value for owners, by age of householder, 2007 to 2013; percentage point change in ownership and percent change in value, 2010–13 and 2007–13; in 2013 dollars)

				percentage point change	
PERCENT OWNING BUSINESS EQUITY	2013	2010	2007	2010–13	2007–13
Total households	**11.7%**	**13.3%**	**13.6%**	**–1.6**	**–1.9**
Under age 35	6.5	8.4	8.0	–1.9	–1.5
Aged 35 to 44	15.6	11.2	18.2	4.4	–2.6
Aged 45 to 54	14.6	16.8	17.2	–2.2	–2.6
Aged 55 to 64	15.5	19.6	18.1	–4.1	–2.6
Aged 65 to 74	11.0	15.9	11.2	–4.9	–0.2
Aged 75 or older	4.4	6.0	4.5	–1.6	–0.1

				percent change	
MEDIAN VALUE OF BUSINESS EQUITY	2013	2010	2007	2010–13	2007–13
Total households	**$67,500**	**$84,400**	**$103,500**	**–20.0%**	**–34.8%**
Under age 35	23,800	32,200	39,300	–26.1	–39.4
Aged 35 to 44	50,000	53,600	66,200	–6.7	–24.5
Aged 45 to 54	93,200	85,700	86,200	8.8	8.1
Aged 55 to 64	110,000	107,200	112,300	2.6	–2.0
Aged 65 to 74	100,000	107,200	336,800	–6.7	–70.3
Aged 75 or older	157,500	236,700	252,600	–33.5	–37.6

Source: Federal Reserve Board, Survey of Consumer Finances, Internet site http://www.federalreserve.gov/econresdata/scf/scfindex .html; calculations by New Strategist

Most Households Are in Debt

Among households with debt, the amount they fell between 2010 and 2013.

Three out of four households are in debt, owing a median of $60,400 in 2013. The median amount of debt owed by the average debtor household fell 20 percent between 2010 and 2013, after adjusting for inflation. Householders aged 35 to 54 are most likely to be in debt, with 82 to 85 percent owing money. Debt declines with age, falling to a low of 41 percent among householders aged 75 or older. The percent of householders aged 75 or older who are in debt has climbed by a hefty 10 percentage points since 2007.

Four types of debt are relatively common—mortgage debt, which is held by 41.5 percent of households; credit card debt (38 percent); vehicle loans (31 percent); and education loans (20 percent). Mortgages account for the largest share of debt. The average homeowner with a mortgage owed $116,000 in 2013. Education loans are second in size, the average household with education loans owing a median of $16,000—more than the $11,900 owed by (the more numerous) households with vehicle loans. Credit card debt is tiny by comparison, the average household with a credit card balance owing only $2,300.

■ Americans have paid off a substantial portion of their debt, but household net worth continues to decline because asset values are falling faster than debt.

Education loans are common among young and middle-aged householders

(percentage of households with education loans, by age of householder, 2013)

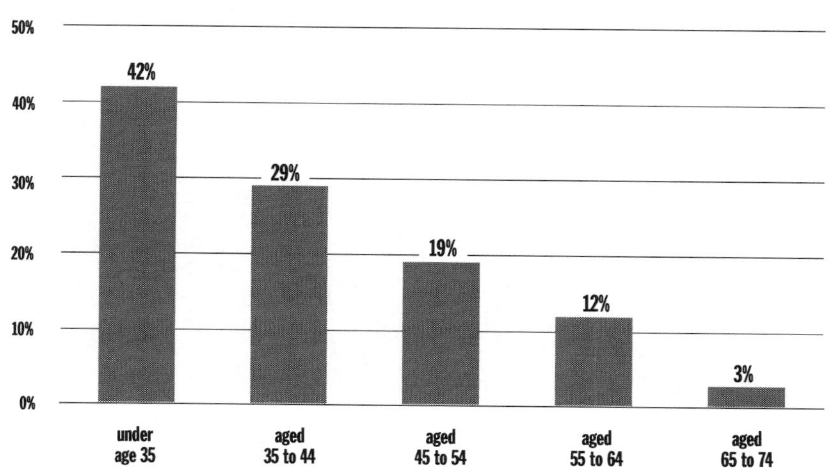

Table 11.15 Debt of Households, 2007 to 2013

(percentage of households with debt and median amount of debt for debtors, by age of householder, 2007 to 2013; percentage point change in households with debt and percent change in amount of debt, 2010–13 and 2007–13; in 2013 dollars)

				percentage point change	
PERCENT WITH DEBT	**2013**	**2010**	**2007**	**2010–13**	**2007–13**
Total households	**74.5%**	**74.9%**	**77.0%**	**–0.4**	**–2.5**
Under age 35	77.1	77.8	83.6	–0.7	–6.5
Aged 35 to 44	84.8	86.0	86.2	–1.2	–1.4
Aged 45 to 54	82.3	84.1	86.8	–1.8	–4.5
Aged 55 to 64	78.7	77.7	81.8	1.0	–3.1
Aged 65 to 74	66.4	65.2	65.5	1.2	0.9
Aged 75 or older	41.4	38.5	31.4	2.9	10.0

				percent change	
MEDIAN AMOUNT OWED	**2013**	**2010**	**2007**	**2010–13**	**2007–13**
Total households	**$60,400**	**$75,800**	**$75,600**	**–20.3%**	**–20.1%**
Under age 35	31,100	42,500	40,600	–26.8	–23.4
Aged 35 to 44	96,500	115,700	119,200	–16.6	–19.0
Aged 45 to 54	100,000	98,400	107,700	1.6	–7.1
Aged 55 to 64	63,400	82,500	67,700	–23.2	–6.4
Aged 65 to 74	44,000	48,300	45,100	–8.9	–2.4
Aged 75 or older	20,000	32,200	14,600	–37.9	37.0

Source: Federal Reserve Board, Survey of Consumer Finances, Internet site http://www.federalreserve.gov/econresdata/scf/scfindex .html; calculations by New Strategist

Table 11.16 Households with Mortgage Debt, 2007 to 2013

(percentage of households with mortgage debt and median amount of debt for debtors, by age of householder, 2007 to 2013; percentage point change in households with debt and percent change in amount of debt, 2010–13 and 2007–13; in 2013 dollars)

				percentage point change	
PERCENT WITH MORTGAGE DEBT	2013	2010	2007	2010–13	2007–13
Total households	**41.5%**	**45.2%**	**46.3%**	**–3.7**	**–4.8**
Under age 35	28.6	33.9	37.2	–5.3	–8.6
Aged 35 to 44	52.7	57.3	59.3	–4.6	–6.6
Aged 45 to 54	55.3	58.5	63.8	–3.2	–8.5
Aged 55 to 64	45.8	50.6	50.2	–4.8	–4.4
Aged 65 to 74	38.9	36.6	35.5	2.3	3.4
Aged 75 or older	18.6	21.2	11.0	–2.6	7.6

				percent change	
MEDIAN AMOUNT OWED	2013	2010	2007	2010–13	2007–13
Total households	**$116,000**	**$117,900**	**$123,500**	**–1.6%**	**–6.1%**
Under age 35	120,000	128,600	149,300	–6.7	–19.6
Aged 35 to 44	140,000	146,100	140,300	–4.2	–0.2
Aged 45 to 54	120,000	120,000	120,100	0.0	–0.1
Aged 55 to 64	107,000	101,800	101,100	5.1	5.8
Aged 65 to 74	87,000	84,700	95,100	2.7	–8.5
Aged 75 or older	59,000	62,200	56,100	–5.1	5.2

Source: Federal Reserve Board, Survey of Consumer Finances, Internet site http://www.federalreserve.gov/econresdata/scf/scfindex .html; calculations by New Strategist

Table 11.17 Households with Home Equity Line of Credit Debt, 2007 to 2013

(percentage of households with home equity line of credit debt and median amount of debt for debtors, by age of householder, 2007 to 2013; percentage point change in households with debt and percent change in amount of debt, 2010–13 and 2007–13; in 2013 dollars)

				percentage point change	
PERCENT WITH HELOC DEBT	**2013**	**2010**	**2007**	**2010–13**	**2007–13**
Total households	**5.0%**	**7.2%**	**8.5%**	**–2.2**	**–3.5**
Under age 35	–	2.3	4.0	–	–
Aged 35 to 44	5.2	5.6	8.8	–0.4	–3.6
Aged 45 to 54	5.7	10.9	11.7	–5.2	–6.0
Aged 55 to 64	8.8	10.6	12.6	–1.8	–3.8
Aged 65 to 74	6.8	8.7	9.6	–1.9	–2.8
Aged 75 or older	2.3	4.9	3.4	–2.6	–1.1

				percent change	
MEDIAN AMOUNT OWED	**2013**	**2010**	**2007**	**2010–13**	**2007–13**
Total households	**25,000**	**28,300**	**26,900**	**–11.7%**	**–7.1%**
Under age 35	–	16,100	26,900	–	–
Aged 35 to 44	25,000	32,200	22,500	–22.4	11.1
Aged 45 to 54	20,000	32,200	28,100	–37.9	–28.8
Aged 55 to 64	27,000	22,500	22,500	20.0	20.0
Aged 65 to 74	30,000	31,100	16,800	–3.5	78.6
Aged 75 or older	16,000	21,400	28,100	–25.2	–43.1

Note: "–" means sample is too small to make a reliable estimate.
Source: Federal Reserve Board, Survey of Consumer Finances, Internet site http://www.federalreserve.gov/econresdata/scf/scfindex.html; calculations by New Strategist

Table 11.18 Households with Credit Card Debt, 2007 to 2013

(percentage of households with credit card balances and median amount of debt for debtors, by age of householder, 2007 to 2013; percentage point change in households with debt and percent change in amount of debt, 2010–13 and 2007–13; in 2013 dollars)

				percentage point change	
PERCENT WITH CREDIT CARD BALANCES	**2013**	**2010**	**2007**	**2010–13**	**2007–13**
Total households	**38.1%**	**39.4%**	**46.1%**	**–1.3**	**–8.0**
Under age 35	36.8	38.7	48.5	–1.9	–11.7
Aged 35 to 44	41.7	45.7	51.7	–4.0	–10.0
Aged 45 to 54	44.3	46.2	53.6	–1.9	–9.3
Aged 55 to 64	43.4	41.3	49.9	2.1	–6.5
Aged 65 to 74	32.8	31.9	37.0	0.9	–4.2
Aged 75 or older	21.1	21.7	18.8	–0.6	2.3

				percent change	
MEDIAN AMOUNT OWED	**2013**	**2010**	**2007**	**2010–13**	**2007–13**
Total households	**$2,300**	**$2,800**	**$3,400**	**–17.9%**	**–32.4%**
Under age 35	1,500	1,700	2,000	–11.8	–25.0
Aged 35 to 44	2,500	3,800	3,900	–34.2	–35.9
Aged 45 to 54	2,600	3,800	4,000	–31.6	–35.0
Aged 55 to 64	3,000	3,000	4,000	0.0	–25.0
Aged 65 to 74	2,300	2,300	3,400	0.0	–32.4
Aged 75 or older	1,900	1,900	900	0.0	111.1

Source: Federal Reserve Board, Survey of Consumer Finances, Internet site http://www.federalreserve.gov/econresdata/scf/scfindex.html; calculations by New Strategist

Table 11.19 Households with Education Loans, 2007 to 2013

(percentage of households with education loans and median amount of debt for debtors, by age of householder, 2007 to 2013; percentage point change in households with debt and percent change in amount of debt, 2010–13 and 2007–13; in 2013 dollars)

				percentage point change	
PERCENT WITH EDUCATION LOANS	2013	2010	2007	2010–13	2007–13
Total households	**20.0%**	**19.2%**	**15.2%**	**0.8**	**4.8**
Under age 35	41.7	40.1	33.8	1.6	7.9
Aged 35 to 44	28.7	26.5	14.9	2.2	13.8
Aged 45 to 54	18.6	17.6	14.5	1.0	4.1
Aged 55 to 64	12.0	9.3	10.6	2.7	1.4
Aged 65 to 74	3.1	4.2	–	–1.1	–
Aged 75 or older	–	–	–	–	–

				percent change	
MEDIAN AMOUNT OWED	2013	2010	2007	2010–13	2007–13
Total households	**$16,000**	**$13,900**	**$13,500**	**15.1%**	**18.5%**
Under age 35	17,200	13,900	14,600	23.7	17.8
Aged 35 to 44	17,000	14,400	13,500	18.1	25.9
Aged 45 to 54	13,200	12,900	13,500	2.3	–2.2
Aged 55 to 64	17,200	16,100	7,900	6.8	117.7
Aged 65 to 74	17,000	12,900	–	31.8	–
Aged 75 or older	–	–	–	–	–

Note: "–" means sample is too small to make a reliable estimate.
Source: Federal Reserve Board, Survey of Consumer Finances, Internet site http://www.federalreserve.gov/econresdata/scf/scfindex .html; calculations by New Strategist

Table 11.20 Households with Vehicle Loans, 2007 to 2013

(percentage of households with vehicle loans and median amount of debt for debtors, by age of householder, 2007 to 2013; percentage point change in households with debt and percent change in amount of debt, 2010–13 and 2007–13; in 2013 dollars)

				percentage point change	
PERCENT WITH VEHICLE LOANS	**2013**	**2010**	**2007**	**2010–13**	**2007–13**
Total households	**30.9%**	**30.2%**	**34.9%**	**0.7**	**–4.0**
Under age 35	35.2	32.2	44.3	3.0	–9.1
Aged 35 to 44	37.0	40.8	42.6	–3.8	–5.6
Aged 45 to 54	36.5	35.9	39.1	0.6	–2.6
Aged 55 to 64	30.8	28.2	35.2	2.6	–4.4
Aged 65 to 74	24.4	22.8	21.6	1.6	2.8
Aged 75 or older	10.7	8.1	6.1	2.6	4.6

				percent change	
MEDIAN AMOUNT OWED	**2013**	**2010**	**2007**	**2010–13**	**2007–13**
Total households	**$11,900**	**$10,700**	**$13,000**	**11.2%**	**–8.5%**
Under age 35	11,000	10,600	13,000	3.8	–15.4
Aged 35 to 44	12,500	11,900	13,900	5.0	–10.1
Aged 45 to 54	12,100	10,500	13,000	15.2	–6.9
Aged 55 to 64	11,700	10,100	12,100	15.8	–3.3
Aged 65 to 74	10,500	10,600	13,400	–0.9	–21.6
Aged 75 or older	13,400	10,800	9,900	24.1	35.4

Source: Federal Reserve Board, Survey of Consumer Finances, Internet site http://www.federalreserve.gov/econresdata/scf/scfindex.html; calculations by New Strategist

Americans of All Ages Are Worried about Retirement

The expected age of retirement is climbing.

Only 18 percent of American workers are "very" confident in having enough money to live comfortably throughout retirement, according to the Employee Benefit Research Institute's Retirement Confidence Survey. Workers should be worried about their retirement security. More than one-third (36 percent) have less than $1,000 in savings and the 52 percent majority has less than $10,000 saved. Among workers aged 55 or older, one in four has saved less than $1,000 and one in three has saved less than $10,000. Only 42 percent of the oldest workers have saved $100,000 or more.

Among all workers, the share expecting to retire at age 65 or earlier has fallen from 65 percent in 2007—before the start of the Great Recession—to 50 percent in 2014. Among workers aged 55 or older, the percentage expecting to retire at age 66 or later climbed from 37 to 52 percent during those years.

■ Although most workers say they are saving for retirement, only about one-third contribute to a workplace retirement savings plan.

Most workers aged 55 or older expect to retire at age 66 or later

(percent of workers aged 55 or older who expect to retire at age 66 or older, including never retire, 2007 and 2014)

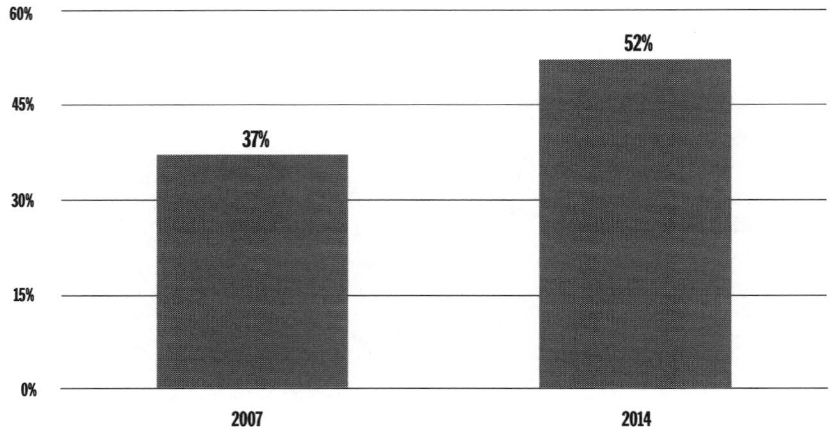

Table 11.21 Retirement Attitudes and Planning by Age, 2014

(percentage of workers aged 25 or older responding by age, 2014)

	total workers	25 to 34	35 to 44	45 to 54	55 or older
Percent very confident in having enough money to live comfortably throughout retirement	18%	21%	15%	17%	21%
Worker and/or spouse are currently saving for retirement	57	42	57	60	71
Have an IRA (includes rollover IRA)	43	27	48	42	57
Contribute to a workplace retirement savings plan	34	26	33	37	44
TOTAL SAVINGS AND INVESTMENTS (NOT INCLUDING VALUE OF PRIMARY RESIDENCE OR DEFINED BENEFIT PLANS)					
Less than $1,000	36%	43%	37%	34%	24%
$1,000 to $9,999	16	27	15	11	10
$10,000 to $24,999	8	11	7	8	7
$25,000 to $49,999	9	8	8	13	9
$50,000 to $99,999	9	8	11	7	8
$100,000 to $249,999	11	4	8	15	19
$250,000 or more	11	0	15	12	23

Source: Employee Benefit Research Institute, American Savings Education Council, and Mathew Greenwald & Associates, Inc., 2014 Retirement Confidence Survey, Internet site http://www.ebri.org/surveys/rcs/2014/

Table 11.22 Expected Age of Retirement by Age, 2007 and 2014

(percentage of workers aged 25 or older by expected age of retirement, by age, 2007 and 2014)

	2014	2007	percentage point change
Total workers			
Under age 60	9%	17%	–8
Aged 60 to 64	18	21	–3
Aged 65	23	27	–4
Aged 66 or older	33	24	9
Never retire	10	6	4
Don't know/refused	8	6	2
Workers aged 25 to 34			
Under age 60	12	26	–14
Aged 60 to 64	19	19	0
Aged 65	26	24	2
Aged 66 or older	28	19	9
Never retire	8	6	2
Don't know/refused	7	6	1
Workers aged 35 to 44			
Under age 60	13	16	–3
Aged 60 to 64	13	20	–7
Aged 65	25	30	–5
Aged 66 or older	31	22	9
Never retire	10	5	5
Don't know/refused	6	7	–1
Workers aged 45 to 54			
Under age 60	7	16	–9
Aged 60 to 64	20	20	0
Aged 65	20	28	–8
Aged 66 or older	34	26	8
Never retire	8	6	2
Don't know/refused	11	3	8
Workers aged 55 or older			
Under age 60	2	8	–6
Aged 60 to 64	21	25	–4
Aged 65	19	22	–3
Aged 66 or older	38	32	6
Never retire	14	5	9
Don't know/refused	6	7	–1

Source: Employee Benefit Research Institute, American Savings Education Council, and Mathew Greenwald & Associates, Inc., 2014 Retirement Confidence Survey, Internet site http://www.ebri.org/surveys/rcs/2014/

The iGeneration

Americans Born 1995 to present

CHAPTER

12

Education

■ Most young children today are in school. The percentage of 3-to-4-year-olds enrolled in nursery school or kindergarten has grown substantially over the decades, from 36.7 percent in 1980 to 53.5 percent in 2012.

■ Among the nation's elementary, middle, and high school students, 8 to 9 percent attend private school. Only 3 percent of children aged 5 to 17 are homeschooled.

■ In the nation as a whole, nearly half (48 percent) of public school students are Asian, Black, Hispanic, or another minority. In the South and West, the majority of public school students are minority.

■ Most of today's parents are actively involved in their children's education. The parents of 74 percent of the nation's elementary and secondary school children attended a class event during the past year.

■ Complaints about the nation's schools are commonplace, but the parents of most children in kindergarten through 12th grade are "very satisfied" with various aspects of their child's school.

Most Young Children Attend School

The percentage of 3- and 4-year-olds enrolled in school rises with mother's education.

Most young children today are in school. The percentage of 3-to-4-year-olds enrolled in nursery school or kindergarten has grown substantially over the decades, from 36.7 percent in 1980 to the 53.5 percent majority in 2012.

A mother's labor force status has a surprisingly small effect on the school enrollment of young children. Among 3-to-4-year-olds whose mother works full-time, 57 percent were enrolled in school in 2012. Among those whose mother is not in the labor force, 48 percent were in school. A mother's educational attainment is a more important factor in the school enrollment of young children. Among 3-to-4-year-olds whose mother has a bachelor's degree, nearly two-thirds are enrolled in school compared with a much smaller 39 percent of children whose mother did not graduate from high school.

■ Enrolling children in preschool has become the norm, especially for college graduates.

The school enrollment of young children has grown substantially

(percentage of 3-to-4-year-olds enrolled in nursery school or kindergarten, 1980 and 2012)

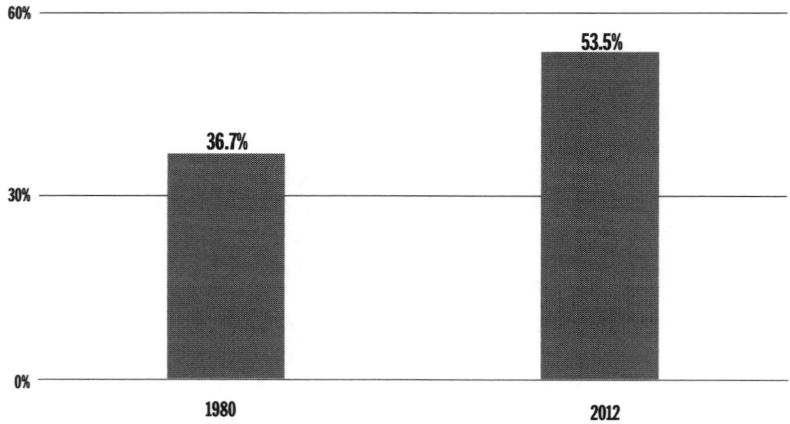

Table 12.1 Three- and Four-Year-Olds Enrolled in School, 1980 to 2012

(percentage of three- and four-year-olds enrolled in nursery school or kindergarten, 1980 to 2012)

2012	53.5%
2011	52.4
2010	53.2
2009	52.4
2008	52.8
2007	54.5
2006	55.7
2005	53.6
2004	54.0
2003	55.1
2002	54.5
2001	52.2
2000	52.1
1990	44.4
1980	36.7

Source: Bureau of the Census, School Enrollment, Historical Tables, Internet site http://www.census.gov/hhes/school/data/cps/historical/index.html

Table 12.2 School Enrollment Status of Children Aged 3 to 4 by Characteristics of Mother, 2012

(number and percent distribution of children aged 3 to 4 by labor force status and educational attainment of mother, and number and percent enrolled in school, 2012; numbers in thousands)

	total		enrolled in school	
	number	percent distribution	number	share of total
EMPLOYMENT STATUS OF MOTHER				
Total children	**8,014**	**100.0%**	**4,289**	**53.5%**
Mother employed full-time	2,913	36.3	1,674	57.5
Mother employed part-time	1,221	15.2	739	60.5
Mother unemployed	482	6.0	244	50.6
Mother not in the labor force	2,635	32.9	1,264	48.0
EDUCATIONAL ATTAINMENT OF MOTHER				
Total children	**8,014**	**100.0**	**4,289**	**53.5**
Not a high school graduate	893	11.1	350	39.2
High school graduate	1,746	21.8	796	45.6
Some college or associate's degree	2,213	27.6	1,219	55.1
Bachelor's degree or more	2,400	29.9	1,557	64.9

Source: Bureau of the Census, School Enrollment—CPS October 2012 Detailed Tables, Internet site http://www.census.gov/hhes/school/data/cps/2012/tables.html; calculations by New Strategist

Diversity in Public Schools Is on the Rise

In some states minority students are in the majority.

School attendance has become common even for "preschoolers." Among children aged 5, nearly 90 percent attended school in 2012. The figure is 66 percent among children aged 4 and exceeds 40 percent among 3-year-olds.

Among children enrolled in nursery through high school, 11 percent are in private school. At the elementary, middle, and high school level, 8 to 9 percent of students are in private school. Only 3 percent of the nation's school-aged children are homeschooled.

Nearly half (48 percent) of the nation's public school students are Asian, Black, Hispanic, or another minority. By region, most public school students in the South and West are minority. The minority share of public school students exceeds 50 percent in 12 states and the District of Columbia.

■ The minority share of public school students is less than 10 percent in Maine, Vermont, and West Virginia.

Minorities are the majority of public school students in the South and West

(percent of students who are minority, by region, 2010)

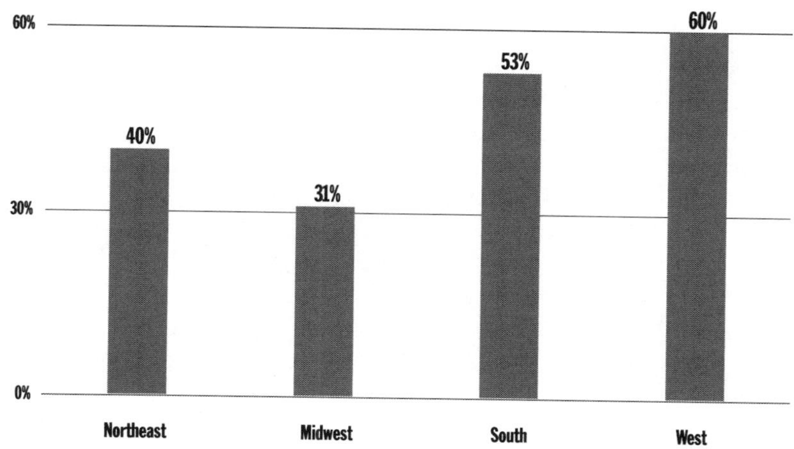

Table 12.3 School Enrollment of Children, 2012

(number and percent of people aged 3 or older and aged 3 to 18 enrolled in school by age, 2012; numbers in thousands)

	number	percent
Total enrolled	**78,426**	**26.4%**
Total aged 3 to 18	59,597	90.4
Aged 3	1,614	40.5
Aged 4	2,675	66.4
Aged 5	3,812	89.8
Aged 6	3,916	96.8
Aged 7	3,966	98.1
Aged 8	4,023	98.2
Aged 9	3,962	97.9
Aged 10	3,959	97.9
Aged 11	4,051	97.8
Aged 12	4,155	98.3
Aged 13	4,031	98.1
Aged 14	4,021	98.0
Aged 15	4,065	98.4
Aged 16	3,962	97.1
Aged 17	4,108	94.6
Aged 18	3,277	77.0

Source: Bureau of the Census, School Enrollment—CPS October 2012 Detailed Tables, Internet site http://www.census.gov/hhes/school/data/cps/2012/tables.html; calculations by New Strategist

Table 12.4 Enrollment in Nursery School through High School, 2012

(number and percent distribution of people attending nursery school through high school, fall 2012; numbers in thousands)

	number	percent distribution
Total, nursery school through 12th	**58,497**	**100.0%**
Nursery school	**4,628**	**7.9**
Kindergarten	**4,138**	**7.1**
Elementary and middle, total	**32,683**	**55.9**
1st grade	4,042	6.9
2nd grade	4,139	7.1
3rd grade	4,095	7.0
4th grade	3,879	6.6
5th grade	4,256	7.3
6th grade	4,098	7.0
7th grade	4,212	7.2
8th grade	3,962	6.8
High school, total	**17,048**	**29.1**
9th grade	4,249	7.3
10th grade	4,096	7.0
11th grade	4,248	7.3
12th grade	4,455	7.6

Source: Bureau of the Census, School Enrollment—CPS October 2012 Detailed Tables, Internet site http://www.census.gov/hhes/school/data/cps/2012/tables.html; calculations by New Strategist

Table 12.5 Enrollment in Nursery School through High School by Control of School, 2012

(number of students enrolled in nursery school through high school by control of school, and private school share of total, fall 2012; numbers in thousands)

			private	
	total	public	number	percent
Total enrolled	**58,497**	**51,985**	**6,511**	**11.1%**
Nursery school	4,628	2,732	1,896	41.0
Kindergarten	4,138	3,684	454	11.0
Elementary and middle school	32,683	29,865	2,818	8.6
High school	17,047	15,704	1,343	7.9

Source: Bureau of the Census, School Enrollment, Historical Tables, Internet site http://www.census.gov/hhes/school/data/cps/historical/index.html

Table 12.6 Homeschooling, 2011–12

(number and percent of children aged 5 to 17 who are homeschooled by selected characteristics, 2011–12)

	homeschooled	
	number	percent
Total children aged 5 to 17	**1,770**	**3.4%**
Locale of student's household		
City	489	3.2
Suburb	601	3.1
Town	132	2.7
Rural	548	4.5
Race and Hispanic origin of student		
Asian	73	2.6
Black	139	1.9
Hispanic	267	2.3
Non-Hispanic White	1,201	4.5
Student's grade equivalent		
Kindergarten to 2nd grade	415	3.1
3rd to 5th grade	416	3.4
6th to 8th grade	425	3.5
9th to 12th grade	514	3.7

Note: Asians and Blacks are those who identify themselves as being of the race alone and not Hispanic.
Source: National Center for Education Statistics, Parent and Family Involvement in Education, from the National Household Education Surveys Program of 2012, Internet site http://nces.ed.gov/pubsearch/pubsinfo.asp?pubid=2013028; calculations by New Strategist

Table 12.7 Enrollment in Public Elementary and Secondary School by Region, Race, and Hispanic Origin, 2010

(number and percent distribution of students enrolled in public elementary and secondary school by region, race, and Hispanc origin, 2010; numbers in thousands)

		minority students							
	total	total	American Indian	Asian or Pacific Islander	Black	two or more races	Hispanic	non-Hispanic White
Total public school children	**49,484**	**23,554**	**566**	**2,467**	**7,918**	**1,161**	**11,442**	**25,930**
Northeast	8,071	3,195	27	500	1,208	96	1,364	4,876
Midwest	10,610	3,282	94	312	1,505	294	1,077	7,327
South	18,805	9,937	207	555	4,545	424	4,206	8,869
West	11,998	7,140	237	1,100	661	347	4,795	4,859
PERCENT DISTRIBUTION BY RACE AND HISPANIC ORIGIN								
Total public school children	**100.0%**	**47.6%**	**1.1%**	**5.0%**	**16.0%**	**2.3%**	**23.1%**	**52.4%**
Northeast	100.0	39.6	0.3	6.2	15.0	1.2	16.9	60.4
Midwest	100.0	30.9	0.9	2.9	14.2	2.8	10.2	69.1
South	100.0	52.8	1.1	3.0	24.2	2.3	22.4	47.2
West	100.0	59.5	2.0	9.2	5.5	2.9	40.0	40.5

Note: American Indians, Asians, and Blacks are those who identify themselves as being of the race alone. Numbers do not sum to total because Hispanics may be of any race.
Source: National Center for Education Statistics, Digest of Education Statistics: 2012, Internet site http://nces.ed.gov/programs/digest/2012menu_tables.asp; calculations by New Strategist

Table 12.8 Enrollment in Public Elementary and Secondary School by State, Race, and Hispanic Origin, 2010

(percent distribution of students enrolled in public elementary and secondary school by state, race, and Hispanc origin, 2010)

		minority students						
	total	total	American Indian	Asian or Pacific Islander	Black	two or more races	Hispanic	non-Hispanic White
Total public school children	**100.0%**	**47.6%**	**1.1%**	**5.0%**	**16.0%**	**2.4%**	**23.1%**	**52.4%**
Alabama	100.0	41.7	0.8	1.3	34.6	0.3	4.7	58.3
Alaska	100.0	47.8	23.0	8.0	3.6	7.2	5.9	52.2
Arizona	100.0	57.1	5.2	3.0	5.6	1.2	42.2	42.9
Arkansas	100.0	35.2	0.7	1.9	21.5	1.3	9.8	64.8
California	100.0	73.4	0.7	11.7	6.7	2.9	51.4	26.6
Colorado	100.0	43.2	0.9	3.1	4.8	2.8	31.6	56.8
Connecticut	100.0	38.0	0.4	4.3	13.2	1.4	18.6	62.0
Delaware	100.0	49.9	0.5	3.4	32.3	1.4	12.4	50.1
District of Columbia	100.0	92.9	0.1	1.4	77.8	1.0	12.6	7.1
Florida	100.0	57.0	0.4	2.6	23.0	3.0	28.0	43.0
Georgia	100.0	55.6	0.2	3.4	37.0	3.0	11.9	44.4
Hawaii	100.0	85.5	0.6	69.6	2.5	8.4	4.5	14.5
Idaho	100.0	21.5	1.4	1.7	1.0	1.5	15.9	78.5
Illinois	100.0	48.7	0.3	4.2	18.4	2.9	22.9	51.3
Indiana	100.0	26.9	0.3	1.6	12.1	4.4	8.4	73.1
Iowa	100.0	18.5	0.5	2.1	5.1	2.2	8.5	81.5
Kansas	100.0	32.0	1.3	2.6	7.4	4.3	16.4	68.0
Kentucky	100.0	18.1	0.1	1.4	10.8	1.8	3.9	81.9
Louisiana	100.0	51.5	0.9	1.5	45.4	1.0	2.6	48.5
Maine	100.0	7.5	0.7	1.1	1.8	2.5	1.5	92.5
Maryland	100.0	57.1	0.4	5.9	35.8	3.5	11.5	42.9
Massachusetts	100.0	32.0	0.2	5.6	8.2	2.4	15.4	68.0
Michigan	100.0	30.2	0.8	2.7	19.0	1.9	5.8	69.8
Minnesota	100.0	26.2	1.9	6.1	9.2	1.8	7.2	73.8
Mississippi	100.0	54.0	0.2	0.9	49.9	0.5	2.5	46.0
Missouri	100.0	25.3	0.5	2.0	17.1	1.3	4.5	74.7
Montana	100.0	18.3	11.1	1.1	1.0	1.6	3.5	81.7
Nebraska	100.0	29.2	1.5	2.1	6.7	2.9	16.0	70.8
Nevada	100.0	61.3	1.3	7.1	9.9	4.2	38.7	38.7
New Hampshire	100.0	10.2	0.3	2.8	2.0	1.5	3.7	89.8
New Jersey	100.0	48.5	0.1	8.9	16.7	0.7	22.1	51.5
New Mexico	100.0	74.0	10.2	1.3	2.1	1.0	59.4	26.0
New York	100.0	50.8	0.5	8.3	19.0	0.6	22.4	49.2
North Carolina	100.0	46.8	1.5	2.5	26.5	3.7	12.6	53.2
North Dakota	100.0	16.3	9.1	1.3	2.4	3.3	0.1	83.7
Ohio	100.0	25.8	0.1	1.7	16.3	4.2	3.4	74.2
Oklahoma	100.0	45.4	17.7	2.1	10.2	3.2	12.3	54.6
Oregon	100.0	33.7	1.9	4.5	2.6	4.2	20.5	66.3
Pennsylvania	100.0	28.8	0.2	3.2	15.7	1.5	8.3	71.2
Rhode Island	100.0	34.8	0.7	3.0	8.0	2.4	20.8	65.2
South Carolina	100.0	46.6	0.3	1.4	36.2	2.3	6.4	53.4
South Dakota	100.0	20.2	11.6	1.5	2.5	1.1	3.5	79.8

		minority students						
	total	total	American Indian	Asian or Pacific Islander	Black	two or more races	Hispanic	non-Hispanic White
Tennessee	100.0%	32.7%	0.2%	1.7%	23.9%	0.7%	6.1%	67.3%
Texas	100.0	68.8	0.5	3.6	12.9	1.6	50.3	31.2
Utah	100.0	22.0	1.3	3.4	1.4	0.8	15.1	78.0
Vermont	100.0	7.2	0.3	1.6	1.8	2.1	1.3	92.8
Virginia	100.0	45.9	0.3	6.0	24.1	4.1	11.4	54.1
Washington	100.0	37.2	1.7	8.1	4.8	4.6	18.0	62.8
West Virginia	100.0	8.0	0.1	0.7	5.2	0.8	1.1	92.0
Wisconsin	100.0	25.6	1.3	3.6	9.9	1.5	9.3	74.4
Wyoming	100.0	19.0	3.3	0.9	1.1	1.4	12.3	81.0

Note: American Indians, Asians, and Blacks are those who identify themselves as being of the race alone. Numbers do not sum to total because Hispanics may be of any race.
Source: National Center for Education Statistics, Digest of Education Statistics: 2012, Internet site http://nces.ed.gov/programs/digest/2012menu_tables.asp; calculations by New Strategist

Parents Are Involved in Their Children's Education

During a given year, most parents attend school events.

Most of today's parents are actively involved in their children's education. The parents of 87 percent of the nation's elementary and secondary school children say they attended a PTA or general school meeting during the past year, according to a 2011–12 survey by the National Center for Education Statistics. Seventy-six percent attended a parent–teacher conference, 74 percent attended a class event, and 42 percent volunteered.

Parental involvement in enrichment activities with children rises with the educational attainment of the parent. The percentage of children whose parents took their child to a play, concert, or other live show in the past year, for example, climbs from 20 percent among parents who did not graduate from high school to 43 percent among parents with a graduate degree. Surprisingly, however, the most educated parents are no more likely than the least educated to check their children's homework.

■ Poor parents are slightly more likely than those who are not poor to make sure their child has done his homework.

Educated parents are most likely to attend their children's class events

(percent of children whose parents attended a class event in the past year, by educational attainment of parent, 2011–12)

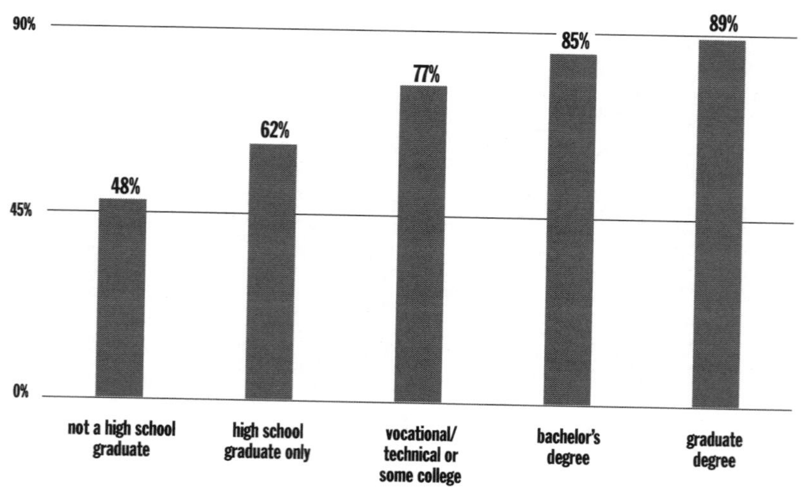

Table 12.9 Parental Involvement in School Functions, 2011–12

(total number and percent of children in kindergarten through 12th grade whose parents reported participation in school functions, by selected characteristics of child and parent, 2011–12)

	total		parent attended a PTA or general school meeting	parent attended a parent–teacher conference	parent attended a school or class event	parent volunteered at school	parent participated in school fundraising
	number (in 000s)	percent					
Total children	**52,211**	**100%**	**87%**	**76%**	**74%**	**42%**	**58%**
Race and Hispanic origin of child							
Asian	2,871	100	84	72	65	37	47
Black	7,466	100	85	76	68	31	52
Hispanic	12,110	100	86	73	64	32	46
Two or more races	2,827	100	88	78	76	44	58
Non-Hispanic White	26,938	100	89	77	82	50	67
Educational attainment of parent							
Not a high school graduate	6,335	100	77	64	48	19	31
High school graduate	10,571	100	82	72	62	28	46
Vocational/technical or some college	15,810	100	88	77	77	41	61
Bachelor's degree	11,839	100	92	80	85	55	71
Graduate degree	7,656	100	95	82	89	61	75
School type							
Public, assigned	40,097	100	86	74	73	38	56
Public, chosen	7,448	100	89	76	75	44	57
Private, religious	3,271	100	96	85	88	69	84
Private, nonreligious	788	100	95	89	91	66	78
Student's grade level							
Kindergarten through 2nd grade	13,610	100	93	89	79	56	67
3rd through 5th grade	12,243	100	92	89	82	51	69
6th through 8th grade	11,717	100	87	71	70	32	53
9th through 12th grade	14,642	100	79	57	66	28	47
Poverty status							
Poor	10,333	100	82	71	60	27	41
Not poor	41,878	100	89	77	78	45	63

Note: Asians and Blacks are those who identify themselves as being of the race alone and not Hispanic. The multiracial are not Hispanic.
Source: National Center for Education Statistics, Parent and Family Involvement in Education, from the National Household Education Surveys Program of 2012, Internet site http://nces.ed.gov/pubsearch/pubsinfo.asp?pubid=2013028; calculations by New Strategist

Table 12.10 Parental Involvement in Activities with Children, 2011–12

(total number and percent of children in kindergarten through 12th grade whose parents reported engaging in activity with children, by selected characteristics of child and parent, 2011–12)

	total								
	number (in 000s)	percent	visited library	visited bookstore	attended play, concert, or other live show	visited art gallery, museum, or historical site	visited zoo or aquarium	attended community religious or ethnic event	attended sporting event
Total children	**52,211**	**100%**	**39%**	**38%**	**31%**	**21%**	**19%**	**54%**	**42%**
Race and Hispanic origin of child									
Asian	2,871	100	53	42	33	22	25	52	30
Black	7,466	100	47	37	32	21	21	65	43
Hispanic	12,110	100	38	36	26	20	24	52	39
Two or more races	2,827	100	40	37	29	23	17	55	41
Non-Hispanic White	26,938	100	36	38	33	22	15	53	44
Educational attainment of parent									
Not a high school graduate	6,335	100	37	30	20	17	25	46	33
High school graduate	10,571	100	38	26	24	15	17	48	36
Vocational/technical or some college	15,810	100	35	36	30	20	18	54	41
Bachelor's degree	11,839	100	41	46	37	25	18	60	47
Graduate degree	7,656	100	48	50	43	30	18	65	49
School type									
Public, assigned	40,097	100	38	36	30	20	18	53	41
Public, chosen	7,448	100	44	41	33	25	19	55	42
Private, religious	3,271	100	44	47	39	25	17	72	50
Private, nonreligious	788	100	40	48	46	41	23	49	46
Student's grade level									
Kindergarten through 2nd grade	13,610	100	48	38	31	28	29	56	38
3rd through 5th grade	12,243	100	46	41	33	24	21	59	45
6th through 8th grade	11,717	100	38	39	32	19	15	55	44
9th through 12th grade	14,642	100	27	33	29	15	10	48	40
Poverty status									
Poor	10,333	100	42	28	23	17	22	51	35
Not poor	41,878	100	39	40	33	22	18	55	43

Note: Asians and Blacks are those who identify themselves as being of the race alone and not Hispanic. The multiracial are not Hispanic.
Source: National Center for Education Statistics, Parent and Family Involvement in Education, from the National Household Education Surveys Program of 2012, Internet site http://nces.ed.gov/pubsearch/pubsinfo.asp?pubid=2013028; calculations by New Strategist

Table 12.11 Parental Involvement in Child's Homework, 2011–12

(percent of children aged 6 to 17 participating in specified extracurricular activities, by selected characteristics of child and parent, 2009)

	total		student does homework outside of school		
	number (in 000s)	percent	total	place in home set aside for homework	adult in household checks that homework is done
Total children	**52,211**	**100%**	**96%**	**86%**	**67%**
Race and Hispanic origin of child					
Asian	2,871	100	98	91	65
Black	7,466	100	96	89	71
Hispanic	12,110	100	97	84	69
Two or more races	2,827	100	96	87	70
Non-Hispanic White	26,938	100	95	85	65
Educational attainment of parent					
Not a high school graduate	6,335	100	94	83	67
High school graduate	10,571	100	95	86	65
Vocational/technical or some college	15,810	100	96	87	69
Bachelor's degree	11,839	100	97	85	67
Graduate degree	7,656	100	97	86	66
School type					
Public, assigned	40,097	100	97	86	67
Public, chosen	7,448	100	94	88	69
Private, religious	3,271	100	87	85	65
Private, nonreligious	788	100	95	83	64
Student's grade level					
Kindergarten through 2nd grade	13,610	100	94	87	94
3rd through 5th grade	12,243	100	98	89	85
6th through 8th grade	11,717	100	97	86	58
9th through 12th grade	14,642	100	95	82	34
Poverty status					
Poor	10,333	100	94	84	72
Not poor	41,878	100	96	86	66

Note: Asians and Blacks are those who identify themselves as being of the race alone and not Hispanic. The multiracial are not Hispanic.

Source: National Center for Education Statistics, Parent and Family Involvement in Education, from the National Household Education Surveys Program of 2012, Internet site http://nces.ed.gov/pubsearch/pubsinfo.asp?pubid=2013028; calculations by New Strategist

Most Parents Are Satisfied with Their Child's School

Most are also satisfied with their child's teachers and the amount of homework.

Complaints about the nation's schools are commonplace, but in fact the parents of most children in kindergarten through 12th grade are "very satisfied" with various aspects of their child's school. Fifty-nine percent of school children have parents who are very satisfied with their child's school. Sixty percent are very satisfied with their child's teachers. Similar proportions are very satisfied with their school's academic standards and discipline. Seventy-seven percent say the amount of homework assigned to their child is "about right."

The biggest difference in satisfaction levels is by type of school and grade level. Typically, private school parents are happier than public school parents, and the parents of younger children are happier than the parents of children in middle or high school. Nevertheless, the majority of parents, regardless of type of school or grade level, say they are very satisfied with their child's school.

■ Although most parents are very satisfied with their child's school, a substantial minority is not. Unhappy parents are one factor driving the push for school reform.

Blacks are least likely to be very satisfied with their child's school

(percent of children in kindergarten through 12th grade whose parents are "very satisfied" with their child's school, by race and Hispanic origin, 2011–12)

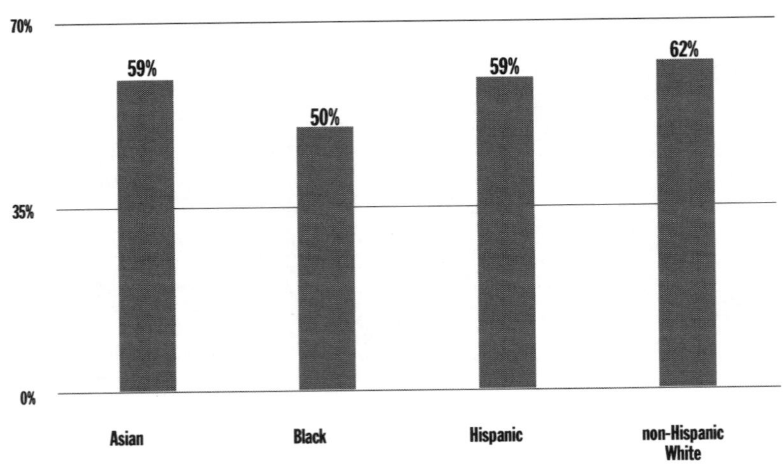

Table 12.12 Parental Satisfaction with School, 2011–12

(total number and percent of children in kindergarten through 12th grade whose parents reported being "very satisfied" with school characteristics and amount of homework, by selected characteristics of child and parent, 2011–12)

	total		parent reports being "very satisfied"					
	number (in 000s)	percent	with the school	with teachers student had this year	with academic standards of the school	with order and discipline at the school	with the way school staff interacts with parents	amount of homework assigned is "about right"
Total children	**52,211**	**100%**	**59%**	**60%**	**59%**	**60%**	**52%**	**77%**
Race and Hispanic origin of child								
Asian	2,871	100	59	57	58	60	51	75
Black	7,466	100	50	53	51	54	47	77
Hispanic	12,110	100	59	60	58	61	52	80
Two or more races	2,827	100	57	57	59	59	53	75
Non-Hispanic White	26,938	100	62	61	62	61	54	77
Educational attainment of parent								
Not a high school graduate	6,335	100	60	61	58	60	55	81
High school graduate	10,571	100	55	57	57	56	48	78
Vocational/technical or some college	15,810	100	54	55	55	55	48	76
Bachelor's degree	11,839	100	64	64	64	64	57	77
Graduate degree	7,656	100	66	64	65	66	57	75
School type								
Public, assigned	40,097	100	56	58	56	56	49	77
Public, chosen	7,448	100	62	59	64	63	56	76
Private, religious	3,271	100	80	76	80	82	72	85
Private, nonreligious	788	100	82	82	84	81	78	81
Student's grade level								
Kindergarten through 2nd grade	13,610	100	70	75	68	71	66	85
3rd through 5th grade	12,243	100	63	67	62	66	60	78
6th through 8th grade	11,717	100	53	52	53	54	45	73
9th through 12th grade	14,642	100	50	44	52	49	39	73
Poverty status								
Poor	10,333	100	55	59	55	56	51	78
Not poor	41,878	100	60	60	60	60	53	77

Note: Asians and Blacks are those who identify themselves as being of the race alone and not Hispanic. The multiracial are not Hispanic.
Source: National Center for Education Statistics, Parent and Family Involvement in Education, from the National Household Education Surveys Program of 2012, Internet site http://nces.ed.gov/pubsearch/pubsinfo.asp?pubid=2013028; calculations by New Strategist

CHAPTER

13

Health

■ The 57 percent majority of children under age 18 is in excellent health, according to their parents. Only about 2 percent of parents rate their child's health as only fair or poor.

■ A government study of high school students found 17 percent of girls to be overweight. A larger 36 percent of girls thought they were overweight, and 63 percent were trying to lose weight.

■ Among boys, 54 percent are sexually experienced by 11th grade. The figure rises to 65 percent in 12th grade. The statistics are almost identical for girls.

■ In a government survey of high school students, 35 percent say they used alcohol in the past month and 23 percent used marijuana.

■ Among all Americans, 13 percent did not have health insurance at any time in 2013. The figure was a smaller 7 percent among children.

■ Nearly 10 million children (13.2 percent) have taken prescription medications regularly for at least three months during the past year.

■ Among children aged 1 to 14, accidents are by far the leading cause of death.

Most Children Are in Excellent Health

Many are obese, however.

The 57 percent majority of children under age 18 is in excellent health, according to their parents. Only about 2 percent of parents rate their child's health as fair or poor.

In a study that measures the prevalence of obesity among children based on physical examinations, the federal government found a substantial 10 percent of 2-to-5-year-olds to be obese. The figure was an even larger 18 to 19 percent among older children. In a separate study of high school students, about 17 percent of girls and boys were found to be overweight. A larger 36 percent of girls and 26 percent of boys thought they were overweight. Most girls were trying to lose weight.

The percentage of high school students who are in physical education class falls from a high of 64 percent among 9th graders to just 35 percent by 12th grade. The 57 percent majority of high school boys reports being physically active for at least one hour a day, five days a week. The figure is just 37 percent among high school girls.

■ Although most teenage girls are weight conscious, few are physically active.

Many girls think they are overweight

(percent of girls in 9th to 12th grade who are overweight, think they are overweight, and trying to lose weight, 2013)

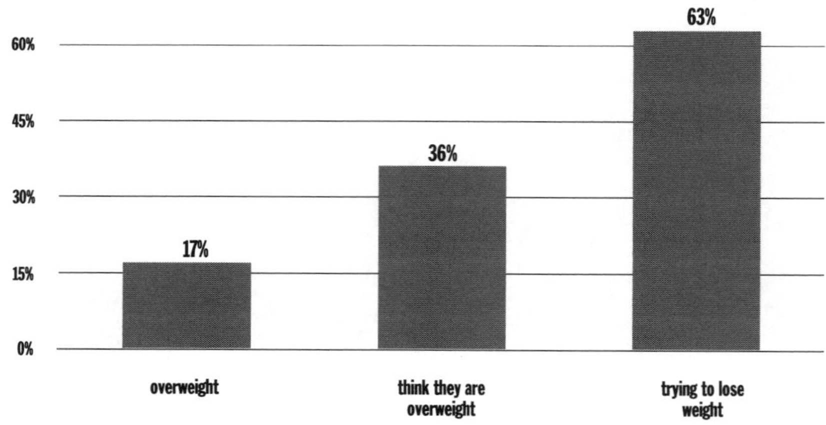

Table 13.1 Health Status of Children under Age 18, 2012

(parent-reported health status of people under age 18, by age, 2012)

	total	excellent	very good	good	fair/poor
Total children	**100.0%**	**57.0%**	**25.8%**	**15.0%**	**2.1%**
Under age 5	100.0	61.2	24.6	12.8	1.4
Aged 5 to 11	100.0	57.2	25.7	15.1	2.0
Aged 12 to 17	100.0	53.5	27.0	16.7	2.7

Source: National Center for Health Statistics, Summary Health Statistics for U.S. Children: National Health Interview Survey, 2012, Series 10, No. 258, 2013, Internet site http://www.cdc.gov/nchs/products/series/series10.htm

Table 13.2 Obesity among Children, 2009–12

(percent of children aged 2 to 19 who are obese, by age and sex, 2009–12)

	total	boys	girls
Aged 2 to 5	10.2%	12.0%	8.4%
Aged 6 to 11	17.9	18.3	17.4
Aged 12 to 19	19.4	20.0	18.9

Note: Data are based on physical examinations. "Obese" is defined as a body mass index at or above the sex- and age-specific 95th percentile BMI cutoff points from the 2000 CDC growth charts.
Source: National Center for Health Statistics, Health, United States, 2013, Internet site http://www.cdc.gov/nchs/hus.htm

Table 13.3 Weight Status of 9th to 12th Graders by Sex, 2013

(percent of 9th to 12th graders by weight status, by sex and grade, 2013)

	overweight*	described themselves as overweight	trying to lose weight
Total students	**16.6%**	**31.1%**	**47.7%**
9th grade	18.2	30.2	48.7
10th grade	16.1	30.4	46.7
11th grade	15.6	32.5	48.6
12th grade	16.2	31.5	47.0
Boys	**16.5**	**25.9**	**33.0**
9th grade	18.6	26.1	37.1
10th grade	15.7	26.7	31.2
11th grade	15.5	25.4	32.1
12th grade	16.1	25.4	31.2
Girls	**16.6**	**36.3**	**62.6**
9th grade	17.9	34.5	60.5
10th grade	15.6	34.3	62.8
11th grade	15.8	39.3	64.7
12th grade	16.2	37.5	62.6

** Students who were overweight were at or above the 85th percentile for body mass index, by age and sex, based on reference data.*
Source: Centers for Disease Control and Prevention, Youth Risk Behavior Surveillance—United States, 2013, Internet site http://www.cdc.gov/HealthyYouth/yrbs/index.htm

Table 13.4 Participation of High School Students in Physical Education Classes, Team Sports, and Physical Activity, 2013

(percent of 9th through 12th graders who attended a physical education class at least one day a week, participated in at least one sports team, and who were physically active at least 60 minutes a day for five of the past seven days, by sex and grade, 2013)

	attended PE class	played on sports team in past year	physically active at least one hour/day five days/week
Total students	**48.0%**	**54.0%**	**47.3%**
9th grade	64.3	56.4	50.6
10th grade	50.5	58.4	49.1
11th grade	39.6	51.9	44.7
12th grade	35.2	48.5	43.9
Boys	**53.3**	**59.6**	**57.3**
9th grade	67.8	61.6	60.5
10th grade	55.3	61.3	57.2
11th grade	46.9	59.5	56.8
12th grade	40.6	55.5	53.9
Girls	**42.8**	**48.5**	**37.3**
9th grade	60.8	51.2	40.7
10th grade	45.5	55.4	40.7
11th grade	32.6	44.7	33.1
12th grade	29.9	41.7	34.1

Source: Centers for Disease Control and Prevention, Youth Risk Behavior Surveillance—United States, 2013, Internet site http://www.cdc.gov/HealthyYouth/yrbs/index.htm

Majority of 11th and 12th Graders Have Had Sex

Most sexually active teens use birth control.

Among boys, 54 percent of 11th graders have had sexual intercourse. The figure rises to 65 percent among boys in 12th grade. The statistics are almost identical for girls—54 percent of 11th graders and 63 percent of 12th graders have had sexual intercourse. A smaller share of teens is currently sexually active—meaning they have had sexual intercourse in the past three months.

Among sexually active teens, most used birth control the last time they had sex. Among sexually active boys, 66 percent say they used a condom and 15 percent say their partner was on the pill. Among sexually active girls, 53 percent say their partner used a condom and 22 percent say they were taking the pill.

■ With teenagers being sexually active, preventing pregnancy and sexually transmitted diseases is of prime concern to parents and schools.

Girls and boys are almost equally sexually active

(percent of 9th to 12th graders who have had sexual intercourse, by sex, 2013)

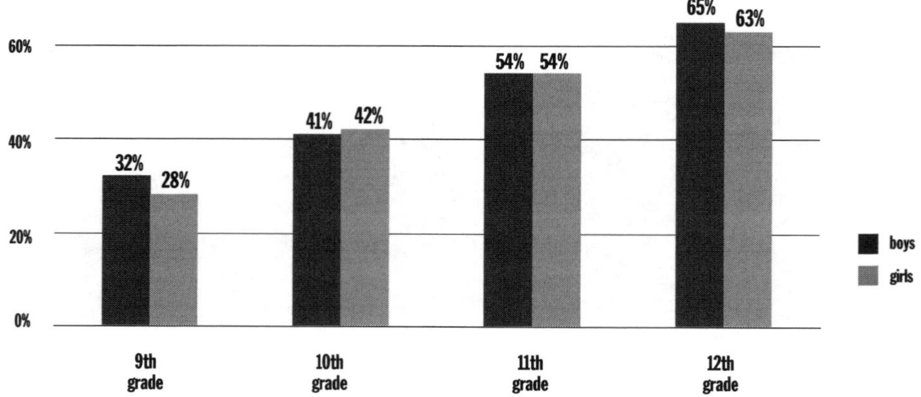

Table 13.5 Sexual Behavior of 9th to 12th Graders by Sex, 2013

(percent of 9th to 12th graders engaging in selected sexual activities, by sex and grade, 2013)

	ever had sexual intercourse	currently sexually active*	condom use during last sexual intercourse**	birth control pill use before last sexual intercourse**
Total students	**46.8%**	**34.0%**	**59.1%**	**19.0%**
9th grade	30.0	19.6	62.7	11.4
10th grade	41.4	29.4	61.7	16.7
11th grade	54.1	40.2	62.3	19.3
12th grade	64.1	49.3	53.0	23.7
Boys	**47.5**	**32.7**	**65.8**	**15.1**
9th grade	32.0	19.3	69.5	7.7
10th grade	41.1	27.0	69.3	13.7
11th grade	54.3	39.6	70.6	15.1
12th grade	65.4	47.8	58.0	19.3
Girls	**46.0**	**35.2**	**53.1**	**22.4**
9th grade	28.1	19.8	56.5	14.7
10th grade	41.7	31.8	55.5	19.2
11th grade	53.9	40.7	54.8	23.2
12th grade	62.8	50.7	48.4	27.6

* *Sexual intercourse during the three months preceding the survey.*
** *Among those who are currently sexually active.*
Source: Centers for Disease Control and Prevention, Youth Risk Behavior Surveillance—United States, 2013, Internet site http://www.cdc.gov/HealthyYouth/yrbs/index.htm

Many Teens Smoke Cigarettes

But teens are more likely to smoke marijuana than cigarettes.

Cigarette smoking remains stubbornly high among teenagers. Overall, 22 percent of people aged 12 or older smoked a cigarette in the past month, according to a 2012 survey. The proportion of teenagers who have smoked a cigarette in the past month rises steadily with age to 25 percent among 18-year-olds.

Sixteen percent of high school students report having smoked a cigarette in the past month. Interestingly, a larger 23 percent of high school students report having used marijuana in the past month.

■ Nearly half of teens have tried a cigarette by 11th grade and some will make smoking a lifelong habit.

Cigarette smoking doubles between ages 16 and 18

(percent of people aged 12 to 18 who have smoked a cigarette in the past month, by age, 2012)

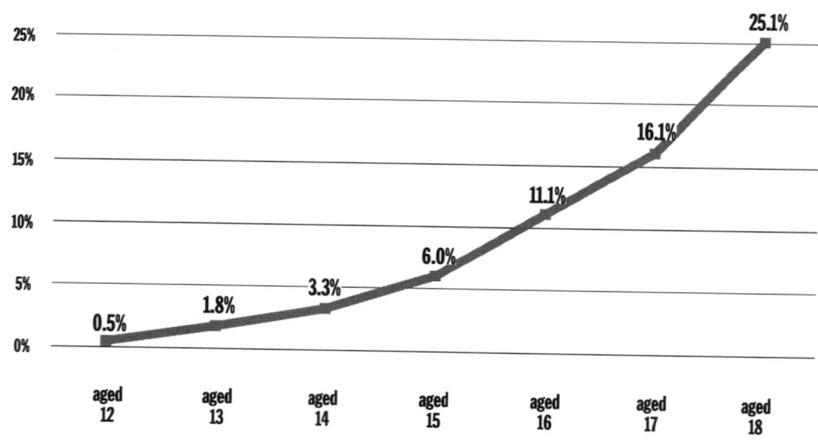

Table 13.6 Cigarette Smoking among People Aged 12 to 18, 2012

(percent of people aged 12 or older and people aged 12 to 18 reporting any, past year, and past month use of cigarettes, 2012)

	ever smoked	smoked in past year	smoked in past month
Total people aged 12 or older	**61.9%**	**26.1%**	**22.1%**
Aged 12 to 17	17.4	11.8	6.6
Aged 12	3.1	1.6	0.5
Aged 13	6.4	3.9	1.8
Aged 14	12.0	7.5	3.3
Aged 15	19.9	12.9	6.0
Aged 16	27.6	19.2	11.1
Aged 17	34.1	24.8	16.1
Aged 18	47.3	36.1	25.1

Source: SAMHSA, Office of Applied Studies, 2012 National Survey on Drug Use and Health, Detailed Tables, Internet site http://www.samhsa.gov/data/NSDUH/2012SummNatFindDetTables/Index.aspx

Table 13.7 Cigarette Use by 9th to 12th Graders, 2013

(percent of 9th to 12th graders who have ever tried cigarette smoking or who have smoked cigarettes in the past 30 days, by sex, 2013)

	lifetime cigarette use	past month cigarette use
Total students	**41.1%**	**15.7%**
9th grade	31.7	10.2
10th grade	39.0	13.2
11th grade	47.0	21.1
12th grade	48.1	19.2
Boys	**42.5**	**16.4**
9th grade	33.1	10.3
10th grade	40.2	13.6
11th grade	49.1	23.4
12th grade	49.7	19.6
Girls	**39.6**	**15.0**
9th grade	30.3	10.0
10th grade	37.7	12.6
11th grade	45.2	18.9
12th grade	46.5	18.7

Source: Centers for Disease Control and Prevention, Youth Risk Behavior Surveillance—United States, 2013, Internet site http://www.cdc.gov/HealthyYouth/yrbs/index.htm

Many Teens Drink Alcohol

Nearly 40 percent of 18-year-olds have had an alcoholic beverage in the past month.

The percentage of teenagers who have consumed alcohol in the past month rises from just 1 percent among 12-year-olds to 40 percent among 18-year-olds. It surpasses 50 percent among 20-year-olds, despite the fact that the legal drinking age is 21.

Many teens and young adults are binge drinkers, meaning they have had five or more drinks on one occasion in the past month. Among people aged 19 and 20, more than one in 10 participated in heavy drinking during the past month—meaning they binged at least five times.

In a survey of high school students, 35 percent say they used alcohol in the past month. The figure rises by grade level to nearly half of boys and girls in 12th grade.

■ Heavy drinking is a bigger problem than drug use among teenagers.

Many teens drink alcohol

(percent of people aged 16 to 20 who have consumed alcoholic beverages in the past month, by age, 2012)

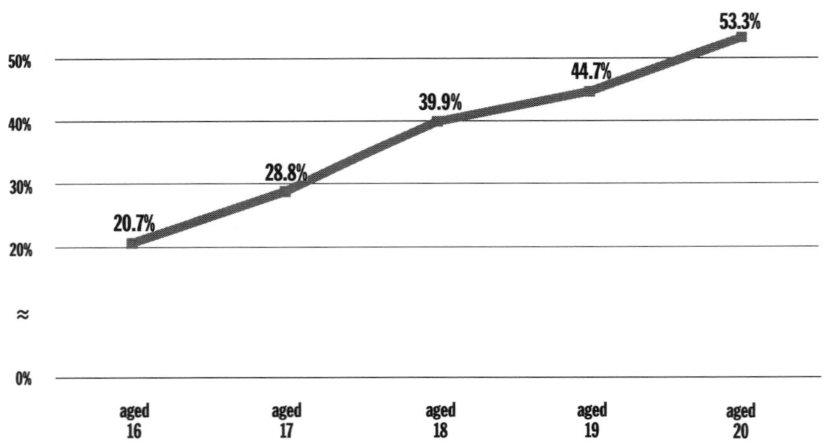

Table 13.8 Alcohol Use by People Aged 12 to 20, 2012

(percent of people aged 12 or older and people aged 12 to 20 who drank alcoholic beverages during the past month, by level of alcohol use, 2012)

	drank at any time during past month	binge drinking during past month	heavy drinking during past month
Total people aged 12 or older	**52.1%**	**23.0%**	**6.5%**
Aged 12 to 17	12.9	7.2	1.3
Aged 12	1.2	0.5	0.0
Aged 13	3.3	1.3	0.4
Aged 14	8.7	4.0	0.3
Aged 15	13.6	6.8	0.9
Aged 16	20.7	11.8	2.4
Aged 17	28.8	18.2	3.7
Aged 18	39.9	26.0	6.6
Aged 19	44.7	30.7	11.1
Aged 20	53.3	35.3	12.6

Note: "Binge drinking" is defined as having five or more drinks on the same occasion on at least one day in the 30 days prior to the survey. "Heavy drinking" is having five or more drinks on the same occasion on each of five or more days in 30 days prior to the survey.

Source: SAMHSA, Office of Applied Studies, 2012 National Survey on Drug Use and Health, Detailed Tables, Internet site http://www.samhsa.gov/data/NSDUH/2012SummNatFindDetTables/Index.aspx

Table 13.9 Alcohol Use by 9th to 12th Graders, 2013

(percent of 9th to 12th graders who have ever drunk alcohol or who have drunk alcohol in the past 30 days, by sex, 2013)

	lifetime alcohol use	past month alcohol use
Total students	**66.2%**	**34.9%**
9h grade	55.6	24.4
10th grade	64.0	30.9
11th grade	71.2	39.2
12th grade	75.6	46.8
Boys	**64.4**	**34.4**
9th grade	52.4	22.7
10th grade	61.9	28.6
11th grade	70.3	41.0
12th grade	74.9	48.0
Girls	**67.9**	**35.5**
9th grade	58.8	26.2
10th grade	66.1	33.2
11th grade	72.0	37.5
12th grade	76.3	45.7

Source: Centers for Disease Control and Prevention, Youth Risk Behavior Surveillance—United States, 2013, Internet site http://www.cdc.gov/HealthyYouth/yrbs/index.htm

Marijuana Use Is Common among Teens

More than 40 percent of 18-year-olds have ever used marijuana.

Among Americans aged 12 or older, only 9 percent have used an illicit drug in the past month. Teens and young adults are much more likely than the average person to be current drug users. Among 18-year-olds, 22.5 percent have used an illicit drug in the past month. Marijuana is by far the most commonly used illicit drug. Among 18-year-olds, 20 percent have used marijuana in the past month.

In a survey of high school students, 41 percent say they have used marijuana in their lifetime and 23 percent have used it in the past month. The percentage who have used marijuana in the past month rises with grade level to 31 percent of 12th grade boys and 25 percent of 12th grade girls.

■ Teens are more likely to smoke marijuana than cigarettes.

Twenty percent of 18-year-olds have used marijuana in the past month

(percent of people aged 12 to 18 who have used marijuana in the past month, by age, 2012)

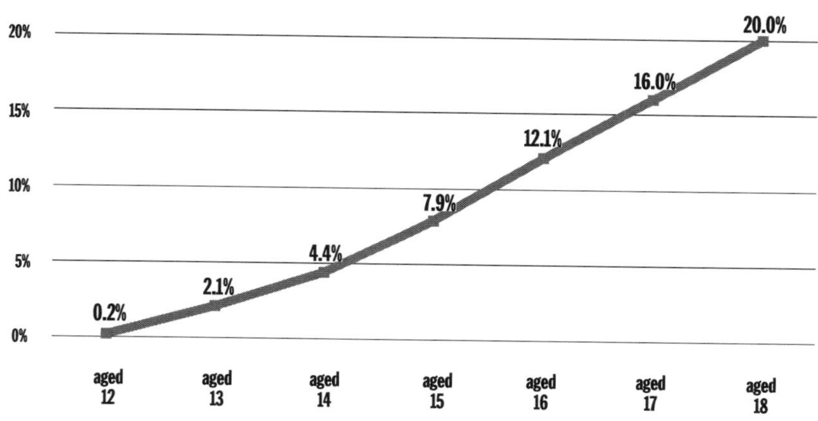

Table 13.10 Illicit Drug Use by People Aged 12 to 18, 2012

(percent of people aged 12 to 18 who ever used any illicit drug, who used an illicit drug in the past year, and who used an illicit drug in the past month, 2012)

	ever used	used in past year	used in past month
Total people aged 12 or older	**48.0%**	**16.0%**	**9.2%**
Aged 12 to 17	24.2	17.9	9.5
Aged 12	8.1	5.0	2.5
Aged 13	12.9	8.8	4.6
Aged 14	19.1	13.3	6.8
Aged 15	27.1	19.3	9.5
Aged 16	34.8	27.5	14.7
Aged 17	42.1	32.4	18.4
Aged 18	49.3	38.4	22.5

Note: Illicit drugs include marijuana, hashish, cocaine (including crack), heroin, hallucinogens, inhalants, or any prescription-type psychotherapeutic used nonmedically.
Source: SAMHSA, Office of Applied Studies, 2012 National Survey on Drug Use and Health, Detailed Tables, Internet site http://www.samhsa.gov/data/NSDUH/2012SummNatFindDetTables/Index.aspx

Table 13.11 Marijuana Use by People Aged 12 to 18, 2012

(percent of people aged 12 or older and people aged 12 to 18 who ever used marijuana, who used marijuana in the past year, and who used marijuana in the past month, 2012)

	ever used	used in past year	used in past month
Total people aged 12 or older	**42.8%**	**12.1%**	**7.3%**
Aged 12 to 17	17.0	13.5	7.2
Aged 12	1.4	1.1	0.2
Aged 13	5.1	4.1	2.1
Aged 14	10.4	8.4	4.4
Aged 15	18.8	14.7	7.9
Aged 16	28.7	23.0	12.1
Aged 17	36.0	28.5	16.0
Aged 18	43.3	34.2	20.0

Source: Centers for Disease Control and Prevention, Youth Risk Behavior Surveillance—United States, 2013, Internet site http://www.cdc.gov/HealthyYouth/yrbs/index.htm

Table 13.12 Marijuana Use by 9th to 12th Graders, 2013

(percent of 9th to 12th graders who have ever used marijuana or who have used marijuana in the past 30 days, by sex, 2013)

	lifetime marijuana use	past month marijuana use
Total students	**40.7%**	**23.4%**
9th grade	30.1	17.7
10th grade	39.1	23.5
11th grade	46.4	25.5
12th grade	48.6	27.7
Boys	**42.1**	**25.0**
9th grade	31.1	17.7
10th grade	40.7	24.3
11th grade	47.8	28.4
12th grade	50.9	30.9
Girls	**39.2**	**21.9**
9th grade	29.0	17.6
10th grade	37.4	22.7
11th grade	45.1	22.8
12th grade	46.4	24.6

Source: Centers for Disease Control and Prevention, Youth Risk Behavior Surveillance—United States, 2013, Internet site http://www.cdc.gov/HealthyYouth/yrbs/index.htm

Most Children Are Covered by Health Insurance

More than 5 million children do not have health insurance, however.

Among all Americans, 42 million were without health insurance coverage at any time in 2013—or 13 percent of the population. The figure is a smaller 7 percent among children. The majority of children with health insurance is covered by an employment-based plan (their parents'). Medicaid, the government's health insurance program for the poor, covers a substantial 41 percent of children with health insurance.

Nearly 87 percent of children had health expenses in 2012, with a median cost of $541. Private insurance covered 51 percent of the cost, Medicaid paid another 27.5 percent, and parents paid 15 percent of the cost out-of-pocket. Most parents are satisfied with the health care their children receive. Seven out of 10 parents rated their child's last health care visit a 9 or 10 on a scale of 0 (worst) to 10 (best).

■ Providing health insurance coverage to all children is a political problem because many without health insurance are children of undocumented immigrants.

Most children with health insurance are covered by an employment-based plan

(percent of children with health insurance by type, 2013)

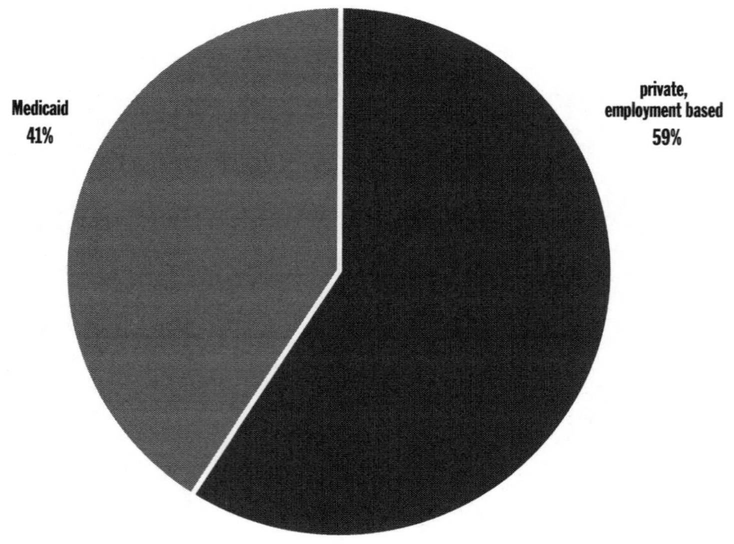

Table 13.13 Health Insurance Coverage of People under Age 18, 2013

(number and percent distribution of people under age 18 by health insurance coverage status, 2013; numbers in thousands)

	total	covered by some type of health insurance during the year	not covered at any time during the year
Total people	**313,395**	**271,442**	**41,953**
Under age 18	74,055	68,613	5,441
Under age 6	23,997	22,182	1,815
Aged 6 to 11	24,559	22,909	1,650
Aged 12 to 17	25,499	23,522	1,977
PERCENT DISTRIBUTION BY COVERAGE STATUS			
Total people	**100.0%**	**86.6%**	**13.4%**
Under age 18	100.0	92.7	7.3
Under age 6	100.0	92.4	7.6
Aged 6 to 11	100.0	93.3	6.7
Aged 12 to 17	100.0	92.2	7.8
PERCENT DISTRIBUTION BY AGE			
Total people	**100.0**	**100.0**	**100.0**
Under age 18	23.6	25.3	13.0
Under age 6	7.7	8.2	4.3
Aged 6 to 11	7.8	8.4	3.9
Aged 12 to 17	8.1	8.7	4.7

Source: Bureau of the Census, Health Insurance, Internet site http://www.census.gov/hhes/www/hlthins/; calculations by New Strategist

Table 13.14 Health Insurance Coverage of People under Age 18 by Type of Coverage, 2013

(number and percent distribution of people under age 18 with health insurance by type of coverage, 2013; numbers in thousands)

	total with coverage	total with private	employment based		direct purchase	total with government	Medicaid	Medicare	military
			total	own					
Total people	**271,442**	**201,064**	**169,015**	**87,097**	**34,531**	**107,581**	**54,081**	**48,977**	**14,147**
Under age 18	68,613	44,429	40,556	64	4,828	30,410	27,814	264	2,970
Under age 6	22,182	13,013	12,188	0	1,239	11,131	10,224	66	1,054
Aged 6 to 11	22,909	14,827	13,755	0	1,654	10,293	9,487	86	921
Aged 12 to 17	23,522	16,589	14,613	64	1,935	8,986	8,103	112	996
PERCENT DISTRIBUTION BY TYPE OF COVERAGE									
Total people	**100.0%**	**74.1%**	**62.3%**	**32.1%**	**12.7%**	**39.6%**	**19.9%**	**18.0%**	**5.2%**
Under age 18	100.0	64.8	59.1	0.1	7.0	44.3	40.5	0.4	4.3
Under age 6	100.0	58.7	54.9	0.0	5.6	50.2	46.1	0.3	4.8
Aged 6 to 11	100.0	64.7	60.0	0.0	7.2	44.9	41.4	0.4	4.0
Aged 12 to 17	100.0	70.5	62.1	0.3	8.2	38.2	34.4	0.5	4.2
PERCENT DISTRIBUTION BY AGE									
Total people	**100.0**	**100.0**	**100.0**	**100.0**	**100.0**	**100.0**	**100.0**	**100.0**	**100.0**
Under age 18	25.3	22.1	24.0	0.1	14.0	28.3	51.4	0.5	21.0
Under age 6	8.2	6.5	7.2	0.0	3.6	10.3	18.9	0.1	7.4
Aged 6 to 11	8.4	7.4	8.1	0.0	4.8	9.6	17.5	0.2	6.5
Aged 12 to 17	8.7	8.3	8.6	0.1	5.6	8.4	15.0	0.2	7.0

Note: Numbers do not add to total because some people are covered by more than one type of health insurance.
Source: Bureau of the Census, Health Insurance, Internet site http://www.census.gov/hhes/www/hlthins/; calculations by New Strategist

Table 13.15 Spending on Health Care for Children, 2012

(percent of children under age 18 with health care expense, median expense per child, total expenses, and percent distribution of total expenses by source of payment, by age, 2012)

				total expenses	
	total (thousands)	percent with expense	median expense per person	amount (millions)	percent distribution
Total children	**73,913**	**86.7%**	**$541**	**$133,951**	**100.0%**
Under age 6	24,067	88.8	477	45,817	34.2
Aged 6 to 11	24,303	86.6	476	36,144	27.0
Aged 12 to 17	25,543	84.7	699	51,991	38.8

	percent distribution by source of payment				
	total	out of pocket	private insurance	Medicare	Medicaid
Total children	**100.0%**	**15.0%**	**50.6%**	**1.3%**	**27.5%**
Under age 6	100.0	6.2	46.9	1.0	37.0
Aged 6 to 11	100.0	16.0	56.9	0.2	23.2
Aged 12 to 17	100.0	22.1	49.5	2.5	22.0

Note: Source of payment does not sum to 100 because "other" is not shown.
Source: Agency for Healthcare Research and Quality, Medical Expenditure Panel Survey, 2012, Internet site http://meps.ahrq .gov/mepsweb/survey_comp/household.jsp; calculations by New Strategist

Table 13.16 Parents' Rating of Health Care Received by Children at Doctor's Office or Clinic, 2012

(number of children under age 18 visiting a doctor or health care clinic in past 12 months, and percent distribution by rating given by parents for health care received by children on a scale from 0 (worst) to 10 (best), 2012; children in thousands)

	with health care visit		rating		
	number	percent	9 to 10	7 to 8	0 to 6
Total children	**57,159**	**100.0%**	**70.4%**	**25.4%**	**4.0%**
Under age 6	19,510	100.0	71.1	25.1	3.7
Aged 6 to 11	18,487	100.0	69.5	26.0	4.0
Aged 12 to 17	19,161	100.0	70.4	25.2	4.2

Source: Agency for Healthcare Research and Quality, Medical Expenditure Panel Survey, 2012; Internet site http://meps.ahrq .gov/mepsweb/survey_comp/household.jsp; calculations by New Strategist

Asthma and Allergies Affect Many Children

Boys are more likely than girls to have learning disabilities.

Asthma is a problem for many children. A substantial 14 percent have been diagnosed with asthma. Nine percent have had asthma in the past year. Black children are most likely to have ever had asthma (22 percent).

Nearly 5 million children aged 3 to 17 (8 percent) have been diagnosed with a learning disability. An even larger 6 million have been diagnosed with attention deficit hyperactivity disorder. Boys are more likely than girls to have these conditions and account for 64 percent of those with learning disabilities and 72 percent of those with attention deficit hyperactivity disorder.

Many children use prescription medications. Nearly 10 million have taken prescription medications regularly for at least three months in the past year—a substantial 13 percent of the nation's children. Among 12-to-17-year-olds, the figure is an even higher 17 percent.

■ Prescription drug use is growing, even among children.

Among Black children, asthma is a common health condition

(percentage of people under age 18 who have been diagnosed with asthma, by race and Hispanic origin, 2012)

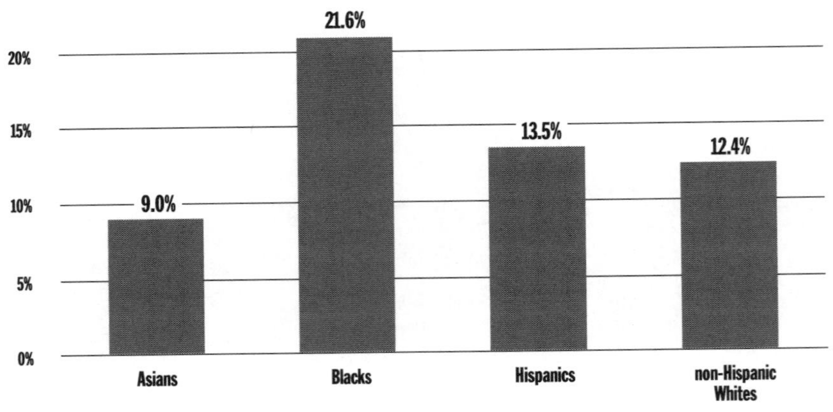

Table 3.17 Health Conditions among Children by Selected Characteristics, 2012

(number of children under age 18 with selected health conditions, by selected characteristics and type of condition, 2012; numbers in thousands)

	total children	diagnosed with asthma	still have asthma	experienced in last 12 months: hay fever	respiratory allergies	food allergies	skin allergies
Total children	**73,661**	**10,322**	**6,834**	**6,641**	**7,826**	**4,099**	**8,808**
Sex							
Female	36,033	4,333	3,085	2,800	3,318	1,995	4,138
Male	37,628	5,988	3,748	3,841	4,507	2,104	4,671
Age							
Aged 0 to 4	20,006	1,406	1,080	888	1,500	1,126	2,893
Aged 5 to 11	28,829	4,483	3,162	2,666	3,492	1,804	3,642
Aged 12 to 17	24,827	4,433	2,591	3,086	2,833	1,169	2,274
Race and Hispanic origin							
Asian	3,403	310	173	303	310	196	368
Black	10,591	2,265	1,675	741	1,037	758	2,014
Hispanic	17,663	2,344	1,552	1,201	1,393	749	1,668
Non-Hispanic White	39,057	4,881	3,079	4,124	4,648	2,152	4,271
Family structure							
Mother and father	50,442	6,006	3,853	4,585	5,101	2,765	5,491
Mother, no father	18,115	3,552	2,480	1,578	2,053	1,140	2,912
Father, no mother	2,695	430	260	166	334	96	165
Neither mother nor father	2,410	333	240	311	339	98	240
Parent's education							
Less than high school diploma	8,802	1,356	995	508	525	368	866
High school diploma or GED	13,990	2,061	1,400	855	1,223	622	1,535
More than high school	48,248	6,555	4,191	4,958	5,739	3,000	6,161
Household income							
Less than $35,000	23,433	4,054	2,849	1,577	2,270	1,392	3,208
$35,000 to $49,999	9,019	1,183	813	757	1,006	435	1,062
$50,000 to $74,999	11,818	1,376	862	1,128	1,125	460	1,387
$75,000 to $99,999	9,133	1,256	838	901	1,129	531	1,086
$100,000 or more	16,644	2,009	1,227	2,009	1,989	1,124	1,785

Note: "Mother and father" includes biological, adoptive, step, in-law, or foster relationships. Legal guardians are classified as "neither mother nor father." Parent's education is the education level of the parent with the higher level of education. Race/Hispanic origin, education, and income categories do not sum to total because not all races are shown and those not reporting education or income are not shown.

Source: National Center for Health Statistics, Summary Health Statistics for U.S. Children: National Health Interview Survey, 2012, Series 10, No. 258, 2013, Internet site http://www.cdc.gov/nchs/nhis.htm

Table 3.18 Percent of Children with Health Conditions by Selected Characteristics, 2012

(percent of children under age 18 with selected health conditions, by type of condition and selected characteristics, 2012)

				experienced in last 12 months			
	total children	diagnosed with asthma	still have asthma	hay fever	respiratory allergies	food allergies	skin allergies
Total children	**100.0%**	**14.0%**	**9.3%**	**9.0%**	**10.6%**	**5.6%**	**12.0%**
Sex							
Female	100.0	12.1	8.6	7.8	9.2	5.6	11.5
Male	100.0	15.9	10.0	10.2	12.0	5.6	12.4
Age							
Aged 0 to 4	100.0	7.0	5.4	4.5	7.5	5.6	14.5
Aged 5 to 11	100.0	15.6	11.0	9.3	12.1	6.3	12.6
Aged 12 to 17	100.0	17.9	10.5	12.5	11.4	4.7	9.2
Race and Hispanic origin							
Asian	100.0	9.0	4.9	8.8	9.0	5.8	10.9
Black	100.0	21.6	16.0	7.0	9.9	7.1	18.9
Hispanic	100.0	13.5	8.9	6.9	8.0	4.3	9.4
Non-Hispanic White	100.0	12.4	7.9	10.4	11.9	5.6	11.0
Family structure							
Mother and father	100.0	12.1	7.7	9.2	10.2	5.5	10.8
Mother, no father	100.0	19.5	13.7	8.6	11.3	6.3	16.2
Father, no mother	100.0	16.1	10.1	5.7	11.5	4.1	6.2
Neither mother nor father	100.0	14.5	10.8	12.9	14.3	4.1	10.3
Parent's education							
Less than high school diploma	100.0	15.4	11.3	5.8	6.0	4.2	9.8
High school diploma or GED	100.0	14.8	10.1	6.1	8.8	4.5	11.0
More than high school	100.0	13.6	8.7	10.3	11.9	6.2	12.8
Household income							
Less than $35,000	100.0	17.9	12.5	7.0	9.9	5.9	13.5
$35,000 to $49,999	100.0	13.0	9.0	8.4	11.1	4.8	11.9
$50,000 to $74,999	100.0	11.7	7.4	9.6	9.6	3.9	11.8
$75,000 to $99,999	100.0	13.5	9.1	9.7	12.3	5.9	12.0
$100,000 or more	100.0	11.7	7.2	11.6	11.8	6.8	10.8

Note: "Mother and father" includes biological, adoptive, step, in-law, or foster relationships. Legal guardians are classified as "neither mother nor father." Parent's education is the education level of the parent with the higher level of education. Race/Hispanic origin, education, and income categories do not sum to total because not all races are shown and those not reporting education or income are not shown.

Source: National Center for Health Statistics, Summary Health Statistics for U.S. Children: National Health Interview Survey, 2012, Series 10, No. 258, 2013, Internet site http://www.cdc.gov/nchs/nhis.htm

Table 3.19 Distribution of Health Conditions among Children by Selected Characteristics, 2012

(percent distribution of children under age 18 with health conditions, by selected characteristics, 2012; numbers in thousands)

				experienced in last 12 months			
	total children	diagnosed with asthma	still have asthma	hay fever	respiratory allergies	food allergies	skin allergies
Total children	**100.0%**	**100.0%**	**100.0%**	**100.0%**	**100.0%**	**100.0%**	**100.0%**
Sex							
Female	48.9	42.0	45.1	42.2	42.4	48.7	47.0
Male	51.1	58.0	54.8	57.8	57.6	51.3	53.0
Age							
Aged 0 to 4	27.2	13.6	15.8	13.4	19.2	27.5	32.8
Aged 5 to 11	39.1	43.4	46.3	40.1	44.6	44.0	41.3
Aged 12 to 17	33.7	42.9	37.9	46.5	36.2	28.5	25.8
Race and Hispanic origin							
Asian	4.6	3.0	2.5	4.6	4.0	4.8	4.2
Black	14.4	21.9	24.5	11.2	13.3	18.5	22.9
Hispanic	24.0	22.7	22.7	18.1	17.8	18.3	18.9
Non-Hispanic White	53.0	47.3	45.1	62.1	59.4	52.5	48.5
Family structure							
Mother and father	68.5	58.2	56.4	69.0	65.2	67.5	62.3
Mother, no father	24.6	34.4	36.3	23.8	26.2	27.8	33.1
Father, no mother	3.7	4.2	3.8	2.5	4.3	2.3	1.9
Neither mother nor father	3.3	3.2	3.5	4.7	4.3	2.4	2.7
Parent's education							
Less than high school diploma	11.9	13.1	14.6	7.6	6.7	9.0	9.8
High school diploma or GED	19.0	20.0	20.5	12.9	15.6	15.2	17.4
More than high school	65.5	63.5	61.3	74.7	73.3	73.2	69.9
Household income							
Less than $35,000	31.8	39.3	41.7	23.7	29.0	34.0	36.4
$35,000 to $49,999	12.2	11.5	11.9	11.4	12.9	10.6	12.1
$50,000 to $74,999	16.0	13.3	12.6	17.0	14.4	11.2	15.7
$75,000 to $99,999	12.4	12.2	12.3	13.6	14.4	13.0	12.3
$100,000 or more	22.6	19.5	18.0	30.3	25.4	27.4	20.3

Note: "Mother and father" includes biological, adoptive, step, in-law, or foster relationships. Legal guardians are classified as "neither mother nor father." Parent's education is the education level of the parent with the higher level of education. Race/Hispanic origin, education, and income categories do not sum to total because not all races are shown and those not reporting education or income are not shown.

Source: National Center for Health Statistics, Summary Health Statistics for U.S. Children: National Health Interview Survey, 2012, Series 10, No. 258, 2013, Internet site http://www.cdc.gov/nchs/nhis.htm

Table 3.20 Children with a Learning Disability or Attention Deficit Hyperactivity Disorder by Selected Characteristics, 2012

(number, percent, and percent distribution of children aged 3 to 17 who have ever been told by a school representative or health professional that they had a learning disability or attention deficit hyperactivity disorder, by selected characteristics, 2012; numbers in thousands)

	learning disability			attention deficit hyperactivity disorder		
	number with condition	percent with condition	percent distribution	number with condition	percent with condition	percent distribution
Children with disability	**4,943**	**8.0%**	**100.0%**	**5,876**	**9.5%**	**100.0%**
Sex						
Female	1,796	6.0	36.3	1,636	5.4	27.8
Male	3,146	10.0	63.6	4,239	13.5	72.1
Age						
Aged 3 to 4	192	2.4	3.9	136	1.7	2.3
Aged 5 to 11	2,338	8.1	47.3	2,726	9.5	46.4
Aged 12 to 17	2,413	9.7	48.8	3,014	12.2	51.3
Race and Hispanic origin						
Asian	65	2.2	1.3	77	2.6	1.3
Black	671	7.7	13.6	769	8.8	13.1
Hispanic	1,020	7.1	20.6	839	5.8	14.3
Non-Hispanic White	2,888	8.7	58.4	3,834	11.5	65.2
Family structure						
Mother and father	2,881	7.0	58.3	3,433	8.3	58.4
Mother, no father	1,623	10.5	32.8	1,911	12.4	32.5
Father, no mother	227	8.8	4.6	248	9.5	4.2
Neither mother nor father	211	10.2	4.3	283	13.1	4.8
Parent's education						
Less than high school diploma	814	11.0	16.5	537	7.2	9.1
High school diploma or GED	1,126	9.7	22.8	1,267	10.9	21.6
More than high school	2,783	6.9	56.3	3,779	9.4	64.3
Household income						
Less than $35,000	2,115	11.4	42.8	2,167	11.7	36.9
$35,000 to $49,999	719	9.4	14.5	874	11.5	14.9
$50,000 to $74,999	770	7.8	15.6	788	8.0	13.4
$75,000 to $99,999	381	4.8	7.7	611	7.7	10.4
$100,000 or more	839	5.7	17.0	1,311	8.8	22.3

Note: "Mother and father" includes biological, adoptive, step, in-law, or foster relationships. Legal guardians are classified as "neither mother nor father." Parent's education is the education level of the parent with the higher level of education. Race/Hispanic origin, education, and income categories do not sum to total because not all races are shown and those not reporting education or income are not shown.
Source: National Center for Health Statistics, Summary Health Statistics for U.S. Children: National Health Interview Survey, 2012, Series 10, No. 258, 2013, Internet site http://www.cdc.gov/nchs/nhis.htm

Table 3.21 Children Taking Prescription Medication by Selected Characteristics, 2012

(number, percent, and percent distribution of children under age 18 with who have taken prescription medication regularly for at least three months, by selected characteristics, 2012; numbers in thousands)

	number	percent of total children	percent distribution
Children taking prescription medication	**9,715**	**13.2%**	**100.0%**
Sex			
Female	4,086	11.3	42.1
Male	5,629	15.0	57.9
Age			
Aged 0 to 4	1,328	6.6	13.7
Aged 5 to 11	4,089	14.2	42.1
Aged 12 to 17	4,298	17.3	44.2
Race and Hispanic origin			
Asian	257	7.6	2.6
Black	1,664	15.9	17.1
Hispanic	1,536	8.9	15.8
Non-Hispanic White	5,760	14.6	59.3
Family structure			
Mother and father	5,858	11.8	60.3
Mother, no father	3,134	17.2	32.3
Father, no mother	372	12.5	3.8
Neither mother nor father	351	14.7	3.6
Parent's education			
Less than high school diploma	995	11.3	10.2
High school diploma or GED	1,816	13.1	18.7
More than high school	6,544	13.6	67.4
Household income			
Less than $35,000	3,491	15.4	35.9
$35,000 to $49,999	1,335	14.7	13.7
$50,000 to $74,999	1,417	12.0	14.6
$75,000 to $99,999	1,141	12.3	11.7
$100,000 or more	2,021	11.6	20.8

Note: "Mother and father" includes biological, adoptive, step, in-law, or foster relationships. Legal guardians are classified as "neither mother nor father." Parent's education is the education level of the parent with the higher level of education. Race/Hispanic origin, education, and income categories do not sum to total because not all races are shown and those not reporting education or income are not shown.

Source: National Center for Health Statistics, Summary Health Statistics for U.S. Children: National Health Interview Survey, 2012, Series 10, No. 258, 2013, Internet site http://www.cdc.gov/nchs/nhis.htm

Among Children, Accidents Are the Leading Cause of Death

Homicide is an important cause of death as well.

Once children have grown past infancy, accidents cause the largest share of deaths among children under age 15—which means a large portion of deaths in the age group are preventable. Among infants, congenital malformations are the leading cause of death.

In the 1-to-4 age group, accidents account for 32 percent of deaths, while congenital malformations rank second. Disturbingly, homicide is the third leading cause of death in the age group. Among 5-to-14-year-olds, accidents are the leading cause of death followed by cancer, congenital malformations, and suicide. Homicide ranks fifth as a cause of death among 5-to-14-year-olds.

■ As medical science tamed ailments that once killed many infants and children, accidents have become a more important cause of death.

Accidents are by far the leading cause of death among children aged 1 to 14

(percent of deaths due to the four leading causes of death among children by age, 2011)

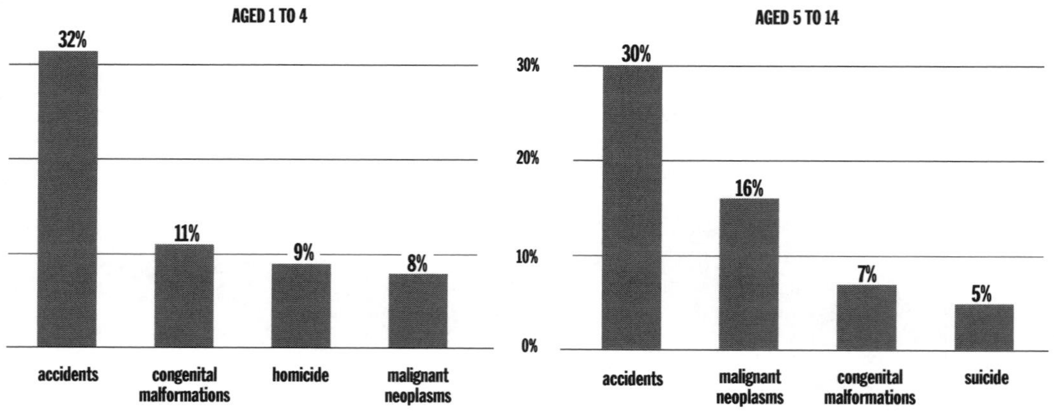

Table 3.22 Leading Causes of Death for Infants, 2011

(number and percent distribution of deaths accounted for by the 10 leading causes of death for children under age 1, 2011)

	number	percent distribution
All causes	**23,907**	**100.0%**
1. Congenital malformations	4,984	20.8
2. Disorders related to short gestation and low birth weight	4,116	17.2
3. Sudden infant death syndrome	1,711	7.2
4. Newborn affected by maternal complications of pregnancy	1,578	6.6
5. Accidents (5)	1,089	4.6
6. Newborn affected by complications of placenta, cord, or membranes	992	4.1
7. Bacterial sepsis of newborn	526	2.2
8. Respiratory distress of newborn	514	2.1
9. Diseases of circulatory system	496	2.1
10. Neonatal hemorrhage	444	1.9
All other causes	7,457	31.2

Note: Number in parentheses shows rank for all Americans if the cause of death is in top 10.
Source: National Center for Health Statistics, Deaths: Preliminary Data for 2011, National Vital Statistics Report, Vol. 61, No. 6, 2012, Internet site http://www.cdc.gov/nchs/deaths.htm; calculations by New Strategist

Table 3.23 Leading Causes of Death for Children Aged 1 to 4, 2011

(number and percent distribution of deaths accounted for by the 10 leading causes of death for children aged 1 to 4, 2011)

	number	percent distribution
All causes	**4,214**	**100.0%**
1. Accidents (5)	1,346	31.9
2. Congenital malformations	483	11.5
3. Homicide	370	8.8
4. Malignant neoplasms (cancer) (2)	352	8.4
5. Diseases of the heart (1)	158	3.7
6. Influenza and pneumonia (8)	96	2.3
7. Septicemia	59	1.4
8. Chronic lower respiratory diseases (3)	44	1.0
9. In situ neoplasms, benign neoplasms	43	1.0
10. Cerebrovascular diseases (4)	43	1.0
All other causes	1,220	29.0

Note: Number in parentheses shows rank for all Americans if the cause of death is in top 10.
Source: National Center for Health Statistics, Deaths: Preliminary Data for 2011, National Vital Statistics Report, Vol. 61, No. 6, 2012, Internet site http://www.cdc.gov/nchs/deaths.htm; calculations by New Strategist

Table 3.24 Leading Causes of Death for Children Aged 5 to 14, 2011

(number and percent distribution of deaths accounted for by the 10 leading causes of death for children aged 5 to 14, 2011)

	number	percent distribution
All causes	**5,395**	**100.0%**
1. Accidents (5)	1,613	29.9
2. Malignant neoplasms (cancer) (2)	865	16.0
3. Congenital malformations	356	6.6
4. Suicide (10)	281	5.2
5. Homicide	269	5.0
6. Diseases of the heart (1)	185	3.4
7. Chronic lower respiratory diseases (3)	134	2.5
8. Influenza and pneumonia (8)	112	2.1
9. Cerebrovascular diseases (4)	83	1.5
10. In situ neoplasms, benign neoplasms	72	1.3
All other causes	1,425	26.4

Note: Number in parentheses shows rank for all Americans if the cause of death is in top 10.
Source: National Center for Health Statistics, Deaths: Preliminary Data for 2011, National Vital Statistics Report, Vol. 61, No. 6, 2012, Internet site http://www.cdc.gov/nchs/deaths.htm; calculations by New Strategist

CHAPTER

14

Housing

■ Most families with children under age 18 own their home. The homeownership rate differs by age of child, however, and families with preschoolers have the lowest rate.

■ Youth under age 19 have a slightly higher mobility rate than the average person. Among Americans aged 1 or older, 11.7 percent moved from one house to another between March 2012 and March 2013. Among youth under age 19, the mobility rate was 13.1 percent.

■ Among children under age 16 who moved between 2012 and 2013, more than half (51 percent) moved for housing reasons.

Most Families with Children Are Homeowners

The rate is lowest among families with young children.

The homeownership rate of families with children is slightly below the overall homeownership rate. But the rate differs by age of children at home.

Among all families with children under age 18, 60.4 percent owned their home, slightly below the 63.9 percent of all households that were homeowners, according to the 2012 American Community Survey. The rate is lowest (50.1 percent) for families with preschoolers and no older children at home—in other words, the youngest parents. The rate peaks at 66.6 percent among families with school-aged children and no preschoolers—in other words, among older parents.

■ Families with children under age 18 account for 32 percent of renters and 27 percent of homeowners.

Among households with children, homeownership varies by age of child

(homeownership rate of families with children under age 18, by age of child, 2012)

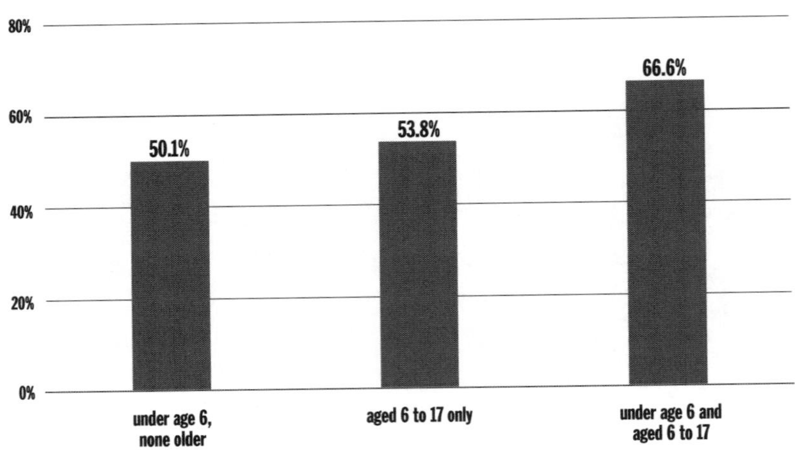

Table 14.1 Homeownership among Families with Children, 2012

(number and percent distribution of households by presence of own children under age 18 and homeownership status, 2012; numbers in thousands)

	total	owners	renters
Total households	**115,970**	**74,119**	**41,850**
With children under age 18	33,613	20,296	13,317
Under age 6 only	7,404	3,711	3,692
Under age 6 and aged 6 to 17	6,805	3,659	3,146
Aged 6 to 17 only	19,404	12,925	6,479
Without children under age 18	82,357	53,824	28,533
PERCENT DISTRIBUTION BY TENURE			
Total households	**100.0%**	**63.9%**	**36.1%**
With children under age 18	100.0	60.4	39.6
Under age 6 only	100.0	50.1	49.9
Under age 6 and aged 6 to 17	100.0	53.8	46.2
Aged 6 to 17 only	100.0	66.6	33.4
Without children under age 18	100.0	65.4	34.6

Source: Bureau of the Census, 2012 American Community Survey, Internet site http://factfinder2.census.gov/faces/nav/jsf/pages/index.xhtml; calculations by New Strategist

Older Children Are Less Likely to Move

Families try to stay put as children enter middle and high school.

Children under age 18 have a slightly higher mobility rate than the average person. Among all Americans aged 1 or older, 11.7 percent moved from one house to another between March 2012 and March 2013. Among youth under age 19, the mobility rate was 13.1 percent.

The mobility rate is highest for the youngest children because their parents are searching for bigger and better housing before their children start school. Seventeen percent of children aged 1 to 4 moved between 2012 and 2013. The figure falls as children age, bottoming out at 10 percent among 15-to-17-year-olds. The household mobility statistics confirm this pattern, with the mobility rate highest among families with preschoolers (20 percent) and lowest among families with school-aged children only (10 percent). The mobility rate rises among 18-to-19-year-olds because some are beginning to establish independent households.

Most moves are local, with movers remaining in the same county. Among children under age 16 who moved between 2012 and 2013, more than half (51 percent) moved for housing reasons. Family reasons ranked second, at 31 percent. The pattern is similar for teens aged 16 to 19, the largest share (47 percent) moving for housing reasons.

■ Among children who moved between 2012 and 2013, the single biggest reason was that their parents wanted a better home or apartment.

Among children, mobility rate is highest for preschoolers

(percent of people aged 1 to 17 who moved between March 2012 and March 2013, by age)

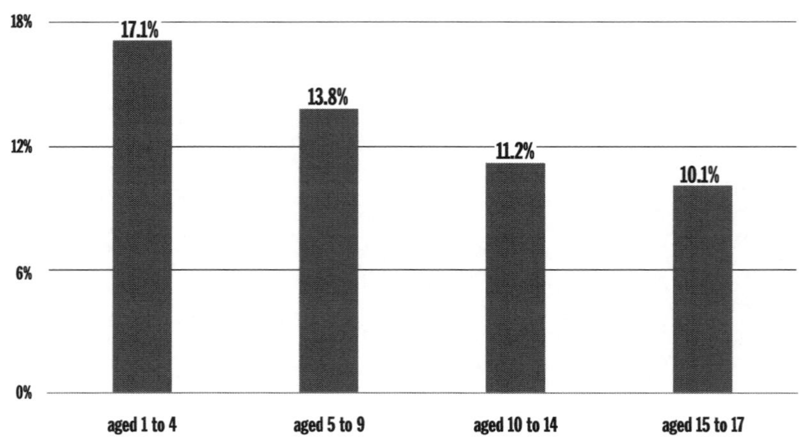

Table 14.2 Geographic Mobility by Generation, Age, and Type of Move, 2012–13

(number and percent distribution of people aged 1 or older, under age 19, and in age groups that include the iGeneration, by mobility status between March 2012 and March 2013; numbers in thousands)

	total	total movers	same county	different county, same state	different state: total	different state: same region	different state: different region	movers from abroad
Total, aged 1 or older	**307,243**	**35,918**	**23,150**	**6,961**	**4,770**	**2,323**	**2,447**	**1,036**
iGeneration (under age 19)	**74,252**	**9,735**	**6,627**	**1,677**	**1,167**	**598**	**570**	**263**
Aged 1 to 4	16,044	2,739	1,807	519	342	175	167	71
Aged 5 to 9	20,536	2,830	1,938	472	325	155	170	95
Aged 10 to 14	20,640	2,309	1,633	345	276	156	120	54
Aged 15 to 17	13,094	1,316	886	240	165	81	84	25
Aged 18 to 19	7,876	1,081	726	202	118	61	57	36
PERCENT DISTRIBUTION BY MOBILITY STATUS								
Total, aged 1 or older	**100.0%**	**11.7%**	**7.5%**	**2.3%**	**1.6%**	**0.8%**	**0.8%**	**0.3%**
iGeneration (under age 19)	**100.0**	**13.1**	**8.9**	**2.3**	**1.6**	**0.8**	**0.8**	**0.4**
Aged 1 to 4	100.0	17.1	11.3	3.2	2.1	1.1	1.0	0.4
Aged 5 to 9	100.0	13.8	9.4	2.3	1.6	0.8	0.8	0.5
Aged 10 to 14	100.0	11.2	7.9	1.7	1.3	0.8	0.6	0.3
Aged 15 to 17	100.0	10.1	6.8	1.8	1.3	0.6	0.6	0.2
Aged 18 to 19	100.0	13.7	9.2	2.6	1.5	0.8	0.7	0.5

Source: Bureau of the Census, Geographic Mobility: 2012 to 2013, Internet site http://www.census.gov/hhes/migration/data/cps/cps2013.html; calculations by New Strategist

Table 14.3 Movers among Children by Type of Move, 2012–13

(number and percent distribution of people aged 1 or older, under age 19, and in age groups that include the iGeneration who moved between March 2012 and March 2013, by type of move; numbers in thousands)

	total movers	same county	different county, same state	different state: total	different state: same region	different state: different region	movers from abroad
Total movers aged 1 or older	**35,918**	**23,150**	**6,961**	**4,770**	**2,323**	**2,447**	**1,036**
iGeneration (under age 19)	**9,735**	**6,627**	**1,677**	**1,167**	**598**	**570**	**263**
Aged 1 to 4	2,739	1,807	519	342	175	167	71
Aged 5 to 9	2,830	1,938	472	325	155	170	95
Aged 10 to 14	2,309	1,633	345	276	156	120	54
Aged 15 to 17	1,316	886	240	165	81	84	25
Aged 18 to 19	1,081	726	202	118	61	57	36
PERCENT DISTRIBUTION BY MOBILITY STATUS							
Total movers aged 1 or older	**100.0%**	**64.5%**	**19.4%**	**13.3%**	**6.5%**	**6.8%**	**2.9%**
iGeneration (under age 19)	**100.0**	**68.1**	**17.2**	**12.0**	**6.1**	**5.9**	**2.7**
Aged 1 to 4	100.0	66.0	18.9	12.5	6.4	6.1	2.6
Aged 5 to 9	100.0	68.5	16.7	11.5	5.5	6.0	3.4
Aged 10 to 14	100.0	70.7	14.9	12.0	6.8	5.2	2.3
Aged 15 to 17	100.0	67.3	18.2	12.5	6.2	6.4	1.9
Aged 18 to 19	100.0	67.2	18.7	10.9	5.6	5.3	3.3

Source: Bureau of the Census, Geographic Mobility: 2012 to 2013, Internet site http://www.census.gov/hhes/migration/data/cps/cps2013.html; calculations by New Strategist

Table 14.4 Geographic Mobility of Families with Children, 2012–13

(total number and percent distribution of family householders aged 15 to 54 by mobility status and presence of own children under age 18 at home, March 2012 to March 2013; numbers in thousands)

	total	total movers	same county	different county, same state	different state	movers from abroad
Total family householders	**51,011**	**6,679**	**4,433**	**1,210**	**872**	**164**
With children under age 18	33,176	4,529	3,074	810	536	110
Under age 6 only	7,946	1,625	1,067	312	208	38
Under age 6 and aged 6 to 17	6,872	993	674	179	113	28
Aged 6 to 17 only	18,358	1,911	1,333	319	215	44
Without children under age 18	17,834	2,149	1,359	400	337	53
PERCENT DISTRIBUTION BY MOBILITY STATUS						
Total family householders	**100.0%**	**13.1%**	**8.7%**	**2.4%**	**1.7%**	**0.3%**
With children under age 18	100.0	13.7	9.3	2.4	1.6	0.3
Under age 6 only	100.0	20.5	13.4	3.9	2.6	0.5
Under age 6 and aged 6 to 17	100.0	14.4	9.8	2.6	1.6	0.4
Aged 6 to 17 only	100.0	10.4	7.3	1.7	1.2	0.2
Without children under age 18	100.0	12.1	7.6	2.2	1.9	0.3
PERCENT DISTRIBUTION OF MOVERS BY TYPE OF MOVE						
Total family householders	–	**100.0**	**66.4**	**18.1**	**13.1**	**2.5**
With children under age 18	–	100.0	67.9	17.9	11.8	2.4
Under age 6 only	–	100.0	65.7	19.2	12.8	2.3
Under age 6 and aged 6 to 17	–	100.0	67.9	18.0	11.4	2.8
Aged 6 to 17 only	–	100.0	69.8	16.7	11.3	2.3
Without children under age 18	–	100.0	63.2	18.6	15.7	2.5

Note: "–" means not applicable.
Source: Bureau of the Census, Geographic Mobility: 2012 to 2013, Internet site http://www.census.gov/hhes/migration/data/cps/cps2013.html; calculations by New Strategist

Table 14.5 Reason for Moving among Children under Age 16, 2012–13

(number and percent distribution of movers under age 16 by primary reason household head moved and share of total movers between March 2012 and March 2013; numbers in thousands)

	total movers	movers under age 16		
		number	percent distribution	share of total
Total movers	**35,918**	**8,28**	**100.0%**	**23.2%**
Family reasons	10,871	2,565	30.8	23.6
Change in marital status	1,817	425	5.1	23.4
To establish own household	3,753	782	9.4	20.8
Other family reasons	5,301	1,358	16.3	25.6
Employment reasons	6,979	1,440	17.3	20.6
New job or job transfer	3,242	714	8.6	22.0
To look for work or lost job	750	165	2.0	22.0
To be closer to work/easier commute	1,941	351	4.2	18.1
Retired	237	14	0.2	5.9
Other job-related reason	809	196	2.4	24.2
Housing reasons	17,225	4,210	50.6	24.4
Wanted own home, not rent	2,099	543	6.5	25.9
Wanted better home/apartment	5,332	1,511	18.1	28.3
Wanted better neighborhood/less crime	1,135	308	3.7	27.1
Wanted cheaper housing	2,989	676	8.1	22.6
Foreclosure/eviction	654	160	1.9	24.5
Other housing reasons	5,016	1,012	12.2	20.2
Other reasons	844	113	1.4	13.4
To attend or leave college	215	5	0.1	2.3
Change of climate	20	6	0.1	30.0
Health reasons	136	10	0.1	7.4
Natural disaster	11	4	0.0	36.4
Other reasons	462	88	1.1	19.0

Source: Bureau of the Census, Geographic Mobility: 2012 to 2013, Internet site http://www.census.gov/hhes/migration/data/cps/cps2013.html; calculations by New Strategist

Table 14.6 Reason for Moving among People Aged 16 to 19, 2012–13

(number and percent distribution of movers aged 16 to 19 by primary reason for move and share of total movers between March 2012 and March 2013, by age; numbers in thousands)

	total movers	movers aged 16 to 19: number	percent distribution	share of total
Total movers	**35,918**	**1,948**	**100.0%**	**5.4%**
Family reasons	10,871	673	34.5	6.2
Change in marital status	1,817	98	5.0	5.4
To establish own household	3,753	207	10.6	5.5
Other family reasons	5,301	368	18.9	6.9
Employment reasons	6,979	285	14.6	4.1
New job or job transfer	3,242	124	6.4	3.8
To look for work or lost job	750	38	2.0	5.1
To be closer to work/easier commute	1,941	100	5.1	5.2
Retired	237	1	0.0	0.0
Other job-related reason	809	22	1.1	2.7
Housing reasons	17,225	913	46.9	5.3
Wanted own home, not rent	2,099	98	5.0	4.7
Wanted better home/apartment	5,332	237	12.2	4.4
Wanted better neighborhood/less crime	1,135	65	3.3	5.7
Wanted cheaper housing	2,989	167	8.6	5.6
Foreclosure/eviction	654	49	2.5	7.5
Other housing reasons	5,016	297	15.2	5.9
Other reasons	844	80	4.1	9.5
To attend or leave college	215	33	1.7	15.3
Change of climate	20	3	0.2	15.0
Health reasons	136	14	0.7	10.3
Natural disaster	11	0	0.0	0.0
Other reasons	462	30	1.5	6.5

Source: Bureau of the Census, Geographic Mobility: 2012 to 2013, Internet site http://www.census.gov/hhes/migration/data/cps/cps2013.html; calculations by New Strategist

CHAPTER

15

Income

■ The median income of households with children under age 18 ranged from a low of $26,148 for those in a female-headed family to a high of $84,916 for those in a married-couple family.

■ Regardless of family type, median income is higher for those without preschoolers in the household. Among couples with children aged 6 to 17 and none younger, median income exceeds $90,000.

■ The poverty rate of children under age 18 was 19.9 percent in 2013, much higher than the 14.5 percent national rate. The iGeneration accounts for about one-third of the nation's poor.

Families with Children Have Been Losing Ground

Families without children at home have also seen their median income decline.

Between 2000 and 2013, the median income of married couples with children under age 18 fell 3 percent, after adjusting for inflation. The median income of married couples without children at home fell 2 percent. The declines were even greater for male- and female-headed families with and without children.

Until 2007, the median income of married couples had been rising. When the Great Recession hit, the incomes of married couples began to fall. In contrast, the median income of male-headed families was declining well before the Great Recession, which exacerbated the loss. The median income of female-headed families with children under age 18 also began to decline before the Great Recession, but the incomes of female-headed families without children at home had been rising until 2007.

■ Some recovery may be evident in the 2013 income statistics, with higher incomes for married couples and male-headed families with children.

Among families with children under age 18, married couples have lost less than others

(percent change in median income of families with children under age 18 by family type, 2007 to 2013; in 2013 dollars)

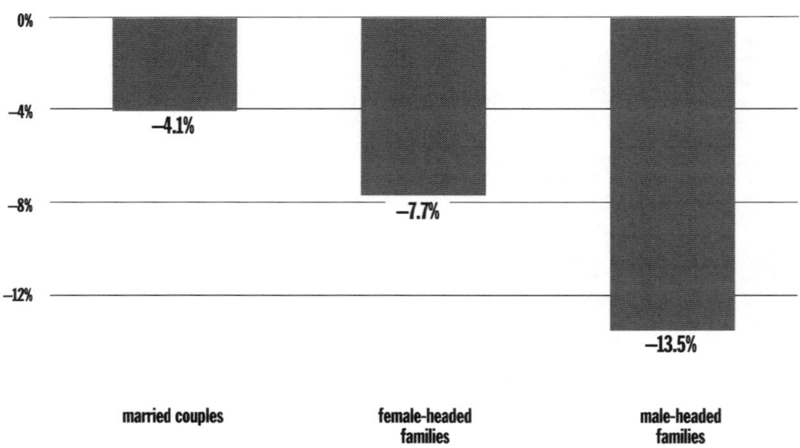

Table 15.1 Median Income of Married-Couple Families by Presence of Children, 2000 to 2013

(median income of married-couple families by presence of related children under age 18 at home, 2000 to 2013; percent change for selected years; in 2013 dollars)

	married couples		
	total	no children under age 18	with children under age 18
2013	$76,339	$70,803	$84,916
2012	76,633	71,932	82,639
2011	76,426	72,556	81,511
2010	77,182	73,204	82,668
2009	77,789	73,172	83,243
2008	78,701	74,153	84,081
2007	81,552	77,472	86,183
2006	80,186	74,361	85,553
2005	78,641	73,392	84,544
2004	78,466	73,410	83,634
2003	78,883	74,112	84,124
2002	79,154	73,671	84,682
2001	79,387	72,921	85,792
2000	79,944	73,401	85,391
PERCENT CHANGE			
2007 to 2013	–6.0%	–7.2%	–4.1%
2000 to 2013	–4.1	–2.0	–3.2

Note: Median incomes in this table are slightly different from the figures shown in the household income tables because these figures include the incomes of only the family members and not any unrelated members of the household.
Source: Bureau of the Census, Historical Income Data, Internet site http://www.census.gov/hhes/www/income/data/historical/index.html; calculations by New Strategist

Table 15.2 Median Income of Female-Headed Families by Presence of Children, 2000 to 2013

(median income of female-headed families by presence of related children under age 18 at home, 2000 to 2013; percent change for selected years; in 2013 dollars)

	female-headed families, no spouse present		
	total	no children under age 18	with children under age 18
2013	$31,408	$43,546	$26,148
2012	31,132	42,759	25,863
2011	31,340	43,278	26,259
2010	31,149	41,920	26,037
2009	32,331	42,763	27,338
2008	32,597	44,705	27,656
2007	34,037	49,890	28,030
2006	33,308	47,967	28,184
2005	32,508	46,695	27,601
2004	33,259	45,689	28,868
2003	33,627	46,137	28,656
2002	34,214	46,518	29,312
2001	33,874	46,402	28,943
2000	34,786	46,562	29,645
PERCENT CHANGE			
2007 to 2013	–8.5%	–14.3%	–7.7%
2000 to 2013	–10.5	–8.2	–12.8

Note: Median incomes in this table are slightly different from the figures shown in the household income tables because these figures include the incomes of only the family members and not any unrelated members of the household.
Source: Bureau of the Census, Historical Income Data, Internet site http://www.census.gov/hhes/www/income/data/historical/index .html; calculations by New Strategist

Table 15.3 Median Income of Male-Headed Families by Presence of Children, 2000 to 2013

(median income of male-headed families by presence of related children under age 18 at home, 2000 to 2013; percent change for selected years; in 2013 dollars)

	male-headed families, no spouse present		
	total	no children under age 18	with children under age 18
2013	$44,475	$47,891	$40,868
2012	42,974	50,055	37,001
2011	44,608	52,820	39,531
2010	46,161	55,327	38,846
2009	45,071	53,158	39,189
2008	47,140	53,725	41,404
2007	49,835	57,811	42,786
2006	48,345	56,075	43,196
2005	49,055	57,780	43,634
2004	49,775	55,855	44,889
2003	48,170	56,936	40,420
2002	48,866	57,410	41,635
2001	48,144	57,720	42,015
2000	51,034	60,279	43,940
PERCENT CHANGE			
2007 to 2013	−13.8%	−13.4%	−13.5%
2000 to 2013	−15.8	−17.0	−15.8

Note: Median incomes in this table are slightly different from the figures shown in the household income tables because these figures include the incomes of only the family members and not any unrelated members of the household.
Source: Bureau of the Census, Historical Income Data, Internet site http://www.census.gov/hhes/www/income/data/historical/index.html; calculations by New Strategist

Married Couples with Children Have Above-Average Incomes

Single parents have below-average incomes.

The financial wellbeing of children depends greatly on the type of household in which they live. Those living with married parents are far better off than those living in other types of households. Among households with children under age 18, the median income of married couples stood at $84,916 in 2013. This compares with a median of $40,868 for male-headed families and just $26,148 for female-headed families.

Married couples with children aged 6 to 17 and none younger have the highest incomes, a median of $90,898 in 2013. Forty-four percent have incomes of $100,000 or more. The incomes of male- and female-headed families with school-aged children also surpass the incomes of those with preschoolers. Most householders with school-aged children are in their peak earning years, which accounts for their above-average incomes. Female-headed families with a combination of preschoolers and school-aged children have the lowest incomes—a median of just $20,287 in 2013.

■ Regardless of family type, incomes have declined in the aftermath of the Great Recession.

Single-parent families have the lowest incomes

(median income of families with children under age 18 by family type, 2013)

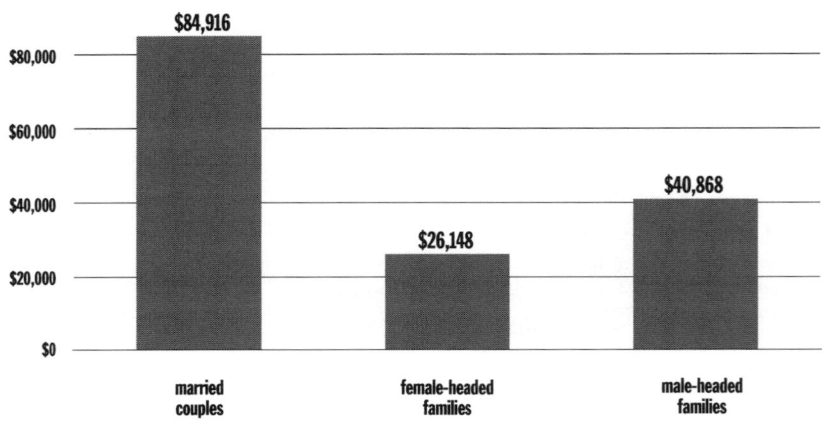

Table 15.4 Income of Households with Children under Age 18 by Household Type, 2013

(number and percent distribution of households with children under age 18 at home, by household income and household type, 2013; households in thousands as of 2014)

	married couples	female-headed families	male-headed families
Total households with children	**25,335**	**9,930**	**3,080**
Under $10,000	421	2,002	230
$10,000 to $19,999	853	1,884	344
$20,000 to $29,999	1,390	1,651	513
$30,000 to $39,999	1,704	1,292	403
$40,000 to $49,999	1,887	848	336
$50,000 to $59,999	1,826	659	231
$60,000 to $69,999	1,833	392	192
$70,000 to $79,999	1,911	360	171
$80,000 to $89,999	1,689	161	128
$90,000 to $99,999	1,587	153	121
$100,000 or more	10,234	528	412
$100,000 to $124,999	3,291	240	167
$125,000 to $149,999	2,134	143	88
$150,000 to $174,999	1,572	56	70
$175,000 to $199,999	844	28	16
$200,000 or more	2,393	61	70
Median income	**$84,916**	**$26,148**	**$40,868**
PERCENT DISTRIBUTION			
Total households with children	**100.0%**	**100.0%**	**100.0%**
Under $10,000	1.7	20.2	7.5
$10,000 to $19,999	3.4	19.0	11.2
$20,000 to $29,999	5.5	16.6	16.7
$30,000 to $39,999	6.7	13.0	13.1
$40,000 to $49,999	7.4	8.5	10.9
$50,000 to $59,999	7.2	6.6	7.5
$60,000 to $69,999	7.2	4.0	6.2
$70,000 to $79,999	7.5	3.6	5.5
$80,000 to $89,999	6.7	1.6	4.2
$90,000 to $99,999	6.3	1.5	3.9
$100,000 or more	40.4	5.3	13.4
$100,000 to $124,999	13.0	2.4	5.4
$125,000 to $149,999	8.4	1.4	2.9
$150,000 to $174,999	6.2	0.6	2.3
$175,000 to $199,999	3.3	0.3	0.5
$200,000 or more	9.4	0.6	2.3

Note: The median income of married couples in this table is slightly different from the figure shown in the household income tables because this figure includes the incomes only of family members and not any unrelated members of the household.
Source: Bureau of the Census, 2014 Current Population Survey, Internet site http://www.census.gov/hhes/www/income/data/index.html; calculations by New Strategist

Table 15.5 Married Couples with Children by Family Income and Age of Children, 2013

(number and percent distribution of total married couples and married couples with related children under age 18 by family income and age of related children, 2013; married couples in thousands as of 2014)

		one or more children under age 18			
	total	total	all under 6	some under 6, some 6 to 17	all 6 to 17
Total married couples	**59,692**	**25,335**	**5,976**	**5,356**	**14,003**
Under $10,000	1,206	421	116	104	200
$10,000 to $19,999	2,481	853	220	224	409
$20,000 to $29,999	3,999	1,390	362	349	679
$30,000 to $39,999	4,790	1,704	397	495	811
$40,000 to $49,999	4,944	1,887	506	508	873
$50,000 to $59,999	4,824	1,826	426	453	946
$60,000 to $69,999	4,588	1,833	447	418	968
$70,000 to $79,999	4,546	1,911	474	375	1,062
$80,000 to $89,999	3,848	1,689	387	355	947
$90,000 to $99,999	3,467	1,587	370	335	882
$100,000 or more	20,998	10,234	2,270	1,738	6,225
$100,000 to $124,999	6,775	3,291	761	598	1,933
$125,000 to $149,999	4,377	2,134	498	346	1,290
$150,000 to $174,999	3,234	1,572	347	260	964
$175,000 to $199,999	1,840	844	179	148	517
$200,000 or more	4,772	2,393	486	387	1,520
Median income	**$76,339**	**$84,916**	**$80,783**	**$72,664**	**$90,898**
PERCENT DISTRIBUTION					
Total married couples	**100.0%**	**100.0%**	**100.0%**	**100.0%**	**100.0%**
Under $10,000	2.0	1.7	1.9	2.0	1.4
$10,000 to $19,999	4.2	3.4	3.7	4.2	2.9
$20,000 to $29,999	6.7	5.5	6.1	6.5	4.8
$30,000 to $39,999	8.0	6.7	6.6	9.2	5.8
$40,000 to $49,999	8.3	7.4	8.5	9.5	6.2
$50,000 to $59,999	8.1	7.2	7.1	8.5	6.8
$60,000 to $69,999	7.7	7.2	7.5	7.8	6.9
$70,000 to $79,999	7.6	7.5	7.9	7.0	7.6
$80,000 to $89,999	6.4	6.7	6.5	6.6	6.8
$90,000 to $99,999	5.8	6.3	6.2	6.3	6.3
$100,000 or more	35.2	40.4	38.0	32.5	44.5
$100,000 to $124,999	11.4	13.0	12.7	11.2	13.8
$125,000 to $149,999	7.3	8.4	8.3	6.5	9.2
$150,000 to $174,999	5.4	6.2	5.8	4.9	6.9
$175,000 to $199,999	3.1	3.3	3.0	2.8	3.7
$200,000 or more	8.0	9.4	8.1	7.2	10.9

Note: The median income of married couples in this table is slightly different from the figure shown in the household income tables because this figure includes the incomes only of family members and not any unrelated members of the household.
Source: Bureau of the Census, 2014 Current Population Survey, Internet site http://www.census.gov/hhes/www/income/data/index .html; calculations by New Strategist

Table 15.6 Female-Headed Families with Children by Family Income and Age of Children, 2013

(number and percent distribution of total female-headed families and female-headed families with related children under age 18 by family income and age of related children, 2013; female-headed families in thousands as of 2014)

		one or more children under age 18			
	total	total	all under 6	some under 6, some 6 to 17	all 6 to 17
Total female-headed families	**15,195**	**9,930**	**2,179**	**1,950**	**5,801**
Under $10,000	2,356	2,002	605	532	865
$10,000 to $19,999	2,558	1,884	436	429	1,018
$20,000 to $29,999	2,330	1,651	304	361	986
$30,000 to $39,999	1,991	1,292	245	220	827
$40,000 to $49,999	1,468	848	158	139	551
$50,000 to $59,999	1,123	659	117	59	483
$60,000 to $69,999	828	392	74	45	274
$70,000 to $79,999	695	360	94	47	218
$80,000 to $89,999	382	161	17	22	122
$90,000 to $99,999	301	153	34	13	107
$100,000 or more	1,163	528	94	84	351
$100,000 to $124,999	525	240	32	30	178
$125,000 to $149,999	317	143	31	31	82
$150,000 to $174,999	136	56	14	17	25
$175,000 to $199,999	67	28	6	2	20
$200,000 or more	118	61	11	5	45
Median income	**$31,408**	**$26,148**	**$21,235**	**$20,287**	**$30,287**
PERCENT DISTRIBUTION					
Total female-headed families	**100.0%**	**100.0%**	**100.0%**	**100.0%**	**100.0%**
Under $10,000	15.5	20.2	27.8	27.3	14.9
$10,000 to $19,999	16.8	19.0	20.0	22.0	17.5
$20,000 to $29,999	15.3	16.6	14.0	18.5	17.0
$30,000 to $39,999	13.1	13.0	11.2	11.3	14.3
$40,000 to $49,999	9.7	8.5	7.3	7.1	9.5
$50,000 to $59,999	7.4	6.6	5.4	3.0	8.3
$60,000 to $69,999	5.4	4.0	3.4	2.3	4.7
$70,000 to $79,999	4.6	3.6	4.3	2.4	3.8
$80,000 to $89,999	2.5	1.6	0.8	1.1	2.1
$90,000 to $99,999	2.0	1.5	1.5	0.6	1.8
$100,000 or more	7.7	5.3	4.3	4.3	6.0
$100,000 to $124,999	3.5	2.4	1.5	1.5	3.1
$125,000 to $149,999	2.1	1.4	1.4	1.6	1.4
$150,000 to $174,999	0.9	0.6	0.6	0.9	0.4
$175,000 to $199,999	0.4	0.3	0.3	0.1	0.3
$200,000 or more	0.8	0.6	0.5	0.2	0.8

Note: The median income of female-headed families in this table is slightly different from the figure shown in the household income tables because this figure includes the incomes only of family members and not any unrelated members of the household.
Source: Bureau of the Census, 2014 Current Population Survey, Internet site http://www.census.gov/hhes/www/income/data/index .html; calculations by New Strategist

Table 15.7 Male-Headed Families with Children by Family Income and Age of Children, 2013

(number and percent distribution of total male-headed families and male-headed families with related children under age 18 by family income and age of related children, 2013; male-headed families in thousands as of 2014)

		one or more children under age 18			
	total	total	all under 6	some under 6, some 6 to 17	all 6 to 17
Total male-headed families	**6,330**	**3,080**	**906**	**394**	**1,780**
Under $10,000	448	230	97	27	105
$10,000 to $19,999	660	344	91	54	199
$20,000 to $29,999	866	513	195	73	245
$30,000 to $39,999	855	403	137	49	217
$40,000 to $49,999	698	336	98	41	196
$50,000 to $59,999	517	231	69	28	134
$60,000 to $69,999	435	192	37	40	115
$70,000 to $79,999	372	171	52	11	108
$80,000 to $89,999	271	128	30	15	82
$90,000 to $99,999	242	121	17	13	91
$100,000 or more	967	412	82	43	287
$100,000 to $124,999	393	167	39	13	115
$125,000 to $149,999	236	88	7	16	65
$150,000 to $174,999	127	70	16	5	50
$175,000 to $199,999	52	16	2	0	14
$200,000 or more	158	70	18	9	43
Median income	**$44,475**	**$40,868**	**$33,029**	**$38,864**	**$45,277**
PERCENT DISTRIBUTION					
Total male-headed families	**100.0%**	**100.0%**	**100.0%**	**100.0%**	**100.0%**
Under $10,000	7.1	7.5	10.7	7.0	5.9
$10,000 to $19,999	10.4	11.2	10.1	13.6	11.2
$20,000 to $29,999	13.7	16.7	21.5	18.5	13.8
$30,000 to $39,999	13.5	13.1	15.1	12.5	12.2
$40,000 to $49,999	11.0	10.9	10.9	10.5	11.0
$50,000 to $59,999	8.2	7.5	7.6	7.0	7.5
$60,000 to $69,999	6.9	6.2	4.1	10.0	6.5
$70,000 to $79,999	5.9	5.5	5.8	2.7	6.1
$80,000 to $89,999	4.3	4.2	3.3	3.9	4.6
$90,000 to $99,999	3.8	3.9	1.9	3.3	5.1
$100,000 or more	15.3	13.4	9.0	10.9	16.1
$100,000 to $124,999	6.2	5.4	4.3	3.3	6.5
$125,000 to $149,999	3.7	2.9	0.7	4.1	3.7
$150,000 to $174,999	2.0	2.3	1.8	1.2	2.8
$175,000 to $199,999	0.8	0.5	0.2	0.0	0.8
$200,000 or more	2.5	2.3	2.0	2.4	2.4

Note: The median income of male-headed families in this table is slightly different from the figure shown in the household income tables because this figure includes the incomes only of family members and not any unrelated members of the household.
Source: Bureau of the Census, 2014 Current Population Survey, Internet site http://www.census.gov/hhes/www/income/data/index.html; calculations by New Strategist

Children Have the Highest Poverty Rate

The iGeneration accounts for nearly one-third of the nation's poor.

Children are much more likely to be poor than middle-aged or older adults. While 14.5 percent of all Americans were poor in 2013, the poverty rate among children under age 18 (the iGeneration was under age 19 in 2013) was a larger 19.9 percent. Black and Hispanic children are much more likely to be poor (36.9 and 30.4 percent, respectively) than non-Hispanic Whites or Asians (10.7 and 9.6 percent, respectively). Non-Hispanic Whites account for only 28 percent of the iGen poor.

Children under age 18 who live in families headed by married couples are much less likely to be poor than those in single-parent families. Only 7.6 percent of children in married-couple families were poor in 2013 versus 39.6 percent of those in female-headed families. Among Black children living in a married-couple family, the poverty rate is 12.9 percent. Among those living in a female-headed single-parent family, the poverty rate is 46.7 percent.

■ The poverty rate for the iGeneration is well above average because many live in female-headed families—the poorest household type.

In the iGeneration, non-Hispanic Whites have the lowest poverty rate

(percent of people under age 18 living below poverty level, by race and Hispanic origin, 2013)

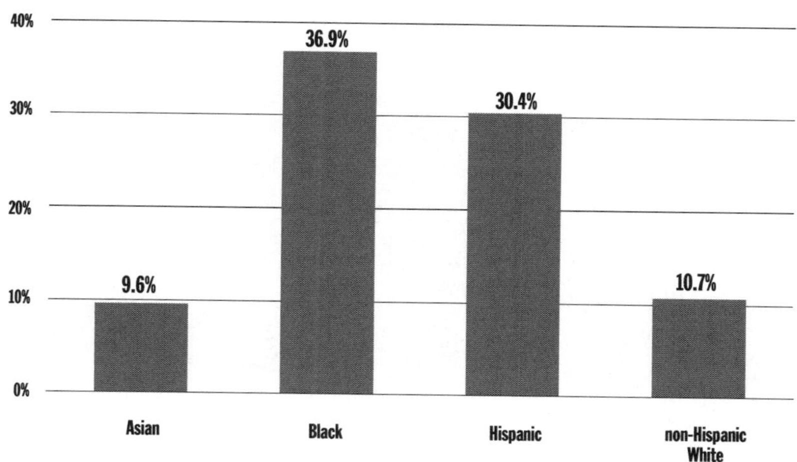

Table 15.8 People below Poverty Level by Age, Race, and Hispanic Origin, 2013

(number, percent, and percent distribution of people under age 18 below poverty level by race and Hispanic origin, 2013; people in thousands as of 2014)

NUMBER IN POVERTY	total	Asian	Black	Hispanic	non-Hispanic White
Total people	**45,318**	**1,974**	**11,959**	**12,744**	**18,796**
Under age 18	14,659	457	4,838	5,415	4,094
Aged 18 to 64	26,429	1,258	6,410	6,654	12,133
Aged 65 or older	4,231	259	712	676	2,569
PERCENT IN POVERTY					
Total people	**14.5%**	**10.4%**	**27.1%**	**23.5%**	**9.6%**
Under age 18	19.9	9.6	36.9	30.4	10.7
Aged 18 to 64	13.6	10.2	23.8	20.2	9.9
Aged 65 or older	9.5	13.6	17.4	19.8	7.4
PERCENT DISTRIBUTION OF POOR BY AGE					
Total in poverty	**100.0**	**100.0**	**100.0**	**100.0**	**100.0**
Under age 18	32.3	23.2	40.5	42.5	21.8
Aged 18 to 64	58.3	63.7	53.6	52.2	64.6
Aged 65 or older	9.3	13.1	6.0	5.3	13.7
PERCENT DISTRIBUTION OF POOR BY RACE AND HISPANIC ORIGIN					
Total in poverty	**100.0**	**4.4**	**26.4**	**28.1**	**41.5**
Under age 18	100.0	3.1	33.0	36.9	27.9
Aged 18 to 64	100.0	4.8	24.3	25.2	45.9
Aged 65 or older	100.0	6.1	16.8	16.0	60.7

Note: Numbers do not add to total because Asians and Blacks are those who identify themselves as being of the race alone and those who identify themselves as being of the race in combination with other races. Non-Hispanic Whites are those who identify themselves as being White alone and not Hispanic. Hispanics may be of any race.
Source: Bureau of the Census, Poverty, Internet site http://www.census.gov/hhes/www/cpstables/032014/pov/toc.htm; calculations by New Strategist

Table 15.9 Families with Children in Poverty by Family Type, Race, and Hispanic Origin, 2013

(number and percent of families with children under age 18 in poverty, and percent distribution of families with children in poverty, by type of family and race and Hispanic origin of householder, 2013; families in thousands as of 2014)

NUMBER IN POVERTY	total	Asian	Black	Hispanic	non-Hispanic White
Total families with children in poverty	**6,482**	**245**	**1,918**	**2,088**	**2,275**
Married couples	1,937	133	302	809	700
Female householders, no spouse present	3,937	86	1,445	1,107	1,337
Male householders, no spouse present	607	26	170	172	238
PERCENT IN POVERTY					
Total families with children	**16.9%**	**10.2%**	**31.9%**	**26.9%**	**10.3%**
Married couples	7.6	6.8	12.9	17.5	4.3
Female householders, no spouse present	39.6	28.1	46.7	46.5	31.6
Male householders, no spouse present	19.7	20.1	28.9	22.6	14.7
PERCENT DISTRIBUTION OF FAMILIES IN POVERTY BY RACE AND HISPANIC ORIGIN					
Total families with children in poverty	**100.0**	**3.8**	**29.6**	**32.2**	**35.1**
Married couples	100.0	6.9	15.6	41.8	36.1
Female householders, no spouse present	100.0	2.2	36.7	28.1	34.0
Male householders, no spouse present	100.0	4.3	28.0	28.3	39.2
PERCENT DISTRIBUTION OF FAMILIES IN POVERTY BY FAMILY TYPE					
Total families with children in poverty	**100.0**	**100.0**	**100.0**	**100.0**	**100.0**
Married couples	29.9	54.3	15.7	38.7	30.8
Female householders, no spouse present	60.7	35.1	75.3	53.0	58.8
Male householders, no spouse present	9.4	10.6	8.9	8.2	10.5

Note: Numbers do not add to total because Asians and Blacks are those who identify themselves as being of the race alone and those who identify themselves as being of the race in combination with other races. Non-Hispanic Whites are those who identify themselves as being White alone and not Hispanic. Hispanics may be of any race.
Source: Bureau of the Census, Poverty, Internet site http://www.census.gov/hhes/www/cpstables/032014/pov/toc.htm; calculations by New Strategist

CHAPTER

16

Labor Force

■ The youthful iGeneration accounted for only 3 percent of the labor force in 2013, the same share as the oldest Americans (aged 68 or older).

■ Most of the iGeneration is under age 18 and most have working parents. Among women with children under age 18, nearly 70 percent were in the labor force in 2013.

■ The 59 percent majority of married couples with children under age 18 are dual earners. Only 31 percent are "traditional," meaning only the father is employed.

■ Among children under age 5 with working mothers, the largest share is in center-based day care. Grandparent care is the second most common arrangement.

■ Among preschoolers with working mothers, those whose mothers are college-educated are most likely to be in center-based care.

Most of the iGeneration Is Too Young to Work

The iGeneration accounts for only 3 percent of the labor force.

In 2013, only 4 million of the 155 million Americans in the labor force were members of the iGeneration. The labor force is defined as people aged 16 or older who are working or looking for work. The oldest members of the iGeneration were aged 18 in 2013, which is why the generation is such a small share of the labor force. Of the 12.6 million iGens aged 16 to 18, only 4.3 million were in the labor force.

Among iGen men, non-Hispanic Whites are most likely to be in the labor force (38 percent) and Asians least likely (23 percent). Among iGen women, the pattern is the same with 40 percent of non-Hispanic Whites in the labor force compared with only 20 percent of Asians.

■ Unemployment is higher in the iGeneration than in any other generation. Among 16-to-18-year-olds in the labor force, 23 percent are unemployed.

The iGeneration and older Americans account for the same small share of the labor force

(percent distribution of the labor force by generation, 2013)

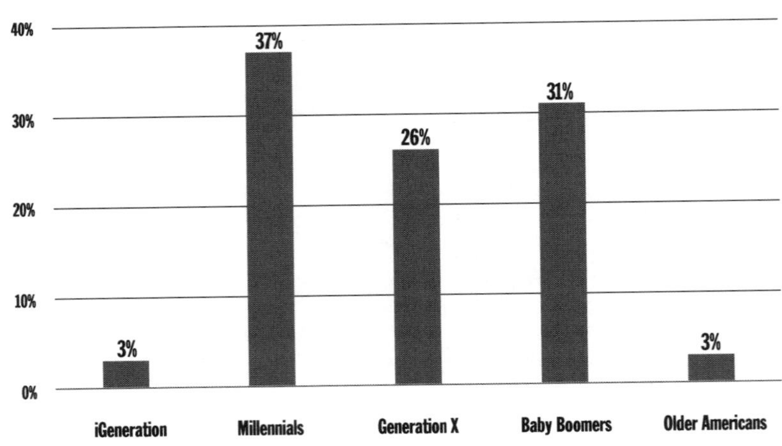

Table 16.1 Employment Status of the iGeneration by Sex, 2013

(number and percent of people aged 16 or older, aged 16 to 18, and in age groups that include the iGeneration, by sex and employment status, 2013; numbers in thousands)

	civilian noninstitutional population	civilian labor force					not in labor force	
					unemployed			
		total	percent of population	employed	number	percent of labor force	number	percent of population
Total aged 16 or older	**245,679**	**155,389**	**63.2%**	**143,929**	**11,460**	**7.4%**	**90,290**	**36.8%**
iGeneration (aged 16 to 18)	**12,590**	**4,339**	**34.5**	**3,344**	**995**	**22.9**	**8,252**	**65.5**
Aged 16 to 17	8,943	2,023	22.6	1,487	536	26.5	6,920	77.4
Aged 18 to 19	7,845	3,762	48.0	2,971	791	21.0	4,082	52.0
Men aged 16 or older	**118,555**	**82,667**	**69.7**	**76,353**	**6,314**	**7.6**	**35,889**	**30.3**
iGeneration (aged 16 to 18)	**6,404**	**2,192**	**34.2**	**1,633**	**560**	**25.5**	**4,211**	**65.8**
Aged 16 to 17	4,532	987	21.8	700	287	29.1	3,545	78.2
Aged 18 to 19	4,006	1,936	48.3	1,477	459	23.7	2,071	51.7
Women aged 16 or older	**127,124**	**72,722**	**57.2**	**67,577**	**5,146**	**7.1**	**54,401**	**42.8**
iGeneration (aged 16 to 18)	**6,187**	**2,147**	**34.7**	**1,711**	**436**	**20.3**	**4,040**	**65.3**
Aged 16 to 17	4,410	1,036	23.5	787	249	24.0	3,375	76.5
Aged 18 to 19	3,838	1,826	47.6	1,494	332	18.2	2,012	52.4

Source: Bureau of Labor Statistics, Labor Force Statistics from the Current Population Survey, Internet site http://www.bls.gov/cps/tables.htm#empstat; calculations by New Strategist

Table 16.2 Employment Status of iGeneration Men by Race, Hispanic Origin, and Age, 2013

(number and percent of men aged 16 or older, aged 16 to 18, and in age groups that include the iGeneration, by race, Hispanic origin, and employment status, 2013; numbers in thousands)

	civilian noninstitutional population	civilian labor force					not in labor force	
					unemployed			
		total	percent of population	employed	number	percent of labor force	number	percent of population
Asian men aged 16 or older	**6,225**	**4,547**	**73.0%**	**4,294**	**253**	**5.6%**	**1,678**	**27.0%**
Asian iGeneration (aged 16 to 18)	**308**	**70**	**22.7**	**55**	**15**	**21.5**	**238**	**77.3**
Aged 16 to 17	191	17	9.1	13	4	–	173	90.6
Aged 18 to 19	219	75	34.3	60	15	20.3	144	65.8
Black men aged 16 or older	**13,747**	**8,733**	**63.5**	**7,497**	**1,236**	**14.2**	**5,014**	**36.5**
Black iGeneration (aged 16 to 18)	**957**	**260**	**27.2**	**144**	**116**	**44.4**	**697**	**72.8**
Aged 16 to 17	685	105	15.3	51	54	51.2	580	84.7
Aged 18 to 19	591	242	40.9	141	101	41.6	349	59.1
Hispanic men aged 16 or older	**18,798**	**14,341**	**76.3**	**13,078**	**1,263**	**8.8**	**4,457**	**23.7**
Hispanic iGeneration (aged 16 to 18)	**1,403**	**460**	**32.8**	**330**	**130**	**28.2**	**943**	**67.2**
Aged 16 to 17	988	169	17.1	111	58	34.5	819	82.9
Aged 18 to 19	882	444	50.4	329	115	25.8	438	49.7
Non-Hispanic White men aged 16 or older	**76,067**	**52,501**	**69.0**	**49,244**	**3,257**	**6.2**	**23,567**	**31.0**
Non-Hispanic White iGeneration (aged 16 to 18)	**3,391**	**1,293**	**38.1**	**1,028**	**265**	**20.5**	**2,098**	**61.9**
Aged 16 to 17	2,425	652	26.9	497	155	23.8	1,773	73.1
Aged 18 to 19	2,096	1,072	51.1	874	198	18.5	1,025	48.9

Note: Race is shown only for those who identify themselves as being of the race alone. People who selected more than one race are not included. Hispanics may be of any race. Non-Hispanic Whites are estimated by subtracting Hispanics from Whites. "–" means data are not available.
Source: Bureau of Labor Statistics, Labor Force Statistics from the Current Population Survey, Internet site http://www.bls.gov/cps/tables.htm#empstat; calculations by New Strategist

Table 16.3 Employment Status of iGeneration Women by Race, Hispanic Origin, and Age, 2013

(number and percent of women aged 16 or older, aged 16 to 18, and in age groups that include the iGeneration, by race, Hispanic origin, and employment status, 2013; numbers in thousands)

		civilian labor force					not in labor force	
					unemployed			
	civilian noninstitutional population	total	percent of population	employed	number	percent of labor force	number	percent of population
Asian women aged 16 or older	**7,071**	**4,037**	**57.1%**	**3,842**	**195**	**4.8%**	**3,034**	**42.9%**
Asian iGeneration (aged 16 to 18)	**306**	**62**	**20.3**	**51**	**11**	**18.1**	**244**	**79.7**
Aged 16 to 17	226	28	12.5	24	4	–	198	87.6
Aged 18 to 19	181	55	30.2	44	11	19.3	127	70.2
Black women aged 16 or older	**16,629**	**9,846**	**59.2**	**8,654**	**1,192**	**12.1**	**6,783**	**40.8**
Black iGeneration (aged 16 to 18)	**967**	**278**	**28.7**	**185**	**93**	**33.5**	**689**	**71.3**
Aged 16 to 17	659	113	17.2	66	47	41.6	546	82.9
Aged 18 to 19	630	257	40.8	180	77	29.8	373	59.2
Hispanic women aged 16 or older	**18,719**	**10,430**	**55.7**	**9,437**	**994**	**9.5**	**8,289**	**44.3**
Hispanic iGeneration (aged 16 to 18)	**1,336**	**390**	**29.2**	**286**	**104**	**26.7**	**946**	**70.8**
Aged 16 to 17	923	159	17.2	107	52	33.0	764	82.8
Aged 18 to 19	858	361	42.0	274	86	23.9	497	57.9
Non-Hispanic White women aged 16 or older	**80,748**	**46,141**	**57.1**	**43,620**	**2,519**	**5.5**	**34,608**	**42.9**
Non-Hispanic White iGeneration (aged 16 to 18)	**3,245**	**1,313**	**40.5**	**1,109**	**204**	**15.5**	**1,931**	**59.5**
Aged 16 to 17	2,354	689	29.3	558	131	19.0	1,665	70.7
Aged 18 to 19	1,972	1,062	53.9	921	142	13.4	910	46.1

Note: Race is shown only for those who identify themselves as being of the race alone. People who selected more than one race are not included. Hispanics may be of any race. Non-Hispanic Whites are estimated by subtracting Hispanics from Whites. "–" means data are not available.

Source: Bureau of Labor Statistics, Labor Force Statistics from the Current Population Survey, Internet site http://www.bls.gov/cps/tables.htm#empstat; calculations by New Strategist

Most Children Have Working Parents

For the iGeneration, working mothers are by far the norm.

Most of the iGeneration is children, and most of those children have working mothers. Among women with children under age 18, nearly 70 percent were in the labor force in 2013 (the iGeneration was aged 5 to 18 in that year). Sixty-five percent of women with children under age 18 are employed, most working full-time. Even among women with preschoolers, 64 percent are in the labor force, and most workers have a full-time job.

Fifty-nine percent of married couples with children under age 18 are dual earners. In just 31 percent, the father is the only employed parent. Children in single-parent families also have parents who work. Sixty-eight percent of women who head single-parent families have a job, as do 81 percent of their male counterparts.

■ With working parents the norm, family life is highly scheduled.

For most children in a married-couple family, both mom and dad work

(percent distribution of married couples with children under age 18 by labor force status, 2013)

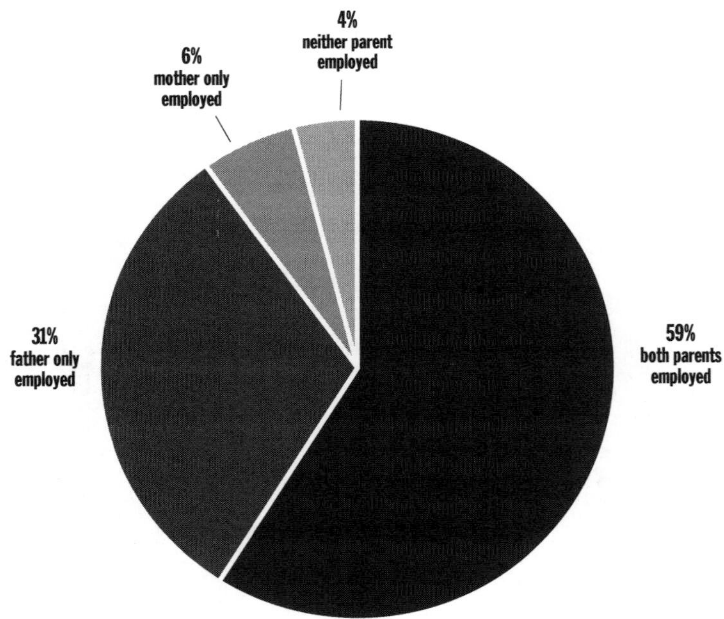

Table 16.4 Labor Force Status of Women by Presence of Children, 2013

(number and percent distribution of women aged 16 or older by labor force status and presence and age of own children under age 18 at home, 2013; numbers in thousands)

		civilian labor force				
			employed			
	civilian population	total	total	full-time	part-time	not in labor force
Total women	**127,124**	**72,722**	**67,577**	**49,979**	**17,598**	**54,402**
No children under age 18	90,686	47,256	43,971	32,342	11,629	43,430
With children under age 18	36,438	25,466	23,606	17,637	5,969	10,972
Children aged 6 to 17, none younger	20,212	15,101	14,169	10,819	3,349	5,111
Children under age 6	16,226	10,365	9,437	6,817	2,620	5,861
Children under age 3	9,211	5,626	5,113	3,615	1,497	3,585
Children under age 1	3,069	1,757	1,593	1,124	469	1,312
PERCENT DISTRIBUTION BY LABOR FORCE STATUS						
Total women	**100.0%**	**57.2%**	**53.2%**	**39.3%**	**13.8%**	**42.8%**
No children under age 18	100.0	52.1	48.5	35.7	12.8	47.9
With children under age 18	100.0	69.9	64.8	48.4	16.4	30.1
Children aged 6 to 17, none younger	100.0	74.7	70.1	53.5	16.6	25.3
Children under age 6	100.0	63.9	58.2	42.0	16.1	36.1
Children under age 3	100.0	61.1	55.5	39.2	16.3	38.9
Children under age 1	100.0	57.2	51.9	36.6	15.3	42.8

Source: Bureau of Labor Statistics, Employment Characteristics of Families, Internet site http://www.bls.gov/news.release/famee.nr0.htm; calculations by New Strategist

Table 16.5 Labor Force Status of Families with Children under Age 18, 2013

(number and percent distribution of families with children under age 18 by employment status of parent, by family type, 2013; numbers in thousands)

	with children under age 18	
	number	percent
Married couples with children under age 18	**23,259**	**100.0%**
One or both parents employed	22,408	96.3
Mother employed	15,200	65.4
Both parents employed	13,746	59.1
Mother employed not father	1,454	6.3
Father employed, not mother	7,208	31.0
Neither parent employed	851	3.7
Female-headed families with children under age 18	**8,575**	**100.0**
Mother employed	5,851	68.2
Mother not employed	2,724	31.8
Male-headed families with children under age 18	**2,558**	**100.0**
Father employed	2,077	81.2
Father not employed	481	18.8

Source: Bureau of Labor Statistics, Employment Characteristics of Families, Internet site http://www.bls.gov/news.release/famee.nr0.htm; calculations by New Strategist

Table 16.6 Labor Force Status of Families with Children under Age 6, 2013

(number and percent distribution of families with youngest child under age 6 by employment status of parent, by family type, 2013; numbers in thousands)

	with children under age 6	
	number	percent
Married couples with children under age 6	**10,076**	**100.0%**
One or both parents employed	9,732	96.6
Mother employed	5,987	59.4
Both parents employed	5,455	54.1
Mother employed not father	532	5.3
Father employed, not mother	3,745	37.2
Neither parent employed	344	3.4
Female-headed families with children under age 6	**3,450**	**100.0**
Mother employed	2,124	61.6
Mother not employed	1,326	38.4
Male-headed families with children under age 6	**1,100**	**100.0**
Father employed	889	80.8
Father not employed	210	19.1

Source: Bureau of Labor Statistics, Employment Characteristics of Families, Internet site http://www.bls.gov/news.release/famee.nr0.htm; calculations by New Strategist

Table 16.7 Labor Force Status of Families with Children Aged 6 to 17, 2013

(number and percent distribution of families with youngest child aged 6 to 17 by employment status of parent, by family type, 2013; numbers in thousands)

	with children aged 6 to 17	
	number	percent
Married couples with children aged 6 to 17	**13,183**	**100.0%**
One or both parents employed	12,676	96.2
Mother employed	9,213	69.9
Both parents employed	8,291	62.9
Mother employed, not father	922	7.0
Father employed, not mother	3,463	26.3
Neither parent employed	507	3.8
Female-headed families with children aged 6 to 17	**5,125**	**100.0**
Mother employed	3,727	72.7
Mother not employed	1,398	27.3
Male-headed families with children aged 6 to 17	**1,459**	**100.0**
Father employed	1,188	81.4
Father not employed	271	18.6

Source: Bureau of Labor Statistics, Employment Characteristics of Families, Internet site http://www.bls.gov/news.release/famee.nr0.htm; calculations by New Strategist

Many Preschoolers Depend on Grandparents for Day Care

The children of educated mothers are most likely to be in center-based care.

Among the nation's preschoolers with working mothers, the largest share (24 percent) are in center-based care during their mother's work hours. The second most common care arrangement is grandparent care, with 20.5 percent under the watchful eye of a grandparent while their mother works. Father care comes in third at 19.5 percent. The importance of grandparent care has grown over the past two decades, while the importance of family day care and in-home babysitting has declined.

The children of mothers with a bachelor's degree are much more likely than those with less-educated mothers to be in center-based care while their mother is at work. Nearly one-third of preschoolers with college-educated mothers are in center-based care versus only 18 percent of children whose mother has no more than a high school diploma.

■ Educated mothers are most likely to use center-based care because they can better afford the expense.

College-educated mothers are most likely to have their preschoolers in center-based care

(percent of children under age 5 with working mothers who are in center-based care while their mother works, by educational attainment of mother, 2011)

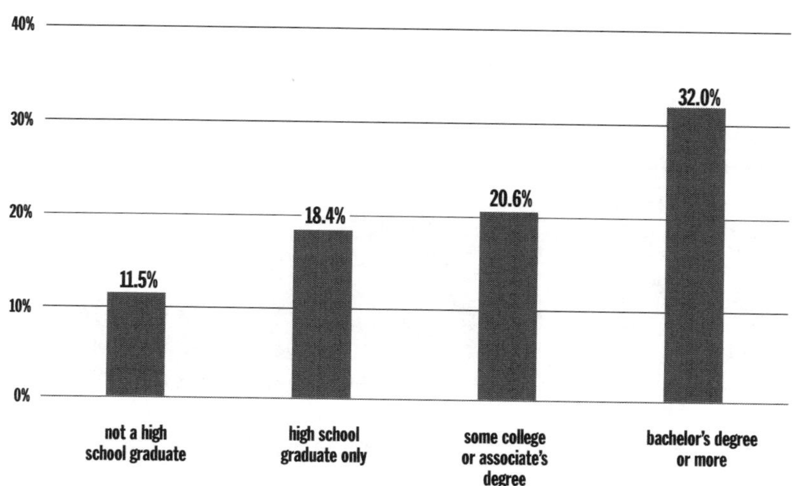

Table 16.8 Primary Childcare Arrangement of Preschoolers with Working Mothers, 1991 and 2011

(percent distribution of children aged 0 to 4 with employed mothers by primary type of care arrangement during mother's work hours, 1991 and 2011; percentage point change, 1991–2011)

	2011	1991	percentage point change
Total preschoolers with working mothers	**100.0%**	**100.0%**	–
Mother care	3.6	8.7	–5.1
Father care	19.5	20.0	–0.5
Grandparent care	20.5	15.8	4.7
Other relative care	5.3	7.7	–2.4
Center-based care	24.1	23.1	1.0
Other nonrelative care	13.1	23.3	–10.2
Other care	14.0	–	–

Note: Other relatives include siblings. Center-based care includes day care centers, nursery schools, preschools, and Head Start. Other nonrelative care includes family day care providers and in-home babysitters. Other care includes children in kindergarten or with no regular arrangement. Numbers may sum to more than 100 because of multiple arrangements. "–" means data are not comparable or inapplicable.
Source: Forum on Child and Family Statistics, America's Children: Key National Indicators of Children's Well-Being, 2013, Internet site http://www.childstats.gov/

Table 16.9 Primary Childcare Arrangement of Preschoolers with Working Mothers by Educational Attainment of Mother, 2011

(percent distribution of children aged 0 to 4 with employed mothers by primary type of care arrangement during mother's work hours, by educational attainment of mother, 2011)

	total	less than high school	high school graduate	some college or associate's degree	bachelor's degree or more
Total preschoolers with working mothers	**100.0%**	**100.0%**	**100.0%**	**100.0%**	**100.0%**
Mother care	3.6	4.0	2.3	3.4	4.4
Father care	19.5	17.0	21.8	22.3	16.2
Grandparent care	20.5	18.2	24.0	21.8	18.0
Other relative care	5.3	16.4	8.5	6.0	1.2
Center-based care	24.1	11.5	18.4	20.6	32.0
Other nonrelative care	13.1	8.3	11.7	13.2	14.7
Other care	14.0	24.5	13.4	12.7	13.5

Note: Other relatives include siblings. Center-based care includes day care centers, nursery schools, preschools, and Head Start. Other nonrelative care includes family day care providers and in-home babysitters. Other care includes children in kindergarten or with no regular arrangement. Numbers may sum to more than 100 because of multiple arrangements.
Source: Forum on Child and Family Statistics, America's Children: Key National Indicators of Children's Well-Being, 2013, Internet site http://www.childstats.gov/

CHAPTER

17

Living Arrangements

■ The Great Recession created a new baby bust. The number of births has declined since 2007, and the number of nuclear families (married couples with children under age 18) has fallen by more than 2 million.

■ Only 29 percent of the nation's households include children under age 18. Among households headed by married couples, the figure is 40 percent.

■ Among the nation's 74 million children, about one in five is the only child in the household. Another 39 percent have one sibling, and 40 percent have two or more siblings in the home.

■ Sixty-nine percent of children under age 18 lived with two parents in 2013—down from 85 percent in 1970.

■ The proportion of children who live with two parents (married or unmarried) ranges from a low of 41 percent among Black children to a high of 83 percent among Asian children.

■ Fathers who live with their children participate in their care. Most fathers with preschoolers bathe, diaper, or dress their child every day.

Most Married Couples Do Not Have Children under Age 18 at Home

Among those who do, few have more than two.

Among the nation's 122 million households, only 29 percent include children under age 18. When children of any age are included in the count, the figure rises to 39 percent. Among married couples, only 40 percent have children under age 18 at home. Female-headed families are more likely to have children, 56 percent including children under age 18. A much smaller 41 percent of male-headed families include children under age 18.

Among married couples with children under age 18, one child lives in the home of 38 percent, and another 40 percent have two. Female-headed families are more likely to have only one child under age 18 (48 percent), and male-headed families are most likely to have only one (58 percent).

■ Many young adults are postponing marriage and children because of the Great Recession. Consequently, the number of married couples with children under age 18 has declined.

The number of nuclear families has fallen by more than 2 million since 2007

(number of married-couple households with children under age 18, 2000 to 2013)

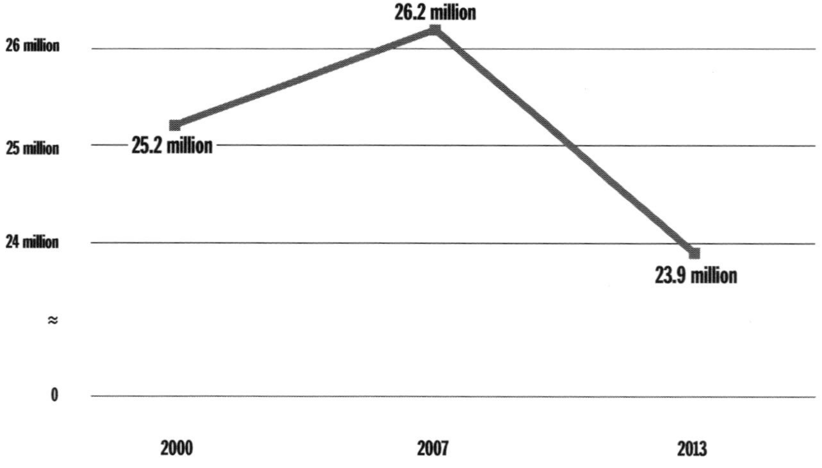

Table 17.1 Households by Type, 2000 to 2013

(number and percent distribution of households by household type, 2000 to 2013; percent change in number for selected years; numbers in thousands)

NUMBER	2013	2010	2007	2000	percent change 2007–13	percent change 2000–13
Total households	**122,459**	**117,538**	**116,011**	**104,705**	**5.6%**	**17.0%**
Family households	80,902	78,833	78,425	72,025	3.2	12.3
Married couples	59,204	58,410	58,945	55,311	0.4	7.0
With own children under age 18	23,870	24,575	26,158	25,248	–8.7	–5.5
Female householders, no spouse present	15,469	14,843	14,416	12,687	7.3	21.9
With own children under age 18	8,627	8,419	8,585	7,571	0.5	13.9
Male householders, no spouse present	6,229	5,580	5,063	4,028	23.0	54.6
With own children under age 18	2,560	2,224	2,015	1,786	27.0	43.3
Nonfamily households	41,558	38,705	37,587	32,680	10.6	27.2

PERCENT DISTRIBUTION	2013	2010	2007	2000	percentage point change 2007–13	percentage point change 2000–13
Total households	**100.0%**	**100.0%**	**100.0%**	**100.0%**	–	–
Family households	66.1	67.1	67.6	68.8	–1.5	–2.7
Married couples	48.3	49.7	50.8	52.8	–2.5	–4.5
With own children under age 18	19.5	20.9	22.5	24.1	–3.1	–4.6
Female householders, no spouse present	12.6	12.6	12.4	12.1	0.2	0.5
With own children under age 18	7.0	7.2	7.4	7.2	–0.4	–0.2
Male householders, no spouse present	5.1	4.7	4.4	3.8	0.7	1.2
With own children under age 18	2.1	1.9	1.7	1.7	0.4	0.4
Nonfamily households	33.9	32.9	32.4	31.2	1.5	2.7

Note: "–" means not applicable.
Source: Bureau of the Census, Current Population Survey Annual Social and Economic Supplement, Internet site http://www.census.gov/hhes/www/income/dinctabs.html; calculations by New Strategist

Table 17.2 Total Households by Presence and Age of Children, 2013

(number and percent distribution of households by presence and age of own children under age 18 and type of family, 2013; numbers in thousands)

	total	married couples	female householder, no spouse present	male householder, no spouse present
Total households	**122,459**	**59,204**	**15,469**	**6,229**
With children of any age	48,105	31,156	13,131	3,818
With children under age 18	35,058	23,870	8,627	2,560
With children under age 12	25,623	17,586	6,184	1,853
With children under age 6	15,046	10,409	3,496	1,141
With children under age 1	2,743	1,929	545	269
PERCENT DISTRIBUTION BY PRESENCE AND AGE OF CHILDREN				
Total households	**100.0%**	**100.0%**	**100.0%**	**100.0%**
With children of any age	39.3	52.6	84.9	61.3
With children under age 18	28.6	40.3	55.8	41.1
With children under age 12	20.9	29.7	40.0	29.7
With children under age 6	12.3	17.6	22.6	18.3
With children under age 1	2.2	3.3	3.5	4.3
PERCENT DISTRIBUTION BY FAMILY TYPE				
Total households	**100.0**	**48.3**	**12.6**	**5.1**
With children of any age	100.0	64.8	27.3	7.9
With children under age 18	100.0	68.1	24.6	7.3
With children under age 12	100.0	68.6	24.1	7.2
With children under age 6	100.0	69.2	23.2	7.6
With children under age 1	100.0	70.3	19.9	9.8

Source: Bureau of the Census, America's Families and Living Arrangements: 2013, Internet site http://www.census.gov/hhes/families/data/cps2013.html; calculations by New Strategist

Table 17.3 Families by Number of Children under Age 18, 2013

(number and percent distribution of family households with own children under age 18 by number of children and type of family, 2013; numbers in thousands)

	total	married couples	female householder, no spouse present	male householder, no spouse present
Total families with children under age 18	**35,058**	**23,870**	**8,627**	**2,560**
One child	14,784	9,157	4,144	1,482
Two children	13,187	9,597	2,825	766
Three children	5,086	3,707	1,148	231
Four or more children	2,001	1,410	510	81
PERCENT DISTRIBUTION BY NUMBER OF CHILDREN				
Total families with children under age 18	**100.0%**	**100.0%**	**100.0%**	**100.0%**
One child	42.2	38.4	48.0	57.9
Two children	37.6	40.2	32.7	29.9
Three children	14.5	15.5	13.3	9.0
Four or more children	5.7	5.9	5.9	3.2
PERCENT DISTRIBUTION BY FAMILY TYPE				
Total families with children under age 18	**100.0**	**68.1**	**24.6**	**7.3**
One child	100.0	61.9	28.0	10.0
Two children	100.0	72.8	21.4	5.8
Three children	100.0	72.9	22.6	4.5
Four or more children	100.0	70.5	25.5	4.0

Source: Bureau of the Census, America's Families and Living Arrangements: 2013, Internet site http://www.census.gov/hhes/families/data/cps2013.html; calculations by New Strategist

Most Children Have Siblings in the Household

The largest share of children has a parent with a bachelor's degree or more education.

Among the nation's 74 million children, about one in five is the only child in the household. Thirty-nine percent are sharing their living quarters with one brother or sister, and a substantial 40 percent have two or more siblings in the home.

Most children live in a family with a household income of $50,000 or more. A substantial 26 percent live in a family with an annual income of $100,000 or more.

More than one-third of the nation's children under age 18 have a parent with a bachelor's degree or even more education. Another 28 percent have a parent with some college experience or an associate's degree. Combining these two categories reveals that the 65 percent majority of children have parents with college experience.

■ Because so many children have parents with college experience, the pressure on children to attend college themselves is intense.

Many children must share a bathroom with brothers and sisters

(percent distribution of children under age 18 by number of siblings in the home, 2013)

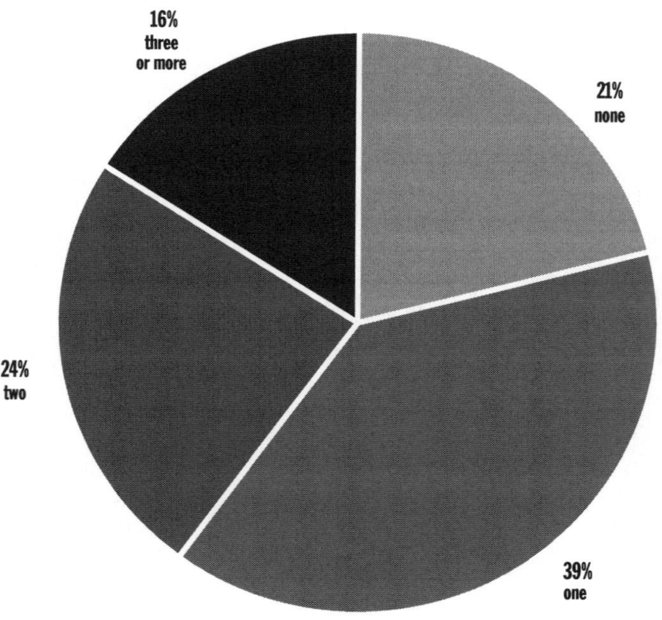

Table 17.4 Children under Age 18 by Family Characteristics, 2013

(number and percent distribution of children under age 18 by child and family characteristics, 2013; numbers in thousands)

	number	percent distribution
Total children under age 18	**73,910**	**100.0%**
Age of child		
Under age 1	3,873	5.2
Aged 1 to 2	7,994	10.8
Aged 3 to 5	12,171	16.5
Aged 6 to 8	12,290	16.6
Aged 9 to 11	12,224	16.5
Aged 12 to 14	12,491	16.9
Aged 15 to 17	12,866	17.4
Number of siblings in household		
None	15,238	20.6
One	28,971	39.2
Two	18,027	24.4
Three or more	11,675	15.8
Family income		
Under $20,000	13,338	18.0
$20,000 to $29,999	7,059	9.6
$30,000 to $39,999	6,813	9.2
$40,000 to $49,999	5,673	7.7
$50,000 to $74,999	12,274	16.6
$75,000 to $99,999	9,277	12.6
$100,000 or more	19,475	26.3
Highest education of either parent		
Not a high school graduate	7,246	9.8
High school graduate	15,535	21.0
Some college or associate's degree	20,761	28.1
Bachelor's degree	15,719	21.3
Professional or graduate degree	11,916	16.1
No parents present	2,733	3.7
Parents' labor force status		
Two parents, both in labor force	30,402	41.1
Two parents, father only in labor force	16,131	21.8
One parent, mother in labor force	13,167	17.8
One parent, mother not in labor force	4,365	5.9
No parents present	2,733	3.7
One parent, father in labor force	2,678	3.6
Two parents, mother only in labor force	2,527	3.4
Two parents, neither in labor force	1,586	2.1
One parent, father not in labor force	321	0.4

Source: Bureau of the Census, America's Families and Living Arrangements: 2013, Internet site http://www.census.gov/hhes/families/data/cps2013.html; calculations by New Strategist

Most Moms Are in the Labor Force

Stay-at-home mothers are not the norm, even among couples with preschoolers.

Among married couples with children under age 15, the 68 percent majority has a mom in the labor force. Only 27 percent have a mom who stays home to care for her family. Stay-at-home dads are even less common. Only 1.6 percent of married couples with children under age 15 have a dad who is not in the labor force because he is caring for the family.

Couples with preschoolers are only slightly more likely than average to have a stay-at-home mother, at 32 percent. They are about equally as likely to have a stay-at-home father, at 1.9 percent.

■ Perhaps no characteristic distinguishes today's children from those in the past more than working parents. With both mother and father in the labor force, family life has become much more complicated.

One-third of couples with preschoolers have a stay-at-home mom

(percent distribution of married-couple family groups with children under age 6 by labor force status of mother during past year, 2013)

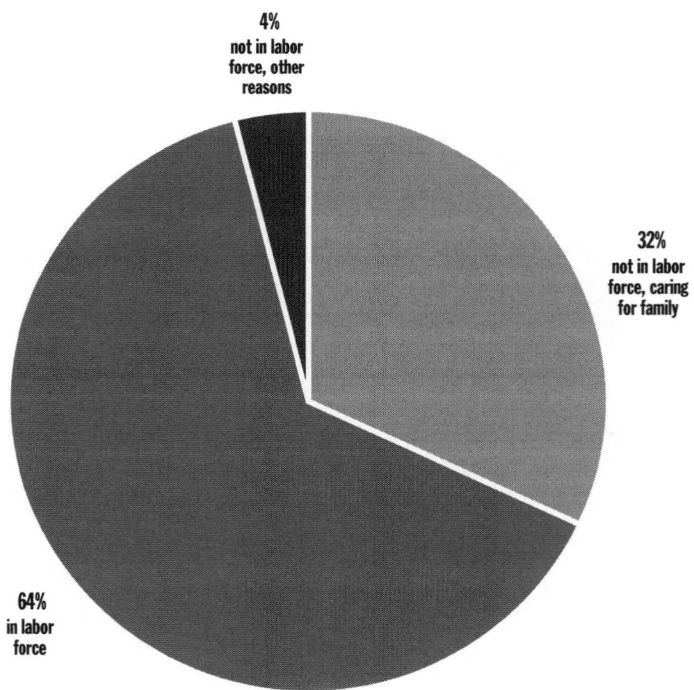

Table 17.5 Stay-at-Home Parents among Married Couples, 2013

(number and percent distribution of married-couple family groups with children under age 15 by stay-at-home status of mother and father and age of child, 2013; numbers in thousands)

	with own children under age 15		with own children under age 6	
	number	percent distribution	number	percent distribution
Total married-couple family groups	**21,547**	**100.0%**	**10,867**	**100.0%**
Mother's labor force status in past year				
In labor force one or more weeks	14,650	68.0	6,968	64.1
Not in labor force, caring for family	5,824	27.0	3,447	31.7
Not in labor force, other reason	1,073	5.0	452	4.2
Father's labor force status in past year				
In labor force one or more weeks	20,190	93.7	10,229	94.1
Not in labor force, caring for family	340	1.6	203	1.9
Not in labor force, other reason	1,017	4.7	435	4.0

Note: Married-couple family groups include married-couple householders and married couples living in households headed by others.

Source: Bureau of the Census, America's Families and Living Arrangements: 2013, Internet site http://www.census.gov/hhes/families/data/cps2013.html; calculations by New Strategist

Sixty-Nine Percent of Children Live with Two Parents

Fewer than 4 percent live with their father only.

Among the nation's 74 million children under age 18, the 69 percent majority lived with two parents in 2013—down from 85 percent in 1970. The proportion of children who live with two parents (married or unmarried) ranges from a low of 41 percent among Black children to a high of 83 percent among Asian children. A smaller share of children lives with their married biological parents, ranging from 31 percent of Blacks to 76 percent of Asians.

The proportion of children who live with their mother only ranges from a low of 12 percent among Asians to a high of 49 percent among Blacks. Few children live only with their father regardless of race or Hispanic origin.

■ The poverty rate among children is unlikely to decline significantly until fewer children live in single-parent families.

Children's living arrangements vary greatly by race and Hispanic origin

(percent of children living with two married biological parents, by race and Hispanic origin, 2013)

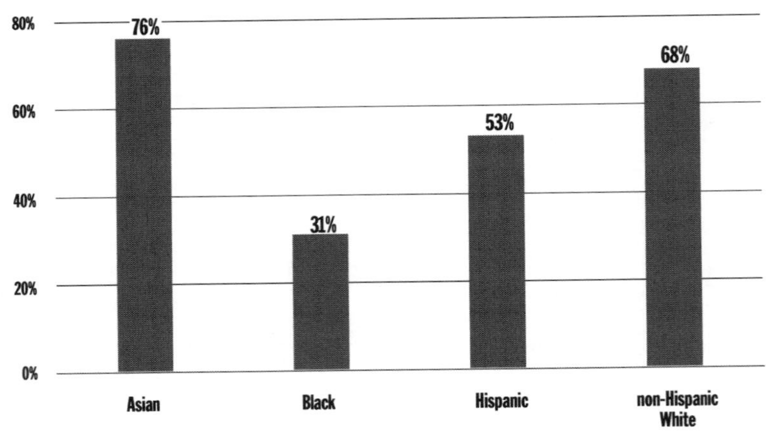

Table 17.6 Living Arrangements of Children, 1970 to 2013

(number and percent distribution of children under age 18 by living arrangement, 1970 to 2013; numbers in thousands)

	total		children living with			
TOTAL CHILDREN	number	percent	two parents	mother only	father only	neither parent
2013	73,910	100.0%	68.5%	23.7%	4.1%	3.7%
2012	73,817	100.0	68.1	24.4	4.0	3.6
2011	74,002	100.0	68.7	23.8	3.5	4.0
2010	74,718	100.0	69.4	23.1	3.4	3.5
2009	74,230	100.0	69.8	22.8	3.4	3.4
2008	74,104	100.0	69.9	22.8	3.5	3.8
2007	73,746	100.0	70.7	22.6	3.2	3.5
2007	73,746	100.0	67.8	24.2	4.5	3.5
2006	73,664	100.0	67.4	23.3	4.7	4.6
2005	73,523	100.0	67.4	23.4	4.7	4.5
2000	72,012	100.0	69.1	22.4	4.2	4.2
1990	64,137	100.0	72.5	21.6	3.1	2.8
1980	63,427	100.0	76.7	18.0	1.7	3.7
1970	69,162	100.0	85.2	10.8	1.1	2.9

Note: The methodology changed in 2007, allowing two parents to be either married or unmarried and increasing the number of children in two-parent families.
Source: Bureau of the Census, Families and Living Arrangements, Historical Tables—Households, Internet site http://www.census .gov/hhes/families/data/children.html; calculations by New Strategist

Table 17.7 Living Arrangements of Children, 2013: Total Children

(number and percent distribution of total children under age 18 by living arrangement, 2013; numbers in thousands)

	number	percent distribution
Total children	**73,910**	**100.0%**
Living with two parents	50,645	68.5
Married parents	47,611	64.4
Unmarried parents	3,034	4.1
Biological mother and father	45,814	62.0
Married parents	43,230	58.5
Biological mother and stepfather	2,837	3.8
Biological father and stepmother	896	1.2
Biological mother and adoptive father	147	0.2
Biological father and adoptive mother	34	0.0
Adoptive mother and father	695	0.9
Other	224	0.3
Living with one parent	20,531	27.8
Mother only	17,532	23.7
Father only	2,999	4.1
Living with no parents	2,733	3.7
Grandparents	1,431	1.9
Other	1,302	1.8

Source: Bureau of the Census, America's Families and Living Arrangements: 2013, Internet site http://www.census.gov/hhes/families/data/cps2013.html; calculations by New Strategist

Table 17.8 Living Arrangements of Children, 2013: Asian Children

(number and percent distribution of Asian children under age 18 by living arrangement, 2013; numbers in thousands)

	number	percent distribution
Asian children	**4,551**	**100.0%**
Living with two parents	3,800	83.5
Married parents	3,708	81.5
Unmarried parents	92	2.0
Biological mother and father	3,563	78.3
Married parents	3,478	76.4
Biological mother and stepfather	61	1.3
Biological father and stepmother	43	0.9
Biological mother and adoptive father	4	0.1
Biological father and adoptive mother	1	0.0
Adoptive mother and father	121	2.7
Other	9	0.2
Living with one parent	669	14.7
Mother only	543	11.9
Father only	125	2.7
Living with no parents	83	1.8
Grandparents	27	0.6
Other	56	1.2

Note: Asians are those who identify themselves as being of the race alone and those who identify themselves as being of the race in combination with other races.
Source: Bureau of the Census, America's Families and Living Arrangements: 2013, Internet site http://www.census.gov/hhes/families/data/cps2013.html; calculations by New Strategist

Table 17.9 Living Arrangements of Children, 2013: Black Children

(number and percent distribution of Black children under age 18 by living arrangement, 2013; numbers in thousands)

	number	percent distribution
Black children	**13,132**	**100.0%**
Living with two parents	5,379	41.0
Married parents	4,746	36.1
Unmarried parents	634	4.8
Biological mother and father	4,562	34.7
Married parents	4,035	30.7
Biological mother and stepfather	493	3.8
Biological father and stepmother	126	1.0
Biological mother and adoptive father	28	0.2
Biological father and adoptive mother	12	0.0
Adoptive mother and father	123	0.9
Other	35	0.3
Living with one parent	6,979	53.1
Mother only	6,373	48.5
Father only	606	4.6
Living with no parents	774	5.9
Grandparents	432	3.3
Other	342	2.6

Note: Blacks are those who identify themselves as being of the race alone and those who identify themselves as being of the race in combination with other races.
Source: Bureau of the Census, America's Families and Living Arrangements: 2013, Internet site http://www.census.gov/hhes/families/data/cps2013.html; calculations by New Strategist

Table 17.10 Living Arrangements of Children, 2013: Hispanic Children

(number and percent distribution of Hispanic children under age 18 by living arrangement, 2013; numbers in thousands)

	number	percent distribution
Hispanic children	**17,709**	**100.0%**
Living with two parents	11,521	65.1
Married parents	10,300	58.2
Unmarried parents	1,221	6.9
Biological mother and father	10,500	59.3
Married parents	9,438	53.3
Biological mother and stepfather	692	3.9
Biological father and stepmother	167	0.9
Biological mother and adoptive father	29	0.2
Biological father and adoptive mother	4	0.0
Adoptive mother and father	95	0.5
Other	34	0.2
Living with one parent	5,504	31.1
Mother only	4,935	27.9
Father only	570	3.2
Living with no parents	684	3.9
Grandparents	291	1.6
Other	393	2.2

Source: Bureau of the Census, America's Families and Living Arrangements: 2013, Internet site http://www.census.gov/hhes/families/data/cps2013.html; calculations by New Strategist

Table 17.11 Living Arrangements of Children, 2013: Non-Hispanic White Children

(number and percent distribution of non-Hispanic White children under age 18 by living arrangement, 2013; numbers in thousands)

	number	percent distribution
Non-Hispanic White children	**38,880**	**100.0%**
Living with two parents	30,092	77.4
Married parents	28,935	74.4
Unmarried parents	1,157	3.0
Biological mother and father	27,332	70.3
Married parents	26,363	67.8
Biological mother and stepfather	1,597	4.1
Biological father and stepmother	562	1.4
Biological mother and adoptive father	84	0.2
Biological father and adoptive mother	17	0.0
Adoptive mother and father	352	0.9
Other	147	0.4
Living with one parent	7,631	19.6
Mother only	5,938	15.3
Father only	1,692	4.4
Living with no parents	1,158	3.0
Grandparents	655	1.7
Other	503	1.3

Note: Non-Hispanic Whites are those who identify themselves as being White alone and not Hispanic.
Source: Bureau of the Census, America's Families and Living Arrangements: 2013, Internet site http://www.census.gov/hhes/families/data/cps2013.html; calculations by New Strategist

Most Fathers Eat Meals with Their Children Every Day

Not surprisingly, fathers who do not live with their children are less involved.

In a unique study carried out in 2006–2010, the National Center for Health Statistics included in the National Survey of Family Growth a nationally representative sample of men aged 15 to 44. In the survey, fathers of children under age 19 were asked about their involvement with their children during the past four weeks. The results show that most fathers who live with their children (85 percent of fathers) participate extensively in caring for them.

Among fathers who live with children under age 5, a substantial 81 percent play with their child every day, 72 percent eat meals with or feed their child every day, and 58 percent bathe, diaper, or dress their child on a daily basis. The figures are much lower for nonresident fathers, although the majority participates at least occasionally in most of these activities. Among fathers who live with children aged 5 to 18, two-thirds eat meals with their children on a daily basis and also talk with their children about their day. The typical nonresident father with children aged 5 to 18 does not eat meals with his children but does occasionally talk with them about their day.

■ Overall, 88 percent of fathers who live with their children say they are doing a good or very good job as a father. Among fathers who do not live with their children, the figure is smaller 54 percent.

Most resident fathers are involved in caring for their preschoolers

(percent of fathers aged 15 to 44 who live with a child under age 5 who say they have done the selected activity with their child every day in the past four weeks, 2006–2010)

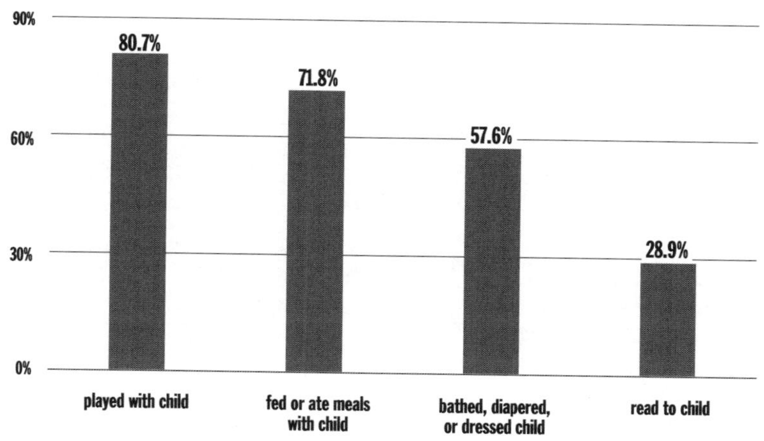

Table 17.12 Father's Involvement with Their Children under Age 5, 2006–2010

(percent of fathers aged 15 to 44 with children under age 5 by how often they engaged in selected activities with their children in the past four weeks, by living arrangement with children, 2006–2010)

	fed or ate meals with his children	bathed, diapered, or dressed his children	played with his children	read to his children
Living with one or more children under age 5	**100.0%**	**100.0%**	**100.0%**	**100.0%**
Every day	71.8	57.6	80.7	28.9
Several times a week	24.1	32.0	17.6	30.9
Once a week or less	3.2	6.4	1.3	24.5
Not at all	0.8	4.0	0.4	15.7
Not living with one or more children under age 5	**100.0**	**100.0**	**100.0**	**100.0**
Every day	7.9	8.3	10.4	4.9
Several times a week	22.1	22.8	28.5	17.6
Once a week or less	27.2	21.4	24.1	25.5
Not at all	42.8	47.4	37.0	52.0

Source: National Center for Health Statistics, Fathers' Involvement with Their Children: United States, 2006–2010, National Health Statistics Reports, No. 71, 2013; Internet site http://www.cdc.gov/nchs/nsfg.htm

Table 17.13 Father's Involvement with Their Children Aged 5 to 18, 2006–2010

(percent of fathers aged 15 to 44 with children aged 5 to 18 by how often they engaged in selected activities with their children in the past four weeks, by living arrangement with children, 2006–2010)

	ate meals with his children	took his children to or from activities	talked with his children about their day	helped with or checked his children's homework
Living with one or more children aged 5 to 18	**100.0%**	**100.0%**	**100.0%**	**100.0%**
Every day	65.5	20.5	65.3	29.7
Several times a week	27.5	34.0	27.2	33.1
Once a week or less	5.7	31.0	6.3	23.2
Not at all	1.4	14.5	1.1	14.1
Not living with one or more children aged 5 to 18	**100.0**	**100.0**	**100.0**	**100.0**
Every day	2.9	3.9	15.5	6.0
Several times a week	13.0	7.3	20.1	7.6
Once a week or less	31.5	17.4	27.0	17.2
Not at all	52.5	71.4	37.3	69.1

Source: National Center for Health Statistics, Fathers' Involvement with Their Children: United States, 2006–2010, National Health Statistics Reports, No. 71, 2013; Internet site http://www.cdc.gov/nchs/nsfg.htm

CHAPTER

18

Population

■ The iGeneration numbers 62 million, a figure that includes everyone born from 1995 through 2009. The iGeneration accounts for 20 percent of the total population.

■ The annual number of births fell below 4 million in 2010. That marked the beginning of the Recession generation, which was aged 0 to 3 in 2013.

■ America's children are much more diverse than middle-aged or older people. While non-Hispanic Whites accounted for 63 percent of all Americans in 2013, their share is a smaller 53 percent of the iGeneration.

■ Among children aged 5 to 17, more than 22 percent do not speak English at home. Most of those who do not speak English at home are Spanish speakers, and most also speak English "very well."

■ In Utah, the iGeneration accounts for fully 25 percent of the state's population, and the Recession generation is an additional 7 percent.

The iGeneration Is Larger than Gen X

One in five Americans is in the iGeneration.

The iGeneration numbers 62 million, a figure that includes everyone born from 1995 through 2009. The iGeneration accounts for 20 percent of the total population, making it larger than Generation X.

Another generation may be in the making, based on the decline in births that followed the Great Recession. Generations typically are defined by the rise and fall of births. Births peaked in 2007 and began to decline. In 2010, the annual number of births fell below 4 million for the first time since 1999. That marked the beginning of the Recession generation, which was aged 0 to 3 in 2013 and accounted for 5 percent of the population.

■ The iGeneration is more diverse than Millennials or Gen Xers, which will make it a difficult market to target.

The iGeneration outnumbers Gen X

(number of people by generation, 2013)

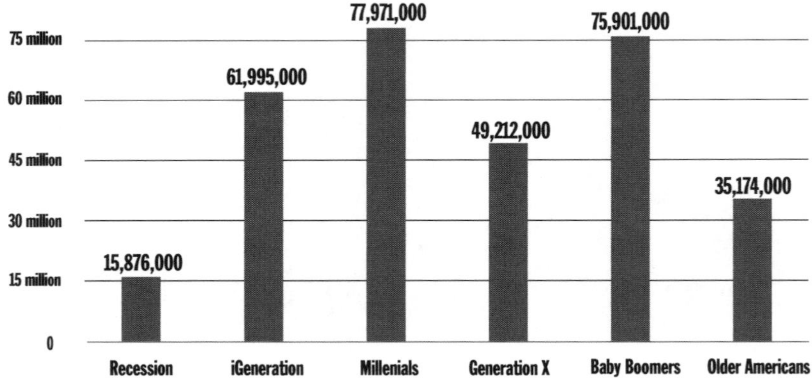

Table 18.1 Population by Age and Generation, 2013

(number and percent distribution of people by age and generation, 2013; numbers in thousands)

	number	percent distribution
Total people	**316,129**	**100.0%**
Under age 5	19,868	6.3
Aged 5 to 9	20,571	6.5
Aged 10 to 14	20,650	6.5
Aged 15 to 19	21,159	6.7
Aged 20 to 24	22,795	7.2
Aged 25 to 29	21,580	6.8
Aged 30 to 34	21,264	6.7
Aged 35 to 39	19,604	6.2
Aged 40 to 44	20,849	6.6
Aged 45 to 49	21,208	6.7
Aged 50 to 54	22,559	7.1
Aged 55 to 59	21,194	6.7
Aged 60 to 64	18,122	5.7
Aged 65 to 69	14,609	4.6
Aged 70 to 74	10,608	3.4
Aged 75 to 79	7,678	2.4
Aged 80 to 84	5,769	1.8
Aged 85 or older	6,041	1.9
Total people	**316,129**	**100.0**
Recession (aged 0 to 3)	15,876	5.0
iGeneration (aged 4 to 18)	61,995	19.6
Millennial (aged 19 to 36)	77,971	24.7
Generation X (aged 37 to 48)	49,212	15.6
Baby Boom (aged 49 to 67)	75,901	24.0
Older Americans (aged 68 or older)	35,174	11.1

Source: Bureau of the Census, Population Estimates, Internet site http://www.census.gov/popest/; calculations by New Strategist

Table 18.2 Younger Generations by Single Year of Age, 2013

(number of people under age 19 by single year of age and sex, and sex ratio by age, 2013; numbers in thousands)

	total	female	male	sex ratio
Total Recession generation	**15,876**	**7,761**	**8,116**	**105**
Aged 0	3,942	1,925	2,017	105
Aged 1	3,956	1,934	2,022	105
Aged 2	3,989	1,949	2,040	105
Aged 3	3,990	1,953	2,036	104
Total iGeneration	**61,995**	**30,300**	**31,695**	**105**
Aged 4	3,992	1,955	2,037	104
Aged 5	4,122	2,018	2,104	104
Aged 6	4,142	2,025	2,117	105
Aged 7	4,108	2,008	2,100	105
Aged 8	4,095	2,003	2,092	104
Aged 9	4,103	2,008	2,095	104
Aged 10	4,073	1,994	2,079	104
Aged 11	4,056	1,986	2,070	104
Aged 12	4,156	2,033	2,123	104
Aged 13	4,218	2,059	2,158	105
Aged 14	4,147	2,026	2,122	105
Aged 15	4,147	2,026	2,122	105
Aged 16	4,158	2,032	2,126	105
Aged 17	4,191	2,043	2,148	105
Aged 18	4,286	2,085	2,201	106

Note: The sex ratio is the number of males per 100 females.
Source: Bureau of the Census, Population Estimates, Internet site http://www.census.gov/popest/; calculations by New Strategist

The Nation's Children Are Diverse

Hispanics outnumber Blacks in the younger generations.

America's children are much more diverse than middle-aged or older people. While non-Hispanic Whites accounted for 63 percent of all Americans in 2013, their share is a smaller 53 percent among the iGeneration (aged 4 to 18) and just half of the Recession generation (aged 0 to 3).

Among Boomers and older Americans, Blacks outnumber Hispanics. In the younger generations, Hispanics are a larger share of the population than Blacks. Twenty-four percent of the members of the iGeneration are Hispanic and 17 percent are Black. The figures are similar for the Recession generation.

■ Racial and ethnic differences between young and old may divide the nation in the years ahead.

In the iGeneration, about one in four is Hispanic

(percent distribution of people aged 4 to 18 by race and Hispanic origin, 2013)

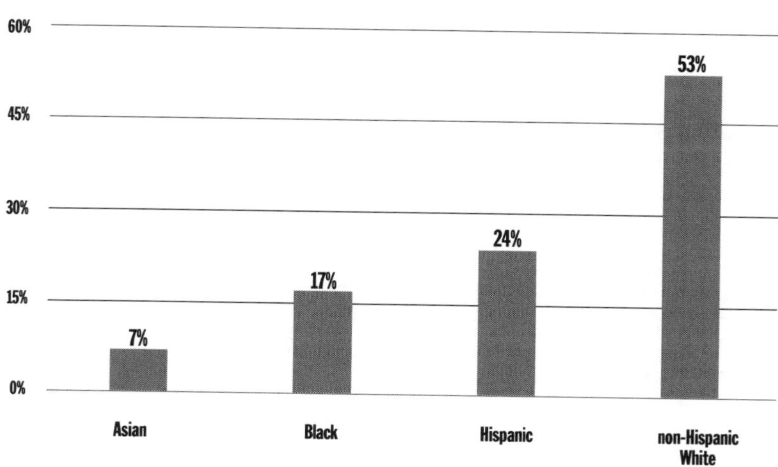

Table 18.3 Population by Generation, Race, and Hispanic Origin, 2013

(number and percent distribution of people by generation, race, and Hispanic origin, 2013; numbers in thousands)

	total	Asian	Black	Hispanic	non-Hispanic White
Total people	**316,129**	**19,437**	**45,004**	**54,071**	**197,836**
Recession (aged 0 to 3)	15,876	1,139	2,928	4,101	7,926
iGeneration (aged 4 to 18)	61,995	4,048	10,825	14,575	32,987
Millennial (aged 19 to 36)	77,971	5,564	12,258	16,020	44,314
Generation X (aged 37 to 48)	49,212	3,446	6,806	8,798	30,117
Baby Boom (aged 49 to 67)	75,901	3,811	9,074	8,011	54,592
Older Americans (aged 68 or older)	35,174	1,429	3,112	2,567	27,900
PERCENT DISTRIBUTION BY RACE AND HISPANIC ORIGIN					
Total people	**100.0%**	**6.1%**	**14.2%**	**17.1%**	**62.6%**
Recession (aged 0 to 3)	100.0	7.2	18.4	25.8	49.9
iGeneration (aged 4 to 18)	100.0	6.5	17.5	23.5	53.2
Millennial (aged 19 to 36)	100.0	7.1	15.7	20.5	56.8
Generation X (aged 37 to 48)	100.0	7.0	13.8	17.9	61.2
Baby Boom (aged 49 to 67)	100.0	5.0	12.0	10.6	71.9
Older Americans (aged 68 or older)	100.0	4.1	8.8	7.3	79.3
PERCENT DISTRIBUTION BY GENERATION					
Total people	**100.0**	**100.0**	**100.0**	**100.0**	**100.0**
Recession (aged 0 to 3)	5.0	5.9	6.5	7.6	4.0
iGeneration (aged 4 to 18)	19.6	20.8	24.1	27.0	16.7
Millennial (aged 19 to 36)	24.7	28.6	27.2	29.6	22.4
Generation X (aged 37 to 48)	15.6	17.7	15.1	16.3	15.2
Baby Boom (aged 49 to 67)	24.0	19.6	20.2	14.8	27.6
Older Americans (aged 68 or older)	11.1	7.4	6.9	4.7	14.1

Note: Asians and Blacks are those who identify themselves as being of the race alone and those who identify themselves as being of the race in combination with other races. Non-Hispanic Whites are those who identify themselves as being White alone and not Hispanic. Numbers do not add to total because not all races are shown and Hispanics may be of any race.
Source: Bureau of the Census, Population Estimates, Internet site http://www.census.gov/popest/; calculations by New Strategist

Table 18.4 Younger Generations by Single Year of Age, Race, and Hispanic Origin, 2013

(number and percent distribution of people under age 19 by single year of age, race, and Hispanic origin, 2013; numbers in thousands)

	total	Asian	Black	Hispanic	non-Hispanic White
Total Recession generation	**15,876**	**1,139**	**2,928**	**4,101**	**7,926**
Aged 0	3,942	279	731	1,015	1,972
Aged 1	3,956	285	734	1,020	1,973
Aged 2	3,989	288	733	1,035	1,987
Aged 3	3,990	287	729	1,031	1,994
Total iGeneration	**61,995**	**4,048**	**10,825**	**14,575**	**32,987**
Aged 4	3,992	281	731	1,018	2,011
Aged 5	4,122	290	752	1,052	2,077
Aged 6	4,142	285	747	1,052	2,104
Aged 7	4,108	281	725	1,030	2,113
Aged 8	4,095	283	710	1,007	2,131
Aged 9	4,103	281	701	985	2,169
Aged 10	4,073	276	692	967	2,167
Aged 11	4,056	263	699	953	2,168
Aged 12	4,156	269	720	960	2,232
Aged 13	4,218	263	737	959	2,281
Aged 14	4,147	252	718	928	2,269
Aged 15	4,147	253	719	916	2,276
Aged 16	4,158	255	715	911	2,294
Aged 17	4,191	257	714	911	2,323
Aged 18	4,286	258	745	925	2,371
PERCENT DISTRIBUTION BY RACE AND HISPANIC ORIGIN					
Total Recession generation	**100.0%**	**7.2%**	**18.4%**	**25.8%**	**49.9%**
Aged 0	100.0	7.1	18.6	25.7	50.0
Aged 1	100.0	7.2	18.6	25.8	49.9
Aged 2	100.0	7.2	18.4	25.9	49.8
Aged 3	100.0	7.2	18.3	25.8	50.0
Total iGeneration	**100.0**	**6.5**	**17.5**	**23.5**	**53.2**
Aged 4	100.0	7.0	18.3	25.5	50.4
Aged 5	100.0	7.0	18.2	25.5	50.4
Aged 6	100.0	6.9	18.0	25.4	50.8
Aged 7	100.0	6.8	17.6	25.1	51.4
Aged 8	100.0	6.9	17.3	24.6	52.0
Aged 9	100.0	6.9	17.1	24.0	52.9
Aged 10	100.0	6.8	17.0	23.7	53.2
Aged 11	100.0	6.5	17.2	23.5	53.4
Aged 12	100.0	6.5	17.3	23.1	53.7
Aged 13	100.0	6.2	17.5	22.7	54.1
Aged 14	100.0	6.1	17.3	22.4	54.7
Aged 15	100.0	6.1	17.3	22.1	54.9
Aged 16	100.0	6.1	17.2	21.9	55.2
Aged 17	100.0	6.1	17.0	21.7	55.4
Aged 18	100.0	6.0	17.4	21.6	55.3

Note: Asians and Blacks are those who identify themselves as being of the race alone and those who identify themselves as being of the race in combination with other races. Non-Hispanic Whites are those who identify themselves as being White alone and not Hispanic. Numbers do not add to total because not all races are shown and Hispanics may be of any race.
Source: Bureau of the Census, Population Estimates, Internet site http://www.census.gov/popest/; calculations by New Strategist

Many Children Do Not Speak English at Home

Most are Spanish speakers, and most also speak English very well.

Sixty-two million residents of the United States speak a language other than English at home, according to the Census Bureau's 2012 American Community Survey—21 percent of the population aged 5 or older. Among those who do not speak English at home, 62 percent speak Spanish.

More than one in five children aged 5 to 17 does not speak English at home. Among them, 72 percent are Spanish speakers. Most children who do not speak English at home are able to speak English "very well." Only 21 percent of the Spanish speakers aged 5 to 17, for example, cannot speak English very well. Among all U.S. residents who speak Spanish at home, a much larger 42 percent cannot speak English very well.

■ The language barrier is a bigger problem for adults than for children.

Few children who speak Spanish at home cannot speak English "very well"

(percent of people who speak Spanish at home who do not speak English "very well," by age, 2012)

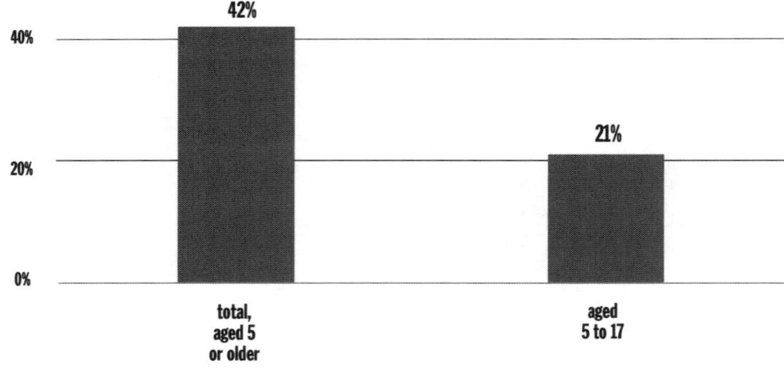

Table 18.5 Language Spoken at Home by People Aged 5 to 17, 2012

(number and percent distribution of people aged 5 or older and aged 5 to 17 who speak a language other than English at home by language spoken at home and ability to speak English "very well," 2012; numbers in thousands)

	total		aged 5 to 17	
	number	percent distribution	number	percent distribution
Total, aged 5 or older	**294,004**	**100.0%**	**53,800**	**100.0%**
Speak only English at home	232,126	79.0	41,806	77.7
Speak a language other than English at home	61,877	21.0	11,994	22.3
Speak English less than "very well"	25,088	8.5	2,498	4.6
Total who speak a language other than English at home	**61,877**	**100.0**	**11,994**	**100.0**
Speak Spanish at home	38,325	61.9	8,587	71.6
Speak other Indo-European language at home	11,035	17.8	1,595	13.3
Speak Asian or Pacific Island language at home	9,752	15.8	1,306	10.9
Speak other language at home	2,765	4.5	506	4.2
Speak Spanish at home	38,325	100.0	8,587	100.0
Speak English less than "very well"	16,149	42.1	1,775	20.7
Speak other Indo-European language at home	11,035	100.0	1,595	100.0
Speak English less than "very well"	3,462	31.4	291	18.2
Speak Asian or Pacific Island language at home	9,752	100.0	1,306	100.0
Speak English less than "very well"	4,618	47.4	334	25.6
Speak other language at home	2,765	100.0	506	100.0
Speak English less than "very well"	859	31.1	98	19.4

Source: Bureau of the Census, 2012 American Community Survey, Internet site http://factfinder2.census.gov/faces/nav/jsf/pages/index.xhtml; calculations by New Strategist

Largest Share of Children Lives in the South

One in four residents of Utah is a member of the iGeneration.

The South is home to the largest share of the population, and consequently to the largest share of the iGeneration. In 2013, 38 percent of Americans ranging in age from 4 to 18 lived in the South, according to Census Bureau estimates. In the South, the iGeneration accounts for 20 percent of the population.

The iGeneration is a substantial 25 percent of the population of Utah, and the Recession generation is another 7 percent of Utah's population. At the other extreme, the iGeneration is only 17 percent of Maine's population and the Recession generation only 4 percent.

■ The iGeneration will be a growing force in every state and region in the years ahead.

The Northeast is home to just 17 percent of the iGeneration

(percent distribution of people aged 4 to 18 by region, 2013)

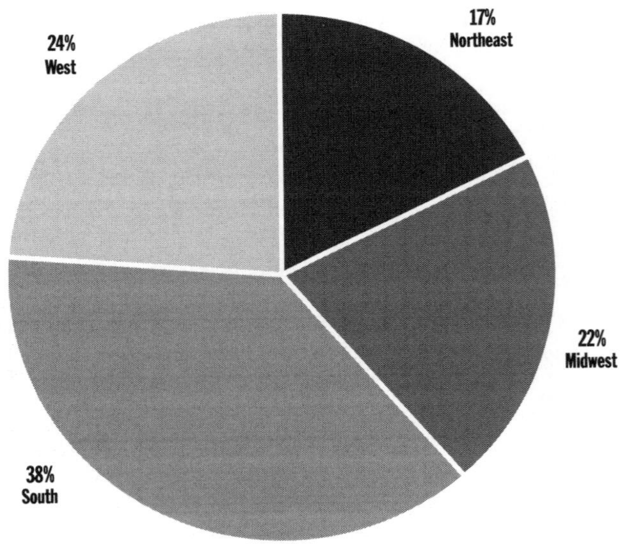

Table 18.6 Population by Generation and Region, 2013

(number and percent distribution of people by generation and region, 2013; numbers in thousands)

	total	Northeast	Midwest	South	West
Total people	**316,129**	**55,943**	**67,548**	**118,383**	**74,254**
Recession (aged 0 to 3)	15,876	2,557	3,349	6,085	3,903
iGeneration (aged 4 to 18)	61,995	10,306	13,380	23,486	14,949
Millennial (aged 19 to 36)	77,971	13,398	16,121	29,085	19,108
Generation X (aged 37 to 48)	49,212	8,897	10,300	18,689	11,692
Baby Boom (aged 49 to 67)	75,901	13,934	16,466	27,656	16,826
Older Americans (aged 68 or older)	35,174	6,850	7,931	13,382	7,776
PERCENT DISTRIBUTION BY GENERATION					
Total people	**100.0%**	**100.0%**	**100.0%**	**100.0%**	**100.0%**
Recession (aged 0 to 3)	5.0	4.6	5.0	5.1	5.3
iGeneration (aged 4 to 18)	19.6	18.4	19.8	19.8	20.1
Millennial (aged 19 to 36)	24.7	24.0	23.9	24.6	25.7
Generation X (aged 37 to 48)	15.6	15.9	15.2	15.8	15.7
Baby Boom (aged 49 to 67)	24.0	24.9	24.4	23.4	22.7
Older Americans (aged 68 or older)	11.1	12.2	11.7	11.3	10.5
PERCENT DISTRIBUTION BY REGION					
Total people	**100.0**	**17.7**	**21.4**	**37.4**	**23.5**
Recession (aged 0 to 3)	100.0	16.1	21.1	38.3	24.6
iGeneration (aged 4 to 18)	100.0	16.6	21.6	37.9	24.1
Millennial (aged 19 to 36)	100.0	17.2	20.7	37.3	24.5
Generation X (aged 37 to 48)	100.0	18.1	20.9	38.0	23.8
Baby Boom (aged 49 to 67)	100.0	18.4	21.7	36.4	22.2
Older Americans (aged 68 or older)	100.0	19.5	22.5	38.0	22.1

Source: Bureau of the Census, State Population Estimates, Internet site http://www.census.gov/popest/data/state/asrh/2013/index .html; calculations by New Strategist

Table 18.7 Younger Generations by State, 2013

(number of total people, people aged 0 to 3 and 4 to 18, and in age groups that include the Recession and iGeneration, by state, 2013; numbers in thousands)

	total population	Recession (0 to 3)	iGeneration (4 to 18)	0 to 4	5 to 9	10 to 14	15 to 19
Total population	**316,129**	**15,876**	**61,995**	**19,868**	**20,571**	**20,650**	**21,159**
Alabama	4,834	238	940	297	308	316	321
Alaska	735	44	153	55	52	50	49
Arizona	6,627	345	1,363	432	460	456	451
Arkansas	2,959	154	593	193	200	199	196
California	38,333	2,006	7,719	2,508	2,562	2,528	2,659
Colorado	5,268	268	1,042	335	355	348	340
Connecticut	3,596	154	689	192	215	232	254
Delaware	926	45	173	56	57	57	60
District of Columbia	646	33	93	41	30	25	38
Florida	19,553	863	3,398	1,078	1,113	1,133	1,171
Georgia	9,992	535	2,099	669	704	706	695
Hawaii	1,404	73	251	91	86	82	80
Idaho	1,612	91	358	113	123	121	114
Illinois	12,882	639	2,562	799	842	858	877
Indiana	6,571	337	1,344	421	444	451	456
Iowa	3,090	156	616	195	205	202	213
Kansas	2,894	160	606	200	205	201	201
Kentucky	4,395	220	851	275	285	285	283
Louisiana	4,625	247	926	308	314	309	302
Maine	1,328	52	227	65	72	76	83
Maryland	5,929	294	1,133	367	373	376	390
Massachusetts	6,693	292	1,217	366	380	398	457
Michigan	9,896	458	1,929	573	614	652	685
Minnesota	5,420	278	1,075	348	363	355	359
Mississippi	2,991	159	623	198	210	206	208
Missouri	6,044	301	1,178	377	392	392	398
Montana	1,015	49	189	61	63	62	64
Nebraska	1,869	104	388	130	133	127	127
Nevada	2,790	143	550	178	188	184	177
New Hampshire	1,323	53	239	66	73	80	91
New Jersey	8,899	427	1,705	533	558	576	582
New Mexico	2,085	111	426	139	145	141	140
New York	19,651	939	3,587	1,174	1,149	1,179	1,280
North Carolina	9,848	490	1,939	612	645	650	651
North Dakota	723	39	137	49	47	42	49
Ohio	11,571	553	2,257	691	734	761	780
Oklahoma	3,851	212	788	264	269	261	256
Oregon	3,930	184	723	230	240	240	246
Pennsylvania	12,774	573	2,339	716	746	772	847
Rhode Island	1,052	44	191	55	59	61	75
South Carolina	4,775	234	916	292	306	303	311
South Dakota	845	48	173	60	60	55	57

	total population	Recession (0 to 3)	iGeneration (4 to 18)	0 to 4	5 to 9	10 to 14	15 to 19
Tennessee	6,496	320	1,256	400	418	423	419
Texas	26,448	1,553	5,857	1,941	1,996	1,963	1,887
Utah	2,901	203	735	254	261	245	224
Vermont	627	24	111	30	33	36	45
Virginia	8,260	410	1,575	512	523	520	537
Washington	6,971	356	1,325	445	446	438	439
West Virginia	1,854	82	324	102	106	108	112
Wisconsin	5,743	275	1,115	344	367	372	385
Wyoming	583	31	115	38	40	37	38

Source: Bureau of the Census, State Population Estimates, Internet site http://www.census.gov/popest/data/state/asrh/2013/index .html; calculations by New Strategist

Table 18.8 Younger Generation Share of State Populations, 2013

(percent of population aged 0 to 3 and 4 to 18, and in age groups that include the Recession and iGeneration, by state, 2013)

	total population	Recession (0 to 3)	iGeneration (4 to 18)	0 to 4	5 to 9	10 to 14	15 to 19
United States	**100.0%**	**5.0%**	**19.6%**	**6.3%**	**6.5%**	**6.5%**	**6.7%**
Alabama	100.0	4.9	19.4	6.1	6.4	6.5	6.6
Alaska	100.0	6.0	20.8	7.5	7.1	6.9	6.7
Arizona	100.0	5.2	20.6	6.5	6.9	6.9	6.8
Arkansas	100.0	5.2	20.1	6.5	6.8	6.7	6.6
California	100.0	5.2	20.1	6.5	6.7	6.6	6.9
Colorado	100.0	5.1	19.8	6.4	6.7	6.6	6.4
Connecticut	100.0	4.3	19.2	5.3	6.0	6.5	7.1
Delaware	100.0	4.9	18.7	6.1	6.1	6.2	6.5
District of Columbia	100.0	5.1	14.4	6.3	4.6	3.9	5.8
Florida	100.0	4.4	17.4	5.5	5.7	5.8	6.0
Georgia	100.0	5.4	21.0	6.7	7.0	7.1	7.0
Hawaii	100.0	5.2	17.9	6.5	6.1	5.9	5.7
Idaho	100.0	5.6	22.2	7.0	7.6	7.5	7.0
Illinois	100.0	5.0	19.9	6.2	6.5	6.7	6.8
Indiana	100.0	5.1	20.5	6.4	6.8	6.9	6.9
Iowa	100.0	5.0	19.9	6.3	6.6	6.5	6.9
Kansas	100.0	5.5	20.9	6.9	7.1	6.9	6.9
Kentucky	100.0	5.0	19.4	6.3	6.5	6.5	6.4
Louisiana	100.0	5.3	20.0	6.7	6.8	6.7	6.5
Maine	100.0	3.9	17.1	4.9	5.4	5.7	6.2
Maryland	100.0	5.0	19.1	6.2	6.3	6.3	6.6
Massachusetts	100.0	4.4	18.2	5.5	5.7	6.0	6.8
Michigan	100.0	4.6	19.5	5.8	6.2	6.6	6.9
Minnesota	100.0	5.1	19.8	6.4	6.7	6.6	6.6
Mississippi	100.0	5.3	20.8	6.6	7.0	6.9	7.0
Missouri	100.0	5.0	19.5	6.2	6.5	6.5	6.6
Montana	100.0	4.8	18.6	6.0	6.2	6.1	6.3
Nebraska	100.0	5.6	20.8	7.0	7.1	6.8	6.8
Nevada	100.0	5.1	19.7	6.4	6.7	6.6	6.3
New Hampshire	100.0	4.0	18.1	5.0	5.5	6.1	6.9
New Jersey	100.0	4.8	19.2	6.0	6.3	6.5	6.5
New Mexico	100.0	5.3	20.4	6.7	6.9	6.8	6.7
New York	100.0	4.8	18.3	6.0	5.8	6.0	6.5
North Carolina	100.0	5.0	19.7	6.2	6.6	6.6	6.6
North Dakota	100.0	5.4	19.0	6.7	6.4	5.8	6.8
Ohio	100.0	4.8	19.5	6.0	6.3	6.6	6.7
Oklahoma	100.0	5.5	20.5	6.9	7.0	6.8	6.7
Oregon	100.0	4.7	18.4	5.9	6.1	6.1	6.3
Pennsylvania	100.0	4.5	18.3	5.6	5.8	6.0	6.6
Rhode Island	100.0	4.2	18.2	5.2	5.6	5.8	7.1
South Carolina	100.0	4.9	19.2	6.1	6.4	6.4	6.5
South Dakota	100.0	5.7	20.4	7.1	7.1	6.5	6.8

	total population	Recession (0 to 3)	iGeneration (4 to 18)	0 to 4	5 to 9	10 to 14	15 to 19
Tennessee	100.0%	4.9%	19.3%	6.2%	6.4%	6.5%	6.5 %
Texas	100.0	5.9	22.1	7.3	7.5	7.4	7.1
Utah	100.0	7.0	25.3	8.8	9.0	8.4	7.7
Vermont	100.0	3.9	17.7	4.9	5.3	5.7	7.1
Virginia	100.0	5.0	19.1	6.2	6.3	6.3	6.5
Washington	100.0	5.1	19.0	6.4	6.4	6.3	6.3
West Virginia	100.0	4.4	17.5	5.5	5.7	5.8	6.1
Wisconsin	100.0	4.8	19.4	6.0	6.4	6.5	6.7
Wyoming	100.0	5.3	19.7	6.6	6.9	6.3	6.5

Source: Bureau of the Census, State Population Estimates, Internet site http://www.census.gov/popest/data/state/asrh/2013/index .html; calculations by New Strategist

CHAPTER

19

Spending

■ The oldest members of the iGeneration turned 19 in 2013. Spending trends among households with children helps to reveal their economic status.

■ The spending of married couples with preschoolers fell by a substantial 10 percent between 2006 and 2013, after adjusting for inflation. This household type reined in its spending on most products and services as the cost of health insurance and other necessities climbed.

■ Married couples with school-aged children rank among the nation's biggest spenders, but they cut their spending by 9 percent between 2006 and 2013 after adjusting for inflation. Their spending on food away from home fell 14 percent, and their spending on mortgage interest was down 20 percent.

■ Single parents with children under age 18 spent 8 percent less in 2013 than in 2006, after adjusting for inflation. But their out-of-pocket spending on health insurance climbed by a stunning 52 percent during those years.

Spending of Married Couples with Children Has Stabilized since 2010

Their spending plunged on most items between 2006 and 2013.

Married couples with children spend much more than the average household because they have the highest incomes and the largest households. In 2013, couples with children of any age at home spent an average of $72,518, much greater than the $51,100 spent by the average household.

Between 2000 and 2006 (the year overall household spending peaked), couples with children boosted their spending by 9 percent, after adjusting for inflation. Between 2006 and 2013, however, couples with children reduced their spending by 8 percent. Between 2010 and 2013, spending by this household type stabilized, rising by a tiny 0.7 percent. In the 2006-to-2013 time period, couples with children cut their spending on many discretionary items such as alcoholic beverages (down 22 percent), household furnishings and equipment (down 23 percent), and entertainment (down 7 percent). They were forced to boost their spending on out-of-pocket health insurance costs by a stunning 41 percent.

■ Spending by households with children began to recover in the 2010-to-2013 time period for items such as new cars and trucks (up 20 percent), cash contributions (up 4 percent), and food away from home (up 2 percent).

Married couples with children spent less on many items

(percent change in spending by married couples with children of any age at home on selected items, 2006 and 2013; in 2013 dollars)

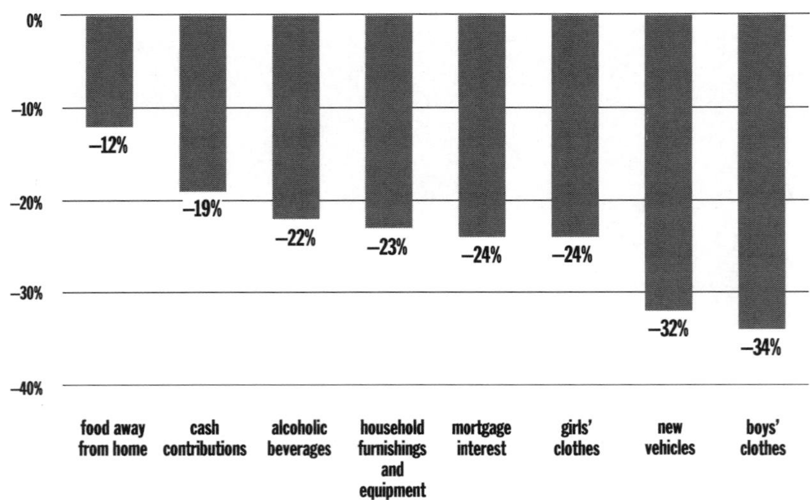

Table 19.1 Average Spending by Married Couples with Children at Home, 2000 to 2013

(average annual spending of consumer units headed by married couples with children of any age at home, 2000 to 2013; percent change for selected years; in 2013 dollars)

	average spending				percent change		
	2013	2010	2006	2000	2010–13	2006–13	2000–06
Number of consumer units headed by married couples with children at home (in 000s)	**28,668**	**28,172**	**29,381**	**28,777**	**1.8%**	**–2.4%**	**2.1%**
Average annual spending of consumer units	**$72,518**	**$71,988**	**$78,986**	**$72,493**	**0.7**	**–8.2**	**9.0**
FOOD	**9,572**	**9,483**	**10,243**	**9,809**	**0.9**	**–6.5**	**4.4**
Food at home	**5,674**	**5,677**	**5,815**	**5,894**	**–0.1**	**–2.4**	**–1.4**
Cereals and bakery products	814	811	779	920	0.4	4.5	–15.3
Cereals and cereal products	279	276	254	325	1.2	9.7	–21.7
Bakery products	535	535	525	595	0.0	2.0	–11.9
Meats, poultry, fish, and eggs	1,201	1,195	1,331	1,506	0.5	–9.8	–11.6
Beef	314	328	387	453	–4.3	–18.9	–14.6
Pork	236	218	257	306	8.3	–8.0	–16.1
Other meats	177	187	186	200	–5.3	–4.9	–7.1
Poultry	245	220	247	280	11.3	–0.9	–11.7
Fish and seafood	155	174	200	207	–11.0	–22.5	–3.4
Eggs	75	68	55	60	9.7	35.2	–6.8
Dairy products	606	619	642	651	–2.0	–5.7	–1.3
Fresh milk and cream	228	237	253	272	–3.9	–9.9	–6.9
Other dairy products	378	381	389	379	–0.9	–2.9	2.8
Fruits and vegetables	1,065	1,045	1,004	961	1.9	6.1	4.5
Fresh fruits	393	368	333	292	6.9	18.1	13.9
Fresh vegetables	325	313	334	285	3.8	–2.7	17.0
Processed fruits	165	174	184	222	–5.2	–10.2	–17.2
Processed vegetables	181	191	153	161	–5.4	18.7	–5.3
Other food at home	1,989	2,007	2,059	1,857	–0.9	–3.4	10.9
Sugar and other sweets	204	210	203	233	–3.1	0.3	–12.6
Fats and oils	161	153	140	153	5.4	15.1	–8.5
Miscellaneous foods	1,055	1,090	1,104	916	–3.2	–4.4	20.5
Nonalcoholic beverages	512	488	543	482	4.9	–5.7	12.8
Food prepared by consumer unit on trips	58	65	68	73	–11.0	–14.9	–6.7
Food away from home	**3,898**	**3,805**	**4,427**	**3,915**	**2.4**	**–11.9**	**13.1**
ALCOHOLIC BEVERAGES	**452**	**453**	**578**	**536**	**–0.2**	**–21.8**	**7.8**
HOUSING	**23,678**	**24,029**	**26,002**	**23,177**	**–1.5**	**–8.9**	**12.2**
Shelter	**13,597**	**13,960**	**14,972**	**13,113**	**–2.6**	**–9.2**	**14.2**
Owned dwellings	9,937	10,457	11,856	10,264	–5.0	–16.2	15.5
Mortgage interest and charges	5,756	6,239	7,590	6,683	–7.7	–24.2	13.6
Property taxes	2,765	2,833	2,740	2,189	–2.4	0.9	25.2
Maintenance, repair, insurance, other expenses	1,415	1,385	1,526	1,392	2.2	–7.3	9.7
Rented dwellings	2,745	2,566	2,241	2,032	7.0	22.5	10.3
Other lodging	916	937	876	817	–2.2	4.6	7.2

	average spending				percent change		
	2013	2010	2006	2000	2010–13	2006–13	2000–06
Utilities, fuels, and public services	**$5,009**	**$5,031**	**$5,121**	**$4,302**	**–0.4%**	**–2.2%**	**19.0%**
Natural gas	528	614	768	536	–14.0	–31.3	43.4
Electricity	1,814	1,892	1,872	1,571	–4.1	–3.1	19.2
Fuel oil and other fuels	176	172	203	162	2.3	–13.5	25.3
Telephone services	1,783	1,672	1,662	1,484	6.6	7.3	12.0
Residential telephone, VOIP, and phone cards	411	532	795	1,235	–22.7	–48.3	–35.6
Cellular phone service	1,372	1,140	867	249	20.4	58.3	248.2
Water and other public services	708	681	616	548	4.0	15.0	12.4
Household services	**2,084**	**1,922**	**2,072**	**1,652**	**8.4**	**0.6**	**25.4**
Personal services	1,088	1,016	1,297	1,015	7.1	–16.1	27.8
Other household services	996	906	775	637	9.9	28.5	21.7
Housekeeping supplies	**869**	**887**	**1,070**	**951**	**–2.0**	**–18.8**	**12.5**
Laundry and cleaning supplies	215	234	261	275	–8.1	–17.7	–4.9
Other household products	479	471	589	457	1.7	–18.7	28.9
Postage and stationery	176	182	220	219	–3.1	–19.8	0.2
Household furnishings and equipment	**2,119**	**2,231**	**2,764**	**3,160**	**–5.0**	**–23.3**	**–12.5**
Household textiles	149	155	223	219	–3.8	–33.2	1.8
Furniture	528	535	770	823	–1.4	–31.4	–6.4
Floor coverings	23	56	80	96	–58.6	–71.2	–17.0
Major appliances	309	313	413	392	–1.3	–25.1	5.2
Small appliances and miscellaneous housewares	131	158	156	165	–17.1	–16.0	–5.5
Miscellaneous household equipment	979	1,014	1,123	1,464	–3.4	–12.8	–23.3
APPAREL AND RELATED SERVICES	**2,461**	**2,605**	**3,241**	**3,719**	**–5.5**	**–24.1**	**–12.8**
Men and boys	**608**	**641**	**849**	**924**	**–5.1**	**–28.4**	**–8.1**
Men, aged 16 or older	442	452	599	632	–2.2	–26.2	–5.3
Boys, aged 2 to 15	166	189	251	292	–12.2	–33.8	–14.2
Women and girls	**913**	**1,018**	**1,302**	**1,423**	**–10.3**	**–29.9**	**–8.5**
Women, aged 16 or older	652	756	958	1,053	–13.8	–31.9	–9.0
Girls, aged 2 to 15	261	262	344	371	–0.3	–24.2	–7.1
Children under age 2	**168**	**199**	**217**	**234**	**–15.5**	**–22.7**	**–7.2**
Footwear	**515**	**456**	**514**	**649**	**12.9**	**0.2**	**–20.8**
Other apparel products and services	**257**	**292**	**358**	**488**	**–11.9**	**–28.3**	**–26.7**
TRANSPORTATION	**13,057**	**11,735**	**14,776**	**15,000**	**11.3**	**–11.6**	**–1.5**
Vehicle purchases	**4,971**	**4,241**	**6,417**	**7,258**	**17.2**	**–22.5**	**–11.6**
Cars and trucks, new	2,346	1,949	3,441	3,352	20.4	–31.8	2.7
Cars and trucks, used	2,606	2,234	2,880	3,811	16.7	–9.5	–24.4
Gasoline and motor oil	**3,840**	**3,266**	**3,751**	**2,542**	**17.6**	**2.4**	**47.6**
Other vehicle expenses	**3,510**	**3,527**	**3,907**	**4,535**	**–0.5**	**–10.2**	**–13.8**
Vehicle finance charges	330	394	574	722	–16.3	–42.5	–20.5
Maintenance and repairs	1,144	1,170	1,107	1,151	–2.2	3.3	–3.8
Vehicle insurance	1,261	1,327	1,427	1,484	–5.0	–11.6	–3.8
Vehicle rentals, leases, licenses, other charges	776	636	798	1,178	22.1	–2.8	–32.2
Public transportation	**737**	**700**	**703**	**664**	**5.3**	**4.9**	**5.8**

	average spending				percent change		
	2013	**2010**	**2006**	**2000**	**2010–13**	**2006–13**	**2000–06**
HEALTH CARE	**$4,436**	**$3,998**	**$3,620**	**$3,120**	**11.0%**	**22.5%**	**16.0%**
Health insurance	2,641	2,227	1,875	1,530	18.6	40.8	22.6
Medical services	1,172	1,073	1,006	944	9.3	16.4	6.6
Drugs	467	528	569	488	–11.5	–17.9	16.4
Medical supplies	157	171	169	157	–8.2	–6.9	7.5
ENTERTAINMENT	**3,630**	**3,875**	**3,903**	**3,874**	**–6.3**	**–7.0**	**0.7**
Fees and admissions	1,022	1,163	1,128	1,150	–12.2	–9.4	–1.9
Audio and visual equipment and services	1,223	1,261	1,381	1,155	–3.0	–11.4	19.5
Pets, toys, and playground equipment	776	865	662	674	–10.3	17.2	–1.7
Pets	556	610	456	372	–8.9	21.8	22.7
Toys, hobbies, and playground equipment	220	255	206	302	–13.8	7.0	–31.8
Other entertainment products and services	608	587	734	896	3.7	–17.1	–18.1
PERSONAL CARE PRODUCTS AND SERVICES	**791**	**848**	**939**	**1,040**	**–6.8**	**–15.8**	**–9.7**
READING	**112**	**120**	**158**	**238**	**–6.4**	**–29.3**	**–33.5**
EDUCATION	**2,223**	**2,242**	**2,044**	**1,523**	**–0.9**	**8.7**	**34.2**
TOBACCO PRODUCTS AND SMOKING SUPPLIES	**299**	**357**	**359**	**484**	**–16.2**	**–16.8**	**–25.8**
MISCELLANEOUS	**798**	**1,064**	**1,091**	**1,208**	**–25.0**	**–26.8**	**–9.7**
CASH CONTRIBUTIONS	**1,955**	**1,883**	**2,407**	**1,650**	**3.8**	**–18.8**	**45.8**
PERSONAL INSURANCE AND PENSIONS	**9,053**	**9,298**	**9,626**	**7,112**	**–2.6**	**–5.9**	**35.3**
Life and other personal insurance	441	565	579	813	–22.0	–23.8	–28.8
Pensions and Social Security*	8,611	8,733	9,047	6,299	–1.4	–4.8	*
GIFTS FOR PEOPLE IN OTHER HOUSEHOLDS	**1,248**	**1,173**	**1,486**	**1,713**	**6.4**	**–16.0**	**–13.2**

**Recent spending on pensions and Social Security is not comparable with 2000 because of changes in methodology.*
Note: The Bureau of Labor Statistics uses consumer unit rather than household as the sampling unit in the Consumer Expenditure Survey. For the definition of consumer unit, see the glossary. Spending on gifts is also included in the preceding product and service categories.
Source: Bureau of Labor Statistics, 2000, 2006, 2010, and 2013 Consumer Expenditure Surveys, Internet site http://www.bls.gov/cex/; calculations by New Strategist

Spending Has Stabilized among Couples with Preschoolers

The spending of married couples with preschoolers fell sharply between 2006 and 2013.

The spending of married couples with preschoolers fell 9.6 percent between 2006 (the year overall household spending peaked) and 2013, after adjusting for inflation—greater than the 8.6 percent decline in spending by the average household. Between 2010 and 2013, however, spending by this household type stabilized with a small 0.4 percent gain.

Couples with preschoolers cut their spending sharply on many items between 2006 and 2013. They reduced their spending on food away from home by 13 percent during those years, after adjusting for inflation. There was some recovery in this category in the 2010-to-2013 time period, with a 5 percent increase in spending. Couples with preschoolers spent 13 percent more on new cars and trucks in 2013 than in 2010. Despite this gain, their 2013 spending on this category was a stunning 40 percent below the 2006 level. As the housing market collapsed and some couples lost their home and others decided not to buy, spending on mortgage interest fell 33 percent between 2006 and 2013, and spending on rent increased 48 percent. Couples with preschoolers spent 27 percent more out-of-pocket on health insurance in 2013 than they did in 2006.

■ Couples with preschoolers were badly hurt by the Great Recession and its aftermath, and it will take them years to recover.

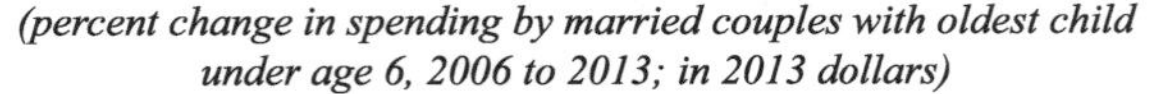

(percent change in spending by married couples with oldest child under age 6, 2006 to 2013; in 2013 dollars)

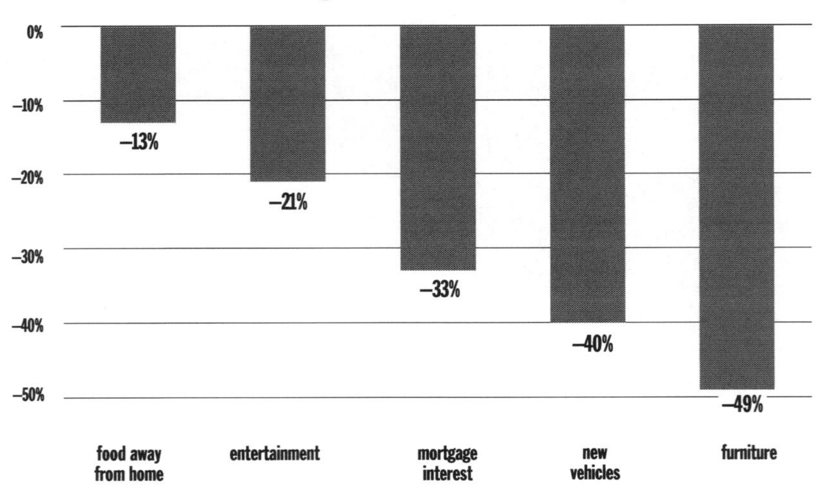

Table 19.2 Average Spending of Married Couples with Preschoolers, 2000 to 2013

(average annual spending of married-couple consumer units with oldest child under age 6, 2000 to 2013; percent change for selected years; in 2013 dollars)

	average spending				percent change		
	2013	2010	2006	2000	2010–13	2006–13	2000–06
Number of consumer units headed by married couples with preschoolers (in 000s)	**5,559**	**5,185**	**5,763**	**5,291**	**7.2%**	**–3.5%**	**8.9%**
Average annual spending of consumer units	**$66,247**	**$65,976**	**$73,280**	**$68,664**	**0.4**	**–9.6**	**6.7**
FOOD	**8,001**	**7,538**	**8,229**	**7,869**	**6.1**	**–2.8**	**4.6**
Food at home	**4,921**	**4,606**	**4,683**	**4,950**	**6.8**	**5.1**	**–5.4**
Cereals and bakery products	679	603	588	733	12.7	15.4	–19.8
Cereals and cereal products	236	222	193	252	6.2	22.3	–23.3
Bakery products	444	380	395	482	16.7	12.3	–17.9
Meats, poultry, fish, and eggs	962	854	911	1,108	12.7	5.6	–17.8
Beef	249	200	283	331	24.6	–12.0	–14.6
Pork	154	135	169	204	14.4	–8.7	–17.4
Other meats	148	169	117	146	–12.3	26.8	–20.1
Poultry	197	174	178	231	13.1	10.7	–23.1
Fish and seafood	144	124	125	147	16.2	15.4	–15.4
Eggs	70	51	39	45	36.5	78.2	–12.0
Dairy products	566	519	599	561	9.0	–5.4	6.6
Fresh milk and cream	227	214	250	238	6.2	–9.1	4.8
Other dairy products	339	304	349	323	11.3	–2.9	7.9
Fruits and vegetables	932	896	852	837	4.0	9.4	1.7
Fresh fruits	352	329	300	254	7.0	17.2	18.1
Fresh vegetables	293	269	250	249	8.8	17.4	0.3
Processed fruits	144	156	179	206	–7.7	–19.6	–12.9
Processed vegetables	143	142	122	127	0.6	16.7	–3.7
Other food at home	1,783	1,734	1,733	1,711	2.8	2.9	1.3
Sugar and other sweets	181	135	151	172	34.5	19.6	–11.9
Fats and oils	137	105	102	100	30.9	34.7	1.6
Miscellaneous foods	1,012	1,085	997	992	–6.8	1.5	0.6
Nonalcoholic beverages	410	364	418	387	12.5	–2.0	8.1
Food prepared by consumer unit on trips	44	46	64	61	–4.2	–30.8	4.4
Food away from home	**3,080**	**2,933**	**3,545**	**2,919**	**5.0**	**–13.1**	**21.4**
ALCOHOLIC BEVERAGES	**516**	**470**	**550**	**507**	**9.8**	**–6.2**	**8.4**
HOUSING	**25,385**	**25,874**	**28,700**	**25,301**	**–1.9**	**–11.6**	**13.4**
Shelter	**13,904**	**15,146**	**16,284**	**14,067**	**–8.2**	**–14.6**	**15.8**
Owned dwellings	9,194	10,714	12,807	10,639	–14.2	–28.2	20.4
Mortgage interest and charges	5,930	6,970	8,833	7,420	–14.9	–32.9	19.0
Property taxes	2,190	2,357	2,685	2,035	–7.1	–18.5	32.0
Maintenance, repair, insurance, other expenses	1,074	1,388	1,287	1,182	–22.6	–16.6	8.9
Rented dwellings	4,245	3,716	2,869	2,925	14.2	48.0	–1.9
Other lodging	465	716	609	503	–35.0	–23.6	21.0

	average spending				percent change		
	2013	2010	2006	2000	2010–13	2006–13	2000–06
Utilities, fuels, and public services	**$3,811**	**$4,059**	**$4,311**	**$3,793**	**–6.1%**	**–11.6%**	**13.7%**
Natural gas	422	550	700	487	–23.3	–39.7	43.8
Electricity	1,368	1,476	1,566	1,293	–7.3	–12.6	21.1
Fuel oil and other fuels	114	127	154	154	–10.3	–25.8	–0.3
Telephone services	1,376	1,354	1,381	1,414	1.7	–0.4	–2.3
Residential telephone, VOIP, and phone cards	238	332	663	1,163	–28.4	–64.1	–43.0
Cellular phone service	1,137	1,021	718	250	11.3	58.4	186.7
Water and other public services	532	552	511	445	–3.7	4.2	14.8
Household services	**4,523**	**3,992**	**4,027**	**3,220**	**13.3**	**12.3**	**25.1**
Personal services	3,569	3,162	3,269	2,692	12.9	9.2	21.4
Other household services	954	830	758	528	14.9	25.9	43.7
Housekeeping supplies	**887**	**701**	**871**	**836**	**26.6**	**1.8**	**4.2**
Laundry and cleaning supplies	205	170	235	203	20.7	–12.6	15.6
Other household products	482	415	438	409	16.3	10.1	7.2
Postage and stationery	200	116	199	225	71.7	0.6	–11.5
Household furnishings and equipment	**2,260**	**1,977**	**3,207**	**3,385**	**14.3**	**–29.5**	**–5.3**
Household textiles	165	114	222	242	44.3	–25.6	–8.4
Furniture	565	566	1,114	977	–0.2	–49.3	14.0
Floor coverings	24	58	79	62	–58.4	–69.5	26.3
Major appliances	293	323	425	358	–9.2	–31.1	18.6
Small appliances and miscellaneous housewares	166	148	118	169	11.8	40.8	–30.3
Miscellaneous household equipment	1,046	768	1,250	1,576	36.2	–16.3	–20.7
APPAREL AND RELATED SERVICES	**2,519**	**2,317**	**3,081**	**3,504**	**8.7**	**–18.2**	**–12.1**
Men and boys	**439**	**381**	**681**	**728**	**15.1**	**–35.5**	**–6.5**
Men, aged 16 or older	332	268	504	528	23.8	–34.1	–4.5
Boys, aged 2 to 15	107	113	177	200	–5.5	–39.5	–11.7
Women and girls	**763**	**724**	**1,082**	**1,051**	**5.3**	**–29.5**	**2.9**
Women, aged 16 or older	564	538	864	843	4.7	–34.7	2.6
Girls, aged 2 to 15	200	186	217	208	7.6	–7.9	4.3
Children under age 2	**524**	**655**	**638**	**674**	**–20.0**	**–17.9**	**–5.3**
Footwear	**481**	**247**	**378**	**607**	**94.9**	**27.3**	**–37.8**
Other apparel products and services	**312**	**311**	**304**	**444**	**0.4**	**2.7**	**–31.5**
TRANSPORTATION	**11,696**	**9,996**	**12,928**	**14,536**	**17.0**	**–9.5**	**–11.1**
Vehicle purchases	**4,822**	**4,018**	**6,022**	**7,568**	**20.0**	**–19.9**	**–20.4**
Cars and trucks, new	2,129	1,885	3,542	3,571	13.0	–39.9	–0.8
Cars and trucks, used	2,643	2,114	2,462	3,810	25.0	7.3	–35.4
Gasoline and motor oil	**3,068**	**2,618**	**3,015**	**2,156**	**17.2**	**1.8**	**39.8**
Other vehicle expenses	**3,210**	**2,819**	**3,361**	**4,261**	**13.9**	**–4.5**	**–21.1**
Vehicle finance charges	363	425	600	745	–14.6	–39.5	–19.5
Maintenance and repairs	884	958	746	963	–7.8	18.4	–22.5
Vehicle insurance	1,227	802	1,094	1,295	52.9	12.1	–15.5
Vehicle rentals, leases, licenses, other charges	736	634	921	1,257	16.2	–20.1	–26.7
Public transportation	**597**	**541**	**530**	**551**	**10.4**	**12.6**	**–3.7**

	average spending				percent change		
	2013	2010	2006	2000	2010–13	2006–13	2000–06
HEALTH CARE	**$3,503**	**$3,337**	**$3,150**	**$2,566**	**5.0%**	**11.2%**	**22.7%**
Health insurance	2,123	1,898	1,674	1,387	11.8	26.8	20.8
Medical services	956	1,001	988	741	–4.5	–3.2	33.3
Drugs	309	324	388	326	–4.5	–20.4	19.1
Medical supplies	116	115	99	114	0.5	16.7	–12.5
ENTERTAINMENT	**2,629**	**3,065**	**3,327**	**2,964**	**–14.2**	**–21.0**	**12.2**
Fees and admissions	513	578	662	657	–11.2	–22.5	0.7
Audio and visual equipment and services	1,003	1,129	1,249	970	–11.2	–19.7	28.8
Pets, toys, and playground equipment	668	853	683	651	–21.6	–2.2	5.0
Pets	331	569	339	221	–41.9	–2.2	53.5
Toys, hobbies, and playground equipment	337	283	344	430	19.0	–2.1	–20.0
Other entertainment products and services	445	504	731	685	–11.8	–39.2	6.9
PERSONAL CARE PRODUCTS AND SERVICES	**708**	**679**	**863**	**878**	**4.2**	**–18.0**	**–1.7**
READING	**77**	**83**	**121**	**235**	**–7.6**	**–36.5**	**–48.5**
EDUCATION	**743**	**697**	**659**	**568**	**6.7**	**12.8**	**15.9**
TOBACCO PRODUCTS AND SMOKING SUPPLIES	**184**	**262**	**248**	**372**	**–29.7**	**–25.9**	**–33.2**
MISCELLANEOUS	**629**	**1,209**	**894**	**929**	**–48.0**	**–29.7**	**–3.8**
CASH CONTRIBUTIONS	**1,482**	**1,297**	**1,557**	**1,147**	**14.3**	**–4.8**	**35.7**
PERSONAL INSURANCE AND PENSIONS	**8,174**	**9,149**	**8,974**	**7,289**	**–10.7**	**–8.9**	**23.1**
Life and other personal insurance	267	500	419	652	–46.6	–36.3	–35.7
Pensions and Social Security	7,907	8,649	8,554	6,637	–8.6	–7.6	28.9
GIFTS FOR PEOPLE IN OTHER HOUSEHOLDS	**506**	**662**	**1,045**	**1,242**	**–23.6**	**–51.6**	**–15.9**

Note: The Bureau of Labor Statistics uses consumer unit rather than household as the sampling unit in the Consumer Expenditure Survey. For the definition of consumer unit, see the glossary. Spending on gifts is also included in the preceding product and service categories.

Source: Bureau of Labor Statistics, 2000, 2006, 2010, and 2013 Consumer Expenditure Surveys, Internet site http://www.bls.gov/cex/; calculations by New Strategist

Spending of Couples with School-Aged Children Continues to Fall

They cut their spending sharply on most categories between 2006 and 2013.

Married couples with school-aged children rank among the most affluent households in the nation, and their spending—at $72,639 in 2013—is far above average. Because of the Great Recession, however, these households cut their spending by 9 percent between 2006 and 2013, after adjusting for inflation. Unlike some other household types, the spending of these couples did not show any sign of recovery in the 2010-to-2013 time period.

Couples with school-aged children cut their spending on most items between 2006 and 2013. They spent 3 percent less on food at home (groceries), after adjusting for inflation. Their spending on food away from home fell by a much larger 14 percent. They spent 4 percent less on entertainment, 32 percent less on alcoholic beverages, and 28 percent less on new cars and trucks. Their spending on new vehicles recovered somewhat in the 2010-to-2013 time period, with a gain of 12 percent. Couples with school-aged children cut their spending on mortgage interest by 20 percent between 2006 and 2013 as some lost their home and others chose not to buy. Meanwhile, their spending on rent climbed 19 percent.

Couples with school-aged children spent 47 percent more out-of-pocket on health insurance in 2013 than in 2006, after adjusting for inflation. They spent 14 percent more on education.

■ The spending of married couples with school-aged children will remain muted until these families feel more economically secure.

Couples with school-aged children are spending more for health insurance

(percent change in spending by married couples with children aged 6 to 17 on selected items, 2006 to 2013; in 2013 dollars)

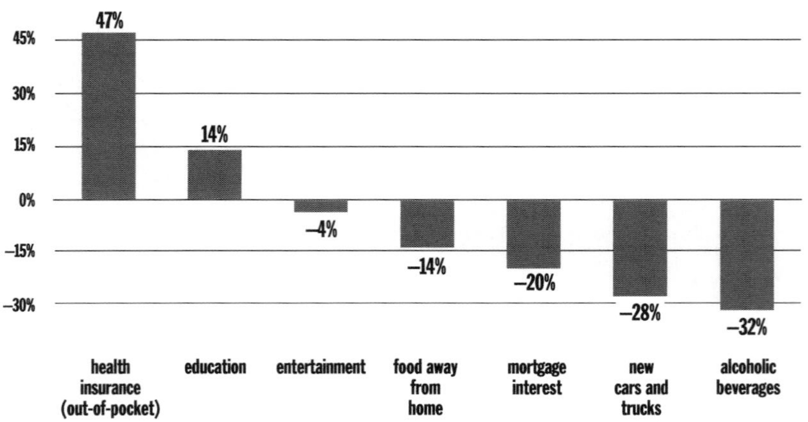

Table 19.3 Average Spending of Married Couples with School-Aged Children, 2000 to 2013

(average annual spending of married-couple consumer units with oldest child aged 6 to 17, 2000 to 2013; percent change for selected years; in 2013 dollars)

	average spending				percent change		
	2013	2010	2006	2000	2010–13	2006–13	2000–06
Number of consumer units headed by married couples with school-aged children (in 000s)	**14,066**	**14,242**	**15,166**	**15,396**	**–1.2**	**–7.3**	**–1.5**
Average annual spending of consumer units	**$72,639**	**$74,288**	**$79,914**	**$73,283**	**–2.2**	**–9.1**	**9.0**
FOOD	**9,825**	**10,027**	**10,644**	**10,157**	**–2.0**	**–7.7**	**4.8**
Food at home	**5,715**	**5,850**	**5,879**	**6,031**	**–2.3**	**–2.8**	**–2.5**
Cereals and bakery products	833	866	818	950	–3.9	1.8	–13.9
Cereals and cereal products	292	297	266	346	–1.7	9.9	–23.3
Bakery products	541	569	552	602	–5.0	–2.1	–8.2
Meats, poultry, fish, and eggs	1,203	1,222	1,329	1,563	–1.6	–9.5	–15.0
Beef	311	326	374	467	–4.6	–16.9	–19.8
Pork	232	229	253	319	1.5	–8.3	–20.7
Other meats	179	187	192	207	–4.3	–6.7	–7.3
Poultry	252	232	250	284	8.7	1.0	–12.1
Fish and seafood	153	175	203	227	–12.7	–24.8	–10.5
Eggs	77	74	57	60	4.5	36.0	–4.9
Dairy products	630	645	662	672	–2.4	–4.9	–1.5
Fresh milk and cream	243	247	266	283	–1.5	–8.6	–6.0
Other dairy products	387	398	396	390	–2.9	–2.4	1.7
Fruits and vegetables	1,096	1,061	1,003	970	3.3	9.3	3.4
Fresh fruits	422	381	330	291	10.6	27.7	13.6
Fresh vegetables	330	313	330	288	5.4	–0.1	14.7
Processed fruits	165	174	181	229	–5.2	–9.1	–20.6
Processed vegetables	179	192	161	162	–6.9	11.4	–1.1
Other food at home	1,952	2,057	2,066	1,878	–5.1	–5.5	10.0
Sugar and other sweets	202	232	208	238	–12.9	–2.9	–12.6
Fats and oils	153	156	138	160	–1.9	11.3	–13.9
Miscellaneous foods	1,030	1,101	1,107	917	–6.5	–7.0	20.7
Nonalcoholic beverages	508	494	548	483	2.9	–7.3	13.4
Food prepared by consumer unit on trips	59	74	67	80	–20.0	–12.0	–16.0
Food away from home	**4,111**	**4,177**	**4,764**	**4,126**	**–1.6**	**–13.7**	**15.5**
ALCOHOLIC BEVERAGES	**399**	**450**	**585**	**494**	**–11.3**	**–31.8**	**18.4**
HOUSING	**23,840**	**24,673**	**26,263**	**23,584**	**–3.4**	**–9.2**	**11.4**
Shelter	**14,216**	**14,538**	**15,592**	**13,576**	**–2.2**	**–8.8**	**14.9**
Owned dwellings	10,346	10,903	12,342	10,737	–5.1	–16.2	14.9
Mortgage interest and charges	6,319	6,704	7,941	7,143	–5.7	–20.4	11.2
Property taxes	2,763	2,911	2,859	2,170	–5.1	–3.4	31.7
Maintenance, repair, insurance, other expenses	1,264	1,287	1,543	1,425	–1.8	–18.1	8.3
Rented dwellings	2,897	2,661	2,427	2,087	8.9	19.4	16.3
Other lodging	973	974	824	752	–0.1	18.1	9.5

	average spending				percent change		
	2013	2010	2006	2000	2010–13	2006–13	2000–06
Utilities, fuels, and public services	**$5,008**	**$5,105**	**$5,186**	**$4,320**	**–1.9%**	**–3.4%**	**20.1%**
Natural gas	526	611	779	537	–13.9	–32.5	45.0
Electricity	1,857	1,943	1,901	1,583	–4.4	–2.3	20.1
Fuel oil and other fuels	123	166	221	160	–25.7	–44.3	38.3
Telephone services	1,788	1,674	1,647	1,483	6.8	8.6	11.1
Residential telephone, VOIP, and phone cards	396	546	800	1,231	–27.5	–50.5	–35.0
Cellular phone service	1,392	1,128	847	252	23.4	64.3	236.6
Water and other public services	714	712	639	557	0.3	11.7	14.6
Household services	**1,789**	**1,755**	**1,832**	**1,600**	**1.9**	**–2.3**	**14.4**
Personal services	746	779	1,004	894	–4.2	–25.7	12.3
Other household services	1,043	976	826	708	6.8	26.2	16.8
Housekeeping supplies	**854**	**943**	**1,089**	**979**	**–9.5**	**–21.5**	**11.1**
Laundry and cleaning supplies	193	260	255	306	–25.7	–24.4	–16.5
Other household products	483	495	617	467	–2.4	–21.7	32.2
Postage and stationery	178	189	216	207	–5.9	–17.6	4.4
Household furnishings and equipment	**1,973**	**2,331**	**2,564**	**3,107**	**–15.4**	**–23.1**	**–17.5**
Household textiles	123	163	174	212	–24.8	–29.5	–17.8
Furniture	487	575	727	859	–15.3	–33.0	–15.4
Floor coverings	26	71	83	81	–63.1	–68.7	2.5
Major appliances	293	293	361	371	0.1	–18.7	–2.7
Small appliances and miscellaneous housewares	109	131	141	162	–17.1	–22.7	–13.2
Miscellaneous household equipment	936	1,099	1,078	1,423	–14.9	–13.2	–24.2
APPAREL AND RELATED SERVICES	**2,540**	**2,855**	**3,296**	**3,839**	**–11.0**	**–22.9**	**–14.2**
Men and boys	**650**	**718**	**902**	**970**	**–9.5**	**–28.0**	**–7.0**
Men, aged 16 or older	402	442	540	570	–9.1	–25.5	–5.3
Boys, aged 2 to 15	248	276	363	400	–10.0	–31.7	–9.4
Women and girls	**973**	**1,185**	**1,329**	**1,480**	**–17.9**	**–26.8**	**–10.2**
Women, aged 16 or older	630	793	848	940	–20.5	–25.7	–9.8
Girls, aged 2 to 15	344	392	482	541	–12.3	–28.6	–11.0
Children under age 2	**109**	**123**	**141**	**138**	**–11.3**	**–22.7**	**2.2**
Footwear	**557**	**536**	**544**	**726**	**3.9**	**2.3**	**–25.1**
Other apparel products and services	**250**	**293**	**379**	**525**	**–14.6**	**–34.0**	**–27.8**
TRANSPORTATION	**12,715**	**11,948**	**14,755**	**14,400**	**6.4**	**–13.8**	**2.5**
Vehicle purchases	**4,793**	**4,527**	**6,456**	**6,902**	**5.9**	**–25.8**	**–6.5**
Cars and trucks, new	2,562	2,289	3,557	3,218	11.9	–28.0	10.5
Cars and trucks, used	2,225	2,193	2,789	3,596	1.4	–20.2	–22.4
Gasoline and motor oil	**3,879**	**3,289**	**3,751**	**2,524**	**17.9**	**3.4**	**48.6**
Other vehicle expenses	**3,266**	**3,354**	**3,843**	**4,318**	**–2.6**	**–15.0**	**–11.0**
Vehicle finance charges	346	378	571	699	–8.5	–39.4	–18.4
Maintenance and repairs	1,100	1,159	1,150	1,119	–5.1	–4.3	2.8
Vehicle insurance	1,022	1,235	1,314	1,328	–17.2	–22.2	–1.1
Vehicle rentals, leases, licenses, other charges	799	581	808	1,172	37.5	–1.1	–31.1
Public transportation	**777**	**779**	**705**	**656**	**–0.2**	**10.2**	**7.4**

	average spending				percent change		
	2013	2010	2006	2000	2010–13	2006–13	2000–06
HEALTH CARE	**$4,344**	**$3,879**	**$3,511**	**$3,045**	**12.0%**	**23.7%**	**15.3%**
Health insurance	2,660	2,136	1,814	1,458	24.6	46.6	24.4
Medical services	1,120	1,090	998	989	2.8	12.2	1.0
Drugs	422	478	518	442	–11.6	–18.5	17.0
Medical supplies	143	175	180	156	–18.4	–20.7	15.9
ENTERTAINMENT	**4,154**	**4,460**	**4,319**	**4,397**	**–6.9**	**–3.8**	**–1.8**
Fees and admissions	1,351	1,555	1,420	1,419	–13.1	–4.9	0.1
Audio and visual equipment and services	1,303	1,326	1,434	1,241	–1.7	–9.1	15.6
Pets, toys, and playground equipment	861	874	669	740	–1.5	28.7	–9.6
Pets	618	572	447	400	8.1	38.2	11.7
Toys, hobbies, and playground equipment	243	302	222	340	–19.6	9.5	–34.7
Other entertainment products and services	639	705	796	996	–9.4	–19.7	–20.0
PERSONAL CARE PRODUCTS AND SERVICES	**772**	**875**	**905**	**1,047**	**–11.8**	**–14.7**	**–13.6**
READING	**115**	**125**	**166**	**235**	**–8.0**	**–30.9**	**–29.3**
EDUCATION	**2,150**	**2,169**	**1,887**	**1,396**	**–0.9**	**13.9**	**35.2**
TOBACCO PRODUCTS AND SMOKING SUPPLIES	**280**	**328**	**369**	**455**	**–14.6**	**–24.0**	**–18.9**
MISCELLANEOUS	**727**	**995**	**1,114**	**1,299**	**–26.9**	**–34.7**	**–14.2**
CASH CONTRIBUTIONS	**1,880**	**1,969**	**2,445**	**1,718**	**–4.5**	**–23.1**	**42.3**
PERSONAL INSURANCE AND PENSIONS	**8,897**	**9,535**	**9,656**	**7,216**	**–6.7**	**–7.9**	**33.8**
Life and other personal insurance	435	557	603	798	–21.8	–27.9	–24.4
Pensions and Social Security	8,462	8,978	9,053	6,418	–5.8	–6.5	41.1
GIFTS FOR PEOPLE IN OTHER HOUSEHOLDS	**1,203**	**1,303**	**1,662**	**1,552**	**–7.7**	**–27.6**	**7.1**

Note: The Bureau of Labor Statistics uses consumer unit rather than household as the sampling unit in the Consumer Expenditure Survey. For the definition of consumer unit, see the glossary. Spending on gifts is also included in the preceding product and service categories.

Source: Bureau of Labor Statistics, 2000, 2006, 2010, and 2013 Consumer Expenditure Surveys, Internet site http://www.bls.gov/cex/; calculations by New Strategist

Single Parents Are Spending Less

Spending fell 8 percent between 2006 and 2013, after adjusting for inflation.

Single parents with children under age 18 at home spent an average of $37,752 in 2013—7.9 percent less than they spent in 2006, after adjusting for inflation. This spending decline was somewhat less than the 8.6 percent cut made by the average household, but the spending of single parents fell well more than average in the more recent 2010-to-2013 time period—a 4.3 percent decline for single parents versus an 0.6 percent decline for the average household.

Between 2006 and 2013, single parents cut their spending on food away from home by a substantial 23 percent, after adjusting for inflation. They spent an even larger 33 percent less on alcoholic beverages. They cut their spending on entertainment by 20 percent. Mortgage interest payments fell 15 percent as some lost their home and others were unable or unwilling to buy. Meanwhile, spending on rent climbed 5 percent. Out-of-pocket spending on health insurance increased 52 percent during those years.

■ Single parent families are spending more on necessities such as health insurance and less on discretionary items such as entertainment.

Single parents are cutting corners on many discretionary items

(percent change in spending by single parent families with children under age 18 at home, 2006 to 2013; in 2013 dollars)

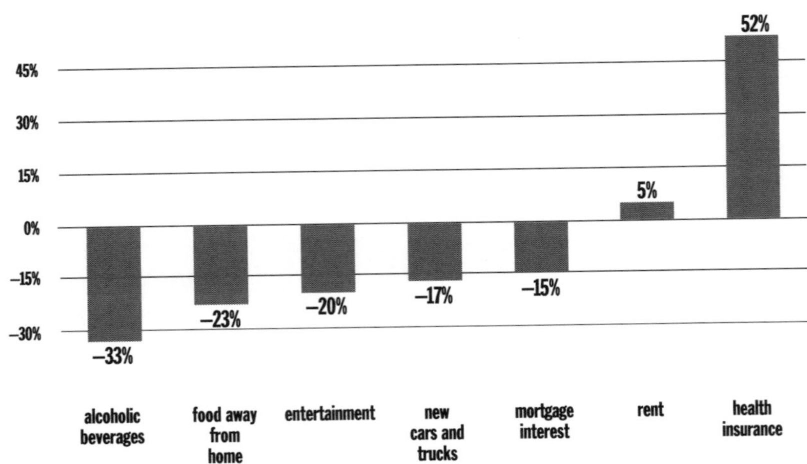

Table 19.4 Average Spending of Single Parents with Children under Age 18 at Home, 2000 to 2013

(average annual spending of consumer units headed by single parents with children under age 18 at home, 2000 to 2013; percent change for selected years; in 2013 dollars)

	average spending				percent change		
	2013	2010	2006	2000	2010–13	2006–13	2000–06
Number of consumer units headed by single parents with children under age 18 at home (in 000s)	**6,777**	**7,141**	**7,225**	**6,132**	**–5.1%**	**–6.2%**	**17.8%**
Average annual spending of consumer units	**$37,752**	**$39,457**	**$41,011**	**$39,128**	**–4.3**	**–7.9**	**4.8**
FOOD	**5,550**	**5,584**	**5,938**	**5,756**	**–0.6**	**–6.5**	**3.2**
Food at home	**3,697**	**3,512**	**3,520**	**3,581**	**5.3**	**5.0**	**–1.7**
Cereals and bakery products	545	482	476	525	13.1	14.5	–9.3
Cereals and cereal products	205	158	176	207	29.7	16.7	–15.1
Bakery products	340	324	299	317	5.0	13.6	–5.5
Meats, poultry, fish, and eggs	823	775	838	1,020	6.3	–1.8	–17.9
Beef	220	199	237	302	10.7	–7.1	–21.5
Pork	153	137	164	215	11.9	–6.8	–23.7
Other meats	113	118	118	123	–3.8	–4.1	–4.3
Poultry	180	168	158	207	7.3	13.7	–23.5
Fish and seafood	106	108	125	126	–1.8	–15.1	–0.8
Eggs	51	46	36	45	11.0	42.4	–19.8
Dairy products	381	340	364	377	12.1	4.7	–3.6
Fresh milk and cream	144	127	156	158	13.3	–7.7	–1.4
Other dairy products	237	213	208	219	11.5	13.9	–5.1
Fruits and vegetables	624	604	515	552	3.4	21.1	–6.6
Fresh fruits	197	208	153	154	–5.4	29.2	–1.1
Fresh vegetables	183	148	142	158	23.2	28.8	–10.2
Processed fruits	108	122	114	142	–11.3	–5.6	–19.5
Processed vegetables	136	125	106	97	8.8	27.9	9.1
Other food at home	1,325	1,314	1,327	1,107	0.8	–0.1	19.9
Sugar and other sweets	135	121	112	145	11.8	20.4	–22.6
Fats and oils	115	97	80	106	18.3	44.2	–24.4
Miscellaneous foods	687	726	706	486	–5.4	–2.7	45.4
Nonalcoholic beverages	365	345	400	326	5.8	–8.7	22.6
Food prepared by consumer unit on trips	23	24	29	43	–2.1	–20.4	–33.3
Food away from home	**1,853**	**2,072**	**2,419**	**2,175**	**–10.5**	**–23.4**	**11.2**
ALCOHOLIC BEVERAGES	**179**	**178**	**268**	**253**	**0.3**	**–33.2**	**6.0**
HOUSING	**14,703**	**15,196**	**15,993**	**14,519**	**–3.2**	**–8.1**	**10.2**
Shelter	**8,803**	**8,828**	**9,308**	**8,565**	**–0.3**	**–5.4**	**8.7**
Owned dwellings	3,758	3,887	4,537	3,784	–3.3	–17.2	19.9
Mortgage interest and charges	2,381	2,461	2,789	2,292	–3.3	–14.6	21.7
Property taxes	963	1,022	1,050	874	–5.8	–8.3	20.2
Maintenance, repair, insurance, other expenses	414	404	697	618	2.5	–40.6	12.7
Rented dwellings	4,789	4,724	4,551	4,485	1.4	5.2	1.5
Other lodging	256	216	220	296	18.6	16.6	–25.9

	average spending				percent change		
	2013	**2010**	**2006**	**2000**	**2010–13**	**2006–13**	**2000–06**
Utilities, fuels, and public services	**$3,351**	**$3,570**	**$3,849**	**$3,159**	**–6.1%**	**–12.9%**	**21.9%**
Natural gas	323	407	569	414	–20.6	–43.2	37.3
Electricity	1,383	1,453	1,481	1,167	–4.8	–6.6	26.9
Fuel oil and other fuels	87	64	69	58	35.7	25.5	19.2
Telephone services	1146	1,219	1,331	1,208	–6.0	–13.9	10.2
Residential telephone, VOIP, and phone cards	206	309	662	1,092	–33.3	–68.9	–39.4
Cellular phone service	940	910	669	116	3.3	40.5	475.1
Water and other public services	411	426	399	311	–3.6	3.1	28.1
Household services	**1096**	**1,265**	**1,120**	**1,063**	**–13.4**	**–2.1**	**5.3**
Personal services	543	744	742	793	–27.0	–26.8	–6.4
Other household services	553	522	378	271	5.9	46.3	39.7
Housekeeping supplies	**451**	**473**	**489**	**498**	**–4.7**	**–7.7**	**–1.8**
Laundry and cleaning supplies	142	168	173	204	–15.3	–18.1	–15.1
Other household products	249	228	205	189	9.4	21.7	8.0
Postage and stationery	61	78	111	104	–21.8	–45.0	6.5
Household furnishings and equipment	**1,002**	**1,059**	**1,228**	**1,234**	**–5.4**	**–18.4**	**–0.4**
Household textiles	75	119	117	81	–36.8	–35.7	43.8
Furniture	243	297	352	368	–18.2	–31.1	–4.2
Floor coverings	7	6	13	30	9.2	–44.9	–57.3
Major appliances	234	151	131	141	55.3	79.2	–7.2
Small appliances and miscellaneous housewares	47	62	80	49	–24.1	–41.1	63.7
Miscellaneous household equipment	396	423	537	564	–6.4	–26.3	–4.8
APPAREL AND RELATED SERVICES	**1,595**	**2,149**	**2,153**	**2,599**	**–25.8**	**–25.9**	**–17.2**
Men and boys	**305**	**438**	**380**	**549**	**–30.4**	**–19.8**	**–30.8**
Men, aged 16 or older	108	230	133	200	–53.0	–18.7	–33.6
Boys, aged 2 to 15	197	208	247	350	–5.4	–20.3	–29.4
Women and girls	**686**	**982**	**938**	**1,098**	**–30.1**	**–26.9**	**–14.6**
Women, aged 16 or older	387	754	616	720	–48.7	–37.2	–14.4
Girls, aged 2 to 15	299	226	322	377	32.0	–7.3	–14.6
Children under age 2	**81**	**119**	**127**	**150**	**–31.7**	**–36.3**	**–15.4**
Footwear	**386**	**415**	**517**	**556**	**–6.9**	**–25.3**	**–7.1**
Other apparel products and services	**136**	**198**	**190**	**244**	**–31.2**	**–28.2**	**–22.2**
TRANSPORTATION	**6,781**	**6,867**	**6,360**	**6,787**	**–1.3**	**6.6**	**–6.3**
Vehicle purchases	**2,537**	**2,430**	**2,215**	**3,163**	**4.4**	**14.5**	**–30.0**
Cars and trucks, new	530	999	639	709	–46.9	–17.1	–9.9
Cars and trucks, used	2,006	1,386	1,563	2,449	44.8	28.3	–36.1
Gasoline and motor oil	**2,045**	**1,833**	**1,961**	**1,209**	**11.5**	**4.3**	**62.1**
Other vehicle expenses	**1,905**	**2,308**	**1,881**	**2,054**	**–17.4**	**1.3**	**–8.4**
Vehicle finance charges	159	238	223	294	–33.3	–28.7	–24.0
Maintenance and repairs	555	635	540	636	–12.5	2.8	–15.1
Vehicle insurance	770	1,116	770	749	–31.0	0.1	2.7
Vehicle rentals, leases, licenses, other charges	422	317	350	373	33.0	20.5	–6.2
Public transportation	**294**	**297**	**302**	**361**	**–1.0**	**–2.5**	**–16.5**

	average spending				percent change		
	2013	2010	2006	2000	2010–13	2006–13	2000–06
HEALTH CARE	**$1,752**	**$1,616**	**$1,509**	**$1,372**	**8.4%**	**16.1%**	**10.0%**
Health insurance	1,134	837	744	613	35.6	52.4	21.4
Medical services	383	487	443	491	–21.4	–13.5	–9.9
Drugs	169	231	242	196	–26.8	–30.0	23.1
Medical supplies	66	62	81	73	6.5	–18.4	10.7
ENTERTAINMENT	**1,724**	**1,826**	**2,148**	**1,939**	**–5.6**	**–19.7**	**10.8**
Fees and admissions	404	436	465	547	–7.3	–13.0	–15.0
Audio and visual equipment and services	795	871	946	800	–8.7	–16.0	18.4
Pets, toys, and playground equipment	391	354	333	345	10.6	17.5	–3.5
Pets	283	236	220	161	19.9	28.9	36.4
Toys, hobbies, and playground equipment	107	118	113	184	–8.9	–5.5	–38.4
Other entertainment products and services	134	165	404	246	–18.6	–66.9	64.3
PERSONAL CARE PRODUCTS AND SERVICES	**548**	**561**	**532**	**770**	**–2.3**	**3.1**	**–30.9**
READING	**58**	**45**	**73**	**103**	**29.3**	**–20.3**	**–29.2**
EDUCATION	**765**	**397**	**871**	**534**	**92.5**	**–12.2**	**63.0**
TOBACCO PRODUCTS AND SMOKING SUPPLIES	**241**	**324**	**299**	**404**	**–25.5**	**–19.5**	**–26.0**
MISCELLANEOUS	**391**	**652**	**744**	**1,061**	**–40.0**	**–47.5**	**–29.8**
CASH CONTRIBUTIONS	**751**	**955**	**847**	**551**	**–21.4**	**–11.3**	**53.8**
PERSONAL INSURANCE AND PENSIONS	**2,715**	**3,107**	**3,276**	**2,481**	**–12.6**	**–17.1**	**32.0**
Life and other personal insurance	125	139	173	203	–10.0	–27.9	–14.6
Pensions and Social Security	2,590	2,968	3,104	2,277	–12.7	–16.6	36.3
GIFTS FOR PEOPLE IN OTHER HOUSEHOLDS	**548**	**480**	**559**	**924**	**14.2**	**–2.0**	**–39.5**

Note: The Bureau of Labor Statistics uses consumer unit rather than household as the sampling unit in the Consumer Expenditure Survey. For the definition of consumer unit, see the glossary. Spending on gifts is also included in the preceding product and service categories.

Source: Bureau of Labor Statistics, 2000, 2006, 2010, and 2013 Consumer Expenditure Surveys, Internet site http://www.bls.gov/cex/; calculations by New Strategist

Married Couples with Children Spend More than Average

Single parents spend less than average on most products and services.

Because married couples with children under age 18 have higher than average incomes and larger than average households, their spending is also above average. Overall, couples with preschoolers spend 30 percent more than the average household, and couples with school-aged children spend 42 percent more. Single-parent families, in contrast, spend 26 percent less than average. Married couples with preschoolers account for 5.7 percent of total household spending, while those with school-aged children account for a much larger 15.9 percent. Single parents control only 4.0 percent of household spending.

Couples with preschoolers spend much more than average on items needed by young children. They spend nearly 10 times the average on household personal services (mostly day care) and about seven times the average on clothes for infants.

Couples with school-aged children spend much more than average on most products and services. Alcoholic beverages, rent, fuel oil, drugs, and tobacco are the only exceptions.

Single parents spend less than average on all but a few categories. They are above average spenders on items such as rent, household personal services (mostly day care), children's clothes, and used vehicles.

■ Many married couples with children bought homes during the housing bubble. This explains why their mortgage interest payments are about twice the average.

Married couples with school-aged children spend the most

(indexed average annual spending of households with children by type of household, 2013; 100 is the index for the average household)

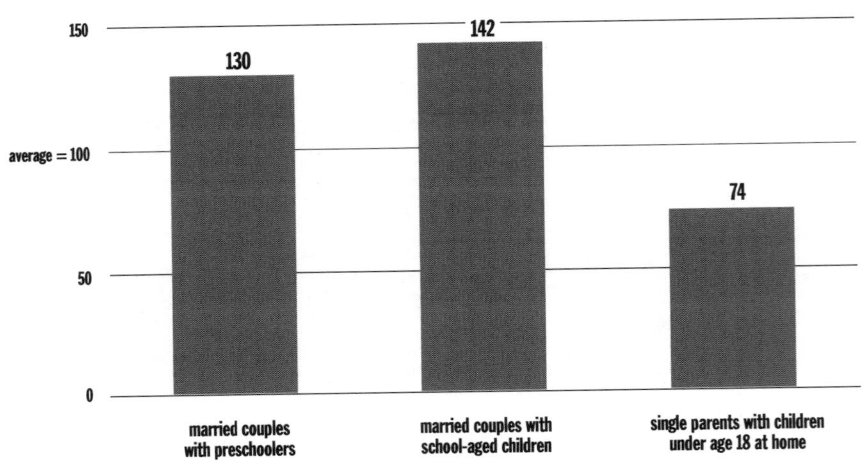

Table 19.5 Indexed Spending of Households with Children, 2013

(indexed spending of total consumer units and consumer units with children under age 18 at home, by type of consumer unit, 2013)

	total consumer units	married couples, oldest child under age 6	married couples, oldest child aged 6 to 17	single parents with children under age 18
Number of consumer units (in 000s)	**125,670**	**5,559**	**14,066**	**6,777**
Average annual spending	**100**	**130**	**142**	**74**
FOOD	**100**	**121**	**149**	**84**
Food at home	**100**	**124**	**144**	**93**
Cereals and bakery products	100	125	153	100
Cereals and cereal products	100	128	158	111
Bakery products	100	124	151	95
Meats, poultry, fish, and eggs	100	112	141	96
Beef	100	114	142	100
Pork	100	91	136	90
Other meats	100	124	150	95
Poultry	100	116	148	106
Fish and seafood	100	118	125	87
Eggs	100	125	138	91
Dairy products	100	137	152	92
Fresh milk and cream	100	149	160	95
Other dairy products	100	129	148	90
Fruits and vegetables	100	124	146	83
Fresh fruits	100	130	156	73
Fresh vegetables	100	124	140	78
Processed fruits	100	125	143	94
Processed vegetables	100	110	138	105
Other food at home	100	126	138	94
Sugar and other sweets	100	127	141	94
Fats and oils	100	117	131	98
Miscellaneous foods	100	139	141	94
Nonalcoholic beverages	100	107	132	95
Food prepared by consumer unit on trips	100	105	140	55
Food away from home	**100**	**117**	**157**	**71**
ALCOHOLIC BEVERAGES	**100**	**116**	**90**	**40**
HOUSING	**100**	**148**	**139**	**86**
Shelter	**100**	**138**	**141**	**87**
Owned dwellings	100	151	169	62
Mortgage interest and charges	100	193	205	77
Property taxes	100	119	150	52
Maintenance, repair, insurance, other expenses	100	91	107	35
Rented dwellings	100	128	87	144
Other lodging	100	72	150	39

	total consumer units	married couples, oldest child under age 6	married couples, oldest child aged 6 to 17	single parents with children under age 18
Utilities, fuels, and public services	**100**	**102**	**134**	**90**
Natural gas	100	107	134	82
Electricity	100	96	131	97
Fuel oil and other fuels	100	80	87	61
Telephone services	100	108	141	90
Residential telephone, VOIP, and phone cards	100	66	111	58
Cellular phone service	100	125	152	103
Water and other public services	100	105	140	81
Household services	**100**	**395**	**156**	**96**
Personal services	100	970	203	148
Other household services	100	123	134	71
Housekeeping supplies	**100**	**138**	**132**	**70**
Laundry and cleaning supplies	100	133	125	92
Other household products	100	138	138	71
Postage and stationery	100	143	127	44
Household furnishings and equipment	**100**	**147**	**128**	**65**
Household textiles	100	170	127	77
Furniture	100	148	127	64
Floor coverings	100	120	130	35
Major appliances	100	137	137	109
Small appliances and miscellaneous housewares	100	166	109	47
Miscellaneous household equipment	100	144	129	54
APPAREL AND RELATED SERVICES	**100**	**157**	**158**	**99**
Men and boys	**100**	**117**	**174**	**82**
Men, aged 16 or older	100	109	132	36
Boys, aged 2 to 15	100	153	354	281
Women and girls	**100**	**120**	**153**	**108**
Women, aged 16 or older	100	107	120	73
Girls, aged 2 to 15	100	183	316	274
Children under age 2	**100**	**699**	**145**	**108**
Footwear	**100**	**157**	**181**	**126**
Other apparel products and services	**100**	**148**	**118**	**64**
TRANSPORTATION	**100**	**130**	**141**	**75**
Vehicle purchases	**100**	**147**	**147**	**78**
Cars and trucks, new	100	136	164	34
Cars and trucks, used	100	158	133	120
Gasoline and motor oil	**100**	**118**	**149**	**78**
Other vehicle expenses	**100**	**124**	**126**	**74**
Vehicle finance charges	100	178	170	78
Maintenance and repairs	100	106	132	66
Vehicle insurance	100	121	101	76
Vehicle rentals, leases, licenses, other charges	100	138	150	79
Public transportation	**100**	**111**	**145**	**55**

	total consumer units	married couples, oldest child under age 6	married couples, oldest child aged 6 to 17	single parents with children under age 18
HEALTH CARE	**100**	**96**	**120**	**48**
Health insurance	100	95	119	51
Medical services	100	120	141	48
Drugs	100	66	90	36
Medical supplies	100	86	106	49
ENTERTAINMENT	**100**	**106**	**167**	**69**
Fees and admissions	100	90	237	71
Audio and visual equipment and services	100	104	135	82
Pets, toys, and playground equipment	100	112	144	66
Pets	100	72	134	62
Toys, hobbies, and playground equipment	100	248	179	79
Other entertainment products and services	100	126	181	38
PERSONAL CARE PRODUCTS AND SERVICES	**100**	**116**	**127**	**90**
READING	**100**	**75**	**113**	**57**
EDUCATION	**100**	**65**	**189**	**67**
TOBACCO PRODUCTS AND SMOKING SUPPLIES	**100**	**56**	**85**	**73**
MISCELLANEOUS	**100**	**98**	**113**	**61**
CASH CONTRIBUTIONS	**100**	**81**	**103**	**41**
PERSONAL INSURANCE AND PENSIONS	**100**	**148**	**161**	**49**
Life and other personal insurance	100	84	136	39
Pensions and Social Security	100	152	162	50
GIFTS FOR PEOPLE IN OTHER HOUSEHOLDS	**100**	**47**	**112**	**51**

Note: The index compares the spending of consumer units with children with the spending of the average consumer unit by dividing the spending of consumer units with children by average spending in each category and multiplying by 100. An index of 100 means the spending of consumer units with children equals average spending. An index of 125 means the spending of consumer units with children is 25 percent above average, while an index of 75 means the spending of consumer units with children is 25 percent below average. The Bureau of Labor Statistics uses consumer unit rather than household as the sampling unit in the Consumer Expenditure Survey. For the definition of consumer unit, see the glossary.
Source: Bureau of Labor Statistics, 2013 Consumer Expenditure Survey, Internet site http://www.bls.gov/cex/; calculations by New Strategist

Table 19.6 Market Share of Spending Controlled by Households with Children, 2013

(percent of total household spending accounted for by consumer units with children under age 18 at home, 2013)

	total consumer units	consumer units with children under age 18			
		total	married couples, oldest child under age 6	married couples, oldest child aged 6 to 17	single parents with children under age 18
Number of consumer units (in 000s)	125,670	26,402	5,559	14,066	6,777
Share of consumer units	100.0%	21.0%	4.4%	11.2%	5.4%
Share of total annual spending	100.0	25.6	5.7	15.9	4.0
FOOD	**100.0**	**26.6**	**5.4**	**16.7**	**4.5**
Food at home	**100.0**	**26.6**	**5.5**	**16.1**	**5.0**
Cereals and bakery products	100.0	28.1	5.5	17.1	5.4
Cereals and cereal products	100.0	29.3	5.6	17.7	6.0
Bakery products	100.0	27.4	5.5	16.9	5.1
Meats, poultry, fish, and eggs	100.0	25.9	5.0	15.7	5.2
Beef	100.0	26.3	5.0	15.9	5.4
Pork	100.0	24.1	4.0	15.3	4.9
Other meats	100.0	27.5	5.5	16.8	5.1
Poultry	100.0	27.4	5.1	16.6	5.7
Fish and seafood	100.0	23.9	5.2	14.0	4.7
Eggs	100.0	25.8	5.5	15.4	4.9
Dairy products	100.0	28.0	6.0	17.0	5.0
Fresh milk and cream	100.0	29.6	6.6	17.9	5.1
Other dairy products	100.0	27.1	5.7	16.5	4.9
Fruits and vegetables	100.0	26.3	5.5	16.3	4.5
Fresh fruits	100.0	27.2	5.8	17.5	3.9
Fresh vegetables	100.0	25.3	5.5	15.7	4.2
Processed fruits	100.0	26.7	5.5	16.1	5.1
Processed vegetables	100.0	25.9	4.9	15.4	5.6
Other food at home	100.0	26.1	5.6	15.5	5.1
Sugar and other sweets	100.0	26.5	5.6	15.8	5.1
Fats and oils	100.0	25.1	5.2	14.6	5.3
Miscellaneous foods	100.0	27.1	6.1	15.8	5.1
Nonalcoholic beverages	100.0	24.7	4.7	14.8	5.1
Food prepared by consumer unit on trips	100.0	23.3	4.6	15.7	3.0
Food away from home	**100.0**	**26.5**	**5.2**	**17.5**	**3.8**
ALCOHOLIC BEVERAGES	**100.0**	**17.3**	**5.1**	**10.0**	**2.2**
HOUSING	**100.0**	**26.7**	**6.5**	**15.6**	**4.6**
Shelter	**100.0**	**26.6**	**6.1**	**15.8**	**4.7**
Owned dwellings	100.0	28.9	6.7	19.0	3.3
Mortgage interest and charges	100.0	35.7	8.5	23.0	4.2
Property taxes	100.0	24.8	5.2	16.7	2.8
Maintenance, repair, insurance, other expenses	100.0	17.9	4.0	12.0	1.9
Rented dwellings	100.0	23.2	5.6	9.8	7.8
Other lodging	100.0	22.1	3.2	16.8	2.1

	total consumer units	consumer units with children under age 18: total	married couples, oldest child under age 6	married couples, oldest child aged 6 to 17	single parents with children under age 18
Utilities, fuels, and public services	**100.0%**	**24.3%**	**4.5%**	**15.0%**	**4.8%**
Natural gas	100.0	24.2	4.7	15.0	4.4
Electricity	100.0	24.1	4.3	14.6	5.2
Fuel oil and other fuels	100.0	16.6	3.6	9.7	3.3
Telephone services	100.0	25.4	4.8	15.7	4.9
Residential telephone, VOIP, and phone cards	100.0	18.4	2.9	12.4	3.1
Cellular phone service	100.0	28.1	5.5	17.1	5.6
Water and other public services	100.0	24.7	4.6	15.7	4.4
Household services	**100.0**	**40.2**	**17.5**	**17.5**	**5.2**
Personal services	100.0	73.5	42.9	22.7	8.0
Other household services	100.0	24.3	5.4	15.0	3.8
Housekeeping supplies	**100.0**	**24.7**	**6.1**	**14.8**	**3.8**
Laundry and cleaning supplies	100.0	24.9	5.9	14.0	5.0
Other household products	100.0	25.4	6.1	15.4	3.8
Postage and stationery	100.0	22.9	6.3	14.2	2.3
Household furnishings and equipment	**100.0**	**24.3**	**6.5**	**14.3**	**3.5**
Household textiles	100.0	25.9	7.5	14.2	4.2
Furniture	100.0	24.2	6.5	14.3	3.4
Floor coverings	100.0	21.7	5.3	14.6	1.9
Major appliances	100.0	27.3	6.1	15.3	5.9
Small appliances and miscellaneous housewares	100.0	22.1	7.3	12.2	2.5
Miscellaneous household equipment	100.0	23.7	6.4	14.4	2.9
APPAREL AND RELATED SERVICES	**100.0**	**30.0**	**6.9**	**17.7**	**5.4**
Men and boys	**100.0**	**29.0**	**5.2**	**19.5**	**4.4**
Men, aged 16 or older	100.0	21.5	4.8	14.8	1.9
Boys, aged 2 to 15	100.0	61.6	6.8	39.7	15.2
Women and girls	**100.0**	**28.2**	**5.3**	**17.1**	**5.8**
Women, aged 16 or older	100.0	22.1	4.7	13.4	4.0
Girls, aged 2 to 15	100.0	58.2	8.1	35.3	14.8
Children under age 2	**100.0**	**53.0**	**30.9**	**16.3**	**5.8**
Footwear	**100.0**	**34.0**	**6.9**	**20.3**	**6.8**
Other apparel products and services	**100.0**	**23.3**	**6.5**	**13.3**	**3.5**
TRANSPORTATION	**100.0**	**25.6**	**5.7**	**15.8**	**4.1**
Vehicle purchases	**100.0**	**27.1**	**6.5**	**16.4**	**4.2**
Cars and trucks, new	100.0	26.2	6.0	18.3	1.8
Cars and trucks, used	100.0	28.4	7.0	14.9	6.5
Gasoline and motor oil	**100.0**	**26.0**	**5.2**	**16.6**	**4.2**
Other vehicle expenses	**100.0**	**23.6**	**5.5**	**14.1**	**4.0**
Vehicle finance charges	100.0	31.1	7.9	19.0	4.2
Maintenance and repairs	100.0	23.0	4.7	14.7	3.6
Vehicle insurance	100.0	20.7	5.4	11.3	4.1
Vehicle rentals, leases, licenses, other charges	100.0	27.2	6.1	16.8	4.3
Public transportation	**100.0**	**24.1**	**4.9**	**16.2**	**3.0**

	total consumer units	consumer units with children under age 18			
		total	married couples, oldest child under age 6	married couples, oldest child aged 6 to 17	single parents with children under age 18
HEALTH CARE	**100.0%**	**20.3%**	**4.3%**	**13.4%**	**2.6%**
Health insurance	100.0	20.3	4.2	13.4	2.7
Medical services	100.0	23.7	5.3	15.7	2.6
Drugs	100.0	14.9	2.9	10.0	1.9
Medical supplies	100.0	18.3	3.8	11.9	2.6
ENTERTAINMENT	**100.0**	**27.2**	**4.7**	**18.7**	**3.7**
Fees and admissions	100.0	34.4	4.0	26.6	3.8
Audio and visual equipment and services	100.0	24.2	4.6	15.1	4.4
Pets, toys, and playground equipment	100.0	24.7	5.0	16.2	3.5
Pets	100.0	21.5	3.2	15.0	3.3
Toys, hobbies, and playground equipment	100.0	35.2	11.0	20.0	4.2
Other entertainment products and services	100.0	27.9	5.6	20.3	2.0
PERSONAL CARE PRODUCTS AND SERVICES	**100.0**	**24.2**	**5.2**	**14.2**	**4.9**
READING	**100.0**	**19.0**	**3.3**	**12.6**	**3.1**
EDUCATION	**100.0**	**27.7**	**2.9**	**21.1**	**3.6**
TOBACCO PRODUCTS AND SMOKING SUPPLIES	**100.0**	**15.9**	**2.5**	**9.5**	**3.9**
MISCELLANEOUS	**100.0**	**20.2**	**4.3**	**12.6**	**3.3**
CASH CONTRIBUTIONS	**100.0**	**17.3**	**3.6**	**11.5**	**2.2**
PERSONAL INSURANCE AND PENSIONS	**100.0**	**27.2**	**6.5**	**18.0**	**2.6**
Life and other personal insurance	100.0	21.1	3.7	15.3	2.1
Pensions and Social Security	100.0	27.6	6.7	18.2	2.7
GIFTS FOR PEOPLE IN OTHER HOUSEHOLDS	**100.0**	**17.3**	**2.1**	**12.5**	**2.7**

Note: Market shares are calculated by multiplying average spending by the total number of households. Using those aggregate figures, the total spending of each segment is divided by the total for all households to determine each segment's share of the total. The Bureau of Labor Statistics uses consumer unit rather than household as the sampling unit in the Consumer Expenditure Survey. For the definition of consumer unit, see the glossary.
Source: Bureau of Labor Statistics, 2013 Consumer Expenditure Survey, Internet site http://www.bls.gov/cex/; calculations by New Strategist

CHAPTER

20

Time Use

■ Most, but not all, of today's young children have working mothers. There are substantial differences in time use depending on a mother's employment status.

■ Employed mothers spend less time caring for children than mothers who are not employed. Fathers spend about the same amount of time caring for children, whether or not their wife works.

■ Among dual-income couples with children under age 18, mothers have less leisure time than fathers—2.91 hours per day for mothers and 3.68 hours per day for fathers.

■ Teenagers aged 15 to 19 have more leisure time per day (4.47 hours) than most adults. Only people aged 55 or older have more leisure time than teenagers.

■ On an average day, 35 percent of boys aged 15 to 19 play games as a primary activity (a category that includes computer games). Only 10 percent of girls play games on an average day.

Among Mothers, Time Use Varies by Employment Status

For fathers, time use varies by their wife's employment status.

Most, but not all, of today's young children have working mothers. Among those mothers, there are substantial differences in time use depending on their employment status. Mothers who are employed full-time spend less time sleeping, doing housework, and shopping than mothers who do not work outside the home. Employed mothers also spend less time caring for children than mothers who are not employed.

Among dual-income couples with children under age 18, wives do three times more housework than husbands. But among couples in which only the husband works, wives do nearly eight times more housework than husbands. Wives in dual-earner couples spend 1.28 hours per day tending to their children's needs, 49 percent more than the 0.86 hours per day their husbands devote to those tasks. Wives in single-earner couples spend a much larger 2.60 hours per day tending to children's needs—more than three times the 0.82 hours per day spent by their husbands.

■ Among dual-income couples with children, mothers have less leisure time than fathers.

Working mothers have less leisure time

(average number of hours per day of leisure time for married couples with children under age 18 in which both spouses work full time, by sex, 2007–11)

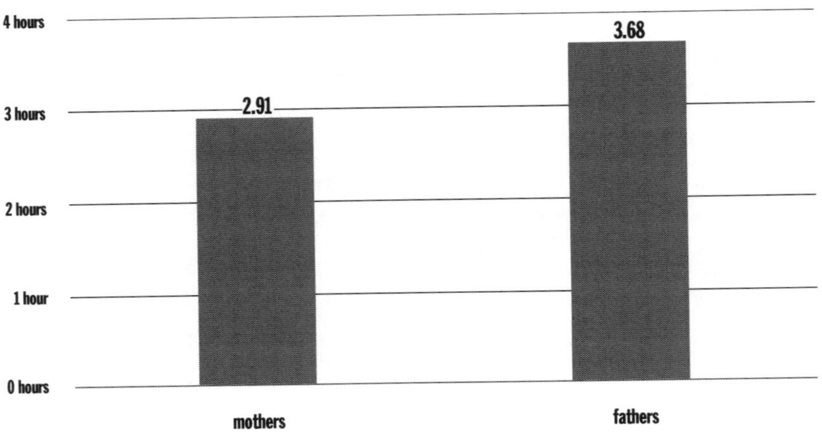

Table 20.1 Time Use of Married Mothers with Children under Age 18 by Employment Status, 2007–11

(average hours per day married mothers with own children under age 18 spend in primary activities, percent participating in primary activities, and index of mothers employed full-time to mothers who are not employed, by employment status, 2007–11)

	average hours			percent participating		
	employed full-time	not employed	index, employed full-time to not employed	employed full-time	not employed	index, employed full-time to not employed
Married mothers with children under age 18						
Total, all activities	**24.00 hrs.**	**24.00 hrs.**	**100**	**100.0%**	**100.0%**	**100**
Personal care activities	8.96	9.46	95	100.0	99.9	100
Sleeping	8.14	8.83	92	99.9	99.9	100
Household activities	1.94	3.47	56	87.9	95.8	92
Housework	0.81	1.55	52	50.2	73.2	69
Food preparation and cleanup	0.80	1.46	55	75.2	88.4	85
Lawn and garden care	0.07	0.13	54	4.6	8.6	53
Purchasing goods and services	0.54	0.71	76	51.5	53.6	96
Grocery shopping	0.12	0.18	67	16.6	21.2	78
Consumer goods purchases, except grocery shopping	0.33	0.39	85	38.2	38.1	100
Caring for and helping household members	1.25	2.51	50	74.3	85.1	87
Caring for and helping household children	1.24	2.49	50	73.3	84.6	87
Physical care	0.55	1.00	55	54.7	70.9	77
Education-related activities	0.10	0.25	40	12.5	19.6	64
Reading to/with children	0.04	0.08	50	10.7	15.0	71
Playing/doing hobbies with children	0.22	0.59	37	15.5	30.0	52
Working and work-related activities	5.34	0.00	–	70.3	0.0	–
Working	5.31	0.00	–	69.9	0.0	–
Leisure and sports	2.92	4.18	70	92.2	95.9	96
Socializing and communicating	0.59	0.85	69	38.0	44.1	86
Watching television	1.55	2.23	70	72.5	79.1	92
Participating in sports, exercise, and recreation	0.17	0.23	74	14.4	17.3	83
Travel	1.33	1.15	116	94.8	82.8	114
Travel related to caring for and helping household children	0.22	0.29	76	41.3	42.2	98
Other activities	1.72	2.43	71	98.1	98.6	99

Note: Primary activities are those respondents identified as their main activity. Other activities done simultaneously are not included. The index is caluclated by dividing time use or participation rate of mothers who are employed full-time by time use or participation rate of mothers who are not employed and multiplying by 100. "–" means divisor is zero.
Source: Bureau of Labor Statistics, Married Parents' Use of Time, 2007–11 American Time Use Survey, Internet site http://www.bls.gov/tus/; calculations by New Strategist

Table 20.2 Time Use of Married Mothers with Children Aged 6 to 17 by Employment Status, 2007–11

(average hours per day married mothers with youngest own child aged 6 to 17 spend in primary activities, percent participating in primary activities, and index of mothers employed full-time to mothers who are not employed, by employment status, 2007–11)

	average hours			percent participating		
	employed full-time	not employed	index, employed full-time to not employed	employed full-time	not employed	index, employed full-time to not employed
Married mothers with youngest child aged 6 to 17						
Total, all activities	**24.00 hrs.**	**24.00 hrs.**	**100**	**100.0%**	**100.0%**	**100**
Personal care activities	8.96	9.43	95	100.0	100.0	100
Sleeping	8.09	8.71	93	99.8	99.9	100
Household activities	2.04	3.69	55	88.2	95.0	93
Housework	0.84	1.68	50	52.3	73.7	71
Food preparation and cleanup	0.81	1.46	55	74.7	87.9	85
Lawn and garden care	0.08	0.16	50	5.7	10.7	53
Purchasing goods and services	0.55	0.77	71	52.0	57.6	90
Grocery shopping	0.12	0.21	57	16.5	25.1	66
Consumer goods purchases, except grocery shopping	0.35	0.41	85	39.4	40.2	98
Caring for and helping household members	0.70	1.48	47	62.3	73.0	85
Caring for and helping household children	0.69	1.45	48	60.5	71.8	84
Physical care	0.20	0.36	56	34.2	47.4	72
Education-related activities	0.12	0.32	38	14.2	22.9	62
Reading to/with children	0.02	0.04	50	5.3	7.0	76
Playing/doing hobbies with children	0.04	0.12	33	3.7	8.7	43
Working and work-related activities	5.50	0.00	–	71.7	0.0	–
Working	5.47	0.00	–	71.2	0.0	–
Leisure and sports	3.11	4.60	68	93.9	96.3	98
Socializing and communicating	0.58	0.85	68	38.8	45.7	85
Watching television	1.68	2.39	70	73.5	80.4	91
Participating in sports, exercise, and recreation	0.17	0.26	65	14.8	20.0	74
Travel	1.35	1.26	107	94.9	84.6	112
Travel related to caring for and helping household children	0.19	0.30	63	36.0	43.0	84
Other activities	1.78	2.64	67	98.1	98.9	99

Note: Primary activities are those respondents identified as their main activity. Other activities done simultaneously are not included. The index is caluclated by dividing time use or participation rate of mothers who are employed full-time by time use or participation rate of mothers who are not employed and multiplying by 100. "–" means divisor is zero.
Source: Bureau of Labor Statistics, Married Parents' Use of Time, 2007–11 American Time Use Survey, Internet site http://www.bls.gov/tus/; calculations by New Strategist

Table 20.3 Time Use of Married Mothers with Children under Age 6 by Employment Status, 2007–11

(average hours per day married mothers with own children under age 6 spend in primary activities, percent participating in primary activities, and index of mothers employed full-time to mothers who are not employed, by employment status, 2007–11)

	average hours			percent participating		
	employed full-time	not employed	index, employed full-time to not employed	employed full-time	not employed	index, employed full-time to not employed
Married mothers with youngest child under age 6						
Total, all activities	**24.00 hrs.**	**24.00 hrs.**	**100**	**100.0%**	**100.0%**	**100**
Personal care activities	8.98	9.48	95	100.0	99.9	100
Aeeping	8.20	8.92	92	100.0	99.9	100
Household activities	1.80	3.31	54	87.4	96.4	91
Housework	0.76	1.46	52	47.4	72.8	65
Food preparation and cleanup	0.77	1.47	52	75.8	88.7	85
Lawn and garden care	0.05	0.11	45	3.2	7.0	46
Purchasing goods and services	0.51	0.66	77	50.8	50.7	100
Grocery shopping	0.13	0.16	81	16.8	18.5	91
Consumer goods purchases, except grocery shopping	0.30	0.38	79	36.5	36.5	100
Caring for and helping household members	2.01	3.26	62	91.0	93.9	97
Caring for and helping household children	1.99	3.25	61	90.8	93.8	97
Physical care	1.05	1.46	72	83.0	87.8	95
Education-related activities	0.08	0.20	40	10.2	17.1	60
Reading to/with children	0.08	0.11	73	18.2	20.8	88
Playing/doing hobbies with children	0.46	0.93	49	31.7	45.3	70
Working and work-related activities	5.11	0.00	–	68.4	0.0	–
Working	5.09	0.00	–	68.2	0.0	–
Leisure and sports	2.65	3.87	68	89.8	95.5	94
Socializing and communicating	0.61	0.85	72	36.8	43.0	86
Watching television	1.37	2.11	65	71.0	78.1	91
Participating in sports, exercise, and recreation	0.17	0.20	85	13.9	15.4	90
Travel	1.31	1.07	122	94.6	81.6	116
Travel related to caring for and helping household children	0.27	0.29	93	48.6	41.7	117
Other activities	1.63	2.28	71	98.2	98.4	100

Note: Primary activities are those respondents identified as their main activity. Other activities done simultaneously are not included. The index is caluclated by dividing time use or participation rate of mothers who are employed full-time by time use or participation rate of mothers who are not employed and multiplying by 100. "–" means divisor is zero.
Source: Bureau of Labor Statistics, Married Parents' Use of Time, 2007–11 American Time Use Survey, Internet site http://www.bls.gov/tus/; calculations by New Strategist

Table 20.4 Time Use of Dual-Earner and Single-Earner Married Couples with Children under Age 18, 2007–11

(average hours per day married couples with children under age 18 spend in primary activities by employment status, and index of mother's time to father's, 2007–11)

	both spouses work full-time			mother not employed, father employed full-time		
	mother	father	index, mother's time to father's	mother	father	index, mother's time to father's
Total, all activities	**24.00 hrs.**	**24.00 hrs.**	**100**	**24.00 hrs.**	**24.00 hrs.**	**100**
Personal care activities	8.96	8.59	104	9.43	8.74	108
Sleeping	8.12	7.98	102	8.80	8.15	108
Household activities	1.95	1.34	146	3.51	1.07	328
Housework	0.82	0.26	315	1.57	0.20	785
Food preparation and cleanup	0.79	0.37	214	1.45	0.28	518
Lawn and garden care	0.07	0.23	30	0.14	0.18	78
Purchasing goods and services	0.55	0.34	162	0.72	0.37	195
Grocery shopping	0.13	0.06	217	0.19	0.08	238
Consumer goods purchases, except grocery shopping	0.34	0.22	155	0.42	0.23	183
Caring for and helping household members	1.29	0.88	147	2.62	0.84	312
Caring for and helping household children	1.28	0.86	149	2.60	0.82	317
Physical care	0.57	0.28	204	1.03	0.25	412
Education-related activities	0.11	0.09	122	0.26	0.04	650
Reading to/with children	0.05	0.03	167	0.09	0.03	300
Playing/doing hobbies with children	0.22	0.24	92	0.63	0.33	191
Working and work-related activities	5.27	6.07	87	0.08	6.20	1
Working	5.24	6.03	87	0.02	6.15	0
Leisure and sports	2.91	3.68	79	4.09	3.55	115
Socializing and communicating	0.60	0.54	111	0.87	0.55	158
Watching television	1.53	2.15	71	2.13	2.06	103
Participating in sports, exercise, and recreation	0.18	0.32	56	0.24	0.27	89
Travel	1.35	1.41	96	1.15	1.40	82
Travel related to caring for and helping household children	0.23	0.16	144	0.30	0.09	333
Other activities	1.73	1.70	102	2.40	1.82	132

Note: Primary activities are those respondents identified as their main activity. Other activities done simultaneously are not included. The index is calculated by dividing mother's time by father's time and multiplying by 100.
Source: Bureau of Labor Statistics, Married Parents' Use of Time, 2007–11 American Time Use Survey, Internet site http://www.bls.gov/tus/; calculations by New Strategist

Teenagers Spend More Time at Play than in School

Watching television is the single biggest leisure-time activity of 15-to-19-year-olds.

Time use varies sharply by age, with teenagers aged 15 to 19 having more leisure time (4.47 hours per day) than most adults. Only people aged 55 or older have more leisure time than teens. On an average day, teenagers spend much more time in leisure activities than they do at work (0.97 hours) or in school (3.23 hours) combined.

Boys aged 15 to 19 spend an average of nearly one hour a day playing games as a primary activity, a category that includes computer games. On an average day, 35 percent of teen boys play games. Only 10 percent of their female counterparts play games on an average day, but girls are almost as likely as boys to use a computer for other leisure pursuits (16 percent of girls and 18 percent of boys).

■ Teenaged girls and boys spend more time than the average person sleeping and grooming.

Among 15-to-19-year-olds, boys and girls spend their time differently

(percent of people aged 15 to 19 who participate in selected primary activities on an average day, by sex, 2013)

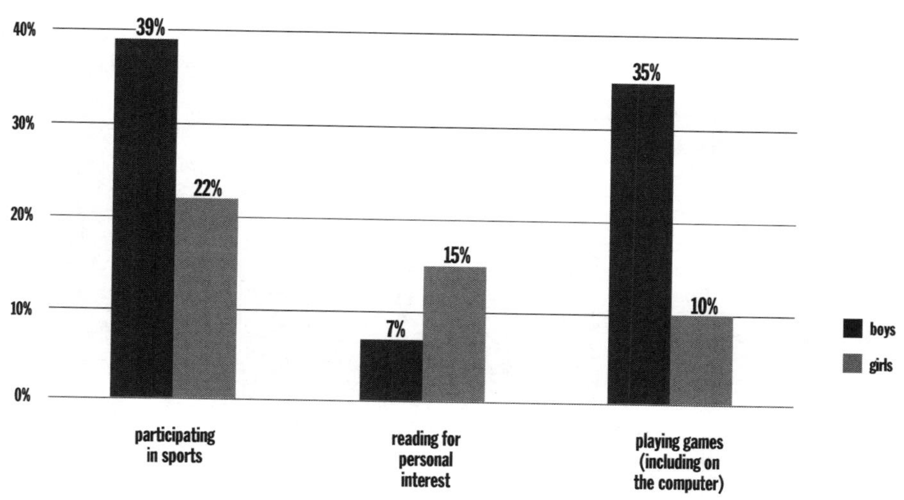

Table 20.5 Detailed Time Use of People Aged 15 to 19, 2013

(hours per day spent in primary activities by total people aged 15 or older and people aged 15 to 19, index of age group to total, and number and percent of people aged 15 to 19 participating in activity on an average day, 2013)

	average hours per day for total people	average hours per day for people aged 15 to 19	index, 15 to 19 to total	people aged 15 to 19 participating in activity: number (in 000s)	percent
Total, all activities	**24.00 hrs.**	**24.00 hrs.**	**100**	**20,913**	**100.0%**
Personal care activities	9.53	10.48	110	20,913	100.0
Sleeping	8.74	9.57	109	20,913	100.0
Grooming	0.70	0.87	124	18,343	87.7
Health-related self-care	0.09	0.05	–	322	1.5
Household activities	1.78	0.72	40	10,529	50.3
Housework	0.57	0.22	39	3,976	19.0
Food preparation and cleanup	0.57	0.18	32	5,944	28.4
Lawn, garden, and houseplants	0.18	0.04	22	604	2.9
Animals and pets	0.10	0.07	70	1,673	8.0
Vehicles	0.04	–	–	284	1.4
Household management	0.18	0.09	50	3,433	16.4
Financial management	0.03	–	–	54	0.3
Household and personal organization and planning	0.10	0.07	70	2,989	14.3
Household and personal mail and messages (except email)	0.01	–	–	167	0.8
Household and personal email and messages	0.03	0.01	33	393	1.9
Caring for and helping household members	0.44	0.13	30	2,463	11.8
Caring for and helping household children	0.36	0.09	25	1,674	8.0
Caring for household adults	0.02	–	–	299	1.4
Helping household adults	0.01	0.01	100	330	1.6
Caring for and helping people in other households	0.14	0.13	93	3,355	16.0
Caring for and helping children in other households	0.07	0.09	129	1,904	9.1
Caring for adults in other households	0.01	–	–	175	0.8
Helping adults in other households	0.05	0.03	60	1,375	6.6
Working and work-related activities	3.20	0.97	30	3,887	18.6
Working	3.14	0.90	29	3,256	15.6
Job search and interviewing	0.04	–	–	284	1.4
Educational activities	0.45	3.23	718	10,635	50.9
Taking class	0.26	2.32	892	7,955	38.0
Homework and research	0.18	0.82	456	7,502	35.9
Consumer purchases	0.37	0.25	68	5,599	26.8
Grocery shopping	0.11	0.02	18	1,034	4.9
Shopping (except groceries, food, and gas)	0.24	0.20	83	3,281	15.7
Professional and personal care services	0.08	0.06	75	1,091	5.2
Medical and care services	0.05	0.03	60	552	2.6

	average hours per day for total people	average hours per day for people aged 15 to 19	index, 15 to 19 to total	people aged 15 to 19 participating in activity	
				number (in 000s)	percent
Eating and drinking	1.11 hrs.	0.92 hrs.	83	20,244	96.8%
Socializing, relaxing, and leisure	4.71	4.47	95	19,806	94.7
Socializing and communicating	0.65	0.75	115	8,811	42.1
Attending or hosting social events	0.07	0.08	114	601	2.9
Relaxing and leisure	3.91	3.51	90	18,683	89.3
Television and movies	2.77	2.17	78	15,348	73.4
Playing games	0.22	0.56	255	4,745	22.7
Computer use for leisure (except games)	0.21	0.32	152	3,547	17.0
Reading for personal interest	0.32	0.13	41	2,300	11.0
Arts and entertainment (other than sports)	0.08	0.12	150	923	4.4
Attending movies	0.03	0.06	200	582	2.8
Sports, exercise, and recreation	0.32	0.75	234	6,762	32.3
Participating in sports, exercise, and recreation	0.30	0.68	227	6,420	30.7
Attending sporting or recreational events	0.03	0.07	233	492	2.4
Religious and spiritual activities	0.14	0.10	71	1,564	7.5
Volunteer activities	0.14	0.14	100	1,063	5.1
Telephone calls	0.10	0.18	180	3,218	15.4
Traveling	1.18	1.14	97	18,736	89.6

Note: Primary activities are those respondents identified as their main activity. Other activities done simultaneously are not included. Travel related to activities is reported separately. Numbers do not sum to total because not all activities are shown. The index is calculated by dividing time spent by age group by time spent by the average person and multiplying by 100. "–" means sample is too small to make a reliable estimate.

Source: Bureau of Labor Statistics, unpublished tables from the 2013 American Time Use Survey, Internet site http://www.bls.gov/tus/home.htm; calculations by New Strategist

Table 20.6 Detailed Time Use of Men Aged 15 to 19, 2013

(hours per day spent in primary activities by total men aged 15 or older and men aged 15 to 19, index of age group to total, and number and percent of men aged 15 to 19 participating in activity on an average day, 2013)

	average hours per day for total men	average hours per day for men aged 15 to 19	index, 15 to 19 to total	men aged 15 to 19 participating in activity	
				number (in 000s)	percent
Total, all activities	**24.00 hrs.**	**24.00 hrs.**	**100**	**10,640**	**100.0%**
Personal care activities	9.29	10.46	113	10,640	100.0
Sleeping	8.65	9.77	113	10,640	100.0
Grooming	0.57	0.66	116	9,072	85.3
Health-related self-care	0.60	–	–	179	1.7
Household activities	1.34	0.73	54	4,689	44.1
Housework	0.25	0.19	76	1,815	17.1
Food preparation and cleanup	0.33	0.12	36	2,566	24.1
Lawn, garden, and houseplants	0.25	0.07	28	487	4.6
Animals and pets	0.09	0.08	89	639	6.0
Vehicles	0.08	–	–	284	2.7
Household management	0.14	0.07	50	1,453	13.7
Financial management	0.02	–	–	–	–
Household and personal organization and planning	0.08	0.06	75	1,264	11.9
Household and personal mail and messages (except email)	0.01	–	–	34	0.3
Household and personal email and messages	0.03	–	–	190	1.8
Caring for and helping household members	0.30	0.11	37	1,109	10.4
Caring for and helping household children	0.24	0.06	25	672	6.3
Caring for household adults	0.01	–	–	156	1.5
Helping household adults	0.01	–	–	224	2.1
Caring for and helping people in other households	0.12	0.05	42	1,428	13.4
Caring for and helping children in other households	0.05	0.02	40	524	4.9
Caring for adults in other households	0.01	–	–	175	1.6
Helping adults in other households	0.06	0.03	50	820	7.7
Working and work-related activities	3.88	1.06	27	1,971	18.5
Working	3.80	1.02	27	1,694	15.9
Job search and interviewing	0.05	–	–	189	1.8
Educational activities	0.45	2.91	647	5,007	47.1
Taking class	0.27	2.20	815	3,797	35.7
Homework and research	0.17	0.62	365	3,505	32.9
Consumer purchases	0.29	0.22	76	2,273	21.4
Grocery shopping	0.07	0.02	29	446	4.2
Shopping (except groceries, food, and gas)	0.19	0.19	100	1,291	12.1
Professional and personal care services	0.06	0.05	83	474	4.5
Medical and care services	0.04	–	–	178	1.7

	average hours per day for total men	average hours per day for men aged 15 to 19	index, 15 to 19 to total	men aged 15 to 19 participating in activity	
				number (in 000s)	percent
Eating and drinking	1.14 hrs.	0.90 hrs.	79	10,242	96.3%
Socializing, relaxing, and leisure	4.94	4.75	96	10,247	96.3
Socializing and communicating	0.60	0.65	108	4,066	38.2
Attending or hosting social events	0.06	0.06	100	214	2.0
Relaxing and leisure	4.20	3.96	94	9,860	92.7
Television and movies	2.98	2.30	77	7,947	74.7
Playing games	0.32	0.92	288	3,695	34.7
Computer use for leisure (except games)	0.22	0.39	177	1,916	18.0
Reading for personal interest	0.26	0.07	27	757	7.1
Arts and entertainment (other than sports)	0.08	0.07	88	324	3.0
Attending movies	0.03	–	–	244	2.3
Sports, exercise, and recreation	0.42	1.05	250	4,279	40.2
Participating in sports, exercise, and recreation	0.40	0.99	248	4,188	39.4
Attending sporting or recreational events	0.02	–	–	194	1.8
Religious and spiritual activities	0.12	0.08	67	649	6.1
Volunteer activities	0.13	0.15	115	398	3.7
Telephone calls	0.06	0.13	217	1,428	13.4
Traveling	1.21	1.06	88	9,534	89.6

Note: Primary activities are those respondents identified as their main activity. Other activities done simultaneously are not included. Travel related to activities is reported separately. Numbers do not sum to total because not all activities are shown. The index is calculated by dividing time spent by age group by time spent by the average man and multiplying by 100. "–" means sample is too small to make a reliable estimate.

Source: Bureau of Labor Statistics, unpublished tables from the 2013 American Time Use Survey, Internet site http://www.bls.gov/tus/home.htm; calculations by New Strategist

Table 20.7 Detailed Time Use of Women Aged 15 to 19, 2013

(hours per day spent in primary activities by total women aged 15 or older and women aged 15 to 19, index of age group to total, and number and percent of women aged 15 to 19 participating in activity on an average day, 2013)

	average hours per day for total women	average hours per day for women aged 15 to 19	index, 15 to 19 to total	women aged 15 to 19 participating in activity: number (in 000s)	percent
Total, all activities	**24.00 hrs.**	**24.00 hrs.**	**100**	**10,273**	**100.0%**
Personal care activities	9.75	10.50	108	10,273	100.0
Sleeping	8.82	9.36	106	10,273	100.0
Grooming	0.82	1.09	133	9,271	90.2
Health-related self-care	0.11	–	–	143	1.4
Household activities	2.20	0.70	32	5,840	56.8
Housework	0.87	0.24	28	2,161	21.0
Food preparation and cleanup	0.80	0.25	31	3,378	32.9
Lawn, garden, and houseplants	0.12	–	–	117	1.1
Animals and pets	0.11	0.06	55	1,034	10.1
Vehicles	0.01	–	–	–	–
Household management	0.21	0.11	52	1,980	19.3
Financial management	0.04	–	–	54	0.5
Household and personal organization and planning	0.12	0.08	67	1,725	16.8
Household and personal mail and messages (except email)	0.02	–	–	133	1.3
Household and personal email and messages	0.04	–	–	202	2.0
Caring for and helping household members	0.58	0.15	26	1,354	13.2
Caring for and helping household children	0.47	0.12	26	1,002	9.8
Caring for household adults	0.03	–	–	143	1.4
Helping household adults	0.01	–	–	106	1.0
Caring for and helping people in other households	0.16	0.20	125	1,927	18.8
Caring for and helping children in other households	0.10	0.17	170	1,380	13.4
Caring for adults in other households	0.01	–	–	–	–
Helping adults in other households	0.05	0.03	60	555	5.4
Working and work-related activities	2.57	0.88	34	1,917	18.7
Working	2.52	0.79	31	1,563	15.2
Job search and interviewing	0.03	–	–	96	0.9
Educational activities	0.45	3.56	791	5,628	54.8
Taking class	0.25	2.44	976	4,158	40.5
Homework and research	0.19	1.02	537	3,997	38.9
Consumer purchases	0.45	0.27	60	3,326	32.4
Grocery shopping	0.14	0.03	21	588	5.7
Shopping (except groceries, food, and gas)	0.28	0.22	79	1,990	19.4
Professional and personal care services	0.10	0.06	60	617	6.0
Medical and care services	0.07	–	–	374	3.6

	average hours per day for total women	average hours per day for women aged 15 to 19	index, 15 to 19 to total	women aged 15 to 19 participating in activity	
				number (in 000s)	percent
Eating and drinking	1.09 hrs.	0.95 hrs.	87	10,001	97.4%
Socializing, relaxing, and leisure	4.50	4.18	93	9,559	93.0
Socializing and communicating	0.70	0.86	123	4,744	46.2
Attending or hosting social events	0.08	0.11	138	386	3.8
Relaxing and leisure	3.63	3.04	84	8,823	85.9
Television and movies	2.56	2.03	79	7,402	72.1
Playing games	0.13	0.18	138	1,050	10.2
Computer use for leisure (except games)	0.20	0.25	125	1,631	15.9
Reading for personal interest	0.38	0.19	50	1,542	15.0
Arts and entertainment (other than sports)	0.09	0.18	200	599	5.8
Attending movies	0.03	–	–	338	3.3
Sports, exercise, and recreation	0.23	0.44	191	2,483	24.2
Participating in sports, exercise, and recreation	0.20	0.37	185	2,233	21.7
Attending sporting or recreational events	0.03	–	–	298	2.9
Religious and spiritual activities	0.17	0.13	76	915	8.9
Volunteer activities	0.15	0.14	93	665	6.5
Telephone calls	0.14	0.24	171	1,790	17.4
Traveling	1.15	1.22	106	9,202	89.6

Note: Primary activities are those respondents identified as their main activity. Other activities done simultaneously are not included. Travel related to activities is reported separately. Numbers do not sum to total because not all activities are shown. The index is calculated by dividing time spent by age group by time spent by the average woman and multiplying by 100. "–" means sample is too small to make a reliable estimate.
Source: Bureau of Labor Statistics, unpublished tables from the 2013 American Time Use Survey, Internet site http://www.bls.gov/tus/home.htm; calculations by New Strategist

Glossary

adjusted for inflation A dollar value that has been adjusted for the rise in the cost of living by use of the consumer price index.

age Classification by age is based on the age of the person at his/her last birthday.

American Community Survey The ACS is an ongoing nationwide survey of 250,000 households per month, providing detailed demographic data at the community level. Designed to replace the census long-form questionnaire, the ACS includes more than 60 questions that formerly appeared on the long form, such as questions about language spoken at home, income, and education. ACS data are available for areas as small as census tracts.

American Housing Survey The AHS collects national and metropolitan-level data on the nation's housing, including apartments, single-family homes, and mobile homes. The Census Bureau conducts the nationally representative survey, with a sample of 55,000 households, for the Department of Housing and Urban Development every other year.

American Indians American Indians include Alaska Natives unless those groups are shown separately.

American Time Use Survey Under contract with the Bureau of Labor Statistics, the Census Bureau collects ATUS information, revealing how people spend their time. The ATUS sample is drawn from U.S. households completing their final month of interviews for the Current Population Survey. One individual from each selected household is chosen to participate in the ATUS. Respondents are interviewed by telephone about their time use during the previous 24 hours.

Asian The term "Asian" includes Native Hawaiians and other Pacific Islanders unless those groups are shown separately.

baby boom Americans born between 1946 and 1964.

baby bust Americans born between 1965 and 1976. Also known as Generation X.

Behavioral Risk Factor Surveillance System The BRFSS is a collaborative project of the Centers for Disease Control and Prevention and U.S. states and territories. It is an ongoing data collection program designed to measure behavioral risk factors in the adult population aged 18 or older. All 50 states, three territories, and the District of Columbia take part in the survey, making the BRFSS the primary source of information on the health-related behaviors of Americans.

Black The Black racial category includes those who identified themselves as "Black" or "African American."

Consumer Expenditure Survey The CEX is an ongoing study of the day-to-day spending of American households administered by the Bureau of Labor Statistics. The CEX includes an interview survey and a diary survey. The average spending figures shown are the integrated data from both the diary and interview components of the survey. Two separate, nationally representative samples are used for the interview and diary surveys. For the interview survey, about 7,500 consumer units are interviewed on a rotating panel basis each quarter for five consecutive quarters. For the diary survey, 7,500 consumer units keep weekly diaries of spending for two consecutive weeks.

consumer unit *(on spending tables only)* For convenience, the terms consumer unit and household are used interchangeably, although consumer units are somewhat different from the Census Bureau's households. A consumer unit includes all the related members of a household or any financially independent member of a household. A household may include more than one consumer unit.

Current Population Survey The CPS is a nationally representative survey of the civilian noninstitutional population aged 15 or older. It is taken monthly by the Census Bureau for the Bureau of Labor Statistics, collecting information from 60,000 households on employment and unemployment. In March of each year, the survey includes the Annual Social and Economic Supplement, which is the source of most national data on the characteristics of Americans, such as educational attainment, living arrangements, and incomes.

disability The National Health Interview Survey estimates the number of people aged 18 or older who have difficulty in physical functioning, probing whether respondents could perform nine activities by themselves without using special equipment. The categories are walking a quarter mile; standing for two hours; sitting for two hours; walking up 10 steps without resting; stooping, bending, kneeling; reaching over one's head; grasping or handling small objects; carrying a 10-pound object; and pushing/pulling a large object. Adults who reported that any of these activities was very difficult or they could not do it at all were defined as having physical difficulties.

dual-earner couple A married couple in which both the householder and the householder's spouse are in the labor force.

earnings A type of income, earnings is the amount of money a person receives from his or her job. *See also* Income.

employed All civilians who did any work as a paid employee or farmer/self-employed worker or who worked 15 hours or more as an unpaid farm worker or in a family-owned business during the reference period. All those who have jobs but are temporarily absent from their jobs due to illness, bad weather, vacation, labor management dispute, or personal reasons are considered employed.

expenditure The transaction cost including excise and sales taxes of goods and services acquired during the survey period. The full cost of each purchase is recorded even though full payment may not have been made at the date of purchase. Average expenditure figures may be artificially low for infrequently purchased items such as cars because figures are calculated using all consumer units within a demographic segment rather than just purchasers. Expenditure estimates include money spent on gifts for others.

family A group of two or more people (one of whom is the householder) related by birth, marriage, or adoption and living in the same household.

family household A household maintained by a householder who lives with one or more people related to him or her by blood, marriage, or adoption.

female/male householder A woman or man who maintains a household without a spouse present. May head family or nonfamily household.

foreign-born population People who are not U.S. citizens at birth.

full-time employment Full-time is 35 or more hours of work per week during the majority of weeks worked.

full-time, year-round Indicates 50 or more weeks of full-time employment during the previous calendar year.

General Social Survey The GSS is a biennial survey of the attitudes of Americans taken by the University of Chicago's National Opinion Research Center. NORC conducts the GSS through face-to-face interviews with an independently drawn, representative sample of 1,500 to 3,000 noninstitutionalized people aged 18 or older who live in the United States.

generation X Americans born between 1965 and 1976. Also known as the baby-bust generation.

Hispanic Because Hispanic is an ethnic origin rather than a race, Hispanics may be of any race. While most Hispanics are White, there are Black, Asian, American Indian, and even Native Hawaiian Hispanics.

household All the persons who occupy a housing unit. A household includes the related family members and all the unrelated persons, if any, such as lodgers, foster children, wards, or employees who share the housing unit. A person living alone is counted as a household. A group of unrelated people who share a housing unit as roommates or unmarried partners is also counted as a household. Households do not include group quarters such as college dormitories, prisons, or nursing homes.

household, race/ethnicity of Households are categorized according to the race or ethnicity of the householder only.

householder The householder is the person (or one of the persons) in whose name the housing unit is owned or rented or, if there is no such person, any adult member. With married couples, the householder may be either the husband or wife. The householder is the reference person for the household.

householder, age of The age of the householder is used to categorize households into age groups such as those used in this book. Married couples, for example, are classified according to the age of either the husband or wife, depending on which one identified him- or herself as the householder.

housing unit A housing unit is a house, an apartment, a group of rooms, or a single room occupied or intended for occupancy as separate living quarters. Separate living quarters are those in which the occupants do not live and eat with any other persons in the structure and that have direct access from the outside of the building or through a common hall that is used or intended for use by the occupants of another unit or by the general public. The occupants may be a single family, one person living alone, two or more families living together, or any other group of related or unrelated persons who share living arrangements.

Housing Vacancy Survey The HVS is a supplement to the Current Population Survey, providing quarterly and annual data on rental and homeowner vacancy rates, characteristics of units available for occupancy, and homeownership rates by age, household type, region, state, and metropolitan area. The Current Population Survey sample includes 60,000 occupied housing units and about 9,000 vacant units.

housing value The respondent's estimate of how much his or her house and lot would sell for if it were for sale.

iGeneration Americans born between 1995 and 2009.

immigrants Aliens admitted for legal permanent residence in the United States.

income Money received in the preceding calendar year by a person aged 15 or older from any of the following sources: earnings from longest job (or self-employment), earnings from jobs other than longest job, unemployment compensation, workers' compensation, Social Security, Supplemental Security income, public assistance, veterans' payments, survivor benefits, disability benefits, retirement pensions, interest, dividends, rents and royalties or estates and trusts, educational assistance, alimony, child support, financial assistance from outside the household, and other periodic income. Income is reported in several ways in this book. Household income is the combined income of all household members. Income of persons is all income accruing to a person from all sources. Earnings are the money a person receives from his or her job.

industry Refers to the industry in which a person worked longest in the preceding calendar year.

job tenure The length of time a person has been employed continuously by the same employer.

labor force The labor force tables in this book show the civilian labor force only. The labor force includes both the employed and the unemployed (people who are looking for work). People are counted as in the labor force if they were working or looking for work during the reference week in which the Census Bureau fields the Current Population Survey.

labor force participation rate The percent of the civilian noninstitutional population that is in the civilian labor force, which includes both the employed and the unemployed.

male householder *See* Female/Male Householder.

married couples with or without children under age 18 Refers to married couples with or without own children under age 18 living in the same household. Couples without children under age 18 may be parents of grown children who live elsewhere or they could be childless couples.

median The median is the amount that divides the population or households into two equal portions: one below and one above the median. Medians can be calculated for income, age, and many other characteristics.

median income The amount that divides the income distribution into two equal groups, half having incomes above the median, half having incomes below the median. The medians for households or families are based on all households or families. The median for persons are based on all persons aged 15 or older with income.

metropolitan statistical area To be defined as an MSA, an area must include a city with 50,000 or more inhabitants, or a Census Bureau–defined urbanized area of at least 50,000 inhabitants and a total metropolitan population of at least 100,000 (75,000 in New England). The county (or counties) that contains the largest city becomes the "central county" (counties), along with any adjacent counties that have at least 50 percent of their population in the urbanized area surrounding the largest city. Additional "outlying counties" are included in the MSA if they meet specified requirements of commuting to the central counties and other selected requirements of metropolitan character (such as population density and percent urban). In New England, MSAs are defined in terms of cities and towns rather than counties. For this reason, the concept of New England County Metropolitan Area is used to define metropolitan areas in the New England division.

millennial generation Americans born between 1977 and 1994.

mobility status People are classified according to their mobility status on the basis of a comparison between their place of residence at the time of the March Current Population Survey and their place of residence in March of the previous year. Nonmovers are people living in the same house at the end of the period as at the beginning of the period. Movers are people living in a different house at the end of the period from that at the beginning of the period. Movers from abroad are either citizens or aliens whose place of residence is outside the United States at the beginning of the period, that is, in an outlying area under the jurisdiction of the United States or in a foreign country. The mobility status for children is fully allocated from the mother if she is in the household; otherwise it is allocated from the householder.

National Health and Nutrition Examination Survey The NHANES is a continuous survey of a representative sample of the U.S. civilian noninstitutionalized population. Respondents are interviewed at home about their health and nutrition, and the interview is followed up by a physical examination that measures such things as height and weight in mobile examination centers.

National Health Interview Survey The NHIS is a continuing nationwide sample survey of the civilian noninstitutional population of the United States conducted by the Census Bureau for the National Center for Health Statistics. In interviews each year, data are collected from more than 100,000 people about their illnesses, injuries, impairments, chronic and acute conditions, activity limitations, and use of health services.

National Household Education Survey Sponsored by the National Center for Education Statistics, the NHES provides descriptive data on the educational activities of the U.S. population, including after-school care and adult education. The NHES is a system of telephone surveys of a representative sample of 45,000 to 60,000 households in the United States.

National Survey of Family Growth Sponsored by the National Center for Health Statistics, the NSFG is a periodic nationally representative survey of the civilian noninstitutionalized population aged 15 to 44. In-person interviews are completed with men and women, collecting data on marriage, divorce, contraception, and infertility. The 2006–10 survey updates previous NSFG surveys taken in 1973, 1976, 1988, 1995, and 2002.

National Survey on Drug Use and Health The NSDUH is an annual survey of a nationally representative sample of people aged 12 or older living in households, noninstitutional group quarters (such as college dorms), and military bases in the United States. It is the primary source of information about illegal drug use in the United States and has been conducted since 1971. Interviews are held in person and incorporate procedures (such as anonymity and computer-assisted interviewing) that will increase respondents' cooperation and willingness to report honestly about their illicit drug use behavior.

Native Hawaiian and Other Pacific Islander The 2000 census identified this group for the first time as a separate racial category from Asians. In most survey data, however, the population is included with Asians.

nonfamily household A household maintained by a householder who lives alone or who lives with people to whom he or she is not related.

nonfamily householder A householder who lives alone or with nonrelatives.

non-Hispanic People who do not identify themselves as Hispanic are classified as non-Hispanic. Non-Hispanics may be of any race.

non-Hispanic White People who identify their race as White and who do not indicate a Hispanic origin.

nonmetropolitan area Counties that are not classified as metropolitan areas.

occupation Occupational classification is based on the kind of work a person did at his or her job during the previous calendar year. If a person changed jobs during the year, the data refer to the occupation of the job held the longest during that year.

occupied housing units A housing unit is classified as occupied if a person or group of people is living in it or if the occupants are only temporarily absent—on vacation, for example. By definition, the count of occupied housing units is the same as the count of households.

outside principal city The portion of a metropolitan county or counties that falls outside of the principal city or cities; generally regarded as the suburbs.

own children Own children are sons and daughters, including stepchildren and adopted children, of the householder. The totals include never-married children living away from home in college dormitories.

owner occupied A housing unit is "owner occupied" if the owner lives in the unit, even if it is mortgaged or not fully paid for. A cooperative or condominium unit is "owner occupied" only if the owner lives in it. All other occupied units are classified as "renter occupied."

part-time employment Part-time is less than 35 hours of work per week in a majority of the weeks worked during the year.

percent change The change (either positive or negative) in a measure that is expressed as a proportion of the starting measure. When median income changes from $20,000 to $25,000, for example, this is a 25 percent increase.

percentage point change The change (either positive or negative) in a value that is already expressed as a percentage. When a labor force participation rate changes from 70 percent to 75 percent, for example, this is a 5 percentage point increase.

poverty level The official income threshold below which families and people are classified as living in poverty. The threshold rises each year with inflation and varies depending on family size and age of householder.

principal city The largest city in a metropolitan area is called the principal or central city. The balance of the metropolitan area outside the principal or central city is regarded as the "suburbs."

proportion or share The value of a part expressed as a percentage of the whole. If there are 4 million people aged 25 and 3 million of them are White, then the White proportion is 75 percent.

race Race is self-reported and can be defined in three ways. The "race alone" population comprises people who identify themselves as being of only one race. The "race in combination" population comprises people who identify themselves as being of more than one race, such as White and Black. The "race, alone or in combination" population includes both those who identify themselves as being of one race and those who identify themselves as being of more than one race.

recession generation Americans born from 2010 to the present.

regions The four major regions and nine census divisions of the United States are the state groupings as shown below:
Northeast:
—New England: Connecticut, Maine, Massachusetts, New Hampshire, Rhode Island, and Vermont
—Middle Atlantic: New Jersey, New York, and Pennsylvania
Midwest:
—East North Central: Illinois, Indiana, Michigan, Ohio, and Wisconsin
—West North Central: Iowa, Kansas, Minnesota, Missouri, Nebraska, North Dakota, and South Dakota
South:
—South Atlantic: Delaware, District of Columbia, Florida, Georgia, Maryland, North Carolina, South Carolina, Virginia, and West Virginia
—East South Central: Alabama, Kentucky, Mississippi, and Tennessee
—West South Central: Arkansas, Louisiana, Oklahoma, and Texas
West:
—Mountain: Arizona, Colorado, Idaho, Montana, Nevada, New Mexico, Utah, and Wyoming
—Pacific: Alaska, California, Hawaii, Oregon, and Washington

renter occupied *See* Owner Occupied.

Retirement Confidence Survey The RCS—sponsored by the Employee Benefit Research Institute, the American Savings Education Council, and Mathew Greenwald & Associates—is an annual survey of a nationally representative sample of 1,000 people aged 25 or older. Respondents are asked a core set of questions that have been included in the survey since 1996, measuring attitudes and behavior toward retirement, as well as additional questions about current retirement issues.

rounding Percentages are rounded to the nearest tenth of a percent; therefore, the percentages in a distribution do not always add exactly to 100.0 percent. The totals, however, are always shown as 100.0. Moreover, individual figures are rounded to the nearest thousand without being adjusted to group totals, which are independently rounded; percentages are based on the unrounded numbers.

self-employment A person is categorized as self-employed if he or she was self-employed in the job held longest during the reference period. Persons who report self-employment from a second job are excluded, but those who report wage and salary income from a second job are included. Unpaid workers in family businesses are excluded. Self-employment statistics include only nonagricultural workers and exclude people who work for themselves in incorporated business.

sex ratio The number of men per 100 women.

suburbs *See* Outside Principal City.

Survey of Consumer Finances The Survey of Consumer Finances is a triennial survey taken by the Federal Reserve Board. It collects data on the assets, debt, and net worth of approximately 6,000 nationally representative American households.

Survey of Income and Program Participation The SIPP is a continuous, monthly panel survey of up to 36,700 households conducted by the Census Bureau. It is designed to measure the effectiveness of existing federal, state, and local programs and to measure economic well-being, including wealth, asset ownership, and debt.

unemployed Unemployed people are those who, during the survey period, had no employment but were available and looking for work. Those who were laid off from their jobs and were waiting to be recalled are also classified as unemployed.

White People who identify their race as White. The "White" racial category includes many Hispanics (who may be of any race) unless the term "non-Hispanic White" is used.

Youth Risk Behavior Surveillance System The Centers for Disease Control created the YRBBS to monitor health risks being taken by young people at the national, state, and local level. The national survey is taken every two years based on a nationally representative sample of 16,000 students in 9th through 12th grade in public and private schools.

Bibliography

Agency for Healthcare Research and Quality

Internet site http://www.ahrq.gov/

—Medical Expenditure Panel Survey, Internet site http://meps.ahrq.gov/mepsweb/survey_comp/household.jsp

Bureau of Labor Statistics

Internet site http://www.bls.gov

—2013 American Time Use Survey, Internet site http://www.bls.gov/tus/home.htm

—College Enrollment and Work Activity of 2012 High School Graduates, Internet site http://www.bls.gov/news.release/hsgec.nr0.htm

—Consumer Expenditure Surveys, various years, Internet site http://www.bls.gov/cex/home.htm

—Employee Tenure, Internet site http://www.bls.gov/news.release/tenure.toc.htm

—Employment Characteristics of Families, Internet site http://www.bls.gov/news.release/famee.toc.htm

—Employment Projections, Internet site http://www.bls.gov/emp/

—Labor Force Statistics from the Current Population Survey—Annual Averages, Internet site http://www.bls.gov/cps/tables.htm#empstat

—*Monthly Labor Review*, "Labor Force Projections to 2020: A More Slowly Growing Workforce," January 2012, Internet site http://www.bls.gov/opub/mlr/

—Table 15. Employed persons by detailed occupation, sex, and age, Annual Average 2013 (Source: Current Population Survey), unpublished table received from the BLS by special request

Bureau of the Census

Internet site http://www.census.gov

—2010 Census, American Factfinder, Internet site http://factfinder2.census.gov/faces/nav/jsf/pages/index.xhtml

—American Community Survey, American Factfinder, Internet site http://factfinder2.census.gov/faces/nav/jsf/pages/index.xhtml

—America's Families and Living Arrangements, Current Population Survey Annual Social and Economic Supplement, Internet site http://www.census.gov/hhes/families/

—Current Population Survey Annual Social and Economic Supplement, Internet site http://www.census.gov/hhes/www/income/data/

—Educational Attainment, CPS Historical Time Series Tables, Internet site http://www.census.gov/hhes/socdemo/education/data/cps/historical/index.html

—Educational Attainment, Current Population Survey Annual Social and Economic Supplement, Internet site http://www.census.gov/hhes/socdemo/education/

—Families and Living Arrangements, Historical Tables—Households, Internet site http://www.census.gov/hhes/families/data/historical.html

—Fertility of American Women: 2012, Detailed Tables, Internet site http://www.census.gov/hhes/fertility/data/cps/2012.html

—Geographic Mobility/Migration, Current Population Survey Annual Social and Economic Supplements, Internet site http://www.census.gov/hhes/migration/

—Health Insurance, Current Population Survey Annual Social and Economic Supplements, Internet site http://www.census.gov/hhes/www/hlthins/

—Historical Income Data, Current Population Survey Annual Social and Economic Supplements, Internet site http://www.census.gov/hhes/www/income/data/historical/index.html

—Housing Vacancy Survey, Internet site http://www.census.gov/housing/hvs/

—Income, Current Population Survey Annual Social and Economic Supplements, Internet site http://www.census.gov/hhes/www/income/data/index.html

—Number, Timing, and Duration of Marriages and Divorces: 2009, Detailed Tables, Internet site http://www.census.gov/hhes/socdemo/marriage/data/sipp/2009/tables.html

—Population Estimates, Internet site http://www.census.gov/popest/data/index.html

—Population Projections, Internet site http://www.census.gov/population/projections/

—Poverty, Current Population Survey Annual Social and Economic Supplements, Internet site http://www.census.gov/hhes/www/poverty/index.html

—School Enrollment, CPS Historical Time Series Tables on School Enrollment, Internet site http://www.census.gov/hhes/school/data/cps/historical/index.html

—School Enrollment, CPS October 2013, Detailed Tables, Internet site http://www.census.gov/hhes/school/data/cps/2013/tables.html

—Voting and Registration, Internet site http://www.census.gov/hhes/www/socdemo/voting/index.html

Centers for Disease Control and Prevention

Internet site http://www.cdc.gov

—Behavioral Risk Factor Surveillance System, Prevalence and Trends Data, Internet site http://apps.nccd.cdc.gov/brfss/

—Diagnosis of HIV Infection in the United States and Dependent Areas, 2011, Internet site http://www.cdc.gov/hiv/surveillance/resources/reports/2011report/index.htm

—Youth Risk Behavior Surveillance—United States, 2013, Internet site http://www.cdc.gov/HealthyYouth/yrbs/index.htm

Employee Benefit Research Institute

Internet site http://www.ebri.org/

—Retirement Confidence Surveys, Internet site http://www.ebri.org/surveys/rcs/

Federal Interagency Forum on Child and Family Statistics

Internet site http://childstats.gov

—America's Children: Key National Indicators of Well-Being, 2013, Internet site http://www.childstats.gov/

Federal Reserve Board

Internet site http://www.federalreserve.gov

—Survey of Consumer Finances, Internet site http://www.federalreserve.gov/econresdata/scf/scfindex.htm

Homeland Security

Internet site http://www.dhs.gov/index.shtm

—Yearbook of Immigration Statistics, Internet site http://www.dhs.gov/yearbook-immigration-statistics

National Center for Education Statistics

Internet site http://nces.ed.gov

—Digest of Education Statistics: 2013, Internet site http://nces.ed.gov/programs/digest/2013menu_tables.asp

—Parent and Family Involvement in Education, from the National Household Education Surveys Program of 2012, Internet site http://nces.ed.gov/pubsearch/pubsinfo.asp?pubid=2013028

—Projections of Education Statistics to 2021, Internet site http://nces.ed.gov/programs/projections/projections2021/

National Center for Health Statistics

Internet site http://www.cdc.gov/nchs

—*Anthropometric Reference Data for Children and Adults: United States, 2007–2010*, National Health Statistics Reports, Series 11, No. 252, 2012, Internet site http://www.cdc.gov/nchs/nhanes.htm

—Birth Data, Internet site http://www.cdc.gov/nchs/births.htm

—*Births: Preliminary Data for 2013*, National Vital Statistics Reports, Vol. 63, No. 2, 2014, Internet site http://www.cdc.gov/nchs/births.htm

—*Current Contraceptive Use in the United States, 2006–2010, and Changes in Patterns of Use since 1995*, National Health Statistics Reports, No. 60, 2012, Internet site http://www.cdc.gov/nchs/nsfg.htm

—*Deaths: Preliminary Data for 2011*, National Vital Statistics Reports, Vol. 61, No. 6, 2012, Internet site http://www.cdc.gov/nchs/deaths.htm

—*Fathers' Involvement with Their Children: United States, 2006–2010*, National Health Statistics Reports, No. 71, 2013, Internet site http://www.cdc.gov/nchs/nsfg.htm

—*First Marriages in the United States: Data from the 2006–2010 National Survey of Family Growth*, National Health Statistics Reports, No. 49, 2012, Internet site http://www.cdc.gov/nchs/nsfg.htm

—*Health, United States, 2013*, Internet site http://www.cdc.gov/nchs/hus.htm

—Mortality data, Internet site http://www.cdc.gov/nchs/deaths.htm

—*Sexual Behavior, Sexual Attraction, and Sexual Identity in the United States: Data from the 2006–2008 National Survey of Family Growth*, National Health Statistics Reports, No. 36, 2011, Internet site http://www.cdc.gov/nchs/nsfg/new_nsfg.htm

—*Summary Health Statistics for the U.S. Population: National Health Interview Survey, 2012*, Series 10, No. 259, 2013, Internet site http://www.cdc.gov/nchs/nhis.htm

—*Summary Health Statistics for U.S. Adults: National Health Interview Survey, 2012*, Series 10, No. 260, 2014, Internet site http://www.cdc.gov/nchs/products/series/series10.htm

—*Summary Health Statistics for U.S. Children: National Health Interview Survey, 2012*, Series 10, No. 258, 2013, Internet site http://www.cdc.gov/nchs/nhis.htm

Substance Abuse and Mental Health Services Administration

Internet site http://www.samhsa.gov

—National Survey on Drug Use and Health, 2012, Internet site http://www.samhsa.gov

Survey Documentation and Analysis, Computer-assisted Survey Methods Program, University of California, Berkeley

Internet site http://sda.berkeley.edu/

—General Social Surveys, 1972–2012 Cumulative Data Files, Internet site http://sda.berkeley.edu/cgi-bin/hsda?harcsda+gss12

Index